THE COMPARATIVE RUSSIAN-ENGLISH DICTIONARY OF

RUSSIAN PROVERBS & SAYINGS

WITH 5543 ENTRIES
1900 MOST IMPORTANT PROVERBS HIGHLIGHTED
ENGLISH PROVERB INDEX

Peter Mertvago

Hippocrene Books
New York

To the memory of Galina Markov

for her invaluable help in preparing this book

Посвящается доброй памяти Галины Софроновны Марковой,

оказавшей автору ценную помощь в составлении этого издания

For information, address:
HIPPOCRENE BOOKS, INC.
171 Madison Ave.
New York, NY 10016

ISBN 0-7818-0424-8

Printed in the United States of America.

TABLE OF CONTENTS

INTRODUCTION

The proverb as cliché.

Language is a semiotic system whose essential function is the communication of information. The units which convey or vehiculate this communication vary in length and may be morphemes, words, phrases or complete sentences and groups of sentences. Depending on the particular circumstance and linguistic facility of the author, a communication may either be an original utterance, produced at the time of speaking and made up of language units arranged at the author's discretion, or it may be cast in the form of a ready-made grammatical structure that is easily assimilated by the members of a given language and cultural group, and which dispenses the author from any need of prior formulation.

Proverbs and proverbial sayings offer precisely this convenience by making it possible to convey entire thoughts or concepts in an encapsulated, code-like manner and by functioning as *signs* of situations or of a certain type of relationship between objects.[1] Many have viewed this as a praiseworthy property which over time transmits the oral tradition of a culture and provides an unwritten language for the applied arts and morality to be passed down the ages on the lips of successive generations. But it has also aroused the disdain of those who consider that the vulgar philosophy disseminated by proverbs is more appropriate for the street or market than the parlour, and that such immediacy of expression is incompatible with the subtle inventiveness expected of an educated mind, much in the way that fast food today is despised by fine gourmets. This attitude was epitomized in Lord Chesterfield's admonition that "a man of fashion never has recourse to proverbs and vulgar aphorisms."[2] Whereas such an attitude may have occasioned a certain decline in the accepted use of proverbs among some members of the intelligentsia in England, this is not necessarily true of other countries. In Russia certainly, proverbs and proverbial sayings have formed an integral part of the spoken and written language, and occupy a rank somewhere

---

[1] G.L.Permiakov, *From Proverb to Folk Tale. Notes on the General Theory of Cliché* (Moscow: Nauka Publ. 1979), p.20.

[2] *Letters*, 27 Sept.1749. Still echoed in the next century by William Hazlitt: "To repeat what has been said a thousand times is commonplace." *Works*, 1.381.

between the oral and literal traditions, offering a common basis for both. Vladimir Dal, the Russian compiler of proverbs, defined proverbs as a circumlocution or periphrasis, himself citing the Russian proverb that *stark (direct) speech is not a proverb* - «голая (прямая) речь не пословица», which indicates that there is more to proverbs than a mere concatenation of words. It is as if, as Disraeli had observed, there were no occurrence in human affairs to which some proverb might not be applied, and "all knowledge had been long aphoristical and traditional, pithily contracting the discoveries which were to be instantly comprehended and easily retained." [3]

Indeed many paremiological theories have been expounded to demonstrate how proverbs may have originated: either from simple apothegms and platitudes, metaphoric uses of observation, or from generalizations of simple scenes or fables.[4] Inasmuch as human nature and experience are by and large universal, similar situations and similar objects ellicit a similar response in terms of the way people think and act and express themselves. Hence it is inevitable for there to be an inchoate resemblance between certain proverbs of different nations.[5] This commonality of experience and expression has also been expanded through borrowing, such as that which resulted from rampant translation of proverbs in Europe following the publication in 1500 of Erasmus' *Adagia*, much of which produced what Seiler has termed the *gemeinmittelalterlich* (international medieval) class of proverbs which derive from Latin and evidently owe their currency to that international language of the Middle Ages.[6]

It is often impossible and always somewhat futile to try to unravel which proverb derives from which source, especially as literary history frequently runs parallel to or draws upon the oral vernacular tradition. The difficulty is further compounded when dealing with proverbs of different languages, and the most pragmatic solution may simply be to identify the similarities and correspondence without attempting to make any absolute judgment as to who got what from whom, unless chronology and word-for-word semantic concordance otherwise permit.[7] This is the approach that has been followed in this dictionary, in which equivalent and similar proverbs and sayings from Greek, Latin and the scriptures have been included to suggest possible provenance.

---

[3] Isaac Disraeli, "The Philosophy of Proverbs," in *The Curiosities of Literature* (London: Routledge, 1834), p.402.

[4] See A.Taylor, *The Proverb* (Hatboro Pennsylvania, 1962), pp. 3ff., 27-31, 141ff., who points out that it is difficult to determine which came first, the specific proverb or the fable. Also, that not all nations have regarded fables and proverbs as distinct forms: the Greek αἶνος, for example, means both. Similarly, in cases of proverbs deriving from generalizations, it is irrelevant whether the perception of the scene and its appreciation are simultaneous or separated in time.

[5] Permiakov, *op. cit.*, p.20 regards concrete situations as *invariants* of which proverbs of different peoples are specific image variants, irrespective of their language material.

[6] F.Seiler, *Deutsche Sprichwörterkunde* (Handbuch des deutschen Unterrichts IV.III) Munich 1922, cited in Taylor, *op.cit.* pp.50-51.

[7] Thus, for example, the American proverb recorded in the ODAP, p.96.29 *with seven nurses a child will be without eyes* can be safely assumed to derive from the Russian «у семи нянек дитя без глазу» which therefore one may infer had been brought to America by Russian immigrants in the late 19th - early 20th centuries, since no trace of this proverb exists in England.

The Russian Proverb

To the extent then that there is a uniform pool of human experience and derivational interborrowing from common historical and cultural antecedents, many Russian and English proverbs parallel each other.[8] When expressing a similar experience or phenomenon through a proverbial cliché, many of the differences between Russian and English proverbs can be accounted for by differences in the prevailing rhythms of the languages in addition to the inherent grammatical differences in the languages themselves. These are then supplemented by topical local colour, which Permiakov calls the *realia.*[9] Thus, for example, *carrying coals to Newcastle* in Russian becomes *carrying samovars to Tula*, and we have the expression *Moscow wasn't built in a day* for the proverb about Rome.

The Russian language differentiates a *proverb*, пословица, from a *saying*, поговорка - a distinction that has frequently been blurred in English. The term *proverb* in English is often used loosely and before the 18th century it had even been applied to descriptive epithets, similes, and metaphorical expressions. Requiring proverbs to be complete sentences does not obviate the conceptual difficulty since any such epithet or metaphorical phrase can be easily recast into sentence form, as for example *penny wise and pound foolish* can be restated *One must not be penny wise and pound foolish*, and thus acquire the aura of a proverb.

The difference in the Russian usage is itself explained by means of a Russian proverb:

Поговорка - цветок, пословица - ягодка.
A saying is a flower, a proverb a berry.

Thus a *saying* may be any widely used metaphor, simile or the like which aptly describes a specific occurrence or concept and which is admired for its charm, while a *proverb* is something that can, as it were, be eaten and digested - an aphorism or *sententia* which confers a benefit beyond its sensory appeal. In Russian, however, as well as in English, it is often counterproductive to belabour this distinction, and many proverbial sayings have been included in this dictionary, selected on the basis of their frequency of use among native speakers of the language.

The relative brevity of many Russian proverbs stems directly from the fact that the Russian language has no article, does not employ the present of the verb *to be*, and idiomatically resorts to frequent participial condensation. Also, the inflected nature of the Russian language offers ample opportunities for grammatical rhyme which are more rare in English.

It is rhyme together with alliteration that make up the dominant characterisitic of Russian proverbs and sayings, so much so that one frequently may wonder whether certain expressions have any purpose other than their rhyming or alliterative magnetism. Indeed, rhymes like «без капусты щи не густы», «где лад, там и склад», or «снегу нету и следу нету» abound in colloquial Russian, and may usually be labelled as поговорки rather than proverbs, though, as indicated above, such a distinction is often neither apparent nor productive. The effect of rhyme had already been noted in an early anonymous

---

[8] For the purposes of this dictionary, *English proverbs* means either *English* or *American* proverbs. British spelling has been used throughout, with the exception of those proverbs and sayings which can be identified as exclusively American.

[9] *op.cit.* pp.28-31, and "The object content of Proverbs," *Proverbium* 12 (1969), pp.324ff.

study of Russian proverbs published in 1875.   In deploring the impossibilities of translating Russian proverbs because of their rhyme and alliteration, it observed, "Even where reason remains, the want of rhyme in a popular saying is often fatal.   We recognize a magic force in *a stitch in time saves nine* which *a stitch in time saves eight* would never have exercised." [10]   When rhyme plays such a primordial role, the task of translating Russian proverbs indeed becomes akin to translating poetry, which may strip the original of much of its point if not significance.   Consequently, this dictionary does not include those sayings which display this characteristic *alone*, and which therefore may be better viewed as simple rhymes rather than even as sayings.[11]

There has been a considerable amount of recent scholarship devoted to the structure of proverbs in general and Russian proverbs in particular.[12]   Knowledge of grammatical structure does not necessarily enhance a native speaker's ability to understand his language, and similarly an awareness of proverb structure will not automatically confer any immediate understanding or command of specific proverbs. It is analogous to the plight of Monsieur Jourdain in *Le Bourgeois Gentilhomme* who had been speaking prose all his life without knowing it.   But for the linguist or scholar, structural analysis is an excellent means of gaining insight into the mechanical interface between language, thought and cultural influences and helps gauge the extent to which the medium may be the message in the case of certain proverbs. Appendix 2 arranges numerous Russian proverbs and sayings by structural type and seeks to incorporate them within the general structural scheme described by Dundes for all proverbs.[13]   This scheme is summarized in Table 1, p. 380.

---

[10] *The Quarterly Review,* 139 (1875), p.262.

[11] Additional examples of some common rhymes of this type are: Беда, что с гор вода. Без друга в жизни туго. В зимний холод всякий молод. Всякому нужен и обед и ужен. Где пьют, там и льют. Днем тихо, ночью лихо. Другие дни, другие сны. Зимою шубка не шутка. Мышь гложет что может. Офицер без шпаги хуже бабы. Пить пиво - сидеть криво. Разбойник живой покойник... But there are so many of these used colloquially in Russian that one could easily compile a separate volume without ever exhausting the supply.

[12] See Bibliography. Of particular importance are the seminal studies of A.Taylor and A.Dundes on the proverb, and for Russian proverbs, those of M.I.Levin and G.L.Permiakov (*From Proverb to Folk Tale*).

[13] *Op.cit.* pp.961-971. Of course this is but one possible type of structural classification. Permiakov, *op.cit.* pp.17-31, analyses Russian proverbs from three different angles or aspects which he argues must form the core of any meaningful classification. These are what he terms the logico-semiotic aspect, in which proverbs are regarded as signs for situations or logical relationships, the linguistic aspect based on syntax and grammatical considerations, and the object-image or *realia* aspect, which focuses on the specific ethnic, geographical, historical or other unique "local colour" features of proverbs.

How to Use this Dictionary

The *Comparative Dictionary* is by no means an exhaustive compilation of all Russian proverbs and sayings, but includes only those which are most common either in contemporary spoken Russian or in literature. It has been designed to serve, *inter alia* as a translator's tool and therefore has treated proverbs and sayings as units within a semiotic system as described above. Such an approach has been indicated and followed intuitively by paremiographers since antiquity because, while it may be open to criticism regarding the aptness of any particular correspondence between proverbs in different languages, it nevertheless seeks to convey in the idiom and mindset of the target language the meaning and emotion of the proverb of the source language. Literal translations are included for all but the most easily understood entries, and citations of related or similar proverbs and sayings and comparative cross-references are provided to assist readers in deciding whether the correspondence proposed is suitable for their purpose.

The entries in the *Dictionary* are arranged in Russian alphabetical order by first word of the Russian proverb, cited in its most usual form. Proverbs commonly existing in several word orders are cross-referenced, as are similar proverbs. Where alternate variations of proverbs exist, they are indicated in parentheses under the entry for the most common form of the proverb. Similarly, alternate words or phrases within the proverbs themselves are placed in parentheses. The most common and important Russian proverbs used in modern spoken Russian have been marked with an asterisk (*) to assist students and non-native speakers of the language.

Within each entry, English **bold-faced** text indicates an equivalent English proverb. Equivalence, for the purposes of this dictionary means lexical and conceptual correspondence. English proverbs that correspond in concept or meaning but not lexically are set in normal type following a literal translation of the Russian proverb which stands in square brackets [ ]. Where no corresponding English proverb exists, only a literal translation of the Russian proverb is provided within square brackets. The symbol *Cf.* introduces proverbs and sayings that bear a similarity to the entry either in subject, imagery, or structure, and are included for purposes of comparison and to minimize explanatory comments. Proverbs and sayings that have a meaning opposite to that of the entry are preceded by an dagger (†) and have also been included for comparison. All explanatory remarks are given in *italics*. An index of corresponding or equivalent English proverbs arranged by key word is provided in the end for quick reference.

Sources

Russian:

Богданов А.И. *Сборник пословиц и присловиц Российских.* 1741.
Даль В.И. *Пословицы русского народа.* Москва 1861-1862.
Княжевич Д.М.   Полное собрание русских пословиц и поговорок, расположенных по азбучному порядку. Москва 1822.
Снегирев И.М.   Русские народные пословицы и притчи. Москва 1848.

English:

ODEP	*The Oxford Dictionary of English Proverbs.* Oxford 1970.
ODAP	*The Oxford Dictionary of American Proverbs.* Oxford 1992.

Greek and Latin:

EA   Erasmus *Veterum Maximeque Insignium Paroemiarum, id est Adagiorum Collectanea*

SPL   *Nemecko-latinskii i russkii leksikon kupno s pervymi nachalami russkago jazyka.* St. Petersburg 1731.[14]

Plan   Planudes Maximus (14th cent) in ed. Kurz, *Sprichwörtersammlung des Maximus Planudes,* Leipzig 1886; selected proverbs also in Altenkirch, R. "Die Beziehungen zwischen Slaven und Griechen in ihren Sprichwörten." *Archiv für slavische Philologie.* 30 (1908-1909), 1-47, 321-364.

The following Greek paroemiographers in E.L. von Leutsch & F.G. Schneidewin, *Corpus Paroemiographorum Graecorum* (Göttingen, 1839-51):

Apost.   Apostolius (15 cent.)
Diogen.   Diogenianus of Heraclea (early 2nd cent.)
Zen.   Zenobius (2nd cent.)

Abbreviations

Cf.	*confer (compare)*
hum.	*humorous*
idiom.	*idiomatic*
obs.	*obsolete*
sarc.	*sarcasm*
v.	*vide (see)*
vulg.	*vulgar*

---

[14] This is a trilingual dictionary of proverbs published in the early 18th century aligning Russian proverbs with Latin and German proverbs. It is a document of exceptional interest because it offers insight into how Russians themselves understood their own proverbs, and is therefore particularly helpful in identifying their semiotic meaning; *eg:* трудно природу переменить - die Katz lasste Mausen nicht - naturae sequitur femina quisque suae. For a modern edition of the text, with detailed analysis, see Bibliography, Geyr H.

A

1   **А где тот хлеб что вчера съели?**   *v.* Б366, О41, Т2, У91
[And where's the bread we ate yesterday?]   Eaten bread is soon forgotten. You can't have your cake and eat it.

2   **Август каторга, да после будет мятовка.**
[August drudgery brings feasts and abundance.]   A dry summer never made a dear peck.

3   **Август крушит, да после круглит.**
[August destroys, then restores.]   Dry August and warm doth harvest no harm.

4   **Августа капуста, а марта осетр.**   *v.* В635,644,655
[August cabbage and March sturgeon.]   *Cf.* Everything in its season.

5   **Авось да небось - хоть вовсе брось.**   *v.* Е21, К6,232, *Ар.*1.24
If ifs and an's were pots and pans, there'd be no trade for tinkers.

6   **Авось задатка не дает.**   *v.* К232
[There's no banking on "maybe."]   What may be, may not be. Every maybe hath a may not be.

7   **Авось и к нам взойдет солнышко на двор.**   *v.* Б373, В288, П256
[Maybe the sun will shine on our yard too.]   Our day too will come some day.

8   **Авось и рыбака толкает под бока.**   *v.* С284
["Maybe" goads on the fisherman.]   Still he fishes that catches one.

9   **Авось попадет, что заяц в тенета.**
[Maybe, like the hare that *may be* snared.]   *Cf.* May bees don't fly this month.

10   **Авоськины детки не рождены (авосевы города не горожены).**
["Maybe's" children are unborn (cities are unguarded).]   May-bee was ne'er a good honey bee.

11*   **Ад вымощен благими намерениями.**   *v.* Д353
Hell is paved with good intentions. *Lat.* Undique ad inferos tantundem viae est.

12   **Азбуки не знает а читать садится.**   *v.* В54, Х94
Learn to say before you sing.

13   **Алмаз алмазом гранится (плут плутом губится).**   *v.* К106, Л80
Diamond cut diamond [and cheat swindle cheat.]

14*   **Алмаз алмазом решится.**   *v.* К106
Diamond cut diamond.

15   **Алтарю служить, от алтаря и жить.**   *v.* Г189
[He that serves the altar, must live from the altar.]
Practice what you preach. *Cf.* No penny, no paternoster.

16   **Алтын сам ворота отпирает и путь очищает.**
Money is wise, it knows the way. Money recommends a man everywhere.

17   **Алтынная кошка полтинную часть тянет.**
[A penny cat draws a pound portion.]   *Cf.* To bit off more than one can chew.

18   **Алтынного вора (малых воров) вешают, полтинного (больших) чествуют.**
Little thieves are hanged, but great ones are honoured.   *v.* Б330, З75, Н268, Ш6
SPL. Dat veniam corvis, vexat censura columbas. *Cf.* A thief passes for a gentleman
when stealing has made him rich.

19   **Алчешь чужого, потеряешь свое.**   *v.* В522, З4, М132, Н303,318,338, Ч126
[Covet others' and lose your own.]
Cf. Covet not that which belongs to others. All covet all lose.

20   **Аминем лихого (беса) не избудешь.**   *v.* М138, Х14
[Amens (*i.e.* prayers) alone won't ward off evil (the devil).]
It is too late to pray when the devil comes. Prayers plough not.

21*   **Аппетит приходит во время еды.**   *v.* Б239
Appetite comes with eating.

22*   **Апрель с водой, а май с травой.**
April showers bring may flowers.

23   **Аптека и лечит как калечит.**
[Medicines both cure and cripple.] *Cf.* Physicians kill more than they cure.

24   **Аптека не прибавит века.**   *v.* О122
There is no medicine against death. *Lat.* Contra malum mortis, non est medicamentum
in hortis. *Cf.* A deadly disease neither physician nor physic can cure.

25   **Аптека улечит на полвека.**
[Medicines will lay you up for a half a lifetime.]
Medicines are not meant to live on. *Cf.* A pitiful physician spoileth a sore.

26   **Аптекам предаться - деньгами не жаться.**
[To indulge in medicines is to loosen your purse.]
Ready money is ready medicine. *Cf.* Who pays the physician does the cure.

27   **Артельный (общий) горшок гуще кипит.**   *v.* †У51
[The common pot boils thickest.] *Cf.* †A pot that belongs to many is ill stirred and worst
boiled. †The common horse is worst shod.

28   **Аршин на кафтан, а два на заплаты.**   *v.* Д345
[A yard or the coat and two for the patches.] The tailor must cut three sleeves to every
woman's gown.

29   **Ахи да охи не дадут подмоги.**   *v.* Б219, И140, О4, П27,278, Ч92
[Moans and groans won't help.]   It's no use crying over spilt milk. *Cf.* A laugh is
worth a thousand groans in any market.

Б

1   **Баба без характера что хлеб без соли.**
    [A woman without character is like salt-free bread.]   A fair woman without virtue is like palled wine.

2   **Баба блудит а деду грех.**   *v.* Н386
    A light wife doth make a heavy husband.

3   **Баба в избу - мухи вон.**
    A woman at home and the flies are gone.

4* **Баба с возу - кобыле легче.**
    [A woman off, so much lighter for the mare.]   One less, one lighter.

5   **Баба с печи летит, семьдесят семь дум передумает.**   *v.* Д110, С105
    [As a woman alights from a stove, she changes her mind 77 times.]   A woman's mind and winter wind change oft. A woman is a weathercock.

6   **Баба слезами беде помогает.**   *v.* Ж84
    [Women console themselves with tears.]   *Cf.* Women laugh when they can and cry when they will. A woman's tears are silent orators.

7   **Бабе дорога - от печи до порога.**   *v.* Д318, Ж60
    [A woman's place is between the stove and doorstep.]   A woman's place is in the home.

8* **Бабушка (старуха) надвое сказала (гадала).**   *v.* В503, Э1
    [Grandmother said (foretold) it ambiguously.] *i.e.: "You never can tell."* We shall see what we shall see.

9   **Базар цену скажет.**
    [The market sets the price.]   A man must sell his ware after the rates of the market.

10 **Баран бараном, а рога даром.**
    [Whoever takes the lamb gets the horns free.]   Let the horns go with the hide.

11 **Барская хворь - мужицкое здоровье.**   *v.* В410, И133, К157,186, О43, *Ap.*1.23
    A falling master makes a standing servant.

12 **Барский двор - хуже петли.**
    A rich man's garden is his servant's prison.

13 **Барский приказчик и в лохани указчик.**
    [The master's steward gives the orders in the kitchen.]   Everyone is a master and a servant.

14 **Барскую просьбу почитай за приказ.**
    The master's wish is his command.

15   **Бархатный весь, а жальце есть.**
[Smooth as velvet, but with a stinger.]   Flies like a butterfly but stings like a bee.

16   **Бары дерутся а у холопов чубы болят.**   *v.* К186, П4, С185
[The rich fight and the poor feel the blows.]   The humble suffer from the folly of the great.   The pleasures of the mighty are the tears of the poor.   *SPL.* quando delirant reges, plectuntur Achivi.

17   **Барыш барышом, а магарычи даром.**   *v.* Л126
[Profits may be earned, but gifts are free.]   Nothing freer than a gift.

18   **Барыш с накладом на одних санях ездят (в одних сапожках ходят) (в одном кармане живут) (двор обо двор живут).**   *v.* Б19,80, Г61, Д73, К273
[Profit and risk go together (on one sled) (in the same shoes) (in one pocket) (in adjoining yards).]   Nothing ventured, nothing gained.   Those who take the profits should also bear the expense.   Where profit is, loss is hidden near by.

19   **Барышу наклад большой (родной) брат.**   *v.* Б18, П240, У72
[Profit is risk's big (true) brother.]   Nothing ventured, nothing gained.   Nothing stake, nothing draw.

20   **Баснями закрома не наполнятся (соловья не кормят).**   *v.* Б21,В376, М138, С236
Bare words buy no barley.   A thousand words won't fill a bushel.   *SPL.* peculium re non verbis augetur.

21   **Баснями сыт не будешь.**   *v.* Б367, Г184,226,Е45, Р24, С29, С236, У7,Ш14
Fair words fill not the belly.   Fair (fine) words butter no parsnips (cabbage).

22*   **Беда беду накликает (родит).**   *v.* Б25, О48
Trouble breeds trouble.

23*   **Беда - глупости сосед.**
[Trouble is folly's neighbour.]   Folly has a fall before it.

24   **Беда за бедой как волна за волной.**   *v.* Б29,44, О67, Т1, Ч51
[Woe upon woe as a wave upon wave.]   Ill comes on worse's back.

25*   **Беда не приходит одна.**   *v.* Б22,44, О48, П251
Misfortunes never come alone.   *SPL.* nulla calamitas sola.   *Cf.* Shakes.*Ham.*4.7.164: When sorrows come, they come not single spies, But in batallions.

26   **Беда не с бубенцами приходит.**   *v.* Б27
Trouble enters unannounced.

27   **Беда приспела, наперед не сказала.**   *v.* Б26,41, П255
[Trouble appears without prior notice.]   Trouble enters unannounced.   *Cf.* Sorrow comes unsent for.   Sorrow is soon enough when it comes.

28   **Беда приходит пудами а уходит золотниками.**
Mischief comes by the pound and goes away by the ounce.   Misfortunes come on wings and depart on foot.   Ill comes in ells and goes out by inches.

29   **Беда семь бед приводит.**   *v.* Б24, О67, Т1
[One misfortune carries with it seven more.]   One misfortune comes on the neck of another.   *Cf.* He that lives not well one year, sorrows seven after.

30   **Беда сшибши руки ходит.**   *v.* Б43
[Misfortune strikes with swift hands.] Mischief has swift wings. *Cf.* Ill weeds grow apace.

31*   **Бедному везде бедно.**   *v.* Н1
The poor man is aye put to the worst. *Lat.* pauper ubique iacet.

32   **Бедному все в глаза ветер дует.**   *v.* Б31, Н1
[The wind is always blowing in the poor man's eyes.] The poor man is aye put to the worst. The poor suffer all the wrong. *Cf.* Want of money, want of comfort. The wind in one's face makes one wise.

33*   **Бедному жениться - ночь коротка.**
[The night is too brief to warrant marrying poor.] Who marries for love without money has good nights and sorry days.

34   **Бедность и мудрого смиряет.**   *v.* Г222, П308
[Poverty brings even the wise man down.] There is no virtue that poverty destroyeth not. *Cf.* Wisdom without wealth is worthless.

35*   **Бедность не грех (а до греха доводит).**
Poverty is no sin (crime) [but leads to sin (crime).]

36*   **Бедность не порок (стыд).**
Poverty is no vice (shame) (+ but an inconvenience) Poverty is no shame (+ but the being ashamed of it is). *Lat.* Paupertas non est vitium.

37*   **Бедность плачет а богатство скачет.**   *v.* Б287,288
[Poverty laments, wealth dances.] The rich feast, the poor fast; dogs dine, the poor pine.

38   **Бедность учит а счастье портит.**
[Poverty teaches while fortune spoils.] *Cf.* Poverty is the mother of all arts.

39   **Бедный знает и друга и недруга.**   *v.* Д447
Poverty shows us who our friends are and who are our enemies. The rich man knows not his friend.

40*   **Бедный песни поет, а богатый только слушает.**
[The poor sing, the rich listen.] The poor must dance as the rich pipe.

41   **Беду не ждут - она сама приходит.**   *v.* Б27
[Sorrow is not expected - it comes itself.] Sorrow (and ill weather) come(s) unsent for. *Lat.* Mala ultro adsunt.

42   **Беду скоро наживешь да не скоро выживешь.**   *v.* Г271, З115,123, С320
Misfortunes come on wings but depart on foot.

43   **Беды да печали на почтовых примчали.**   *v.* Б30
[Trouble and sorrow travel express.] Mischief has swift wings.

44   **Беды как гряды - считать станешь, устанешь.**   *v.* Б24,25
[Sorrows, like furrows, are too tiresome to count.] A man cannot have but one loss, more will follow.

45   **Беды мучат, да уму учат.**   *v.* В82, Н583,588
Adversity makes men wise. *Cf.* Adversity is the first path to truth. There is no education like adversity.

46* **Бежал от волка, а попал медведю в зубы.** *v.* Б46, И93, О117
[Fled the wolf and fell into the maw of the bear.] From pillar to post.

47* **Бежал от дыма и упал в огонь.** *v.* И76,93, О146
[Out of the smoke and into the fire.]   Out of the frying pan and into the fire.
Gr. καπνόν φεύγων εἰς τὸ πῦρ ἐνέπεσον.   *Lat.* fumum fugiens in ignem incidit.

48* **Без беды друга не узнаешь.** *v.* Д412,419,420, З164
A friend is never known until needed. A friend in need is a friend indeed. Adversity is
the touchstone of friendship.

49* **Без беды и добра не бывает.** *v.* Б35,127, В174,616, Г281,297, Л173, Н73
No pains, no gains. No cross, no crown. The way to bliss lies not on beds of down. No
rose without a thorn.

50* **Без болезни и здоровью не рад.**
Health is not valued till sickness comes.

51* **Без брата проживу, а без соседа не проживу.**
We can live without our friends [brother] **but not our neighbours.**

52 **Без вина правды не скажешь.** *v.* В544
[You will not tell the truth without wine.] In wine there is truth.   *Lat.* in vino veritas.

53 **Без волнения, без заботы, не жди радости от работы.** *v.* Б49
[Without cares, vexation, work yields little satisfaction.]   Never was good work done
without much trouble. *Cf.* Care and diligence bring luck.

54 **Без глаз рожа не пригожа.**
The eye is the pearl of the face.

55 **Без дела жить - только небо коптить.** *v.* Б104,151, В505, О144, С167
[To live idly is to kill time.]   Idle men are dead all their life long. *Cf.* An idle head
is a box for the wind.

56 **Без денег - везде худенек.** *v.* Б273
He that wants money wants everything.   A man without money is no man at all.
Lat. homo sine pecunia est imago mortis.

57* **Без денег и разума нет.**
[No cents, no sense.] *Cf.* He that has money in his purse cannot want a head for his
shoulders.

58 **Без денег на базар не ходят.**
A moneyless man goes fast through market.

59 **Без денег сон крепче.** *v.* Б290, Г243, К278, М166
Little goods, little cares. Much coin, much care. *Lat.* Hor.*Od.*3.16: crescentem
sequitur cura pecuniam.

60 **Без детей горе (сухота) - а с детьми вдвое (перхота).** *v.* Д214,382, Ж35
[Dreary without children, weary with.] *Cf.* Children bring with them innumerable cares.
Children are certain cares but uncertain comforts.

61 **Без друга жить, самому себе постылым быть.** *v.* Ж112,151
[Live without friends and hate yourself.] Life without a friend is death without a witness.

62   **Без друга на сердце вьюга.**   *v.* K9
[Lone man, cold heart.]   Woe to him that is alone.

63   **Без друга сирота, а с другом семьянин.**   *v.* Б224, Д336,450, K234
[Friendless - an orphan, with friends - a family man.]   A good friend is my nearest relation.

64*   **Без дураков скучно.**
More fools, more fun.

65   **Без жены как без шапки (шпаги).**   *v.* H300
[A man without a wife is like a man without his hat (sword).]   No lack to lack a wife.
He that has not got a wife is not yet a complete man.

66   **Без жены прожить - ошибка, без детей - пытка.**
(Без жены - скука, без детей - мука.)   *v.* У33, X57
[Life without a wife is a mistake (dull), but without children, it is an ordeal.]
Cf. Who has no children knows not what is love. It takes children to make a happy home.

67   **Без забора, без запора, не уйдешь от вора.**
[Only locks and fences fend off thieves.]   It's easy to rob an orchard when none keeps it.

68   **Без запасу не станет припасу.**   *v.* Б84,446, З86,89, У35
[No savings, no reserve.]   Provision in season makes a rich house.

69   **Без клещей кузнец что без рук.**   *v.* Б110,123,200
[A blacksmith's forceps are his arms.]   What's a workman without his tools. *Cf.* A tool is but the extension of a man's hand.

70*   **Без копейки рубля нет.**   *v.* Г330, Д164, K167,168
[No *kopek*, no *ruble*.]   Take care of the pence and the pounds will take care of themselves.

71   **Без костей мясо не живет (вешают).**   *v.* Б466, B101
[There's no (weighing) meat without bones.]   Bones bring meat to town. *Cf.* No land without stones, no meat without bones.

72*   **Без кота мышам масленица (раздолье).**   *v.* Г63, K127
When the cat's away, the mice will play. *Lat.* mus debaccatur ubi catus non dominatur.

73   **Без крыльев (хвоста) птица - ком.**   *v.* Б74
[What's a bird without wings.]   No flying without wings.

74   **Без крыльев не летай - упадешь.**   *v.* Б73
[Don't fly without wings, you'll fall.] *Cf. Lat.* Plaut.*Poen.*4.2: sine pennis volare haud facile est. Unused wings cannot soar.

75*   **Без меня меня женили.**   *v.* Б332, C97,121, Ч29
[They married me off without me.] *i.e. decide for someone without asking.* The absent are always wrong. *Cf.*Tennyson *CLB.*17: Their's not to reason why, Their's but to do and die.

76   **Без молока сливок не бывает.**
[No milk, no cream.] *Cf.* Don't expect to enjoy the cream of life if you keep your milk of human kindness bottled up.

77   **Без мужа, жена всегда сирота.**
[Without her husband, a wife's aye an orphan.] If the husband be not at home, there is nobody.

78* **Без муки нет и науки.** *v.* Б93, Д403, Т72, У120
[There is no science without toil.] Much science, much sorrow. *Cf.* No toil, no treasure.

79 **Без надежды что без одежды - и в теплую погоду замерзнешь.** *v.* Г38, П130
[Going hopeless is like going naked - you freeze even in warm weather.] *Cf.* He that lives on hope has a slender diet.

80* **Без накладу барыш не живет.** *v.* Б18, Г61, Д73,246, Л176, К273
Nothing ventured, nothing gained.

81 **Без народа - не воевода.** *v.* Б95,123,200
[Without a people to command, there's no commander.] *Cf.* Like prince, like people.

82 **Без наук как без рук.** *v.* Б69,108,110,123
[Uneducated, unarmed.] Ignorance is blister. *Cf.* Ignorance is a voluntary misfortune.

83* **Без начала и конца не бывает.** *v.* Б471
Where there's no beginning there's no end. Whatever begins also ends. *Cf.* Everything must have a beginning.

84 **Без нужды живет кто деньги бережет.** *v.* Б68, З89, П239, Т55
Of saving comes having.

85 **Без обеда не красна (и) беседа.** *v.* Б113
[Without a meal the talk is lean.] A dinner lubricates business. *Cf.* It is good to be merry at meat (meals).

86 **Без обручьев нет клепкам державы.** *v.* С213
[Without a hoop, rivets have no hold.] For want of a nail the shoe is lost. Thirteen staves and a hoop will not make a barrel. The loss of a nail, the loss of an army.

87 **Без огня овина не высушишь.**
[Without a fire you can't dry the barn.] *Cf.* The fire which lights (warms) us at a distance will burn us when near.

88* **Без одежды но не без надежды.** *v.* Ж29, Н13,33
[Without clothes but not without hope.] Hope is the poor man's bread. *Lat.* spes servat afflictos.

89* **Без одной не сотня.** *v.* В244, И90, П58, 82
[You can't have a hundred without ones.] Many a little makes a mickle. *Cf.* Chauc.*Parsons.T.*362: Many small make a great.

90 **Без осанки и конь корова.**
[Without a carriage, a horse is just like a cow.] *Cf.* If you can't ride a horse, ride a cow. Every horse is an animal but not every animal is a horse. You may know a horse by its harness.

91 **Без отваги нет и браги.** *v.* Т64
[No spunk, no moonshine.] He was a bold man that first ate an oyster.

92* **Без охоты нет работы.**
[No inclination, no occupation.] Interest will not lie.

93* **Без палки нет учения.** *v.* Б78, Ж11, Т72
[No rod, no learning.] Spare the rod and spoil the child. *Cf.* A whip for a fool and a rod for a school is always in good season.

94 **Без пары не живут и гагары.**   *v.* B584
   [Even loons pair off.]   It takes two birds to make a nest.

95 **Без пастуха и овцы не стадо.**   *v.* Б81
   [Without a shepherd the sheep are not a flock.]   *Cf.* It is a sorry (silly) flock where the ewe bears the bell.

96 **Без перевясла и веник рассыпается.**
   [Without a knot a garland comes undone.]   Where the knot is loose, the string slippeth.

97 **Без подвоху (подводу) вор (тать) не крадет.**   *v.* Г49, K251
   [Without a ruse the thief won't steal.]   Show me a liar and I will show you a thief.
   Lat. da mihi mendacem et ego ostendam tibi furem.

98 **Без поджоги и дрова не горят.**
   [Without kindling the logs won't burn.]   Little sticks kindle the fire (great ones put it out).

99 **Без порчи и дела не сделаешь.**   *v.* H314,358, O197, П17
   [Success is impossible without error.]   He who makes no mistakes, makes nothing.
   Cf. Failure teaches success. A hard beginning makes a good ending.

100 **Без правды веку не изживешь.**   *v.* B456, Л103
    [Life is short without truth.]   Lies have short legs (wings).   *Cf.* He that trusts in a lie shall perish in truth.

101 **Без привязи лошадь не будет стоять.**   *v.* 383, H83
    [Unhaltered, a horse won't stay put.]   A boisterous horse must have a rough bridle.

102 **Без причины и прыщ не вскочит.**   *v.* И10
    [There's a reason even for a pimple.]   There is reason in the roasting of eggs.

103* **Без причины ничего не бывает.**   *v.* Ч99
     There is a reason for everything. There's reason in all things.

104 **Без работы день годом станет.**   *v.* Б55, B505, O144, C167
    [Without work, days stretch into years.]   Work makes life pleasant.   *Cf.* †The day is short and the work is long.

105 **Без работы нудно а без денег трудно.**
    [Out of work - a bore; broke - sore.]   *Cf.* Idleness is the key of beggary. Nothing is gained without work.

106* **Без раны зверя не убьешь.**   *v.* B369, Д410, И71, Л54
     [The beast cannot be killed without inflicting a wound.]   Omelettes are not made without the breaking of eggs.

107 **Без рассуждения не делай осуждение.**
    [Do not judge without careful thought.]   He that soon deemeth, shall soon repent.

108 **Без ремесла - без рук.**   *v.* Б82
    [No trade, no arms.]   *Cf.* He that hath no good trade, it is to his loss.

109* **Без смелости не возмешь крепости.**   *v.* C192
     [Fear never stormed a citadel.]   Faint heart never won fair lady.

110   **Без снаряда что без рук.**   *v.* Б69,123,200
     A tool is but the extension of a man's hand.   What's a workman without his tools?

111   **Без сноровки и ложку мимо уха пронесешь.**
     [Unskilled hands can guide a spoon past the ear.] All things require skill but appetite.

112   **Без собаки зайца не поймаешь.**
     [You can't catch a hare without a dog.]   *Cf.* A hare is not caught with a drum.

113*   **Без соли, без хлеба худая беседа.**   *v.* Б85
     [Without a meal the conversation is lean.]   A dinner lubricates business.

114*   **Без соли стол кривой.**
     [A table is incomplete without salt.]   Salt seasons all things.

115   **Без соли хлебать, что немилого целовать.**
     [Food without salt is like a kiss without love.] An apple pie without cheese is like a kiss without a squeeze.

116*   **Без смерти не умрешь.**   *v.* П230, Р39
     No man dies before his time.   *Cf.* Death is but death, and all in time shall die.

117*   **Без спотычки и конь не пробежить.**   *v.* И35, К165
     A horse stumbles that has four legs.   *Cf.* Even Homer sometimes nods.

118   **Без старых не проживешь.**
     [You cannot get by without elders.]   An old man in a house is a good sign.

119   **Без стыда лица (без позору рожи) не износишь.**
     [No shame (disgrace), no wrinkles.]   *Cf.* There is never a foul face, but there's a foul fancy. *Lat.* Juv.*Sat.*6.199: facies tua comptat annos.

120   **Без счету и денег нету.**   *v.* С333
     [No accounts, no money]   Misreckoning (wrong reckoning) is no payment.

121*   **Без терпения нет умения (учения).**
     [No skill without patience.]   *Cf.* Only those who have the patience to do simple things perfectly will acquire the skill to do difficult things easily.

122   **Без толку молитесь, без меры согрешаете.**
     [Pointless to pray when you sin without measure.] He has much prayer and little devotion.

123   **Без топора не плотник, без иглы не портной.**   *v.* Б69,81,110,200
     [What's a carpenter without his bench-axe or a tailor without his needle?]   What's a workman without his tools?

124*   **Без тройцы дом не строится.**   *v.* Б263,Т71
     [It takes three go's to build a house.] *said to justify doing something a third time.* Good things come in threes.

125*   **Без труда и отдых не сладок.**
     [Without toil, even leisure is no pleasure.]   Of sufferance cometh ease (rest).

126*   **Без труда не вынешь рыбку из пруда.**   *v.* М213
     [Without toil, you cannot angle the fish from the stream.] A cat in gloves catches no mice.   *Lat.* sine labore non erit panis in ore.

127* **Без (хорошего) труда нет добра (плода).**   *v.* Б49, В616, Г281,297, Л173, Н73
No pains, no gains. Good things are hard. *Gr.* Pl.*Crat*.1.384A: χαλεπὰ τὰ καλά.

128 **Без ужина подушка в головах вертится.**   *v.* С336
Who goes to bed supperless, all night tumbles and tosses. *Cf.* When a man sleeps, his head is in his stomach.

129 **Без ужина спать - собачья стать.**
[Go to bed supperless and arise like a dog.] *Cf.* Who goes to bed supperless, all night tumbles and tosses.

130 **Без ума голова - кочка.**   *v.* Г212
[An empty head is just a bump on a log.] You have a head and so has a pin (nail). *Cf.* Use your head for something besides a hat rack.

131* **Без ума голова ногам покою не дает.**   *v.* Г134
If you don't use your head, you must use your feet (legs) (heels). Little wit in the head makes much work for the feet (heel). Little wit makes mickle travel.

132 **Без ума голова - пивный котел.**   *v.* Г204
An idle head is a box for the wind.

133 **Без ума житье - рай.**
Ignorance is bliss.

134 **Без ума не в пользу и сума.**   *v.* Б289, Д149,504, У118
[What good is a purse without wit.] Better an empty purse than an empty head. *Prov*.16.16: Without wisdom, wealth is worthless.

135 **Без ума ни топором тяпать, ни ковырять лапоть.**   *v.* Д149
[Neither wield an axe nor weave a sandal without thinking.] Want of wit is worse than want of gear. It's all in knowing how. *Cf.* A steady head means a good job.

136 **Без ума проколотишься, а без хлеба не проживешь.**   *v.* Н160
[You'll muddle through without a brain, but without bread you can't survive.] Better fed than taught.

137 **Без ума пьет, без угла живет.**
[Mindless drinking, homeless living.] *Cf.* A drunkard's purse is a bottle.

138 **Без ума суму таскать, а с умом деньги считать.**
[Fools beg and wise men count money.] Better wit than wealth.

139 **Без ума торговать - только деньги терять (долги наживать).**   *v.* Г137, У25
A fool and his money are soon parted.

140 **Без умения и сило ни причем.**   *v.* И49, Н410, Р28, С120
Skill will accomplish what is denied to force. Wisdom goes beyond strength. It's not strength but art that obtains the prize. Force without forecast is of little avail.

141 **Без формы кирпичу не быть, без расчета - делу.**
[A brick requires a mold, an enterprise - a plan.] An examined enterprise goes boldly.

142 **Без хвоста и ворона некрасива.**   *v.* В310
[Even a crow is ugly without its tail.] Fine (fair) feathers make fine birds (fair fowls).

143 **Без хлеба и медом сыт не будешь.**
[Even honey alone cannot satisfy without bread.] *Cf.* Bread is the staff of life.

144 **Без хлеба куска везде тоска.** *v.* Б679, Г224, М196
[Without bread, there is but grief everywhere.] All griefs with bread are less.

145* **Без хлеба не жить, да не от хлеба жить.**
Man must eat to live but not live to eat.

146 **Без хлопот - зажать лучше рот.** *v.* В348, Н257
[No cares - better keep your mouth shut.] Do not cry roast meat.

147* **Без хозяина дом сирота.** *v.* В615, Д379, Н289, П128
[The master away, the house is an orphan.] The master absent and the house is dead.

148 **Без языка и колокол нем (колокольчик ни к чему).**
[Even a bell is dumb (useless) without its clapper.] *Cf.* A cracked bell is never sound.

149 **Безгрешного человека на свете нет.** *v.* И39, Ч30
[No man on earth is free of sin.] *Lat.* peccare humanum est. None of us are perfect.

150* **Безделье - мать пороков.** *v.* Л52, П225
Idleness is the mother (root) of all evil (sin) (vice).

151 **Безделье - сестра болезни.** *v.* Б55
[Idleness is illness' sister.] *Cf.* Sloth, like rust, consumes faster than labour wears.

152 **Бездельнику и чужая смерть - праздник.** *v.* Б205, К252, Л44
[For the sluggard even someone's death means a day off.] Idle folks lack no excuses.
Cf. Every day is a holiday with sluggards.

153 **Бездетной женщине колыбель не утеха.** *v.* У45
[A cradle is litttle comfort to a childless woman.] *Cf.* Name not a rope in the house of
a hanged man.

154 **Бездетный умрет - и собака не взвоет.** *v.* Ж112
[Die childless and not even a dog will stir.] *Cf.* Life without a friend is death without a witness.

155 **Бездна бездну призывает.**
*Psalms.*42.7: Deep calleth unto deep.

156 **Бездомного осла съедят волки.** *v.* Б187, У105
[A homeless ass will fall prey to wolves.] The lone sheep is in danger of the wolf.

157* **Бездонной кадки водой не наполнишь.** *v.* В128,320, К22, Н362, Р56
[You can't fill a bottomless tub.] *Cf.* Carry water in a sieve. *EA.* cribro aquam haurire.

158 **Бездушное слово сердце заморозит.** *v.* С180, Я22
[Callous words chill the heart.] *Cf.* Words cut (hurt) more than swords.

159 **Беззаконным закон не писан.** *v.* †378, †П224
[Laws are not written for the lawless.] *Cf.* The more laws, the more offenders.
Much law, little justice. Ambition obeys no law.

160 **Безмену пест не замена.**
[The pestle is no substitute for the balance.]

Force is no argument.   *Cf.* The balance distinguishes not between gold and lead.

161   **Безмерная хвала чести вредит.**   *v.* П197
[Excessive praise injures honour.] Praise none too much, for all are fickle. *Cf.* Praise to the face is open disgrace.

162   **Безобычному человеку с людьми не жить.**   *v.* Б230, Л112
[Ill-mannered people must live alone.]   The best remedy against an ill man is much ground between.

163* **Безрогая корова хоть шишкою боднет.**   *v.* Б298, Н277
[A hornless cow will still bump you with its knobs.] *Cf.* A curst cow has short horns.

164   **Безумен с ученым не пирует.**   *v.* Д481, †И108
[Fools and wise men feast not together.] *Cf.* Fools make feasts and wise men eat them.

165   **Безумного волей не научишь.**
[Will alone cannot teach the fool.] *Cf.* He that is born a fool is never cured.

166   **Безумный и разумных ума лишает.**   *v.* Г142, Д501, И17, О33, С9
[A fool strips even the wise of reason.]   One fool makes many. *Lat.* unius dementia dementes efficit multos.

167* **Безумие и на мудрого бывает.**   *v.* Б420,В160,353, Е9, И37, Н24,246
No man is wise at all times.   None is so wise but the fool overtakes him. Everyman is a fool sometimes (and none at all times). *Lat.* Plin.*H.N.*7.40.2: nemo mortalium omnibus horis sapit.

168* **Бей быка что не дает молока.**   *v.* Д364, Н399, О150, Я3
[Beat the bull for not giving milk.]   To ask pears of an elm tree.

169* **Бей в решето когда в сито не пошло.**   *v.* Г17, Н224. Х78
[Try a larger mesh if the sieve is to fine.]   If at once you don't succeed, try and try again.

170   **Бей галку (сороку) и ворону,   добьешься и до ясного сокола (белого лебедя).**
[Set your sights on daws (magpies) and crows, hawks   *v.* П56,150, Х27
(white swans) will follow.] Use the little to get to the big. *Cf.* He will shoot higher who shoots at the moon (sun) than he who aims at a tree. Aim for a star, even though you hit a cow on the hillside. You can't kill an elephant by shooting at a mousehole.

171* **Бей своих и чужие бояться будут.**   *v.* Г329
[Spare not your nearest and all others will fear.]   A dog scourged can bid a lion fear. When the dog is beaten, the lion is tamed.   *Lat.* quando canis flagellatur, leo domesticatur. He threatens many that injures one.

172   **Бел снег, да ногами топчут - черен мак, да люди едят.**   *v.* Б344, Н226
[White snow gets trampled and black poppies get eaten.]   Spice is black but it has a sweet smack. *Cf.* A black plum (raisin)(grape) is as sweet as a white.

173   **Бела береста да деготь черен.**   *v.* К173, М208
[White birchbark produces black tar.]   White silver draws black lines. A black hen lays a white egg.

174* **Белая деньга про черный день.**   *v.* Б180, В83, О180, Х60
Lay up for a rainy day.   Keep something for the sore foot.

175* **Белая стена дуракам бумага.**
A white wall is a fool's paper.

176 **Белила не делают мила.** *v.* Н238
[Whiting is not righting.]   All that glitters is not gold.

177 **Белые ручки чужие труды любят.** *v.* М213

178* **Белый свет не клином сошелся.** *v.* С52

179* **Белый свет не околица, а пустая речь не пословица.** *v.* Г135,204, О55, П183
[The wide world's no village, nor empty talk a proverb.] A proverb comes not from nothing.

180 **Береги денежку про черный день.** *v.* Б174, В83, О180
Lay up (keep something) for a rainy day.

181* **Береги платье снову а честь смолоду.** *v.* Ч46, У123
[Preserve a dress when new and honour from youth.] Learn young, learn fair. The mark must be made in youth. *Cf.* Youth must store up, age must use.

182 **Береги чужое, а свое - как знаешь.** *v.* О173
[Take care of others' belongings but do what you like with your own.] Be bold with what is thine own.

183* **Берегись бед пока их нет.** *v.* К221, О112,141, Р33
[Prepare for trouble ere it comes.] Advisement is good before the need. Prevent rather than repent. A stitch in time saves nine.

184 **Берегись козла спереди, коня сзади, а лихого человека со всех сторон.** *v.* Н213
[Trust not a goat before, a horse from behind, and an evil man from all sides.] *Cf.* Beware of a mule's hind foot, a dog's tooth, and a woman's tongue. Trust not a horse's heel nor a dog's tooth.

185* **Береженая вещь два века живет.** *v.* Б415, С269
[An object cared for has two lives.] An old cart well used may outlast a new one abused.

186 **Бережение лучше вороженья.** *obs.* *v.* О141, П226
[Provision is better than prediction.] *Cf.* Prevention is better than cure. Forewarned, forearmed.

187 **Береженого барашка волк не съест.** *v.* Б156, О22, У105
[The wolf won't eat a guarded sheep.] The lone sheep is in danger of the wolf. Wolves rend sheep when shepherds fail.

188* **Береженого (и) Бог бережет.** *v.* Б265, К295
God (heaven) helps them that help themselves. *Lat.* dii facientes adiuvant.

189* **Бережливость лучше прибытка.**
[Prevention (care) is better than profit.] Providence is better than rent.

190 **Бережливость - не скупость.** *v.* Т55
[Thrift is not avarice.] *Cf.* Thrift is a great revenue. *Lat.* Cic.*Paradox*.6.3.49: magnum vectigal parsimonia.

191 **Березовицы на грош, а лесу и рублем не уплатишь.** *v.* З22, О15
[A penny's worth of birch sap at the cost of a forest.] *Cf.* Penny wise and pound foolish.

192* **Берет руками а отдает ногами.**   *v.* В31, Д13,71, К170, С164
[Takes with the hands and returns with the feet.] *i.e. easy at taking but difficult at returning.* Some have a short arm for giving and a long arm for getting. *Cf.* Greedy folks have long arms. Lend sitting and you will run to collect.

193 **Берешь - об отдаче помни.**   *v.* В293, К31
[When you borrow, remember to return.] Pay with the same dish you borrow.

194* **Бери жену не дородную, а природную.**   *v.* Б431, Ж48, Л142, Н229
Better a portion (treasure) in a wife than with a wife.

195 **Берись дружно - не будет грузно.**
Good will and welcome is the best cheer. *Gr.* Ξενίων δέ τε θυμὸς ἄριστος.

196 **Берись за то чему ты сроден (за то к чему ты годен).**   *v.* П289, Т74
[Do what comes natural.] He that follows nature is never out of his way. Go not against the grain.

197 **Берут завидки за чужие пожитки.**   *v.* З64, У27
[People envy others' gains.] *Cf.* Envy never dies.

198 **Бес беса (и) хвалит (а людям беды ладит).**   *v.* Д469,471
[One devil praises another (and raises hell for people).] One fool praises another. *Cf.* The devil is a busy bishop in his own diocese.

199* **Беседа дорогу коротает (а песня - работу).**   *v.* В213, Р22, У103
[Talk shortens a journey (as a song eases work).] No road is long with good company. A merry companion is a wagon in the way. *Lat.* facetus comes in via pro vehiculo est.

200 **Бескосый не косец.**   *v.* Б69,81,110,123
[No scythe, no mower.] What's a workman without his tools?

201 **Беспечальному сон сладок.**
[Sweet, the sleep of the innocent.] The sleep of the just.

202* **Бесплодная курица много кудахчет.**   *v.* Е29, К330
[The barren hen cackles the most.] You cackle often, but never lay an egg. *Cf.* Empty barrels make the most noise.

203 **Бесстрашны сердца у тех кто трудятся сообща.**   *v.* Д441, Е31, С213
[They are intrepid who make common cause.] Union is strength.

204 **Бесстыжему город велик.**

[The city is great for the shameless.] He who is without shame, all the world is his.

205 **Бесстыжему каждый день праздник.**   *v.* Б152, Л44
Every day is a holiday with sluggards.

206 **Бестолков да памятлив.**
[No brains, but a good memory.] *Cf.* A man of great memory without learning has a distaff and spindle and no stuff to spin.

207 **Бестолкового учить - только себя трудить.**
[Teach a fool and put yourself out for nothing.] He that teaches a scorner, does an injury to himself.

208 **Бесцельно сил на ветер не пускай.**
  Don't waste your strength on the wind. Puff not against the wind.

209 **Бесчестье в бороду не упрячешь.**   *v.* П215
  [You cannot hide dishonour in your beard.] *Cf.* A good heart cannot lie.

210* **Бесчестье хуже смерти.**   *v.* Г289
  Better death than dishonour.

211* **Бешена собака и хозяина кусает.**   *v.* З125, И139
  The mad dog bites his master.

212 **Бешеному (дитяти) ножа не давати.**
  Children (and fools) must not play with edged tools.

213 **Бивщись с козой (коровой) - не удой (молоко).**
  [You cannot milk a goat (cow) by beating it.] You may beat a horse till he be sad and a cow till she be mad.

214* **Бил дед жабу грозясь на бабу.**
  [He beat the toad out of wrath at the woman.] He that cannot beat the horse beats the saddle.

215 **Бил жену денечек, сам плакал годочек.**   *v.* Г167
  [He beat his wife one day then cried alone all year.] *Cf.* He that passes judgment as he runs, overtakes repentance.

216 **Бился, колотился, а доброй жены не добился.**
  [Though he struggled and pined, a good wife he couldn't find.] It's hard to wive and thrive both in a year.

217* **Бит небитого на руках носит.**   *v.* З2, Л145, О92
  [The veteran carries the rookie.] Experience is the best teacher.

218* **Битая посудина два века живет.**   *v.* Л82, С133,160
  Ill vessels seldom miscarry. Nought is never in danger. *Lat.* malum vas non frangitur.

219 **Битого, пролитого да прожитого не воротишь.**   *v.* А29, О4,85, П27,278,279, Ч93,105
  [What's broken, spilt or done can ne'er be undone.] It is no use crying over spilt milk.

220* **Битому коту лишь лозу покажи.**   *v.* Б349, Н55
  A beaten dog escheweth the whip. *Cf.* A scalded cat (dog) fears cold water.

221 **Благодеяние свершить никогда не поздно.**
  It's never too late to do good. *Cf.* †Good that comes too late is as good as nothing.

222 **Благословенный баран лучше неблагословенного быка.**   *v.* И55
  [Better a blessed lamb than an unblessed bull.] Better (do) a little good than a great dealbad. *Cf.* Better some of a pudding than none of a pie.

223 **Ближе живешь - уреживаешь, дальше живешь - учащиваешь.**
  [You make yourself scarce when near and a frequent visitor when afar.] *Cf.* Distance lends enchantment. He goes far that never returns.

224* **Ближний сосед лучше дальней родни.**   *v.* Б231, Д336
  A near friend is better than a far-dwelling kinsman. Better a neighbour near than a brother far. A friend at hand is better than a relative at a distance.

225*   Ближний счет - дальняя дружба.   *v.* Д44, К175, С332, Ч10
Short reckonings (accounts) make long friends.

226*   Ближнюю дорогу вдалеке не ищут.   *v.* Д50, Н505
Don't go round the world for a shortcut.

227   Ближняя - ворона, дальняя - соколина.   *v.* Д57, С168
[A crow nearby, a falcon afar.] Far fowls have fair feathers.

228   Ближняя копеечка дороже дальнего рубля.   *v.* Б417
[Better a *kopek* in hand than a ruble afar.] A penny at a pinch is worth a pound.
Cf. Better is one *accipe*, than twice to say *dabo tibi*.

229   Ближняя родня - на одном солнышке онучи сушили.   *v.* Д450, К234
[Close kin dried clothes on the same line.] *Cf.* A good friend is my nearest relation.

230   Ближняя собака скорее укусит.   *v.* Б162,244
[The nearer dog is likelier to bite.] *Cf.* †Dogs that bark at a distance bite not at hand.

231*   Ближняя соломка лучше дальнего сенца.   *v.* Б224,232, Д393, Ж169, Л152, С122
[Better a nearby straw than a distant haystack.] A bird in the hand's worth two in the bush.

232   Ближняя хаянка лучше дальней хваленки.   *v.* Б231
[Better an insult near than a compliment far.] A friend's frown is better than a foe's smile.

233   Близ границы не строй светлице.   *v.* П233, Р52
[Don't build your cottage near a border.] Choose not a house near an inn or in a corner.

234   Близ норы лиса на промыслы не ходит.   *v.* Х106
The fox preys farthest from home.

235   Близ царя - близ смерти.
Nearest the king (highest in court), nearest the gallows (widdie). *SPL.* procul ab Iove, procul a fulmine. potentum amicitiae pericolosae.

236*   Близко церкви да далеко от Бога.   *v.* Г8, И122, Н434, О73
The nearer the church, the farther from God.

237*   Близок локоть, да не укусишь. *v.*   Л105

238   Блин не клин, брюха не расколет.
[A *blin* won't split your belly like a spit.] *said as an excuse for eating.* *Cf.* †Too much pudding will choke a dog.

239   Блин съешь, а два вымечешь.   *v.* А21
[Eat one *blin,* get two ready.] New meat begets new appetite. Appetite comes with eating.

240   Блоха блоху не ест.   *v.* В389,435, И21, К155, С221
[Flea does not eat flea.] Dog does not eat dog. *Lat.* canis caninum non edit.
Cf. Juv.*Sat.*15.160: parcit cognatis maculis similis fera.

241   Блоха проскачила, стол повалила.
[A flea skipped by and tripped the table.] *Cf.* Like a bull in a China shop.

242* **Блоху на цепь приковали.**
[To rivet a chain to a flea.] Flay a flea for the hide and tallow. *Cf.* To square the circle.

243 **Блудливая свекровь и невестке не верит.**
[A licentious mother-in-law mistrusts the bride.] The mother-in-law remembers not that she was a daughter-in-law.

244 **Блудливой чушке полено на шею.**   *v.* Б101, З383
[Yoke the errant pig to a stake.] A mischievous dog must be tied short.

245 **Блюди хлеб на обед (про еду), а слово на (про) ответ(а).**   *v.* В494
[Keep your bread for lunch and your words for talk.] *Cf.* First think and then speak. Speak by the card.

246 **Бог ведает кто как обедает.**   *v.* 38
[God shall determine how men dine.] *Cf.* They are well guided that God guides.

247 **Бог да город, черт да деревня.**
[God (made) the city and the devil the country.] *Cf.* †God made the country and man made the town. †*Lat.* Varro: divina natura dedit agros, ars humana aedificavit urbes.

248* **Бог дал, Бог и взял.**
The Lord giveth and the Lord taketh away.

249* **Бог дал два уха а один язык.**   *v.* И11, У97
[God gave (man) two ears and one tongue.] Nature has given us two ears, two eyes, and but one tongue. *Cf.* Man was born with two eyes and only one tongue in order that he may see twice as much as he says.

250 **Бог дал родню а черт вражду.**
[God chooses your relations and the devil your enemies.] *Cf.* He to whom God gave no sons, the devil gives nephews.

251* **Бог даст, (и) в окно подаст.**   *v.* 38, Ч61
[What God gives He serves through the window.] *i.e. "on a silver platter."* God's always opening his hand. *Cf.* Whom God loves, his bitch brings forth pigs.

252* **Бог даст день, даст и пищу.**   *v.* Д38, Н28, Р63
[God has given the day and will provide the bread thereof.] God never sends mouth but he sends meat. *SPL.* vitae dator et dator escae est. *Cf.* Have God, have all.

253 **Бог долго ждет, да больно бьет.**
[God waits long and strikes strong.] God comes with leaden feet but strikes with iron hands. God's mill grinds slow but sure. *Gr.* Sext.Emp. ὀψὲ ϑεῶν ἀλέουσι μύλοι,ἀλέουσι δὲ λεπτά.

254 **Бог дурака поваля кормит.**
[God jostles but feeds the fool.] God builds the nest of the blind bird.

255 **Бог лучше знает что дать, чего не дать.**
[God knows best what to give and not to give.] God complains not, but does what is fitting.

256 **Бог любит смирение.**
[God loves the meek.] *Cf. Matt.*5.5: Blessed are the meek, for they shall inherit the earth.

257 **Бог напитал, никто не видал (а кто видел, тот не обидел).**   *obs.*

[God hath nourished and none hath seen (but whosoever hath seen, complained not.] *archaic; said jocularly after meals.* Cf. All good and God say Amen.

258   **Бог не без милости (казак не без счастья).**   **(Бог милостив.)**
[God is not unmerciful (and a Cossack not unlucky).] **The Lord is merciful.**

259*   **Бог (Господь) не выдаст, свинья не съест.**
[The swine won't eat what God won't provide.] *i.e. things work out in the end.* Nothing with God is accidental. All is for the best.

260*   **Бог по силе крест налагает.**   *v.* H28
God shapes the back for the burden. God sendeth cold after clothes. God sends men cloth according to their cold. God tempers the wind to the shorn lamb.

261   **Бог пугает громом, черт рогом, а поп снова Богом, и так без конца.**   *v.* Г91
[God instils fear with thunder, the devil with his horns, the preacher with God, and so it goes without end.] *Cf.* Danger past, God is forgotten.

262   **Бог сотворил два зла - приказного и козла.**
[God made two evils: tax collectors and goats.] *Cf.* Nothing's certain but death and taxes.

263*   **Бог троицу любит.**   *v.* Б124, Т71
All good things come in threes. *Lat.* omne trinum perfectum.

264*   **Бог шельму (плута) метит.**   *Cf.* †Wickedness with beauty is the devil's hook baited.
[God marks the wicked.]

265   **Бог-то Бог, да и сам не будь плох.**   *v.* Б188,297, К295, H6
Pray to God, but keep hammering (but hammer away). *Cf.* Work as if everything depended on you, pray as if everything depended on God.

266   **Богат дивится - чем голь живится.**
Little knows the fat man what the lean man thinks. One half the world doesn't know how the other half lives.

267*   **Богат, что церковная мышь.**
Poor (hungry) as a churchmouse.

268   **Богата, хоть дурака, всяк почитает.**   *v.* Г33, Д178
[Even a fool is respected if he's rich.] Wealth makes worship. *Cf.* Money will do more than my lord's letter. Who has a full purse never wanted a friend.

269   **Богатого и вчуже знают, убогий и в своих невидим.**   *v.* Д184,186,447
[A rich man is known abroad while a poor man is unnoticed even at home.] *Lat.* Ov.*A.A.*2.276: dummodo sit dives, barbarus ipse placet. Everyone's akin to the rich man.

270   **Богатого от тороватого не отличишь.**
[You can't tell the rich from the liberal.] *Cf.* The prodigality of the rich is the providence of the poor. Generosity is more charitable than wealth. †Poor and liberal, rich and covetous.

271   **Богатого по отчеству, убогого по прозвищу.**   *v.* H1
[Address the rich with respect, the poor with any sobriquet.] *Cf.* Wealth makes worship.

272   **Богатому богатство и вяжется.**   *v.* Д173,183, К164
The rich get richer. *Cf.* Money draws (begets)(breeds)(gets) money.

273* **Богатому везде дом.**   *v.* А16, Б56
    Money makes a man free (recommends a man) everywhere.

274* **Богатому завсе праздник.**   *v.* Б205
    [Every day is a holiday for the rich.] The rich man has the world by the tail. *Cf.* Rich
    men may have what they will.

275 **Богатому и в раю тесно.**   *v.* Д35, Ж3, Л92, М128
    [A rich man finds even heaven cramped.] *Cf.* Abundance of things engenders
    disdainfulness.

276 **Богатому не спится, богатый вора боится.**   *v.* Б279,290, Д152, К278, М166
    [A rich man cannot sleep for fear of thieves.] Little wealth, little care. Small riches have
    most rest.

277* **Богатому телята, бедному ребята.**   *v.* У5

278* **Богатство добыть - и братство забыть.**
    [Get rich and forget brotherhood.] The beggar ennobled does not know his own kinsman.

279 **Богатство и спокойствие редко живут вместе.**   *v.* Б276
    [Wealth and peace are seldom bedfellows.] *Cf.* Riches and cares are inseparable. Wealth
    and power don't give peace of mind. If we have not the world's wealth, we have the
    world's ease.

280 **Богатство родителей - порча детям.**   *v.* Г140
    [Wealthy parents - spoiled children.] The abundance of money ruins youth.

281 **Богатство - скор путь на зло.**   *v.* Д150
    [Wealth is the quick road to evil.] More money - more sin. Muck and money go together.

282 **Богатство ум рождает, а бедность последний отнимает.**   *v.* Д177
    [Wealth engenders wit, poverty robs the last of it.] A rich man's foolish sayings pass for
    wise ones. Wealth makes wit waver. *Cf.* Bought wit is best.

283 **Богатство человека от смерти не избавит.**   *v.* Б310, З114
    [Wealth cannot bribe death.] Wealth can buy no health. *Cf.* Poverty is the mother of
    health. There is a remedy for all things but death.

284* **Богатством ума не купишь.**   *v.* Д505, Н291, У118
    Better wit than wealth. *Cf.* It's not wealth but wisdom that makes a man rich.

285 **Богатую взять - станет попрекать.**   *v.* Ж48, Л142
    [Marry for riches and reap reproaches.] A great dowry is a bed full of brambles. *Cf.* He
    that marries for wealth sells his liberty.

286* **Богаты не будем а сыты будем.**   *v.* Н447, Т56,59, Х76
    He is rich enough who lacks not bread. The greatest wealth is contentment with little.
    Enough is great riches.

287* **Богатый бедного не разумеет.**   *v.* Б288
    [The rich don't understand the poor.] Poverty and wealth do not agree.

288* **Богатый бедному не брат.**   *v.* Б37,287,350, Д401
    [A rich man is no brother to the poor man.] *Cf.* †Poverty and wealth are twin sisters.

289   **Богатый без ума - туло без головы.**   *v.* Б134, Г140, Д149, Н291, У118
[Mindless wealth is a headless torso.] Without wisdom, wealth is worthless. *Cf.* Nobility without ability is like pudding wanting suet.

290*   **Богатый всегда в страхе.**   *v.* Б59,276, Г243, Д179, К278, М166
[The rich are always in fear.] Much coin, much care.

291   **Богатый золото не ест, а бедный камень гложет.**   *v.* Б293
[The rich man cannot eat his gold but the poor man must gnaw at a stone.] *Cf.* Poor men seek meat for their stomachs, rich men stomach for their meat.

292   **Богатый и в будни пирует, а бедный и в праздник горюет.**
[The rich feast on weekdays whilst the poor hunger even on holidays.] *Cf.* The rich man may dine when he will, the poor man when he may.

293*   **Богатый как хочет, а бедный как может.**   *v.* Б291, Ж117
Rich men may have what they will poor men what they can.

294*   **Богатый на деньги, голь на выдумки.**
[The rich man accomplishes with money what the poor man does through craft.] He that have no honey in his pot, let him have it in his mouth.

295   **Богатый совести не купит, а свою погубит.**   *v.* Г32, Ч56
[The rich man may only ruin, not buy, a clean conscience.] Riches and virtue do not often keep each other company. *Cf.* Honour and profit lie not in one sack.

296   **Богатый, что бык рогатый - в тесные ворота не влезет.**
[A rich man, like a horned steer, won't fit through a narrow gate.] *Cf. Mark* 10.25: It is easier for the camel to go through an eye of a needle than for the rich man to enter into the kingdom of God.

297*   **Богу молись, а сам трудись.**   *v.* Б265, Ж16, Н6,119
[Pray to God, but continue to work.] Trust in God and do something. *Cf.* Trust in God but keep your powder dry. God gives the milk, but not the pail. Get thy spindle and distaff ready, and God will send the flax.

298*   **Бодливой корове Бог рог не дает.**   *v.* Б163, Н277, С329
[God doesn't bestow horns upon an ill-tempered cow.] Curst cow has short horns.

299*   **Божбой прав не будешь.**   *v.* Б313, Д407, П208, Ш13
[Swearing will not make you right.] *Cf.* He who swears, swears in vain. Swear till one is black (blue) in the face.

300   **Бойко наскочил, да напоролся на копыл.**   *v.* В287, Г90, З103, Н155,223, П188,202,
[He bolted boldly but ran on a stake.]   С155,159
Hasty climbers have sudden falls. *Cf.* Haste may trip up its own heels.

301*   **Бойся козы что базар повидала.**
[Beware the goat that's been to market.] Where an ass falls, there he'll never fall again.

302   **Бойся лисьего раскаяния и жалоб плута.**   *v.* П146
[Beware a fox's remorse and a knave's lament.] When the fox preaches, beware of your geese.

303   **Болезнь входит пудами а выходит золотниками.**   *v.* Б304
A man is not so soon healed as hurt. *Plan.* 1.29: εἴσοδος νόσου ἐν σάκκῳ, ἔξοδος δὲ βελόνῃ. *Lat.* citius venit malum quam revertitur.

304* **Болезнь к нам верхом, а от нас пешком.**   *v.* Б42,303, Г271, З123
        Diseases come on horseback but depart on foot.

305* **Болезнь человека не красит.**
        [Man is not embellished by disease.] *Cf.* Sickness shows (tells) us what we are.

306 **Боль без языка, а сказывается.**
        [Pain has no voice yet is heard.] *Cf.* Sorrow makes silence her best orator. Small pain is
        eloquent.

307 **Боль отбудешь и так помрешь.**   *v.* О155
        [Though you recover, you'll still die.] *Cf.* Death defies the doctor.

308 **Боль приживчива, приурочлива.**
        [Pain endures and inures.] What pains us, trains us. What can't be cured must be endured.

309* **Больной от могилы бежит, а здоровый в могилу спешит.**
        [The sick run from the grave, but the healthy run to it.] *Cf.* Old men go to death, death
        comes to young men.

310* **Больному и золотая кровать не поможет.**   *v.* Б283, З114
        [Not even a bed of gold can help the sick.] *Cf.* Health is better than wealth.

311* **Больны раны на своих плечах.**   *v.* В657, К10, Н162, П300
        [One's own wounds always hurt more.] Everyone can master a grief but he that has it.
        Cf. Everyone thinks his sack heaviest.

312 **Большая лошадь хозяину не ко двору - травы недостанет.**   *v.* Т17
        [A horse that's too big for the yard leaves no grass.] *Cf.* To a greedy eating horse, a
        short halter.

313 **Большая река течет спокойно, умный человек говорит без крика.**   *v.* Б299,В164,
        [Great rivers flow quietly, wise men speak softly.]   Г136,П208, Ш13
        Striking manners are bad manners. *Cf.* Soft words and hard arguments.

314 **Большая рыба маленькую целиком глотает.**   *v.* К249, Н96, Р89
        The great fish eat up the small. *Lat.* piscem vorat maior minorem.

315 **Большая сыть брюху вредит.**
        [Overindulgence is bad for the belly.] Gluttony kills more than the sword. *Lat.* plures
        necat gula quam gladius.

316* **Больше верь делам нежели словам.**   *v.* Г185, Д117,294, М60, С206
        [Trust in deeds rather than words.] Judge a man by his deeds, not by his words. Deeds,
        not words.

317* **Больше верь своим очам нежели чужим речам.**   *v.* Г113, Л123,146, Н215, О194
        [Trust your own eyes more than others' words.] It is better to trust the eye than the ear.
        Cf. Believe only half of what you see and nothing that you hear.

318* **Больше говоришь (жить), больше грешишь (грешить).**   *v.* В357, Г176, Л90, М61,
        [Talk (live) much, sin more.] Talk much and err much.   О196

319 **Больше дерутся так смирнее живут.**   *v.* М90
        [The more they fight, the more peaceably they live.] The quarrel of lovers is the renewal
        of love.

320* Больше друзей - больше и врагов.   *v.* Д446
      [More friends, more foes.] He makes no friend who never made a foe. *Cf.* He who has many friends, has no friends.

321* Больше (много) знать так меньше спать.   *v.* М109, Н149, С34
      [Know more and sleep less.] Much learning, much sorrow. *Cf.* Wise fear begets care.

322* Больше плачешь, меньше скачешь.
      [The more you cry, the less you dance.] *Cf.* Shakes.*AWEW*.1.1.48: excessive grief is the enemy of the living.

323* Больше почет, больше хлопот.   *v.* В234, Н29, Ч7
      Great honours are great burdens. *SPL.* onus est honos. *Cf.* High places have their precipices.

324* Больше слушай, меньше говори.   *v.* М21
      Hear much, speak little.

325   Больше той любви не бывает, как друг за друга умирает.
      John 15.13: Greater love hath no man than this, that a man may lay down his life for his friend(s). *Cf.* †They love too much that die for love.

326* Большие порядки доводят до больших беспорядков.   *v.* В675, С319
      [Great orders lead to great disorders.] The greater the man, the greater the crime. Great fortune brings with it great misfortune.

327   Большого пламени не задуешь а пуще раздуешь.
      [Blowing will not extinguish, but only fan a great flame.] *Cf.* †A little wind kindles, much puts out the fire.

328   Большое вяканье доводит до даканья.
      [Much chatter leads to blabber.] Chatting to chiding is not worth a chute.

329   Большой болтун, большой врун.   *v.* Б338, Г184, Д210
      [Great talkers are great liars.] Great talkers, little doers. In many words, the truth goes by.

330* Большой вор малого воришку вешает.   *v.* А18, З75, Н268
      Great thieves hang little ones.

331   Большой вырос а ума не вынес.   *v.* Г209
      [Grown great in body but not in mind.] Seldom is a long man wise.

332   Большой меньшего не дожидается.   *v.* Г216, С96,117, У54
      [The greater waits not for the lesser.] *Cf.* The tail does not shake the dog.

333* Большому - большая дорога.   *v.* Б336, В243, К68,321
      [A great road for a great man.] *Cf.* A great shoe fits not a little foot.

334* Большому больше и надобно.   *v.* Б336
      [Great men have great needs.] *Cf.* Great men have great faults.

335   Большому вытью не верь.   *v.* В318,319, К207,261
      [Don't believe shrill talk.] Great cry and little wool. Great strokes make not sweet music.

336* Большому кораблю - большое (и) плавание.   *v.* Б333, В243, К68, У82
      A great ship asks deep waters. *SPL.* in magno mari pisces, in urbibus magnis magna scelera. Mart.10.104.19: magna navis magnam fortitudinem habet.

337   **Большому простор, малому теснота.**
[Space for the great, straitss for the small.] Great winds blow upon high hills.

338   **Борится, коробится - как подметка на огне.**   *v.* Б329, Д210
[Talks bravely but shrivels like shoeleather on a flame.] *Cf.* The greatest talkers (braggarts) are (always) the least doers.

339   **Борода апостольская, а усек дьявольский.**   *v.* Г73, О82, П146
[An apostolic beard with devilish whiskers.] *Cf.* The cross on the breast and the devil in the heart. A wolf in sheep's clothing.

340*   **Борода в честь, а усы и у кошки есть.**   *v.* В400, М171, У107, *Ар.*1.1
[A beard may be becoming, but any cat has whiskers.] If the beard were all, the goat might preach.

341   **Борода велика (выросла), а ума не на лыко (не вынесла).**   *v.* В400, М171, П60
[A thick beard and scant wit.] More hair than wit. You cannot grow hair and brains in the same head. *Cf.* It's not the beard that makes the philosopher. *Lat.* non barbam facit philosophum.

342   **Борода уму (глазам) не замена.**   *v.* М171
[A beard is no substitute for brains (eyes).] Brains don't lie in the beard.

343   **Борода широка, да душа молода.**   *v.* В401,402, Г214, П99, С89
[A mature beard but a young heart.] Old head on young shoulders. *Cf.* Old head and young hands.

344   **Бортник горек, да мед его сладок.**   *v.* Б172, В8, Г281, Л171, Н221,363
[A bitter beekeeper may have sweet honey.] Spice is black, yet it has a sweet smack. The bitter must come before the sweet. *Cf.* A black hen lays a white egg.

345   **Борьба и охота похвальбу любят.**   *v.* М107
[Fighting and hunting thrive on praise.] *Cf.* War, hunting and love (law) are as full of trouble as pleasure.

346   **Борьба не на жизнь, а на смерть.**   *v.* В384
[Not a life but a death struggle.] War to the knife.

347   **Бос лаптей не износит.**
[A barefoot man will not wear out shoes.] A beggar can never be bankrupt.

348*   **Бочка пахнет чем что в ней раньше было.**   *v.* В73
The cask savours of the first fill. *Lat.* sapiunt vasa quicquid primum acceperunt.

349   **Боязливый не переступит через пеструю веревку.**   *v.* В394, Н55
[A coward won't step over a motley rope.] He that has been bitten by a serpent (snake) is afraid of a rope.

350   **Боярин и в рубище не брат.**   *v.* Б287,288, И22
[A lord in plain clothes is still not the commoner's brother.] *Cf.* It is not the gay coat that makes the gentleman.

351   **Боярская ласка - до порога.**   *obs.*
[An aristocrat's kindness extends to the doorstep.] Great men's favours are uncertain. *Cf.* A king's favour is no inheritance.

352 **Бояться воров - не держать коров.** *v.* Г239, Н558
[He that fears thieves should not keep cattle.] *Cf.* The beggar may sing before the thief.

353* **Бояться несчастья - и счастья не видать.** *v.* Б49, В616, Г297,281, Н221,363
[He that fears misfortune misses fortune.] No pains, no gains.
Cf. He that fears death, lives not.

354 **Бояться себя заставишь, а любить не принудишь.** *v.* И105, К199, М92, Н145, С112
[People can be forced to fear, but not to love.]
Cf. Love cannot be compelled. Love rules his kingdom without a sword.

355* **Боящийся воробьев не сеет проса.** *v.* В393, Д451, Т66
[He that fears sparrows should not sow seeds.] He that fears every bush must never go a-birding. He that fears every grass must not walk in a meadow.

356* **Брань на вороту не виснет.** *v.* Н134, С297, Я19
[Insults won't stick to your collar.] *i.e. like dirt or mud.* Words may pass but blows fall heavy. *Cf.* Sticks and stones may break your bones but names will never hurt you.

357 **Брань - не дым, глаза не ест.** *v.* С297
[Insults won't sting the eyes like smoke.] Hard words break no bones.

358 **Брань правды не любит.** *v.* С256
[Derision hates precision.] In too much dispute, truth is lost.
Cf. Abusive language is abuse of language.

359* **Брат за брата не ответчик (плательщик).** *v.* Б361
Not his brother's keeper.

360 **Брат на брата - пуще супостата.**
[A brother may be his own brother's worst adversary.] *Cf.* Between two brother's - two witnesses and a notary. *Lat.* fratrum concordia rara, discrepatio crebra.

361 **Брат он мой, а ум его свой.** *v.* Б359
[He's is my brother yet he is his own man.] I'm not my brother's keeper.

362 **Братчина так и складчина.** *v.* Д242, С59
[Brothers' goods are in common.] Friends' goods are in common. *Lat.* Cic.*Off.*16.51: amicorum communia omnia. *Gr.* Diog.Laert.4.53: κοινὰ τὰ φιλῶν.

363 **Брови пригожи, а дровни угожи.** *v.* Н44, С16
[Eyebrows may be pretty but firewood is useful.] Prettiness makes no pottage. Beauty is a fine thing but you can't live on it.

364* **Брось псу кусок, так не лает.** *v.* И51, Н173, Ч34
[Throw a dog a piece and he won't bark.] Anything for a quiet life. Into the mouth of a bad dog often falls a good bone. *Cf.* A dog will not howl if you beat him with a bone.

365 **Брюхо больного умнее лекарской головы.** *v.* Ж84
[A patient's belly is wiser than a doctor's head.] *Cf.* The belly teaches all arts.

366 **Брюхо, злодей - старого добра (старой дружбы) не помнит.** *v.* А1
[The belly is a knave that forgets past benefits (old friends).] Eaten bread is soon forgotten.

367* **Брюхо не насыщается словами.** *v.* Б21, В376, Г184, Е45, Р24, С186,236, У7, Ш14
Fair words fill not the belly. *Lat.* difficile est vacuo verbis imponere ventri.
Cf. Hungry bellies have no ears. It's a good story that fills the belly.

368* **Брюхо сыто да глаза голодны.** *v.* В275, Г111,116, Д507, З161
[The belly's full but the eyes are hungry.] The eye is bigger than the belly.

369 **Брюхом добра не наживешь.**
Never good that mind the belly too much.

370 **Брюшко да головка - семинарская отговорка.**
[A seminary repudiates the belly and the scarf.] *i.e. gluttony and women. Cf.* A belly full
of gluttony will never study willingly. *Lat.* impletus venter non vult studere libenter.

371* **Будет день, будет и ночь.** *v.* Д159,160, Н529
Every day cometh night. As sure as night follows day.

372* **Будет друг коли хлеба есть круг.** *v.* Б428,429, Д447, Е42, Ж10, З16,
No longer foster, no longer friend. Н64, П236, Х23

373* **Будет и на нашей улице праздник.** *v.* А7, В288, И20, П256, С234
[Our street too will have its fair.] Our day will come. Every dog has its day.

374 **Будет имение, будет и умение.** *v.* Б422, Н591
[If you have property, you will have skill.] *Cf.* Necessity is the mother of invention.
Ability is of little account without opportunity.

375 **Будет корова, будет подойник.** *v.* Б374,425,447,475, В292, Д39, К303
[He who has a cow will have a pail.] *Cf.* God gives the cow but not the pail.

376 **Будешь богат, будешь и скуп.** *v.* Н132
[Be rich, be miserly.] Poor and liberal, rich and covetous. *SPL.* quo plus sunt potae,
plus sitiuntur aquae.

377 **Будешь лукавить так черт задавит.** *v.* Д456, Ж153, К29,238, Л76, С78,81,224, Т14
[The devil suppresses the man who transgresses.] Rake hell and skim the devil.
Cf. They that deal with the devil get a dear pennyworth.

378* **Будешь меня любить, так и собаку мою люби (не бей).** *v.* К128,229,254
Love me, love my dog. *Lat.* qui me amat, amat et canem meum.

379 **Будешь сладок - разлижут, будешь горек - расплюют.** *v.* Б394,398, Л81
[Affability invites kisses, austerity - hisses.] *Cf.* He that all men will please, shall never
find ease.

380 **Будешь трудиться - будешь кормиться.** *v.* В113, Д12,127, К75, Л39, Р7
[If you work, you shall eat.] Those who will not work, shall not eat. *Cf. Thessal.*3.10:
He that will not work, shall not eat.

381 **Будто тяп-ляп, да и корабль.** *v.* Т87

382 **Буду есть мякину, а фасон не кину.** *v.* В10, Г88, М174, Н9
[I'll dine on chaff but I won't abandon fashion.] Silks and satins put the fire out in the
chimney. *Cf.* Do not be a slave to fashion. For fashion's sake, as dogs go to church.

383* **Будут голодные, съедят и холодное.** *v.* Г230,231, К227, *Ap.*1.91

[If they're hungry, they'll even eat it cold.]
Hunger finds no fault with the cookery. Hungry dogs will eat dirty puddings.

384   **Будут дожди, будет и ведро.**   *v.* Г23, Ж32, П166
        After black clouds, clear weather.   After a storm comes a calm.

385*   Будут целы овцы коли волк стережет.   *sarc.*   *v.* В395, Д359, Н211,389
        Set the wolf to keep the sheep.

386   Будут штаны но не знаю когда.
        [I will have trousers, but I don't know when.] *i.e. money, wherewithal.* A day will come
        shall pay for all.

387*   Будь без хвоста, да не кажись кургуз(а).   *v.* Н446
        [Be a bobtail, but don't look docked.] *i.e. never betray your weaknesses.* Cry not before
        you are hurt. A short-tailed dog wags his tail same as a long one.

388   Будь большой а слушайся меньших.   *v.* З111
        [Be great but heed the small.] Great without small makes a bad wall. *Cf.* If great men
        would have care of little ones, both would last long.

389   Будь в голубятине корм, голуби слетятся.   *v.* Б394,428, Е42
        [Stock the dovecote and the birds will flock.] A dog returns to where he has been fed.

390*   Будь друг, да не вдруг.   *v.* В214, У78, Ч108
        [Make friends slowly.] *Cf.* Before you make a friend, eat a bushel of salt with him.
        Lat. nemini fidas nisi cum quo prius modium salis absumperis.

391   Будь друг (знаком), отойди прочь (а ходи дальше).   *v.* Д58, М205, Н219
        Friends agree but at a distance.

392   Будь жена хоть коза - лишь золотые рога.
        [Let the bride look like a goat as long as the horns are gilt.] Old woman's gold is not
        ugly. *Cf.* Money makes marriage.

393   Будь красив, да не будь списив.
        [Be gorgeous, not supercilious.] *Cf.* There is many a fair thing full false.

394   Будь лишь мед, много мух нальнет.   *v.* Б379,389,398,461, Г51,290
        [Wherever there's honey, the flies will swarm.] A fly followeth the honey. *Cf.* Make
        yourself all honey and the flies will devour you.

395*   Будь малым доволен - больше получишь.   *v.* †П121
        [Be content with little and get more.] *Cf.* He has enough who is content with little. He
        who is content in his poverty is wonderfully rich.

396   Будь не из умных, да не из безумных.
        [Be neither too sensible nor too senseless.] He is not a wise man who cannot play the
        fool on occasion.

397*   Будь ниже травы, тише воды.   *v.* Ж123
        [Be lower than grass, more silent than water.] *Cf.* Back the wind and front the sun. Be
        still and have thy will.

398   Будь овцой, а волки готовы.   *v.* Б379,394, С83
        [Be a sheep, the wolves are ready.] He that makes himself a sheep shall be eaten by the wolf.

399   **Будь своему слову господин.**   *v.* К73,92
[Be master of your word.] *Cf.* An honest man's word is as good as his bond. While the word is in your mouth it is your own, when it's spoken it is another's.

400   **Будь так коли пометил дьяк.**
We all have our cross to bear.   *SPL.* ferendum est quod mutari non potest.

401   **Будь умен а не силен.**   *v.* И49, Р28, С119
[Be wise rather than strong.] Wisdom goes beyond strength. Better brains than brawn.

402   **Будь хоть дураком, да не болтай языком.**
[Be a fool but hold your tongue.] *Cf.* Let not your tongue run at rover.

403   **Будь хоть каналья, только бы добрый человек.**   *v.* В421, И13
[Be a rogue, but be kind.] There isn't a rascal or a thief that doesn't have his devotion.

404*   **Буквы кривые да смысл прямой.**   *v.* Г126, Д411, И23, С287, У75
[Cursive letters have straight meaning.] Crooked logs make straight fires.

405   **Булавку на себя концом не подымай.**   *v.* Л69, Н421
[Don't pick up a pin by the point.] Never catch at a falling knife.

406   **Булат железо и кисель режет.**   *v.* И94
[The sword can cut both steel and jelly.] The same knife cuts bread and fingers.

407   **Бумага без души - что угодно пиши.   (Бумага все терпит.)**
Paper is patience - you can put anything on it. Paper won't blush.   *Lat.* Cic.*Fam.*5.12.1: epistula non erubescit.

408   **Бумажки клочок в суд волочет.**   *v.* И41, М5
[A scrap of paper can drag you into court.] A small leak will sink a great ship.
Cf. Paper and ink and little justice.

409*   **Буря в стакане воды.**
A storm in a teacup. *Lat.* Cic.*Leg.*3.16.36: excitare fluctus in simpulo.

410   **Бутылочки да рюмочки доведут до сумочки.**
[Bottles and glasses unfasten purses.] A penny in the purse will bid me drink.

411   **Бывает добрая овца и от беспутного отца.**
[Sometimes dissolute fathers have resolute sons.] No man is responsible for his father.
Cf. †Many a good father has a bad son.

412*   **Бывает и виноватый прав.**   *v.* В465, И16,129
[Sometimes even the guilty may be right.]   *Cf.* A fool may sometimes speak to the purpose. *Gr.* πολλάκι τοι καὶ μωρὸς ἀνὴρ καταίριον εἶπε. *Lat.* interdum stultus opportuna loquitur.

413   **Бывает и прок, коль работает в срок.**   *v.* В635
[There is benefit from work done on time.] Timely blossom, timely ripe.

414   **Бывает и простота хуже воровства.**   *v.* Д491
[Sometimes stupidity is worse than thievery.] The fools do more hurt in this world than the rascals.

415   **Бывает и так - и стар да петух, и молод да протух.**   *v.* Б185, Н545

[Sometimes an old man crows vigorously whilst a young man cowers drained.]
Cf. Old young and old long.

416   **Бывает иногда от рюмки водки и до могилы путь короткий.**
[From glass to grave is often a short pass.] *Cf.* Wine has drowned more men than the sea. Bacchus has drowned more men than Neptune.

417*   **Бывает копейка дороже рубля.**   *v.* Б228
[At times a *kopek* may be worth more than a ruble.] **A penny at a pinch is worth a pound.**

418   **Бывает порою - течет вода горою.**   *v.* К118, М63, П265, С86
When it rains it pours.

419*   **Бывает что и вошь кашляет (и курица петухом поет).**   *v.* И28,54
[Even a louse may cough (and a chicken crow).] *Cf.* A fly hath a spleen (anger).
Lat. EA. habet et musca splenem. formicae inest sua bilis.

420   **Бывает что и дурак умного надувает.**   *v.* Б167, Е9, И37, Н24
[Sometimes a fool can fool a wise man.] None so wise but the fool overtakes him.

421   **Быка берут за рога, а человека ловят на слове.**
An ox is taken by the horns, a man by the tongue. Take a man by his word, and a cow by her horn.

422   **Был бы горшок, а покрышка найдется. (Был бы крюк, а веревку найдем).**
[First get the pot (hook), then the lid (rope).]   *v.* Б374,472
Cf. First catch your hare. *Lat.* primum oportet cervum capere.

423   **Был бы друг (дружок), а время будет (найдем и досуг) (найдется и часок).**
[First find the friend, then the time.] *Cf.* Friends are thieves of time. *Lat.* amici fures temporis.

424   **Был бы запевала, а подголоски найдутся.**
[First find the soloist, then the chorus.] *Cf.* Put first things first. Learn to say before you sing. First catch your hare.

425   **Был бы конь, а сбруя найдется.**   *v.* Б375,447
[First find the horse, then the harness.] *Cf.* †Give a Yorkshireman a halter, and he'll find a horse.

426*   **Был бы лес, а волки будут.**   *v.* Б468, Г37,102, Д510
[If there are woods, there are wolves.] *Cf.* Cut down the woods and you'll catch the wolf.

427   **Был бы лес, а топор сыщем.**
[First find the trees, then the axe.] *Cf.* Put first things first.

428   **Был бы ломоть, собак много (будет).**   *v.* Б372,389, Е42, Ж10
[If you have the bread, dogs will follow you.] *Cf.* If you would wish the dog to follow you, feed him. Who hath no more bread than need, must not keep a dog.

429   **Был бы мед да пиво, а дружков не звать.**   *v.* Б372, Е42, Ж10, З16
[When you've got beer and honey, friends don't wait for an invitation.] *Cf.* Good cheer and good cheap gars many haunt the house. In times of prosperity, friends will be plenty.

430   **Был бы мешок а деньги будут.**
[If you have the purse, you'll have the money.] Don't fling away the empty wallet.
Cf. †He that has no money, needs no purse.

431* **Был бы милый по душе, проживем и в шалаше.** *v.* Б194, Ж48, Н404, С20
[If he's kind at heart, we'll get by in a hut.] Content lodges oftener in cottages than palaces.

432 **Был бы сад, соловьи прилетят.** *v.* Г51,79,104
[Where there's a garden, nightingales will roost.] *Cf.* Destroy the nests and the birds will fly away.

433 **Был бы сам хорош, так бы люди не испортили.**
[If you are good yourself, others can't corrupt you.] He cannot be virtuous that is not rigorous. *Cf.* Virtue and vice cannot dwell under the same roof.

434 **Был бы сокол а вороны налетят.** *v.* К325
[Where there's a falcon, the crows will follow.] *Cf.* When the crow flies, her tail follows.

435 **Был бы ум, будет и рубль (+ не будет ума, не будет и рубля).** *v.* Н516
[If you had sense, you'd have cents (+ if you don't, you won't).] *Cf.* He that has money in his purse, cannot want a head for his shoulders.

436 **Был бы хлеб, а зубы сыплются.** *v.* Б252,475, Д38, Р63
[First find the bread, then the teeth.] *Cf.* God never sendeth mouth but He sendeth meat.

437 **Был головастиком, стал лягушкой.** *v.* Б458, М25
[Out of little tadpoles large frogs grow.] Out of little acorns mighty oak trees grow.

438 **Был дом, да оборотился вверх дном.** *v.* В273, П204
Throw (fling) the house out of the window.

439 **Был конь, да изъездился.** *v.* Н553, У80
[The old horse has been ridden out.] The ole' gray mare ain't what she used to be. *Cf.* The old horse must die in someone's hand. Nothing lasts forever.

440 **Был обык, теперь стал перевык.** *v.* И30, К94, Н123
[Every habit can be broken.] *Cf.* The command of custom is great.

441* **Был он и в кольях, и в мяльях.** *v.* И4, С41
[He's been on stakes and (executioner's) blocks.] He's been through thick and thin. Passed (through) the pikes.

442* **Был полковник - стал (помер) покойник.** *v.* Ж152

443 **Был свой и стал чужой.** *v.* В13, К120
[Exchanged independence for dependence.] A married man turns his staff into a stake.

444 **Был со всем а стал ни с чем.** *v.* Б476,479, К47
[Had everything and then - nothing.] Here one minute, gone the next.

445 **Был такой что торопился да скоро умер.** *v.* К29, С197, Ч3
[There once was one who hurried so that he died anon.] *Cf.* Haste trips up its own heels. The man in a hurry is in a hurry to go nowhere.

446 **Была бы в сусеке рожь, будет и в кармане грош.** *v.* Б68, *Ар.*1.17
[Rye in the silo - money in the pocket.] Provision in season makes a rich house.

447 **Была бы корова, найдем и подойник.** *v.* Б375,475, В292, Д39, К303
[If we had the cow, we would find the pail.] *Cf.* God gives the milk, but not the pail.

448   **Была бы кость да тело, а платье сам делай.**   E27
[If you have life and limb, you must provide the clothes.] God makes and the tailor (apparel) shapes.

449   **Была бы кутья, а кутейники сами придут (а плакуши будут).**   *v.* Б372,429, E42,
[Where there's a wake, the wakers (mourners) will come.]   Ж10
Cf. At marriages and funerals, friends are discerned (from kinfolk).

450   **Была бы нитка, дойдем до клубка.**   *v.* Б451, П62
[First mind the thread, then wind the ball.] Step after step the ladder is ascended.

451   **Была бы основа, а уток найдем.** *v.* П63

452   **Была бы охота, а возможность найдется (заладится всякая работа)**
(а впереди еще много работы) (найдем доброхота).   *v.* Г101, Д76, Х74
Where there's a will, there's a way [there's work to be done.]

453   **Была бы рыба, а хлеб будет.**   *v.* E53, K101
[If there were fish, the bread could be found.] *Cf.* They that have no other meat, bread and butter are glad to eat.

454   **Была бы собака, а палка будет (камень найдется).**   *v.* Г302, K122, C109
[If you have a dog, you'll find a staff (stone).] A staff is quickly found to beat a dog.

455*   **Была бы спина - найдется вина.**   *v.* Г302, H495
[First find the man, then the fault.] You would find fault if you knew how.

456   **Была бы шея, а веревку сыщем (хомут найдется).**
[A rope (yoke) can be found if there's a neck to put it on.] For every dog there is a leash.

457   **Была вина, да прощена.**   *v.* Б482, П271, Ч62
[There was fault and there was pardon.] Forgive and forget. Let bygones be bygones.

458   **Была кучка, стал ворошок.**   *v.* Б437, В684, Д125, И73
[There was a small pile, now it's a heap.] Make a mountain out of a molehill.

459   **Была не была.**   *v.* Г58, Л67, Р55
Win or lose. Come hell or high water. Come what may.

460   **Была у двора масленица, да в избу не зашла.**   *v.* В210,218, H309, O76, C310
[The carnival got as far as the yard but didn't enter the house.] No telling which way luck is going to turn. *Cf.* Some have the hap, others stick in the gap.

461   **Были бы бобры, а ловцы будут.**   *v.* Б394, K37
[Where there are beavers, there are trappers.] *Cf.* It takes two to tango.

462   **Были бы бумажки, будут и милашки.**
[Who has a roll of bills, attracts a lot of babes.] Money wants no followers. *Cf.* †Dally not with women or money.

463   **Были бы враки, а что врать - сыщут.**
[Liars will always find things to lie about.] A false tongue will hardly speak truth.

464   **Были бы денежки святые, грешная помощь будет.**   *v.* Б281, Д150
[Where money is sacred, there's always sinful help.] *Cf.* Money is the root of all evil.

465   **Были бы деньги, а честь найдем.**   *v.* Д193, Ж148
[Money first, then honour.] Jack would be a gentleman if he had money.

466   **Были бы кости, а мясо будит.**   *v.* Б71
[Where there are bones, there is meat.] *said encouragingly to thin people.* Bones bring meat to town.

467   **Были бы пирожки, будут и дружки.**   *v.* Д447, Е42, Ж10,
        Были бы хоромцы, будут и знакомцы (питомцы).   З16, Н64, П236
[Where there are *piroshki*, there will be friends.] [Where there are banquets, there are freeboarders.] *Cf.* At dinner my man appears.

468   **Было бы болото, а за лягушками дело не станет (а черти будут).**   *v.* Б426
[Where there's a bog, there's plenty of frogs (evil).] *Cf.* A frog cannot out of her bog.

469   **Было бы вино, а пьяны будут.**
[Where there is drink, there are drunks.] The more one drinks, the more one may. *Cf.* One drink leads to another.

470   **Было бы кому врать, а слушать станут.**
[When someone lies, others listen.] There's a sucker born every minute.

471*   **Было бы начало, будет и конец.**   *v.* Б83, Е37, Н553, С136
[Where there's a beginning there's an end.] Everything must have a beginning and an end.

472   **Было бы поле, найдем и сошку.**   *v.* Б422
[First find the field, then the lot.] *Cf.* First catch your hare.

473   **Было бы суслице, доживем и до бражки.**   *v.* Б437
[If there is must, there will be wine.] *Cf.* From small beginnings come great things.

474   **Было бы толоконце, а толоконнички будут.**   *obs.*   *v.* К111, Н355, О35
[Where there are oatmeal tarts, there are oatmeal lovers.] All fasten where there is gain. *Cf.* Where there is a store of oatmeal, you may put enough in the crock.

475   **Было бы хлебово, а хлебалку найдем.**   *v.* Б375,436,447, В292, Д39
[First find the gruel, then the bowl.] God gives the cow, not the pail.

476*   **Было густо, стало пусто.**   *v.* Б444
        Ever busy, ever bare.

477   **Было, да быльем поросло.**   *v.* Д140
[What has been is long forgotten.] Done and forgotten. *Cf.* Long absent, soon forgotten.

478   **Было добро да давно, опять будет да уж нас не будет.**   *v.* Д371
[What happened a long time ago will happen again when we are long gone.] Time is, time was, and time is past.

479*   **Было - сплыло.**   *v.* Б444,476, В662, К47, Ч80
        Easy come, easy go.

480   **Быль за сказкой не угоняется.**
[Truth cannot keep up with falsehood.] Give a lie a twenty-four hour start and you can never overtake it.

481   **Быль как смола (трава), небыль как вода.**   *v.* В209, Ф1

[Truth sticks like resin, lies like water.] *Cf.* Truth and oil are ever above. Facts are stubbourn things. Truth has always a fast bottom.

482   **Быль молодцу не укор.**   *v.* Б457, П271, Ч62
[Truth rebukes not the competent.] Truth may be blamed, but cannot be shamed. Let bygones be bygones. *Cf.* What's done is done (and cannot be undone).

483   **Быль не сказка - из нее слова не выкинешь.**   *v.* Н78
[Fact is not fiction - you cannot edit it.] *Cf.* Fact (truth) is stranger than fiction.

484*   **Быстрая вода до моря не доходит.**   *v.* Б486, Д47
[Rapid waters reach not the sea.] He that runs fast will not run long. *Cf.* †A still river never finds the ocean. †All rivers run into the sea.

485   **Быстрая вошка первая попадает на гребешок.**
[Fleety lice are quickly caught by the comb.] *Cf.* The more the bird caught in lime strives, the faster he sticks.

486   **Быстрая лошадь скорее станет.**   *v.* Б484, Д47
[The faster horse tires sooner.] He that runs fast will not run long.

487*   **Быстроногий осел не сравнится с хромой лошадью.**   *v.* Г285, Л149, П129
[Better a swift ass than a lame horse.] *Cf.* Better the head of an ass than the tail of a horse. Better ride an ass that carries me than a horse that throws me.

488   **Быть бычку на веревочке.**   *v.* В375, Ж69,76, З32, Р44
[Time for the bullock to be put on a leash.] Wedlock is a padlock. After a collar comes the halter. Pay the piper (devil) his due. *Cf.* They that dance must pay the fiddler. The married man exchanges a staff for a stake.

489   **Быть по-сказанному, как по-писанному.**
[Spoken and written should be the same.] *Cf.* Don't say it, write it. Never write what you dare not say.

490   **Бюрократ любой бумажке рад.**   *v.* Д500
[Any scrap of paper will please a bureaucrat.] *Cf.* The greatest clerks are not the wisest men.

В

1   **В августе серпы греют, вода холодит.**
[In August, sickles heat and waters cool.] *Cf.* Dry August and warm does harvest no harm.

2   **В богатстве сыто брюхо, голодна душа.**   *v.* T16
[Wealth has a full but a hungry soul.] The body is more (sooner) dressed than the soul.

3   **В болоте тихо, да жить (там) лихо.**
[A swamp is peaceable, but uninhabitable.] *Cf.* He would live in a gravel pit.

4   **В большом месте сидеть - много надо ума иметь.**
[It takes great wit to sit in a high place.] *Cf.* Authority without wisdom is like a heavy axe without an edge: fitter to bruise than to polish.

5   **В бор не по груши - по еловы шишки.**   *v.* З101, H399
[Look not for pears, but cones in a pine forest.] Look not for musk in a dog's kennel.

6   **В борьбе силу одолевает учение.**   *v.* B203
[In combat, training prevails over strength.] Skill and confidence are an unconquered army. *Cf.* Using our brains is often wiser than depending on our strength.

7*   **В бочку меду ложку дегтя (+ все портит).**   *v.* Г51, K8,203, O54,148, Ш3
[A spoonful of tar will ruin a barrel of honey.] One bad apple spoils the lot. A fly in the ointment. *Cf.* Dying flies spoil the sweetness of the ointment.

8   **В бою горько, зато потом сладко.**   *v.* Б344, Г281, H221,363
[Bitter in the fray, sweet the next day.] That which was bitter to endure may be sweet to remember. *Lat.* Sen.*H.F.*656: quae fuit durum pati, meminisse dulce est.

9   **В брюхе простор - что ни день, то сыпь и лей.**
[An empty stomach accepts anything - just pour.] A bellyful is a bellyful, whether it be meat or drink.

10   **В брюхе солома (шелк), а шапка с заломом (а на брюхе шелк).**   *v.*Б382,Г88,Л3,M174
[An empty belly but a cocked hat.] [Nothing *in* the belly but a silk wrap *over* it.] Silks and satins put out the kitchen fire. Were it not for the belly, the back might wear gold.

11   **В вознесение, когда будет оно в воскресение.**   *v.* П168
[When Ascension Day falls on a Sunday.] *i.e.never.* At Latter Lammas. *Cf.* At (on) the Greek Calends. *Lat.* ad calendas graecas. The road of by-and-by leads to the town of nowhere.

12   **В воре что в море, а в дураке что в пресном молоке.**   *v.* B35, П286
[A thief's like the high seas, but a sot is tepid milk.] I'd rather have a knave than a fool. *Cf.* † Better be a fool than a knave.

13   **В восемнадцать лет жениться, чтоб на тягло садиться.**   *v.* Б443, В294, Ж70, К119
[Marry at eighteen and become a hitched pack-team.] *Cf.* It is time to yoke when the cart comes to the caples (horses). Marry late or never.

14*   **В воскресение веселье, в понедельник похмелье.**   *v.* В15
[Sunday's highs bring Monday's lows.] Drunken days have all their tomorrows. St. Monday. *Cf.* Sunday's wooing draws to ruin.

15   **В воскресение (песни) орет, в понедельник кобылы ищет.**   *v.* В14
[Drunk on Sunday and can't find his horses on Monday.] Drunken days have all their tomorrows. *Cf.* Monday religion is better than Sunday procession.

16   **В глаза ласкает (льстят) (любит) (мил) (не льсти),**
а за глаза лает (ругают) (губит) (постыл) (не брани).   *v.* В100, З36, О86
Laugh in one's face and cut his throat. *Cf.* He has honey in the mouth and a razor at the girdle. A stab in the back is worse than a kick in the face.

17   **В глупом сыне и отец не волен.**   *v.* И47
[Not even a father delights in a fool for a son.] A foolish son is the calamity of his father. *Cf.* He that hath one son makes him a fool.

18   **В голове нет, и в шапку не накладешь.**
[You won't hide under your cap what you haven't got in your head.] It makes little difference what's on the outside of your head if there's nothing on the inside.
Cf. He that has no head, needs no hat. A hat will never be worn without a head.

19   **В голове нет, так в аптеке не купишь.**   *v.* В496, У85
[What you haven't got in your head you won't buy in a pharmacy.] *Cf.* Send a fool to market and a fool he will return again.

20*   **В город ехать - толчки принимать.**   *v.* В68, Г284, Л173,178, С78, Х28
[Driving to town means taking the bumps.] If you don't like the heat, get out of the kitchen. *Cf.* Drive gently over the stones.

21   **В гости ходить - надо и к себе водить.**   *v.* О8
[Guests must in turn be hosts.] A host's invitation is expensive.

22*   **В гостях воля хозяйская (в гостях что в неволе).**   *v.* Г307, Н409, У50, Х30
[The host's will prevails over the guest's.] [A guest is a prisoner.] He that reckons without his host, must reckon again.

23*   **В гостях хорошо, а дома лучше.**   *v.* Д51, *Ap.*1.83
[It's nice to be a guest but home is best.] East or west, home is best. *SPL.* domi manere oportet belle fortunatum. *Lat.* nullus est locus domestica sede iucundior.

24   **В гроб смотрит, а деньги коптит.**   **(В могилу глядит а над копейку дрожит.)**
[Hoards money at death's door.] He'd reach out his hand if he were dying.

25   **В длинной дороге и сумка говорлива.**   *v.* Р22
[On a long journey even a bag is talkative.] *Cf.* Cheerful company shortens the miles.
†In a long journey, straw weighs.

26   **В добром житье краснеют, а в чуждом - бледнеют.**
[Virtue blushes, evil pales.] A blush on the face is better than a blot on the heart.
Cf. Blushing is virtue's color. *Lat.* rubor est virtutis color.

27   **В добрую голову - сто рук.**   *v.* Г210, З13, О46, Р31, У93
        One good head is better than a thousand [hundred] **hands.**

28   **В добрый час молвить, в худой промолчать.**
        [Speak in good times, keep silent in bad.] *Cf. Eccles.*3.7: There is a time to keep silence and a time to speak.   Silence in time of suffering is best.

29   **В дождь избы не кроют, а в ведро и сама не капнет.**
        [Roofs are not repaired in the rain, but they won't leak in good weather either.] The roof doesn't need mending when it's not raining. *Cf.* Thatch your roof before the rain begins.

30   **В дождь коси, в ведро греби.**   *v.* К180, С252
        [Mow in the rain and rake in the sunshine.] *Cf.* Make hay while the sun shines. If there were no rain, there'd be no hay to make when the sun shines.

31*   **В долг брать легко, а платит тяжело.**   *v.* Б192, Д13,71, К170
        A good borrower is a lazy payer.

32*   **В долг давать - дружбу терять.**   *v.* Д426, *Ap.*1.25
        Lend your money and lose your friend.

33   **В долг давать - под гору метать.**
        [To lend is to bury deep.] Lend and lose is the game of fools.

34   **В долгах что в репьях.**
        [In debt, in a thicket.] A man in debt is a man caught in a net. *Cf.* He that goes a-borrowing goes a-sorrowing.

35   **В долгу, что в море - ни дна, ни берегов.**   *v.* В12, Д367
        [Being in debt is like being adrift at sea: neither shores nor bottom.] *Cf.* Out of debt, out of danger.

36*   **В доме повешенного не говорят о веревке.**   *v.* З53, С13
        Name not a halter in the house of the hanged. *Lat.* ne restim memores apud ipsum reste neccatum.

37   **В дороге хлеб не помеха.** *v.* Х21

38*   **В драке волос не жалеют.**   *v.* В104, К124, П304
        [In a fight, you forget about your hair.] Never wear your best trousers when you go out to fight. *Cf.* He that handles thorns shall prick his fingers.

39   **В драке нет умолоту.**   *v.* В385
        [Fighting yields nothing.] War begets no good offspring. *Cf.* In war all suffer defeat, even the victors. War is a business that ruins those who succeed in it.

40*   **В дружбе правда.**   *v.* Д439
        [There is truth in friendship.] *Cf.* Nothing spoils friendship sooner than the exaggeration of friends. †There is falsehood (fraud) in fellowship.

41   **В душу влезет, а за грош продаст.**
        [Gains your trust and betrays you for a farthing.] In trust is treason. *Cf.* Trust is the mother of deceit.

42*   **В жизни все меняется.**   *v.* В515,532
        [In life everything changes.] All things change, and we with them.

43* **В закрытый рот муха не залетит.**   *v.* Н398
   A closed mouth catches no flies. Flies fly not into a shut mouth.

44 **В запас не наглядишься.**   *v.* В532
   [One cannot forestall all.] Nothing is certain but the unforeseen.

45* **В здравом теле здравый ум (дух).**   *v.* З112
   A sound mind in a sound body. *Lat.* Juv.*Sat.*10.356: mens sana in corpore sano.

46 **В игре да в дороге узнают людей.**
   In sports and journeys men are known. A man knows his companions in a long journey and a small inn.

47 **В кабаке родился, в вине крестился.**
   [Born in a tavern, christened in wine.] Christened with pump water.

48* **В каждой шутке есть доля правды.**   *v.* В202
   Many a true word is spoken in jest. *Cf.* The sting of reproach is the truth of it.

49 **В какой мешок свинью не суй, ее все равно слышно.** *v.* В361, С54, Ш7
   [In whatever bag the pig is put, his grunt is heard.] You can't take the grunt out of the pig. The voice of a pig cannot be disguised. *Cf.* A pig in a parlour is still a pig. Fire cannot be hidden in flax.

50* **В какой народ попадешь (приедешь), такую и шапку наденешь (надень).**
   (В каком народе живешь, такого обычья и держись.)   *v.* В154,187,541, Г31
   [Don the cap of the people around you.] [Observe the customs of the people among whom you live.] When in Rome, do as the Romans do. *Lat.* si fueris Romae, Romano vivito more. *Cf.* A wise man esteems every place to be his own country. Whose bread I eat, his song I sing.

51 **В камень стрелять - только стрелы терять.**
   [Shoot at a stone and lose your arrows.] He is a fool that makes a hammer of his fist. *Cf.* It is better to have an aim and miss than to hit and not have an aim.

52* **В карете цугом по грибы не ездят.**   *v.* В120, Г160, И63
   [One doesn't harness a dual team to go picking mushrooms.] Make not your sail too big for the ballast. *Cf.* Don't put marble tops on cheap furniture.

53 **В кармане диплом, а в голове лом.**   *v.* И108
   [Diploma in the pocket, scrap in the head.] A mere scholar, a mere ass. *Cf.* Wisdom doesn't always speak in Greek or Latin.

54* **В карты играет а мастей не знает.**   *v.* А12, Х94
   [Plays cards without knowing the suits.] *Cf.* Many carry cards that cannot play.

55 **В ком добра нет, в том и правды мало. (В ком честь, в том и правда.)** *v.* Г77
   [He that is unkind is untrue.] [A man of honor is a man of truth.] Without truth, there can be no virtue. *Cf.* Cowards are cruel. Honour is the reward of virtue.

56 **В ком есть бог, в том есть и стыд (страх). (В ком стыд, в том и совесть.)** *v.* Д483
   [The godly have a sense of shame (fear).] [He who has shame, has a conscience.]
   He who has no shame, has no honour. *Cf.* He that lives ill, fear follows him.
   Gr. Diog.5.30/ Apost.9.6: ἵνα δέος, ἔνθα αἰδώς. *Lat.* ubit timor, ibi pudor, ubi pudor, ibi honos.

57 **В которой посудине деготь побывает, и огнем не выжжешь.** *v.* Г333, О81, Ч135
[Once tar has stained a pot, it can't even be burned out.] *Cf.* He that touches pitch shall be defiled.

58 **В кривом зеркале и рот набоку.** *v.* К205
[In a warped mirror even your mouth is awry.] A straight stick is crooked in the water.

59* **В лес дров не возят, а в колодец воды не льют.** *v.* В377,378, *Ap.*1.85
[Take neither lumber to the woods nor water to a well.] To carry wood into the forest. *EA.* in sylvam importat ligna. *Cf.* Fuel is not sold in a forest, nor fish on a lake. To cast water into the sea. To take owls to Athens. To take pepper to Hindustan.

60 **В лесу лес не ровен, в миру - люди.** *v.* В69, У16
[As trees in the wood stand unequal in height, so too do men in the world.] It takes all kinds of trees to make a forest. It takes all sorts to make a world.

61* **В лесу рубят, а к нам щепки летят.** *v.* Т8

62 **В лихости и зависти нет ни проку ни радости.** *v.* З67
[In envy and conceit there is neither benefit nor bliss.] Envy never enriched any man. *Cf.* The envious man grows lean.

63 **В лукавом правды не сыщешь.** *v.* В148
[Truth is not found in wiles.] An ill deed cannot bring honour. *Cf.* We cannot come to honour under coverlet.

64* **В людях ангел (добро), а дома черт (вольно).** *v.* В65, Д390, П79, *Ap.*1.4
An angel on the street, a devil at home.

65 **В людях тороватым казался, а дома никому не сказался.**
(В людях форсит, а дома без соли сидит.) *v.* В64, Д390
[Big spender in public, penniless at home.] He that gives to be seen will relieve none in the dark. *Cf.* He that spends more than he should shall not have to spend when he would.

66* **В мае жениться - век маятся.**
Marry in May, repent alway (rue for aye). *Lat.* Ov.*Fas.*5.490: mense malum maio nubere vulgus ait.

67* **В мелких словах и большое дело утопить можно.** *v.* Л90, О149
[A great enterprise may be drowned in shallow words.] Loose talk costs lives. *Cf.* A fool's tongue is long enough to cut his own throat.

68* **В мире жить - с миром жить.** *v.* В20, Л177
[To live in this world means to live with this world.] Life means strife. *Cf.* Life lies not in living, but in liking. *Lat.* Mart. non est vivere sed valere vita. You get out of the world just what you put into it.

69 **В мире, как в море, все есть.** *v.* В60, У16
[The world, like the sea, has everything.] It takes all sorts (kinds of people) to make a world.

70* **В миру виноватого нет.**
[No one in the world is ever guilty.] The fault is always someone else's. *Cf.* All are presumed good till they are found at fault.

71 **В миру что на пиру, кто скачет, а кто плачет.**   v. B210,218,611, K176, O62,76,
[The world is a feast where some dance and some cry.]   C310,330
There is no great banquet but some fare ill. The world is a ladder for some to go up and
some down.

72 **В молодости охотою, в старости перхотою.** v. C207

73 **В молоке не было, и в сыворотке не найдешь.**   v. Б348, Г94
[If it wasn't in the milk, you won't find it in the whey.] The husk often tells what the
kernel is. What is bred in the bone will come out in the flesh. *Cf.* The cask savours of
the first fill.

74 **В мошне густо, так и дома не пусто.**   v. Д155, E35
[When the purse is full the home is not empty either.]   A full purse begets a stout
stomach. A heavy purse makes a light heart.

75 **В мужицком брюхе и долото сгниет.**
[A hearty stomach can digest a chisel.] A stomach (digestion) like an ostrich.
Cf. Shakes.*Hen*.IV.iv.10.27: I'll make thee eat iron like an ostrich.

76* **В мутной воде хорошо рыбу ловить.**
It is good fishing in troubled waters.   *Lat.* aqua turbida piscosior est.

77 **В напраслине, что в деле, погибают.**   v. B651
[As many die in vain as for a cause.] Death is not chosen. *Cf.* Graves are of all sizes.
Some men die before they begin to live.

78 **В наряде пригож, а без него на пень похож.**   v. H144
[Handsome in a suit, but like a tree stump without it.] Dress up a stick and it does not
appear to be a stick.

79 **В наш огород камни бросают.**
[They're throwing stones into our garden.] *i.e.* casting aspersions. *Cf.* Throw enough
pitch and some is sure to stick. To poke another man's fire.

80 **В нем уже смерть гнездо свила.**
[Death has already made its nest in him.] Like death upon wires.

81* **В ногах правды нет.**
[No honour in standing] *used as an invitation to take a seat.* It is as cheap sitting as
standing.

82* **В нужде и кулик соловьем свищет.**   v. Б45, Г220, H583,589, П274
[Need makes a sandpiper sing like a nightingale.] Needs must when necessity drives.

83 **В нужде сберечь - на ухабе подпречь.**   v. Б174,180, X60
[To save in need is like tightening the reins on an uneven road.]   Save today, safe
tomorrow. *Cf.* Sparing is the first gaining.

84 **В нынешние годы мудрены народы.**
[In this day and age people are wiser.] The world is wiser than it was. *Cf.* †The world
is full of fools. *Lat.* Cic.*Fam*.9.22: stultorum plena sunt omnia.

85 **В объезд - так к обеду, а прямо - так дай Бог к ночи.**   v. Д53, П294
[By noon the long way, and by the direct route by nightfall with any luck.] The longest
way round is the shortest way home.

86* В один день по две радости не живет. *v.* H508

[One day cannot bring two joys.] You cannot have two forenoons in the same day.
Cf. †No day passes without some grief.

87 В одиночку не сдвинешь и кочку. *v.* O28,37

[Alone, one cannot even move a mound.] Not even Hercules could contend against two.

88* В одно перо и птица не родится. *v.* Г193, H392, P20, *Ap.*1.93

[Not all birds have the same feathers.] No like is the same.

89* В одно ухо влетает, в другое вылетает.
In one ear and out the other.

90 В одной берлоге два медведя не живут. *v.* Д84

91* В одной руке двух арбузов не удержишь. *v.* Д86,99, З1, Л88, Ч96

[One hand cannot hold two watermelons.] Two bigs will not go into one bag.
Cf. Take no more than you're able to bear.

92* В одной руке пусто, а в другой ничего. *v.* B93

[One hand is empty and there's nothing in the other.] Flat broke. *Cf.* Six of one and half
a dozen of the other.

93 В одном кармане вошь на аркане, в другом блоха на цепи. *v.* B92

[A louse on a leash in one pocket and a flea on a chain in the other] *i.e. empty pockets.*
Cf. The devil dances in an empty pocket.

94 В одну петелку всех пуговок не устегнешь. *v.* H66,222

[One buttonhole cannot accommodate all buttons.] Every shoe fits not every foot.

95 В одну руку (лапу) всего не загребешь. *v.* B91,523

[You cannot grab everything with one hand.] *Cf.* Covetousness brings nothing home.

96* В окно всего света не увидишь. *v.* C52

[You can't see the whole world through a window.] *i.e. you can't see everything.*
Cf. The world is a wide place (long journey).

97 В опорках ходить да с милым жить. *v.* C20

[Better to live in rags but with a kind man.] *Cf.* He who is content in his poverty is
wonderfully rich.

98* В отпертые двери лезут звери. *v.* K126

At open doors dogs come in.

99 В очах мило, да в сердце постыло. *v.* Г112, Л85, H258, P65, C51

[Kind eyes, cold heart.] Fair face, foul heart. An angel on top but a devil underneath.
Cf. The face is no index to the heart. *Lat.* Juv.*Sat.*2.8: frontis nulla fides. †The heart's
letter is read in the eyes. †Cold hand, warm heart.

100 В очи хвала, что (по)заочно хула. *v.* B16, З36, O86

[Praise face to face, insults behind the back.] *Cf.* To laugh (smile) in one's face and cut
one's throat.

101 В пашне огрехи - и на кафтане прорехи. *v.* Б71

[A garment has flaws, as a field has faults.] No land without stones, or meat without
bones.

102 В первый день гость - цветок, во второй - соловей, а в третий - палку бери и бей.

v. Г305, Д337

[On the first day, a guest is like a flower; on the second, like a nightingale, but on the third day, take a stick to him!] Guests, like fish, (begin to) spoil after three days.

103 В плохого друга - послуга упруга. *v.* Н103

[A bad friend's help is lax.] *Cf.* Friendship cannot always stand on one side.

104 В пляске сапог не жалеют. *v.* В38

[Spare not your shoes when dancing.] Throw your bonnet over the windmill.

105 В подметки ему не годится.

He's not fit to shine his shoes.

106 В подпечье и помело большак. *v.* В52, Г160, И63

[In the cupboard, the mop is boss.] Everyone excels in something in which someone fails.

107 В подрукавных рукавицах за кодол не берись. *v.* Г310, И1, О81

[Do not seize a tow-line with kid gloves.] *Cf.* A cat in gloves catches no mice.

108* В пожар квартир не разводят. *v.* О19

[Do not lay out flats in a fire.] To play chess when the house is on fire.

109* В поле две воли (чья сильнее). *v.* Д82,250

[Two opposing wills in the field (which is the stronger)] *i.e. a duel.* It takes two to make a quarrel.

110* В поле за ветром не угоняешься. *v.* 35

111* В поле (степи) и жук мясо. *v.* Е56, Л139, М197, Н31

[Even a beetle is meat in the field (steppe).] Better a louse (mouse) in the pot than no flesh at all. Anything's good in a famine.

112 В поле пшеница годом родится, а добрый человек всегда пригодится.

[Wheat grows all year in the fields but a good man is ever in demand.] *Cf.* Good folks are scarce.

113 В поле серпом да вилой, так дома ножом да вилкой. *v.* Б380, Г131, Р7, О95

[Whoever wields a scythe and pitchfork in the fields will have use for knives and forks at home.] *Cf.* Plough deep, while sluggards sleep, and you'll have corn to sell and keep.

114 В понедельник любит, а во вторник губит.

[Monday love, Tuesday loathe.] Hot love is soon cold. Hot love, hasty vengeance.

115 В пороховом погребе не курят. *v.* З10, К281, О81, С25

[Do not smoke in a powder magazine.] If you play with fire, you get burnt.

116* В правде счет не теряется. *v.* З49

[Honesty does not lose accounts.] No honest man ever repented of his honesty. *Cf.* Short accounts (reckonings) make long friends.

117 В просьбе поклон не в потерю. *v.* П133

[Deference detracts not from a request.] Respect a man and he will do the more.

118 В протоколе густо, а на деле пусто. *v.* Б335, В319, К207, Н76, П2

[Much ceremony but little action.] More show than substance.

119* В пустой бочке звону больше.   *v.* Г136, П306, Х103, Ш13
Empty barrels (vessels) make the greatest noise (sound).

120 В пустой чердак двойных стекол не вставляют.   *v.* В52
[Double windows are not installed in an empty garret.] They don't put marble tops on cheap furniture.

121 В пустую хоромину вор не подламывается.   *v.* Г237,241, З9, Н125, С5
[A thief does not break into an empty house.] *Cf.* The beggar may sing before the thief. No naked man is sought after to be rifled.

122 В работе отстаем, а за едой обгоняем. (В работе «ох» а ест за трех.)   *v.* К1, Л49,
To have two stomachs to eat and only one to work.   Н80, Р4
To tremble at doing and to sweat at eating.

123 В радости сыщут, а в горести забудут.   *v.* В318, К255
When we laugh everyone sees, when we cry, no one sees. When you laugh, the world laughs with you, but when you cry, you cry alone.

124 В разгладицу дело не поладится.   *v.* Г311, З131, И81, К201
[It doesn't always come out in the wash.] *Cf.* Two wrongs don't make a right.

125 В рай за волосы не тянут.   *v.* Л180
[No one is dragged to heaven by the hair.] There's no going to heaven in a sedan.

126 В рай просят, а сами в ад лезут.   *v.* Г180
[They seek Heaven but they flock toward Hell.] He looks one way and rows another. *Cf.* Hopers go to Hell.

127 В расплохе и медведь труслив.
[Even a bear cowers when taken by surprise.] A man surprised is half beaten (taken).

128 В решете воду черпать (носить).   *v.* Б157, В320, К22, Н362, Р56, Х13
To carry (draw) (fetch) water in a sieve. *EA.* cribro aquam haurire.

129 В решете густо (много высевок) а в закроме пусто (весной).
[The sieves are full (with chaff) and the silos are empty (in Spring).] Sift him grain by grain, and he proves but chaff.

130* В роде дураков старшего нет.
[In the family of fools there is no elder.] The family of fools is very old. *Cf.* No fool to the old fool. A fool always finds a greater fool to admire.

131 В роспуск веселее, а с зажимкой прибыльнее.
[Extravagance is fun, but thrift is profitable.] *Cf.* Spare well and spend well.

132 В рукавицу ветра не изловишь.   *v.* В215, З5, И143, Н12
[One cannot catch the wind in a mitten.] To catch the wind in a net.

133 В своей земле (избе) никому пророком не быть.
No man is a prophet in his own country. *Matt.*13.57: A prophet is not without honour, save in his own country and in his own house.

134 В своей семье сам большой.   *v.* В137,557,607
[He is a big man at home.] Every dog is a lion at home.

135   В своей хате и углы помогают.   *v.* Д387
         [At home every corner helps.]   At home everything is easy.

136   В своем доме все судьи (как хочу, так и ворочу).   *v.* В194,579, С72, Т14
         [Everyone is the judge in his own home (at home I give the orders).]   Every man is a king
         (master) in his own house.   A man's home is his castle.

137*   В своем курятнике петух хозяин.   *v.* В134,557,562,607
         A cock is master of his coop. *Cf.* A cock is bold on his own dunghill.
         Lat. Sen.*Claud.Mort.* gallus in sterquilinio suo plurimum potest.

138   В своем ломте - своя воля.   *v.* С65
         [Do what you like with your own (piece).]   Own is own. *Cf.*. Paddle your own canoe.

139   В семье и каша гуще.   *v.* Д386, Н116, С61, Ч128
         [At home even the porridge is thicker.] Dry bread at home is better than roast meat broad.

140*   В семье не без урода.   *v.* В159, И18, С131
         Accidents will happen in the best regulated families. There are black sheep in every
         flock.   Skeletons in the closet. *SPL.* terra salutiferas herbas eadem quae nocentes nutrit,
         et urticae proxima saepe rosa est.

141*   В сене огня не скроешь.   *v.* С237, Ш7
         Fire cannot be hidden in straw (flax).

142*   В сердце нет окна.   *v.* В184, Л85, Ч112
         [The heart hath no window.]   You can look in the eyes, but not in the heart. *Cf.* Don't
         wear your heart on your sleeve.

143   В суде убогий с богатым, хотя и прав бывает виноватым.
         [In court against a rich man, the pauper is guilty even though he may be right.] *Cf.* One
         law for the rich and another for the poor.

144*   В супрядках (супрядке) не пряжа, (а) в складчине не торг.
         [Little spinning at sewing circles, little money in junk.] *Cf.* No mill no meal, no will no deal.

145   В счастье всякий умеет попеть, а умный умеет и горе терпеть.   *v.* В151, К162, С316,
         [Anyone can sing when fortune smiles, but a wise man also knows   Т65, Х71
         how to bear adversity.] He dances well to whom fortune pipes. Any man can be a sailor
         on a calm sea.

146*   В счете правда не теряется. *v.* В116

147   В схватке счастье великое дело.
         [In war, luck is paramount.] *Lat.* Tac. in rebus bellicis maxime dominatur fortuna.

148   В тайном деле чести нет.   *v.* В63, Ч20
         We cannot come to honour under coverlet.   Wherever there is a secret, there must be
         something wrong.

149*   В темноте и гнилушка светит. *v.* В448

150*   В тесноте, да не в обиде. (В тесноте люди живут, а в обиде гибнут.)   *v.* Л204
         [It's tight but all right.] [One can live in tight quarters but not in shame.] *said to make*
         light of a lack of space, as in the expression "The more the merrier!" Where there's room

in the heart, there's room in the house. The more the merrier. *Cf.* Home is home though it never be so homely. Content lodges oftener in cottages than palaces.

151* **В тихое время, всяк может править.** *v.* B145, X71
Anyone can be a sailor (pilot) on a calm sea. *SPL.* quilibet tranquillo mari gubernare potest.

152* **В тихой воде (тихих омутах) (тихом озере) -**
омуты глубоки (черти в омутах) (черти водятся). *v.* E3, 32, T29, Ч112
Still waters run deep. *SPL.* altiora flumina, minimo sono labuntur.
Cf. Shakesp.*2Hen.VI*.III.1.53: Smooth runs the water where the brook is deep.

153 **В тихой губке больше рыбки.**
[There are more fish in a placid inlet.] *Cf.* The best fish keep near the bottom. †*Lat.* aqua turbida piscosior est.

154 **В траве идет - с травою вровен, в лесу - с лесом.** *v.* B50,187,541, Г39, T34,86
[In the grass as a blade, in the forest as a tree.] *Cf.* A wise man esteems every place to be his own country. When in Rome, do as the Romans.

155* **В трех соснах заблюдился.** *v.* П203
[He lost his way around three firs.] *Cf.* †A man never got lost on a straight road.

156 **В трубе углем не запишешь.**
[One cannot write with charcoal in a chimney.] Black will take no other hue.

157 **В тюрьму широка дорога, а из тюрьмы тесна.** *v.* Ш9
[The way to jail is wide, the way out narrow.] *Cf.* Verg.*Aen*.6.1.126: facilis descensus Averno (easy is the descent to hell) †Cic.*Tusc*.1.43.104: undique ad inferos tantundum viae est.

158 **В убогой гордости дьяволу утеха.**
[A wretch's pride is the devil's solace.] The devil wipes his tail with a poor man's pride.

159 **В уйме (чернолесье) не без зверя, в людях не без лиха.** *v.* B140
[Every horde (forest) has its beast, every people its villain.] There is a black sheep in every flock.

160 **В умницы попал а из дураков не вышел.** *v.* Б167, B353, E9, И37,38, H24
No man is wise at all times. *Lat.* Pliny *H.N.*7.40.2: nemo mortalium omnibus horis sapit. *Cf.* A wise man may sometimes play the fool.

161 **В умной беседе ума набраться, в глупой - свой растерять.** *v.* З136
[Intelligent conversation is mind-expanding, foolish chatter mind-boggling.] Evil is soon learnt. Evil communications corrupt good manners. *Cf.* Think with the wise but talk with the vulgar. *Lat.* loquendum ut vulgus, sentiendum ut sapientes.

162 **В уханье не слыхать и оханье.**
[You cannot hear the moans for the groans.] The noise is so great one cannot hear God thunder.

163 **В хваленой капусте много гнилых кочанов.** *v.* B352,354
[The best cabbage may have rotten heads.] The best cloth may have a moth in it.

164 **В хороший барабан не надо бить с силой.** *v.* Б313, B232
[A good drum doesn't have to be struck with force.] Great strokes make not sweet music.

165   **В хороший год хорош и приплод.**
[In a good year the issue is good.] Cherry (pear) year, a merry year; (+ a plumb year, a dumb year).

166   **В худого коня корм травить (тратить) - что в худую корзину воду лить.**
[Wasting feed on a lame horse is like pouring water into a broken bucket.] *Cf.* Old mare would have new crupper. As fit as a shoulder of mutton for a sick horse.

167* **В царстве слепых, кривой царь (и кривому честь).**   *v.* B448, З30, M54
In the kingdom of the blind, the one-eyed is king. *Gr. Plan.*253: ἐν τῇ τυφλῶν πόλει καὶ ὁ ἑτερόφθαλμος ὡραῖος δοκεῖ.

168   **В человеке важен не чин а начин.**
[Birth, not position makes the man.] Breed is stronger than pasture. *Cf.* †It is not what is he but what has he.

169* **В чем грех, в том и спасение.**   *v.* Г24, Ч43
Seek your salve where you get your sore.

170   **В чем деду стыд, в том бабе смех.**
[What is shameful for the old man is funny for the lady.] One man's meat is another man's poison. *Cf.* Every white has its black and every sweet its sour.

171   **В чем же призван, в том и пребывай.**
[Go where you are summoned.] Come not to counsel uncalled.

172   **В чем застану, в том и сужу.**
[The judgment depends on the crime.] The punishment should fit the crime.

173* **В чем молод похвалится, в том стар покается.**   *v.* B72, C207, Ч39
Young mens' knocks old men feel. *Lat.* quae peccamus iuvenes ea luimus senes. We pay when we are old for the misdeeds of our youth.

174   **В чем (живет) смех, в том и грех.**   *v.* Б49, B616, П29
No joy without annoy. *Cf. Lat.* extrema gaudii luctus occupat (grief borders on the extremes of gladness).

175   **В чем смолода охота, в том под старость неволя.**   *v.* M147, C280, Ч8
[What the young man craves, the old man cannot do.] *Cf.* If the young man would and the old man could, there would be nothing undone.

176   **В честь вино пьют, а не в честь, льют.**
[Wine is toasted in honour and spilt in dishonour.] *Cf.* Spilt wine is worse than water.

177   **В чины протрешься, а в ум не вотрешься.**   *v.* B536
[One may advance in rank but not in intelligence.] The greatest clerks are not the wisest men. *Lat.* magis magni clerici non sunt magis sapientes.

178   **В чужих руках краюха (кус) за ковригу (ломоть).**
В чужих руках (чужой руке) ломоть велик (всегда пирог шире) (кус и больше).
[A lump looks like a loaf in another's hands.]   *v.* B179,186,583, H118, П122,
[The portion is always greater in another's hands.]   C168,Ч118,129, X43
Cf. Our neighbour's cow (ground) yields better milk (corn) than ours. The grass is greener (on the other side). The hills are green far away. *Lat.* fertilior seges est alieno semper in arvo. Pub.Syr. aliena nobis nostra plus aliis placent.

179   **В чужих руках ноготок с локоток.**   *v.* B178
[Another's inch looks like a foot.] Your pot broken seems better than my pot whole.

180   **В чужое горло не напьешься.**   *v.* B185,198,200, Г128, H111, Ч127
[One cannot drink one's fill vicariously.] You can't get warm in another's fur coat.
Cf. He that is fed at another's hand (table) may stay long ere he be full.

181*   **В чужое счастье не мухой пасть.**   *v.* 365, Ч121
[Don't denigrate others' good luck.] *Cf.* Envy shoots at others and wounds itself. Never interfere with anything that doesn't bother you. Meddle not with another man's matter.

182   **В чужой азбуке по толкам читаешь, а в своей и складов не разберешь.**   *v.* B192,
[You read another's alphabet well, but cannot even discern   309, Ч116
syllables in your own.] If we can tell others what to do, we should know what to do ourselves. *Cf.* The eye that sees all things else sees not itself. We do not always see what is in the wallet behind.

183   **В чужой беседе всяк ума (не) купит.**
[(Not) everyone learns from others' talk.] *Cf.* He that nothing questions, nothing learns.

184   **В чужой душе, не вода в ковше - не разглядишь сразу.**   *v.* B142, Ч112
[One can't read another's mind as clearly as one sees through a pitcher of water.]
Cf. Cic.*Rep.*6.24.26: mens cuiusque is est quisque.

185   **В чужой загородке скота не наплодишь.**   *v.* B180,198,199,200, Г128
[One cannot breed a herd in another's corral.] Build not up a fortune on the labours of others. *Cf.* A man must plough with such oxen as he has.

186*   **В чужой лодке всегда больше рыбки.**   *v.* B178, T10
[There are always more fish in another's boat.] Our neighbour's ground yields better corn than ours.

187*   **В чужой монастырь со своим уставом не ходи.**   *v.* B50,154, 353,107, H87
[Go not to another's monastery with your own dogma.] Measure not another's corn by your own bushel. When in Rome, do as the Romans.

188   **В чужой мошне, не в своей квашне - не смекнешь есть ли тесто аль пусто место.** Ч130
[Another's purse isn't your kneading tray - no telling if there's any dough or not.]
You cannot know the wine by the barrel. You cannot tell a book by its cover.
Cf. Neither eyes on letters nor hands on coffers.

189   **В чужой огород не пустят козла полоть.**   *v.* H114,201,283,400, X97
[A goat is not permitted to graze in another's orchard.] Pluck not where you never planted. *Cf.* The goat must browse where she is tied.

190   **В чужой прудок не кидай неводок (не закинешь неводок).**   *v.* H114,197,201
[Cast not your net into another's stream.] Pluck not where you never planted.
Cf. It is in vain to cast your net where there is no fish.

191*   **В чужой рот не поставишь ворот.**   *v.* B404,528, H113
[One cannot muzzle another's mouth.] Everyone to his own opinions. *SPL.* non est arbitrii nostri quid quisque loquatur.

192*   **В чужом глазу сучок велик (видим) а в своем (у себя) и бревня не видит (видим).**
*Matt.*7.3: **You see a mote in another's eye but not a beam in your own.**   *v.* B182
SPL.   qui ne tuberibus propriis offendat amicum postulat, ignosct verrucis illius.

193   **В чужом доме не будь приметлив, а будь приветлив.**
[Be gracious, not observant in another's home.] Curiosity is ill manners in another's house.

194*   **В чужом доме не указывают.**   *v.* В136,579, С72, Х30
[Do not give commands in another's house.] *Cf.* Every man is a king (master) in his own house.

195   **В чужом доме побывать - в своем гнилое бревно увидать.**
[Visit another's house and you'll see the spoiled woodwork of your own.] *Cf.* Some people can see no good near home.

196*   **В чужом огороде капусту садить.**   *v.* Н201, Н400
[To plant cabbage in another's garden] *i.e. to mind other people's business.*
Cf. Everyman should cultivate his own garden. Hoe your own row. Skeer your own fire.

197*   **В чужом пиру похмелье (наживешь).**   *v.* З24, С1, Т8, *Ap.*1.77
[You'll get drunk at another man's feast.] *Lat.* Plaut.*Mil.*3.2: alii ebrii sunt, alii poscam potitant. One does the harm, another bears the blame. *Cf* The best wine is that drunk at another's cost.

198   **В чужом платье не накрасоваться.**   *v.* В180,,185,200
[Do not dress up in another's gown.] *Cf.* Do not take credit that is due others.

199   **В чужом хлеву овец не считают.**   *v.* В185, Ч131
[Don't count the sheep in another's barn.] Count not four, except when you have them in a wallet.

200   **В чужую дудку не наиграешься.**   *v.* В180,185,198, Н111, Ч127
[No fun in playing another's horn.] Toot your own horn (lest the same be never tooted).

201   **В шубе жарко а в кафтане сквозь несет.**
[Too hot with the fur, too cold without.] Over hot, over cold.

202*   **В шутках правды бывает (слово молвится).**   *v.* В48
Many a true word is spoken in jest.

203   **Важна смелость, да нужна и умелость.**   *v.* В6
[Valour is important, but so is skill.] Skill and assurance are an invincible couple.

204   **Важно знать не то каким ты родился, а каким умрешь.**   *v.* С313, Т44, Х6
[What matters is not who you are at birth, but at death.] Count no man successful until he is dead. Praise no man till he be dead. *Lat.* vitae finem spectato.

205   **Вали валом, после разберем.**
[Go all the way and sort it out later.] *Cf.* Come what may. It'll all come right in the wash.

206   **Вали на серого - серый все свезет.**   *v.* К184,218, Р54
[Let the obliging fool carry it.] All lay load on the willing horse.

207*   **Валить с больной головы на здоровую.**   *v.* З24, Л202, С1, Т8
[Shift blame from the guilty to the innocent.] Have the wrong sow by the ear. Beg at the wrong door. *Cf.* Bark up the wrong tree. One does the harm and another bears the blame.

208   **Вам Бог дал, а нам посулил.**
[God gave unto you, but promised unto us.] A gift is better than a promise.

209 **Вари не вари, а масло поверху.** *v.* Б481
[No matter how you cook the oil floats to the top.] Truth and oil are ever above.

210 **Ваши играют (скачут) (пляшут) а наши рыдают (плачут).** *v.* Б460,В71,218,
Some of us have the hap, others stick in the gap. K186, O62,76, C310,330
Cf. There is no great banquet but some fare ill.

211 **Ваши пьют, а наши(х) пьяных бьют (у наших с похмеля голова болит).**
[Some drink while other drunks get beaten (get the hangover).] *v.* В197,210, O63
Cf. One sows and another reaps.

212* **Вашими (твоими) бы устами (да) мед пить.**
[One might drink honey with you lips.] May your words come true. Were it only true.

213* **Вдвоем, дорогой веселее.** *v.* Б199, Р22, У103
[Two make the road more fun.] No road is long with good company. A merry
companion is a wagon in the way. Cheerful company shortens the miles.
Lat. P.Syr: comes iucundus in via pro vehiculo.

214* **Вдруг не станешь друг.** *v.* Б390, У78, Ч108
[One cannot become a friend immediately.] It takes a year to make a friend. Before you
make a friend, eat a bushel of salt with him. *Lat.* nemini fidas nisi cum quo prius
modium salis absumpseris.

215 **Ведрами ветра не смеряешь.** *v.* В110,132,320, З5, И143, Н12
[One cannot measure the wind with buckets.] To catch the wind in a net. *Cf.* The sea
cannot be scooped up in a tumbler.

216* **Ведрами разольешь, так каплями не соберешь.** *v.* П277
[What's spilled by buckets is irretrievable by drops.] Spilled water cannot be gathered up.

217* **Веером тумана не разгонишь.**
[One cannot fan away the fog.] You cannot hinder the wind from blowing.

218 **Везде скачут а у нас плачут.** *v.* Б460, В71,210,460, K186, O62,76, C310,330
[All are cheerful while we weep.] Some have the hap, others stick in the gap. *Cf.* He
that is warm thinks all so. He whose belly is full believes not him who is fasting.

219 **Век дожил а ума не нажил.** *v.* В403
[He lived long but didn't get any wiser.] Live a fool, die a fool.

220 **Век - долга неделя.** *v.* В226
[A liftime is a long week.] *Cf.* Life is a span.

221 **Век долог да час дорог.** *v.* Г195, Д376, Ж140
[Life is long but the hour dear.] Life is short and time is swift. *Cf.* He that has (gains)
time, has (gains) life.

222* **Век живи, век учись (а дураком помрешь).** *v.* Д254, П118
Live and learn. *Gr.* Zen.304: γηράσκω δ'αιεί διδασκόμενος. *Lat.* vivere tota vita
discendum est. *SPL.* nulla aetas ad discendum sera.

223 **Век изжил, все прожил, горб нажил.**
[He lived to a ripe old age, suffered all and has the hump to show for it.] To live long
is to suffer long. *Cf.* To work hard, live hard, die hard and go to hell after all would be
hard indeed.

224 **Век мелет а посыпать не умеет.** *v.* B319, K207
[He grinds forever but knows not how to sprinkle.] Long mint, little dint.

225 **Век на смеху живет.**
Live happy, live long.

226 **Век не веревкой мерян.** *v.* B20
[Life is not measured by a strand.] *Cf.* Life is but a span.

227 **Век прожить (пережить) - не поле перейти (переехать).** *v.* Г194, Ж147,164
[Living a lifetime is more than just crossing a field.] Life is not a bed of roses. Life is not all beer and skittles.

228 **Веку мало да горя много.**
[Life is short, but misery long.] Life's short and full of blisters. Long life has long misery. *Cf. Lat.* P.Syr.438: o vita misero longa, felici brevis. A long harvest for a little corn.

229 **Велеречие часто наносит увечье.** *v.* B357, Ж95, Л90
[Bombast often bombs.] Many words, many buffets. *Cf.* In many words, the truth goes by.

230 **Велик баклан, да есть изъян.**
[The head is great, yet it has its flaw.] Have a soft place in one's head. It's a sound head that hasn't a soft piece in it.

231 **Велик воин за стаканом вина.** *v.* M107,130, П313,316
[Great is the warrior behind his drink.] Many soldiers are brave at the table who are cowards in the field. Whiskey made the rabbit hug the lion.

232 **Велик звон да не красен.** *v.* B164
Great strokes make not sweet music.

233 **Велик карман да пуст.**
[The pocket is large but empty.] Great as beggars.

234 **Велик почет не живет без хлопот.** *v.* Б323, Ч7
Great honours are great burdens.

235 **Велик рот, а ничего не видит.**
[The mouth is great but it can't see.] *Cf.* Every commodity has its discommodity.

236 **Велик телом да мал делом.**
Great bodies move slowly.

237 **Велика тюрма, да тесно жить.** *v.* K198
[A large prison is still tight.] There are no ugly loves nor handsome prisons.
Cf. A bean in liberty is better than a comfit in prison.

238 **Велика хоромина, да пуста.**
[A great mansion, but empty.] A great city, a great solitude. A big heart is better than a big house.

239 **Велика честь, да нечего есть.**
[A great honour, but nothing to eat.] Nothing agrees worse than a lord's heart and a beggar's purse. *SPL.* gloria quantalibet quid erit, si gloria tantum est.

240* **Великие умы сходятся.**
Great minds think alike.

241 **Великим правду говорить - не легче лжи.**
[Great men find it equally difficult to tell the truth as to lie.] *Cf.* The greater the truth, the greater the libel.

242 **Велико ли перо, а большие книги пишет.**
[Small is the pen, yet it writes big books.] The pen conveys one's meaning a thousand miles. *Cf.* From small beginnings come great things.

243 **Великое дело великой помощи требует.** *v.* Б333,336, К68
[A great enterprise requires great assistance.] *Cf.* Three helping one another bear the burden of six. Earnest effort leads to success.

244 **Великое число из единиц составляется.** *v.* Б89, И90, П58,82
[A large number consists of single digits.] Many small make a great. *Cf.* Add little to little and there will be a great heap. Many drops make a shower.

245* **Венец всему делу конец.** *v.* Д338, К163
The end crowns all (the work). *Lat.* finis coronat opus.

246 **Веника не сломишь, а прутья по одному все переломаешь.** *v.* Д441,445
[A bundle holds whereas twigs break easily one by one.] Weak things united become strong. *Cf.* Willows are weak but they bind other wood.

247 **Верен, что золото в огне.**
[True as gold in the flame.] *Cf.* Gold is tried in the fire.

248 **Верная любовь ни в огне не горит, ни в воде не тонет.**
[True love cannot be burned by fire nor drowned by water.] *Cf.* Love will go through stone walls. Sound love is not soon forgotten. †Salt water and absence wash away love.

249 **Верная указка - не кулак а ласка.** *v.* Д315,354, Ж40, Л8,147, М49, П137
[Good advice: a caress is better than a fist.] Kindness is the strongest weapon to conquer with. Power itself has not one half the might of gentleness. *Cf.* Speak gently: it is better to rule by love than by fear.

250 **Верно как дважды два четыре.**
[As sure as two times two is four.] As sure as eggs is eggs.

251 **Верному другу цены нет.** *v.* Д413, Л130
[A true friend has no price.] Loyalty is worth more than money.

252 **Верный друг лучше сотни слуг.** *v.* Д298,413
[Better a true friend than a hundred servants.] They are rich who have true friends.

253 **Верный друг любит до смерти.** *v.* Д444, Л189
[A true friend is a friend until death.] *Cf.* True love never grows old.

254 **Верный слуга царю всего дороже.**
[A loyal servant is a king's greatest asset.] The subject's love is the king's lifeguard.

255 **Вертит языком, что корова хвостом.**
[He moves his tongue like a cow wags its tail.] The tongue of idle persons is never still.

256* **Вертится как белка в колесе.** *v.* К16

257 **Вертится как черт перед заутреней.** *v.* В587
[He's fidgety like the devil before matins.] *Cf.* The faulty stands on his guard.

258 **Верь волчьим слезам.**
[Believe lupine tears.] *Cf.* Crocodile tears. *EA.* crocodili lacrimae.

259 **Верь не болезни а врачу.**
[Trust the doctor, not the disease.] *Cf.* †The doctor is often more to be feared than the disease.

260* **Верь приданому после свадьбы.** *v.* Д126, Ж34, М48, Н460,477, Т45, Ц10
[Count the dowry after the wedding.] *Cf.* Don't count your chickens before they are hatched. Don't count fish till on dry land.

261 **Верю кошке и ежу, а тебе погожу.** *v.* Л121
[I trust a cat or a hedgehog, but for you I demur.] I will trust you no further than I can see you. *Cf.* You can't trust your best friend.

262 **Веселись, играй, да дело знай.**
[Be merry, play, but know your way.] It is good to be merry and wise.

263 **Веселого нрава не купишь.** *v.* В267, Д360, Н104,195
[You cannot buy a happy disposition.] Money can't buy happiness.

264* **Веселый гость - дому радость.**
[The happy guest is a joy to the house.] *Cf.* The company makes the feast.

265 **Веселье делает безделье.** *v.* О126
[Merriment breeds idleness.] Laugh and grow fat.

266 **Веселье - делу не помеха.** *v.* В269
[Mirth only helps.] *Cf.* Laughter's the best medicine. A cheerful look makes a dish a feast.

267 **Веселье лучше богатства.** *v.* В263, Д360, Н104,194
[Better be happy than wealthy.] Content is more than a kingdom. *Cf.* Happiness does not consist of riches alone.

268 **Веселье не вечно, и печальное конечно.** *v.* Д290
[Mirth is not eternal, melancholy is.] The mirth of the world, dureth but a while.

269 **Веселье - от всех бед спасение.** *v.* В266
[Mirth is the cure for all ills.] Laughter is the best medicine.

270 **Весна да осень - на дню погод восем.**
[In Spring and Fall, eight different kinds of weather in a day.] *Cf.* An English summer - two fine days and a thunderstorm.

271 **Весна красная а лето страдное.**
[Spring is handsome, summer toilsome.] *Cf.* Summer is a seemly time.

272 **Вести-то пустили, а колокола не отлили.**
[The news was leaked before the bells were forged.] *i.e. to announce them.* *Cf.* We cannot control the news we get, but we can control the news we start.

273 **Весь дом вверх дном.** *v.* Б438, П204
    [The entire house is topsy-turvy.] To throw the house out the window.

274 **Весь как есть, с начинкой и с потрохами.**
    [Complete with stuffing and giblets.] Lock, stock and barrel.

275 **Весь сыт, а глаза голодны.** *v.* Б368, Г111,116, Д507, З161
    The eyes are bigger than the belly.

276 **Ветер горы разрушает, слово народы поднимает.**
    [Winds erode mountains, words rouse people.] *Cf.* The tongue is the rudder of our ship.

277 **Ветер не дует, так и осока не шумит.**
    [If the wind is still, the grass won't rustle.] Straws show which way the wind blows.
    Cf. To pluck the grass to see where the wind sits.

278 **Ветр с ветром и знается.** *v.* В417
    [One wind knows another.] One thief knows another. One swine recognizes another.

279 **Вечер плач а заутра радость.**
    [Tears may linger at nightfall but joy comes in the morning.] *Psalm.*29.6 ad vesperum demorabitur fletus et ad matutinum laetitia. A blustering night, a fair day.

280* **Вечер покажет каков был день.** *v.* Д171
    [Night reveals the day.] Praise a fair day at night. *SPL.* ante obitum neminem beatum dixeris.

281 **Вешний день целый год кормит.**
    [A spring day feeds the entire year.] *Cf.* April and May are the keys of the year.

282 **Вещий сон не обманет.**
    [Prophetic dreams don't lie.] *Cf.* Morning dreams come true. †Dreams are lies.

283* **Вещь хороша когда новая, а друг - старый.** *v.* Д415, Л160
    New things are the best things, but old friends are the best friends.
    Cf. Old friends and old wine and old gold are best.

284 **Взаймы брать - других учить, взаймы давать - себя казнить.**
    (Взявши у других поучишь, отдавши сам в науку поидешь).
    [Borrow (take) and teach others, lend and punish (learn) yourself.] *Cf.* Lend and lose (is the game of fools).

285 **Взаймы не брал - хоть гол, да прав.** *v.* Л159, М168
    [Better be poor than borrow.] Better to go to bed supperless than to rise in debt.

286 **Взглянет - огнем опалит, молвит - рублем подарит.** *v.* К259
    His bark is worse than his bite.

287* **Взлетел орлом, прилетел голубем.** *v.* Б300, В430, З103, Н155
    [He took off an eagle but landed a pigeon.] To go up like a rocket and come down like a stick. *Cf.* Attempt not to fly like an eagle with the wings of a wren.

288* **Взойдет солнце и над нашими воротами (к нам на двор) (к нам в окно).**
    [The sun will also shine on our gates (yard) (window).] *v.* А7, Ж118, П256
    The sun shines on all the world. Every dog has his day. *Cf.* Tomorrow is another day.
    †The sun does not shine on both sides of the hedge at once.

289   Взывать к помощи нечистой силы.
      To hold a candle to the devil.

290   Взяв (взял) лычко, отдашь (отдай) ремешок.   *v.* В381, Д367, З12
      [Borrow a rope, return a strap.] He that borrows binds himself with his neighbour's rope.

291*   Взявши (взялся) за гуж, не говори что не дюж.   *v.* В342, Ж14, К170,213, Л70,
      Don't say go but gaw.   Н133,440, П201, С84
      In for a penny, in for a pound. *Cf.* Never make a promise if you don't intend to keep it.

292*   Взял корову, возьми и подойник.   *v.* Б375,447,475, К303
      [When you take the cow, take also the pail.] If you buy the cow, take the tail into the bargain. *Cf.* God gives the milk but not the pail.

293   Взял на час, дай в добрый час.   *v.* Б193, К31
      [Having borrowed, return promptly.]   *Cf.* Pay with the same dish you borrowed.

294   Взял с сердцем, так и ешь с перцем.   *v.* Ж70, К119
      [Married for love, now live with all the trimmings.] Marry in haste and repent at leisure.

295*   Взял топор - возьми и топорище.   *v.* Д40
      Take the helve with the axe.

296   Взялась собака мясом торговать.   *v.* В395, Д359
      [The dog has become a meat dealer.] *Cf.* The cat is honest when the meat is out of her reach. The blind man's peck should be well measured. Set the wolf to watch the sheep.

297   Взяло разумье глядя на безумие.
      [Reason won out when it looked at folly.] *Cf.* It is a great point of wisdom to find out one's own folly.

298*   Взятки гладки.   *v.* В693
      [Nothing more is to be had.] *i.e. from someone.* *Cf.* You cannot get blood from a stone. Squeezed dry. Slippery as an eel.

299*   Взять легко, вернуть трудно.   *v.* Б192, Д13,71
      [Easier to borrow than to return.] Some men have a short arm for giving and a long arm for taking. *Cf.* Sweet appears sour when we pay.

300*   Виденное лучше сказанного.   *v.* Г165
      Better seen than heard. *Cf.* Seeing is believing.

301*   Видеть легко, предвидеть трудно.
      [Seeing is easier than foreseeing.] He is wise that is ware in time. *Cf.* Foresight is better than hindsight.

302*   Видим и сами что кривы наши сани.
      [We don't need anyone to tell us our sledge is bent.] The land's never void of counsellors. After advice is fool's advice. Don't add insult to injury (rub salt in the wound).

303   Видимая беда, что у старого жена молода.
      [An old man with a young bride is a foreseeable disaster.] *Cf.* Old men, when they marry young women, make much of death. There's nothing worse than an old lover.

304   Видимая смерть страшна.
      Death hath not so ghastly a face at a distance as it hath at hand.

305 **Видит, да не там где надо.**
[He sees, but not what he should.] *Cf.* To have eyes yet see not.

306 **Видит и кривой на ком кафтан плохой.** *v.* О70, У40
[Even the one-eyed can see whom the *caftan* doesn't fit.] *Cf.* None so blind as those who will not see.

307 **Видит корова что за рекой солома.** *v.* Д272
[The cow can see the straw across the river.] What we see depends mainly on what we look for. *Cf.* A hungry man sees far. We soon believe what we desire.

308 **Видит кот (собака) молоко, да рыло коротко (да в кувшине глубоко).**
(Видит око, да зуб неймет.) *v.* В362, Г109
[The cat (dog) sees the milk, but its neck is too short (but the jug is deep).]
[The eye sees but the tooth cannot touch.] *Cf. Lat.* Cato *ap.Aul.Gell.*13.17.1: inter os atque offam multa intervenire posse. Many a slip 'twixt the cup and the lip.

309* **Видишь глаз чужой, да не видишь свой.** *v.* В659, С77, Ч116
The eye that sees all things else sees not itself.

310* **Видна птица по перьям, а человек по речам.** *v.* Б142, В314, З158, О98
The bird is known by his note [feathers], the man by his words. *Lat.* qualis homo ipse est, talis eius est oratio.

311* **Видна птица по полету.** *v.* К49, П54
[A bird is known by its flight.] A bird is known by his note.

312 **Видно, не той ногой (невпопад) порог переступил.**
[He obviously crossed the threshold on the wrong foot (inopportunely).] *Cf.* To rise on the wrong side.

313 **Видно непряха коли утла рубаха.** *v.* В602, Д145
[The seamstress is known by the delicacy of the shirt.] *Cf.* A bad seamstress uses a long thread. The workman is known by his work.

314 **Видно совушку по перышку, а сироту по одеже.** *v.* В310
[An owl is known by its feathers, and an orphan by his clothes.] *Cf.* Fine feathers make fine birds.

315 **Видом внушительный, да в работе нерешительный.** *v.* Р37
[Impressive in appearance but indecisive at task.] *Cf.* They that are booted are not always ready. Be what you appear to be.

316 **Видом орел, а умом тетерев. (Видом сокол, голосом ворона.)** *v.* К191, Н143,237
[The appearance of an eagle (falcon), the brain (call) of a grouse (crow).] *Cf.* Appearances (one's looks) are deceiving. If you have good looks, you don't need any brains.

317 **Видя на море волны не суйся.** *v.* Н56
Never go to sea when a storm is coming.

318 **Вижу кто скачет, а не вижу кто плачет.**
Все видят как веселюсь, а никто не видит как плачу (крушусь). *v.* В123, К255
When we laugh, everyone sees, when we cry, no one sees.
Cf. Suffering doesn't manifest itself.

319* **Визгу много а шерсти нет.**   *v.* Б335, В118,224, К207,261, М204
   Great cry and little wool.   *Lat.* multum clamoris, parum lanae.

320* **Вилкой щи хлебать.**   *v.* Б157, В128,215, М160, Р56, Х13
   [Eat soup with a fork.]   *Cf.* To empty the sea with a spoon. To carry water in a sieve.
   To catch the wind in a net.

321 **Вина голову клонит.**   *v.* В426, Н18
   [Guilt bows the head.]   *Cf.* A guilty conscience feels continual fear.

322 **Вино веселит, да от вина голова болит.**   *v.* В14,15
   Drunken days have all their tomorrows.

323 **Вино веселит сердце человеку.**
   Wine is the whetstone to wit.

324 **Вино вину творит.**
   [Wine engenders guilt.]   *Cf.* Wine is a turncoat.

325* **Вино входит, ум выходит.**   *v.* Д55, К294
   When wine is in, wit is out.   *Lat.* dum vinum intrat, exit sapientia.

326* **Вино на пиво диво (+ а пиво на вино г...).** *vulg.(2nd part which is usually left unsaid)*
   Wine on beer brings good cheer (but beer on wine is not so fine).

327 **Вино надвое растворено - на веселье и на горе.**
   [Wine has two parts: one for mirth and the other for grief.]   *Cf.* The vine brings forth
   three grapes: the first of pleasure, the second of drunkenness, the third of sorrow. Wine
   is a turncoat.

328 **Вино не винит (а пьянство).**   *v.* Н220

329 **Вино ничего не изобретает, оно только выбалтывает.**
   Drunkenness does not produce faults, it discovers them.   *Cf.* Wine wears no breeches.

330 **Вино с водой хуже воды с вином.**
   [Wine with water is worse than water with wine.]   *Cf.* Never mix your liquor. Better to
   have bread left over than run out of wine.

331* **Вино с разумом не ладит.**   *v.* В338
   Counsels in wine seldom prosper.   *SPL.* vinum obumbrat sapientiam.

332 **Вино сперва веселит, а потом безумным творит.**
   [Wine first gladdens, then maddens.]   Wine is a turncoat (first a friend, then an enemy).
   Cf. A man takes a drink and then the drink takes the man. Sweet is the wine but sour is
   the payment.

333 **Виноват волк (медведь) что козу ободрал (корову сьел),**
   не права и коза (корова) что в лес зашла (за поля ходила).   *v.* Н512
   [The wolf (bear) is to blame for eating the goat (cow), but the goat (cow) was wrong to
   enter the wood (leave the field.)]   How can the cat help it if the maid be a fool?

334* **Виноватому все кажется что про него говорят.**   *v.* Н18
   He that commits a fault thinks everyone speaks of it.

335   **Виноватый винится, а правый ничего не боится.**   *v.* Д276, К241
      A guilty conscience is a self-accuser. A clear conscience is like a coat of mail.

336   **Вином горя не зальешь, а новое наживешь.**   *v.* Г298
      [Wine cannot wash sorrows out, it only brings them in.] Drink does not drown care, but waters it and makes it grow faster.

337   **Вином жажды не запьешь, разве больше наживешь.**
      A drunken man is always dry. Ever drunk, ever dry.

338   **Вином разум не промоешь.**   *v.* В331
      [Wine does not refresh the mind.] Drinking and thinking don't mix.

339   **Винцо да игра не доведут до добра.**
      Wine, women and song will do a man wrong. *Cf.* Play, women and wine undo men laughing. Gaming, women and wine, while they laugh, they make men pine.

340   **Вкусив сладкого, не захочешь горького.**   *v.* Н363
      [Having tasted the sweet, you will not want the sour.] *Cf.* He deserves not the sweet that will not taste the sour.

341   **Влажна рука торовата, сухая - скуповата.**
      [A moist hand affirms a generous nature, a dry hand - avarice.] *Cf.* A moist hand argues an amorous nature. A cold hand, a warm heart.

342   **Влез по пояс (горло), полезай и по горло (уши).**   *v.* В291, Ж14, К170, Л70
      In for a penny, in for a pound.

343   **Вместе и горе легче переносить.**   *v.* В546, Г266, Н53, С21
      It is good to have company in trouble. Misery loves company. Two in distress make sorrow less.

344   **Вместе тошно (тесно), порознь скучно (а розно грустно).**   *v.* Р67

345   **Вместо калача (спасибо), да кукиш (шею бьют). (Вместо ореха да свищ.)**   *v.* К93,171
      [Instead of pie (thanks), nothing.] [A knot instead of a nut.] Ask for bread and be given a stone.

346   **Во время брани добра не говорят.**
      [Good is not said in anger.] *Cf.* When wrath speaks, wisdom veils her face.

347   **Во время поры точи топоры, а пройдет пора - не надо и топора.**   *v.* П172

348   **Во время счастья не возносись, а больше Богу молись.**   *v.* Б146, Н257
      [Vaunt not your fortune but pray to God.] *Cf.* He that talks much of his happiness, summons grief.

349   **Во всем доля, а ни в чем воля.**
      There is measure in all things [but freedom in none].

350   **Во всякой гордости черту радость.**
      [The devil takes pleasure in every conceit.] Pride is a flower that grows in the devil's garden.

351*   **Во всякой избушке свои погремушки.**   *v.* Х29

352   **Во всякой реке есть мели.**   *v.* В159,163,354
         [Every river has its shoals.] No garden without its weeds.

353*   **Во всяком мудреце довольно простоты.**   *v.* Б167,420, В160, Е9, Н24
         [Every wise man is fool enough.] No man is wise at all times.

354   **Во всяком хлебе есть мякина.**
         Every grain has its bran.

355*   **Во всяком худе не без добра.**   *v.* Н192,531, Т17
         Nothing so bad in which there is not something of good. *Lat.* malum quidem nullum esse sine aliquo bono.

356   **Во лжи постоянства нет.**
         [There is no constancy in lies.] *Cf.* False with one can be false with two.

357   **Во многом глаголании нет спасения.**   *v.* Б318, В229, Л90
         [No salvation in much talk.] *Cf.* The tongue talks at the head's cost.

358   **Во сне счастье, наяву ненастье.**
         [Blissful sleep, sorrowful wakening.] Dreams are what you hope for, reality is what you plan for.

359   **Во что кто влюбился, в то преобразился.**   *v.* З15, С12,28,123
         [What one loves, one becomes.] *Cf.* Congruity is the mother of love.

360   **Во что метил, в то и попал.**   *v.* К88,318, П55,192, Ч97
         He that sows thistles shall reap prickles.

361   **Во что черт ни нарядится, а все чертом останется.**   *v.* В49, Л42, О9, С54
         [However the devil is clad, he's still the devil.] An ape's an ape, a varlet's a varlet though they be clad in silk or scarlet.

362   **Вода близко, да гора (ходить) склизка(о).**   *v.* В308, Г109, И2
         [The water's near but the slope is slippery.] There's many a slip 'twixt the cup and the lip.

363   **Вода и землю точит и камень долбит.**   *v.* В473, Д513, К98, М11
         Constant dripping wears away the stone.

364   **Вода не замутит живота.**
         [Water won't spoil your stomach.] *Cf.* Adam's ale is the best brew.

365   **Вода путь найдет.**
         [Water will find a way.] *Cf.* The strong man and the waterfall channel their own path.

366   **Водка портит все кроме посуды.**
         [Vodka spoils everything but the glasses.] Wine is the best liquor to wash glasses in.

367   **Водке - рюмка, пиву - стакан, а столу - веселая компания.**
         [A glass for the vodka, a mug for the beer, and cheerful company for the table.] The company makes the feast. *Cf.* Choose thy company before thy drink.

368*   **Воду варить (толочь), вода и будет.**   *v.* Г296, К50, С137
         [Boil (beat) water and it's still water.] Whether you boil snow or pound it, you can have but water of it.

369 **Воду жалеть - каши не сварить.**   *v.* Б106, Д410, Л54
[He who saves water cannot cook *kasha.*] He who does not kill hogs will not get black puddings. You must lose a fly to catch a trout.

370 **Воды много, а почерпнуть нечего.**
[There's much water but none to draw.] Many are called but few are chosen.

371 **Военное дело не учить - битым быть.**
[Inadequate military training means defeat.] *Cf.* In war it is not permitted twice to err.

372 **Воз под горою а вожжи в руках.**   *v.* К323, П206
[The cartload is down the hill, but the reins are in the hand.] Up the creek without a paddle. To leave one holding the bag.

373 **Воз рассыпал, а два нагреб.**   *v.* Н372
[Dropped one load and gathered up two.] What you lose on the swings, you gain on the roundabouts.

374 **Возвышает жену не наряд, а домостройство.**
[It is not the gown that embellishes the bride, but her housekeeping.] The best furniture in a house is a virtuous woman.

375 **Воздавай должное и дьяволу.**   *v.* Б488
Give the devil his due.

376 **Воздух словами не наполнить.**   *v.* Б20,21,367, Р24, С236
[You can't fill the air with words.] Good words fill not a sack.

377* **Возить дрова в лес.**   *v.* В59, *Ap.*1.85
[To carry wood to the woods.] *Lat.* ligna in silvam portare (stultum est). To carry coals to Newcastle.

378* **Возить песок к морю.**   *v.* В59,377, *Ap.*1.85
[To carry sand to the sea.] *Lat.* Ov.*Tr.*5.6.43: in litus harenas. To cast water into the sea. Salt to Dysart.

379 **Возле людей потирайся, да ума набирайся.**   *v.* Д496
[Mingle and learn.] A learned assembly is a living library. *Cf.* Wise men learn from others' harms. Learn wisdom from others' folly.

380* **Возьмет голод - явится и голос.**   *v.* Г232
[When hunger strikes, you'll find your voice.] The hungry man often talks of bread. *Cf.* He that cannot ask, cannot live.

381 **Возьмешь лычко, а отдашь веревочку.**   *v.* В290, Д368, З12
[Borrow bast but return a rope.] Repay kindness with kindness. *Cf.* To give as good as one gets.

382 **Возьмешь с жаром - отдашь даром.**   *v.* Г90, П188, Ч102
[Take capriciously and you'll give it away for nothing.] *Cf.* In giving and taking there may be mistaking.

383 **Воин погибает а счастливый подбирает.**
[While one soldier perishes, another lucky one cleans up.] Soldiers fight, and kings are the heroes.

384 **Война кровь любит.**   *v.* Б346
[War loves blood.] War is death's feast.

385 **Война не лечит а калечит.**   *v.* В39
[War does not cure but butchers.] Wars bring scars.

386 **Войной да огнем не шутят.**   *v.* Х24
[Don't joke with fire or war.] Do not jest in serious matters.

387 **Войну хорошо слышать, да тяжело видеть.**
[War is good to hear about but harsh to see.] War is sweet to them that know it not.

388 **Волк в монашеской рясе. (Волк и в овечьей шкуре не укроется.)**   *v.* В437, Г163
[A wolf in a monk's tunic.] A wolf in sheep's clothing. *Cf. Matt.*vii.15: Beware of false prophets which come to you in sheep's clothing, but inwardly they are ravening wolves.

389 **Волк волка не съест.**   *v.* Б240, В435, И21, К155, С221
[Wolf does not eat wolf.] Dog does not eat dog.

390 **Волк и больной овце не корысть.**   *v.* В392, К23
[Even a sick wolf is a bane to sheep.] A wolf may lose his teeth but never his nature.

391* **Волк кается, а за овцу хватается.**
[A wolf bewails the sheep, then eats it.] Carrion crows bewail the dead sheep, then eat them.

392* **Волк (и каждый год) линяет, но нрав не меняет (а все сер бывает).**   *v.* Н17, С138,
[The wolf sheds his fur each year, but his colours do not change.]   Т66, У8
The wolf may lose his teeth, but never his nature. *Gr. Plan.*178: ὁ λύκος τὴν τρίχα ἀμείβει,τὴν γνώμην οὐκ ἀμείβει. *Lat.* lupus pilum mutat, non mentem. *Cf.* The fox may grow grey, but never good.

393 **Волка (волков) бояться - (так) в лес не ходить.**   *v.* Б355, Д451, Т66
[Those who fear wolves should not venture into the woods.] He that fears leaves must not go into the wood. *Lat.* folias qui timet, silvas non adeat.

394* **Волка бояться и от белки бежать.**   *v.* Б349
[He who fears wolves also flinches from squirrels.] When a serpent has bitten, a lizard alarms. *Cf.* He that has been bitten by a serpent is afraid of a rope.

395 **Волка в пастухи поставили.**   *v.* Б385, Д359, Н211,389, П303
To set the wolf to keep the sheep. *Lat.* Ter.*Eun.*v.i.16: ovem lupo commisisti.

396 **Волка ноги кормят.**   *v.* Б380, В113, К75, Л39
[The legs feed the wolf.] *Gr. Plan.*147: τὸν λύκον οἱ πόδες αὐτοῦ τρεφοῦσιν. The dog that trots about finds the bone. A man has to work for a living.

397* **Волки (бы были) сыты и овцы целы.** *v.* И12

398* **Волком родился (родясь) - лисой (лисицей) не бывать.**   *v.* В439, И74,106,
[What is born a wolf cannot become a fox.]   Н194, С135,227
He who is born round cannot die square. *Cf.* A carrion kite (buzzard) will never make a good hawk. The wolf must die in his own skin. He that comes of a hen must scrape.

399 **Волку верь убитому, а врагу разбитому.**
[Trust only dead wolves and defeated enemies.] The only good wolf (enemy) is a dead wolf (enemy).

400*   **Волос долог да ум короток.**   *v.* Б340,341, П60, У2
Long hair, short wit. Long hair and short sense. *Gr.* μαλὰ μακρια, γνόον ὀλιγον.

401   **Волос седой, а голова шалит.**   *v.* Б343, В402, Г214, Р64, С89
Hoar head and green tail. *Cf.* Grey hairs are nourished with green thoughts.

402   **Волосом бел, а крепостью цел.**   *v.* Б343, В401, Р64
A grey head is often placed on green shoulders.

403   **Волосом сед, а совести нет.**   *v.* В219
He is grey before he is good.

404   **Вольно всякому на своей земле яму копать.**   *v.* В136,191,406,579, С72, Т14
[Everyone is free to dig a ditch on their own land.] It's a free country. Every man is master in his house.

405   **Вольно собаке и на владыку (месяц) брехать (лаять).**
[A dog is free to bark at the bishop (moon).] A cat may look at a king.

406*   **Вольному воля, спасенному рай.**   *v.* В191,Д490, Н369
[Freedom for the free, and heaven for the survivors.] It's a free country. To each his own. As the fool thinks, so the bell clinks.

407*   **Вольному воробью и соловей в клетке завидует.**   *v.* В411
[Even a caged nightingale will envy a free sparrow.] Poor freedom is better than rich slavery. *Cf.* Better hand loose than an ill tethering. It's the pretty bird that gets caged.

408   **Вольность всего лучше.**
[Freedom is best.] Freedom comes before silver and gold. *Cf.* Freedom is a fair thing.

409*   **Волю неволя учит.**   *v.* К215, Ч76
[Bondage teaches freedom.] *Cf.* The worth of a thing is best known by the want of it.

410   **Воля господину - неволя рабу.**   *v.* Б11, К157, О43
[The master's liberty is servitude for the slave.] Fortune to one is mother, to another, stepmother. *Cf.* He who serves is not free.

411*   **Воля птичке дороже (лучше) золотой клетки.**   *v.* В407
[Better free than in a gilt cage.] A golden cage is still a cage. *Cf.* A bean in freedom is better than a comfit in prison.

412   **Воля и добрую жену (доброго мужа) (коня) портит.**   *v.* Д32
[Too much liberty spoils a good wife (husband)(horse).] *Cf.* Too much liberty spoils all.

413*   **Вон из глаз, вон из сердца.**   *v.* Д48, Н218, С4, Ч14
Out of sight, out of mind. *Gr.* τὰ ἔξω ὀφθαλμῶν, ἔξω φρενῶν.

414   **Вор беду избудет - опять на воровстве будет.**   *v.* З6, П249
[An escaped thief will steal again.] Once a thief, always a thief.

415   **Вор божится - недоброе затевает.**   *v.* Б97, З95
[The thief swears innocence and schemes evil.] Show me a liar and I will show you a thief. He that will swear will lie.

416   **Вор вора терпит (кроет) (за вора стоит).**   *v.* В421
Thick as thieves. *Cf.* There is honour among thieves.

417* Вор вора узнает и темной ночью. *v.* B278
[A thief knows a thief even in the darkest night.] A thief knows a thief as a wolf knows a wolf. *SPL.* graculus graculo assidet. fur furem cognoscit, lupus lupem.

418 Вор ворует да стены оставляет, а пожар ничего не оставляет.
[Thieves take everything but the walls, fires take everything.] *Cf.* Three removes are as bad as a fire.

419* Вор думает что все на свете воры. *v.* B425, K205
The thief thinks that everyone else is a thief. *Cf.* Ill doers are ill deemers.

420 Вор на вора не челобитчик. *v.* B425, Д357
[A thief does not bow to another thief.] *Cf.* One thief robs another.

421* Вор на воре не ищет. *v.* B416
There is honour among thieves.

422 Вор не бывает богат, а бывает горбат. *v.* B432,434
[Thieves don't get rich, they get beaten.] All thieves come to some bad end. Crime doesn't pay.

423 Вор не всегда крадет, а всегда его берегутся. *v.* H241

424 Вор с мошенника шапку снял. (Вор у вора дубинку украл). *v.* B420, Д357
[A thief stole the swindler's hat (club).] One thief robs another. The biter is sometimes bit.

425 Вор честному не верит. *v.* B419, K205
[The thief distrusts an honest man.] Who is in fault suspects everybody.

426 Вор что заяц, и тени своей боится. *v.* B257,587, H18, У10
[A thief and a rabbit fear their own shadow.] *Cf.* The thief does fear each bush an officer.

427 Вора миловать - доброго погубить.
Pardoning the bad is injuring the good. *Lat.* bonis nocet qui malis pascet.

428 Вора на виселицу ведут, а он все правится.
[The thief protests his innocence all the way to the gallows.] *Cf.* The thief is sorry to be hanged, but not that he is a thief.

429 Вора принять - самому в беду попасть. (Вору потакать - что самому воровать.)
[Abet a thief and get yourself into trouble (you are yourself a thief).] *v.* K220, H456
The receiver is as bad as the thief. He who holds the ladder is as bad as the thief.

430 Воробей, а метит в орлы. *v.* B287
[A sparrow that would be an eagle.] Attempt not to fly like an eagle with the wings of a wren. *Cf.* Every ass thinks himself worthy to stand with the king's horses.

431 Воров в лесу сторожили, а они из дому выносили.
[Guarded the wood against thieves while they plundered the house.] *Cf.* The back door robs the house.

432 Воровать, не торговать - наклад больше нежели прибыль. *v.* B422
[Stealing doesn't pay - the risk is greater than the profit.] *Cf.* Crime doesn't pay. Who knows what may be gained in a day never steals.

433 Воровство - последнее ремесло.
Of all crafts, theft is the worst.

434   **Воровством каменных палат не наживешь (села не наполнишь).**   *v.* B422
[You won't build stone mansions by stealing.]   *Cf.* He who steals will always fail.

435*   **Ворон ворону глаза не выклюет.**   *v.* Б240, B389, И21, K155, C221
Crows will not pick out crows' eyes.   *Lat.* corvus oculem corvi non eruet.
SPL. aequalis aequalem delectat.   lupus lupum non edit.

436   **Ворон каркает - к покойнику.**
The croaking raven bodes death (misfortune).

437*   **Ворона в павлиных перьях.**   *v.* B388
[A crow in peacock's feathers.]   *Cf.* Wolf in sheep's clothing. Putting feathers on a
buzzard won't make it an eagle.

438   **Ворона за море летала, а умнее не стала (да вороной и вернулась).**   *v.* Г337, У85,
[The crow flew overseas but still returned a crow (none the smarter).]   *Ap.* 1.32,61
If an ass goes a-travelling, he'll not come home a horse. *Cf.* Send a fool to the market,
and a fool he will return again.

439*   **Вороне соколом не бывать.**   *v.* B398, И74,106, H194, C135,227
A carrion kite will never make a good hawk.

440*   **Вороны везде черные.**
Crows are black the world over. *Cf.* A crow is never the whiter for washing herself
often. In every country dogs bite.

441   **Ворчаньем наскучишь, примером научишь.**   *v.* Д335
[Grumbling bores, example teaches.] A good example is the best sermon. *Cf.* Example
is the best precept.   Constant complaints never get pity.

442*   **Вот где собака зарыта.**
[That's where the dog is buried.] To hit the nail on the head.   There's the rub.

443*   **Вот такие (какие) пироги.**   *v.* T6
That's the way the cookie crumbles.

444   **Вошедши в службу, терпи и нужду.**   *v.* C188
He that serves, must serve.

445*   **Вперед идет а назад дорогу ищет.**
[He goes forward but loses the way back.] If you leap into a well, providence is not
bound to fetch you out. *Cf.* Look one way and row the other.

446*   **Впереди стояла затрещина, а сзади - тычок.**   *v.* K323, H566
[Between a blow and a sharp object.] Between a rock and a hard place.   Between the
devil and the deep blue sea.

447   **Вполплеча работа тяжела, оба подставишь - легче справишь.**   *v.* O51
Two hands are better than one.

448*   **Впотьмах и гнилушка светит.**   *v.* B167,498, И32, K152, H3, X42
[Even stumps illuminate the darkness.] A bad bush is better than the open field. *Cf.* Every
light is not the sun. Little is the light will be seen far in a mirky night. All the darkness
in the world cannot put out a single candle.

449   Врага (по)щадить - себя губить (в беду угодить).
        He that dallies with an enemy dies by his own hand.

450   Врагу места много.
        [Give an enemy much room.]   For a flying enemy, make a golden bridge.

451   Вражда с дураком не умнее дружбы.   *v.* Д479, С8
        [Enmity with a fool is not wiser than friendship.]   He is not the fool that the fool is, but he that with the fool deals.

452   Враки доводят до драки.
        [Enemies spawn battles.]   *Cf.* The war is not done so long as my enemy lives.

453   Врал в детстве - не поверят и в старости.   *v.* В666, К24, Л64, С215
        [He who lies as a child is not believed when an elder.]   He that once deceives is ever suspected.   *Cf.* A liar is not believed when he tells the truth.   He who lies once is never believed again.

454   Вранье не введет в добро.
        [Lying leads to no good.] *Cf.* Cheats never prosper. Lying's the first step to the prison gates.

455   Вранье не споро, попутает скоро.   *v.* Л63
        [Lying is difficult, it's easy to get mixed up.]   *Cf.* Liars have need of good memories. *Lat.* Quint.4.2.91: mendacem memorem esse oportet.

456*   Вранью короткий век.   *v.* Б100, Л103
        Lies have short (no) legs (wings).   *Cf.* Though a lie be swift, truth overtakes it.

457   Вранья на зуб не наложишь.
        A lie will give blossoms but no fruit.   *Cf.* A blister will rise upon one's tongue that tells a lie.

458   Врать - не деньги брать.
        [Lying is not like stealing money.]   *Cf.* †A liar is worse than a thief.

459   Врать - своя неволя.
        [Lying is bondage.]   *Cf.* Liars begin by imposing upon others, but end by deceiving themselves.

460   Врать - так с людми не знаться.
        [Lying is a disregard for others.]   *Cf.* Misunderstandings bring lies to town.   The liar and the murderer are children of the same village.

461   Врать, что лыки драть - лыко за лыком тянется.   *v.* К292, Л102
        [Lying is like stripping lime bark: one strip draws another.]   One lie makes many (leads to another).   *Cf.* He that tells a lie must invent twenty more to maintain it.

462*   Врач - исцели себя самого.
        Luke.iv.23: **Physician heal thyself**.

463   Временем в горку, а временем в норку.   *v.* Л179, П8
        [Sometimes up the hill, sometimes in the hole.]   *Cf.* What you lose on the swings you gain on the roundabouts.   There is a time to wink as well as to see.

464   Временем гони, а временем и сам беги.   (Время гнать и время бежать.)
        [There's a time to chase, a time to run.]   *Cf.* There's a time to fish and a time to dry nets.

465* **Временем и дурак правду скажет (умно говорит).**   *v.* Б412, И16, У95
     A fool may sometimes tell the truth (speak to the purpose.) *Lat.* interdum stultus bene loquitur.

466* **Времени не (по)воротишь.**   *v.* П194
     Time lost (past) cannot be recalled.

467 **Времени (погоды) дома не выберешь.**
     Take the weather as it comes. *Cf.* Man is never satisfied with the weather. He that forecasts all perils will never sail the sea.

468 **Время бежит, как вода.**   *v.* В475, Г199
     [Time runs out like water.] *Cf.* Time flees away without delay.

469 **Время - воробей, упустишь - не поймаешь.**
     [Time is a sparrow that will fly away if you let it go.] Time has wings. Time lost cannot be recalled. *Cf. Lat.* Verg.*G*.3.284: fugit inreparabile tempus.

470 **Время все излечивает (изнуряет).**   *v.* Д61
     Time cures all things.

471 **Время всему научит.**   *v.* В481, Д5
     Time reveals (discloses) all things.   *Lat.* tempus omnia revelat.

472* **Время дороже денег (золота).**
     [Time is more precious than money (gold).] *Cf.* Time is money.

473 **Время и камень долбит.**   *v.* В363, К98, М11
     [Time wears away even a stone.] *Cf.* Time devours all things. Constant dripping wears away the stone. *Lat.* Ov.*Met*.15.234: tempus edax rerum.

474 **Время и случай разум дают.**
     [Time and circumstance dispense reason.] *Cf.* Time is the best teacher.

475* **Время летит.**   *v.* В468
     Time flies.   *Lat.* tempus fugit.

476* **Время - лучший лекарь (врач) (советчик).**   *v.* Ж98
     Time is the best healer [(physician)(adviser)].   *Lat.* tempus dolorem lenit.

477* **Время на время не приходит.**   *v.* В88, Г193, Д165, Н392, Р20
     All times are not alike. *SPL.* horae non ulli similis produciter hora. *Cf.* Now is now and then was then.

478 **Время не деньги, потеряешь - не найдешь.**
     [Time is not money: once you lose it, you won't find it.] *Cf.* Time is like money: once spent, it can never be spent again.

479* **Время не ждет.**   *v.* Н488
     Time waits for no man.

480 **Время подойдет, так и лед пройдет.**   *v.* Б471, В535,646, Н553, Т19
     [When the time's right, the ice too will pass.] *Cf.* Time ends all things. All things have an end.

481* **Время покажет.**   *v.* Д5
     Time will tell.   *SPL.* annus producit, non ager.

482   **Время придет - слезы утрет (и час пробьет).**   *v.* В634
[Time will dry the tears (and strike the hour).] *Cf.* Time tames the strongest grief.

483*   **Время разум дает.**   *v.* К307, С265, Ч42
Older and wiser. *Lat.* senis venit usus ab annis.

484   **Время - судья.**   *v.* Д5
Time tries truth. *Cf.* Time is the father of truth.

485   **Время человека красит.**
[Time decorates the man.] *SPL.* tempus largitur omnia. *Cf.* Time ripens all things. Time is the sire of fame. Time and patience change the mulberry leaf to satin.

486   **Врет и глазом не моргнет (смигнет).   (Врет как сивый мерин.)**
[He lies without batting an eye.] [He lies like a grey gelding] *i.e. inveterate liar.*
Cf. A false tongue will hardly speak the truth.

487   **Все бобры, все равны.**   *v.* В506, Е14, З7, Т3
[All beavers are alike.] Another yet the same. You've seen one, you've seen them all.

488   **Все бондаря, да немногих благодарят.**   *v.* К133
[Not all coopers are thanked.] Many a man serves a thankless master. *Cf.* It's easier to be generous than grateful.

489   **Все видят как веселюсь, а никто не видит как плачу (крушусь).**   *v.* В318

490   **Все детки о одной матки.**
[All children of the same mother.] Children are what their mothers are.

491   **Все добро да не все на пользу.**   *v.* В552, И19
[Not all good is beneficial.] None so good that it's good to all.

492   **Все доброхоты, а в нужде помочь нет охоты.**
When need is highest, help is nighest.

493   **Все за одного, один за всех.**
All for one and one for all.

494*   **Все идет в свой черед (своим чередом).**   *v.* Б245
Everything in turn.

495*   **Все имеет начало.**   *v.* Б471
Everything has a beginning.

496*   **Все кузни исходил, а не кован воротился.**   *v.* В19, Д488, УУ96
[He made the round of blacksmiths but returned untempered.] Send a fool to market and a fool he will return.

497   **Все лучше бывает когда все заранее осмотрено и уготовлено.**
[Things go better with planning and preparation.] Great success is always preceded by great preparation. *Cf.* He is wise who looks ahead.

498   **Все лучше того как нет ничего.**   *v.* В448, З63, К152, Н3, П50
Something is better than nothing.

499* Все люди, все человеки.   *v.* В508,625, Е14, Л200
   We are all Adam's children. We are only human.

500 Все минется, одна правда останется.
   [Everything passes but truth remains.] Truth never grows old.

501 Все может случиться - и богатый к бедному стучится.
   [Anything can happen - even a rich man may knock at the pauper's door.] He that falls today may rise tomorrow. *SPL.* irus est subito, qui modo Croesus erat. *Cf.* The highest spoke in fortune's wheel may soon turn lowest.

502 Все мои приборы - лапти да оборы.   *v.* Г238
   [All my accessories: shoes and laces.] *Cf. Lat.* omnia mea mecum porto.

503 Все мы говорим, да не все по говоренному выходит. *v.* Б8, Н98,231, О153, Э1
   [We all talk, but] from word to deed is a great space. Saying so don't make it so. *Cf.* Talk is easy, work is hard.

504* Все на одну карту поставить.   *v.* В94, Н66, Х88
   [Stake everything on one card.] To put all your eggs in one basket.

505 Все надоедает кроме работы.   *v.* Б55,104, О144, С167
   [Everything but work is dull.] Business is the salt of life. Labour is the law of happiness. Work makes life pleasant.

506 Все одно - что дерево, что бревно.   *v.* В487, З7, Т3
   [It's all the same, wood or a log.] Another yet the same. Seen one, seen all. *Cf.* †No like is the same. *Lat.* nullum simile est idem.

507 Все одно, что в лоб, что в голову.
   [It's all the same, on the forehead or the head.] It is as broad as it is long.

508* Все под Богом ходим.   *v.* В499,514,625
   All men are mortal.

509* Все познается в сравнении.   *v.* К280
   [Everything is learned through comparison.] Nothing is good or bad but by comparison.

510* Все приходит вовремя для того кто умеет ждать.   *v.* И24
   Everything comes to him who waits.

511 Все равно что восемнадцать, что без двух двадцать. *v.* Е14, К277, С108,
   Six of one and half a dozen of the other.   Х85, Ч64,69

512* Все скоро сказывается, да не все скоро делается. *v.* Г186, Л27, Н231, О153
   Easier said than done.

513* Все столом и скатертью.   *v.* Д142
   It's a piece of cake.

514* Все там будем.   *v.* В508
   We'll all be there someday. All men must die.

515* Все течет, все изменяется.   *v.* В42,532
   [Everything flows, everything changes.] All things change and we with them. *Cf. Gr.*

Heracl. ap.Pl.*Crat*.402A: πάντα χωρεῖ καὶ οὐδὲν μένει. *Lat.* Ov.*Met*.15.165: omnia mutantur, nihil interit. Time changes everything.

516* **Все хорошое не сразу.**   *v.* В537, И40,116, М212,Х52
[All the good not at once.] You can have too much of a good thing.

517* **Все хорошо что есть, чего нет то худо.**
[All that we have is good, but what we don't have is bad.] Everything that happens, happens for the best. *Cf.* Nothing is to be presumed on or despaired of.

518* **Все хорошо что хорошо кончается.**   *v.* В637
All's well that ends well. *Lat.* si finis bonus est, totum bonus est.

519 **Всегда жди беды, сидя у морской воды.**   *v.* К265
[Expect misfortune, sitting by the sea.] *Cf.* Worse things happen at sea.

520* **Всего вдруг не сделаешь.**   *v.* В537
[A man cannot do everything at once.] *Cf.* Doing everything is doing nothing. A man can't whistle and drink at the same time.

521 **Всего говорить, себе норовить.**   *v.* В67, Л90, О149
[Tell all and injure yourself.] *Cf.* Tell not all you know, all you have, or all you can do.

522 **Всего желать - всего потерят.**   *v.* З54, К222, М132
All covet, all lose. *Lat.* totum vult, totum perdit.

523 **Всего не перенять что по реке плывет.**   *v.* В95, Н203,248
[One cannot fish everything from a river.] *Cf.* None says his garner is full.

524 **Всем давать - много будет.**   *v.* М97, П82, С22
[If all give, there will be much.] *Cf.* Little and often fills the purse. Add little to little and there'll be a great heap.

525 **Всем деревня не выйдет - вода близко, так лес далеко.**   *v.* З159, Н19, О74
[The village never suits everyone: either the water's too near or the forest too far.] There was never a good town but had a mire at one end of it. *Cf.* You can't please everyone. Every path has a puddle.

526 **Всем известно что лукавые живут лестно.**
[Everyone knows that the deceitful love flattery.] When the flatterer pipes, the devil dances.

527 **Всем по сем, а мне по восем.**   *v.* В551,567, С225, Х12
[Seven for everyone, eight for me.] *Cf.* Look after number one.

528 **Всем своего ума не вложишь.**   *v.* В191, Н57,113
[You cannot instill your own mind in everyone else.] Everyone to his own opinion. *Cf.* Our own opinion is never wrong.

529 **Всем сытым быть, так и хлеба не станет.**
[If everyone has their fill, the bread will run out.] Where every hand fleeces, the sheep goes naked. There's little for the rake after the besom.

530 **Всем угодлив, так никому не пригодлив.**   *v.* Д446
A friend to all is a friend to none.

531   **Всем угождать - самому в дураках сидеть.**   *v.* Н19, О74
         [Please everyone and play the fool.] He that would please all and himself too, undertakes
         what he cannot do.

532   **Всему бывает перемена (причина).**   *v.* В42, 515
         [Everything changes (has a cause).] There is nothing permanent except change.

533*   **Всему есть свой предел.**   *v.* В523,534, Ч95
         There's a limit to everything. *Cf.* Everything has an end.

534   **Всему есть счет, мера и граница.**   *v.* В533
         [There is a tally, measure and limit to everything.] There is a measure in all things.
         Lat. est modus in rebus.

535*   **Всему свое время (свой век) (свой черед).**   *v.* В480,646
         Everything has its time. All in good time. *Lat.* habent omnia tempora sua. *SPL.* alia
         aestate, alia hyeme fiunt. *Cf.* Appoint a time for everything and do everything in its time.

536   **Всему учен, только не изловчен.**   *v.* Б217, В177, Д362, Л145, У86,92
         [Educated but not smart.] *Cf.* The greatest clerks are no the wisest men. A handful of
         common sense is worth a bushel of learning.

537   **Вскачь не напашешься.**   *v.* В516, 520,
         [You cannot get your fill quickly.] *Cf.* Who hastens a glutton, chokes him.

538   **Вскорми ворона, он тебе очи выклюет.**   *v.* В676, Н245
         He has brought up a crow to pick out his own eyes.

539   **Вспылил - дело погубил.**   *v.* Г90, П188, Ч102
         Haste makes waste.

540   **Встать пораньше да шагнуть подальше.** *v.* К223

541   **Встретил низкое - перешагни, встретил высокое - нагнись.**   *v.* В50,154, Н280, Т86
         [If it's low - step over it, if it's high - stoop.] Sail with the wind and the tide.

542*   **Встретил с радостью, а проводил с жалостью.**
         Sorrow is at parting if at meeting there be laughter.

543   **Встречают по платью, провождают по уму.** *v.* П64

544   **Вся правда в вине.**   *v.* Б52
         In wine there is truth. *Lat.* in vino veritas.

545   **Вся свадьба песни не стоит.**   *v.* И66, К172, О25, П291
         [Not every wedding is worth the music.] It is a poor dog that is not worth the whistling.

546   **Всяк в беде бывает, а на другом видя, забывает.**   *v.* В343, Г266, Н53, С21
         Two in distress make sorrow less. Misery loves company.

547*   **Всяк в своем добре волен.**   *v.* В578,629
         Men are blind in their own cause.

548   **Всяк годится, да не на всякое дело.**   *v.* В558, Н84,198
         Every man has his (proper) gift. Every man must walk (labour) in his own calling
         (trade) (vocation).

549* Всяк дар в строку. *v.* Д11,74
Benefits bind. *Cf.* Nothing costs so much as what is given us.

550 Всяк держи свои рубежи. *v.* В563, З152,154
Know your limitations and go not beyond them. *Cf.* Every man to his trade.

551 Всяк для (про) себя, а Бог (Господь) для (про) всех. *v.* В527, С225, Х12
Every man for himself and God for us all.

552 Всяк добр, да не до всякого. *v.* В491, И19
None is so good that it's good to all.

553 Всяк дом хозяйкой хорош. *v.* Ж54,91, Х33
The wife is the key of the house. Woeful is the household that wants a woman.

554* Всяк дурак на свой лад с ума сходит. *v.* К12,211, У12,17
Every man is mad on some point.

555 Всяк дурак хвалит свой колпак. *v.* В621,622,652, Т12,38
Every fool likes his own bauble best. Every man likes his own thing best.

556* Всяк (всякий) кузнец своего счастья. *v.* Ч123
Every man is architect of his own fortune. *Lat.* Sall.Rep.1.1: faber est suae quisque fortunae.

557* Всяк кулик на своем болоте велик. *v.* В137,562,607,612
[Every sandpiper is master in its own swamp.] Every dog is a lion at home.

558* Всяк мастер на свой лад. (Всяк своему нраву работает.) *v.* В548,626,628, У13, *Ap.*1.90
Every man (one) after his fashion. *Cf.* Every man's censure is first moulded in his own nature.

559* Всяк на свой аршин меряет. *v.* В187, Н87
To measure everyone by your own yard. Every man should measure himself by his own foot rule.

560 Всяк (всякий) на себя свой хлеб добывает (про себя постельку стелет). *v.* В604
Every man will have his own turn served.

561 Всяк от своих дел (слов) осудится и оправдится. *v.* Д294, С127
[Every man shall be judged and vindicated by his deeds (words).] Our actions are our security, not others' judgments.

562* Всяк петух (всякая курица) на своем пепелище хозяин. *v.* В137,557,612, Д389, И43
A cock is bold on his own dunghill. *Lat.* Sen.Mort.Claud. gallus in sterquilinio suo plurimum potest.

563* Всяк (всякий) портной на свой покрой. *v.* В569, З154, Н84, П293, *Ap.*1.21
Let the cobbler [tailor] stick to his last [garment]. *Cf.* Every man as his business lies.

564 Всяк потужит а никто пособить не может.
[All will complain but none will help.] Those who are free with complaints have little else to offer. *Cf.* A little help is worth a deal of pity.

565 Всяк правду знает, да не всяк правду дает.
Всяк правду хвалит (любит), да не всяк ее хранит (скажет). *v.* Г189, Н228
[All know (praise) (love) the truth but few will speak it.] All truths are not to be told.

566* Всяк рассказ не без прикрас. *v.* P40
A tale never loses in the telling.

567* Всяк (всякий) сам себе ближе (дороже). *v.* B527,658, Л183, P60,73, C74
Every man is nearest himnself. *SPL.* Ter.*And.*4: proximus sum egomet mihi. *Cf.*
Charity begins at home. Near is my shirt, but nearer is my skin.

568* Всяк сам себе и друг и недруг. *v.* B556, H193
[Every man is his own friend and enemy.] *SPL.* quilibet fortunae suae faber. *Cf.* Every
man is his own worst enemy.

569* Всяк сверчок знай свой шесток. *v.* З154

570 Всяк (всякий) своим разумом кормится (умом живет) (голосом поет). *v.* H88, *Ap.*1.13
[Every man lives by his wit.] Everyone is witty for his own purpose. *Cf.* Every man
must stand on his own two feet.

571* Всяк свят пока черти спят.
[All are saints while the devils sleep.] Who avoids temptation avoids sin. *Cf.* The less
the temptation, the greater the sin. †When the voyage is over, the saint is forgot.
†All are not saints that go to church.

572* Всяк себя хвалит. *v.* B590,601, *Ap.*1.88
There is no such flatterer as a man's self. *Cf.* Every bird likes to hear itself sing.

573 Всяк секи дерево по себе. *v.* Г160, Ч13
[Cut the tree to your measure.] Cut your sail according to your cloth. *Cf.* Make not your
sail too large for your ship.

574 Всяк (всякий) спляшет, да не всяк (как) скоморох. *v.* H239,240,469
[Not all who dance are clowns.] All are not merry that dance lightly. *RA*1.30 πολλοί
τοι ναρθηκοφόροι,παῦροι δέ τε βάκχοι. *SPL.* multi thyrsigeri, pauci Bacchi.

575 Всяк страх изгоняет любовь. *v.* K139
Fear is stronger than love.

576 Всяк того обидит, кто дальше носу не видит. *v.* Б139, Г137, У25
[He who cannot see past his nose, shall often be led by the nose.] An easy fool is a
knave's tool.

577 Всяк умен - кто сперва, кто после. *v.* Д467, K313
[Everyone is smart, though some are sooner smart than others.] What the fool does in
the end, the wise man does at the beginning.

578 Всяк (всякий) хлопочет, добра себе хочет. *v.* B547,609, И34
A shrewd man feathers his own nest. No one fouls his hands in his own business.

579 Всяк хозяин в своем доме (царствует в доме своем). *v.* B136,194, C72, T14
Every man is a king (master) in his own home. *Lat.* quilibet est rex in domo sua.

580 Всяк хромает на свою ногу. *v.* B559, H17
[Each limps according to his foot.] Let every tub stand on its own bottom. *Cf.* Measure
yourself by your own foot. Every man should measure himself by his own foot rule.

581* Всяк цыган свою кобылу хвалит. *v.* B555,595,600,604, T38, Ч28
[Every gypsy praises his mare.] Each priest praises his own relics. Each bird likes his

own nest best. Every doctor thinks his pills the best. Every man likes his own thing best. *Cf.* †Never praise your cider or your horse.

582* **Всяк человек лож, и мы тож.** *v.* Н43,495
[Every man is untrue, we too.] *Cf. Psalms*.15.2 omnis homo mendax.

583 **Всяк чужую сторону хвалит, а сам ни ногой.** *v.* В178, Д57, П122, С168, Т10, Ч129
The grass is always greener on the other side of the fence. The apples on the other side of the wall are the sweetest.

584* **Всякая вещь о двух концах.** *v.* У30,47
There are two sides to every question. *Cf.* There are faults on both sides.

585 **Всякая вещь перед царем не утаится.**
[Nothing can be concealed from the king.] *Cf.* Kings have many ears and many eyes.

586* **Всякая вещь хороша на своем месте.**
A place for everything and everything in its place.

587* **Всякая вина виновата.** *v.* В257,426, М2
The faulty stands on his guard. The smaller the wrong, the greater the guilt.

588 **Всякая дешевизна перед дороговизной.** *v.* Г34, Д224,225
[First cheap then dear.] Good cheap is dear. *Cf.* Many have been ruined by buying good pennyworths.

589 **Всякая дорога вдвоем веселей.** *v.* В213

590* **Всякая жаба себя хвалит.** *v.* В572,595,600,601, *Ap.*1.88
[Every toad croaks its own praise.] Every bird loves to hear himself sing. Every ass loves to hear himself bray.

591 **Всякая земная сладость обращается в плач.** *v.* И40, С169
Every sweet has its bitter. Every commodity has its discommodity.

592* **Всякая козявка лезет в букашки. (Всякая кляча мнит себя рысаком.)**
(Всякая мокрица хочет летать как птица.) *v.* В606, С31
[Every gnat (nag) (wood-louse) yearns to be a bug (thoroughbred) (bird).] Every sprat now-a-days calls itself a herring. Every ass thinks himself worthy to stand among the king's horses.

593* **Всякая коляска любит помазку.** *v.* Д346
[Every cart likes to be greased.] *Cf.* To make a cart go, you grease the wheels. Who greases well, drives well.

594 **Всякая копейка алтынным гвоздем прибита.** *v.* З22, О16, П116
[Every *kopek* is riveted with three-*kopek* nails.] Penny wise and pound foolish. Don't waste ten dollars looking for a dime.

595* **Всякая лиса (лисица) свой хвост хвалит.** *v.* В555,590,600,621,652, *Ap.*1.88
[Every fox praises its tail.] *SPL.* suum cuique pulchrum. quisque sibi placet et sapiens sibi videtur. *Cf.* Every man likes his own thing best.

596 **Всякая могила травой зарастает (задернеет).**
[Every grave grows over with grass.] Time erases all sorrows. *Cf.* Grass and hay, we are all mortal. The grave levels all distinctions.

597 **Всякая молодость резвости полна.**
Youth is reckless (never casts for peril). *Cf.* Boys will be boys.

598 **Всякая небылица (тряпица) в три года пригодится.**
[Every rag may come in handy in three years.] Keep a thing seven years and it's bound to come in handy. *Cf.* A wonder lasts but nine days. Everything is of use to a housekeeper.

599 **Всякая невеста для своего жениха родится.** *v.* Ж47, *Ap.*1.5
Every Jack must have his Jill. A true wife is her husband's better half (flower of beauty) (heart's treasure).

600* **Всякая птица свое гнездо любит.** *v.* В581,590,595,621
Every bird likes his own nest best. *Cf. Lat.* sua cuique patria iucundissima.

601 **Всякая птица свои песни (своим голосом) поет.** *v.* В572,590, Н128
Each bird loves to hear himself sing.

602* **Всякая работа мастера хвалит.** *v.* В313, Д145, К336
The work shows the workman. *Lat.* opus laudat (commendat) artificem.

603 **Всякая ржавчина очищается.**
[Any corrosion can be scrubbed.] It will all come out in the wash.

604* **Всякая рука к себе загребает.** *v.* В560,624,629
Every man will have his own turn served. Every man (miller) draws water to his own mill.

605* **Всякая рыба хороша, коли на уду пошла.**
[Any fish is good, if it bites the line.] Anything is fish that comes to net. *Cf.* Small fish are better than no fish.

606 **Всякая свинка лезет в скотинки.** *v.* В592, С31
[Every swine seeks to join the herd.] *Cf.* Every sprat thinks itself a herring. Every little fish would become a whale.

607* **Всякая собака в доме львом кажется. (Всякий пес в своей конуре.)** *v.* В557,562,612, Д389, И43
Every dog is a lion at home. *SPL.* quivis canis domi suae ferox.

608 **Всякая сорока от своего языка погибает (гинет).**
[Every magpie perishes by its own voice.] A fool's tongue is long enough to cut his own throat.

609* **Всякая сосна своему бору шумит.** *v.* В578
[Every pine rustles to its wood.] Feather your own nest.

610 **Всякая страна человеку отечество.** *v.* Ж113, Н445, Т9
A wise man esteems every place to be his own country.

611 **Всякая шутка надвое растворена - коту потешно, а мышке за беду.** *v.* В71, О62
[Every jest is double-edged: what's good for the cat is bad for the mouse.] Everything gives cause for either laughter or tears. *Lat.* Sen.*Ir.*2.10.5: aut ridenda omnia aut flenda sunt. *Cf.* There is no great banquet but some fare ill.

612 **Всякий бугай в своем болоте голосист.** *v.* В134,557,562,607, И43
Every wren is loud in its fen.

613* **Всякий бык был теленком.**
[Every bull was once a calf.] Every oak has been an acorn. *Cf.* The cow has forgotten she was once a calf.

614* **Всякий гриб в руки берут (подымают), да не всякий в кузов (лукошко) кладут.**
(Всякую ягодку в руки берут, да не всякую в кузов кладут.) *v.* К325, Н235
[Not every mushroom (berry) you pick winds up in the basket.] *Cf.* Every block will not make a Mercury.

615 **Всякий дом (добрым) хозяином (держится).** *v.* Б147, Д379, Н289, П128
[The (good) master sustains the house.] *Cf.* The master absent and the house dead.

616* **Всякий доход не живет без забот (хлопот).** *v.* Б49,127,353, В174, Г281,297, Л173,
No pains, no gains. Н73, С201

617* **Всякий дурак красному рад (любит красненькое).** *v.* К195
[Any fool likes beauty.] Beauty and folly go often in company. *Cf.* Beauty draws more than oxen.

618* **Всякий знает где его что колет.**
I know best where the shoe pinches me. *Lat.* nemo scit praeter me ubi me premat.

619 **Всякий знает себя по делам своим.** *v.* В602, Д116,145
[Every man is known by his deeds.] *Cf.* The workman is known by his work.

620* **Всякий избирает друга по своему нраву.** *v.* К266, М164, П109, Т7
[Every man chooses friends according to his like.] Like will to like.

621* **Всякий кулик свое болото хвалит.** *v.* В581,600,652, Х62
[Every sandpiper praises his swamp.] Every cook praises his own broth.

622* **Всякий купец свой товар хвалит.** *v.* В555,581, Н352,383,487
Every peddlar praises his needles. *SPL.* laudat venales, qui vult extrudere merces.

623 **Всякий льстится чтоб добра добиться.** *v.* О136, Н120, Ч24
Every man bows to the bush he gets bield of. *Cf.* Whose bread I eat, his song I sing.

624 **Всякий мастер свою плешь маслит.** *v.* В581,604
[Every master greases his bald patch.] *Cf.* Every man drags water to his own mill. Every doctor thinks his pills the best. Each priest praises his own relics.

625 **Всякий мирянин своему брату семьянин.** *v.* В499,509
[We are all brothers in one family.] *Cf.* We are all Adam's children.

626* **Всякий молодец (скворец) на свой образец.** *v.* В558, У13,17, *Ap.*1.90
Every man [starling] after his fashion. *Lat.* suis quisque fingitur moribus. *SPL.* quot capita, tot sensus.

627* **Всякий подъем имеет и свой спуск.**
Whatever goes up must come down. *Lat.* quo altior mons, tanto profundior vallis.

628 **Всякий поп по-своему поет.** *v.* В558,626, У13
[Every priest chants his own way.] *Cf.* Every man after his fashion.

629* **Всякий сам себе лучший слуга.** *v.* В604, Н313
If you want a thing well done, do it yourself. Self-help is the best help.

630* Всякий совет к разуму хорош.   *v.* М173, У98
Good counsel never comes amiss.   A word to the wise is sufficient.
SPL. sapienti sat dictum.

631* Всякий трус о храбрости беседует.   *v.* К302
[Every coward talks of bravery.]   Cowards prattle more than men of worth.   *Cf.* They can
do least who boast loudest.   Great boaster, little doer.

632* Всякий человек у дела познается.   *v.* Д145,294
'Tis action makes the hero.

633 Всякого слушай, а никому не поддавайся.
[Heed all but yield to none.]   Fear no man and do justice to all men.

634 Всякое горе с временем забывается.   *v.* В482
Time tames the strongest grief.

635 Всякое дело делается во время.   *v.* А4, Б413, В644,655
Everything is good in its season.

636* Всякое дело до искуса.   *v.* К336, Л99, О7
[Everything must be put to the test.]   The proof of the pudding is in the eating.

637 Всякое дело концом хорошо.   *v.* В518
All's well that ends well.

638* Всякое дело мастера боится.   *v.* Д135

639 Всякое дело человеком ставится, человеком и славится.
Whatever is made by the hand of man, by the hand of man may be overturned [gains its glory.]

640 Всякое дерево из той же земли растет.   *v.* Д365, И56
[All trees grow from the same earth.] Human blood is all of a colour. The sun shines on
all alike.

641 Всякое зло терпением одолеть можно.   *v.* Д375, П232, Т23
Patience is a remedy for every grief.   Patience is a plaster for all sores.

642* Всякое начало трудно.   *v.* Д308, З106, Л75, П17, С292
All beginnings are hard (difficult).   *Lat.* omne initium difficile.

643 Всякое полузнание хуже всякого незнания.   *v.* П140

644* Всякое семя знает (сеют в) свое время.   *v.* В535,635,655
[Every seed knows its time.] *Eccles.*iii.1:There is a time for all things.*Lat.* omnia tempus
habent.

645 Всякое умение трудом дается.   *v.* М135
[Every skill is hard.]   There is no royal road to learning.   *Cf. Gr.* χαλεπὰ τὰ καλά.

646* Всякой вещи - свое время.   *v.* В480,535,635,644, П253
Everything has its time.   *Lat.* habent omnia tempora sua.   *Cf.* Pindar ὁ καὶ καιρὸς
ὁμοίως παντὸς ἔχει κορυφῶν.

647* Всякой матери свое дитя мило.   *v.* П235, С57, *Ap.*1.6
No mother has a homely child.   *Cf.* The owl thinks her own young the fairest.
Lat. noctuae pullus suus pulcherrimus.

648* Всякому дню (подобает) забота своя.
  Matt.6.34: **Sufficient unto the day is the evil thereof.**

649 Всякому зерну своя борозда.   *v.* Г15, К225, Ч99
  [Each seed in its furrow.] A place for everything and everything in its place.
  Cf. If you want to raise corn, plant corn seed, not cotton seed.

650 Всякому мертвецу земля - гроб.   *v.* П252
  [The earth is a grave for every dead man.] *Cf.* The grave will receive us all. Six feet of
  earth make all men equal.

651 Всякому мертвому своя могила.
  Graves are of all sizes.

652 Всякому мила своя сторона (свое мило).   *v.* В555,595,621, К11, Т12,38, Х62, Ч28
  Every man likes his own thing best. *Lat.* suum cuique pulchrum est.

653 Всякому молодцу ремесло к лицу.   *v.* В548,558,626
  [Every lad gets the trade he deserves.] He that blows best, bears away the horn.

654 Всякому мужу своя жена милее.
  [Every husband prefers his own wife.] *Cf.* There is one good wife in the country and
  every man thinks he has her.

655* Всякому овощу свое время.   *v.* А4, В535,635,644
  Everything is good in season.

656* Всякому свое и не мыто бело.   *v.* В581,652, Т38
  [Every one thinks his own dirty linen white.] Every man thinks his own geese swans.

657* Всякому свои слезы (сопли) солены.   *v.* Б311, К10, Н162,
  Всякому своя болячка (рана) больна (обида горька).   П300, Ч114
  [Every one's own tears (phlegm) (hurts) are bitter (painful).] Every one thinks his sack
  heaviest. Every horse thinks its own pack heaviest. *Apost.*6.98: ἕκαστος αὑτοῦ τὸ
  βδέλος μήλου γλύκιον ᾀγεῖται. *Lat.* in cuiuslibet ore mucus nasi sui dulcis est.

658* Всякому своя рубаха к телу ближе.   *v.* В567, Л183, Р60,73, С74
  Near is my shirt, but nearer is my skin. Every man is nearest himself.

659 Всякому своя худоба не кажется. *v.* С76

660* Всякому терпению бывает конец.   *v.* В533
  Patience has its limits.

661* Всякому товару цена есть.   *v.* И9
  There is no good that does not cost a price.

662 Вчера варена, вчера и выхлебана.   *v.* Б479, К47, Ч80
  [Yesterday cooked and yesterday eaten.] Easy come, easy go. Cookie today, crumb
  tomorrow. What is quickly done is quickly undone.

663 Вчера гряды копал, а ныне в восводы попал.   *v.* Н190
  [From farmer to statesman.] From rags to riches.

664   **Вчера не догонишь, а от завтра не уйдешь.**
      (Вчерашнего не воротишь, а от завтрашнего не уйдешь.)
      [The past cannot be recalled nor the future avoided.] The time to come is no more ours than the time past.

665   **Вчера с кистенем, сегодня с четками.**
      [A bludgeon yesterday, a rosary today.] No rogue like to the godly rogue. *Cf.* All are not saints that go to church.

666   **Вчера солгал а сегодня лгуном обзывают.**   *v.* В453, К224, С215
      [Told a lie yesterday and branded a liar today.] He that once deceives is ever suspected. *Cf.* Do wrong once and never hear the end of it. Old sins cast long shadows.

667*   **Вчерашней славой на войне не живут.**
      [Yesterday's glory does not keep you alive in war.] Every day is not yesterday.

668   **Выбирай епанчу по своему плечу.**   *v.* П81
      [Fit the cloak to the shoulders.] If the coat fits, put it on. If the shoe (cap) fits, wear it. *Cf.* You must cut your coat according to your cloth.

669   **Выбирай жену не в хороводе, а в огороде.**   *v.* Г161, Ж86
      [Choose a wife in an orchard rather than at a dance.] Choose a wife on a Saturday rather than a Sunday. Choose not a wife by eye only.

670*   **Выбирай жену не глазами но ушами.** *v.* Ж87

671   **Выбирай корову по рогам а девку по родам.**   *v.* Г162
      [Choose cattle by the horn and a wife by the stock.] Take a vine of a good soil and a wife of a good mother.

672*   **Выбирай удилище по лову, а крючок по рыбе.**
      [Choose the rod for the catch, and the hook for the fish.] Bait the hook well and the fish will bite. *Cf.*. You can't kill flies with a spear.

673*   **Выгода на миг, доброе имя на век.**   *v.* Д153,273,305, Л113, Х77
      [Fame lasts longer than gain.] A good name is better than riches.

674   **Выгонит голод на холод.**   *v.* Г218, Н580
      [Hunger will drive one out into the cold.] *Cf.* Hunger drives the wolf out of the wood. Hunger and cold deliver a man up to his enemy.

675   **Выигрыш с проигрышем на одних санях ездят.**   *v.* С319,328
      [Gain and loss ride the same sleigh.] Great fortune brings with it great misfortune.

676   **Выкормить змейку на свою шейку.**   *v.* В538, Н245
      To nourish a snake (viper) in one's bosom. *Gr. Phaedr.* ἐφέρμανεν ἔχιν'ἐν τῷ ἑαυτοῦ κόλπῳ.

677   **Выменял кукушку на ястреба (ястребца).**   *v.* З19
      Give a lark to catch a kite.

678   **Выменял слепой у глухого зеркало на гусли.**
      [The blind man traded his mirror for the deaf man's zither.] *Cf.* A fair exchange is no robbery. A blind man needs no looking glass.

679 Вышей чайку - забудешь тоску. *v.* Б144, Г224
[Drink some tea and forget your sorrows.] All griefs with bread are less. *Cf.* Love and scandal are the best sweeteners of tea.

680* Выплеснуть из ванны вместе с водой и ребенка.
To throw the baby out with the bath water.

681 Выпустил словечко, не догонишь и на крылечке. *v.* С125, Ч83
Words have wings, and cannot be recalled.

682 Выроешь колодец глубоко, вода будет стоять высоко. *v.* Д60
[The deeper the well, the deeper the water.] The deeper the well, the colder the water. *Cf.* The higher the plum-tree, the riper (sweeter) the plum.

683* Вырос лес, так выросло (будет) и топорище. *v.* Л53
[As the tree grows, so grows the axe handle.] The axe goes to the wood from whence it borrowed its helve.

684 Вырос жук больше медведя. *v.* Б458, Д125, И73
[The bug grew bigger than a bear.] To make a mountain out of a molehill.

685 Высока гора, но шапки перед ней не снимают. *v.* О107
[The mountain is high, but one doesn't tip one's hat to it.] The parrot has fine feathers, but he doesn't go to the dance. *Cf.* Goodness is not tied to greatness, but greatness to goodness.

686 Высоко летает да низко садится. *v.* В687, Н223,371, Ч7
The higher standing, the lower fall.

687* Высоко поднял, да низко опустил. *v.* В686, Н223,371
The higher the mountain, the greater descent. *SPL.* tolluntur in altum, ut lapsu graviora ruant. *Cf.* The higher they go, the lower they fall.

688 Высохло море, а все (да) не луже брат.
[A sea may dry up, but it's still not akin to a puddle.] Cut off a dog's tail and he will be a dog still.

689 Выстрелив, пулю не схватишь - а слово сказав не поймаешь. *v.* С125,178,182
A word and a stone let go [bullet shot] cannot be called back.

690* Выше головы не прыгнешь (носа не поднимешь). *v.* В691, И57, Л11, Н546, Р12
[You cannot jump (raise your nose) higher than your head.] A man can do no more than he can.

691 Выше лба не живут глаза (уши не растут). *v.* В691, Н546
[The eyes (ears) are not higher than the forehead.] However high the eye may rise, it will find the eyebrow above. *Cf.* There is no building a bridge across the ocean.

692* Выше себя не вырастешь (прыгнешь). *v.* Р12
[A man will not grow taller than he is.] The stream cannot rise above its source.

693 Вьюн - вокруг вьется, а в руки не дается. *v.* В298
As slippery as an eel. *Cf. Lat.* anguila est: elabitur.

Г

1 **Гад гада блудит - гад и будет.** *v.* Г142, К266
Bad companions corrupt good morals. *Cf.* I.*Cor*.XV.33: Evil communications corrupt good manners.

2 **Где бабка ни бери, а внука корми.**
Good mother asks not "will you?" but gives.

3 **Где бабы гладки, там никогда нет воды в кадке.** *v.* В10. Г88, М174
[Where the women are fine, there's never any water in the tub.] The more women look in their glass, the less they look to their house. Silks and satins put out the fire in the chimney. *Cf.* Dawted daughters make daidling wives.

4 **Где беда не ходила, да к нам пришла.** *v.* Г260,270
[Wherever troubles lurk, they find their way to us.] Misfortunes come of themselves.

5 **Где беде бывать, там ее не миновать.** *v.* 328
He that seeks trouble never misses.

6 **Где бес (черт) не сможет, туда бабу пошлет.** *v.* К138

7* **Где блины, там и мы - где с маслом каша, тут и место наше. (Где кисель, там и присел.) (Где пирог с грибами , там и мы с руками.)** *v.* Н445, Т9
[Home is where the cakes and buttered porridge are.] [Dessert is where you'll find me.] [Wherever there's mushroom pie, our hands are outstretched.] Not where one is bred, but where one is fed. *Lat.* non ubi nascor, sed ubi pascor. *Cf.* Home is where the heart is. Where it's well with me, there is my country.

8* **Где Бог себе строит церковь, там дьявол часовню.** *v.* Б236, Г103
Where God has his church, the devil will have his chapel.

9 **Где больно - хвать-похвать (тут рука), где мило - глядь-поглядь (тут глаза).**
[Touch what hurts, admire what's pretty.] *Cf. Gr.* ὅπου τις ἀλγεῖ κεῖδε τὴν χεῖρ ἔχει. *Lat.* naturale est manum saepius ad id referre quod dolet.

10* **Где больше двух, там говорят в слух.**
[Don't whisper if there's more than two.] To whisper proclamations is ridiculous.

11 **Где бумажное царство, там волокита - король.** *v.* Б490
[In a paper kingdom, red tape is king.] It is the clerk makes the justice. *Cf.* Paper and ink and little justice.

12 **Где бы ни работать, лишь бы не работать.**
[One will work anywhere just not to work.] *Cf.* Think of ease but work on.

13* **Где веревка тонка, там и рвется.** *v.* Г98, Д199
The thread breaks where it is weakest. A chain's only as strong as its weakest link.

14   Где вода была, там опять вода и будет. (+ куда деньга пошла, там и копится).   *v.* Г83
[Where water's been, it'll come again (+ where there's money, there'll be more).]
It always rains in the ocean. What happened once can happen again. *Cf.* All water that
goes up must come down.

15   Где возу быть, там и поставят. (Где выросла сосна, там она и красна.)   *v.* B515,649
[The load is wherever they put it.] [The pine is loveliest wherever it has grown.]
A place for everything and everything in its place.

16   Где волк, тут стада не паси.   *v.* B395, Д359
[Where there's a wolf, don't graze the flock.] *Cf.* Wolves rend sheep when the shepherds
fail. To leave wolves in charge of the sheep. *Lat.* lupus apud ovis linquere.

17*   Где волчий рот, а где лисий хвост.   *v.* Б169, Н224
Где в волчей нагольной шубе (волчьи зубы), где в лисьей под плисом (лисий хвост).
If the lion's skin cannot, the fox's shall. *Gr.* Plut. ἀν ἡ λεοντὴ μὴ ἐξίκηται τὴν
ἀλοπεκὴν πρόσαψον. *EA.* si leonina pellis non satis est, vulpina addenda.

18*   Где ворона ни летала, а к ястребу в когти попала.
(Где заяц ни бегал, а в тенето попал.)   *v.* Г48, Ж168, О157, Р62
[Wherever the crow flies, the hawk catches it.] [Wherever the hare runs, it falls into the
snare.] *Cf.* A duck never flies so high but that it has to come down for water. A bird
never flew so high but it will fly just as low (but someone can tame it). There's no flying
from fate.

19*   Где все виноваты, там никто не виноват.
When everyone is wrong, everyone is right. *Cf.* Count the thing wrong which would
be wrong if everybody did it. One is not smelt where all stink.

20   Где гнев, там и милость.
He that sharply chides is the most ready to pardon. *Cf.* Those that have much
business must have much pardon.

21   Где голова, там и ноги будут.   *v.* Г216, К40, Л108, П23
[Where the head goes the feet will follow.] Where the crow flies, her tail follows.

22*   Где горе там и смех (радость) (слезы) (увы).   *v.* К301,С85
[Where there's grief there is also laughter (glee) (tears) (sighs).] Our greatest joys and
our greatest sorrows grow on the same vine. After laughter tears.

23*   Где гроза тут и ведро.   *v.* Б384, Г26, Ж32, П166
After a storm comes the calm. After black clouds, clear weather.

24*   Где грех тут и спасение.   *v.* B169, Ч43
Seek your salve where you get your sore.

25   Где грозно там и розно (честно).
[There's no love lost between those who always argue.] *Cf.* In a hundred ells of
contention there is not an inch of love.

26   Где гром, тут и ведро.   *v.* Г23
[Where there's thunder, there's clear weather too.] Every cloud has a silver lining.

27*   Где дают там и бери.   *v.* Д79, Н280, О165, Т43
Take while the taking's good. All is fish that comes to net. Take as falleth in the sheaf.

28 Где два там не один.   *v.* Д89, О51
    [Two is not alone.] *Cf.* Two to one is odds. Two heads are better than one.

29* Где двое бранятся (говорят), тут (там) третий не суйся (приставай).
    (Где свои собаки грызутся, чужая не приставай.)   *v.* М182, С60
    [When two dispute, a third should stay away.] [When our dogs are at play, the stranger's
    should stay away.] Put not thy hand between the bark and the tree. *Cf.* Meddle not in
    another man's matter. †Two dogs strive for a bone, and a third runs away with it.

30* Где двое (стоят), там третий лишний (третьему дела нет).   *v.* Т67
    Two's company but three is none (a crowd).

31 Где деготь побывает, не скоро дух выведешь.   *v.* Г332, О81
    [Where tar has stuck, the odour lingers.] He that has to do with foul, never comes away
    clean.

32 Где деньги замешались, там правды не жди.   *v.* Б295, Ч56
    [Don't expect the truth where money is involved.] Honour and profit lie not in one sack.

33 Где деньги там и честь.   *v.* Б268, Д178
    Wealth makes worship.

34* Где дешево там и дорого.   *v.* В588, Д221,224
    Good cheap is dear.

35* Где дрова рубят, там и щепы летят.   *v.* Г92, Л54, Н396
    [Where logs are chopped, chips will fly.] He that would have eggs must endure the
    cackling of hens. *Cf.* You can tell a woodsman by his chips.

36 Где дураков семья, там своя земля.
    [One feels at home in a company of fools.] *Cf.* Every one has a fool in his sleeve.

37* Где дым там и огонь.   *v.* Б426, Г68, Д510
    Where there's smoke, there's fire. *SPL.* flamma fumo proxima.

38* Где жизнь там и надежда.   *v.* П130
    While there's life, there's hope. *Lat.* dum spiro, spero.

39 Где жить, там (тем) и слыть (богам и молиться).   *v.* В50,154, Н120,409,Ч24
    [Heed (worship) the customs (gods) of your hosts.] When in Rome, do as the Romans.
    Whose bread I eat, his song I sing.

40 Где забор там и вор (раздор).   *v.* Г42
    [Where there are fences there are thieves (discord).] *Cf.* Good fences make good
    neighbours. The greater number of laws, the greater number of thieves.

41 Где зависть есть, там не спи заслуга.
    [Where there is envy, merit should keep awake.] Envy never has a holiday. *Cf.* The dog
    of envy barks at celebrity.

42* Где закон (заповед), там и преступление (обида) (страх).   *v.* Е24, Н186, П227, С296
    [Where there's a law (commandment), there is crime (injury) (fear).] *Cf.* The more laws,
    the more offenders (sins).

43* Где зудит там и чешут.
    Scratch where it itches.

44   Где клятва, тут и преступление.   *v.* З355,85, К258
        He that will swear, will lie.

45*   Где кончается ум, там начинается глупость.
        Where intelligence ends, folly begins.

46*   Где конь катается (поваляется), так (там) и шерсть останется.
        Where the horse lies down, there some hairs will be found.

47   Где ладья ни рыщет, а на якоре (у якоря) будет.   *v.* И59
        [Wherever a boat may sail, it always comes to anchor.] Even the weariest river winds somewhere safe to sea.

48   Где ласточке ни летать, а к весне опять прибывать.   *v.* Г18, Ж168, О157
        [Wherever swallows fly, in spring they'll always return.] There was never a bird who flew so high but that he came down again. *Cf.* The tide never goes out so far but it always comes in again.

49   Где лукавство, там и обманство.   *v.* Б97, К251
        [Deceit and cunning go together.] He that will lie, will steal.

50   Где мед да пиво, туда всякий с рылом - а где лом да пешня, тут говорят
        «я нездешний».   *v.* Б372,467, Д448, Е18, З16, Н64, П236
        [Come food and drink, all follow - but come grind and toil, then "see you tomorrow."] When good cheer is lacking, your friends will be packing.

51   Где мед там и муха.   *v.* Б394,432, Г80,104, К37, Л2
        A fly follows the honey. Where a gull dives in the sea, there are fish for you and me.

52   Где мило, сем верст не криво.   *v.* Д241, Е30, К2
        [I'd walk seven furlongs for some kindness.] *Cf.* He goes not out of his way that goes to a good inn. For a good friend, the journey is never too long.

53   Где много говорят, там машины стоят.   *v.* Ж50
        [Where there is chatter, machines idle.] House goes mad when women gad.

54   Где много гончих, там зайцу смерть.
        [A multitude of hounds signals death for the hare.] *Lat.* multitudo canum mors leporis Many hounds may soon worry one hare.

55   Где много лекарей, там много и больных (недугов).
        The more doctors, the more diseases. *Cf.* One doctor makes work for another.

56   Где много пастухов, там овцы дохнут.   *v.* Д212, У52,53
        [Too many shepherds kill the sheep.] *Cf.* Where every man is master, the world goes to wrack. Too many cooks spoil the broth.

57*   Где много слов, там мало правды (дела).   *v.* Д233, М57, С101
        [Many words, little truth.] A flow of words is not always a flow of wisdom. *Cf.* In many words, a lie or two may escape.

58*   Где наше не пропадало.   *idiom.*   *v.* Б459, Р58, С100
        [Where haven't we lost.] Nothing stake, nothing draw. *Cf.* A man can die but once. Over shoes, over boots.

59   Где не было начала, не будет и конца.   *v.* Б83,471
Where there's no beginning, there's no end.

60   Где не сеют, там не жнут.   *v.* К88, П192
No sowing, no reaping.

61   Где нет борьбы, там нет победы.   *v.* Б80, Д73, Л176
Nothing ventured, nothing gained.

62   Где нет знаний, там нет и смелости.   *v.* З157
[No know-how, no pluck.] Knowledge is power. *Cf.* Action is the proper fruit of knowledge.

63*   Где нет кошки, там мыши резвятся.   *v.* Б72, К127, С233
When the cat's away, the mice will play.

64   Где нет опасения, там нет и спасения.
[No fear, no salvation.] *Cf.* Fear is one part of prudence.

65   Где ни стал, тут и стань.
Stand by your guns.

66*   Где ногой ступить - трава не растет.   *v.* Н5, Р52
[Wherever the foot trods, grass will not grow.] Grass doesn't grow on a busy street.
You can't grow grass on a beaten track. No grass grows under his (my) heel (foot).

67*   Где нянек много, там дитя без глазу. *v.* У52

68*   Где огонь там и дым. *v.* Д510

69   Где одна вода лед положит, там другая снесет.   *v.* Г84, И20, К157
[Where some water freezes, other water sweeps it away.] One man's loss is another man's
gain. Somewhere the sun is shining, somewhere a little rain is falling. *Cf.* One plows,
another sows, who will reap - no one knows.

70   Где песьня льется, там легче живется.
Sing your troubles away.

71   Где пиво пьют, тут и наш приют. (Где пиво там и диво.)   *v.* Б474, О35
[The beer hall is our haven (heaven).] *Cf.* Every one has a penny to spend at a new ale
house.

72   Где плохо лежит, туда вор глядит.   *v.* Н48,320,444
The hole calls the thief. *SPL.* malitiam suadet occasio.

73   Где поп, тут не надобен и черт.   *v.* Б339, О82, П146
[Where there's a priest there's no need for the devil.] The devil lurks behind the cross.

74   Где потеряешь - не чаешь, где найдешь - не знаешь.   *v.* К59, С3, Ч100
For a lost thing care not [you never know where it will turn up].

75   Где похвала, там и хула.   *v.* Г290
[Where there's praise there's blame.] Blame-all and praise-all are two blockheads.
Cf. Some praise at morning what they blame at night. Praises are admonitions, well dressed out.

76   Где право сило, там бесправно право.   *v.* Г87, С118, Ч136
Where force is law, there the law has no force.

77 **Где правда, там и счастье.** *v.* B55
[Where there is truth, there is happines.] Without truth, there can be no virtue.
Cf. Beauty is truth, truth beauty.

78 **Где правит раб господинский дом, хозяин сам живет рабом.**
[When the slave's in charge, the master becomes the slave.] *Cf.* Servants make the worst masters.

79* **Где пруд, там и лягушки.** *v.* Б432, Г51,104
[Where there's a pond, there are frogs.] The frog cannot out of her bog. Where there are reeds, there is water.

80* **Где радость, там и горе.** *v.* Г263,Н543, Р18, С85
Sadness and gladness succeed each other. *Lat.* laetitiae proximus fletus.

81 **Где растяпа да тетеря, там не прибыль а потеря.** *v.* З157
[Where there's a careless laggard, there are losses instead of gain.] If you lose your time, you cannot get money or gain.

82 **Где росла трава, там и будет.** *v.* Г14
[Where grass has grown once, it'll grow again.] Grass is immortal. What has been, may be.

83* **Где рука, там и голова.**
[When you sign, you're responsible.] *Cf.* Read carefully, sign cautiously. The written word remains. If you don't write, you're wrong.

84 **Где свинья умирает, там и ворон играет.** *v.* Г69, И133, К157, О43
[Where the swine dies, the crow dances.] Fortune to one is mother, to another a stepmother. One's loss is another's gain.

85* **Где сердце лежит, туда и око бежит.** *v.* Г76,87
The heart's letter is read in the eye. *Lat.* oculi sunt in amore duces.

86* **Где сило владеет, там закон уступает.** *v.* Б332, С117,121, У54, Ч136
[Where force rules, laws capitulate.] Where drums beat, laws are silent. *Lat.* inter arma silent leges.

87* **Где сило, там и закон.** *v.* С118
[Where there is force, there is law.] Might makes right. *Lat.* violentia praecidit ius.

88 **Где слуги в шелках, там баря в долгах.** *v.* Б382, В10, Г3, М174
[When the maids wear silk, milady's in the red.] Silks and satins put out the fire in the chimney.

89 **Где совет, там и свет. (Где советно, там и любовно.)** *v.* М100
[Where there is harmony, there is light (love).] Order makes for peace. *Cf.* Where there is peace, God is. A harvest of peace is produced from a seed of contentment.

90* **Где спех, там и смех.** *v.* Б300, Д123,146, П188, С159, Ч102
Haste makes waste. *Cf.* Haste trips up its own heels.

91 **Где страх, там и благочестие.** *v.* Б261, Г327, Д334
Danger makes men devout. It was fear first created gods in the world. *Gr.* ἱνα δέος, ἐνθα καὶ αἰΔώς (where there is fear, there is propriety). *Lat.* Stat.*Theb*.3.661: primus in orbe deos fecit timor. *Cf.* Fear is the beadle of the law. Fear of God makes the heart shine. Where there is fear, there is shame (modesty).

92*   **Где строят, там и роют.**   *v.* Г35
    [Where there's building, there is digging.] High buildings have a low foundation.

93   **Где суд, там и неправда.**
    [Where there is a court, there is perjury.] Much law, little justice.

94   **Где сусло хорошо, там и пиво не дурно будет.**   *v.* В73
    [When the wort is good, so is the beer.] The husk often tells what the kernel is. What is bred in the bone will come out in the flesh. *Cf.* Sour grapes never make sweet wine. Good can never grow out of evil.

95   **Где счастье плодится, там и зависть родится.**   *v.* С312, Ч121
    [Fortune engenders envy.] *SPL.* perflant altissima venti, summa petit livor. Envy doesn't enter an empty house.

96   **Где тому бывать, свинье небо видать.**   *v.* Г192, П198
    [As unlikely as a pig seeing the sky.] Pigs might fly, if they had wings.

97   **Где тому случится что безрукий постучится?**   *v.* Ч44
    [As unlikely as the armless knocking.] *Cf.* The age of miracles is past. No man can flay a stone.

98*   **Где тонко, там и рвется (а где худо, тут и порется).**   *v.* Г13, Д199
    The thread breaks where it is thinnest. The chain is no stronger than its weakest link.

99   **Где хвост рассуждает, там голова плутает.**   *v.* Г207
    [When the tail commands, the head strays.] That which is good for the back is bad for the head.

100*   **Где хозяин ходит, там земля родит.**   *v.* С62, Х34
    The master's footsteps fatten the soil.

101*   **Где хотение, там и умение (сило).**   *v.* Б452, Д76, Х74
    Where there's a will there's a way. *Lat.* volenti nil impossibile.

102*   **Где цветок, там и медок.**   *v.* Б426, Г37, Д510
    [Where there are flowers, there's honey.] *Cf.* Where bees are, there is honey.

103   **Где церковь - там корчма близка.**   *v.* Б236, Г8
    [Where there's a church, there's a pub nearby.] *Cf.* Where God has his church, the devil will have his chapel. New churches and new bars are well patronized.

104   **Где чайка там и рыба.**   *v.* Б432, Г51,79
    When a gull dives in the sea, there are fish for you and me.

105   **Где человек не сможет, там и Бог не поможет.**   *v.* Б187, К295
    [Where man cannot, God will not help.] *Cf.* God helps those who help themselves. God reaches us good things by our own hands.

106   **Где я лисой пройду, там три года куры не несутся.**   *v.* П298
    [Where the fox has been, there chickens will not lay eggs for three years.] *Cf.* Once bitten, twice shy. Once the bird has been snared, it fears all bushes.

107   **Герой в бою думает не о смерти, о победе.**   *v.* М188
    [The hero does not think of death in battle, but of victory.] A brave man may fall, but he cannot yield. *Cf.* In victory the hero seeks the glory, not the prey.

108* Гладко было на бумаге, да забыли про овраги. *v.* V113
[It was smooth on paper, but we forgot about the ravines.] It is one thing to plan a deed and another to carry it out.

109* Глаз видит, да зуб неймет. *v.* В308,362, И2
[The eye sees but the tooth has not seized.] There's many a slip 'twixt the cup and the lip.

110* Глаз мал, да далеко видит. *v.* М1
[The eye is small, but it sees far.] One may see day at a little hole.

111 Глаз не накормишь. *v.* Б368, В275, Г116,121,158, Д507, З161, Н343
[The eyes cannot be fed their fill.] Better fill a man's belly than his eye. The eye is bigger than the belly.

112 Глаза - бирюза, а душа - сажа. *v.* В99, Л85, Н258, Р65, С51,211
[Eyes of turquoise, heart of soot.] Fair face, foul heart.

113 Глаза верят самим себе, уши - другим людям. *v.* Б317, Л123,146, Н215, О194
[Eyes believe what they see, ears - what others tell them.] *Cf.* One eye witness is better than two hear-so's.

114* Глаза глядят (боятся) (страшатся), а руки делают. *v.* Г158
[The eyes look (dread), but the hands accomplish.] Looking at a hill won't move it. *Cf.* It's not by saying "honey, honey" that sweetness will come into the mouth.

115 Глаза да мера, то прямая вера. *v.* Л123,146, О194
Seeing is believing.

116* Глаза ели бы, да живот не принимает. (Глаза шире брюха.) *v.* Б368, В275, Г111,
The eyes are bigger than the belly. Д507, З161

117 Глаза завидущие, руки загребущие. (Глаза - ямы, а руки - грабли.) *v.* В604
[Covetous eyes, greedy hands.] [The eyes are like furrows, the hands like rakes.] Neither eyes on letters nor hands on coffers.

118* Глаза - зеркало души. *v.* К77
The eye is the mirror (window) of the soul. *Lat.* oculus animi index.

119 Глаза золотом запорошат, ничего не увидишь. *v.* Д67,75, М85
[Once gold dust gets in the eye, it is blinded.] Gifts blind the eyes.

120 Глаза на мокром месте.
[Eyes in a wet place.] *i.e. easily moved to tears.* *Cf.* Cry before one is hurt.

121* Глаза одни не сыты. *v.* Г111,158, Д507, Н343
The eyes are not satisfied with seeing.

122 Глаза проворны, да руки неловки. *v.* Г109, И2
[Sprightly eyes but clumsy hands.] *Cf.* The eye of the master will do more work than both his hands.

123 Глаза с поволокой, роток с позевотой.
[Languorous eyes, yawning mouth.] *Cf.* Eyes draw (pick) straws. To cast a sheep's eye.

124 Глаза - человеку вороги (неприятели).
[The eyes can be one's enemy (foe).] The eye is a shrew.

125   **Глазам стыдно, а душа радуется.**   *v.* Г127
[The eyes are ashamed but the heart happy.] Little troubles the eye, but far less the soul. *Cf.* To cry with one eye and laugh with the other.

126   **Глазами кос, да душою прям.**   *v.* Б404, Д411, И23, К204, С287, У75
[Cross-eyed but straight-laced.] *Cf.* A straight stick is crooked in the water.

127*   **Глазами плачет а сердцем смеется.**   *v.* Г125
[He grieves with his eyes but laughs in his heart.] To cry with one eye and laugh with the other.

128   **Глазами чужого пива не выпьешь (выпить).**   *v.* В180,185, Г121,158, Н111, Ч119
[You cannot drink another's beer with your eyes.] You can't get warm in another's fur coat. Please the eye and plague the heart.

129   **Глас народа - глас Божий.**
The voice of the people, the voice of God. *Lat.* vox populi, vox dei.

130   **Глину не мять - горшков не видать.**   *v.* Д60, Н174,363, У65
Unless the clay is well-pounded, no pitcher can be made.

131   **Глубже пахать - больше хлеба жевать (ждать).**
(Глубоко пашешь, веселей пляшешь.)   *v.* В113, Д60, О95
[Plough deeper and enjoy more bread.] [Furrow deep and you'll dance sprightly.] Plow deep and you will have plenty of corn. *Cf.* No sweet without sweat.

132   **Глуп да ленив одно дважды делает.**   *v.* Д467
[The lazy fool must do everything twice.] *Cf.* What the fool does in the end, the wise man does at the beginning. Fool's haste is no speed.

133   **Глуп совсем кто не знается ни с кем.**   *v.* Б62
[He is a complete fool who associates with no one.] *Cf.* A solitary man is either a beast or an angel.

134*   **Глупая голова и ногам покою не дает.**   *v.* Б131, Г215
[A foolish mind gives the feet no rest.] What your head forgets, your heels must remember. What you haven't got in your head, you have in your heels. *Cf.* Fools are fain of flitting.

135*   **Глупая речь не пословица.**   *v.* Б179, Г204, О55, П183
[Gibberish does not a proverb make.] A proverb comes not from nothing.

136   **Глупая собака громко лает.**   *v.* Б313, В119, К206, П307, Х103
[Loud is the stupid dog's bark.] *Cf.* An empty barrel makes the most noise.

137   **Глупого долю наперед едят.**   *v.* Б139, В576, У25
A fool and his money are soon parted.

138   **Глупому лучше молчать, нежели много болтать.**
Fools are wise as long as silent.

139   **Глупому сыну и родной отец ума не пришьет.**
[Not even a fool's own father can get him a brain.] *Cf.* A wise man commonly has foolish children.

140   **Глупому сыну не в помощь (прок) и богатство (наследство).**   *v.* Б280,284,289, У118
[Even wealth is no asset to the foolish son (heir).] Without wisdom, wealth is worthless.
Cf. Knowledge is better than riches.

141   **Глупость завидует богатому, а смеется бедному.**
[Folly envies the rich and scoffs at the poor.] *Cf.* A nod from a lord is breakfast for a
fool. The skillfullest wanting money is scorned.

142*   **Глупость заразительна.**   *v.* Б166, Г1, Д501, И17, О33, С9
[Folly is contagious.] One fool makes many (a hundred). *Lat.* unius dementia dementes
efficit multos.

143   **Глупость и чванство неразрывны.**
Ignorance is the mother of impudence. *Lat.* inscitia mater arrogantiae.

144*   **Глупость не порок, а несчастье.**
[Foolishness is not a vice but a calamity.] *Cf.* Folly is an incurable disease.

145   **Глупые друг другу губят да потопляют, а умные друг дружку любят да подсобляют.**
Fools bite one another, but wise men agree together.   *v.* Д493, С33
Fools fight one another, wise men agree.

146   **Глупые речи - что пыль на ветру.**   *v.* У26
[Foolish talk is just dust in the wind.] *Cf.* The mouths of fools pour out foolishness.
Save your breath to cool your porridge.

147*   **Глупый да малый всегда говорят правду.**
Children and fools speak the truth (cannot lie). *Lat.* stultus puerque vera dicunt.

148   **Глупый да малый, что не увидят то и просят.**
[Fools and children ask for everything they see.] Children and princes will quarrel for
trifles. *Cf.* Little things please little minds.

149*   **Глупый завяжет, а умный не скоро развяжет.**   *v.* Д475, О31, У102
[What the fool ties up, the wise man cannot quickly untie.] Fools tie knots and wise men
loosen them. *Cf.* A fool may throw a stone in a well which a hundred wise men cannot
pull out.

150   **Глупый ищет большого места, а разумного и в углу видно (знают).**   *v.* Ж30, П162
[A fool seeks (a great) space, while the wise man is noticed even in the corner.]
A fool always rushes to the fore.

151   **Глупый киснет, а умный все промыслит.**
[The fool sulks, but the wise man understands.] A fool says I can't, a wise man says I'll
try. *Cf.* What the fool does in the end, the wise man does at the beginning.

152   **Глупый много просит, а умный много дает.**   *v.* Д24, Л153
[The fool asks much, the wise man grants much.] *Cf.* The fool asks much, but he is more
fool that grants it.

153   **Глупый осудит, а умный рассудит.**
Wise men propose and fools determine. People condemn what they do not understand.

154*   **Глупый погрешит один, а умный соблазнит многих.**
The fool errs alone whereas the wise man corrupts many.

155*   **Глупым словам - глухое (глупое) ухо.**
        For mad words deaf ears.

156   **Глухой всему виной.**
        Deaf men go away with the blame.

157*   **Глухому (поп) две обедни не поют (служит).**
        Глухому песен не пой (+ не услышит).   *v.* Д236
        [Mass is not repeated for the deaf.] [Don't sing for the deaf (+ they won't hear).]
        Whistle (sing) psalms to the taffrail (a dead horse). *Cf.* Sing (knock) at a deaf man's door.

158*   **Гляденьем сыт не будешь.**   *obs.*
        (Глядя на чужую работу сыт не будешь.)   *v.* Г111,121,128, Д507, Н343
        [Looking won't fill the belly.] [Watching others work will not sate your appetite.] The
        eye is not satisfied with seeing. Looking at a hill won't move it. *Cf.* He that would have
        the fruit must climb the tree.

159   **Глядеть глядим, а видеть ничего не видим.**
        [Looking is not necessarily seeing.] One is not bound to see more than he can.

160*   **Гляди налет на свой полет.**   *v.* В52,573, Ч13
        Make not your sail too big for the ballast.

161   **Гляди невесту не в народе, а в ляде.**   *v.* В669, Ж85
        [Choose a wife in the country, not in town.] Choose a wife on a Saturday rather than a
        Sunday.

162   **Гляди семью, отколь берешь жену.**   *v.* В671
        [Look to the family whence you choose a wife.] Take a vine of a good soil, and the
        daughter of a good mother.

163   **Глядит лисой а пахнет волком.**   *v.* Б302, В388
        [Looks like a fox but smacks of a wolf.] *Cf.* As a wolf is like a dog, so is a flatterer like
        a friend.

164   **Глядя на людей, хоть и не вырастешь, а тянешься.**
        [You may not grow up observing people, but you'll grow taller.] It is good to learn at
        other mens' cost.

165   **Гляженое лучше хваленого.**   *v.* В300, Л146, Н215
        Better seen than heard.

166*   **Гляженый конь лучше хваленого.**   *v.* Л146,154, Н215
         [Better the horse that you see than the one you hear about.] Pedigree won't sell a lame
        horse. *Cf.* Better to have than to wish.

167*   **Гнев - недолгое безумие.**   *v.* Н65
        Anger is a short madness. *Lat.* ira furor brevis est.

168*   **Гнев - плохой советник.**
        [Wrath is a poor advisor.] Anger and haste hinder good counsel.

169   **Гнев человеку сушит кости и рушит сердце.**
        [A man's wrath destroys his heart and parches his bones.] *Cf.* Anger punishes itself.
        Sorrow is always dry.

170   Гневайся, да не согрешай.
However angry your heart, do not do wrong. *Psalm*.4.5: irascimini et nolite peccare.

171   Гневлив с горшками не ездит.
[A choleric person should not travel with crockery.] Anger is a brief madness, but it can do damage that lasts forever.

172   Гневливое слово пороги не держат.
[Thresholds brook not angry words.] When you enter a house, leave anger at the door.

173   Гнездо цело, а птицы улетели.   *v.* Ч57
[The nest is intact but the birds have flown.] There are no birds in last year's nests.

174*   Гнет (дуги) - не парит, переломит - не тужит.   *v.* К60,299, Н485, С75, 109, Х81
[He bends the wood without soaking, if it breaks - too bad.] Such as are careless of themselves are seldom mindful of others. A strong man and waterfall channel their own path.

175   Говори да не заговаривайся, ходи да оглядывайся.
[Talk sense and look where you're going.] Spare to speak and spare to speed.

176*   Говори меньше, умнее будет.   *v.* Б318, Л90, К176, Р47
Few words are best.

177   Говори по делу, живи по совести.
[Speak to the point and live by your conscience.] Speak fair and think what you will.

178   Говори с другими поменьше, а с собою побольше.   *v.* С177
[Speak less with others and more with yourself.] Say little but think the more.

179   Говорила мне своячинка что на дороге бывает всячинка.   *v.* Г192
[My sister-in-law was reminding me about the winding road.] "They say so" is half a lie.

180*   Говорит бело а делает черно. (Говорит на право а глядит на лево.)
(Говорит прямо а делает криво.)   *v.* В126, О152
[He says white and does black.] [He says right and looks left.] [Speaks straight but acts deviously.] Too much courtesy, too much craft. Saying and doing are two things. *Cf.* Fine words dress ill deeds. Saying's one thing, doing another. He looks one way, rows another.

181   Говорит день до вечера, а слушать нечего.   *v.* В503, Г57, К192, Р25
Говорит красиво (красно), да слушать тоскливо (а поглядишь - пестро).
[He talks all day, but nothing worth listening to.] *Cf.* Great talkers are like leaky pitchers, everything runs out of them. The mill that is always going grinds coarse and fine.

182*   Говорит как слепой о краске (красном). *v.* К54

183   Говорит (говоришь) по секрету, а выйдет по всему свету.   *v.* Н411, Ш5
[Say something in secret and the world will know.] Confide in an aunt and the world will know.

184   Говорит что дипломат, да дела нейдут на лад.   *v.* Б21,329,367, К192, Р24,42
[He speaks like a diplomat, but there are no public improvements.] He who gives you fair words, feeds you with an empty spoon.

185   Говорить без дела - что на воде писать.   *v.* Б316, Д117, С127
[Talk and no action is like writing on water.] Words are mere bubbles of water, but deeds are drops of gold.

186* Говорить легко, делать трудно. *v.* В512, Л27,36, Н231, С156
Easier said than done.

187 Говорить не думая что стрелять не целясь. *v.* Г181
Great talkers fire too fast to take aim.

188* Говорить правду - (по)терять дружбу. *v.* Н263, Ш21
[Speak the truth and lose your friend.] Truth finds foes where it makes none.

189* Говоришь правду, правду и делай. *v.* А15, В565, И70
Live truth instead of professing it. Practice what you preach.

190 Говоря, всего договоришься. *v.* Д229, М158
[Agreement may be reached on anything through discussion.] By talking, people understand one another. *Cf.* The lame tongue gets nothing. Good words cool more than cold water.

191 Говоря про чужих, услышишь и про своих.
[Speak of others and you'll hear about your own.] A gossip speaks ill of all and all of her. He who speaks evil, hears worse.

192* Говорят, (что) кур доят. *v.* Г96,179, *Ар.*1.41
[They say chickens can be milked.] They say is a tough old liar. They say so is half a lie.

193 Год году не равен (год на год не приходится). *v.* В88, Д165, И45, Н392, Р20
[Not all years are the same.] *Cf.* No two like are the same.

194* Год прожить - не реку переплыть. *v.* В227, Ж147,164
[Living a year is more than just forging a river.] Life is not all beer and skittles.

195 Год тих, да час лих. *v.* Д376, Ж140
[The year is quiet, the hour frenzied.] *Cf.* Life would be too smooth if it had no rubs in it.

196 Год торгуй, два воруй, а три в яме сиди.
[One year to trade, two to cheat, and three in the slammer.] After your fling, watch for the sting.

197 Года как вода, пройдут не увидишь. *v.* В468,475, Г199
[Like water, years flow by unnoticed.] *Cf.* Noiseless falls the foot of time. Time is a file that wears and makes no noise.

198 Год кончается, другой начинается.
[One year ends, another begins.] Our years roll on. *SPL.* in se sua per vestigia volvitur annus.

199 Года текут как вода. *v.* В468, С235
Time and tide wait for no man.

200 Годами молода, нравом стара. *v.* М139
[Young in years but not in character.] *Cf.* Grey, but not from years.

201 Годы хребет горбят.
Time undermines us.

202 Годы что горе - борозды прокладывают. *v.* Г274, М101, Н225
[Years and tears add wrinkles.] *Cf.* Time is the rider that breaks youth. Misfortunes hasten age. Time consumes the strongest (devours all things).

203   Гол да не вор (беден да честен).
        Better beg than steal.   *v.* Л151, Х104, Х75

204*   Голая речь не пословица.   *v.* Б179, Г135, О55, П183
        [Mere words don't make a proverb.] A proverb is an ornament to language.

205   Голова без ума, что фонарь без огня (свечи).   *v.* Б132
        [An empty head is a lamp without a flame.] An idle head is a box for the wind.

206   Голова болит, все тело скорбит.
        When the head aches, all the body is worse. *Lat.* si caput dolet, omnia membra languent.

207   Голова болит, заду легче.   *v.* Г99
        [When the head aches, the back is better.] What is good for the back is bad for the head.

208   Голова в шляпке а сам в тряпке.
        [A cap on his head but the rest in rags.] My cap is better at ease than my head.

209   Голова велика да мозгу мало. (Голова с пивной котел, а ума ни ложки.)
    (Голова-то есть, да в голове-то нет.)   *v.* Б331
        [A big head but a small brain.] [A head like a beer keg but not a drop of brains.]
        [A head there is, but with nothing in it.] **Mickle head, little wit. Big head, little sense.**

210*   Голова всему начало. (Добрая голова сто голов кормит.)   *v.* B27, O46, P31
        [Everything begins in the head.] [One good head can feed a hundred.] The thought is
        father to the deed. *Cf.* Every revolution was first a thought in one man's mind.

211   Голова как у вола, а все, вишь, мала.
        [A head like an ox, but still too small.] You have a head and so has a pin (nail).

212   Голова не колышек, не шапку на нее вешать.   *v.* Б130
        [The head is not just a stand on which to hang your hat.] Use your head for something
        besides a hat rack.

213   Голова приросла, а уму воля дана.   *v.* Н57, С24
        [The head is attached, but the mind is free.] *Cf.* Thought is free.

214*   Голова седая, да душа молодая.   *v.* Б343,401,402, П99, Р64
        [Grey head, young heart.] Old head on young shoulders. *Cf.* Grey hairs are nourished
        with green thoughts.

215*   Голова у ног ума не просит.   *v.* Б131, Г134
        [The head does not look to the feet for advice.] Don't use your feet, use your head.
        Cf. Look not for musk in a dog's kennel.

216*   Голова хвоста не ждет.   *v.* Б332, Г21, С97
        [The head does not wait for the tail.] *Cf.* Let the tail follow the skin.

217   Голод да холод дорогу в кабак протоптали.
        [Hunger and cold have trodden a path to the pub.] *Cf.* Hunger and cold deliver a man
        up to his enemy.

218*   Голод и волка из лесу (колка) гонит.   *v.* B674, H580
    Голод в мир гонит (морит) (по свету) гонит.
        Hunger drives the wolf out of the woods. *Lat.* fames pellit lupum e silvis. [Hunger
        drives one out into (all over) the world.]

219* **Голод - лучший повар (соус).** *v.* Г230,235
Hunger is the best chef (sauce). *Lat.* fames optimum (cibi) condimentum.

220* **Голод научит говорить.** *v.* В82, Н588, П276, Ч22
[Hunger teaches speech.] Ask and have. Bashfulness is an enemy to poverty. Needs must when necessity drives. *Cf.* Hunger tames the wild beast.

221 **Голод не тетка.**
[Hunger is not a kindly aunt.] Hunger knows no friend.

222 **Голод принудит красть.** *v.* Б34, Ж131, Н59, П308
[Hunger will drive one to steal.] *Cf.* Where there is hunger, law is not regarded (and where law is not regarded, there will be hunger). Poverty is the mother of crime.

223 **Голод учит жить.** *v.* П274
Hunger increases the understanding.

224 **Голоден при хлебе не будешь.** *v.* Б144, В679
All griefs with bread are less.

225* **Голодная муха больнее кусает.**
Hungry flies bite sore.

226* **Голодного песнями не пресытишь.** *v.* Б21, Е45, Р24, С29, У7
[You cannot satisfy a hungry man with song.] *Cf.* A hungry man is an angry man.

227* **Голодное брюхо к словам глухо (ушей не имеет).**
Hungry bellies have no ears. *Lat.* venter aures non habet.

228* **Голодной курице (все) просо снится.** *v.* Л71, С174,226, Ч84
[A hungry chicken dreams of millet.] Pigs dream of acorns and the goose of maize.

229 **Голодному да заботному долга обедня. (Голодному животу и молебен не в утеху).**
The belly hates a long sermon. *Cf.* A sharp stomach makes short devotion.

230 **Голодному и опенки - мясо. (Голодному и вода, что с яйца, вкусна).**
[Hunger makes meat out of mushrooms] *v.* Г219,236, *Ap.*1.90
[Hunger makes the water from boiled eggs seem tasty.] Hunger makes hard beans sweet. Hunger sweetens what is bitter.

231 **Голодному не стать время разбирать.** *v.* Б383, К227
Hunger finds no fault with the cookery. Hunger never saw bad bread.

232 **Голодному хлеб (не сон) на уме (мысли).** *v.* В380
[A hungry man has bread on his mind.] The hungry man often talks of bread. *SPL.* canis famelicus panes somniat. *Cf.* A hungry man smells meat far off.

233* **Голодный волк силней сытой собаки.** *v.* М69
[A starving wolf is stronger than a sated hound.] *Cf. Eccles.*1.9.4: A living dog is better than a dead lion.

234 **Голодный и владыка (патриарх) хлеба украдет.**
[Even a bishop (patriarch) will steal some bread if he's starving.] *Cf.* The friar preached against stealing and had a goose up his sleeve.

235 **Голодный праздников не считает.** *v.* Н581
[The hungry do not count holidays.] *Cf.* Necessity has no holiday.

236* **Голодный укусил (откусил) бы и (от) камня.**   *v.* Г219,230
    [A hungry man would bite a stone.] Hunger makes hard beans sweet. *Cf.* Hunger breaks stone walls. Hunger makes the monkey eat red pepper.

237 **Голой овцы не стригут.**   *v.* Г241, З9
    [A shorn lamb is not cropped.] There's no use trying to strip a naked man.

238 **Голому одеться - только подпоясаться.**   *v.* В502, М166
    [A beggar dresses only by buckling his belt.] *Cf.* Little gear, less care.

239* **Голому разбой не страшен. (Голый разбою не боится.)**   *v.* Б352, Н558
    The beggar may sing before the thief.

240 **Голосом выть, горя не избыть.**
    [Whining won't relieve sorrow.] *Cf.* †Who suffers much is silent. No remedy but patience.

241* **Голый на голом не ищет.**   *v.* В121, З9, Н125,559, С5, У71
    No naked man is sought after to be rifled.

242 **Голый плачется на Бога, а богатый на свое платье.**   *v.* Г255
    [The poor man complains about God, the rich man about his clothes.] *Cf.* The rich man has his ice in summer, the poor man gets his in winter.

243 **Голый, что святой, не боится беды.**   *v.* Б290, К278, М166
    [The poor man, like the saint, does not fear misfortune.] *Cf.* If we have not the world's wealth, we have the world's ease. Little goods, little care.

244 **Голым родился, гол и умру.**
    [Born poor, die poor.] *Cf.* He that has nought, shall have nought.

245 **Голь на выдумки хитра.**   *v.* Н496,591, Я21
    Necessity is the mother of invention. *Lat.* mater artium necessitas.

246* **Гони природу в дверь, а она в окно войдет (влетит).**   *v.* Ч98
    [You can drive nature out the door and she'll return through the window.] You can drive out nature with a pitchfork, but she keeps on coming back.

247* **Гора родила мышь.**   *v.* Д453, М202
    The mountain has brought forth a mouse. *Gr. Diog.*8.75: ὤδινε ὄρος εἶτα μῦν ἀπέτεκεν. *Lat.* parturiunt montes, nascetur ridiculus mus.

248* **Гора с горой не сходится, а человек с человеком сойдется (столкнется) (свидится) (а горшок с горшком соткнется).**
    Friends may meet, but mountains never greet. *Gr. Apost.*13.2: ὄρος ὄρει οὐ μίγνυται, ἄνθρωπος δ'ἀνθρώπῳ. *SPL.* occurrunt homines, nequeunt occurrere montes. mons cum monte non miscetur.

249 **Горазд на собак брехать.**   *v.* М143, П313, Ш10
    [He's good at barking at dogs.] *Cf.* Great barkers are no biters.

250* **Горбатого исправит могила (а упрямого - дубина).**   *v.* И86, К64
    [The grave will straighten the hunchback (as a rod the obdurate).] That which is crooked cannot be made straight. The crooked log (rod) is not to be straightened. *Lat.* lignum tortum haud umquam rectum. *Cf.* The grave levels all distinctions. You can't spell Yarmouth steeple right.

251 **Гордись не ростом а умом.**
[Take pride in your intelligence, not size.] Success does not depend on size. *Cf.* Seldom is a long man wise.

252* **Гордость - глупости сосед.**
[Pride is folly's neighbour.] Ignorance and pride grow on the same wood. *Cf.* Pride and grace dwelt never in one place.

253 **Гордый петух стареет облезлым.** *v.* Д408
[A proud cock grows old with ruffled feathers.] Quarreling dogs come halting home. *Cf.* Pride feels no pain (pride is painful).

254 **Горе в лохмотьях, беда нагишом.**
[Grief goes in rags but misfortune is stark naked.] *Cf.* I cried because I had no shoes until I met a man who had not feet.

255 **Горе ваше что без масла каша.** *v.* Г242
[Your only problem is *kasha* without butter.] *Cf.* A rich man may dine when he will, the poor man when he may. If you have bread, don't look for cake.

256 **Горе да беда - с кем не была.** *v.* Г313
[Grief and sorrow - none are immune.] Tears and trouble are the lot of all. *Cf.* Man is born into trouble. No day passes without some grief.

257 **Горе да нужду обухом не перешибешь.** *v.* Г312
[You can't chop off indigence and misery with an axe.] Life and misery began together.

258 **Горе - деньги, а вдвое - без денег.** *v.* Д148,190
[Misery with money, double misery without.] Fat sorrow is better than lean sorrow. All griefs with bread are less.

259 **Горе есть - не горюй, дело есть - делай.**
[If there's trouble, don't worry, if there's work, get on with it.] If you can do nothing about it, don't worry; if you can do something about it, do it - don't worry.

260* **Горе ждет из-за угла.** *v.* Г4,270, П255
[Grief lurks around the corner.] Trouble arises when you least expect it.

261* **Горе женится - нужда замуж идет.** *v.* Ж71
[Sorrow has taken poverty for his bride.] *said when two poor people marry.* Marriage is a game best played by two winners.

262 **Горе и крушит и сушит.**
[Sorrow devastates and dries.] Sorrow is always dry.

263* **Горе и радость ходят вместе.** *v.* Г80, Н543, Р18, С85
Sadness and gladness succeed each other.

264 **Горе легкое - болтливое, тяжелое - безмолвно.**
Small sorrows speak, great ones are silent.

265* **Горе молчать не будет. (Горе не молчит.)** *v.* Г282
[Sorrow will not be silent.] *Cf.* Grief is lessened when imparted to others. A cure for all sorrows is conversation. †Sorrow makes silence her best orator. †Who suffers much is silent.

266   **Горе на двоих - полгоря, радость на двоих - две радости.**   *v.* В343,546, Н53
Trouble shared is trouble halved [but happiness shared is doubled.] *Cf.* Two in distress make sorrow less. *Lat.* solamen miseris socios habuisse malorum.

267   **Горе на чужой стороне безъязыкому.**   *v.* Н110, П300, Ч110,114,132
It is easy to bear the misfortunes of others.

268   **Горе - не горе, лишь бы не было боле.**
[If there be grief, may there be little.] *Cf.* Sorrow is soon enough when it comes.

269   **Горе не задавит, а с ног свалит.**   *v.* П30
Sorrow kills not, but it blights.

270*   **Горе не ищут, само приходит.**   *v.* Г4,260, Н191, П255
[Grief is not sought, it comes itself.] Misfortunes come of themselves.

271   **Горе не сживешь (изживешь) скоро.**   *v.* Б28,42, З115,123, С320
Ill comes in by ells and goes out by inches.

272*   **Горе одного только рака красит.**
[Misfortune makes only crabs blush.] *i.e. by turning red in boiling water.* *Cf.* Sorrow is good for nothing but sin.

273   **Горе по горю, беды по бедам.**
[Take grief and misfortune one by one.] Never trouble trouble till trouble troubles you. Don't meet troubles half way. *Cf.* Don't cross your bridges till you come to them. Take things as they come.

274   **Горе с сединкою, а годы с лысинкою.**   *v.* Г202, М101, Н225
[Grief greys, but years thin the hair.] *Cf.* Care brings grey hair. After a hundred years we shall all be bald.

275*   **Горе с тобою, беда без тебя.**   *v.* Д440, Р67
[Grief with you and without you.] *Cf.* The greatest hate springs from the greatest love.

276   **Горе старит, радость молодит (красит).**   *v.* Р19
[Grief ages, happiness rejuvenates.] Misfortune hastens age.

277   **Горе тому дому коим владеет жена.**
It is a sad house where the hen crows louder than the cock.

278   **Горе тому кто в карты играет а козырей не знает.**   *v.* Х94

279   **Горе умереть, а за могилой дело не станет.**
[It's sad to die -] **death is the end of all.** *Cf.* Death is a remedy for all ills.

280   **Горек хлеб чужой.**   *v.* С61, Ч128
[Bitter is another's bread.] Bitter is the bread of charity. *Cf.* Dry bread at home is better than roast meat abroad.

281*   **Горести не принять, и сладость не видать. (Горько не едать - и сладкого не видать).**
(Горька работа да сладок хлеб).   *v.* Б344,353, В8, Г297, К256,Л171,173, Н73, 221,363,
The bitter must come before the sweet. *Cf.* Suffering is bitter but its fruits are sweet. No sweet without sweat. He is worth no weal that can bide no woe.

282   **Горесть молчать не умеет.** *v.* Г265

283   **Горница хороша, да окна кривы.**
[The living room is fine, just the windows are crooked.] Every house has its dirty corner.
Cf. Wherever a man dwell, he may be sure to have a thorn bush near his door.

284   **Город каменный - люди железные.** *v.* В20
[A city of stone, a people of iron.] *Cf.* A great city, a great solitude.

285   **Городское телятко разумнее деревенского дитятки.** *v.* Б487, П129
[A city calf is smarter than a country kid.] *Cf.* Better the head of the yeomanry than the tail of the gentry. †The city slicker does not always flicker.

286*   **Горстью моря не вычерпать.** *v.* В320, М160, Ч32
[You cannot bail the sea with your hands.] The sea cannot be scooped up with a tumbler. *Cf.* To empty the sea with a spoon (nutshell).

287*   **Горшку с котлом не биться (+ и должно расшибиться).**
(Горшок чугуну не товарищ.) *v.* Е8
The earthen pot must keep clear of the brass kettle.

288*   **Горшок котлу завидует (смеется), а оба черны. (Горшок с котлом не наспорится.)**
The pot calls the kettle black. *v.* И102, О115
SPL. Clodius accusat moechum, Catilina Cathegum.

289   **Горька смерть, а горче злой живот.** *v.* Б210
[An ill life is worse than an ill death.] Better death than dishonour. *Cf.* Better be dead than out of fashion. †An ill life, an ill death.

290   **Горьким быть - расплюют, сладким - проглотят.** *v.* Б394, Г75
[The stern are eschewed, the meek devoured.] Make yourself honey and the flies will devour you. Blame-all and praise-all are two blockheads. *Cf.* Kind hearts are soonest wronged.

291   **Горьким лечат, а сладким портят (калечат).** *v.* П290
[Bitters cure, sweets spoil.] Bitter pills may have blessed effects. *Lat.* in amaritudine salus.

292   **Горько не вечно, а сладко не бесконечно.** *v.* Н553
[Sorrows end, but so too does happiness.] *Cf.* Soon hot, soon cold. Nothing that is violent is permanent.

293   **Горько пить вино, а обнесут - горчее всего.** *v.* Н298
[It hurts to drink wine, but it hurts even more when its passed around.] *Cf.* Spilt wine is worse than water.

294   **Горько проглотишь, а сладко - выплюнешь. (Горько съешь да сладко отрыгнется.)**
[Bitter to swallow, sweet to belch (spit).] Who has bitter in his mouth spits (not all) sweet.

295   **Горько человеку в чужой земле без языку.**
[Woe to the traveller who doesn't speak the language in a foreign land.] Nothing so necessary for travellers as languages.

296   **Горького дерева корень, хоть в меду вари, не будет сладок.** *v.* В368, К50, К52, С137
[A bitter root cannot be sweetened even if cooked in honey.] *Cf.* Whether you boil snow or pound it, you can have but water of it.

297* **Горя бояться - счастья не видать.**   *v.* Б49,127,353, В616, Г281, Л171
[Fear grief and suffer no hapiness.] *Cf.* Take a pain for a pleasure all wise men can. Pain is the price that God puts on all things. He is worth no weal that can bide no woe.

298 **Горя вином не зальешь, а радость пропьешь.**   *v.* В336
[Wine will not drown grief but only wash away happiness.] Drink does not drown care, but waters it and makes it grow faster.

299 **Горя много, да смерть одна.**   *v.* Д91,107, Р39, С98,291, Ш2
[There are many woes, but only one death.] A man can die but once. *Cf. Lat.* morborum medicus omnium mors ultimus.

300 **Горячо сыро не бывает (живет).**
[Heat and damp don't agree.] You cannot strike fire from snow.

301 **Господин гневу своему - господин всему.**
[He that masters his wrath can master anything.] He that is master of himself will soon be master of others. To control others, learn first to control yourself.

302 **Господин сыщет вину, коли захочет ударить (палкою) свою собаку.**   *v.* Б454,
       It is easy to find a stick to beat a dog.   К122, С109

303 **Гостей трое а хозяев семеро.**   *v.* С95
[Seven hosts for three guests.] Too many chiefs and not enough braves.

304 **Гости из кареты а хозяева не одеты. (Гости наехали а ложки не мыты.)** *v.* Ж22, Н452
[The guests are here but the hosts aren't dressed (spoons are not washed).] *Cf.* It's too late to learn to box when you're in the ring. Have not thy cloak to make when it begins to rain. Thatch your roof before rainy weather. Dig your well before you are thirsty.

305* **Гость - до трех дней.**   *v.* В102, Д337
[Be a guest for three days only.] Fish and guests (visitors) smell (stink) in three days. *Lat.* post tres saepe dies vilescit piscis et hospes.

306 **Гость добрый - всегда хозяину приятен.**   *v.* Ж38
[A kind guest is always welcome.] His worth is warrant for his welcome. *Cf.* Good will and welcome is your best cheer.

307* **Гость хозяину не указчик. (Гость - невольник.) (Гость у хозяина в руках.)**
[The guest cannot command the host.]   *v.* В22, Н409, Х30
[A guest is a prisoner.] [A guest is in the hands of his host.] *Cf.* He that reckons without his host, must reckon again (twice). Be deaf and blind in another man's house.

308 **Гостью воле - лучшая честь.**
[The greatest honour for a guest is to feel at home.] Welcome is the best dish.

309* **Готовь летом сани а зимой телегу.**   *v.* Б183
[Prepare your sledge in summer and your cart in winter.] In fair weather prepare for foul.

310 **Грамоте может, а прочесть не умеет.**   *v.* В54, Х94
[He knows how to write, he just can't read.] Easy writing makes hard reading. *Cf.* He knows how many blue beans make five.

311* **Грех греха не целит.**   *v.* В124, З131, И81, К201
       Two wrongs don't make a right.

312 **Грех да беда на кого не живет.**   *v.* Г257, Н43,495
    Life and misery began together. *SPL.* vitiis nemo sine nascitur. *Cf.* Misfortunes find their way even on the darkest nights.

313 **Грех не беда, молва нехороша.**   *v.* И60, Х47
    [Vice is not bad, it has a bad reputation.] The devil is not so black as he is painted. Nothing is good or bad, only thinking makes it so.

314 **Грех скажет правду однажды в год.**
    An enemy may chance to give good counsel. Truth may sometimes come out of the devil's mouth.

315 **Грех сладок а человек падок. (Грехи сладки, а люди падки.)**   *v.* З91, Ч19
    [Temptation is sweet, man weak.] *Cf. Prov.*9:17 Stolen waters (fruit) are sweet. Forbidden fruit is the sweetest.

316 **Грехи любезны доведут до бездны.**   *v.* М10
    Submitting to one wrong brings on another. *Lat.* veterem iniuriam ferendo invitas novem. *Cf.* Sin plucks on sin.

317* **Гречневая каша сама себя хвалит.**   *v.* Д301, Р57
    [*Kasha* praises itself.] *a double-entendre; i.e. through flatulence also.* *Cf.* Good wine needs no bush.

318 **Грешен грех законом.**
    The law grows of sin (and chastises it).

319 **Грешить легко, трудно каяться.**
    [Easier to sin than to repent.] Short pleasure, long repentance.

320 **Грибы растут в деревне, а их и в городе знают.**   *v.* Ч63
    [Mushrooms are grown in the country but are popular in the city.] The chicken is the country's, but the city eats it.

321 **Гроб видя вздыхают, и смертный час воспоминают.**
    When thou dost hear a toll or knell, then think upon thy passing bell.

322 **Гроз твоих не боюсь, а ласка твоя не нужна.**
    [I neither fear your threats nor crave your affection.] *Cf.* Neglect will kill an injury sooner than revenge.

323 **Гроза бьет по высокому дереву.**
    [Lightning strikes the tallest trees.] The highest branch is not the safest roost. *Cf.* High cedars fall when low shrubs remain. A great tree has a great fall.

324* **Гроза в лес не гонит.**   *v.* О119
    [Storms do not drive one into the woods.] To escape the thunder and fall into the lightning. *Cf.* It's the thunder that frights, but the lightning that smites. †A good tree is good shelter.

325 **Грозен враг за горами, а грозней за плечами.**   *v.* Л129,144
    Better an open enemy than a false friend.

326 **Грозит мышь кошке, да издалека.**   *v.* М210
    [The mouse threatens the cat, but from afar.] It's a bold mouse that breeds in a cat's year.

327* **Гром не гранит - мужик не перекрестится (дрогнет).**   *v.* Г91, К134, Т52
       When it thunders, the thief becomes honest. Vows made in storms are forgotten in calms. Danger past, God is forgotten.

328   **Гром раскатистый а дождь мелкий.**   *v.* К259, Н227
       When the thunder is very loud, there's very little rain.

329   **Громи своих, так чужие трясутся.**   *v.* Б171
       [Thunder at home and others will tremble.] A dog scourged may bid a lion fear. *Cf.* Example teaches more than precept.

330   **Грош к грошу - оно и капитал.**   *v.* Б70, К167
       Penny and penny laid up will be many.

331   **Гроша не стоит а глядит рублем.**
       [Looks expensive but isn't worth a penny.] *Cf.* None can guess the jewel by the casket. Looks often deceive.

332* **Грязью играть - руки замарать.**   *v.* Д63, И1, К271, О81,84, Ч38
       He that touches pitch shall be defiled. You can't play in dirt without getting dirty. Who deals in dirt has foul fingers. *SPL.* manus illi inquinantur qui ludit luto.

333   **Губы да зубы - два запора.**   *v.* Д209, У67
       [Lips and teeth - a double barrier.] *Cf.* Good that the teeth guard the tongue. It is very well that the teeth are before the tongue.

334   **Гуляй, да дела не забывай (да не загуливайся).**
       [Take a break, but remember to come back.] Too much rest is rust. *Cf.* All work and no play make Jack a dull boy. Men tire themselves in the pursuit of rest.

335   **Гулять смолоду (гулявши много) - помирать (умрешь) под старость с голоду.** *v.* Щ1
       An idle youth, a needy age. *Lat.* senem iuventus pigra mendicum creat.

336* **Гусь да баба - торг, два гуся, две бабы - ярмарка.**   *v.* Д98
       Three women and a goose make a market. *Lat.* tres mulieres faciunt nundinas.

337* **Гусь за море полетел - гусь, а не лебедь и назад прилетел.** *v.* В438, У85, *Ap.* 1.32,61
       If an ass [goose] **goes a-travelling, he'll not come home a horse** [swan].

338* **Гусь свинье не товарищ.**   *v.* З117
       [Geese and swine don't mix.] Oil and water don't mix.

Д

1   **Давал Бог клад, да не умели взять.**
[God gave the treasure, but we didn't know to take it.] *Cf.* God reaches us good things by our own hands.

2   **Давали убогому холст, а он говорит: толст (+ так сказали: поищи потоне).**
(Дали нагому рубашку, а он говорит: толста.)
[They offered the beggar canvas-cloth and he said it was too thick, so they told him to find some thinner.] [They gave the beggar a shirt, and he complained it was too coarse.] *Cf.* A beggar pays a benefit with a louse. Kindness is lost on an ungrateful man.

3*   **Давно - не причина (оправдание).**
[That it happened long ago is no reason (justification).] *Cf.* The crutch of time does more than the club of Hercules. A precedent embalms a principle.

4   **Давно то пропало, что с воза упало.** *v.* Ч100

5   **Давность - немалый (первый) свидетель.** *v.* В471,481,484
[Time is the first witness.] Time tries truth. Time will tell (show). *Cf.* Time reveals all things. *EA.* tempus omnia revelat. *Gr.* χρόνια βέβαιος μαρτυς ἐς ἀλήθειαν.

6   **Давши кабалку, не тяжутся.** *v.* У73
[Having promised, do not reneg.] An honest man's word is as good as his bond. A promise is a promise.

7*   **Давши слово держись, а не давши крепись.** *v.* Н274,422, О10, Я18
[Keep your word when you give it and keep firm when you don't.] Be slow to promise and quick to perform. *SPL.* nescit vox dicta reverti.

8   **Дадим мертвым (пьяным) покой.**
[Let the dead (drunkards) rest.] *Cf.* Speak well of the dead. *Lat.* de mortuis nil nisi bonum.

9   **Дадут, в мешок - а не дадут, в другой.**
[It's in the bag if it's given, and in th'other if it's not.] Be damned if you do and damned if you don't. *Cf.* Refuse with the right hand and take with the left.

10   **Дадут дураку честь, так не знает где и сесть.**
Give a fool enough rope and he'll hang himself. *Cf..* He that has a choice has trouble.

11   **Дадут ломоть, да заставят неделю молоть.** *v.* В549, Д74
[They'll part with a piece provided you grind away for a week.] *Cf.* Bound is he that gifts taketh. *Lat.* beneficium accipere, libertatem vendere. I was taken by the morsel, says the fish.

12   **Дадут хлебца, дадут и дельца.** *v.* Б380, К75, Л39, Р7
[Where there's bread, there's work.] *Cf.* Corn him well and he'll work better. He that shall not work, shall not eat.

13* **Дает стогом а принимает логом.**   *v.* Б192, В31,299, Д71, С164
[He delivers by the stack and receives by the gully.] Some have a short arm for giving and a long arm for getting.

14* **Даешь руками, а получать ногами.**
[You give with the hands but take back with the feet.] Lend sitting and you will run to collect.

15 **Дай Бог в добрый час сказать, а в худой помолчать.**
[God help one speak and hold one's tongue at the right time.] *Cf.* He cannot speak well that cannot hold his tongue.

16 **Дай Бог воевать, чтобы сабли не вынимать.**
One sword keeps another in the sheath.

17 **Дай Бог и кошке свое лукошко.**
[Every cat should have its basket.] *Cf.* To a good cat a good rat.

18 **Дай Бог кому детей родить, тому бы их и возрастить.**   *v.* Н481
[May those who beget children bring them up.] *Cf.* He that has no children brings them up well.

19 **Дай Бог тому честь кто умеет ее несть.**   *v.* Ч53
[May honour accrue to those who can bear it.] Let him who deserves the palm carry it. Don't ride the high horse. *Cf.* Honour shows the man. *Gr.* Arist.*Eth.*5.3: ἀρχὴ ἄνρα δείκνυσι.

20 **Дай боли волю - умрешь раньше смерти.**
[Give in to pain and die before your time.] Take pains or the pains will take you.

21 **Дай вору золотую гору - он и ту промотает.**
[Give a thief a mound of gold and he'll squander it.] Pour gold on him and he'll never thrive.

22 **Дай глупому (дураку) волю, а он и две возьмет.**   *v.* Д25,26,31
[Give a dolt (fool) a choice and he'll take both.] Give him an inch and he'll take a yard.

23* **Дай глупому лошадь, так он на ней и к черту уедет.**
[Give a fool a horse and he'll gallop on it to Hell.] Beggars mounted run their horse to death. Give a beggar a horse and he'll ride it to death. *Lat.* nihil superbius paupere dum surgit in altum.

24 **Дай дураку простор - наплачешься.**   *v.* Г152
[Let a fool have his way and live to regret it.] The fool asks much, but he is more the fool that grants it.

25* **Дай ему палец - он всю руку откусит.**   *v.* Д22,31,33, К333
Give a clown your finger and he will take your hand. *SPL.* accepta licentia quaeritur nova. *Apost.*8.10: εὐήθει μὴ δείξῃς, ἵνα μὴ τὴν παλάμην καταπίῃ.

26* **Дай курице гряду - изроет весь огород.**   *v.* Д22,31,33
[Give a chicken a flower bed and she'll uproot the entire orchard.] Give him an inch and he'll take a yard. *Cf.* Let an ill man lie in your straw and he looks to be your heir.

27 **Дай мне полтину, я твое дело покину.**   *v.* Т78
Scratch my back and I'll scratch yours.

28   **Дай на прокорм казенную корову - прокормлю и свое стадо.**   *v.* Л25, Ч130
      [Subsidize one cow and I'll feed my entire herd.] *Cf.* He is free of fruit that wants an orchard. To be free (liberal) at another man's cost.

29   **Дай оправиться (справиться), и нам будут кланяться.**   *v.* П64, Н443
      [Dress up and gain respect.] Good clothes open all doors.

30   **Дай отсрочку, будет дело в точку.**
      [Allow more time and the job will come out fine.] Delays are dangerous but they make things sure. *Cf.* After a delay comes a let.

31*   **Дай с ноготок, попросит в локоток.**   *v.* Д25,31, К333, М194
      Give a clown your finger and he'll take your hand.

32   **Дай сердцу (черту) волю - приведет в неволю (живьем проглотит).**   *v.* В412
      Too much liberty spoils all. *Cf.* Shakes.*C.E.*II.1.15: Headstrong liberty is lashed with woe.

33*   **Дай черту ухватить за один волос, а он и за всю голову.**   *v.* Д31
      [Give the devil a hair and he'll have the head.] Give him an inch and he'll take an ell.

34   **Дал Бог живот, даст и здоровье.**   *v.* Б260, Д38, К158, Р63
      [God has given life, so too shall he provide health.] *Cf.* To whom God gives the task, he gives the wit.

35*   **Дал Бог много, а хочется больше.**   *v.* Б275, В583, Ж3, Н8
      [God has given much, but man wants more.] None says his garner is full. *Cf.* If God does not give us what we want, he gives us what we need.

36   **Дал Бог немому речи а нагому улицу.**
      [God gave speech to the dumb and the street to the bum.] *Cf.* God help the rich, the poor can beg.

37   **Дал Бог отца что и родного сына не слушается.**   *v.* И126
      [And God made fathers whom their own flesh and blood won't even obey.] Many a good father has a bad son.

38   **Дал Бог роток (зубы), даст и хлеб (кусок). (Даст Бог утро и день, даст и пищу).**
      [If God gave a man a mouth (teeth) (morning and daytime),   *v.* Б252,436, 38, Р63
      so too shall he provide bread (nourishment).] God never sends mouth but he sends meat.

39*   **Дал Бог руки, а веревки сам вей.**   *v.* Б447,475
      [God gave the hands, but weave the rope yourself.] God gives the milk, but not the pail.

40   **Дал топор, дай же и топорище.**   *v.* В295
      [If you give the hatchet, give the helve also.] *Cf.* Throw the helve after the hatchet.
      Lat. manubrium post securim iacere.

41   **Дал целковый, так и стал знакомой.**   *v.* Д184
      [He gave a silver coin and became a friend.] *Cf.* Money recommends a man everywhere. Money makes the man. *Lat.* divitiae virum faciunt.

42   **Далась дураку одна песня на веку.**
      The cuckoo [fool] has but one song. *Cf.* Beware of a man of one book.

43*   **Дале (дальше) в спор, больше слов.**   *v.* Н7
      [More contention, more words.] Wranglers never want words. *Cf.*The farther in the deeper.

44* **Дале счет, ближе дружба.** *v.* К175, С332, Ч10
[The longer the reckoning, the closer the friendship.] Short reckonings (accounts) make long friends.

45 **Дале в море, больше горя.** *v.* Д64, Е11, К265, Х3
[Farther at sea, nearer to woe.] He that would sail without danger, must never come on the main sea. *Cf.* He who travels not by sea, knows not the fear of God. Learn to pray, go to sea.

46 **Далекая вода жажды не утолит.**
Water from afar quencheth not [thirst] **fire.**

47* **Далеко идти - не беги, а близко - торопись.** *v.* Б484,486, С157
[Going far, don't run; going nearby, hurry.] *Cf.* Make haste slowly. He that runs fast will not run long.

48* **Далеко из очей (от глаз), далеко из (и от) сердца.** *v.* B413, Н218, С4, Ч14
Far from eye, far from heart. *Cf.* Out of sight, out of mind. *Lat.* procul ex oculis, procul ex mente.

49 **Далеко куцему до (за) зайца(-ем).**
[A mongrel has a long way to go for the hare.] *i.e. to become a hunting dog.* The hindmost dog may catch the hare. *Cf.* It takes a lean dog for a long race.

50 **Далеко не загадывай, поближе поглядывай.** *v.* Б226, З20, Н259, П98
You go far about seeking the nearest.

51 **Далеко не родня.** *v.* В23, *Ap.*1.83
[Far from home, far from kin.] *Cf.* Far from home, near they harm.

52 **Далеко шел, а добра не нашел.** *v.* Д60,384, Н306
Go farther and fare worse.

53 **Далеко ехали, да скоро приехали.** *v.* B85
The farthest (longest) way about is the nearest way home.

54* **Дали беззубому (на) орехи. (Дали орехов белке когда у нее зубов не стало.)**
[Gave nuts to a man (squirrel) without teeth.] The gods gave nuts to those who have no teeth.

55 **Дали вина так и стал без ума.** *v.* B325, К294
When wine (ale) (drink) is in, wit is out.

56 **Дали дураку власть, чтоб ему с нею не пропасть.**
The higher the fool, the greater the fall.

57 **Дальные колокола - звонкие, приблизишься к ним - глуше станут.** *v.* Б227, В178,
[Distant bells peal loudly but grow faint as you approach.] В186,583, Т10
Distance lends enchantment. Faraway cows have long horns. Far folk fare best.

58 **Дальные гости не наскучат.** *v.* Б391, Д286, Н219
[Guests from afar do not bore.] A traveller may lie with authority.

59 **Дальные проводы - лишние слезы.**
[Longer farewells mean longer tears.] *Cf.* The best of friends must part.

60* **Дальше в лес, больше дров.** *v.* В682, Г131
[The deeper into the forest, the more wood.] The farther in, the deeper. Go farther and fare worse. *Cf.* Distant stovewood is good stovewood. The best fish swim near the bottom. The deeper the well, the colder the water.

61 **Дальше горя меньше слез.** *v.* В470
[Further from grief, fewer tears.] There's no cure for sorrow but to put it underfoot.

62 **Дальше носу не видит.**
See no farther than the end of one's nose.

63 **Дальше от кузницы, меньше копоти.** *v.* Г332, О81
[The farther from the forge, the less soot.] *Cf.* You can't touch pitch without soiling (blackening) the fingers. He who goes into a mill comes out powdered.

64 **Дальше от моря - меньше горя.** *v.* Д45, Ч36
[Farther from the sea, farther from grief.] *Cf.* He that would sail without danger, must never come on the main sea.

65* **Дальше (далее) положишь, ближе возьмешь.**
[The farther you put it, the quicker you'll find it.] *Cf.* In an orderly house all things are always ready.

66 **Дано добро - и нажить и прожить.**
In spending lies the advantage.

67 **Дарами и праведного судью к неправде приведешь.** *v.* Г119, Д75, М85
[Gifts will corrupt even the righteous judge.] *Cf.* Gifts blind the eyes.

68* **Дареному (даровому) коню в зубы не смотрят.**
Don't look a gift horse in the mouth. *Lat.* noli equi dentes inspicere donati.

69 **Даровое лыко лучше купленого ремня.** *v.* Л126

70* **Даровой рубль дешев, нажитый дорог.**
[A ruble earned is dearer than a ruble received as a gift.] The gear that is gifted is never so sweet as the gear that is won.

71 **Даром брать хорошо, а отдавать худо.** *v.* Б192, В31,299, Д13, К117, С164
[It's easier to take freely than to give.] *Cf.* A good borrower makes a bad lender.

72 **Даром и чирей не сядет.** *v.* Б103, И10
[There's a reason for everything, even a boil.] *Cf.* There's reason in all things. There's reason in the roasting of eggs.

73* **Даром никто ничего не выиграет.** *v.* Б18,80, Г61, Д246, З31, К273
Nothing ventured, nothing gained. Nothing in this life is free. *SPL.* necesse est facere sumptum, qui quaerit lucrum.

74* **Даром только воду пьют.** *v.* В549, Д11, З31
[Only water is free to drink.] The wind is fresh and free. *Cf.* Benefits bind. The best things in life are free.

75* **Дары и мудрых ослепляют.** *v.* Г119, Д67, М85
[Even the wise are blinded by gifts.] *Cf.* Gold dust blinds all eyes.

76   **Даст Бог волю, забудешь и неволю.**   *v.* Б452, Г101, Х74
Where there's a will there's a way.

77   **Дать черту меду, уйдет в воду.**   *v.* Т81
[Give the devil some honey and he'll vanish into water.] The devil is good when he is pleased.

78   **Дашь языку волю - голове тесно будет.**   *v.* З47, П284
[A loose tongue makes for a crammed head.] The tongue talks at the head's expense. *Cf.* A still tongue makes a wise head.

79*   **Дают - бери, бьют - беги.**   *v.* Г27, Н280, О165, Т43, Ч61
Be the first at a feast and the last at a fight. *Cf.* Take the goods the gods provide. Beggars can't be choosers. Get it while the getting's good. Better come at the latter end of a feast than the beginning of a fray.

80   **Дающая рука не оскудеет (придается).**   *v.* У87
*Od.Solom.*28.27: **The hand that gives grows not weary.** *Cf.* Give and take.

81   **Два брата хвалились, да оба никуда не годились.**   *v.* К296, Х11
One fool praises another. *Cf.* Man's praise in his own mouth stinks.

82*   **Два в поле воюют, а один горюет.**   *v.* В109,210,Д262, Н19, О76, С310
[Of two on the battlefield, one grieves.] *Cf.* If two ride on a horse, one must sit behind.

83   **Два века не проживешь, две молодости не перейдешь.**   *v.* В86, Д90, Н508
[Neither two lives to live, nor two youths to experience.] Youth comes but once in a lifetime. You're only young once.

84*   **Два вора в одном лесу не живутся. (Два кота в одном мешке не улежатся.) (Два медведя в одной берлоге не уживутся).**   *v.* Д94,108, С106
[Two thieves (cats) (bears) cannot abide in one wood (bag) (den).] Two sparrows on one ear of corn make an ill agreement. *SPL.* duos fures non alit unus faltus.

85*   **Два вора дерутся - честному польза (пусть оба гибнут).**   *v.* К170
When thieves fall out, honest men come to their own [let them all perish].

86   **Два дела разом не можно взять в руки.**   *v.* В91, З1, Ч96
No man can do two things at once. Two bigs will not go in one bag.

87   **Два друга - мороз да вьюга.**
[Busom buddies - frosts and blizzards.] Hail brings frost in the tail.

88   **Два жестких жернова хорошей муки не намелят.**
[Two hard millstones cannot grind fine flour.] Hard with hard makes not the stone wall. *Lat.* durum et durum non faciunt murum.

89   **Два (двое) одному рать.**   *v.* Д102,445
Two to one is odds. *Cf.* Not even Hercules could contend against two. *Lat.* ne Hercules quidem adversus duos.

90*   **Два раза (дважды) молодому не быть (+ смерти не отбыть).**   *v.* Д83
You only live once. *Cf.* He that is once born, once must die.

91*   **Два раза не умирать.**   *v.* Г299, Д107, Р39, С98
A man can die but once.

92 **Два сапога - пара (+ и оба на левую ногу). (Два хлеста, а ни у одного хвоста).**
[Two shoes make a pair (and both for the left foot).] *Cf.* Every couple is not a pair.

93 **Два свояка, а промеж их (пестрая) собака.**   *v.* С49
[Two brothers-in-law with but a (motley) dog between them.] There's no love lost between them. Two of a trade seldom agree.

94* **Два черта не живут в одном болоте.**   *v.* Д84,103, С106
[Two devils cannot live in the same swamp.] Two kings in one kingdom cannot reign at once. *Cf.* One fool in a house is enough.

95* **Дважды дает кто скоро дает.**   *v.* К300
He gives twice who gives quickly. *Lat.* bis dat qui cito dat.

96 **Дважды жена бывает мила - в избу ведут да вон понесут.**   *v.* Ж62
Two good days for a man in this life: when he weds and when he buries his wife.
Gr. Δὺ᾽ἡμέραι γυναικός εἰσιν ἥδιστα, ὅταν γαμῇ τις κἀκφέρῃ τεθνηκοῖαν.

97* **Дважды лето (в год лета) не бывает.**   *v.* Д90, Н232
[Summer does not come twice in one year.] You can't have two forenoons in the same day. Christmas comes but once a year.

98* **Две бабы - базар, три - ярмарка.**   *v.* Г336
[Two women make a market, three - a fair.] Three women make a market.

99* **Две бараньи головы в один котел не лезут.**   *v.* В91, Д86, Л88
[Two lamb's heads will will not go into one pot.] Two bigs will not go into one bag.

100* **Две головни (головенки) курятся, а одна никогда (гаснет).**   *v.* Д250
[Two logs smolder, one alone - never.] *Cf.* It takes two to tango. Two dry sticks will kindle a green one.

101* **Две любви в одном сердце не поместятся.**
[One heart cannot accommodate two loves.] One love expels another.

102 **Две маленькие собаки большую едят.**   *v.* Д89,445
[Two small dogs can take one big one.] Two to one is odds. *Cf.* †Dog does not eat dog. *Lat.* †canis caninam non est.

103 **Две шпаги в одних ножнах не живут.**   *v.* Д94, С106
[Two swords dwell not in one scabbard.] Two suns cannot shine in one sphere. *Cf.* One sword keeps another in its scabbard.

104 **Дворянское кушанье - два грибка на тарелочке.**
[An aristocratic meal: two mushrooms on a plate.] *Cf.* Great birth is a very poor dish at table.

105 **Двум головам на одних плечах тесно.**   *v.* Н242
[Little room for two heads on the same shoulders.] Never carry (have) two heads (faces) in (under) one hood. If two men ride on a horse, one must ride behind. *Cf.* †Two heads are better than one.

106* **Двум господам не служат.**   *v.* И38
No man can serve two masters. One master in a house is enough. *Lat. EA.* multitudo imperatorum Cariam perdidit.

107* **Двум смертям не бывать, а одной не миновать.**   *v.* Г299, Д91, С98
      A man can die but once [and that's inevitable].

108* **Двум собакам одной кости не поделить.**   *v.* Д84
      Two dogs over one bone seldom agree. *Lat.* discordia duorum canum super ossa.

109 **Девичий стыд до порога - как переступила, так и забыла.**
      [A girl's modesty is forgotten as soon as she's over the threshold.] Maidens should be meek till they be married.

110 **Девичьи думы изменчивы.**   *v.* Б5, С105
      [Girls' minds are changeable.] A woman is a weathercock.

111 **Девка красна до замужества.**
      [A girl's beauty lasts until marriage.] A neat maiden often makes a dirty wife. *Cf.* All are good girls, but where do the bad wives come from?

112 **Девка плачет а белка скачет.**   *v.* Ж83, В71,218, О76, С310
      [A girl cries as the squirrel hops.] It is no more pity to see a woman weep than to see a goose go barefoot. *Cf.* A woman's tears are her strongest weapon. Some have thew hap, some stick in the gap.

113 **Девки, винцо да игра не доведут до добра.**
      Play, women and wine undo men laughing. Women and wine, game and deceit, make the wealth small and the wants great.

114* **Деда как сажа бела.**   *sarc.*
      [Things are as bright as pitch.] *i.e. not good; usually said in answer to the question "how are things (you)?"*

115* **Дела не делай, а от дела не бегай.**
      [Don't do the work, but don't shun it either.] Haste not, rest not.

116* **Дела сильнее слов.**   *v.* Д355, Н270, С230
      Actions speak louder than words. Doing is better than saying.

117* **Дела словом не заменишь.**   *v.* Б316,Г185, О12,152
      [A word is no substitute for deeds.] Saying and doing are two things. There's a big difference between word and deed.

118* **Делай добро и тебе будет добро.**   *v.* Д263,283,319, К137,233,289, Х72
      Do well and have well. *Cf.* Good finds good.

119 **Делай другу добро, да себе без вреда (беды).**   *v.* Д425, Ж17, П195,245
      [Help your friend but injure not yourself.] Mind other men, but most yourself. *Cf.* Kind hearts are soonest wronged. You always help yourself by helping others.

120* **Делай так, что бы хвост не знал что затевает голова.**
      [Make sure the tail is ignorant of what the head is up to.] Never let your left hand know what your right hand is doing.

121* **Делай хорошо, плохо само получится.**   *v.* Д265
      [Do your best, the bad will take care of itself.] God send you joy, for sorrow will come fast enough. *Cf.* Do what you ought and come what may. †Provide for the worst, the best will save itself.

122* Делал дышло, а вышло топорище.   *v.* И78, Л1
[He was fashioning a pole and it came out a helve.] He will make a spoon or spoil a horn.

123 Делали наспех, а сделали насмех.   *v.* Г90, П188, С159, Ч102
[Fast work is funny work.] *Cf.* Hasty work, double work. Haste makes waste.

124 Делать в слепую - унести суму пустую.   *v.* З34,85, К187, Н381, Ч70
[Act blind and walk away with an empty purse.] *Cf.* Keep your eyes open, a sale is a sale.

125* Делать из мухи слона.   *v.* Б458, В684, И73
[To make an elephant out of a fly.] *Lat.* elephantum ex musca facere. To make a mountain out of a molehill.

126* Делить шкуру неубитого медведя.   *v.* В260, М48, Н373,460,477, Ц10
To sell the bear's (lion's) **skin before one has caught the bear (lion).** *Cf.* To count one's chickens before they are hatched.

127 Дело в руках - и хлеб в устах.   *v.* Б380, Д12, Л39, Р7
[Job in hand, bread in the mouth.] *Cf.* If you won't work, you shan't eat.

128* Дело в шляпе.
It's in the bag [hat].

129 Дело веди, а безделье гони.
[Keep busy and shun idleness.] Think of ease but work on.

130* Дело дело погоняет.   *v.* Д134,231
[Work thrives on work.] A going foot is aye getting.

131 Дело делаешь, а рук своих не ведаешь.   *v.* Н85
[You work without the mastery of your hands.] A bad workman quarrels with his tools.

132 Дело делу учит.   *v.* Д144, У124
In doing we learn.

133 Дело забывчиво, а тело заплывчиво.
[It's easy to let your work and yourself go.] *Cf.* Business is like a car, it will not run by itself except downhill.

134 Дело как плесень в погребе - своей силой растет.   *v.* Д130
[Work is like mildew in the cellar: self-propagating.] *Cf.* Parkinson's law: work expands to fill the time available.

135* Дело мастера боится.   *v.* Р2
[Work fears a master.] Work fears a resolute man. *Cf.* The work commends the master.

136* Дело (работа) не медведь (волк), в лес не уйдет (убежит).
[Unlike a bear (wolf), work won't run away into the woods.] The best way to get rid of work is to do it.

137* Дело не в личности, а в наличности.   *v.* Д437, И64, Л5
It's not the principle, but the money.

138 Дело не в споре, а в сговоре.   *v.* Х107
[It's not the dispute but the agreement that matters.] A bad peace is better than a good quarrel. *Cf.* An ill agreement is better than a good judgment.

139   **Дело право, только гляди прямо.**
      The shortest answer is doing. *Cf.* Do the business at hand first. Have one's work cut out.

140   **Дело решено и под лавку брошено.** *v.* Б477
      [The case is closed, filed away and buried.] Done and forgotten.

141   **Дело с бездельем не мешай.**
      You can't mix business with pleasure.

142   **Дело сделал, как пить дал.** *v.* В513
      Easy as pie.

143   **Дело середкой крепко.** *v.* Л140, М62
      Measure is treasure.

144   **Дело учит и кормит.** *v.* Д132
      [Work is a teacher and a provider.] Keep your shop and your shop will keep you.
      Cf. Diligence makes an expert workman.

145* **Дело явит делателя.** *v.* В313,602,632, Д294, К336, О7
      The workman is known by his work.

146* **Делом спеши, да людей не смеши.** *v.* Г90, Д47, П188, С157
      [Make haste, not laughter.] Make haste slowly. *Lat.* festina lente. *Cf.* He that does most
      at once, does least. Hasty work, double work. More haste, less speed.

147* **Делу - время, а отдыху (потехе) - час.**
      [There is time for work, but only an hour for rest.] The day is short and the work is
      much. Business before pleasure. *Cf.* Oft times one day is better than sometimes a whole
      year.

148   **Денег много - великий грех, а денег намале - грешнее того.** *v.* Г258, Д190
      [Wealth is a sin, but poverty more so.] Fat sorrow is better than lean sorrow.

149   **Денег много да разума мало.** *v.* Б134,289
      [Much money and little wit.] Want of wit is worse than want of gear. *Cf.* Better wit than
      wealth.

150* **Денег нет - горе, а есть - вдвое.** *v.* Б281, Н279
      [Not having money is bad, but having it is doubly so.] If a man could have all his wishes
      he'd double his trouble. More money, more sin. *Cf.* Those who have money have trouble
      about it.

151   **Денег нет, зато сами золото.** *v.* Д153,293,305, Х75,77
      [No gold save ourselves.] *Cf.* Virtue is a jewel of great price.

152   **Денег нет - так подушка под головой не вертится.** *v.* Б276
      [The poor man's pillow doesn't turn under his head at night.] Small riches hath most
      rest.

153   **Денег ни гроша, да слава хороша.** *v.* В673, Д273, Х75,77
      [Penniless, but of good repute.] A good name is better than riches.

154   **Денежка без ног (деньги), а весь свет обойдет (а уходят).** *v.* Д176
      [Money has no legs yet travels around the world (yet goes away).] Money is round and
      rolls away.

155   **Денежка в мошне, говядина в горшке.**   *v.* В74, Е35
      [A full purse means a full pot of beef.]   Money makes the pot boil.

156   **Денежка дорожку прокладывает (открывает небеса).**
      A golden key opens every door.

157   **Денежки что голуби - где обживутся, там и ведутся. (Деньги - голуби, прилетят
      и опять улетят.)**   *v.* Д194
      [As pigeons flock, so money amasses.] [Money, like pigeons, comes and goes.] Money
      has wings. Riches have wings. *Cf.* He that has a goose, will get a goose. Money makes
      money.

158* **Денежная беда не беда.**   *v.* К182, Т39, Э1
      [A money problem is not a problem.]   *Cf.* Money can't buy happiness, but it will go a
      long way in helping you. Money isn't everything. Those who have money have trouble
      about it.

159   **День в растяжку, ночь в размашку.**   *v.* Н529
      Be the day never so long, at length comes evensong.

160* **День да ночь - и сутки прочь (+ а все к смерти ближе).**   *v.* Б371, Д162, Н529,
      [Day after day, night after night.] *used to denote monotonous days.*   С145, Ч3
      Every day comes night [+ and nearer death].

161   **День денежку берет, заря денежку кует.**
      [Dawn mints money, the day spends it.]   *Cf.* Every day brings its bread with it.

162   **День долог, а век короток.**   *v.* Д160,169, Ж140, Ч4
      [The day is long, but life short.]   *Cf.* Life is short and time is swift. A day to come
      seems longer than a year that is gone.

163   **День к вечеру, а работа к завтрему.**
      [Day tends toward evening, and work toward tomorrow.] If today will not, tomorrow may.

164* **День кормит год.**   *v.* Б70, К168
      [The day feeds the year.]   *i.e. make every day count.* Take care of the pennies and the
      pounds (dollars) will take care of themselves.

165   **День на день не приходится (придет).**   *v.* В88,477, Г193, Н392, Р20
      [No two days are the same.] Every day is not yesterday. Take each day as it comes.

166   **День пируют, а неделю голова с похмелья болит.**   *v.* С88
      [Party one day and suffer a hangover all week.]   Today's joys may be tomorrow's woes.
      Cf. Drunken days have all their tomorrows. Live only for this day and you will ruin
      tomorrow.

167   **День придет и заботу принесет.**
      No day passes without some grief.

168   **День прозевал, урожай потерял.**   *v.* Д373
      [Missed a day and lost a harvest.] He that lies long abed, his estate feels it. *Cf.* A day
      lost is never found.

169   **День прошел, и к смерти ближе.**   *v.* Д160, Ч3
      [The day is over and death is nearer.]   As soon as a man is born, he begins to die. The
      evening brings all home.

170   День сегодняшний - ученик вчерашнего.
Today is the scholar of yesterday. Today is yesterday's pupil.

171*   День хвалится вечером.   *v.* В280
Praise a fair day at night. The evening praises (crowns) the day.

172   Деньга да живот, так и старуха живет.   *v.* Щ2
[Money and health keep the old girl alive.] Health and wealth go far.

173*   Деньга деньгу достает (деньги идут к деньгам).   *v.* Б272, Д183, К164
Money begets (breeds) (draws) (gets) money.

174   Деньга и камень долбит.
[Money can even hollow a stone.] *Cf.* Money will do anything.

175   Деньга лежит, а шкура дрожит.   *v.* Д179
Riches bring care and fears.

176   Деньга покатна живет.   *v.* Д154,206
Money is round, it rolls away.

177   Деньга ум родит.   *v.* Б282
[Wealth engenders wit.] He is wise that is rich. *Cf.* A rich man's joke is always funny. A rich man's foolish sayings pass for wise ones.

178*   Деньгам все повинуется.   *v.* Б268, Г33
All things are obedient to money.

179   Деньги временем хлопоты.   *v.* Б290, К278, М166
Much coin, much care.

180*   Деньги всему голова.   *v.* К27, С119
Money is the only monarch.

181   Деньги всякого прельстят.
Rich mens' spots are covered with money.

182   Деньги много могут.   *v.* К27, М167
Money will do anything. *Lat.* pecunia impetrat omnia.

183   Деньги наживное дело.   *v.* Б272, Д173
[Money will come with time.] *Cf.* Many means to get money.

184   Деньги найдут друга.   *v.* Б269
Rich folk have many friends. *Gr.* εἰ μὲν γὰρ πλουτεῖς, πολλοὶ φίλοι. *Lat.* Quint. ubi amici, ibi opes.

185   Деньги не Бог, а много милуют.
[Money is not God, yet it pardons much.] *Cf.* A rich man can do nothing wrong.

186   Деньги не люди, лишними не будут.   *v.* Б269, Д447
[Unlike people, money is always welcome.] There is no companion like the penny.

187*   Деньги не пахнут.
Money has no smell. *Lat.* pecunia non olet.

188   **Деньги прах, одежа тоже, а любовь всего дороже.**
[Money's dust, so are clothes, but most precious of all is love.] *Cf.* Gold is but muck.

189   **Деньги приходят и уходят как вода. (Деньги что вода - плывут неизвестно куда.)**
[Money, like water, comes and goes.] Ready money will away.   *v.* Д176

190   **Деньги склока, а без денег плохо.**   *v.* Г258, Д148
Fat sorrow is better than lean sorrow.

191   **Деньги смогут много, а правда - все.**
[Money can do much, truth - everything.] *Cf.* Beauty is potent, but money is omnipotent.

192   **Деньги суть жизнью войны.**
Money is the sinews of war. *Lat.* Cic.*Phil.*5.2: pecunia nervus belli.

193   **Деньги - черви, а без них люди - черти.**   *v.* Б465, Ж148, *Ap.*1.64
[Money is hearts, with it people are devils.] Jack would be a gentleman if he had money.

194   **Деньги что галки - в стаю сбиваются.**   *v.* Д157
[Money flocks together like daws.] *Cf.* Riches have wings.

195   **Деньги что пух - только дунь на них, их нет.**
[Money is like down - just blow and it vanishes.] Money evaporates.

196*   **Дерево гнется пока молодое.**   *v.* Л107
[A tree bends when it is green.] Thraw the wand while it is green.

197*   **Дерево не поранешь - соку не достанешь.** *v.* Д410

198*   **Дерево познается по плодам (смотри в плодах), а человек по делам (человека в делах).**   *v.* Д409, С209
*Matt.*12.33: **A tree is known by its fruit** [and a man by his deeds]. *Cf.* Deeds are fruit, words are but leaves. A man of words and not of deeds, is like a garden full of weeds.

199   **Дерево роняют туда куда оно нагнулось.**   *v.* Г13,98
[A tree is cut where it bends.] The thread is cut where the thread is thinnest.

200*   **Дерево с одного разу не валится.**   *v.* 333, С27
An oak [tree] **is not felled by one stroke.** *SPL.* non uno cadit arbor ictu. *Cf.* Little strokes fell great oaks.

201   **Дерево срубишь - ветви сами упадут.**
[Fell the tree and the branches will fall off themselves.] Where the dam leaps over, the kid follows.

202   **Деревья скоро садят, да не скоро с них плоды едят.**
[Trees are quick to plant but slow to bear fruit.] The man who plants pears is a-planting for his heirs. *Cf.* One generation plants the trees, another sits in the shade.

203   **Держи голову в холоде, живот в голоде, а ноги в тепле.**   *v.* Н565
[Keep your head cold, stomach hungry and feet warm.] *Cf.* The head and feet keep warm, and the rest will take no harm. Dry feet, warm head bring safe to bead.

204   **Держи девку в темноте (+ а деньги в тесноте).**
[Keep girls in the dark (and money snug).] *Cf. Gr.* Phocylid. παρθενικὴν καὶ φύλασσε πολυκλείστοις.

205   **Держи карман шире.**
                                                          v. П163, Э2
      [Keep your pocket wide open.] *sarcastic, to dispel false hopes.* Don't hold your breath.

206   **Держи копеечку чтобы не укатилась.**
                                                    v. Д154,176
      [Hold your penny lest it roll away.] *Cf.* Money is round and rolls away. A penny saved
      is a penny earned.

207   **Держи кулак в кармане, а язык на аркане.**
                                                         v. З149
      [Keep your fist in your pocket and your tongue on a leash.] *Cf.* Speak softly and carry
      a big stick.

208*   **Держи уши пошире а рот поуже.**   *v.* З149, К277, М117, У97
      Wide ears and short tongue.

209   **Держи язык за зубами (замком).**   *v.* Г333, У67
      Keep your tongue within your teeth [locked].

210   **Дерзок на язык, да скромен на почине.**
                                                    v. Б329,338, Р42
      [Quick to speak, slow to act.] The greatest talkers are the least doers.

211*   **Десятая вода на киселе.**
      [Tenfold dilution of jelly.] *said of a very distant relative.*

212   **Десять поваров только щи пересаливают.**   *v.* У52, У53
      [Ten cooks only oversalt the soup.] Too many cooks spoil the broth.

213*   **Десятью примерь (десять отмеряй), однажды (одного) отрежь.**   *v.* О60, С103
      Measure twice [ten times], cut once. *Gr. Plan.*7: δέκα μέτρα καὶ ἓν τέμνε.

214   **Детей годовать, век коротать.**   *v.* Б60, Ж35
      [Bringing up children takes years off your life.] Children are certain cares but uncertain
      comforts.

215   **Детей наказывай стыдом а не кнутом.**
      [Chastise a child with shame rather than with a rod.] *Cf.* Train up a child the way he
      should go.

216   **Дети возмужают, батьку испугают.**
      [Children grow, frightening father.] Boys will be boys (men).

217   **Дети любят ласку, а станок смазку.**   *v.* Д313,316,346
      [The child needs to be caressed just as a machine needs to be greased.] *Cf.* Children are
      to be deceived with comfits, old men with oaths.

218   **Детки маленьки - поесть не дадут, детки велики - пожить не дадут.**   *v.* М29, С17
      [Children disturb your meals when they're small and your life when they're older.]
      A little child weighs on your knee, a big one on your heart.

219   **Детки хороши (добрые дети) - отцу матери (дому) венец,**
      худы (злые) - отцу матери (дому) конец.   *v.* Х57
      [Good children are the father and mother's pride (pride of the house); bad children are
      their (its) undoing.] *Cf.* Happy is he who is happy in his children. Undutiful children
      make wretched parents. A foolish son is the calamity of his father.

220   **Дешев хлеб коли деньги есть.**
      [Bread's cheap for those with money to buy it.] *Cf.* He's rich enough who lacks no bread.

221   **Дешева рыба, дешева и уха.**   *v.* Д226, К71, П51, У38, †У115, Ч41
[The cheaper the fish, the cheaper the chowder.] Garbage in, garbage out (GIGO). You don't get more out of a thing than you put into it. You get what you pay for. *Cf.* You can never make a cheap palace.

222   **Дешева рыба на чужом блюде.**   *v.* Л25, Н118, Ч118
[A fish served on another's plate is cheap.] The wholesomest meat is at another's cost.

223*   **Дешево да гнило, дорого да мило.**
[Cheap and trashy, dear and fine.] Cheap things are not good, good things are not cheap.

224*   **Дешевое наводит на дорогое.**   *v.* В588, Г34, Д221
Good cheap is dear. A good bargain is a pick-purse. *Cf.* Ill ware is never cheap. A bargain usually costs you more in the end. Cheap goods always prove expensive.

225   **Дешевой покупкой не радуйся.**   *v.* В588
[Don't rejoice at a bargain.] *Cf.* Many have been ruined by buying good pennyworths. Never buy what you do not want because it is cheap.

226   **Дешевому товару дешева и цена.**   *v.* К71, П51
[Cheap goods, cheap price.] Light cheap, lither (bad) yield.

227   **Дикая собака и на небо лает.**
[A savage dog barks even at the sky.] *Cf.* Dogs bark as they are bred.

228   **Диплом имеет а дела не разумеет.**   *v.* Д112, М114
[He has a degree but understands nothing.] *Cf.* The greatest clerks are not the wisest men.

229*   **Дитя не плачет - мать не разумеет.**   *v.* Г190, М158
[If the child cries not, the mother knows not.] The lame tongue gets nothing.

230   **Дитятко за ручку, а матку за сердечко.**
Praise the child and you make love to the mother. *Cf.* Many kiss the child for the nurse's sake.

231   **Дли дело дольше, так будет хлеба больше.**   *v.* Д130
[More work, more pay.] A going foot is aye getting. *Cf.* A swift eater, a swift worker.

232   **Длинная нитка - ленивая швея.**
A long thread, a lazy tailor. *Gr. Plan.*168: ἀνοήτου ῥάπτου μακρὸν τὸ ῥάμμα.

233   **Длинный язык - короткие мысли.**   *v.* М57, С101
[Long tongue, short thoughts.] A flow of words is not always flow of wisdom. An empty head, like a bell, has a long tongue. *Cf.* A long tongue has a short hand. Short tempers often go with long tongues.

234   **Для бедного просьбы у богатого ухи глухи.**   *v.* С340
[The rich man is deaf to the poor man's entreaties.] He whose belly is full believes not him who is fasting. *Cf.* A poor man's tale cannot be heard.

235   **Для вестей подводы не нанимают.**   *v.* Д330, Х91,110
[One doesn't hire a conveyance for news.] *Cf.* Stay a little and news will find you.

236*   **Для (про) глухого дважды (две) обедни не поют.**   *v.* Г157
[Matins are not repeated for the deaf.] Whistle (sing) psalms to the taffrail (a dead horse).

237   **Для грешника нет праздника.**   *v.* †Б205, Д325, †Л44
[There are no holidays for sinners.] *Cf.* Every day's a holiday for sluggards. 'Tis not a holiday what's not kept holy.

238   **Для двух готовя, трех (не) накормишь.**
[By cooking for two, you can(not) feed three.] Stretch your arm no further than your sleeve will reach. *Cf.* The more you put into a thing, the more you get out.

239   **Для добра трудиться - есть чем похвалиться.**
[One may take pride in furthering a good cause.] *Cf.* Praise is the reflection of virtue.

240   **Для друга - все не туго.**   *v.* Д242, М91, Р15
A good friend never offends.

241*   **Для друга и семь верст не околица. (Для дружбы нет расстояний.)**
(Для друга нет круга.)   *v.* Г52, Е30, К2
[Even seven miles are not too far for a friend.] [Friendship knows no distance.]
[For a friend, the sky's the limit.] **For a good friend, the journey is never too long.**
To a friend's house, the trail is never long.

242*   **Для друга ничего не жаль.**   *v.* Б362, Р15, С59
Anything for a friend. *Cf.* When a friend asks, there is no tomorrow.

243   **Для заборной надписи хороший почерк не нужен.**
[Graffitti doesn't require calligraphy.] *Cf.* A white wall is a fool's paper.

244   **Для ленивой лошади и дуга в тягость.**   *v.* Л46, Х109
A lazy horse thinks its harness heavy. *Cf.* A lazy sheep thinks its wool heavy.

245*   **Для милого не жаль потерять и многого.**   *v.* Д242, Р15, С59
[No loss is too great for a friend.] *Cf.* Friends tie their purse with a cobweb thread.
What a friend gets isn't lost.

246*   **Для многого не жаль потерять малого.**   *v.* Б80, В369, Д73
Nothing ventured, nothing gained. *Cf.* Venture a small fish to catch a great one.
Throw out a sprat to catch a mackerel.

247*   **Для мыши и кошка - лев. (Для муравья и капля - озеро.)**
[To a mouse, the cat is a lion.] [For an ant, a drop is a lake.] A coconut shell full of water is an ocean to an ant. *Cf.* What may the mouse do against the cat.

248   **Для ностоящих друзей и вода сладка.**   *v.* Д448
[For real friends even plain water tastes sweet.] Real friendship does not freeze in winter.
Cf. The essence of friendship is not getting, but sharing.

249   **Для спасения надобно терпения.**
He that will be served must be patient. No remedy but patience.

250*   **Для ссоры нужны двое.**   *v.* В109,584, Д100
It takes two to quarrel.

251*   **Для счастья ума не надо.**   *v.* Д489, С30, Ф4
[Luck requires no intellect.] You don't need brains if you have luck. *Cf.* Fortune favours fools. Lucky men need no council. A pocketful of luck is better than a sackful of wisdom.

252   **Для того чтобы думать, денег не надо.**   *v.* С23
       [Thinking requires no money.] *Cf.* Wisdom is the least burdensome travelling pack.

253   **Для умелой руки все работы легки.**
       Few things are impossible to diligence and skill.

254   **Для учения нет старости.**   *v.* В222, П118
       Never too old to learn. *Lat.* numquam sera est ad bonos mores via.

255   **Для хорошего друга не жаль ни хлеба, ни досуга.**   *v.* Д242,423
       [For a good friend, begrudge neither time nor food.] Friendship is a plant which must be often watered.

256   **Днем жать душно, а ночью кусаются комары.**   *v.* К252, Л43
       [It's too hot to mow by day and there are too many mosquitos at night.] *Cf.* Idle folks lack no excuses.

257*   **Днем фонарь не нужен.**
       [One doesn't need a lamp by day.] *Cf.* The morning daylight appears planer when you put out your candle. Burn one candle to find another.

258   **Дни проводят в молитве, а ночи в кабаках.**   *v.* Г189, И70, П146
       [They pray by day and carouse by night.] *Cf.* Not all are saints that go to church.

259*   **До двух раз прощают, а в третий бьют.**
       [Twice pardoned, but the third time struck.] Three strikes and you're out. *Cf.* The first faults are theirs that commit them, the second theirs that permit them. Don't make the same mistake twice. Better a mistake avoided than two corrected.

260   **До лысине (старости) дожил, а ума не нажил.**
   (Дожил до седых волос, а до ума все не дорос.)   *v.* Д486, П100
       [Grew bald (old) (grey) but not smart.] *Cf.* Age makes a man whiter but not better. He that's born a fool is never cured.

261   **До поры, до времени не сеют семени.**
       [Do not sow seeds before the season.] There is a time and a place for everything. Everything is good in its season.

262   **До расправы похваляются двое, а после - один.**   *v.* Д82, Н477
       [Of two who boast before a trial, only one boasts after.] *Cf.* Never triumph before victory.

263*   **Добра желаешь, добро и делай.**   *v.* Д118, К137,233, Х72
       Do well and have well.

264   **Добра куча не наскучит.**   *v.* М112, Х51
       You can never have too much of a good thing. What's good was never yet plentiful. *Cf.* †One can have too much of a good thing. †Abundance of things engenders disdainfulness.

265   **Добра ищи, а худо само придет.**   *v.* Д121
       God send you joy, for sorrow will come fast enough. Good is to be sought and evil attended.

266*   **Добра на худо не меняют.**   *v.* Л166, О125, П203
       [Good is not exchanged for bad.] *Cf.* Do not change horses midstream. Leave well enough alone.

267   Добра что клада ищут, а худо под рукой.   *v.* M118
       [Good is sought like a treasure, but evil is everywhere.] Virtue and vice divide the world, but vice has got the greater share.

268   Добрая весть, коли говорят - пора есть.
       [Good tidings are always on time.] **Good news may be told at any time.** *Cf.* Good counsel never comes too late.

269   Добрая жена - веселье, а худая - зелье.   *v.* Ж47
       A man's best fortune or his worst is a wife.

270   Добрая жена да жирные щи - другого добра не ищи.   *v.* H105
       [A good wife and a thick cabbage soup - don't ask for more.] A good wife and health are a man's best wealth. *Cf.* He that has a good wife has an angel by his side; he that has a bad one has a devil at his elbow.

271   Добрая жена дом сбережет, а плохая рукавом разнесет.   *v.* Ж91, X33
       [A good wife preserves the house, a bad one throws it out the window.] *Cf.* The wife is the key of the house. The wife can throw out with a spoon more than the husband can bring in with a shovel.

272   Добрая наседка одним глазом зерно видит, а другим коршуна.   *v.* B307
       [The good hen espies the grain with one eye and the kite with the other.] *Cf.* What we see depends mainly on what we look for.

273*   Добрая слава дороже богатства (золотого ожерелья) (лучше мягкого пирога).
       A good name is better than riches.   *v.* B673, Д153,305, Л113, X75,77
       Lat. melius est nomen bonum quae divitiae multae.

274   Добрая слава лежит (за печкой спит), а худая бежит (по свету бежит).   *v.* Л104
       A good reputation stands still, a bad one runs.

275*   Добрая совесть любит обличение.   *v.* Д302, П215,223
       [A clear conscience enjoys exposure.] Truth's best ornament is nakedness. *Cf.* Craft must have clothes, but truth loves to go naked. Virtue when concealed hath no value. *Lat.* vile latem virtus.

276   Добрая совесть не боится клевет(ы) (лжи).   *v.* B335, K241
       A clear conscience fears not false accusations. *SPL.* conscia mens recti fama mendacia ridet.

277*   Добро делать - доброму не вредит.   *v.* Д352, K243
       [Doing well means not injuring the good.] *Cf.* Who does no good does evil enough. If you help the evil, you hurt the good.

278   Добро наживай, а худо избывай.   *v.* Д265
       Good is to be sought out and evil attended. *Cf.* Cease to do evil, learn to do good.

279   Добро не умрет, а зло пропадет.   *v.* Д300,332, C195, X53
       [Good does not die, but evil shall perish.] *Cf.* A good deed never dies (is never lost).

280*   Добро помни а зло забывай.   *v.* †Л79
       [Remember the good and forget the bad.] *Cf.* Do not forget little kindnesses and do not remember small faults. †Good deeds are easily forgotten, bad deeds never.

281   Добро поощряй, а зло порицай.
       [Encourage the good and censure the bad.] Praise is a spur to the good, a thorn to the evil. *Cf.* Correction does much, but encouragement everything.

282 Добро серебро, а золото лучше.
[Silver is good, but gold is better.] Good is good, but better carries it (is better).

283 Добро творить - себя веселить.   *v.* X72
Do good: you do it for yourself.

284 Добро тогда будет добро, когда люди похвалят.   *v.* 314
[Good becomes good with praise.] *Cf.* Praise is the reflection of virtue. Good deeds bear blessings for fruit.

285 Добро того бить кто плачет.   *v.* X66
[It is good to beat those who cry.] *Cf.* Well beaten cries as much as badly beaten. †It is good to beat proud folks for they'll not complain.

286* Добро тому врать кто за морем бывал.   *v.* Д58, Л104
A traveller may lie with authority.

287 Добро худо переможет.   *v.* C206
Virtue will triumph. A good heart conquers ill fortune.

288 Доброго коня и под старой попоной узнают.
[A good horse is discerned even from under an old horse-cloth.] There's many a good cock come out of a tattered bag. *Cf.* Truth has a good face but bad clothes.

289 Доброго не бегай (бойся), а худого не делай (твори).
[Run not from the good, nor practise the bad.] *Cf.* Never tire of well-doing.

290 Доброго не надолго, сладкого не досыта.   *v.* B268
[Happiness is brief, sweetness insufficient.] The mirth of the world dureth but a while.

291* Доброго пастыря дело овец стричь, а кожи не снимать.
It is the part of a good shepherd is to shear the flock, not flay it. *Gr.* Suid.2.2.1116: κείρεσθαί μου τὰ πρόβατα, ἀλλ'οὐκ ἀποξύρεσθαι βούλομαι. *SPL.* Suet.*Tib.*32.2: boni pastoris est tondere pecus, non deglubere.

292 Доброго человека в красный угол сажают.   *v.* 314, Ч53
[A good man is held in high esteem.] Honour is the reward of virtue. Praise is the reflection of virtue.

293 Добродетель всего дороже (доброму не вредит).   *v.* Д151
[Virtue is priceless.] Virtue is a jewel of great price. *SPL.* virtus omnibus rebus anteit.

294 Добродетель не в словах, а в честных делах.   *v.* Б316, B561,632, Д145, C127
[Virtue lies not in words but in good deeds.] *Cf.* 'Tis action makes the hero.

295 Добродетель не нуждается в награде.
Virtue is its own reward.

296 Добродетель преодолевает силу.   *v.* B249
[Virtue overcomes force.] *Cf.* Kindness is the noblest weapon to conquer with.

297 Добродетельного монарха весь свет любит.
[The world loves a righteous monarch.] *Cf.* He that sows virtue, reaps fame. Virtue is the best title of nobility.

298 Доброе братство - дороже (лучше) богатства.   *v.* Д413, Л130
A true friend is the best possession.

299* Доброе вино не нуждается в этикетке.   *v.* Д301, X59
Good wine needs no bush.

300* Доброе дело без награды не остается.   *v.* Д279, X53
A good deed is never lost. A good deed comes back a thousand fold.

301 Доброе дело само себя хвалит.   *v.* Г317, Д299,301, P57, X59
The good deed will praise itself.

302 Доброе дело скрытности не любит.   *v.* Д275
[Virtue brooks no concealment.] *Cf.* The truth will out. The truth shows best being naked.

303 Доброе злом погубают, а зло добром приучают.   *v.* Д335
[Evil destroys the good, but good rubs off on the evil.] *Cf.* Show a good man his error and he turns it to a virtue, but an ill - it doubles his fault. For ill, do well - then fear no hell.

304 Доброе и во сне хорошо.
[Virtue is good even in a dream.] *Cf.* Virtue is the beauty of the mind. Dreams are wishes your heart makes.

305* Доброе имя дороже богатой одежды.   *v.* B673, Д153,273, Л113, X75,77
[Better a good name than rich clothes.] Better a good name than riches. Better go to heaven in rags than to hell in embroidery. *Cf.* Good fame is better than a good face.

306 Доброе молчание лучше пустого болтания (худого ворчания).   *v.* Л141, M157, H436,
[A good silence is better than empty chatter (ill grumbling).]   У101
Better say nothing than not to the purpose. *Cf.* Wise men silent, fools talk.

307 Доброе молчание чему не ответ.   *v.* M156, П282, У101
[Good silence is an answer to anything.] *Cf.* No wisdom to silence. Silence means consent.

308* Доброе начало - половина дела (полдела откачало).   *v.* B642, З106, Л75, П199
Well begun - half done. *Gr.* Plat.*Leg.*6: ἀρχὴ γὰρ ἥμισυ παντός. *Lat.*
Hor.*Ep.*1.2.40: dimidium facti, qui caepit, habet.

309 Доброе семя - добрый и всход.   *v.* H156, П73
He that sows good seed, shall reap good corn.

310 Доброе сердце лучше хорошего кафтана.   *v.* C51,210
[A good heart is better than a good coat.] Goodness is better than beauty.

311 Доброе скоро забывается, а худое долго в памяти сохраняется (помнится).
Good deeds are easily forgotten, bad deeds never.   *v.* Л79, H102, P16
Cf. The evil that men do lives after them, the good is oft interred with their bones. Bad deeds follow you, the good ones flee. A bad deed never dies. †Write injuries in dust, but kindness in marble.

312 Доброе слово железные ворота отопрет.   *v.* Л7,8
[A kind word will open iron gates.] There is a great force hidden in a sweet command. *Cf.* An iron anvil should have a hammer of feathers.

313 Доброе слово лучше мягкого пирога. *v.* Л7

314* Доброе (ласковое) слово и кошке приятно. (Доброе слово не пропадет даром.)
A kindness is never lost. Kind words go a long way. Good words   *v.* Д217, Л7,8
cost nought. Lip-service costs little yet may bring in much.   †Sympathy killed a cat.

315 Доброе слово обращает лицо, а злое отвращает сердце.   *v.* В249, Д354, Л147, М49
[A kind word turns the head, a bad one repels the heart.] *Cf.* Kindness is the noblest
weapon to conquer with. Kindness begets tenderness.

316 Доброе слово человеку - что дождь в засуху.   *v.* Д217,346
[Fair words for a man are like rainfall during drought.] *Cf.*Kindness can't be bought for gear.

317 Доброе смолчится, худое молвится.   *v.* Х55,91,110
[The good is kept quiet while the bad is talked about.] *Cf.* No news is good news. Ill
news comes apace.

318 Доброй жене домоседство не мука (+ а мучит жену лишь разлука).   *v.* Б7, Ж91, Х33
[A good wife is happy at home (+ and unhappy at parting).] A woman's place is in the
home. *Cf.* The foot on the cradle and the hand on the distaff is the sign of a good
housewife. Home-keeping folks are happiest. Where there's no wife, there is no home.

319* Доброму везде (все) добро.   *v.* В610, Д118, К289, Х72
[A good man does well everywhere.] *SPL.* vitae integritas ubique praevalet. *Cf.* Do well
and have well.

320 Доброму вору все (всякий сапог) впору.   *v.* Т37
[Everything helps a good thief.] *Cf.* Opportunity makes the thief.

321* Доброму добрая и память.   *v.* П55
He that sows virtue, reaps fame.

322 Доброму ночь не в убыток.   *v.* П237
[A good man suffers not at night.] *Cf.* A good conscience is a soft pillow.

323 Доброму одно слово пуще дубины.   *v.* М173, О39, Р32, У98
A word to the wise is sufficient.

324 Доброму сухарь на пользу, а злому и мясное не в прок.   *v.* Л124
[A good man enjoys his cracker more than a bad man his steak.] Dry bread with love is better
than fried chicken with fear and trembling. *Cf.* Lean liberty is better than fat slavery.

325 Доброму человеку всякий день праздник.   *v.* Д237
A good conscience is a continual feast.

326 Доброму человеку и чужая болезнь к сердцу.
[A kind man grieves even for another's illness.] *Cf.* Pity is akin to love.

327 Доброта без разума пуста.
[Kindness without reason is futile.] *Cf.* A man without reason is a beast in season.

328* Доброю женою и муж честен. *v.* Ж80

329 Добрую жену взять - ни скуки, ни горя не знать.
[Marry a kind wife and forget boredom and sorrow.] A cheerful wife is the joy of life.

330* Добрые вести не лежат на месте.   *v.* Д235, Х91,110
[Good news does not stay put.] News spreads like wildfire. *Cf.* †Bad news travels fast.

331 Добрые жернова все мелют.
[Good millers will grind anything.] The miller grinds more men's corn than one.
Cf. Like the miller, he can set to every wind.

332 Добрые умирают, да дела их живут.   *v.* Д279, Ж142, С195, Х53
[Good men die, but their deeds live on.] Good men must die, but death can't kill them quite.

333 Добрые чувства - соседи любви.
[Kindness is love's neighbour.] *Cf.* Kindness consists in loving people more than they deserve. Pity is akin to love.

334 Добрый вор без молитвы не украдет.   *v.* Г91
[The devout thief won't steal without a prayer.] When a thief breaks into a house he calls on God to help him. *Cf.* Danger makes men devout.

335 Добрый добру научивает, а злой на зло наставляет.   *v.* В442, Д303
[The good man teaches virtue, the ill incites to evil.] *Cf. Gr.* Theognid.*Gnom.* ἐσθλᾶν μὲν γὰρ ἄπ'ἐσθλὰ μαθήσεαι. Example is better than precept.

336* Добрый друг лучше ста родственников.   *v.* Б63,224, Д450, К234
[Better one good friend than a hundred relations.] A good friend is my nearest relation.

337 Добрый именинник до трех дней.   *v.* В102, Г305
[A namesday's charm lasts three days.] *Cf.* Fish and guests smell in three days.

338* Добрый конец - всему делу венец.   *v.* В245, К163
The end crowns the work. *Lat.* finis coronat opus. *SPL.* omnia tunc bona sunt, clausula quando bona est. *Cf.* Greg.Nas. ἀρχῆς καλῆς κάλλιστον εἶναι καὶ τέλος. All's well that ends well.

339 Добрый корень скалу дробит.   *v.* В363, Д513, К98, М11, Т25
[A good root shatters stone.] *Cf.* Constant dripping wears away the stone.

340* Добрый пес лучше злого человека.
[Better a kind dog than a mean man.] A grateful dog is better than an ungrateful man. *Cf.* The best thing about man is the dog.

341 Добрый пес на ветер не лает.
[A good dog barks not at the wind.] *Cf.* Dogs bark as they are bred.

342 Добрый плачет от радости, а злой от зависти.   *v.* 360
[The good man cries from joy, the bad man from envy.] *Cf.* The envious man waxes lean with the fatness of his neighbour.

343* Добрый повар стоит доктора.
[A good cook is as good as a physician.] Kitchen physic is the best physic. Better pay the butcher than the doctor.

344 Добрый политик, худой христианин.
[A good politician is a bad Christian.] In politics a man must learn to rise above principle. *Cf.* In politics there is no honour.

345 Добрый портной с запасом шьет.   *v.* А28
[The good tailor sews with thread to spare.] A tailor must cut three sleeves to every woman's gown.

346   **Добрый привет и кошке приятен.**   *v.* В593,Д217,316, М215, П135, У99
[Even a cat enjoys a warm greeting.] A kind word never hurt anyone.

347   **Добрый разум наживают не разом.**   *v.* К239
[Good sense is not acquired all at once.] A man's studies pass into his character.

348*   **Добрый совет ко времени хорош.**   *v.* Д394,395
[Good advice is good if timely.] Slow help is no help. *Cf.* †Good counsel never comes too late (amiss).

349   **Добрый союз тверже каменных стен.**   *v.* Н325
[A good union is stronger than stone walls.] Men, not walls, make a city safe. *Cf.* Union is strength.

350   **Добрый человек в добре проживет век.**   *v.* К314
He lives long that lives well.

351   **Добрым словом и бездомный богат.**   *v.* Л7
[A kind word consoles even the homeless.] A soft word is often worth more than a house and a lot. Good words cost nought.

352*   **Добрым тот вредит, кто злым попущает.**   *v.* Д277, К243
He that helps evil hurts the good.

353*   **Добрыми намерениями дорога в ад устлана.**   *v.* А11
The road to Hell is paved with good intentions.

354   **Добрых людей чрез добро получают.**   *v.* В249, Д315
[People are made kind by kindness.] Kindness always begets kindness. *Cf.* Honey catches more flies than vinegar.

355   **Добывай горбом, а не горлом.**   *v.* Д116,402, С230
[Use your back rather than your throat.] *Cf.* Actions speak louder than words. Elbow grease gives the best polish.

356   **Добыча ловца не ждет (а ловец ее поджидает).**   *v.* С235
[The prey waits not for the hunter (but vice-versa).] The good huntsman must follow the hounds and not give up the chase.

357   **Добычу вора забрал разбойник.**   *v.* В420,424
[A bandit stole the thief's plunder.] One thief robs another.

358   **Доверяй, да знай кому!**   *v.* Д508
First try and then trust. *Lat.* fide, sed cui, vide.

359   **Доверить стадо волку - не видать толку.**   *v.* Б385, В296,395, Г16, Н211,389, П303
To set the wolf to keep the sheep [makes no sense]. *Lat.* Ter.*Eun.*5.1.16: ovem lupo commisisti.

360*   **Довольство - лучшее богатство.**   *v.* В263,267, Н104,194
Content is all. Content is more than a kingdom. *Lat.* contentum suis rebus esse maximae sunt divitiae.

361   **Догадался когда проигрался.**   *v.* Д484
After wit comes ever late. *Cf.* When a fool has bethought himself, the market's over.

362* **Догадка лучше (не хуже) ума (разума).**   *v.* B536, Л145, У86
[Intuition is better than erudition (reason).] A handful of common sense is worth a bushel of learning.

363* **Договор лучше денег.**   *v.* З21, Т82
[An agreement is better than money.] Agree, for the law is costly.

364 **Дождешься как от вербы яблок.**   *v.* Б168, Н399, О150, Я3
[You'll have to wait long for apples from a willow tree.] Seek pears of an elm tree.

365* **Дождь падает на злых и добрых.**   *v.* B640, И56, С234
Rain falls alike on the just and unjust. *Cf.* The sun shines upon all alike.

366* **Доказчику (доносчику) первый кнут.**   *v.* И121, Н287
[The informer gets the first lash.] *Cf.* The informer is the worse rogue of the two.

367 **Долг есть тягостное бремя, отнимает сон и время.**   *v.* B35,290, К286
[A debt is an oppressive burden that robs one of sleep and time.] Debt is a heavy burden to an honest mind. *SPL.* aeris alieni comes miseriae est. *Cf. Prov.*22.7: The borrower is servant to the lender. *Lat.* P.Syr. alienum aes homini ingenuo acerba est servitus.

368* **Долг платежом красен. (Долг долга платит.)**   *v.* B381, Д367,369, З12, Л19, Т78,79,80,
One good (ill) turn deserves another. One hand washes the other.   У108, Ч108

369 **Долги помнет не тот кто берет, а кто дает.**   *v.* С257, У23
Creditors have better memories than debtors. *Lat.* apud creditorem maior quam apud debitorem debiti memoria.

370 **Долго выбирать - замужем не бывать.** *v.* М111

371 **Долго ли, скоро ли, а все будет конец.**   *v.* Б471, Н553, К33, Т19
[Sooner or later, all will end.] Time is, time was, and time is past.

372* **Долго рассуждай да скоро делай.**   *v.* Д458,459, Н334
[Deliberate at length but act swiftly.] Think twice before you act. Score twice before you cut once.

373 **Долго спать - с долгом встать (долгу наспать) (добра не видать).**   *v.* Д168
[Sleep too much and rise in debt (and see no good).] He that lies long abed, his estate feels it. *Cf.* He who sleeps all morning, may go begging all the day after. Sleeping cats catch no mice.

374* **Долго терпеть не беда, лишь было бы чего ждать.**
[A long wait is worth it if there is something to wait for.] *Cf.* If it were not for hope, he heart would break. Bear with evil and expect good. Wait and you will be rewarded.

375 **Долготерпение приносит благословение.**   *v.* B641, П232, Т23
[Patience brings blessings.] Patience is a remedy for every grief (sorrow). Patience is the key of paradise.

376 **Долог летний день, да коротка неделя.**   *v.* B221, Г195
[A summer day is long, but the week is short.] *Cf.* The sun has stood still, but time never did. Some people stay longer in an hour than others in a week.

377 **Дом высок да под ним песок.**
[The house is tall but built on sand.] *Cf. Matt.*7.26: a foolish man which built his house on sand. A house built on sand will surely fall.

378 **Дом для фасада строится.** *v.* П54
[A house is built for a facade.] *Cf.* The house shows the owner. †One should live to build, not to boast.

379 **Дом красится хозяином.** *v.* Б147,В615, Н289, П128
[The master crowns the house.] *Cf.* The master absent and the house is dead.

380 **Дом купи крытый, кафтан шитый, а жену непочатую.**
[Buy a completed house, a sewn suit and a wife untouched.] *Cf.* In choosing a wife and buying a sword, we ought not to trust another.

381 **Дом не велик, да лежать не велит.**
[It's not a large house, yet it won't allow any rest.] *Cf.* A woman's work is never done.

382 **Дом с детьми - базар, без детей - могила.** *v.* Б60
[A house with children is like a bazaar], **a house without children is a cemetery.** *Cf.* The proof of the house is the nursery.

383 **Дом яма - стой прямо.**
[A house is a pit - stand firm.] Building is a sweet impoverishment.

384 **Дома все споро, а вчуже житье хуже.** *v.* Д52, Н306
He that would be well needs not go from his own house.

385 **Дома жить, чина не нажить.**
[Live for the home and forget your promotion.] *Cf.* A career never takes the place of a home where love reigns.

386 **Дома и солома сьедома.** *v.* В139, Н116, С61, Ч128
[Even straw is edible at home.] *Cf.* Dry bread at home is better than roast meat abroad.

387* **Дома и стены помогают.** *v.* В135, Х31
[Even the walls help at home.] At home everything is easy.

388* **Дома как хочешь, а в дюдях как велят.** *v.* Н409, Ч24, У50

389 **Дома петух, на улице - курица.** *v.* В562,607, И43
[A cock at home but a chicken in the street.] *Cf.* A cock is bold on his own dunghill. Every dog is a lion at home.

390 **Дома чертком, зато в люди цветком. (Дома щи без круп, а влюдях шапка в рубль.)**
A saint abroad, a devil at home. [Plain soup at home, *v.* В64,65, *Ap.* 1.4
a fine hat in public.] *Cf.* It is not the gay coat that makes the gentleman.

391 **Домашнего вора не поймаешь (убережешься).** *v.* Н528, О130
[You cannot catch the thief at home.] Nothing worse than a familiar enemy.
*Gr. Plan.*67: ἔσω κλέπτην καὶ ἔσω πόρνον ὅπόσα βούλει ἐνέδρευε.

392 **Домашние мысли в дорогу не годятся.**
[Homespun thoughts don't travel.] Domestic fruit will not grow on a wild tree.

393* **Домашний теленок лучше заморской коровы.** *v.* Б231, Ж169, Л152, С122
[Better domestic veal than imported beef.] *Cf.* Better a mouse in the pot than no flesh at all. Better a small fish than an empty dish. Better some of a pudding than none of a pie.

394* **Дорога ложка к обеду.**   *v.* Д348, *Ар.*1.104
    [A spoon in time for dinner is nice.] Slow help is no help.

395* **Дорого яичко к великому (светлому) дню.**   *v.* Д348, 394, *Ар.*1.101
    [An egg is best in time for Easter.] *i.e. things are best on time.* *Cf.* He doubles his gift who gives on time. The umbrella goes up when the rain comes down.

396 **Дорогой идешь и то споткнешься.**   *v.* Б116, И35,37, К165
    [Walk the road and you may still fall.] *Cf.* The wisest man may fall. Even a monkey may fall from a tree sometime.

397 **Дорожка вместе, табачок пополам.**   *v.* Ч73
    [Who shares a journey, shares the tobacco.] Share and share alike.

398 **Дорожному Бог простит.**
    [God forgives the traveller.] Travellers and poets have leave to lie.

399 **Дорожный ночлега с собою не возит.**
    [The traveller cannot take his lodging with him.] *Cf.* Much spends the traveller more than the abider.

400 **Достав потерять - лучше не иметь.**   *v.* К268
    ['Tis better not to have had than to have had and lost.] You can't lose what you never had.

401 **Достаток - мать, убожество - мачеха.**   *v.* Б288
    [Wealth is like a mother, poverty - a stepmother.] *Cf.* Poverty and wealth are twin sisters.

402 **Достают хлеб горбом, достают и горлом.**   *v.* Д355, П276, Ч22
    [Bread is gotten with one's back or with one's throat.] *Cf.* He that cannot ask, cannot live.

403* **Доход не живет (бывает) без хлопот.**   *v.* Б93, Т63
    No toil, no treasure.

404 **Дочки оставят мать без сорочки.**
    [Daughters will leave their mothers penniless.] Two daughters and a back door are three arrant thieves.

405 **Дочку в колыбельку - приданое в коробейку.**
    [A daughter in the cradle means a dowry in the basket (*i.e.* piggy).] *Cf.* Building and marrying of children are great wasters.

406* **Дочь чужое сокровище.**
    [A daughter is another's prize.] A diamond daughter turns to glass as a wife.

407* **Дракою прав не будешь.** *v.* П208

408 **Драчливый петух голенаст живет (жирен не бывает).**   *v.* Г253
    [A contentious cock lives sprightly (lean).] Brabbling curs never want sore ears. Quarreling dogs come halting home.

409 **Древо и учитель познаются по плоду.**   *v.* Д198, С209
    [A tree and a teacher are known by their fruit.] *Matt.*12.33: **A tree is known by its fruit.**

410 **Древа не поранишь, соку не достанешь.**   *v.* Б106, В369, И71, Л54, Н396
    [No sap without injury to trees.] You can't make an omelette without breaking eggs.

411* Дрова хоть и кривы, да прямо горят.   *v.* Б404, Г126, И23, К204, С287, У75
Crooked logs make straight fires.

412* Друг в нужде - истинный друг.   *v.* Б48, Д419,420
A friend in need is a friend indeed.

413* Друг всего (денег) дороже.   *v.* В251, Д298, Л130
A true friend is the best possession. A faithful friend is better than gold. *SPL.* nihil homini est amico opportuno amicius. ubi amici ibidem opus. *Cf. Gr.* Stob.120: οὐ τὰ χρήματα φίλοι ’αλλ’οἱ φίλοι χρήματα εἴσιν.

414 Друг до поры - тот же недруг.   *v.* Д248,436,448
[A friend up to a point is no friend at all.] Real friendship does not freeze in winter. *Cf.* A friend as far as the altar.

415* Друг лучше старый, а платье новое.   *v.* В283, Л160
[Better an old friend and a new dress.] New things are the best things, but old friends are best friends.

416 Друг льстив корысти желает.   *v.* Н135
[The flattering friend seeks his own advantage.] All are not friends that speak us fair. *SPL.* fortunae amicus est non hominibus. *Cf.* Dogs wag their tails not so much in love to you as to your bread.

417 Друг научит, недруг проучит.   *v.* Д421
[The friend instructs, the foe teaches a lesson.] *Cf.* From the enemy you learn a lot.

418 Друг не испытанный - что орех не расколотый (не надежен).   *v.* Н312,506
[An untried friend is like an unopened nut (unreliable).] *Cf.* Try your friend before you trust. Prove your friend ere you have need.

419* Друг познается (познавается) в несчастье (при рати) (при беде).   *v.* Д412
A friend is best found in adversity. A friend in need is a friend indeed. *Lat.* Amicus certus in re incerta cernitur.

420 Друга в верности без беды не узнаешь.   *v.* Б48
A friend is never known until a man have need.

421 Друга выручи, а он тебя выучит.   *v.* Д417
[Come to a friend's rescue and he'll teach you.] *Cf.* Save a stranger from the sea and he'll turn your enemy.

422 Друга держать не убыточно.   *v.* Н282, Х70
[There's no disadvantage to keeping a friend.] A friend in the market is better than money in the chest (purse).

423 Друга иметь (любить) - себя не жалеть (щадить).   *v.* Д242,255
[To keep a friend is not to spare oneself.] When a friend asks, there is no tomorrow. *Cf.* Friendship is a plant which must often be watered.

424 Друга люби (любить) - себя не губи (губить). (Друг за дружку не хоронись.)
[Do not bury (destroy) yourself for a friend.]   *v.* Д119, Ж17, П195,245
Mind other men, but most yourself.

425*   Друга на деньги не купишь.
        Bought friends are not friends indeed. *Cf.* A friend whom you can buy can be bought
        from you.

426*   Друга не теряй - взаймы не давай.   *v.* B32, *Ap.*1.25
        Lend your money and lose your friend.

427   Друга прилежно ищи, а нашед, береги.
        Be slow in choosing a friend, but slower in changing him. *Cf.* Select your friend with
        a silk-gloved hand and hold him with an iron gauntlet. *Gr.* D.Laert. φίλους μὴ ταχὺ
        κτῶ, οὓς δὲ ἂν κτήσῃ, μὴ ἀποδοκίμαζε.

428   Друга разжалобить - самому заплакать. Другу угодить - себе досадить.
        [Injure a friend and cry yourself.] *Cf.* Make not thy friend thy foe. An injured friend is
        the bitterest of foes. Contend not with a friend lest you make him an enemy.

429*   Другие времена, другие нравы.   *v.* H391
        Other times, other manners.

430   Другие помыслы мудрейшие первых.
        Second thoughts are best. *Gr.* δεύτεραι φρωντίδες σοφώτεραι.

431   Другими дивились, а сами на льду обломились.   *v.* H107,413,414, T13, Ч47,117
        [Laughed at others and slipped on the ice ourselves.] He finds fault with others and does
        worse himself. To laugh at someone is to be laughed back at.

432*   Других не суди, на себя погляди.   *v.* H172
        [Look to yourself before judging others.] We tax our friends with faults but see not our own.

433   Другой головы не приставишь (наставишь).   *v.* Д90
        [You cannot replace your head.]It's not what you have but how you use it. You only live
        once. Life is swell when you keep well.

434   Другу делай добро, как себе равно (что бы тебе убытку не было) (а недруга в добро
        приводи).   *v.* K74, Ч11
        [Treat your friend as you would yourself (without prejudice to yourself) (and teach your
        enemy by good example).] *Cf. Luke* 6.31: Do as you would be done by.

435*   Дружат, как кошка с собакой.   *v.* Ж104
        To agree like cats and dogs.

436*   Дружба до порога.   *v.* Д414,448
        [Friendship as far as the threshold.] *Cf.* A friend as far as the altar. *Lat.* usque ad aras
        amicus. A friend as far as conscience (religion) permits.

437*   Дружба дружбой, а табачок врозь (а служба службой).   *v.* Д137, И64, Л5, X25,*Ap.*1.25
        [Friendship is one thing and tobacco (business) another.] Brotherly love for brotherly
        love, but cheese for money. Duty before pleasure. Don't mix business with pleasure. *Cf.*
        Play while you play and work while you work. A woman's a woman, but a good cigar's
        a smoke.

438*   Дружба как стекло, разобьешь - не сложишь.
        [Friendship and glass, once shatttered, cannot be mended.] One may mend a torn
        friendship but it soon falls in tatters. *Cf.* A broken friendship may be soldered, but will
        never be sound.

439   **Дружба крепка не лестью, а правдой и честью.**   *v.* B40
[Respect and truth do more for friendship than flattery.] I cannot be your friend and your flatterer too.

440*   **Дружба от недружбы близко живет.**   *v.* Г275, P67
[Friendship and animosity are neighbours.] Love and hate are blood relations.

441   **Дружба созидает, вражда разрушает.**   *v.* C213
[Friendship creates, enmity destroys.] *Lat.* concordia parvae res crescunt discordia maximae dilabuntur. United we stand, divided we fall.

442*   **Дружиться дружись, а за саблю держись.**   *v.* H119
[Friendship's fine, but hold on to your sword.] Love your enemy, but put not a gun in his hand. Trust me but look to thyself. *Cf.* Put your trust in God but keep your powder dry.

443*   **Дружно - не грузно, а врозь - хоть брось.**   *v.* B253
[Together work is lighter, apart - forget it.] Many hands make light work. Stick together or get stuck separately. All things work together for the good.

444   **Дружные - водой не разольешь.**   *v.* B253
[Friendship is thicker than water.] A true friend is forever a friend.

445   **Дружные сороки и гуся сьедят (утащат).**   *v.* B246, Д89,102,441
[Magpies in alliance will take the goose.] *Cf.* Weak things united become strong.

446*   **Друзей-то много, да друга нет.**   *v.* Б320, B530
He that has friends has no friend. He who has many friends has no friends. *Gr.* Arist.*E.Eth.*7.12: οὐθεὶς φίλος ᾧ πολλοὶ φίλοι. *Cf.* A friend to everybody is a friend to nobody.

447   **Друзей у богатых - что мякины около зерна.**   *v.* Б269,372,467
[Friends of the wealthy are like so much chaff around corn.] *Cf.* Wealth finds friends. *Lat.* res amicos invenit. A full purse has many friends.

448*   **Друзья - до первой кости (до черного дня).**   *v.* Д248,414,436, З16
[Friends till the first hitch (misfortune).] Sunshine friends. Dinner over and the company is departed. While the pot boils, friendship lasts. *Lat.* fervet olla, vivit amicitia. *Cf.* Friends as far as the altar.

449*   **Друзья наших друзей - наши друзья.**
Any friend of my friends is a friend of mine.

450   **Друзья прямые - братья родные.**   *v.* Б63, Д336, К234
A good friend is my nearest relation.

451   **Дрязгу бояться, так в лес не ходить.**   *v.* Б355, B393, T66
[If you fear annoyances, venture not into the woods.] He that fears leaves, let him not go into the wood.

452   **Дуб - дерево хорошее, да плоды его только свиньям годны.**   *v.* C209
[The oak is a fine tree, yet its fruit befits only swine.] Great trees are good for nothing but shade.

453*   **Дулась гора родами, а родила мышь.**   *v.* Г247, M202
The mountains have brought forth a mouse. *Lat.* Hor.*A.P.*139: parturiunt montes, nascetur ridiculus mus.

454   Дума пьет воду, а отвага - мед.
     [Thought drinks of water, but valour of mead.] *Cf.* Deeds are fruit, words are but leaves.

455   Думает плотник с топором.
     [The carpenter thinks with his axe.] *Cf.* Sailors' fingers must all be fish-hooks. A tool is but the extension of a man's hand.

456   Думаешь поймал, а тут сам попался.   *v.* Б377, П154, Т13
     The biter is sometimes bit. Treachery will come home to the traitor.

457   Думай ввечеру, делай поутру.   *v.* У114
     [Think by night but act in the morning.] The best advice is found on the pillow.

458*   Думай двояко, а делай одинако.   *v.* Д372, Н334
     Think twice before you act (once).

459   Думай медленно, работай быстро.   *v.* Д372,460, Н334
     Deliberate slowly, execute promptly.

460   Думай что делать, а делай что решил.   *v.* Д459
     Whatsoever is well resolved on should be quickly performed. *Cf.* Mind what you do and how you do it.

461*   Думал купить корову, а купил быка.   *v.* Л1
     [He wanted a cow but bought a bull.] It isn't what you want in this world, it's what you can get. *Cf.* He who buys what he doesn't want will want what he cannot buy.

462   Думают думу без шуму.
     [Thinking makes no noise.] Great thought, like great deeds, needs no trumpet.

463*   Думы за горами, а смерть (беда) за плечами.   *v.* С197
     [Thoughts may be over the hills, but death (trouble) is just over the shoulder.] At every hour death is near.

464   Дуплистое дерево скрипит да стоит, а крепкое валится.
     [The hollow tree screeches but stands but the sturdy one falls.] Oaks may fall when reeds stand the storm.

465   Дурак времени не знает.
     [A fool is ignorant of time.] Time stays not the fool's leisure.   *Cf.* Only fools are loafers.

466   Дурак головой вертит, умный смирно сидит.
     [The fool fidgets while the wise man sits still.] Only fools speak or fiddle at the table. Fools are fain of flitting.

467*   Дурак делает все наоборот.   *v.* В577, Г132, К313, М192
     [The fool does everything backwards.] What the fool does in the end, the wise man does at the beginning. *Cf.* A wise man begins at the end, the fool ends in the beginning.

468*   Дурак дом построил, а умница купил.   *v.* Ч108
     Fools build houses and wise men buy (live in) **them.**

469*   Дурак дурака хвалит.   *v.* Б198, Д471
     One fool praises another. *Cf. Lat.* asinus asino pulcherrimus.

470   **Дурак дурака учит, а оба ничего не смыслят.**   *v.* C175
[One fool teaches another and neither will know anything.] An ill master, an ill scholar. *Cf.* If the blind lead the blind, both will fall into the ditch.

471*   **Дурак дураком (дураку) и тешится (потакает) (рад).**   *v.* Д469
[One fool comforts (encourages) another.] *Lat.* asinus asinum fricat. One fool scrubs another. *Cf.* A fool always finds a greater fool to admire.

472*   **Дурак дураком остается.**   *v.* Д486
Fools will be fools still. *SPL.* nunquam sapiunt stulti. *Cf.* He who is born a fool is never cured. Once a fool, always a fool.

473   **Дурак, если бы знал что он дурак, не был бы дурак.**   *v.* Е21
[If the fool knew he was a fool, he would no longer be a fool.] He who knows he is a fool is not a big fool.

474*   **Дурак завяжет а умный не развяжет.**   *v.* †Г149, У102
[A fool may tie a knot that the wise man cannot untie.] *Cf.* Fools tie knots and wise men loose them. Fools set stools for wise folks to stumble at.

475   **Дурак закинет, а умный доставай.**   *v.* Г149, О31, У102
A fool may throw a stone into a well that a hundred wise men cannot pull out.

476   **Дурак и в углу светится.**   *v.* Д483
[The fool stands out even in a corner.] *Cf.* If all fools wore feathers we should all seem a flock of geese.

477   **Дурак и под коровий рев пляшет.**
[A fool will dance even to the sound of a bellowing cow.] A fool can dance without a fiddle.

478*   **Дурак и посуленному рад.**   *v.* Д501
Fools rejoice [even] **at promises.**

479*   **Дурак кто с дураком свяжется.**   *v.* В451, Н265, С10
He is not the fool that the fool is but he that with the fool deals.

480   **Дурак один родится - всему свету беда.**
[One fool born heralds trouble for the whole world.] *Cf.* One fool makes many.

481*   **Дурак пир устроил, а умница наелся.**   *v.* Б164
Fools make feasts, wise men eat them.

482*   **Дурак сам скажется.**   *v.* Д476
[A fool soon gives himself away.] A fool's bell is soon rung.

483*   **Дурак стыда не знает.**   *v.* В56, Д490, П148
[Fools have no shame.] Fools are never uneasy. *Cf.* A knave and a fool never take thought. Do not be proud of being a fool.

484*   **Дурак торгует когда базар кончится.**   *v.* Д361, У83, *Ap.*1.68
[The fool trades when the market closes.] When a fool has bethought himself, the market's over.

485*   **Дурака (дураков) и в алтаре бьют.**   *v.* С9
[Fools are beaten even at the altar.] Fools never prosper.

486* **Дурака никаким лекарством не вылечишь. (Дураков уколами не вылечишь.)**
[No medication to cure a fool.] He that is born a fool is never cured. *v.* Д260,472

487 **Дурака озолотили, а он будет все то же нести.** *v.* Ж150,163, С162
[A decorated fool will still wear the same suit.] An ass laden with gold still eats thistles. *Cf.* Fools live poor to die rich.

488* **Дурака пошлешь, а за ним сам пойдешь.** *v.* У96
He that sends a fool means to follow him.

489* **Дуракам во всем (везде) (всегда) счастье.** *v.* Д251, С30, Ф4
Fortune favours fools. *Lat.* fortuna favet fatuis.

490* **Дуракам закон не писан.** *v.* В406, Д483, Н369
As the fool thinks, so the bell clinks. Forbid a fool a thing and that he'll do. *Cf.* Ignorance of the law excuses no man. *Lat.* ignorantia iuris neminem excusat.

491* **Дураками свет стоит.**
Knaves and fools divide the world.

492 **Дураки дают, умные берут.** *v.* Д468
[Fools give, wise men take.] *Cf.* Fools lade the water and wise men catch the fish. Fools give parties, sensible people go to them.

493 **Дураки о добыче спорят, а умные ее делят.** *v.* Г145, С33
Fools bite one another, but wise men agree together.

494 **Дураков не сеют, умных не веют - и сами они объявляются.**
[Neither are fools sown nor wise men winnowed - they arise on their own.] Foolishness grows by itself, no need to sow it. Fools grow without watering.

495 **Дураком на свете жить - ни о чем не тужить.** *v.* Д483,497, Л203, П306
[Being a fool means never grieving.] He is a fool that is not melancholy once a day. Only a fool's positive. *Cf.* Children and fools have merry lives. Fools are never uneasy.

496 **Дураку вред - умному навет.** *v.* В379
Wise men learn by other mens' harms, fools by their own. *Lat.* casus dementis correctio fit sapientis.

497* **Дураку все смех на уме.** *v.* Д495. Л203
A fool is ever laughing. Too much laughter discovers folly. *Lat.* per risum multum potest cognoscere stultum. *Cf.* Laughter is the hiccup of a fool.

498 **Дураку наука что ребеньку огонь.** *v.* П140, У92, Х89
[Learning to a fool is like fire to a child.] *Cf.* An educated fool is dangerous. Learning makes a good man better and an ill man worse.

499 **Дураку спесь как коровы седло.** *v.* К19, Н384
[A fool's conceit is as meet as a cow with a saddle.] *Cf.* As meet as a cow (sow) to bear a saddle.

500 **Дураку что глупо, то и потешно.** *v.* Б490, Д509, П306, Р14
[Foolishness comforts fools.] Fools are fain of nothing. A little thing pleases a fool.

501* **Дурень (дурни) (и) думкой богатеет (богатеют).** *v.* Д478
[Fools grow rich on thoughts.] Dreams give wings to fools. Fools rejoice at promises.

502* **Дурные примеры заразительные.**   *v.* Б166, Г142, И17, О33
Nothing so contagious (infectious) as a [bad] **example.** *SPL.* mores bonos convictus inficit.

503* **Дух бодр, да плоть немощна.**   *v.* Р12
The spirit is willing but the flesh is weak.

504   Душа Божья, голова царская.
[The spirit is God's, but the body is the Tsar's.] *Cf. Matt.*12.21: Render unto Caesar the things which are Caesar's.

505*   Душа всего дороже.   *v.* Б284, Н291, С68, У118
[The mind is more precious than all else.] A good mind possesses a kingdom. *Cf.* The mind is the man. *Lat.* Cic.*Rep.*6.24.26: mens cuiusque is est quisque.

506   Душа (всему) мера.
Man is the measure of all things. *Gr.* ἄνθρωπος μετρον ἀπάντων.

507   Душа не принимает, а глаза все просят.   *v.* Б368, В275, Г111,116,121,158,
[The heart is sated but the eyes want more.] *Cf.* Better fill a man's belly than his eye. Please your eye and plague your heart.

508   Душой измерь, умом проверь, тогда и верь.   *v.* Д358
[Measure with your heart, try with your mind, then trust.] *Cf.* First try then trust.

509   Душу кашей не приманишь.   *v.* Д500
Do not sell your soul for a mess of pottage. *Cf.* Small minds are lured by trifles.

510*   Дыма без огня не бывает.   *v.* Г37, Н518, О26
No smoke without fire. *Cf.* Plaut.*Curc.*:1.1.53: flamma fumo est proxuma.

511*   Дыра есть, будет и прореха.
[A small hole will cause a large breach.] From small beginnings come great things.

512*   Дырой нельзя заткнуть дыру.   *v.* Н552, П305
[You cannot plug a hole with a hole.] No one can dig up a hole. *Cf.* Nothing comes of nothing. *Lat.* ex nihilo nihil fit. No man can sup and blow together. Like tinkers who in stopping a hole make two.

513   Дятель и дуб продалбливает.   *v.* В363, Д339, К98, М11
[The woodpecker can hollow out even an oak.] *Cf.* Little strokes fell great oaks.

E

1 **Его лучше нет, когда он уйдет.** *v.* Н219, Р50
[He's the greatest, when he's away.] Men are best loved furthest off.

2 **Его муха крылом перешибет.**
[Even a fly can hurt him.] You could have knocked him down with a feather. *Cf.* †He wouldn't even hurt a fly.

3* **Его сразу не раскусишь.** *v.* В152, Т29, Ч112
[He's inscrutable.] *Cf.* Still waters run deep.

4 **Едет, как горшки везет.**
[To ride as if transporting pottery.] *i.e. slowly. Cf.* A full cup must be carried steadily. A slow coach. Slow and sure like Pedley's mare. To go at a snail's gallop (pace).

5 **Едет не скоро, но споро.** *v.* К236, Т31
Slow but sure.

6* **Едешь на день, бери хлеба на неделю.** *v.* Х19
Who goes for a day into the forest should take bread for a week.

7 **Един камень много горнцев избывает.** *v.* Г287
[One stone can break many a jar.] *Cf.* Whether the pitcher strikes the stone or the stone the pitcher, it's bad for the pitcher.

8 **Единственный сын - не сын, два сына - полсына, три сына - сын.**
[Only son - no son, two sons - half a son, three sons - a son.] *Cf.* †One boy's a boy, two boys - half a boy, three boys - no boy at all.

9* **Ежеден не будешь умен (+ дней много, а ум один).** *v.* Б167,420, В160,353, 37, Н24,246
No man is wise at all times. *Cf. Lat.* Plin.1.40: nemo mortalium omnibus horis sapit.

10* **Ежели несчастье бояться, то и счастье не будет.** *v.* К267, Л176
[There will be no fortune if you fear misfortune.] *Cf.* If you fear to suffer, you suffer from fear. Nothing stake, nothing draw.

11 **Ездить морем - не брезговать горем. (Ездя в море, помни горе.)** *v.* Д45, Ж33, К265,
[Go to sea and invite sorrow.] *Cf.* He that will learn to pray, let him go to sea. ХЗ

12* **Еле-еле душа в теле.**
[Barely together, body and soul.] *Cf.* Almost was never hanged. Almost didn't make it.

13 **Елей огня не угасит.** *v.* З69, М33, Н405, О27
[Firs don't extinguish fires.] Pouring oil on the fire is not the way to quench it. *Cf.* Put not fire to flax.

14 **Елье, березье, все то дрова.** *obs.*   *v.* B487,506,511, C108, Ч64,69
[Fir, birch - timber just the same.] All wood is worth logs. You've seen one, you've seen them all.

15 **Ему говорить, что в стену горох лепить.**
[Talking to him is like smearing peas on the wall.] Talking to him's like talking to a wall.

16 **Ему и в чистом поле тесно.**
[He feels confined even in an open field.] A discontented man knows not where to sit easy.

17 **Ему на голодный зуб не попадайся.**
[Don't fall on his hungry tooth.] Don't rub him the wrong way.

18 **Ему о деле, а он - приходи на неделе.**   *v.* Г50, Л44
[Speak to him about business and he'll tell you to come back next week.] The sluggard's convenient season never comes.

19* **Ему показывают на луну, а он смотрит на палец.**
[Point out the moon and he'll stare at your finger.] He cannot say B to a battledore.

20 **Ересь смола, а грех грязь.**
[Heresy is pitch, sin - dirt.] Heresy may be easier kept out than shook off.

21 **Если бы да кабы, то во рту росли бы грибы (бобы) (то был бы не рот - а целый огород).**   *v.* A5, Д473, E25, *Ap.*1.24
[If it weren't for the ifs, mushrooms (beans) could grow in my mouth (my mouth would not be a mouth but an orchard).] If ifs and ans were pots and pans, there'd be no trade for tinkers. If my aunt had been a man, she'd have been my uncle.

22* **Если бы (кабы) знал (знать) где упасть, так соломки подостлал бы.**   *v.* З71
[If I knew where to fall, I'd lay a mat.] *Cf.* If things were to be done twice, all would be wise. It is too late to close the well after the goat has fallen in.

23* **Если бы молодость знала (умела), а (если) старость могла.**   *v.* M148
If youth but knew and age but could do. If only youth had the experience and old age had the strength. If the young man would and the old man could, there'd be nothing undone.

24 **Если бы не закон, не было бы и преступника.**   *v.* Г42, H186, П227, C296
The more laws, the more offenders.

25 **Если были бы денег, воз да год праздников.**
[The whole year would be a holiday if we had money.] If it weren't for the "ifs" you'd be rich. *Cf.* If all were right in the best possible of worlds.

26* **Если вздохнуть всем народам, ветер будет.**   *v.* M97, П82, C22
[If all sighed at once, there would be a wind.] Many drops make a shower.

27 **Если голова на плечах есть, так и шапку достанешь.**   *v.* Б448
[If you've got a head on your shoulders, you'll find a hat.] A good head does not want for hats. *Cf.* A hat will never be worn without a head.

28* **Если золото всплыло, правда утонет.**
[Where gold swims, truth sinks.] When gold speaks, other tongues are dumb.

29* **Если корова много ревет, значит мало молока дает.**   *v.* Б202, K330

It isn't the cow that lows the most that will milk the most.

30* Если мил друг, и десять верст - не крюк.   *v.* Г52, Д241, К2
   To a friend's house the trail is never long.

31* Если народ един, он непобедим.   *v.* Б203, Д441, С213,231
   Union is strength.

32 Если нрав горяч, жди неудач.   *v.* Н89
   An angry man never wants woe. It takes a level head to win.

33* Если косить языком, спина не устанет.   *v.* К302, М126, Р25, Х10
   [Reap with your tongue and your back won't weary.] A long tongue has a short hand.

34* Если хочешь мира, будь готов к войне.
   If you want peace, you must prepare for war.

35 Есть в мошне, будет и в квашне.   *v.* В74, Д155
   [When it's in the purse, it's in the kneading trough too.] A full purse begets a stout stomach. Money makes the pot boil.

36* Есть еще порох в пороховницах.   *v.* Н561
   [There's still powder in the powder-horns.] There's life in the old dog yet. You can't keep a good man down. A man may be down but he's never out.

37* Есть и в море дно.   *v.* Б471, К33, С136
   [Even the sea has a bottom.] Everything has an end. *Cf.* The tide never goes out so far but it always comes in again.

38 Есть копье (шило), да в сумке.
   [To have a spear (awl), but stored away.] I have a good bow, but it is in the castle.
   Cf. Like the Dutchman's anchor, he's got it at home.

39 Есть кус, да гостя нет.
   It is better to want meat than guests or company.

40* Есть нета лучше.
   Better ought than nought.

41* Есть нечего, а жить весело.   *v.* Б286, Н447, Т56,59
   [Poor but content.] He is not rich that possesses much, but he that is content with what he has. Happiness is more than riches.

42* Есть пирожок, есть и дружок. *v.* Б372,389,428,429,467, Ж10, З16, Х23
   [When you have a pie, you've got a friend.] No longer foster, no longer friend. *Cf.* At dinner, my man appears. Trencher friends are seldom good neighbours.

43 Есть привычка, есть и отвычка. **Habit is overcome by habit.** *Lat.* consuetudo consuetudine vincitur.

44* Есть про себя, а пить про людей.
   [Eat for yourself but drink for others.] *Cf.* Eat at pleasure, drink by measure.

45 Есть что слушать, да нечего кушать. *v.* Б21,367, Г226, Р24, С236, Ш14
   [There's plenty to listen to but nothing to eat.] Fair words will not fill the belly.

46   **Есть шуба и на волке, да пришита.**   *v.* В392, Н17
            [Even the wolf has a fur, but it's attached.] A wolf may change his mind but not his fur.

47   **Ехал прямо, да попал в яму.**
            Better to go about than fall into a ditch.

48   **Ешь до сыта, а работай до пота.**
            [Eat till you're full and work till you sweat.] Earn your sauce with sweat.

49*   **Ешь мед да берегись жала.**   *v.* Ж13
            [Eat the honey but beware the sting.] He that steals honey should beware of the sting.
            Honey is sweet, but bees sting.

50   **Ешь пирог с грибами, а (да) держи язык за зубами.**
            [Eat the mushroom pie and keep your tongue still.] Keep your breath to cool your soup
            (broth) (porridge). There is a time to speak and a time to be silent.

51   **Ешь что поставят, делай что заставят.**
            [Eat what you're offerred and do what you're told.] *Cf.* Do as you're bidden and you'll
            never bear blame.

52   **Ешь хлеб коли пирога нет (а колача береги).**   *v.* Х22
            [If there's no pie, eat bread.] A crust is better than no bread.

53   **Ешь щи с мясом, а (когда) нет, так щи (хлеб) с квасом.**   *v.* Б453, К101
            [Have soup with cider when there's no soup with meat.] They that have no other meat,
            bread and butter are glad to eat.

54   **Еще бы воевал, да ружье потерял.**   *v.* Ж22
            [I'd still be fighting had I not lost my gun.] A bad shearer never had a good sickle.

55*   **Еще дни впереди.**
            [There are days still before us.] Everyone has his lot and a wide world before. *SPL.* non
            dum dierum omnium sol occidit.

56*   **Еще ты не сидел у воды без хлеба.**   *v.* В111, М197, Н31
            [You never had to face water without bread.] *Cf.* Beggars can't be choosers.

Ж

1 **Жаба да баба квохчут, да клохчут.**
[Toads and women either croak or cackle.] *Cf.* A woman's tongue wags like a lamb's tail.

2 **Жаворонок к теплу, а зяблица к стуже.**
[The lark darts towards heat, the finch to the cold.] Some like it hot, others prefer it cold.

3 **Жадной собаке много надо.** *v.* Б275, Д35, Н8
[A greedy dog needs much.] Greedy dogs never have enough. *Lat.* canes impudentissimi nescierunt saturitatem. *Cf.* Greedy as a dog.

4 **Жадность да важность - голове помеха.** *v.* Ж129
[Greed and pride obstruct the mind.] *Cf.* A fat belly does not breed a subtle mind.

5 **Жадность последнего ума лишает.**
[Greed drives one mad.] *Cf.* The pleasure of what we have is lost by coveting more. The covetous man is his own tormentor.

6* **Жадность слепа.**
[Covetousness is blind.] Envy is blind. *Cf.* Covetousness is the root of all evil. Avarice (greed) overreaches itself.

7 **Жадность что река - чем дальше тем шире.** *v.* К14
[Covetousness is like a river: the farther you go, the wider it gets.] Covetousness is always filling a bottomless vessel. *Cf.* Avarice (greed) overreaches itself. The more you get, the more you want.

8 **Жалеть будет сусла, так брага кисла.**
[Spare the wort and sour the brew.] Nothing comes out that is not put in. *Cf.* You get out of life (the world) what you put into it. He that measures oil shall anoint his fingers. Better spent than spared.

9 **Жалеть коня - истомить себя.**
[Spare the mount and exhaust yourself.] *Cf.* Better ride a poor horse than go afoot. It's the bridle and spur that makes a good horse.

10 **Жалеть мешка - не видать дружка.** *v.* Б372,429, Е42
[Spare the purse and lose your friend.] No longer foster, no longer friend. *Cf.* He that has a full purse never wanted a friend.

11 **Жалеть сына, учащивать раны.** *v.* Б93
[Spare your child and increase your pain.] Spare the rod and spoil the child. Better children weep than old men.

12 **Жалеющий чужого, свое потеряешь.**
[Spare another's and lose your own.] A man gets little thanks for losing his own.

13 **Жалить пчелка, жаль меду.**   *v.* E49
    [The bee stings, it's stingy with its honey.] He that steals honey should beware of the
    sting.

14 **Жаловал (кормил) до уса, жалуй (корми) и до бороды.**   *v.* B291,342, K170, Л70
    [Complain (eat) up to the whisker, complain (eat) up to the beard.] In for a
    penny, in for a pound.

15 **Жалом пчелка страшит и короля.**   *v.* П297
    [The little bee can terrify even the king with its sting.] No viper so little but has its
    venom. *Cf.* Dynamite comes in small packages.

16 **Жалуйся Богу, а слезы вода.**   *v.* H6
    [Pray to God, tears are but water.] 'Tis easy to sigh, but it's better to pray.

17* **Жаль друга (тебя), да не как себя.**   *v.* Д119,424, П195, P60, C73
    Close sits my shirt, but closer my skin. *Cf.* Mind other men, but most yourself. The shirt
    is nearer than the coat.

18 **Жаль кулака, да бить (ударишь) дурака.**
    [Spare not your fist to beat a fool.] *Cf.* You can't beat somebody with nobody. †He is
    a fool that makes a hammer (wedge) of his fist.

19* **Жаль молока, не видать кошки.**
    [Spare the milk and never see the cat.] *Cf.* Cats eat what hussies spare. A stingy man
    gives an egg for a chicken.

20 **Жаль писцу бумажки, не нажить ему рубашки.**
    [The scribe who spares his paper shall never earn a shirt.] Often for sparing a little cost
    a man has lost the large coat for the hood. *Cf.* Save your life and lose a minute.

21* **Жаренные голуби сами в рот не влетят.**   *v.* M76
    Roasted ducks don't fly into your mouth. *SPL.* non tibi per ventos assa columba venit.

22 **Жатва поспела и серп изострен.**   *v.* Г304, E54
    [Harvest has arrived and the sickle is dull.] A bad reaper never got a good sickle.

23* **Ждал пока сварится, подожди пока остынет.**   *v.* H98
    [You waited for it to cook, now wait for it to cool.] He that will be served must be
    patient.

24 **Ждал убогий теленка, а дал Бог ему ребенка.**   *v.* У5
    [The poor man hoped for a calf, but God gave him a babe.] Children are poor mens'
    riches.

25* **Ждала сова галку, а выждала палку. (Ждет, что сова палицы.)**
    [The owl expected the daw, but all she got was a cudgel.] *Cf.* Many a patient sheep will
    enter one stall. Patience provoked turns to fury.

26 **Ждали обозу, а дождались навозу.**   *v.* Л1
    [They were waiting for the wagon-train, but just got manure.] Expectation always
    surpasses realization. It's not well for a man to pray cream and live skim milk. *Cf.*
    Don't count your chickens before they are hatched.

27* **Ждать да догонять - нет хуже. (Ждать плохо, а догонять хуже.)**
    [Nothing is worse than having to wait and catch up.] A watched pot never boils.

28   **Ждать друга, отбыть плуга.**
         [To wait on a friend is to forsake the plough.] Friends are thieves of time.

29*   **Ждать пирога, спать не евши.**   *v.* З368, Н13,129
         [To wait for a pie means to go to bed hungry.] He who lives by hope will die of hunger.
         Cf. Expect nothing and you won't be disappointed.

30*   **Ждет дурак большого места.**   *v.* Г150, П162
         [The fool waits for a great place.] A fool always rushes to the fore.

31   **Жди беды от весенней большой воды.**
         [Expect trouble from a wet Spring.] A May flood never did any good.

32   **Жди - будут и ясные дни.**   *v.* Б384, Г23,26, П166
         After black clouds, clear weather.

33   **Жди горя с моря, а беды от воды.**   *v.* Е11
         [Expect sorrows from the sea and woe from water.] *Cf.* He that would sail without
         danger, must never come on the main sea. He that would learn to pray, let him go to sea.

34   **Жди пиво пока устоится.**   *v.* В260, Д126, М48, Н460,477, Т45, Ц10
         [Wait until the beer settles.] It is ill prizing of green barley.

35   **Ждущий деток не поскучить от бедок.**   *v.* Б60, Д214
         [Expect children, expect trouble.] Children are certain cares and uncertain comforts.

36   **Ждущий лосины, поглодать и осины.**   *v.* Г281, Л178, М43, Н94,397, О97
         [He who waits for the elk-skin must suffer the hornets.] If you want to gather honey, you
         must bear the stings of bees.

37   **Желание убогих не погибнет до конца.**
         The hope of the destitute shall not always be in vain. *Psalms*.9.36: patientia
         pauperum non peribit in finem.

38   **Желанный гость зова не ждет.**   *v.* Г306
         [The welcome guest doesn't need an invitation.] His worth is warrant for his welcome.

39*   **Желающего судьба ведет, нежелающего - тащит.**
         Fate leads the willing but drives the stubborn.

40*   **Железный кулак в бархатной перчатке.**   *v.* В249
         An iron fist in a velvet glove.

41   **Железа куют, не поймав татя.**   *v.* Б422, Н373, О6, Ц10
         [They forge the irons before catching the thief.] Don't spread the cloth till the pot begins
         to boil. First catch your hare.

42   **Железо ржа поедает, а сердце печаль изнуряет.**
         [As rust eats away steel, so sorrow gnaws away at the heart.] Grief pent up will break
         the heart.

43   **Железо ржа съедает, а завистливый от зависти погибает.**   *v.* Р46
         [As rust eats away steel, envy destroys the covetous.] Envy eats nothing but its own heart.

44   **Железо ржавое не блестит.**
         [Rusty steel doesn't shine.] †The used key is always bright.

45   **Железо уваришь, а злой жены не уговоришь.**
[Steel may be tempered, but not the shrew.] Women will have their wills.

46   **Жена без мужа - вдовы (всему) хуже.**
[A wife without a husband is worse than a widow (anything).] *Cf.* She is neither maid, wife nor widow.

47*   **Жена благонравна венец мужу своему.**   *v.* В599, Д269
A worthy woman is the crown of her husband. A true wife is her husband's flower of beauty (heart's treasure). *Cf.*The wife is the key of the house. A cheerful wife is the joy of life. A good wife's a goodly prize, saith Solomon the wise.

48   **Жена богатая гордится и с мужем часто бранится.**   *v.* Б194,285,431, Л142, Н299
[The rich wife is proud and often scolds her husband.] A great dowry is a bed full of brambles. *Cf.* Better a portion (treasure) in a wife than with a wife.

49   **Жена бранчива - мужу позор.**   *v.* Ж53
[The scold is a husband's shame.] Who has a scold, has sorrow to his hops.

50   **Жена - в гости, а муж - гложи кости.**   *v.* Г53, Х32
[When the wife's 'a visiting, the husband must gnaw bones.] House goes mad when women gad.

51   **Жена верховодит, так муж по соседам ходит.**   *v.* Ж72
[A scolding wife drives the husband to the neighbours.] *Cf.*Three things drive a man out of his house - smoke, rain and a scolding wife.

52   **Жена говорлива мужу не мила.**
[Husbands don't like garrulous wives.] A quiet wife is mighty pretty. *Cf.* Women and hens are lost by gadding.

53   **Жена злонравна мужу погибель. (Жена злословна мучит мужа своего).**   *v.* Ж49
[A malicious wife is the husband's undoing.] *Cf.* Who has a scold, has sorrow to his hops. When a man takes a wife, he ceases to dread Hell.

54   **Жена как на хате труба, а муж как на церкве глава.**   *v.* В553, Ж58, М177, Х33
[The wife is like the chimney of a house; the husband, like the church's head.] The wife is the key of the house. *Cf.* Where there is no wife, there is no home.

55   **Жена красавица безумному (безочному) радость.**
[A fair wife is the fool's (blind man's) joy.] *Cf.* Who has a fair wife needs more than two eyes.

56   **Жена мужа не бьет, а под свой нрав ведет.**   *v.* 326, Н568, Х101
An obedient wife commands her husband. The cunning wife makes her husband her apron.

57*   **Жена мужу говорит - не верь своим очам, верь моим речам.**
Husband, don't believe what you see, but what I tell you.

58   **Жена мужу пластырь, а он ей пастырь.**   *v.* Ж54, М177
[A wife is her husband's plaster, and he her pastor.] In the husband wisdom, in the wife gentleness.

59*   **Жена на мужа не доказчица.**
A wife cannot testify against her husband.

60 **Жена, пряди рубашки, а муж - вези гуж.**   *v.* Б7, Д318, М185
[The wife must mend the shirts while the husband pulls the load.] Men get wealth and women keep it. A woman's place is in the home.

61* **Жена хороша не телом, а делом.**   *v.* Л136, Н475
[A wife's virtue is in her conduct, not her body.] Choose not a wife by the eye only.

62 **Жена умирает, а муж со смеху помирает.**   *v.* Д96
[As the wife dies, so does her husband - from laughter.] A dead wife's the best goods in a man's house.

63* **Жена честнее мужу милее.**   *v.* Д270
[The more honest the wife, the more loving the husband.] *Cf.* A good wife and health is a man's best wealth.

64 **Жена языком, а муж комельком.**   *v.* Ж85
[A woman uses her tongue, a man - his staff.] *Cf.* A woman's strength is in her tongue.

65* **Женатому учиться время ушло.**   *v.* Ж70
[The married man's time to learn is past.] Matrimony is a school in which one learns too late.

66 **Жене и мельнице всегда довольно не бывает.**
Mills and wives are ever wanting.

67 **Жене спускать, то в мошне искать.**
If you sell your purse to your wife, give your breeks into the bargain.

68 **Жене тайны не сказывай.**
[Don't tell secrets to your wife.] He that tells his wife news, is but newly married.

69* **Женился - навек заложился.**   *v.* Б488
Wife and children are bills of charges. Wedlock is a padlock.

70 **Женился скоро (на скорую руку), да на долгое горе (долгую муку).**   *v.* В294, Ж79,
Marry in haste and repent at leisure.   К119

71 **Женится медведь (рак) на корове (лягушке).**   *v.* Г261
[The bear (crab) takes a cow (frog).] *Cf.* When a weasel and cat make a marriage, it's a very ill presage. Like blood, like good and like age make the happiest marriage. †Marry your like.

72 **Женитьба добрая хозяйству научает, а неудачная от дома отлучает.**   *v.* Ж51
[Good marriages teach housekeeping, bad ones keep one away from the house.] Marriage makes or mars a man.

73 **Женитьба - не гоньба, поспеешь.**   *v.* Н82
[Marriage is not a race - there's time.] Before you marry, 'tis wise to tarry. *Cf.* Marry late or never.

74 **Жениться беда, не жениться другая, а третья - не дадут за меня.**   *v.* Л132
[To marry is a problem, not to marry is another, and a third is to be turned down.] He who marries might be sorry, he who does not will be sorry.

75 **Жениться любясь, жить крутясь.**
It is unlucky to marry for love.

76 **Жениться - перемениться (переродиться).**   *v.* Б488
[He (she) will change after marriage (will be reborn).] *Cf.* Marry first and love will follow. Marriage makes or mars a man.

77 **Жених с места, другой на место.**
One wedding brings another. *Cf.* Frequent remarriage gives room for scandal.

78 **Женихом весел, а мужем нос повесил.**
[Merry groom but weary husband.] They that marry in green, their sorrow is soon seen.
Cf. Marriage is like a tub of water, after a while, it's not so hot.

79* **Женишься раз, а наплачешься век.**   *v.* В294, Ж70, К119, Р34
Marry in haste, repent at leisure.

80 **Женою доброю и муж честен.**   *v.* К78, Х90
A good wife makes a good husband.

81* **Женские прихоти не исполнишь.**
[Womens' whims cannot be satisfied.] If a woman were satisfied, she wouldn't be a woman. *Cf.* Women and their wills are dangerous ills. Women, priests and poultry never have enough.

82 **Женские слезы не вода, а невода.**   *pun.*   *v.* У1
[Womens' tears are nets, not water.] Trust not a woman when she weeps. A woman's tears are her strongest weapons.

83 **Женский обычай - слезами беде помогать.**   *v.* Б6, Д112
[Helping with tears is womens' wont.] A woman's tears are her strongest weapon.
Cf. A woman is the weaker vessel. A tear of sympathy brings its own relief.

84* **Женский ум лучше всяких дум.**   *v.* Б6,365
[A woman's mind is above reasoning.] A woman's instinct is often truer than mens' reasoning.

85 **Женское слово что клей пристанет (что рыбый клей).**   *v.* Ж64
[A woman's word sticks like glue (fish glue).] A woman's strength is in her tongue.

86 **Жену бери не дородную а природную.**   *v.* В669, Г161, Н258
[Choose a wife who's natural, not portly.] Choose a wife on a Saturday rather than a Sunday.

87* **Жену выбирай не глазами а ушами.**
Choose a wife by your ear rather than your eye.

88 **Жену выбирать, что жеребей метать - какая попадается.**
[Choosing a wife is like casting dice - whatever comes up.] Marriage is a lottery.

89 **Жену с мужем некому судить кроме Бога.**
[None but God may judge either husband or wife.] *Cf.* Put not thy hand between the bark and the tree.

90 **Жену хорошую взять - много станут знать, а худую - нельзя в люди показать.**
[A fair wife is too popular and an ugly one cannot be taken out.] *Cf.* He that has a white horse and a fair wife never wants trouble.

91* **Женщине красота домоустройство.**　　　　　　　　　　　*v.* В553, Д271,318, Х33
　　　The wife is the key of the house. *Gr.* γυνὴ δε χρηστῦ πηδάλιον ἐς οἰκιάς.
　　　Cf. Men make houses, women make homes.

92 **Женясь, о доме прилежать.**
　　　Before you marry, be sure of a house wherein to tarry.

93 **Жернова сами не едят, а людям муку строят.**　　　　　　*v.* Н326, С47, У42, Ч133
　　　[Millers do not eat but make flour for others.]　The painter never paints his own house.
　　　Cf. †Millers are the last to die of famine.

94 **Жесток нрав не будет прав.**
　　　[Cruelty can never be just.]　Might does not make right. *SPL.* nihil violentum diuturnum.
　　　Cf. A man of cruelty is God's enemy. Violence does even justice unjustly.

95 **Жестоко слово воздвигает гнев.**　　　　　　　　　　　*v.* В229, О149
　　　[A cruel word unleashes anger.]　One hard word brings on another.　Patience provoked
　　　turns to fury. The second word makes the quarrel.

96* **Жива (живая) душа калачика хочет.**
　　　[Every living person wants his piece of the pie.]　Hope springs eternal in the human
　　　breast. *Cf.* Hope is the blossom of happiness.

97* **Живая кляча (собака) лучше мертвого рысака (льва).**　　　*v.* Ж125, М69, П33
　　　[Better a live pack-horse (dog) than a dead thoroughbred (lion).]　Better a live dog than
　　　a dead lion.

98 **Живая кость мясом обрастает.**　　　　　　　　　　　*v.* В476, Н36
　　　[A live bone will be sheathed with meat.]　*i.e. will heal.*　There is aye life for a living
　　　man.　Time heals all wounds. *Cf.* A cat has nine lives.

99 **Живем, только небо коптим.**
　　　We're living the life of Reilly.

100 **Живет в красне - хорошо и во сне.**　　　　　　　　　　*v.* К56
　　　[He's living fine and dandy, even in his dreams.]　To live in clover.

101 **Живет и меньшее лучше большого.**　　　　　　　　　　*v.* Р86
　　　[It sometimes happens that small is better than big.] The greatest crabs be not the best meat.

102* **Живет и на старуху проруха.**　　　　　　　　　　　*v.* И35, К165, *Ap.*1.36
　　　[Even an old hand can slip.]　Even Homer sometimes nods. It is a good horse that never stumbles.

103 **Живет из кулака да в рот.**
　　　He lives from hand to mouth.

104* **Живет (живут) как кошка с собакой.**　　　　　　　　　*v.* Д435
　　　To agree like cats and dogs. *Gr. Plan.*55: φιλοῦσιν ἀλλήλους ὥσπερ γαλῆ καὶ
　　　κύων.

105 **Живет - мучится, а умереть не хочет.**
　　　[One lives and suffers, but doesn't want to die.] None so old that he hopes not for a year
　　　of life.

106* **Живет не родитель, а умрет не человек.**　　　　　　　*v.* Ж112,151
　　　[Live not a parent, die not a man.]　*Cf.* He that has no children knows not what is love.

107 **Живет - ни себе, ни людям.** *v.* Ч25
[He lives neither for himself not for others.] We are not born for ourselves.

108* **Живет себе как рыба в воде.**
[He lives like a fish in water.] He is (lives) in his element.

109 **Живет - хлеб ждет, спит - небо коптит.**
All he does is just eat and sleep.

110 **Живется в чаю а ждет раю.**
Bear with evil and expect good.

111 **Живешь - не оглянешься, помрешь - не спохватишься.** *v.* П292
[Live without looking back, and before you know it you're dead.] Life is half spent before we know what it is.

112 **Живешь - не с кем покалякать, помрешь - некому поплакать.** *v.* Б61,154, Ж151
Life without a friend is death without a witness.

113 **Живешь не с кем родишься, а с кем сдружишься.** *v.* Н445, Т9
[You live not with your kin, but with your friends.] You may choose your friends; your family is thrust upon you. Home is where the heart is. *Cf.* The soul (lover) is not where it (he) lives, but where it (he) loves. Where men are well used, they'll frequent there.

114 **Живи всяк своим умом да своим горбом.**
[Let each live by his mind and by his back.] Let all trades live.

115 **Живи, да и помирать собирайся.**
[Live, but also prepare to die.] Let all live as they would die.

116* **Живи и жить давай другим.** *v.* С39
Live and let live.

117* **Живи не как хочется, а как можется.** *v.* Б293
[Live not how you want but how you can.] Live within your means. *Cf.* The rich man may dine when he will, the poor man when he may.

118* **Живи не прошлым а завтрашним днем.** *v.* В288
[Live not by yesterday but by tomorrow.] Tomorrow is another day. *Cf.* Live for the present, plan for the future.

119 **Живи ни шатко, ни валко, ни на сторону.**
[Live to neither side but in the middle.] A middle course is the safest. *Cf.* Do not all you can, spend not all you have, believe not all you hear and tell not all you know.

120* **Живи по старому, а говори (мели) по новому.**
[Live by the old but speak to the new.] The ancients tell us what is best, but we must learn of the moderns what is fittest. *Cf.* Use the old before getting the new. Out of old fields comes new corn.

121 **Живи просто, проживешь лет со сто.**
[Live simply and you'll live to be a hundred.] Poverty is the mother of health.

122* **Живи своим умом.**
Use your head.

123 **Живи смирнее, так всем будешь милее (тебе же будет прибыльнее).** *v.* Б397
[Live peaceably and others will like you all the more (and you will profit by it).] Be still and have thy will.

124 **Живого не называй мертвым. (Живому могилы нет.)** *v.* Ж138
[Don't call a living man a corpse.] No man is dead till he's dead. Never say die.
Cf. Don't count your corpses before they're cold.

125 **Живое слово дороже мертвой буквы.** *v.* Ж97, М69, П33
[Better a live word than a dead letter.] *Cf.* Better a live dog than a dead lion. Better be a live rabbit than a dead tiger.

126* **Живой живое (о живом) и думает.**
We must live by the quick (living), (not the dead). *Cf.* Gather ye rosebuds while ye may.

127* **Живому именины, мертвому помины.** *v.* М67

128 **Живот подведет - все пойдет.** *v.* З113, П76
He that wants health wants all.

129 **Живот толстой, да лоб пустой.** *v.* Ж4
Fat paunches have lean pates.

130 **Живу как живется, не как люди хотят.**
[Live as best you can, not as the rest would want.] Make your life, don't copy it.

131 **Живут в бедности, не имеют честности.** *v.* Г222, Н587,590, П308
Poverty is the mother of crime. It is a hard task to be poor and leal.

132* **Живут и на воде люди.** *v.* И3, П68,242,244, С282
[People live even on water.] *Cf.* Custom reconciles us to everything. One can get used to everything, even hanging.

133 **Живут скромно, да едят скромно.**
[They live modestly and eat modestly.] A poor man's table is soon spread.

134 **Живучи в соседах, быть в беседах.**
[If you go to your neighbours, be prepared to talk.] *Cf.* A good neighbour, a good morrow. To be a good neighbour, take heed of your tongue.

135 **Живучи за бабою, квакать жабою.** *v.* З15, М50, П152
[Live with a woman, croak like a toad.] Who keeps company with wolves will learn to howl.

136* **Живы будем и сыты будем.**
May we will all live happily ever after. *said as a toast.*

137 **Живы родители - почитай, померли - поминай.**
[Respect your parents while they're alive and honour them when they are dead.] *Cf.* God and parents can never be requited.

138 **Живых не оплакивают.** *v.* Ж124, 126
[Mourn not the living.] *Cf.* We ought to remember the living.

139* **Живых святых не бывает.**
[There's no such thing as a living saint.] A saint has no value in his own house.
Cf. Praise no man till he is dead.

140   **Жизнь бежит, а годы скачут.**   *v.* B221, Г195
      [Life runs but years leap.] Life is short and time is swift.

141   **Жизнь, как луна - то полная, то на ущербе.**
      [Life, like the moon, is either full or waning.] Life is subject to ups and downs. Life's
      race is either forward or backward. *Cf.* Life is a shadow.

142*   **Жизнь короткая, да слава долгая.**   *v.* Д332, X53
      Life is short, fame (art) long. *Lat.* ars longa, vita brevis. *Cf.* Good men must die, but
      death cannot kill them quite.

143   **Жизнь наша - полная чаша.**
      [Our life is a full chalice.] Life is just a bowl of cherries. *Cf.* Life is not a cup to be
      drained, but a measure to be filled.

144*   **Жизнь не по молодости, смерть не по старости.** *v.* H367

145   **Жизнь одинокого - что пасмурный день.**
      [A life of solitude is like a grey day.] *Cf.* The life of man is a winter's day and a
      winter's way.

146*   **Жизнь пережить - что море переплыть (+ побарахтаешься, да и ко дну).**
      [Living life is like crossing the seas (you drift and you sink).] Life is a pilgrimage. Life
      is a voyage that's homeward bound.

147*   **Жизнь прожить - не поле перейти (не лапти сплесть).**   *v.* B227, Г194, Ж164
      [Living life is more than just crossing a field (is not as easy as weaving sandals).] Life
      is not a bed of roses.

148   **Жил бы хорошенько, да денег маленько.**   *v.* Б465, Д193, K329, *Ap.*1.64
      [I'd live the good life, but I can't afford it.] Jack would be a gentleman if he had money.

149   **Жил в лесе, а пеньям кланялся.**   *v.* B448,498, H2,3
      [Live in the woods and greet the stumps.] *Cf.* Live too near a wood to be frightened by owls.

150   **Жил в неге, а ездил в телеге.**   *v.* Д487, Ж163, C162
      [He lived in the lap of luxury but rode a cart.] Fools live poor to die rich. *Cf.* The ass
      loaded with gold still eats thistles.

151   **Жил не сосед (человек), а умер не покойник.**   *v.* Ж106,112
      [Live not a neighbour, die not mourned.] *Cf.* He dies like a beast who has done no good
      while he lived. Life without a friend is death without a witness.

152*   **Жил - полковник, помер - покойник.**   *v.* C87,198, У57, Ц5
      [He lived as a colonel but died a corpse.] Today a man, tomorrow none. *Cf.* Death is the
      great leveller. Six feet of earth make all men equal.

153   **Жил собакой, околел псом.**   *v.* Б377, K29, Л76, C81,224,
      [He lived like a dog and died like a dog.] An ill life, an ill end. Such a life, such a death.

154*   **Жили люди до нас, будут жить и после нас.**   *v.* H341,458
      [Others lived before us and there will be others after us.] I am not the first and shall not
      be the last. There were brave men before Agamemnon.

155   **Жили - не бранились, и ушли - не простились.**
      [Lived without strife, parted without good-byes.] *Cf.* Little intermeddling makes fair parting.

156* **Жирный кот на мышей не охотится.** *v.* H70
[A fat cat does not stalk mice.] The fed hound never hunts.

157* **Жить в разлуке - жить в муке.** [Life apart is a life of misery.] *Cf.* Absence sharpens love, presence strengthens it.

158* **Жить надейся а умирать готовься.** *v.* H20
[Hope for life but prepare for death.] Plan your life as though you were going to live forever, but live today as if you were going to die tomorrow. *Cf.* Hope for the best and prepare for the worst. Live for the present, plan for the future.

159 **Жить - не живет, а проживать - проживает.** *v.* H457
[He doesn't live but he survives.] *Cf.* Life is not in living but but in liking. It's not how long we live, but how.

160 **Жить славно - не жалеть мошны.** [To live well means not sparing the purse.] As the purse is emptied, the heart is filled. *Cf.* The true value of life cannot be measured in dollars.

161* **Жить страшнее чем умереть.** *v.* C200
'Tis more brave to live than to die. *Cf.* Fear of death is worse than death itself.

162 **Жить широко хорошо, но и уже не хуже.** [Living lavishly is fine, but living modestly is no less so.] Spend and be free, but make no waste. *Cf.* Spend not where you may save, spare not where you must spend. Better a humble life in peace and quiet than a splendid one in danger and risk.

163 **Житье скупое платье носит худое.** *v.* Д487, Ж150, C162
[Avarice wears rags.] The ass loaded with gold still eats thistles.

164 **Житье - что падчерица.** *v.* B227, Г194, Ж141,147, H147,232
[Life is a step-daughter.] *Cf.* Life is a shadow (smoke). Life is a queer proposition.

165* **Жмурится как кот на сливки.** [Screws up his eyes like a cat at cream.] The cat shuts its eyes while it steals cream.

166 **Жнем рано а сеем поздно.** [We reap early and sow late.] *Cf.* Early sow, early mow. You shall reap what you sow.

167 **Жнут порою а жуют зимою.** *v.* K88
[Timely reaping for winter eating.] *Cf.* You can't have the ear unless you plant the corn.

168* **Журавль высоко летает, а от реки не отбывает.** *v.* Г18,48
[The crane may fly high, but it won't stray from the river.] A bird may fly high, but he must come down for water.

169* **Журавля (сокола) в небе не сули, дай прежде синицу в руки.** *v.* Д393, Л152, C122
[Instead of promising a crane in the sky, give a titmouse in your hand.] A bird in the hand is worth two in the bush. *Lat.* plus valet in manibus passer quam in nubibus anser.

170 **Журить, бранить есть кому, а жаловаться некому.** [Many to reprove but none to sollicit.] *Cf.* Open rebuke is better than secret hatred. We are born crying, live complaining and die disappointed.

3

1   **За бешеным стадом не крылатым пастырю быть.**   *v.* В91, Д86
       [A shepherd without wings cannot rout a stampeding flock.]   A man cannot be in two places at once. You can't run and bark at the same time.

2*   **За битого (ученого) двух небитых (неученых) (неучей) дают.**   *v.* Б217, Л145, О92,93
       [Better one experienced (educated) man than two inexperienced (ignorami).] A thimbleful of experience is worth a tubful of knowledge. A thorn of experience is worth a wilderness of advice. *Cf.* An old wise man's shadow is better than a young buzzard's sword.

3   **За богатым не угоняешься.**
       [You can't keep up with a rich man.] *Cf.* He that has little shall have less. Resembling the great in some ways does not make us equally great.

4*   **За большим погонишься, и малое потеряешь.**   *v.* В522, Д246, З22,54, К222, М132
       [Pursue the greater and lose the lesser.] *Cf.* Grasp all, lose all. Catch not at the shadow and lose the substance. He that ventures too far, loses all.

5*   **За ветром в поле не угонять (не угоняешься).**   *v.* И143, Н12
       You cannot reap the wind [in the field].

6   **За вора не божись - обманет.**   *v.* В414, П249
       [Don't vouch for a thief, you'll be deceived.] Once a thief, always a thief. *Cf.* Trust not him that has once broken faith. Save a thief from the gallows and he'll be the first to cut your throat.

7   **За ворота, да опять в теже ворота.**   *v.* В487,506, З18, Т3
       [In and out the same gates.] The more it changes, the more it remains the same. *Cf.* Another yet the same. The nature of things doesn't change.

8   **За голодного Бог заплатит.**   *v.* Б246, Д38, Р63
       [God shall pay for the hungry.] God is always opening his hand. *Cf.* God never sends mouth but he sends meat.

9   **За голым гнать - нечего снять.**   *v.* В120, Г237,241, Н125,559, С5, У71
       No naked man is sought after to be rifled. There's no trying to strip a naked man.

10   **За горячее железо не хватайся.**   *v.* В115, К281
       [Do not clutch at hot steel.] If you play with fire you get burnt. Don't stick your hand in burning water to see if it's hot.

11* **За двумя зайцами гонять, ни одного не поймать.**   *v.* П94
       If you run after two hares, you will catch neither. *Apost.*12.33: ὁ δύο πτῶκας διώκων, οὐδέτερον καταλαμβάνει. *Lat.* duos lepores insequens, neutrum capit.

12* **За добро добром и платят.**   *v.* В380, Д368, Т80, У108
       One good turn deserves another. Repay kindness with kindness.

13   **За доброго человека, сто рук.**   *v.* В27, О46, У93
[I'd give a hundred hands for one good man.]   One good head is better than a thousand strong hands. *Cf.* Good men are scarce.

14   **За добрые дела всегда живет похвала.**
Praise is the reflection of virtue.   *v.* Д284,292, Ч53

15*   **За кем жить, за тем и слыть.**   *v.* В359, Ж135, М50, П152, С28,123
One is known by the company one keeps. Tell me with whom you go and I'll tell you what you do. Show me your company and I'll tell you who you are. *Cf.* He who lives with cats will get a taste for mice. He who keeps company with a wolf, learns to howl.

16   **За кем счастье, за тем и люди.**   *v.* Б429,467, Д448, Л116, Н64
All the world loves a winner. *SPL.* quo se fortuna, eo etiam hominum favor inclinat.

17   **За кем что знаешь, про себя разумей.**   *v.* Н93, О116, Ч135, *Ap.*1.21
[What you know about others, find out about yourself.]   Point not at others' spots with a foul finger. *Cf.* Sweep in front of your own door first. The best place for criticism is in front of one's mirror.   Unless you can do better, don't criticize.

18   **За который перст (палец) ни укуси, все больно.**   *v.* Т3
[Whichever finger you bite, it hurts all the same.] *i.e. parents feel the same for all their children.* No matter how but whether. *Cf.* If a child has cut its finger, it has cut its mother's heart.

19   **За курочку гуська отдать.**   *v.* В677,678
[Give away a gosling for a chick.] Goose, gander, gosling are three sounds but one thing. *Cf.* Fair exchange is no robbery.

20*   **За лесом видит, а под носом нет.**   *v.* Д50, Н259, П98
[He sees through the woods but not in front of his nose.] Lose sight of the forest for the trees.

21   **За малое судиться, большое потерять (приложить).**   *v.* Д363, Т82
[Petty litigation engenders major loss.] Agree, for the law is costly.

22*   **За малым гнался - большое упустил.**   *v.* В594, З4,54, О15, П92,116
Penny wise, pound foolish.

23   **За морем корова по деньге (телушка полушка), да перевоз рубль.**   *v.* В558, Г34,224
[Distant cattle (heifers) may be cheaper, but the transport is dear.] *Cf.* Cheap goods always prove expensive. Cheapest is dearest.

24*   **За морем рубят, сюда щепы летят.**   *v.* В197,207, Л202, Н117, С1, Т8, У8, *Ap.*1.77
[When they chop overseas, the chips fly here.] One does the scathe and another has the scorn.

25   **За морем теплее, а у нас веселее.**
[It may be balmier overseas but it's merrier here.] Travellers may change climates, not conditions.

26   **За мужем жена всегда госпожа.**   *v.* Ж56, Н568, Х101
He that has a wife has a master. *Cf.* A woman can't drive her husband, but she can lead him.

27   **За мухой с обухом не гнаться (нагоняешься).**   *v.* М198
[Take not an axe to kill a fly.] Take not a musket (spear) to kill a butterfly. Don't use a cannon to shoot a sparrow.

28   **За недобрым (худым) пойдешь, на беду набредешь (худое и найдешь).** Г5, К238, О177
He that seeks trouble never misses.

29   **За неимением гербовой, пишут и на простой.**   *v.* И25, О18, С107
[In the absence of a letterhead, a plain sheet will do.] A man must plow with such oxen as he has. Make the most of what you have. If you can't get a horse, ride a cow.

30   **За неимением капрала и ефрейтор правит.**   *v.* М54, В167
[When the corporal is absent, the private gives the orders.] In the kingdom of the blind, the one-eyed man is king.

31*   **За ничто ничего не купишь.**   *v.* Д73,74
Nothing in this life is free.

32   **За обедом соловей, а после обеда воробей.**   *v.* Р44, С147
[A nightingale at the table but an old sparrow after.] Merry is the feast-making till we come to the reckoning.

33*   **За один раз дерева не срубишь.**   *v.* Д200, С27
An oak [tree] is not felled at one stroke.

34*   **За очи коня не купят.**   *v.* Д124, К187, Н381, Ч70
[Don't buy a horse unseen.] Never buy anything before you see it. *Cf.* Don't buy a pig in a poke.

35*   **За правое дело говори смело.**   *v.* Н435
Speak the truth bravely. *SPL.* cum recte vivas ne cures verba malorum. *Cf.* The best cause requires a good pleader. Better to speak truth rudely than to lie covertly.

36   **За руки принимают, а за пяты кусают.**   *v.* В16,100, О86
[They shake hands and bite at your heels.] Many kiss the hand they wish cut off.

37   **За свое вступайся, за чужое не хватайся.**   *v.* Н459
[Defend your own but leave others' alone.] Mind no business but your own.
Cf. Covet not that which belongs to others.

38*   **За свое всяк стоит.**   *v.* П245
[All stand up for their own.] Self-preservation is the first law of nature. *Cf.* Every man should cultivate his own garden.

39*   **За словом в карман не полезет.**
[He needn't look in his pocket for words.] His tongue's well hung.

40   **За смерть нет поруки.**   *v.* О122,154
[No guarantee against death.] There is a remedy for everything but death. *Cf.* Nothing so certain as death. Death is deaf to our wailings. Death is deaf and will hear no denial.

41   **За сон ручаться нельзя.**   *v.* Ж29, Н13,41
[You cannot bank on a dream.] Hope is a slender reed for a stout man to lean on.
Cf. Don't feed yourself on false hopes. Who lives by hope will die by hunger.

42   **За спасибо мужик три года (сем лет) служил (работал).**
[The peasant laboured three (seven) years for a thank you.] The more you do, the less thanks you get. *Cf.* Thanks is poor pay.

43   **За спасибо денег не дают.**   *v.* И101, П134, С244
[Thank you's are free.] You can't put thanks into your pocket.

44*   **За спрос денег не берут.**
It costs nothing to ask.

45   **За тем дело стало что денег мало.**
[No money, no progress.] Where coin is not common, commons must be scant.

46   **За худого замуж не хочется, а доброго негде взять.**   *v.* М111
[No one wants a bad husband, but good men are hard to find.] If you always say "no," you'll never be married. *Cf.* If you wish for too much, you will end up with nothing. Who seeks a faultless friend rests friendless.

47   **За худые слова слетит и голова.**   *v.* Д78, П278
The tongue talks at the head's cost.

48*   **За чем пойдешь, то и найдешь.**   *v.* И144, К246
[What you seek you shall find.] *Matt.*7.7: **Seek and ye shall find.**

49   **За честное обхождение всегда получишь почтение.**   *v.* В116
[Good manners always command respect.] No honest man ever repented of his honesty. *Cf.* Courtesy is one habit that never goes out of style. Courtesy pays.

50   **За что батька (один), за то и детки (другой).**   *v.* К62
Like father, like son. *SPL.* oscitante uno oscitat et alter (when one yawns so does the other).

51*   **За что купил, за то и продаю.**   *v.* И100, Л200
[I'm selling my goods at the same price I paid for them.] *i.e. to say exactly what one heard.* To tell it like it is.

52*   **За что поп, за то и приход.**   *v.* И69, К67, Н42
     Like priest, like people. *Lat.* sicut populus, ita et sacerdos.

53   **За чужим кануном (чужими блинами) своих родителей поминать.**   *v.* В36,187,
[Invoke your own forebears at another's wake (table).]   З107, Н87
Cf. Noble ancestry makes a poor dish at table.

54*   **За чужим погонишься, свое потеряешь.** *v.* В522, З4,22, И134, Н109,112,338, О16, П92
[Pursue another's and lose your own.] *Cf.* Don't neglect your own field and plough your neighbour's.

55   **За чужую душу не божиться стать.**   *v.* Г44, К258, Л25, Ч130
[Don't swear on another's head.] *Cf.* He that will swear will lie.

56   **За шутку не сердись, а в обиду не (в)давайся.**   *v.* Т15, Ш15
[Don't take a joke seriously.] *Cf. Lat.* Plaut. si quid per jocum dictum est, nolito in serium convertere. A joke never gains over an enemy but often loses a friend.

57   **Заберешься, худое выберешь.**
[Given a choice, you'll take the worst.] He that has a choice has trouble. *Cf.* A maiden with many wooers often chooses the worst.

58   **Завей горе веревочкой.**
[Tie your sorrows with a string.] Hang care.

59* **Заветный перстенек и поношенный хорош.**
[A cherished ring is valued despite its wear.] Don't value a gem by what it's set in. *Cf.* Cherish some flower, be it ever so lowly.

60* **Завидлив бывает обидлив.**   *v.* Д342
[The envious are easily offended.] Envy has smarting eyes. *Cf.* He who envies admits his inferiority.

61 **Завидливому и свой хлеб не сладок.**   *v.* Ж43, Р46
[An envious man cannot even enjoy his own bread.] The covetous man is his own tormentor. *Cf.* Envy eats nothing but its own heart.

62 **Завидливые глаза все съесть хотят (всегда не сыты).**
Envy and covetousness are never satisfied.

63 **Завидный в поле горох да репа.**   *v.* В448,498, И32, К152, Н3
[Peas and turnips are enviable commodities in the field.] A bad bush is better than an open field. *Cf.* Better a louse in the pot than no flesh at all.

64 **Завистливое око видит далеко.**   *v.* Б197, У27
Nothing sharpens sight like envy.

65 **Завистливый сохнет по чужому счастью.**   *v.* В181, Ч121
An envious man waxes lean with the fatness of his neighbour.

66 **Зависть прежде нас родилась.**
[Envy was born before us.] Envy never dies.

67 **Завистью ничего не сделаешь.**   *v.* В62
[Envy never accomplished anything.] Envy never enriched any man.

68* **Завтрами сыт не будешь.**   *v.* Ж29, З41, М138, Н13,129
[Tomorrows won't fill your belly.] Who lives by hope will die of hunger.

69 **Загорелось в колодце, а соломой тушили.**   *v.* Е13, М33, О27, Н405
[The well's on fire and they're quenching it with straw.] Pouring oil on the fire is not the way to quench it.

70 **Заднего не поминать.**   *v.* К285, О185, П124,127,179
Latecomers are shent.

71 **Задний ум лучше переднего.**   *v.* Е22
Hindsight is better than foresight. *SPL.* curae posteriores semper meliores. *Cf.* A word before is worth two behind.

72 **Заем платить не беда.**   *v.* З90, Р11, Х56
A borrowed loan should come laughing home.

73 **Заемщик заимодавцу всегда виноват.**   *v.* Д368, К286, С36
[The borrower is always wrong before the creditor.] He who owes, is in all the wrong. The borrower is a slave to the lender.

74 **Займом богат не будешь.**
[A debt never made anyone rich.] Debt is the worst poverty. *Cf.* Out of debt is riches enough.

75* **Закон как паутина - шмель (шершень) проскочит, а муха увязнет (увязает).**
Laws catch flies but let hornets go free. *v.* А18, Б330, Н268, Ш6

76* **Закон назад не действует.**
The law has no retroactive force. *Lat.* lex ad praeterita trahi nequit.

77* **Закон, что дышло - куда повернул, туда и вышло.**
[The law is like a shaft - whichever way you turn it, you're shafted.] The law is like an axle - you can turn it whichever way you please if you give it plenty of grease.

78 **Законнику закон не лежит.** *v.* Б159, П224
[Laws are not for lawyers.] He who is a law to himself no law does need. *Cf.* A lawyer never goes to law himself.

79 **Закрытую рану лечить трудно.**
[It is difficult to treat a closed wound.] The wound that bleeds inwardly is most dangerous. The private wound is deepest.

80* **Залез в богатство, забыл и братство.** *v.* Ч55
[Acquired wealth forgets brotherhood.] Honours change manners. Where wealth is established it is difficult for friendship to find a place. *Cf.* Brotherly love for brotherly love, but cheese for money. Sudden wealth is dangerous.

81 **Замуж выходи, а в оба гляди.**
Keep your eyes wide open before marriage (+ and half shut afterwards).

82 **Замуж идет, песни поет - а вышла, и слезы льет.** *v.* В294, Ж70,79, К119
[Songs before marriage and tears after.] Marriage rides upon the saddle and repentance upon the crupper.

83 **Заносчивого коня построже зануздывают.** *v.* Б101,244, Н83
A boisterous horse must have a rough bridle. A scary horse needs a stout bridle.

84 **Заочная брань - не брань (ветер носит).**
[Insults not heard are not offensive (but wind).] What you don't know can't hurt you. *Cf.* What the eye doesn't see, the heart can't grieve over.

85 **Заочно торговать будет горевать.** *v.* Д124, З34, К187, Н381, Ч70
[Buy unseen and be sorry.] *Cf.* The buyer needs a hundred eyes, the seller but one.

86* **Запас беды не чинит.** *v.* Б68, З87, Л94, Т55, У34, Х19
Store is no sore. *Cf.* Providing is preventing. Save today, safe tomorrow.

87 **Запас мешка (человека) не трет (портит).** *v.* З86, П111, Х19
[Provision doesn't spoil the bag (the man).] Store is no sore.

88* **Запасливый лучше богатого.** *v.* Б189, Т55
[Better a provider than a rich man.] Thrift is a great provider. Forecast is better than work-hard.

89 **Запасливый нужды не терпит (знает).** *v.* Б84, З86, Т55
Save and have. *Cf.* Provision in season makes a rich house.

90 **Заплатишь долг скорее, так будет веселее.** *v.* З72, Р10
[The sooner you repay your loan, the happier you'll be.] A borrowed loan should come laughing home. *Cf.* Pay your debts or lose your friends.

91   **Запретный плод сладок, а человек падок.**   *v.* Г315, Н69, Ч19
     Gen.3.6: **Forbidden fruit is sweet** [+ and man a sinner]. Everything forbidden is sweet.
     SPL. quod non licet, acrius urit.

92   **Запрос в карман не лезет.**   *v.* П155
     [A request doesn't reach into your pocket.] There is no harm in asking.

93   **Запрослив да несчастлив.**   *v.* Л195
     [Inquisitive and unfortunate.] Curiosity killed the cat. *Cf.* Foolish curiosity and vanity
     often lead to misfortune.

94   **Запряг прямо а поехал криво.**   *v.* З103, Н155,156
     [Hitched straight but rode crooked.] *Cf.* A horse never goes straight up a hill. Good to
     begin well, better to end well.

95*   **Зарекал козел в огород ходить.**   *v.* Б97, В415, Г44, К258, З6
     [The goat has foresworn going to the orchard.] Show me a liar and I'll show you a thief.
     Once a thief, always a thief. *Cf.* He who lies once is never believed. The dog returns
     to his vomit.

96   **Заря деньгу дает.**   *v.* Ж118, З8
     [Dawn provides money.] Another day, another dollar. *Cf.* With each new dawn, new
     hope. Tomorrow is another day.

97*   **Заставь дурака Богу молиться, он и лоб расшибет (разобьет).**   *v.* В19,496
     [Send a fool to pray and he'll crack his skull when prostrating himself.] He would fall
     on his back and break his nose. *Cf.* The idiot bakes snow in the oven and expects ice
     cream pie. Send a fool to market and a fool he will return again.

98   **Застарелую болезнь трудно лечить.**
     [An ingrained disease is hard to cure.] A deadly disease neither physician nor physic can
     ease. *Cf.* Old wounds soon bleed.

99   **Застой товару цены сбавляет.**   *v.* П281
     [Demurral reduces prices.] Delay breeds loss. After a delay comes a let.

100   **Засыпь правду золотом, а она всплывает.**   *v.* П215
     [Bury a truth in gold and it will resurface.] *Cf.* Though a lie be swift, the truth overtakes
     it. Truth and oil always come to the top. Buy the truth, but never sell it.

101   **Захотел от калашника дрожжей покупать.**   *v.* В5, И83, К45, Н399, Ч75, Щ7
     [Wanted to buy yeast from a *kalachnik*.] *i.e. from a baker who either needs it himself or
     has none left.* You can't get blood out of a turnip. To get (wring) water (blood) (milk)
     from a stone. You seek hot water under cold ice. Look not for musk in a dog's kennel.

102   **Захочешь добра, посыпь больше серебра.**
     [If you want kindness, drop some silver.] *Cf.* All things are obedient to money.

103*   **Зачал (начал) за здравие, а свел за упокой.**   *v.* Б300, В287, Н156, П202
     [He began with "long live" and ended with "rest in peace."] A sweet beginning with a
     sour end. To go up like a rocket and come down like a stick. Good to begin well, better
     to end well. *SPL.* in fundo feces. *Cf.* The cat is mighty dignified until the dog came
     along.

104   **Зачем в люди по печаль, когда дома плачут.**
     [Why make one's sorrow public.] *Cf.* One shouldn't wash one's dirty linen in public.

105* **Зачем туда с ножом, где топор положен.** *v.* П174

[Why use a knife where the axe has been?] There's little left for the broom after the besom. *Cf.* The best is often the enemy of the good. Never fight a knife with an axe.

106* **Зачин дела лучше.** *v.* В642, Д308, Л756 П199

[Beginning is best.] Well begun is half done. *Cf.* The beginning is the hardest.

107 **Зашел в чужую клеть молебен петь.** *v.* В187, З53, Н87,459

[He entered another cloister to officiate a service.] *Cf.* Meddle not in another man's matter. Paddle your own canoe.

108 **Заяц от лисицы а лягушка от зайца бежит.**

[The hare runs from the fox and the frog from the hare.] *Cf.* Great fish eat up the small. Big fish eat little ones, the little ones eat shrimps, and the shrimps are forced to eat mud.

109 **Заботливый не зажмурясь спит.** *v.* Н510

A good conscience is a soft pillow.

110 **Звание вышнего на браки вечные.** *v.* С193,302

Marriages are made in heaven.

111* **Зваться большим, знаться с меньшим.** *v.* Б388

The great and the little have need of one another.

112* **Здоровая душа в здоровом теле.** *v.* В45

A sound mind in a sound body. *Lat.* mens sana in corpore sano.

113* **Здоровье всему голова.** *v.* Ж128

[Health comes first.] Health is the first muse.

114* **Здоровье дороже (богатства) (всего) (золота).** *v.* Б283,310

Health is better than wealth. Good health is priceless. Find health better than gold. *SPL.* si ventri bene, si lateri pedibusque tuis, nil divitiae poterunt regales addere maius.

115* **Здоровье приходит днями а уходит часами.** *v.* Б42, Г271, З123

[Good health comes by days and leaves by hours.] *Cf.* Ill comes in by ells and goes out by inches. Misfortune arrives on horseback but departs on foot.

116* **Зеркало не виновато коли рожа крива.** *v.* К205, Н37, Р93

[Don't blame the mirror for an ugly face.] *Cf.* What your glass tells you will not be told by counsel. An ugly woman dreads the mirror. Blame not others for faults that are in you.

117 **Зиме да лету союзу нету.** *v.* Г338

[Winter and summer never meet.] *Cf.* Hot summer, cold winter. East is east and west is west, and never the twain shall meet. Oil and water don't mix.

118 **Зла коса на камень не наскочит.**

[A wicked scythe never happens on a rock.] The more wicked, the more lucky.

119 **Злая баба не умрет, коли кто не пришибет.**

[The hag won't die unless someone kills her.] Thieves and rogues have the best luck, if they do but 'scape hanging.

120 **Злая жена сведет мужа с ума.** *v.* З138

[A wicked wife will drive her husband mad.] *Cf.* Three things drive a man out of his house: smoke, rain and a scolding wife.

121 **Зле приобретенное, зле и пропадает.** *v.* К188, Н513, Т49, Х96, Ч127
   Ill-gotten, ill-spent. *Lat.* Cic.*Phil*.2.27: mala parta, mala dilabuntur. *Cf.* Ill-gotten goods
   never prosper.

122* **Зло злым и выгоняют (исполнит).** *v.* А13, К106, Л80
   [Evil drives out evil.] *Cf.* Vice is its own punishment and sometimes its cure. Fight fire
   with fire. Desperate evils require desperate remedies.

123* **Зло к нам летит а от нас ползет.** *v.* Б28,42,304, Г271, С320
   Ill comes in by ells and goes out by inches.

124* **Зло тихо лежать не может.**
   [Evil won't lie still.] *Cf.* Ill weeds grow apace.

125 **Злобный пес и господина грызет.** *v.* Б211, И139
   The mad dog bites his master.

126 **Злой (человек) Бога не боится и людей не стыдится.**
   [Knaves feel neither fear before God nor shame before men.] A knave and a fool never
   take thought.

127* **Злой всегда мыслит злобно.**
   Evil doers are evil dreaders.

128 **Злой мыслит ночью а казнит днем.**
   [The wicked plan by night and execute by day.] *Cf.* He that does ill hates the light.
   What is done by night appears by day.

129 **Злой человек в ненависти изживет (не проживет в добре) век.**
   [The wicked spend their lives in loathing.] *Cf.* A wicked man is his own hell. He that
   lives not well one year, sorrows seven after.

130 **Злой человек в очи льстит, а за очи губит.** *v.* К171, С246
   [The wicked flatter to the face, then stab in the back.] He has honey in the mouth and
   a razor at the girdle. *Cf.* Many kiss the hand they wish cut off.

131* **Злом зла не поправишь.** *v.* В124, Г311, И81, К201
   Two wrongs don't make a right. Never do evil for evil. Never do evil hoping that good
   will come of it.

132 **Злому истина крива.**
   [Truth is ugly for the wicked.] Every vice fights against nature.

133 **Злому масло на голову лей, а ему деготь кажется.** *v.* Н18
   [Anoint the head of the wicked with oil, and to him it seems like tar.] *Cf.* A guilty
   conscience feels continual fear.

134 **Злость под видом добродетеля многих обманывает.**
   Vice is often clothed in virtue's habit.

135 **Злую печаль развевай доброю мыслию.** *v.* Д61
   [Dispel grief with good thoughts.] *Cf.* Will is the cause of woe. There's no cure for
   sorrow but to put it underfoot.

136 **Злые беседы тлят обычаи благие.** *v.* В161
   1 *Corinthians* 15:33: **Evil communications corrupt good manners.**

137   **Злые нравы портят добрые дела.**
        [Evil manners corrupt good deeds.] *Cf.* Corruption of the best becomes the worst.

138   **Злых всех злее злая жена.**   *v.* З120, Л131
        [Worst of all evils is a wicked wife.] A wicked woman is worse than the devil.
        Cf. A bad woman is worse than a bad man.

139   **Змея агнца не рождает.**   *v.* Н47,402, О96,156
        [A snake will not give birth to a lamb.] Eagles do not breed doves.
        Cf. Of a thorn springs not a fig.

140*   **Знаем мы и сами что кривы наши сани.**
        [We know ourselves that our sleds are bent.] *Cf.* He that thatches his house with turds
        shall have more teachers than reachers.

141*   **Знает где раки зимуют.**   *v.* З146, Р29
        [He knows where the crabs go in winter.] He knows on which side his bread is buttered.

142*   **Знает где у него башмак жмет.**   *v.* В618, Н549
        [He nows where his shoe rubs.] I know best where the shoe pinches.

143   **Знает грудь (подоплека).**   *v.* З145, К42
        [The inside (lining) knows.] You cannot hide from your conscience. Suffering does not
        manifest itself. *Cf.* Conscience is the court of justice.

144   **Знает и ворона в чем оборона. (Знает сорока где зиму зимовать.)**   *v.* З141,146
        [Even the crow knows where her safety lies.] [A magpie knows where to winter.]
        Cf. Self-preservation is the first law of nature.

145*   **Знает кошка чье мясо съела.**   *v.* З143, К42, Н18
        [The cat knows who's meat it ate.] *i.e. has a guilty conscience.* You cannot hide from
        your conscience. *Cf.* The cat is honest when the meat is out of her reach. The cat knows
        whose beard she licks. *Lat.* ad cuius veniat scit cattus lingere barbam.

146*   **Знает с какой стороны ветер подул (дует).**   *v.* З141, Р29
        To know which way the wind blows.

147*   **Знает свинья свое порося.**
        [The sow knows her brood.] The litter is like to the sire and dam.

148*   **Знай больше да говори меньше.**
        [Know more and speak less.] Who knows most, speaks least.

149*   **Знай да помалчивай.**   *v.* Д207,208, М117, У97
        [Know but be still.] Keep your mouth shut and your ears open. A wise head makes a
        close mouth.

150   **Знай ереси да не твори.**
        [Know heresy but do not practice it.] *Cf.* Heresy may be easier kept out than shook off.

151   **Знай кошурка (кошка) свою конурку (свое лукошко).**
        [A dog (cat) should know its kennel (basket).] Everybody ought to know his own business
        the best. *Cf.* The hare always returns to her form. Everything is good in its place.

152*   **Знай край да не падай.**   *v.* В550
        Know your limitations and go not beyond them.

153 **Знай лапоть лаптя, сапог сапога.** *v.* З154, Н84, *Ар.*1.12
[A sandal should know a sandal and a boot a boot.] Everybody ought to know his own business best. *Cf.* Stick together or get stuck separately.

154* **Знай сверчок свой шесток.** *v.* В563, З153, Н84, П293, *Ар.*1.21
[The cricket should know its hearth.] The cobbler should stick to his last. *Lat.* ne sutor ultra crepidam. *SPL.* quam quisque norit artem, in ea se exerceat.

155* **Знай себя (+ да указывай дома).**
Know thyself [+ be master of your own house]. *Gr.* γνῶθι σαυτόν. *SPL.* aedibus in nostris quae prava aut recta gerantur, curandum.

156 **Знакомым не всякому будь (быть).**
[One cannot (must not) be a friend to everyone.] Have but few friends, though many acquaintances. *Cf.* A friend to everybody is a friend to nobody.

157* **Знание - сило, время - деньги.** *v.* Г62
Knowledge is power. Time is money.

158* **Знать ворону (сокола) по полету (+ а доброго молодца по походке).**
Знать птицу (сову) по перьям (+ а молодца по речам).
Знать скляночное судно по звону, а человека по речам. *v.* В310, О98
[A crow (falcon) is known by its flight (+ and a good lad by his gait.)]
[The bird (owl) is known by its feathers (+ and a fine lad by his words).]
[The glass vessel is known by its ring, and man by his words.]
The bird is known by his note, the man by his words. *SPL.* cauda de vulpe testatur.

159 **Знаться с кумою (женою) расстаться с женою (кумою).** *v.* В525, Н10,19, О30,74
[A man can be on good terms with his wife or godmother, but not both.] *Cf.* It is hard to please all parties. He that all men will please, shall never find ease. I cannot be both your friend and your flatterer.

160 **Знают попа и в рогоже (+ а разбойника по роже).**
[A priest is recognized even in a sheepskin (+ and a bandit by his face).] Once a priest (knave), ever a priest (knave).

161 **Зоб полон а глаза голодны.** *v.* В275,368, Г111,116
[Gullet full yet eyes ravenous.] The eye is bigger than the belly.

162 **Зови гостей меньше так хлеба останется больше.**
[Invite fewer guests and there will be more bread.] Spare and have is better than spend and crave.

163 **Золото и в грязи (мякине) видно (блестит).**
[Gold glitters even in mud (chaff).] Coal doesn't shine around diamonds.

164* **Золото искушается огнем, а человек напастями.** *v.* Б48, И141
Gold is tried in the fire, [and man by adversity]. *Cf.* Adversity is the touchstone of virtue.

165 **Золото не говорит, да много творит.**
[Gold does not speak, yet it does much.] Gold is an unseen tyrant. *Cf.* †Gold is an orator. †You may speak with your gold, and make other tongues dumb. †When gold speaks, other tongues are dumb.

166 **Золотолюб не ест калачей.** *v.* С162
[The miser does not eat cakes.] A miser is an ass that carries gold and eats thistles.

167 **Золотоноша кругом хороша.** *v.* Б392
[The woman that wears gold is ever beautiful.] An old woman's gold is not ugly.

168 **Зубная боль что деревенская родня.**
[A toothache is like country kinfolk.] A toothache is more ease than to deal with ill people. *Cf.* Aching teeth are ill tenants.

169 **Зуй до воды охочь, а плавать не умеет.**
[Plovers are water lovers but can't swim.] Like an anchor of a ship that is always at sea and never learns to swim.

170* **Зять в дом и иконы вон.**
[When the son-in-law moves in, the icons move out.] *i.e. because there will be abusive arguing.* Mother-in-law and daughter-in-law are a tempest and a hailstorm.

И

1   **И белый песок в грязи чернеет.** *v.* В107, Г332, О81,84
[Even white sands blacken from dirt.] Who deals in dirt has foul fingers. *Cf.* He that touches pitch shall be defiled.

2*   **И близко, да слизко.** *v.* В362, Г109
[It's near but slippery.] There's many a slip 'twixt the cup and the lip.

3*   **И в аду люди живут.** *v.* Ж132, П68,242,244, С282
[People will live even in Hell.] One can get used to everything, even hanging. Custom reconciles us to everything.

4*   **И в колье, и в малье.** *v.* Б441, С41
[Through stakes and blocks.] Through thick and thin. To go through fire and water.

5   **И в красне живут, и в черне живут.**
[They live in beauty and they live in gloom.] Happiness and gladness succeed each other.

6   **И в напраслине, что в деле, погибают.** *v.* В77

7   **И в пепле искра бывает.** *v.* К20
[There may be a spark amidst ashes.] In the coldest flint there is hot fire.

8   **И в тюрме не все воры.** *v.* Н241
[All are not thieves who are in jail.] All are not thieves that dogs bark at.

9*   **И в царство небесное даром не пустят.** *v.* В661
[One can't even get into heaven for nothing.] There is no good that does not cost a price. *Cf.* †Gold goes in at any gate except Heaven's.

10   **И в черве толк - от червя шелк.** *v.* Б102, Д72
[Even a worm has a purpose - silk.] There is reason in roasting of eggs. There is reason in all things.

11   **И велик и широк корове язык Бог дал, да говорить заказал.** *v.* Б249
[God gave the cow a great thick tongue, yet forbade it to speak.] *Cf.* Nature has given us two ears, two eyes, but one tongue.

12*   **И волки сыты и овцы целы.** *v.* И38, К146, Н138
[The wolves are sated and the sheep are safe.] Neither pot broken nor water spilt. *Cf.* Run with the hare and hunt with the hounds. Have your cake and eat it.

13   **И вор Богу молится.** *v.* Б403
[The thief too prays to God.] There isn't a rascal or a thief that doesn't have his devotion. *Cf.* When the devil prays, he has booty in his eye.

14   **И выеденного яйца не стоит.**
      Not worth an eggshell.

15   **И гладок да гадок.**
      [Smooth but vicious.] In silk and scarlet walks many a harlot.

16*   **И глуп смолвит слово в лад.**   *v.* Б412, В465, У95
      A fool may sometimes speak to the purpose. *Gr. Diog.*7.81: πολλάκι τοι καὶ μωρὸς κατακαίριον εἶπε.

17*   **И глупый умного дурачит.**   *v.* Б166, Г142, Д501, О33, С9
      It takes the foolish to confound the wise. *Cf.* Fools set stools for wise folk to stumble at. Fools multiply folly. One fool makes many.

18   **И горшок с горшком сталкиваются (столкнется).**   *v.* В140, И36, Н495, С131
      [Even pots sometimes collide.] The best drivers have wrecks. *Cf.* Accidents will happen in the best regulated families.

19*   **И добро худом бывает.**   *v.* В491,552, Н454
      [Even good may be bad.] None so good that it's good to all.

20   **И добрый временем плачет, а худой скачет.**   *v.* Б373,460, Г69, И24,
      (И дурак ездит в карете, и умный ходит пешком.)   О43, П256, С234
      [At times the good must cry while the bad dance.] [Sometimes the fool must ride the cart while the wise man goes on foot.] Somewhere the sun is shining, somewhere a little rain is falling. *Cf.* Every dog has his day. The sun shines on the evil as well as the good.

21   **И змея своих черев не ест.**   *v.* Б240, В389,435, К155, С221
      [Even the snake does not eat her brood.] Dog does not eat dog. A crow doesn't pick out the eye of another crow.

22   **И из грязи бывают князья.**   *v.* Б350
      [Even princes may spring from dirt.] *Cf.* The more noble, the more humble. It's not the fine coat that makes the gentleman.

23*   **И из кривой трубы дым прямо поднимается.**   *v.* Б404, Г126, Д411, К204, С287, У75
      [Crooked chimneys still let smoke out straight.] Crooked logs make straight fires.
      Cf. Crooked furrows grow straight grain.

24*   **И к нам солнышко изойдет на двор.**   *v.* В510, И20, С234
      [The sun will shine on our yard too.] Our day too will come some day. The sun shines on all alike. Fortune knocks at least once at every man's gate. *Cf.* Everything comes to him who waits. Opportunity sooner or later comes to all who work and wish.

25   **И кафтан греет коли шубы нет.**   *v.* З29, И32, Н3, О18, С107
      [In the abence of a fur, a cloak can keep you just as warm.] If thou hast not a capon, feed on an onion.

26   **И комар лошадь повалит, коли медведь (волк) пособит.**
      [A mosquito can down a steed, if a bear helps.] A fly sat on the axletree of the chariot-wheel and said, "What a dust do I raise."

27*   **И крута гора, да забывчива.**   *v.* Г328
      [The hill is steep, but easily forgotten.] The river (danger) past and God is forgotten.

28* **И курица (муха) с сердцем (сердце имеет). (И муха набивает брюхо.)**   *v.* И31,54
[Even a chicken (fly) has a heart.] [Even a fly must fill its belly.] The fly has her spleen, the ant her gall.

29 **И ложь правдою статься может.**   *v.* Н419
[Even a lie may become a truth.] Tell a lie and find a truth.

30* **И лучшее кушанье приестся.**   *v.* Б440, К94, М212, С341
Custom takes the taste from the most savoury foods.

31 **И малому есть счет.**   *v.* И28,54
[Even a small thing has its worth.] No hair so small but has its shadow.

32* **И месяц светит когда солнца нет.**   *v.* В448, И25, К142, Н525, О18, Х42
[Even the moon shines when there is no sun.] The moon is not seen where the sun shines. *Cf.* Every light is not the sun. †The moon is not seen where the stars shine.

33* **И моя (наша) копеечка (денежка) не щербата.**
[My (our) *kopek* is not chipped.] *i.e. as good as anyone's.* I'm just as good as the next person.

34* **И мышь в свою норку тащит корку.**   *v.* В578,609
[Even the mouse brings a crust to its hole.] Every man drags water to his own mill. The hare always returns to her form.

35* **И на доброго коня бывает спотычка.**   *v.* Б117, Д396, Ж102, К165, *Ap.*1.36
It is a good horse that never stumbles.

36* **И на молодца бывает оплох.**   *v.* И18, Н32,43, Ч26
No man is infallible.

37* **И на мудреца бывает простота.**   *v.* Б167,420, В160, Д396
The wisest man may fall. The wise man may sometimes play the fool.

38* **И нашим и вашим (+ под одну дуду спляшем).**   *v.* Д106, И12
[To dance to everyone's tune all at once.] To run with the hare and hunt with the hounds. No man can serve two masters.

39 **И не наши сани подламываются.**   *v.* Б149, Ч30
[Ours are not the only sleds to break.] There is a crook in the lot of everyone. None of us are perfect.

40 **И от меду мухи мрут.**   *v.* В516,591, И116, М211, С169,170,341, Х52
[Even honey can kill flies.] Too much pudding will choke a dog. Too much honey cloys the stomach.

41 **И от маленькой трещины большой котел дребезжит.**   *v.* Б408, К143, М5
[Even a small crack may cause a large pot to shatter.] A small leak may sink a great ship.

42* **И от ума сходят с ума.**
Much learning makes men mad.

43* **И петух на своем пепелище храбрится.**   *v.* В137,557,562, Д389
(И курица петухом поет на своем пепелище.)
Every cock will crow upon his own dunghill. *Plan.*264: καὶ ὁ ἀλέκτωρ ἐν τῇ οἰκείᾳ κοπρίᾳ ἰσχυρός ἐστι. *Lat.* gallus in suo sterquilinio plurimum potest.

44 **И по заячему следу доходят до медвежьей берлоги.** *v.* П56

45* **И птица в одно перо не родится.** *v.* B88

46 **И пчелка летит на красный цветок.**
[Even the bee is attracted by a beautiful flower.] *Cf.* Beauty draws more than oxen.

47 **И свое дитя не мило когда криво.** *v.* B17
[One may wince even at one's own ugly child.] *Cf.* Not even a father delights in a fool for a son.

48 **И сила есть, да воли нет.** *v.* H153, O189
[The strength is there but the will is gone.] Nothing is easy to the unwilling.

49 **И сило уму уступает.** *v.* Б140, Р28, С120
[Even strength yields to wisdom.] Wisdom is better than strength.

50 **И слепая лошадь везет, коли зрячий на возу сидит.**
[A blind horse can pull provided the driver can see.] It doesn't matter if the ox is blind; load the wagon and apply the line.

51* **И собака не лает на того чей хлеб ест. (И собака помнит кто ее кормит.)** *v.* Б364, 389, H173
[Even a dog won't bark at (remembers) the person who feeds it.]
A dog returns to where he has been fed.

52* **И солнце приходит на скверные места, да не оскверняется.**
The sun is never the worse for shining on a dunghill.

53* **И старая корова быка любит.**
[Even an old cow loves a bull.] *SPL.* etiam anus hircisset.

54 **И у курицы (воробья) есть сердце.** *v.* И28
[Even a chicken (swallow) has a heart.] The fly has her spleen, the ant her gall.
SPL. etiam formicis sua bilis est.

55 **И худой квас лучше хорошей воды.** *v.* Б222
[Better some bad *kvas* than good water.] Better some of a pudding than none of a pie.
†Pure water is better than bad wine.

56 **И худой человек проживет свой век.** *v.* B640, Д365, И24, С234
[Even the vile must live their time.] The sun shines on all alike. *Cf.* The balance distinguishes not between gold and lead.

57 **И царь воды не уймет.** *v.* B690, Л11
[Not even the *tsar* can pacify a torrent.] *Cf.* A man can do no more than he can.

58 **И через золото слезы текут.** *v.* H454
[Tears also flow through gold.] Some swim in wealth but sink in tears. *Cf.* Poison is poison though it come in a golden cup.

59 **И через широкую реку можно построить мост.** *v.* Г47
[A bridge can be built even across a wide river.] Where there's a river there's a bridge.
Cf. Even the weariest river winds somewhere safe to sea.

60* **И черт не так страшен как его малюют.** *v.* Г313, X47
The devil is not so black as he is painted.

61* **Игла в стог упала - считай пропала.** *v.* И143, Л95
A needle in a haystack [is as good as lost].

62* **Иголка маленька, да больно уколеть.** *v.* Г108
[A needle is small but can hurt.] A thorn is small, but he who has felt it doesn't forget it. *Cf.* There is no man, though never so little, but sometimes he can hurt. Dynamite comes in small packages

63 **Иголкой (иглой) колодец не роют (дороги не меряют).** *v.* В52, О114, Щ8
[You don't dig a well (measure roads) with a pin.] To cut blocks with a razor. You can't saw wood with a hammer.

64* **Игра игрою, а дело делом. (Играй, играй - да дело знай.)** *v.* Д437, Л5, Х25
Don't mix business with pleasure.

65 **Игра не доведет до добра.**
[Nothing good from games.] The less play, the better. *Cf.* He makes a foe who makes a jest.

66* **Игра не стоит (стоила) свеч.** *v.* В545, К172, О25, П291
The game isn't worth the candle.

67 **Играй да не заигрывайся.**
Don't carry a joke too far. Long jesting was never good.

68 **Игрок кум вору.**
[The gambler is godfather to the thief.] The better gamester, the worser man. *Cf.* A gambler picks his own pocket. The devil goes shares in gaming.

69 **Игумен хорош так и братьи не худы.** *v.* З52, К67, Н42
[When the abbot is good, so are the monks.] Like priest, like people.

70 **Игумен шевелит а братьям не велит.** *v.* Г189, Д258, М159, П146
[The abbot stirs but won't allow the brothers to budge.] Do as the friar says, not as he does.

71 **Идет воевать да не хочет сабли вынимать.** *v.* Б106, К181, Л54, Н396, Х109
[He goes to war but doesn't want to draw his sword.] The cat would eat fish but would not wet her feet.

72 **Идя вперед, знай как воротиться.**
[If you go forward, remember how to return.] If you go into a labyrinth, take a clew with you.

73* **Из блохи (мухи) (комара) делают верблюда (слона).** *v.* Б458, В684, Д125
[Make a camel (elephant) out of a flea (fly)(mosquito).] Make a mountain out of a molehill. To make of a fly an elephant. *Gr.* ἐλέφαντα ἐκ μυίας. *EA.* elephantum ex musca facis.

74* **Из большого осла (все) не выйдет слона.** *v.* В398, И106, Л42, Н194, О105, С135,227
[You cannot make an elephant out of a large ass.] What good can it do an ass to be called a lion? Buzzards never make good hawks.

75 **Из вины твоей не шубу шить.** *v.* И101
[Your faults are not enough to make a fur.] Wink at small faults. *Cf.* His back is broad enough to bear blame.

76 **Из ворот да в воду.** *v.* Б47, И87,93, О147
[Out of the gate and into the moat.] *i.e. to get off to a bad start. Cf.* Out of the frying pan and into the fire.

77* **Из двух зол выбирай меньшее.** *v.* Л133
Choose the lesser of two evils. *Lat.* ex maximis malis minimum eligendum.

78 **Из дуги (уже) оглобли не сделаешь.** *v.* Д122, Л1
[One can no longer make a shaft from a bow.] He will make a spoon or spoil a horn.

79 **Из ежевой кожи шубы не сошьешь.** *v.* И109, 111, О114, Ш8
[You can't make a fur from the hide of a hedgehog.] You cannot make a silk purse out of a sow's ear.

80* **Из избы сор не выноси.** *v.* Н256, С242
Do not wash your dirty linen in public.

81 **Из зла добро не родится. (Из лжи правды не вырастишь.)** *v.* В124, Г311, З131, К201
An ill deed cannot bring honour. Two wrongs don't make a right.

82* **Из кобыл да в клячи.** *v.* И102
[From filly to jade.] General today, common soldier tomorrow. To go down the ladder.

83 **Из козла молока нечего доить.** *v.* З101, К45, Ч75, Щ7
[No point to milking a he-goat.] *Cf.* You go to a goat (ass) for wool. *EA.* de lana caprina.

84 **Из корки мякише не будет.** *v.* А1, О41
[You can't get the inside from a crust.] *Cf.* You can't eat the same bread twice. No man can flay a stone.

85 **Из короба не лезет, в короб нейдет.**
[If it doesn't fit in the basket, it won't go.] You cannot get a quart into a pint box.

86* **Из кривого прямое не сделаешь.** *v.* Г250, К64,200, С130
[You cannot make something straight from what is bent.] You can't make a crooked stick lay straight. You can't make a crab walk straight.

87* **Из кулька в рогожку.** *v.* И76,93
[From the bag onto the mat.] Out of the frying pan and into the fire.

88 **Из лука стреляют по намерению.** *v.* В360, Р80
[A bow is shot deliberately.] Draw not your bow till your arrow is fixed. Nothing is stolen without hands.

89* **Из малого выходит великое.** *v.* М6,25, Н216
Small is the seed of every greatness.

90* **Из многих малых выходит одно большое.** *v.* Б89, В244, П58,82
Many small make a great. Many a little makes a mickle.

91 **Из ничего сыр бор загорается.** *v.* М14, О142
[It takes nothing to start a forest fire.] Green wood makes a hot fire.

92 **Из обрубков бревна не составишь.** *v.* И118, П278, Р82
[You can't make a beam from stumps.] You can always cut more wood off, but you cannot put it on again.

93* **Из огня (сохи) да в полымя (борону).**   *v.* Б46,47, И76,87, О146
[From the fire (plough) into the flame (harrow).] From the frying pan into the fire.

94 **Из одних уст (одного рта) и тепло и холод.**   *v.* Б406, И96
[Hot and cold from the same lips.] The same sun that will melt butter will harden clay.
Cf. The mouth is the executioner and the doctor of the body.

95 **Из одного два сделаешь - оба окоротишь.**
[Split one and both become shorter.] Do not cut the sheet to mend the dishcloth.
Cf. Many irons in the fire, some must cool.

96* **Из одного дерева и икона и лопата (+ да не оба святы).**   *v.* Б406, И94
[The same wood makes an icon and a shovel (+ and not both are holy.] The same knife
cuts bread and fingers.

97 **Из одного места (города) (куста) не одни вести.**
[Not always the same news from the same place (town)(bush).] There are always two
tales to a story.

98 **Из одного теста сделаны.**   *v.* О71
[Made from the same dough.] Cast from the same mould. A bird of the same feather.
Tarred with the same brush.

99 **Из песка веревки не вьют.**
[You can't weave rope from sand.] To make a rope of sand. *Lat. EA.* ex arena
funiculum nectis.

100 **Из песни слова не выкинешь (выгородишь).**   *v.* З51
[You can't drop a word from a song.] *i.e. to be entirely honest.* To tell the truth, the
whole truth and nothing but the truth. One word cannot be changed but for the worse.
Cf. The musician slurs his mistake with a cough. *Gr.* ἀπορία ψάλτου βήξ.

101 **Из поклонов (спасибо) не шубу шить (шапки не сошьешь).**   *v.* З43, И75, Р24, С236
[You can't make a fur (hat) out of compliments (gratitude).] Thanks is poor pay. Fine
words butter no parsnips.

102* **Из попа (попов) (да) в дьяконы.**   *v.* И82
[From priest to deacon.] Out of the hall and into the kitchen. *Cf.* From the horse to the
ass. *EA.* ab equis ad asinos *Gr. Zen.*2.30: ἀφ'ἵππῶν ἐπ'ὄνους.

103 **Из пуста судна ни пьют ни едят.**
To fill the mouth with an empty spoon.

104 **Из сапог да в лапти.**
[From shoes to slippers.] Over shoes, over boots.

105 **Из сердца не выкинешь (вынешь) а в сердце не вложишь.**   *v.* Б354, К199, М92, С113
[Nothing can be forced in or out of the heart.] *Cf.* Love cannot be compelled. He who
forces love where none is found remains a fool the whole year round.

106* **Из совы сокол не будет.**   *v.* В398,439, И74, К219, С135,227
[You cannot make a falcon out of an owl.] A carrion kite will never be a good hawk.
A buzzard never makes a good hawk.

107   **Из стены тени не вырубишь.**
[You can't obliterate a shadow from the wall.] Stand in the sunshine and the shadow will fall behind. *Cf.* No sun without shadow. The sun doesn't shine on both sides of the hedge at once.

108*   **Из ученого глуп бывает.**   *v.* В53, К263
[A scholar may sometimes be a fool.] Folly and learning often dwell together. *Cf.* Even a fool can learn. A mere scholar, a mere ass. Great scholars are not the shrewdest men. Wisdom doesn't always speak in Greek or Latin.

109*   **Из хама не сдедаешь пана. (Из худого хорошего не сделаешь.)**   *v.* И79, К84,89,
[You can't make a gentleman (good) out of a boor (bad).]   М80, О127,167
The king can make a knight, but not a gentleman. *Cf.* Of evil grain, no good seed can come. No good apple on a sour stock. It takes three generations to make a gentleman,

110*   **Из чужого кармана (мешка) платить легко (не жаль).**   *v.* Л25, Н136,441, Ч120
[It's easy to pay out of another's pocket (purse).] *Cf.* The wholesomest meat is at another's cost. He is free of fruit that wants an orchard. He is free of horse that never had one.

111*   **Из шерсти шелка не сделаешь.**   *v.* И79, О114, Ш8
[You cannot make silk from wool.] You cannot make a silk purse out of a sow's ear.

112   **Из-за чужого обеда не стыдно не евши встать.**
[There's no shame in rising from another's table without eating.] *Cf.* †At the table it becomes no one to be bashful. †Never be ashamed to eat your meat.

113   **Избалуется овца не хуже козы.**   *v.* Т84, Ч68,82
[The lamb is pampered no worse than the goat.] What's good for the goose is good for the gander. As is the gander, so the goose.

114*   **Избирай друга по своему нраву.**   *v.* С12
[Choose a friend according to your character.] Have no friends not equal to yourself. *Cf.* A friend is another self. A person is reflected in the friends he chooses.

115   **Избытка убожество ближний наследник.**
[Poverty is the direct heir of excess.] Plenty makes poor.

116   **Избыточная сладость пуще горечи (горькости).**   *v.* В516, И40, М212, С169,170,341
[Excessive sweetness is worse than bitterness.] Too much sweet spoils the best coffee. *Cf.* Too much of a good thing is worse than none at all. Extremes meet. Too far east is west. Too good is stark nought.

117   **Излишняя игрушка доводит до причины.**   *v.* П207, Т15, Ш15,17
[Long jests lead to pretexts.] *Cf.* Dogs begin in jest and end in earnest.

118   **Изломленное не наставишь.**   *v.* И92, П278, Р82
[You cannot make whole what is broken.] Nothing seems quite as good as new after being broken. *Cf.* A cracked bell can never sound well.

119   **Измазанному бедами не измыться водами.**   *v.* И1, О81,84
[He that is besmirched with woe cannot wash clean.] He that deals in dirt has foul fingers. *Cf.* A clean hand needs no washing.

120*   **Изменника терплю, а измену ненавижу.**   *v.* Н294
[I can endure the traitor, but not treason.] You may hate the things a person does, but never hate the person.

121* **Измену любят а изменнику ненавидят.**   *v.* Д366, Н287
We love the treason but we hate the traitor. A king (prince) loves treason but hates the traitor. *Gr.* Plut.*Rom.*17.3: φιλεῖν μὲν προδοσίαν, προδότην δὲ μισεῖν.
Lat. proditionem amo sed proditorem non laudo.

122 **Иконы красит, а людей (церкви) грабит.**   *v.* Б236, О73, С43
[Paints icons but robs people (churches).] The friar preached against stealing and had a goose in his sleeve. *Cf.* Some make a conscience of spitting in church but rob the altar. Who is near the church is often far from God.

123 **Или (либо) в стремя ногой, или (либо) в пень головой.**   *v.* Л6„68
[Either the foot in the stirrup or the head in the tree-stump.] Either win the saddle or lose the horse. The vessel that will not obey her helm will have to obey the rocks. *Cf.* Between the stirrup and the ground, mercy I asked and mercy I found.

124* **Или (либо) в сук, или (либо) в тетерю (стреляй).**
[Either the bough or the grouse.] To shoot at a pigeon and kill a crow. *Cf.* He who shoots may hit at last. He that shoots oft, at last shall hit the mark.

125 **Иногда и лесть лучше правды.**   *v.* Л101,138,144, О13, У94
[Sometimes flattery is better than truth.] Better a lie that heals than a truth that wounds. A necessary lie is harmless.

126 **Иногда и от доброго отца родится бешена овца.**   *v.* Д37, О145
Many a good father has a bad son. Many a good cow has an evil calf.

127 **Иной в лес, иной по дрова.**   *v.* В574, Н239
[Not all who go to the woods go for wood.] There are more ways to the wood than one. All are not hunters that blow the horn. Some love the meat, some love to pick the bone.

128* **Иной любит попа, другой попадью, а иной попову дочку.**   *v.* Н15, О1, П107, У15
[Some like the priest, others the priest's wife, and others the priest's daughter.] There's no accounting for tastes. All meat's to be eaten, all maids to be wed. *Cf.* Every man to his taste, quoth the man when he kissed his cow.

129 **Иной покажется глуп, а слово молвит в путь.**   *v.* В465, И16, У94
[Some may appear foolish but speak to the purpose.] Fools may sometimes speak to the purpose. A fool's bolt may hit the mark.

130 **Иной стреляет редко, да попадает метко.**
[Some seldom shoot yet hit the mark.] It chances in an hour, that happens not in seven years. *Cf.* A blind man may sometimes hit the mark.

131 **Иной хлеб достает горлом, а иной горбом.**   *v.* Н467
[One uses his voice, another his back.] Many means to get money. Who has not silver in his purse, should have silk on his tongue. *Cf.* Some tasks require a strong back and a weak mind.

132 **Иному гром не гром (слон не слон), а страшен барабан (таракан).**
[Some don't fear thunder (elephants) but drums (roaches).] Fear is beyond all arguments.

133* **Иному счастье - мать, а иному - мачеха.**   *v.* Б11, Г84, К157, О43, *Ap.*1.23
Fortune to one is mother, to another is stepmother.

134 **Искав чужого свое потеряешь.**   *v.* З54, Н109,112,338
[Seek another's and lose your own.] *Cf.* All covet, all lose.

135   Искать вчерашний день.
         In search of yesterday.

136   Искра мала велик пламень родит (а велики вещи сжигает).   *v.* M14, O135,142
         Of a small spark, a great fire.

137*   Искра пока в пепле, тогда и туши.
         (Искру туши до пожара, напасть отводи до удара.)   *v.* Л107
         [Extinguish the spark whilst in the ashes.] [Extinguish the spark before a fire, avert disaster before it strikes.] Destroy the lion while he is yet but a whelp. *Cf.* Meet the malady on the way. Nip in the bud. *Lat.* venienti occurite morbe.

138   Исподволь и ольха гнется (согнешь), а круто и береза ломится.   *v.* Л122
         [An alder will bend gradually, but abruptly even a birch will snap.] Better bend than break. *Cf.* Slow things are sure. Easy to bend a twig, harder to bend an oak. Reeds will bend but iron will not. Too much bending breaks the bow.

139   Исподтишка кусает лишь злая собака.   *v.* Б211, З135, Н181,234, С223, Т28
         [Only the mean dog bites surreptitiously.] A cur will bite before he barks. The silent dog bites first. *Cf.* A still dog bites sore. *Lat.* cave tibi a cane muto.

140   Испортя гужи, не тужи.   *v.* А29, К59, О4, П27, Ч92
         [Grieve not over a broken cart.] Don't cry over spilt milk. Past cure, past care.

141   Испытай золото огнем, а дружбу деньгами.   *v.* З164
         Gold is tested by fire, men by gold.

142   Испуган (испуганный) зверь далече бежит.   *v.* С290
         [The frightened beast runs farther.] Fear gives wings. *Lat.* Virg.*Aen.*8.224: pedibus timor addidit alas.

143*   Ищи (лови) ветра в поле.   *v.* В132,215, З5, И61
         [You may as well look for (reap) the wind in the field.] *i.e. to see someone (thing) that has gone or disappeared.* You cannot catch the wind in a net. Look for a needle in a haystack. *Cf.* Sow the wind and reap the whirlwind.

144   Ищите и обрящете.   *v.* З48, К246
         *Matt.*7.7: **Seek and ye shall find.**

К

1   **К каше с ложкой первый, а к делу последний. (К обеду - не к делу - все готовы.)**
[First with the spoon, last at work.]   *v.* В122, Л49, Н80, Р4
[All are eager to eat but not to work.] To have two stomachs to eat and one to work.

2*   **К милому семь верст не околица.**   *v.* Г52, Д241, Е30
[Seven miles is not too far to see someone kind.] For a good friend, the journey is never too long. To a friend's house, the trail is never long.

3   **К мягкому воску печать, а юно человеку учение.**
[Education is for the young mind what an imprint is for soft wax.] Learning in one's youth is engraving in stone. Soft wax will take any impression.

4   **К старой брани немного новой ссоры надо(бно).**
[Old disputes require a little new contention.] An old quarrel is easily renewed.
Cf. To add oil to the fire. †Old praise dies unless you feed it.

5   **К чему охота, к тому и смысл.**
[Willingness finds purpose.] We soon believe what we desire. *Cf.* The wish is the father to the thought.

6   **Кабы мужик на печи лежал, корабли бы за море не плыли.**   *v.* А5, Е21
[If the hands slept by the hearth, ships would never sail the seas.] If ifs and ans were pots and pans, there'd be no trade for tinkers.

7*   **Кабы не клин, да не мох, так бы и плотник издох.**
[Were it not for wedges and hedges, how would the carpenter live.] What is a workman without his tools? If things did not break or wear out, how would tradesmen live.

8*   **Кадка меду да капля дегтю.**   *v.* В7, К203, Л98, О148
[A drop of tar can ruin a keg of honey.] One drop of poison infects the whole tun of wine. *Cf.* One ill weed mars a whole pot of porridge.

9   **Кается богатый что один пил а друга не любил.**   *v.* Б62, С42
[The rich man repents that he drank alone and disliked his friend.] Who eats his cock alone must saddle his horse alone.

10* **Каждому своя болезнь (болячка) тяжка.**   *v.* Б311, В657, Н162,202, П300
[Everyone thinks his illness (ailment) most serious.] Every man thinks his own burden the heaviest. *Cf.* Every horse thinks his sack heaviest.

11   **Каждому своя отчина мила и каждому своего жаль.**   *v.* В652, Т38
[Everyone likes his estate best and spares his own.] *Cf.* Every man likes his own thing best. Everyone prefers his own.

12* **Каждый (всяк) (всякий) по-своему с ума сходит (беситится).** *v.* В554, У12
Every man is mad on some point.

13* **Каждый смотрит со своей колокольни.**
[Everyone looks from his own belfry.] As a man is, so he sees.

14 **Кайся, да опять за то не принимайся.**
[Repent but do not repeat.] Who errs and mends, to God himself commends.
Cf. Amendment is repentance.

15* **Как аукнется (кликнется), так и откликнется.** *v.* Д367,369, К66,72,287,Л200, Н4,
[Such call, such echo.] Н21,35,Т14,78, Ч72, У108
One good turn deserves another. Tit for tat. To give as good as one gets. *Cf.* There are
many echoes in the world, but few voices.

16* **Как белка в колесе.** *v.* В256
Like a rat [squirrel] **in a wheel.** *Cf.* Like a dog in a wheel, always moving and never
advancing.

17 **Как бешеная овца головой вертит.**
[Turns his head like a crazed lamb.] Like a chicken without a head. *Cf.* To look like a
dog that lost its tail.

18 **Как блин с сковороды на подхват.** *v.* †Л29
[Like a pancake off the pan on the uptake.] Slow as molasses. *Cf.* Dull (flat) (dead) as
a block (ditchwater).

19* **Как в корове седло.** *v.* Д499, Н384,594
As a saddle becomes a cow (sow).

20 **Как в кремне огонь не виден.** *v.* И7
[As invisible as a flame in flint.] *Cf.* In the coldest flint there is hot fire.

21* **Как в лесе кликнешь, так и откликнется.** *v.* К15

22 **Как в утлое судно воды лить.** *v.* Б157, В128, Р56, Х13
[Like pouring water into a broken vessel.] To pour water into a sieve. To water a stake.
Lat. Plaut.*Pseud.*369: in pertusam ingerimus dicta dolium.

23* **Как волка ни корми, а он все к лесу глядит.** *v.* С138

24* **Как волк носил - никто не видал, а как волка понесли - всяк видит.***v.* К322, М130
[None see the wolf when he takes, but all see when the wolf is taken.] When the ox is
down, many are the butchers. When the tree is fallen, everyone runs to it with his axe.

25 **Как волка в хлев пустить, так он и овец всех переест.**
[Let a wolf in the sheepfold and he'll eat all the sheep.] Wolves rend the sheep when the
shepherds fail. *Lat.* sub molli pastore capit lanam lupus.

26 **Как вчера меня звали, так и меня сегодня зовут.**
[What my name was yesterday is still my name today.] That's my name - ask me again
and I'll tell you the same.

27* **Как деньги есть, так и все есть.** *v.* Д178,180,182
[When there's money, there's everything.] He that has money has what he wants. Money
will do anything.

28   **Как жестоко лук натянешь, то струна скоро порвется.**
        A bow too much bent will break. A bow long bent at last waxes weak. *EA.* arcus tensus rumpitur.

29*   **Как живет (жил), так и умер (слывет).**   *v.* Б377,445, Ж153, С224
        Such a life, such a death.

30*   **Как жить ни тошно, а умирать еще тошней.**
        [However ghastly it is to live, it's more ghastly to die.] Half life is better than dying altogether. *Cf.* None is so old that he hopes not for another year of life.

31   **Как занял, так и плати.**   *v.* Б193, В293
        Pay with the same dish you borrow.

32*   **Как из лука стрела.**
        Straight as an arrow [shot from a bow].

33   **Как качели ни качай, придет время - остановятся.**   *v.* Д371, Е37, Н553, 136, Т19
        [However much you push the swings, the time will come for them to stop.] *Cf.* All good things come to an end.

34   **Как кто ведает, так и обедает.**   *v.* С38, Ч77
        [As you direct, so shall you dine.] *Cf.* As you bake, so shall you eat.

35*   **Как кто постелет, так и выспится. (Как постелишь, так и поспишь.)**   *v.* К81,247
        As you make your bed, so you must lie on it.

36   **Как месяц ни свети, но все не солнца свет.**   *v.* И32, Н525
        [However the moon may shine, it's still not sunlight.] The moon is a moon still, whether it shine or not. *Cf.* Always the bridesmaid and never the bride.

37*   **Как муха к меду.**   *v.* Б394, Г51
        As a fly to honey.

38*   **Как нет, так и не спрашивай.**   *v.* Н377
        [When there isn't any, don't ask.] Seek what may be found. *Cf.* He is the greatest fool who asks for what he can't have.

39*   **Как ни брось кота на землю, а он все упадет на ноги.**   *v.* С309
        He is like a cat, fling him which way you will and he'll light on his legs. *Cf.* A cat has nine lives.

40*   **Как ни вертись собака, а хвост позади.**   *v.* Г21, К319, Л108, П23
        [Whichever way the dog turns, its tail is always behind.] A bird never flies so far that his tail doesn't follow. *Cf.* Let the tail follow the skin. Cut off a dog's tail, and he will be a dog still.

41*   **Как ни гнись, а поясницы не поцелуешь.**   *v.* Б237, Л105
        [However much you bend, you cannot kiss your waistline.] The elbow is near, but try and bite it. *Cf.* As shortly as a horse may lick his ear.

42   **Как ни мудри, а совесть не перемудришь.**   *v.* З143,145
        [Regardless of how you try, you cannot outsmart your conscience.] You cannot hide from your conscience. You can't kid your conscience. *Cf.* Conscience is a cut-throat.

43 **Как окрепнешь - будешь крепче камня, а как опустишься - будешь слабее воды.**
[You may shape up to be harder than rock; but when you let yourself go you are weaker than water.] One extreme follows another. *Cf.* The higher they go, the lower they fall. Climb not too high lest the fall be greater.

44 **Как осел к волынке.**
[Like an ass to bagpipes.] *SPL.* asinus ad lyram.

45* **Как от козла ни шерсти, ни молока.**   *v.* З101, И83, Ч75, Щ7
You go to a goat for wool. Milk a he-goat. *Lat. EA.* de lana caprina. mulgere hircum. *Cf.* You come to the goat's house to beg wool.

46 **Как поживется, так и почет несется.**
[One's honour is on a par with one's life.] A man's best reputation for his future is his record of the past.

47* **Как пришло, так и ушло.**   *v.* Б444,479. В662, Ч80
Easy come, easy go. *SPL.* male parta, male dilabuntur.

48 **Как про тебя сказывали, таков ты и есть.**   *v.* П81
[What is said about you is what you are.] If one, two or three tell you you are an ass, put on a bridle. When all men say you are an ass, it is time to bray.

49 **Как птица родилась, так она и поет.**   *v.* В311
The bird is known by its note.

50* **Как пустую воду ни вари, а навару не дождешься.**   *v.* В368, Г296, С137
[Boil water all you want, but grease will never appear on the top.] Whether you boil snow or pound it, you can have but water of it. *Cf.* To pour water into a bowl and pound it with an iron pestle. *EA.* aquam in mortario tundere. You cook a stone.

51* **Как рыба без воды.**
Like a fish out of water.

52* **Как с быком не биться, а все молоко от него не добиться.**   *v.* Г296, К45,50, С137
[Whatever you do to a bull, you cannot get milk out of it.] No one can give what he hasn't got. *Cf.* If you breed a partridge, you'll get a partridge.

53* **Как с неба упал.**
[As if just fallen from heaven.] As if just landed from the moon (Mars). *Cf.* †He wasn't born yesterday.

54* **Как слепой о красках рассуждает.**   *v.* Х38
[As a blind man conversing about colour.] Blind men can (should) judge no colours. *Lat.* caecus non iudicat de colore.

55* **Как снег на голову.**   *v.* Н361
[Like snow falling on the head] *i.e. suddenly.* Out of the blue.

56* **Как сыр в масле катается.**   *v.* Ж100
[Like cheese afloat on butter.] In clover.

57 **Как тебе верят, так и мерят.**
[You are judged as you are trusted..] *Cf.* To be trusted is a greater compliment than to be loved.

58* Как (кто) тонет - топор сулить, а вытащат - то и топорища жаль. *v.* Т52

59* Как упало так и пропало. *v.* Г74, Д4, И140, С3, Ч100
[Once dropped - gone for good.] For a lost thing, care not.

60 Как (что) хочу, так и ворочу. *v.* Г174, К299, Н485, С75
I do as I please. *Lat.* Juv.*Sat.*6.223: hoc volo, sic iubeo.

61 Какие сани, таковы и сами.
[We are as are our sleighs.] A small pack becomes a small peddlar.

62* Каков батька (отец), таковы у него и детки. *v.* З50
Like father, like son. *SPL.* ad mores natura recurrit.

63 Каков в воспитании, таков и в состоянии. *v.* К190
[Station is commensurate with education.] Education makes the man.

64 Каков в колыбельку, таков и в могилку. *v.* Г250, И86, С35, Ч46, *Ap.*1.27
[As in the cradle, so too in the grave.] What is learned in the cradle lasts to the grave.
SPL. quo semel est imbuta recens servabit odorem testa diu. mors similis vitae.
Cf. Between the cradle and the grave. No change in circumstances will change a defect
in character.

65 Каков в обращике, таков и в куске.
A chip off the old block.

66 Каков дар, таков и поклон. *v.* К15,72
[Such gift, such gratitude.] A small gift usually gets small thanks. *Cf.* A small sum will
serve to pay a small reckoning.

67* Каков игумен, таковы и братья. (Каков пастырь, таковы и овцы.)
(Каков поп, таков и приход.) *v.* З52, И69, Н42
[Like abbott, like brothers.] [Such shepherd, such flock.]
Like priest, like people. *Lat.* qualis rex, talis grex. *SPL.* qualis Hera, talis pedissequa.

68 Каков корабль, таково и плавание. *v.* Б333,336, В243, У82
[Such ship, such sailing.] A great ship asks deep waters.

69* Каков корень, такова и отрасль. *v.* К84, П52, Щ4
[Such root, such branch.] *Cf.* One cannot gather grapes of thorns or figs of thistles.
He who loves the tree, loves the branch.

70 Каков купец, таков и продавец.
[Like buyer, like seller.] *Cf.* †There are more foolish buyers than foolish sellers.

71 Каков обиход, таков и расход. *v.* Д221,226, П51, У38
You don't get more out of a thing than you put into it. You get what you pay for.

72* Каков привет, таков и ответ. *v.* К15,21,66, Н4,21,35, Я16
As you salute, you will be saluted. Such answer as a man gives, such will he get.

73* Каков разум, таковы и речи (таков ум). *v.* Б399, К92
Speech is the picture of the mind. *SPL.* qualis vir, talis oratio.

74* Каков сам, таковы к тебе и люди. *v.* Д434, Л177, Н315, Т80, Ч11
[As you are, so are others towards you.] Do as you would be done by.

75   **Каков у дела, таков у хлеба.**   *v.* Б380, В396, Д12, Л39, Р7
[As you work, so you eat.] *Cf.* If you won't work you shan't eat. A swift eater, a swift worker.

76   **Каков царь, такова и орда.**
Such a king (prince), such a people. *Lat.* talis rex, talis grex.

77* **Какова глаза, такова и природа.**   *v.* Г118
The eyes are the window of the soul.

78* **Какова жена, таков и муж.**   *v.* Ж80, Х90
[Such wife, such husband.] A good wife makes a good husband.

79* **Какова зима, таково и лето.**   *v.* Л59
[Such winter, such summer.] A good winter brings a good summer.

80* **Какова мать таковы и дочери.**   *v.* К84,91, У21
Like mother, like daughter.

81* **Какова постель, таков и сон.** *v.* К35

82   **Какова сестра, таков и брат.**
[Like sister, like brother.] *Cf.* Blood will tell.

83   **Какова смерть, таковы и похороны.**
[Such a death, such a funeral.] *Cf.* Such a life, such a death.

84* **Какова яблоня, таков и плод (таковы и отростки).**
Каково дерево, такова и отрасль (таковы и сучья).   *v.* И109, К69, М95
[Such apple-tree, such fruit.] [Such tree, such branches (roots).] No good apple on a sour stock. The apple never falls far from the tree. *Cf.* The fruit of a good tree is also good.

85   **Каково время, так и поступай.**
[Act in step with the times.] One should be compliant with the times. One must move with the times. *Lat.* tempori parendum. Cic.*Fam.*9.7.1: tempori serviendum est.

86   **Каково дело, таков и суд.**   *v.* П104, Ч40
A clear case brings the right verdict with it. *Lat.* P.Syr. manifesta causa secum habet sententiam. Like fault, like punishment.

87   **Каково лукошко, таково ему и покрышка.**   *v.* Н22,39, П49
Like (such) cup, like (such) cover. Every pot has its cover. There's a lid for every pot.

88* **Каково посеешь, таково и пожнешь.**   *v.* В160, Г60, Ж167, К287,318, П73,192, Ч97
Galatians 6:7. **As you sow, so you reap.** *Cf.* Cic.: ut sementem feceris, ita et metes.

89* **Каково семя, таков и плод.**   *v.* И109, К69,84, О127,167, П52, Щ4
[Such seed, such fruit.] Of evil grain, no good seed can come. Ill seed, ill weed.

90   **Каковы веки, таковы и человеки.**   *v.* Д429, Н391
[Such times, such people.] Different times, different manners. *Gr.* ἀλλοτ'ἀλλοῖα φρόνει. *Cf.* Times change and we change with them. *Lat.* tempora mutantur nos et mutamur in illis.

91   **Каковы дядки, таковы дитятки.**   *v.* К80, У21
Parents are patterns.

92 **Каковы свойства, таковы и речи.** *v.* Б399, К73
As the man is, so is his talk. Sen.*Lucil.*20: qualis vir, talis oratio. *Cf.* Speech is the picture (index) (mirror) of the mind (soul). *Lat.* index (imago) est animi sermo.

93 **Калач в руки а камень в зубы.** *v.* В345, К171
[It's a cake in the hand but hard as a rock on the teeth.] *i.e. failed.* All our cakes are dough. *Cf.* He asked for bread and he received a stone.

94 **Калач скоро приестся, а хлеб никогда.** *v.* Б440, И30
[One tires of pastry quickly, but of bread never.] *Cf.* Custom takes the taste from the most savoury dishes.

95 **Калач хлебу не замена.**
[Cake is no substitute for bread.] Lacking bread, tarts are good. *Cf.*You give me bread for cake. A good pie wants no bread. Give a bit of your cake to one who's going to eat pie.

96 **Камень за пазухой держать.** *v.* М214
[Keep a stone up your sleeve.] *Cf.* Keep the staff in your own hand. Speak softly and carry a big stick.

97* **Камень на гору тащится, а вниз сам свалится.**
[A stone carried uphill may roll down by itself.] *Cf.* Stone of Sisyphus. To roll the stone. *Lat.* saxum volvere. The man who flings a stone up a mountainside may have it rolled back upon himself.

98* **Капля по капле и камень долбит.** *v.* В363,473, Д513, Т25,27
Constant dripping wears away the stone. *Gr.* σταγόνες γὰρ ὕδατος πέτρας κοιλαίνουσιν. *Lat.* assidua stilla saxum excavat. Ov.*Epist.Pont.*4.10.5: gutta cavat lapidem.

99* **Каша мать наша.** *v.* Щ5
[*Kasha* is our mother.] *Cf.* Bread is the staff of life.

100 **Кашевар живет сытее князя.** *v.* П88
[The cook lives more sated than the prince.] Millers are the last to die of famine. *Cf.* The parson always christens his own child first.

101 **Каши нет - щей больше лей.** *v.* Б453, Е53
[When there's no *kasha*, pour more soup.] They that have no other meat, gladly bread and butter eat. *Cf.* What we lose in the hake we shall have in the herring. It is better to have bread left over than to run out of wine.

102* **Кашу маслом не испортишь.** *v.* С18
[Butter only improves *kasha*.] You can never have too much of a good thing. *Cf.* Boil stones in butter and you may sup the broth. Butter is good for anything but to stop an oven. Anything is good with strawberries and cream.

103 **Кисель зубов не портит (ноги подъел).**
[Jelly won't spoil your teeth.] *Cf.* †Sweet things are bad for your teeth.

104* **Клади в мешок - после разберешь.**
[Bag it first and sort it later.] Shoot first and ask questions later.

105 **Клевета что уголь - не обожжет, так замарает.** *v.* †Б356
Slander [like coal], leaves a score (scar) behind it. *Lat.* calumniare audacter, aliquid adhaeberit. Fling enough dirt and some will stick.

106* **Клин (кол) клином (колом) выбивают (вышибается).** *v.* А13, З122, Л80, Ч43
[A wedge (stake) is used to drive out another wedge (stake).] One nail (peg) drives out another. *Lat.* clavum clavo ejiciendum. *Lat.* Cic. cuneus cuneum trudit. *Gr.* Ar.*Pol.*5.2.3: ἥλῳ ὁ ἧλος. *Cf.* Fight fire with fire. Set a thief to catch a thief.

107 **Ключ сильнее замка.** *v.* Т58
[The key is mightier than the lock.] There's a key for every lock. *Cf.* A silver key can open an iron lock.

108* **Книга в счастье украшает, а в несчастье утешает.**
[A book entertains in good times and consoles in bad.] Books are not seldom talismans and spells. *Cf.* Literature is a good staff but a bad crutch. A book is like a garden carried in the pocket. Books are friends that never fail.

109 **Книги имеют свою судьбу.**
Books have their own destiny. *Lat.* Varro 3.258: habent sua fata libelli.

110* **Книги не говорят, а правду сказывают.**
[Books are silent yet speak the truth.] Books will speak plain. *Cf.* Good books are friends who are always ready to talk to us. Books speak to the mind. The pen is the tongue of the hand.

111 **Книги читать - зря (зла) не плутать.**
[Read books and cease straying pointlessly.] *Cf.* Books are doors to wide new ways. Something is learned every time a book is opened.

112 **Ко времю гость не в убыток.**
[He is not an ill guest that is on time.] He that is welcome fares well.

113 **Кобыла с волком (медведем) тягалась, только хвост да грива осталась.**
[The mare contended with the wolf (bear), nothing but its tail and mane was left.] The strong and weak cannot keep company.

114 **Кобылка мала а седлу место будет.**
[Even a small mare has room for a saddle.] A short horse is soon curried. Many a shabby colt makes a fine horse.

115 **Когда в хвосте начало, то в голове мочало.** *v.* Л56
[If you begin with the tail, there's something wrong with your head.] Begin at the beginning, not the end. *Cf.* Don't be down on something before you're up on it.

116 **Когда гремит оружие, музы молчат.**
When weapons speak, the muses are silent. *Lat.* Inter arma silent musae.

117 **Когда деньги занимает, тогда всегда у меня бывает - а заплатить, кругом обходит.**
(Когда занимает - сокольи очи имеет, а заплатить - и вороньих нет.) *v.* Б192,474,
[Always there to borrow but never around to pay.] Б31,71, Д79, С164
[The eyes of a falcon to borrow, not even those of a crow to pay.] *Cf.* Everyone fastens where there is gain. Some are always giving, others are always taking. First at a feast and last at a fight.

118* **Когда есть, так густо, а нет так пусто.** *v.* Б418, М63, Н408, С86
[Either too much or too little.] It's either a feast or a famine. When it rains, it pours.

119 **Когда женишься скорее, так в доме будет спорее.** *v.* В13,294, Ж70, Р34
Marry in haste and repent at leisure. *Cf.* He that has a wife has strife.

120 **Когда жену будешь иметь, не станешь на других смотреть.** *v.* Б443
[When you marry, you cease to look at others.] *Cf.* A married man turns his staff into a stake. A reformed rake makes the best husband.

121 **Когда жене спускать, так в чужих домах ее искать.**
[He who pardons his wife, must look for her in others' homes.] *Cf.* Who lets his horse drink at every lake and his wife go to every wake, shall never be without a whore and a jade. Who loves his wife should watch her.

122 **Когда захотят бить, так и в степи палку сыщут.** *v.* Б454, Г302, С109
[Who would inflict a beating, even in the steppe shall find a rod.] It is easy to find a stick to beat a dog.

123 **Когда зло кто похочет делать, слуга всегда ему бывает.**
Who would do ill, ne'er wants [helpers] **occasion.**

124* **Когда идешь на драку, волос не жалей.** *v.* В38, П304
[When off to fight, forget about your hair.] Never wear your best trousers when you go out to fight. *Cf.* Only a witless person expects a blacksmith to wear a white silk apron.

125* **Когда идешь с хромым, то поджимай ноги.** *v.* П106
He that dwells next door to a cripple, will learn to halt. Associate with cripples and you learn to halt.

126 **Когда изба без запору, и свинья в нее бродит.** *v.* В98
[When the house has no fence, even a pig may wander in.] At open doors dogs come in.

127* **Когда кошки грызутся, тогда мышам приволье.** *v.* Б72, Г63, Д85
[While the cats quarrel, the mice will play.] *Cf.* Hatred with friends is succour to foes. Two dogs strive for a bone, and a third runs away with it. When thieves fall out, honest men get their due.

128* **Когда меня любишь, и мою собачку люби.** *v.* Б378, К229,254
Love me, love my dog. *Lat.* qui me amat, amat et canem meum.

129* **Когда не видишь дна, не ходи через воду.** *v.* Н310
[Don't cross the waters when you can't see bottom.] Cross the stream where it is ebbest. Do not wade in unknown waters.

130 **Когда не найдешь в себе, не найдешь в других.**
[Don't look to others for what you can't find in yourself.] Be that which you would make others. *Cf.* If you wish to see the best of others, show the best of yourself. Expect to be treated as you have treated others. He finds fault with others and does worse himself.

131 **Когда нет раба, сам поезжай по дрова.** *v.* Н313

132* **Когда пирог с грибами, так все с руками.** *v.* Б372,428,429, Е42, Н64, Х23
[When there's mushroom pie, all come with hands outstretched.] Feast and your halls are crowded. *Cf.* Trencher friends are seldom good neighbours.

133 **Когда поидешь лихому служить, всегда будешь тужить.** *v.* В488
[Serve a wicked master and grieve.] *Cf.* Many a man serves a thankless master.

134 **Когда придет тревога, по неволе ухватишься за Бога.** *v.* Г327, Т52
[When misfortunes descend, one unwittingly calls to God.] When it thunders, the thief becomes honest. *Cf.* He who is always praying has a dangerous life.

135 **Когда станешь пахать, будешь и богат.**
[You'll become rich when you begin to plough.] By labour comes wealth. *Cf.* Plough deep while sluggards sleep, and you'll have corn to sell and to keep.

136 **Когда судью подаришь, то всех победишь.** *v.* Н370, С304
[Give to the judge and take all.] *Cf.* Who greases his way travels easily. When you buy judges, someone sells justice.

137 **Когда хочешь себе добра, то никому не делай худа.** *v.* Д118,263, К233,289, Х72
Do well and fare well.

138* **Когда черт не сможет чего сделать, посылает бабу.** *v.* Г6
When the devil can't go, he sends his grandmother. Where the devil cannot come, he will send [a woman].

139 **Кого боятся, того не могут любить (того и почитают).** *v.* В575
[He that is feared cannot be loved (is respected).] He that fears you present will hate you absent. *Cf.* Fear is stronger than love.

140* **Кого любят, того и бьют (больше наказывают).** *v.* К212,248
We often hurt those whom we love. You always hurt the one you love. *SPL.* quos pater aetherius coelisti destinet aulae, hos gemitu ac damno suppliisque premit.

141 **Кого седина украшает, того больше бес уловляет.** *v.* С267
There's no fool like an old fool.

142* **Кого хочет Бог наказать, у того отнимает разум.**
When God will punish, he will first take away the understanding. *Lat.* quos deus vult perdere, prius dementat. stultum facit fortuna quem vult perdere.

143* **Коготок увяз - всей птички пропасть.** *v.* И41, М13
[One claw snared and the bird is lost.] To come from little good to stark nought. A little stone in the way overturns a great wain. Small leaks sink big ships. Little rogues easily become great ones. *Cf.* Submitting to one wrong brings on another.

144* **Коза бела, коза сера, а все один дух.** *v.* Н236, 570
[A goat may be white or grey, but the smell is the same.] All cats are alike grey (black) in the night.

145 **Коза на горе выше коровы в поле.**
[A goat on a hill stands taller than a cow in a valley.] *Cf.* While the tall maid is stooping, the little one hath swept the house.

146* **Коза сыта а капуста цела.** *v.* В397, И12, Н138
[The goat is sated and the cabbage is intact.] To have both the egg and the hen.
Cf. Neither pot broken nor water spilt.

147* **Козла бойся спереди, коня сзади, а (злого) человека со всех сторон.** *v.* О168
[Take heed of he-goats before, of steeds behind, and of (evil) men from all sides.] Take heed of an ox before, of a horse behind, and a monk on all sides.

148 **Колесо фортуны вертится быстрее мельничнего.** *v.* С324
[The wheel of fortune spins faster than a windmill.] The wheel of fortune is forever in motion. *Cf.* The highest spoke in Fortune's wheel may soon turn lowest. Fortune is fickle.

149 **Коли есть родня, есть с ней и возня.**
[Where there's kin, there are problems.] A lot of relatives, a lot of trouble.

150 **Коли народ согрешит, царь умолит - а коли царь согрешит, народ не умолит.**
[If the people err, the *tsar* pardons, but when the *tsar* errs, the people do not.]
Cf. Take heed of the wrath of a mighty man and the tumult of the people.

151 **Коли не умеешь начальствовать, умей слышать.** *v.* К276,304
[If you don't know how to command, know how to follow orders.] *Cf.* He is not fit to command others that cannot command himself. If you wish to command, learn to obey.

152 **Коли нет сапогов, так и лапти в честь.** *v.* В448,498, З363, И32, Н3
[If you lack boots, make do with sandals.] He that may not do as he would, must do as he may.

153 **Коли хорош, так не хвались - тебя и так заметят.** *v.* С44
[If you're good, don't boast - you'll be noticed just the same.] Neither praise nor dispraise thyself, thy actions serve the turn.

154 **Коли хочешь (кому хочется) много знать, (тому) не надо много спать.** *v.* К262
[If you want to know much, you must sleep little.] Too much bed makes a dull head. Genius is an infinite capacity for taking pains. *Cf.* Sloth wears out the body while it corrodes the mind.

155 **Комар комару ногу не отдавит.** *v.* Б240, В389,435, И21, С221
[Mosquito treads not upon mosquito.] *Cf.* Dog does not eat dog. Hawks will not pick out hawks' eyes. A crow will not pick out the eye of another crow.

156* **Комар носу не подточит.**
Clean as a whistle.

157 **Кому беда горе, другим беда нажив.** *v.* Б11, В410, Г69,84, И133, О43, *Ap.*1.23
One man's fortune is another's misfortune.

158 **Кому Бог даст чин, тому даст и ум.** *v.* Д34
To whom God gives the task, he gives the wit.

159 **Кому Бог поможет, тот все переможет.**
Where God will help, nothing does harm. *Cf.* The tree that God plants, no winds can hurt it.

160* **Кому быть повешенному, тот не утонет.** *v.* Р62
He that is born to be hanged, shall never be drowned.

161* **Кому какое дело, что кума с кумом сидела.** *v.* Н459
[Whose business is it that the godmother and godfather got together?] Everybody's business is nobody's business.

162 **Кому счастье служит, тот ни о чем не тужит.** *v.* В145, С307, Т65
He dances well to whom fortune pipes.

163* **Конец дело венчает (хвалит). (Конец всему делу венец).** *v.* В245
The end crowns the work. *Lat.* finis coronat opus.

164* **Конь конем покупают.** *v.* Д173
[He that has a horse may buy a horse.] He that has a goose, will get a goose. *Cf.* Have a horse of your own and you may borrow another. Money makes money.

165* **Конь на (о) четырех ногах - и то спотыкается.**   *v.* Б117, Д396, Ж102, И35, *Ар.*1.36
[The horse has four legs and still stumbles.] It is a good horse that never stumbles.

166* **Конь над (через) силу не прянет (скачет) (ступит).**
[A horse cannot trot beyond its strength.] You may break a horse's back, be he never so strong. *Cf.* An ass endures his burden, but not more than his burden.

167 **Копейка к копейке - проживется и семейка.**   *v.* Б70, Г331
Penny and penny laid up will be many [will feed a family].

168* **Копейка рубль бережет.**   *v.* Б70, Д164
Take care of the pennies and the pounds will take care of themselves.

169* **Корень учения горек, а плод сладок.**
Knowledge has bitter roots but sweet fruits.

170 **Корми меня весной, а осенью сам сыт буду.**
[Feed me in spring and I'll feed myself in autumn.] *Cf.* Give me a child for the first seven years and you may do what you like with him afterwards.

171 **Кормил калачом, да в спину кирпичом.**   *v.* В345, З130, К93, Н92,122, С246
[Offered me cake to my face but a brick behind the back.] *Cf.* You show bread in one hand and a stone in the other. *Lat.* Plaut.*Aul.*195: altera manu fert lapidem, altera ostendit panem. He has honey in the mouth and a razor at the girdle.

172* **Корм коня дороже.**   *v.* В545, И66, О25, П291
[The feed is costlier than the horse.] A white elephant. *Cf.* It is a poor dog that is not worth the whistling. †A good horse is worth its fodder.

173* **Корова черна, да молоко у ней бело.**   *v.* Б173, М208
[A cow may be black but its milk is white.] A black hen lays a white egg.

174 **Король царствует, но не управляет.**
The king reigns but does not govern. *Lat.* rex regnat sed non gubernat.

175* **Короткий счет - длинная дружба.**   *v.* Б225, Д44, С332, Ч10
Short reckonings make long friends.

176 **Коротко да ясно, оттого и прекрасно.**   *v.* Г176, Р47
Short and sweet. Few words are best.

177* **Короче отруби, легче понесешь.**   *v.* И91, Т85, Ч96
[Cut shorter and carry easily.] *Cf.* Take no more on you than you're able to bear.

178 **Короче птичьего носа.**
[Smaller than a bird's beak.] As small as a wand.

179* **Коса - девичья краса.**   *v.* П59
[A maiden's beauty is in her braid.] A woman's hair is her crowning glory.

180* **Коси коса пока роса (+ роса долой и мы домой).**   *v.* В30, С252
Make hay while the sun shines.

181* **Кот охотник до рыбы, да воды боится.**   *v.* И71, Л45, Н376, Ч107
The cat would eat fish and would not wet her feet. *Lat.* catus amat pisces, sed non vult tingere plantam.

182*   **Которая беда на деньги пошла, то не беда.**   *v.* Д158
[Any problem resolved with money is not a problem.] Money can't buy happiness, but it can go a long way in helping you. Rather a man without money than money without a man. *Cf.* Money lost, nothing lost; courage lost, much lost; honour lost, more lost; soul lost, all lost. Health without money is half an ague.

183   **Которая корова умерла, та и к удою была добра.** *v.* Т2

184*   **Которая лошадь больше везет, на ту больше и наваливают.**   *v.* В206, К218, Р54
All lay load on the willing horse.

185   **Которая птичка раненько запела, той во весь день молчать.**
[The bird that sings early, remains quiet the rest of the day.] *Cf.* An hour in the morning is worth two in the evening.

186*   **Кошке игрушки, а мышки слезки.**   *v.* Б11, В71,210,211,218, П4, О62,76, С310
[Toys for a cat, tears for a mouse.] What's good for one may be bad for another. It is no play where one weeps and another laughs. The pleasures of the mighty are the tears of the poor. The humble suffer from the folly of the great.

187*   **Кошку в мешке не покупают.**   *v.* Д124, 334,85, Н381, Ч70
One doesn't buy a pig [cat] **in a poke.** *Cf.* Never buy anything before you see it.

188   **Краденое богатство исчезает как лед тает.**   *v.* З121, Н513, Т49, Х96, Ч127
[Stolen wealth disappears like melting ice.] Stolen goods never thrive. Ill-gotten goods never prosper. Ill-gotten gain is no gain at all.

189   **Красивый вид человека не портит.**
[Good looks don't hurt.] Fair faces go places. *Cf.* A good face is a letter of recommendation. Beauty is a good letter of introduction. A kind face needs no bond. Merit in appearance is more often rewarded than merit itself.

190   **Красна птица перьем, а человек ученьем.**   *v.* К63
[Feathers decorate a bird, but knowledge adorns the man.] *Cf.* Education polishes good natures, correcteth bad ones.

191   **Красна ягодка, да на вкус горька.**   *v.* В316, Н143,237
[The berry is pretty but its taste bitter.] *Cf.* What is sweet in the mouth is oft bitter in the stomach. †The blacker (darker) the berry, the sweeter the juice.

192   **Красно говорит, а слушать нечего.**   *v.* Б329, Г181,184, М124, Р25
[Speaks well but says nothing.] He who gives you fair words, feeds you with an empty spoon.

193   **Красный день познавается с утра.**
You can tell the day by the morning. *Cf.* Blustering night, fair day.

194   **Красота и глупость часто бывают купно.**   *v.* В617
Beauty and folly go often in company (are old companions).

195   **Красота разума не придаст.**   *v.* Р65
[Beauty will not impart intelligence.] Beauty has no brains.

196*   **Красота без разума пуста.**   *v.* Л85, С51,210,211
[Beauty without wit is barren.] *Cf.* A fair face is half a portion. Beauty's only skin deep. One can't live on beauty alone.

197 **Краткость - сестра таланта.**
[Brevity is the sister of talent.] Brevity is the soul of wit.

198 **Крепка тюрьма, да ее не хвалят (да кто ей рад) (да кто в нее пойдет).** *v.* B237
[Prisons are secure, but none praise them (who likes them)(who goes there).] *Cf.* No love is foul nor prison fair.

199* **Крестом любви не свяжешь.** *v.* И105, М92, Н145, С113
Love cannot be compelled. *Cf.* Love is free.

200 **Криво рак выступает, да иначе не знает.** *v.* И86, С130
You cannot make a crab walk straight.

201 **Кривого (кривое) кривым не исправишь.** *v.* B124, Г311, З131, И81
Two wrongs do not make a right.

202 **Кривое дерево в сук растет.** *v.* М19
Timely crooks the tree, that will good cammock be.

203 **Кривое окно и фасад портит.** *v.* B7, К8, Л98, О54,148, Ш3
[One crooked window spoils an entire facade.] *Cf.* The rotten apple injures its neighbours. One scabbed sheep will mar a whole flock. One ill weed will mar a whole pot of pottage.

204* **Кривы дрова, да прямо горят.** *v.* Б404, Г126, Д411, И23, К204, С287, У75
Crooked logs make straight fires.

205 **Кривым глазом и прямое криво.** *v.* B58,419,425, З116, Н37
[To a crooked eye the straight appears crooked.] A straight stick is crooked in the water. The thief thinks that everyone else is a thief.

206* **Криком ничего не сделаешь (изба не рубится).** *v.* Б313, П208, Х103, Ш13
[Shouting never accomplished anything.] Those who are right need not talk loudly. Striking manners are bad manners. *Cf.* Some people think that the louder they shout, the more persuasive their argument is. Subtlety is better than force.

207 **Кричит целый век, а толку нет.** *v.* Б335, B118,224,319, Г181, М124, Р25
Many speak much who cannot speak well. Great cry and little wool [sense].

208 **Кровь водой не бывает.**
Blood is thicker than water.

209 **Крой кафтан, а к старому примеривай. (Кроят платье, к старому примеривая.)**
[Pattern the new suit (dress) on the old.] Cut your coat *v.* П65, Р76
according to your cloth.

210* **Круглое - катать, плоское - таскать.**
[Roll what's round, stack what's flat.] *said of menial, easy work.* Monkey see, monkey do.

211 **Кстати и поп пляшет.** *v.* B554, У12
[Even the priest dances on occasion.] Every man is mad on some point. Every man has his delight.

212* **Кто больно сечет, тот нежно любит.** *v.* К140,248
[He who strikes painfully, loves tenderly.] We always hurt the ones we love. *Cf.* The quarrel of lovers is the renewal of love.

213* **Кто в кони пошел, тот и воду вози.**   *v.* В291, Н133, П201
[If you go for horses, be prepared to carry water.] If you don't like the heat, stay out of the kitchen. If you don't like my gate, don't swing on it.

214* **Кто в море бывал, тот лужи не боится.**
[He who has been at sea does not fear a puddle.] Live too near the wood to be frightened by owls.

215* **Кто в нужде не бывал, тот ее и не видал.**   *v.* В409, К280, Ч76
[He knows not what want who hasn't experienced it.] We never know the worth of water till the well is dry. *Cf.* No man better knows what good is than he who has endured evil.

216 **Кто в радости живет, того и кручина не берет.**
A man of gladness seldom falls into madness.

217* **Кто везде, тот нигде.**   *v.* К260, М121
[He who is everywhere, is nowhere.] He who begins many things finishes but few.

218 **Кто везет, того и погоняют.**   *v.* В206, К184, Р54
[He who drives is driven.] All lay load on the willing horse.

219 **Кто венец надевает, тот его и снимает.**   *v.* Т83
[He who dons the crown must take it off.] *Cf.* Uneasy lies the head that dons the crown.

220* **Кто вору потакает, тот сам вор.**   *v.* В429, Н168,456
[He who abets a thief is a thief himself.] The receiver is as bad as a thief.

221 **Кто всегда бережется, тот никогда не ожжется.**   *v.* Б183, О112,141, Р33
[He who is always cautious will never be burnt.] The cautious seldom cry. *Cf.* Caution is the parent of safety. Prevention is better than cure.

222 **Кто всего хочет, тот ничего не достанет.**   *v.* В522, З4, М132
All covet, all lose. *Cf.* Grasp all, lose all.

223 **Кто встал раньше, (тот) ушел (по)дальше.**   *v.* Р35
[He who rises early goes farther.] He who rises early makes progress in his work. *Cf.* The early bird catches the worm.

224* **Кто вчера соврал (солгал), тому и завтра не поверят.**   *v.* В453,666,
(Кто говорит иногда ложно, тому никогда верить не можно.)   Л64, С215
He that once deceives, is ever suspected. A liar is not believed when he speaks the truth.

225* **Кто где родился, тот там и пригодился.**   *v.* М6, Ч25
There is no man born into the world whose work is not born with him. *Cf.* Be useful where you live. We are not born for ourselves. It is a fine thing to make oneself needed. Everyone has his lot and a wide world before.

226* **Кто говорит что хочет, услышит чего не хочет.**
He who says what he likes, shall hear what he does not like. *Lat.* Ter.*And.*5.4: qui quae vult dicit, quae non vult audiet. S.Hieronym. cum dixeris quae vis, quae non vis audies.

227 **Кто голоден никогда не скажет что хлеб худ.**   *v.* Б383, Г231, *Ap.*1.91
Hunger never saw bad bread. Hunger finds no fault with the cookery.

228 **Кто голоден, тот и холоден.**
[A hungry man is also a cold man.] A hungry man is an angry man.

229 **Кто гостю рад, тот и собачку его накормит.**   *v.* Б378, К128,254
[The welcome guest's dog is also fed.] *Cf.* Love me, love my dog.

230 **Кто гостям рад, тот будет прежде сам пьян.**
[The convivial host gets drunk first.] Choose your company before your drink. *Cf.* A merry host makes merry guests.

231 **Кто дела не знает, напрасно о нем рассуждает.**
[Judge not what you do not know.] The quickest way to show ignorance is to talk about something you know nothing about. It's profound ignorance that inspires a dogmatic tone.

232 **Кто делает все на авось, у того все хоть брось.**   *v.* А5,6
Every may be has a may not be.

233 **Кто доброе творит, того зло не вредит (Бог наградит).**   *v.* Д118, К137,289, Х72
[He who does good suffers no evil.] *Cf.* Do well and have well.

234 **Кто друг прямой, тот брат родной.**   *v.* Б63,229, Д336,450
A good friend is my nearest relation [true brother].

235 **Кто едет скоро, тому в дороге не споро.**   *v.* С155, Ч102
[Who travels fast, misses out.] The hasty leaps over his opportunities.

236 **Кто живет тихо, тот не увидит лиха.**   *v.* Д129, Е5
Soft pace goes far. Slow but sure wins the race.

237 **Кто за правду стоит смело, тот совершит дело.**   *v.* М188
[He who is bold in a true cause, succeeds.] *Cf.* Courage is the foundation of victory. Courage conquers all things. He who hesitates is lost.

238 **Кто за худым пойдет, тот добра не найдет.**   *v.* Б377, 328, Л76, О177
He that seeks trouble never misses. *Cf.* He that has to do with what is foul, never comes away clean.

239 **Кто за чем ходит, то и знает.**   *v.* Д347
Pursuits become habits.

240 **Кто заспесивеет, тот скоро оплешивеет.**
[The conceited soon grow bald.] Conceited goods are quickly spent. *Cf.* †Conceit grows as natural as the hair on one's head but is longer in coming out.

241 **Кто зла отлучится, тот никого не боится.**   *v.* В335, Д276, П216
[Who departs from evil, fears no one.] Truth fears no trial.

242 **Кто злую жену получит, тот всю жизнь свою погубит.**
An ill marriage is a spring of ill fortune. *Cf.* Marriage makes or mars a man. The day you marry it's kill or cure.

243* **Кто злым попускает, тот сам зло творит.**   *v.* Д277,352
He that helps evil hurts the good. *Lat.* P.Syr. bonis nocet, quisquis pepercerit malis.

244 **Кто играет подбором, тот ходит по дворам.**
[Who cannot make up his mind, roams much.] Between two stools, one falls to the ground. *Cf.* Who seeks a faultless friend, remains friendless.

245 **Кто имеет жену красную и лошадь хорошую, всегда не без мысли бывает.** *v.* Н212
He that has a white [good] **horse and a fair wife, never wants trouble.**

246 **Кто ищет (бежит), тот и найдет (догоняет).** *v.* З48, И144
[He who seeks (runs), finds (catches up).] *Cf. Matthew* 7.7: Seek and ye shall find.

247 **Кто какой работы горазд, тот тем и кормится.** *v.* О189
One's own will is good food. *Cf.* All things are easy that are done willingly. A will of your own will help you succeed better than the will of a rich relative.

248 **Кто кого любит, тот того и наказывает (бьет) (лупит) (слушает).** *v.* К140,212
[One punishes (chastens)(beats)(heeds) one's beloved.] We often hurt the ones we love. *Cf.* The course of true love never did run smooth.

249 **Кто кого сможет, тот того и гложет (в бок).** *v.* Б314, М55, Р89
[Those who can, tread on the next man.] Big fish eat little fish. *Gr.* Diod.Sic. ὁ πλεῖον δυνάμενος, τὸν ἀσθενέστερον κατισχύει. *Cf.* The little cannot be great unless he devour many.

250* **Кто кому миленек, не умывшись беленек.** *v.* Л193
[One's beloved appears clean even unwashed.] *Cf.* In the eyes of the lover, pock-marks are dimples. Blind love mistakes a harelip for a dimple. Love is blind.

251 **Кто лжет, тот и крадет.** *v.* Б97, Г49
He that will lie, will steal.

252 **Кто ленив, тот и соплив.** *v.* Б152, Д256, Л43
Idle folks lack no excuses.

253* **Кто любит попа, кто попадью, а кто попову дочку.** *v.* И128

254 **Кто любит попа, тот ласкает и попову собаку.** *v.* Б378, К128,229
[If you like the priest, be nice to his dog.] He that loves the tree, loves the branch. *Cf.* Love me, love my dog.

255 **Кто людей веселит, за того весь свет стоит.** *v.* В123,318
[All the world loves an entertainer.] Laugh and the world laughs with you, cry and you cry alone. *Cf.* All the world loves a lover.

256* **Кто малым не доволен, тот большого не достоин.** *v.* Г281, Н221,363
[He that is not content with little, does not deserve much.] *Cf.* He that cannot abide in a bad market, deserves not a good one. He deserves not sweet that will not taste of sour.

257 **Кто меньше толкует, тот меньше тоскует.**
Least said soonest mended. *SPL.* silentii tuta praemia.

258 **Кто много божится, тому меньше верят.** *v.* Г44, З55,95
[He that swears much is believed less.] He that will swear will lie.

259* **Кто много грозит, тот мало вредит.** *v.* В286, Г328, Н227,431
[He that threatens much, harms little.] Great barkers are no biters. *Cf.* Long mint, little dint. There are more men threatened than stricken. Threatened folks live long.

260* **Кто много зачинает, мало оканчивает.** *v.* К217, М121, С103
He who begins many things, finishes but few.

261*   Кто много обещает, тот мало дает.   *v.* Б335, В319
          He that promises much, means nothing.

262   Кто много спит, тому денег не скопить.   *v.* К154, М133
          [He who sleeps much will never have money.] *Cf.* He who sleeps all the morning, may go a begging all the day after. Long sleep makes a bare back.

263*   Кто много учен, тот редко умен.   *v.* В53, И108
          [The learned man is rarely wise.] Great scholars are not the shrewdest men. *Cf.* The greatest clerks are not the wisest men. Wisdom doesn't always speak in Greek and Latin. A mere scholar, a mere ass.

264   Кто много целует, редко не укусит.
          [He who kisses much, seldom will not bite.] Many kiss the hand they wish cut off. Many are betrayed with a kiss.

265*   Кто молиться не умеет, тот пойди на море.   *v.* В519, Д45, Е11
          He that would learn to pray, let him go to sea. *SPL.* orare qui nescit, navigare discat.

266*   Кто на кого похож, тот с тем и схож.   *v.* В620, М164, Н418, П109, Р9, С66, Т7, *Ap.*1.5
          Like will to like. Birds of a feather flock together.

267*   Кто на облака поглядывает часто, тот никогда в дорогу не поедет.   *v.* Е10
          [He that pries into every cloud, never sets out.] He that forecasts all perils will never sail the sea. *Cf.* He that pries into every cloud may be stricken with a thunderbolt.

268   Кто находит, тот и теряет.   *v.* Д400, Л179
          [He who finds also loses.] Those that have must lose. *Cf.* You win some, you lose some.

269   Кто не богат, тот и алтыну рад.   *v.* С314
          [The poor man is content with a three-kopek piece.] Poor folk are fain of little. *Cf.* Poor folks are glad of porridge. It's better to have a little than nothing. He enjoys much who is thankful for little.

270*   Кто не видал церкви, тот и печи молится.   *v.* К279, С50
          [He who has never seen a church, prays at his hearth.] *Cf.* Acorns were good until bread was found. He that never ate flesh thinks pudding a dainty.

271   Кто не ел чесноку, тот и не воняет.   *v.* Г332, О81
          [He who has not eaten garlic, doesn't smell.] *Cf.* He that touches pitch shall be defiled. Garlic makes a man wink, drink and stink. They smell best who smell least.

272   Кто не желает власти, на того не приходят и напасти.
          Far from court, far from care.

273*   Кто не играет, тот не выигрывает.   *v.* Б18,80, Д73
          [He who does not play, cannot win.] A card which never appears neither wins nor loses. *Cf.* Nothing ventured, nothing gained. A game's not won till it's been played.

274*   Кто не с нами, тот против нас.
          Whoever is not with us is against us.

275   Кто не слушает советов, тому не чем помочь.
          He that will not be counselled, cannot be helped. *SPL.* consilia bona, si nemo pareat, in usu non sunt.

276   **Кто не умеет повиноваться, тот не умеет повелевать.**   *v.* K151,304
      No man can be a good ruler, unless he has first been ruled. *Gr.*μὴ ἄρχε πρὶν ἄρχεσθαι μάθη.

277*   **Кто ни поп, тот (то) (и) батька.**   *v.* B511, C108, X85, Ч64
      [If it's not a priest, it's a clergyman.] *i.e. same difference.* It's either six of one or half
      a dozen of the other.

278   **Кто ничего не имеет, тот ничего не боится.**   *v.* Б59,276,290, Г243, Д179, M166
      Little wealth, little care. *Cf.* He that has nothing need fear to lose nothing.

279   **Кто новине не видал, тот и ветошке рад.**
      [He is content with the old that hasn't seen the new.] *Cf.* Acorns were good till bread
      was found. Newer is truer. Novelty always appears handsome.

280*   **Кто нужды не видал, тот и счастья не знает.**   *v.* B509, K215
      One does not appreciate happiness unless one has known sorrow. *Cf.* It is comparison
      that makes men happy or miserable. The way to happiness is through tribulation.

281   **Кто огня не бережется, тот скоро обожжется.**   *v.* B115, 310
      [He who is careless with fire is soon burnt.] He who plays with fire could get burned.
      Cf. Kindle not a fire that you cannot extinguish. Those who are easily burned should
      never go near the fire.

282   **Кто открывает тайну, тот погубляет верность.**
      [He that tells a secret, destroys loyalty.] Those who betray their friends must not expect
      others to keep faith with them. *Cf.* He that tells a secret, is another's servant.

283*   **Кто первее, тот и правее.**   *v.* П19
      First come, first served. *SPL.* Anton.*Cod.*8.18: qui prior tempore, prior (potior) iure.

284*   **Кто подслушивает, слышит себе неприятное.**
      Listen at the keyhole and you'll hear bad news about yourself. *SPL.* clam qui
      sermones aliorum sublegit, audit quod non vult. *Cf.* Listeners seldom hear good of
      themselves.

285   **Кто поздно пришел, тому мосол.**   *v.* 370, O185, П124,127,179,275
      Who comes late, lodges ill. Last come, worst served. *Lat.* tarde venientibus ossa.

286   **Кто поручится тот и мучится.**   *v.* B34, Д367, C36
      He that goes a borrowing, goes a sorrowing. *SPL.* sponde, noxa praesto est.

287*   **Кто посеет ветер, пожнет бурю.**   *v.* K15,88,318
      Sow the wind and reap the whirlwind.

288   **Кто посмирней, тот и виноват.**
      Secret guilt by silence is betrayed. *Cf.* Where there is whispering, there is lying.

289   **Кто правдою живет, тот и добро наживет.**   *v.* Д118,319, K137,233, X72
      Do well and have well.

290   **Кто правду делает, всегда прав будет.**
      [Act truthfully and always be right.] If you tell the truth, you won't have to remember
      what you said. *SPL.* sat fautorum habet semper qui recte facit.

291 **Кто правого винит, тот сам себя язвит.**
[Who blames the just, harms himself.] He that hurts another, hurts himself. Malice hurts itself most. Injure others, injure yourself. He who cheats another, cheats himself.

292 **Кто привык врать, тому трудно отстать.** *v.* В461, Л102
[He that is used to lying, can't stop.] One lie makes many. One lie leads to another. A lie begets a lie.

293 **Кто про кого за глаза говорит, тот того боится.** *v.* З127
[The back-biter fears the person he maligns.] *Cf.* A gossip speaks ill of all, and all of her.

294 **Кто пьет много вина, тот скоро сойдет с ума.** *v.* В325, Д55
[He who drinks too much wine, will soon lose his mind.] When wine is in, wit is out.

295* **Кто работает, тому Бог помогает.** *v.* Б188,265, Г105
God helps them that help themselves.

296 **Кто сам себя хвалит, в том пути никогда не бывает.** *v.* Д81, Х11
[Those who praise themselves are never good for anything.] Self-exaltation is the fool's paradise. *Cf.* Vainglory blossoms but never bears. Great braggarts are little doers.

297 **Кто себя не умеет содержать, тому жены и детей не пропитать.**
[He that cannot provide for himself shall never feed a wife and children.] First thrive, then wive.

298 **Кто себя хулит, тот желает похвалы.** *v.* Н142
[He who belittles himself seeks praise.] *Cf.* He who bewails himself has the cure in his hands.

299 **Кто силен, тот и волен.** *v.* Г174, К60, Н485, С75, Х82
[The strong are free.] The strong man and the waterfall channel their own path.

300* **Кто скоро дал (помог), тот дважды дал (помог).** *v.* Д95
He gives twice who gives quickly. *Lat.* bis dat qui cito dat.

301* **Кто скоро смеется, тот скоро и плачет.** *v.* Г22, П79, С85
Laugh before breakfast, you'll cry before supper. After laughter, tears.

302 **Кто словом скор, тот в деле редко спор.** *v.* В631, Е33, М126, Р25, Х7,9
[He that is quick to speak is seldom quick to act.] They can do least who boast loudest. A long tongue is a sign of a short hand. *SPL.* promissum cadit in debitum.

303* **Кто смог купить корову, тот купит и дойник.** *v.* Б375,447, В292, Д39
[He that has bought a cow can afford a pail.] God gives the milk but not the pail.

304 **Кто собою не управит, тот и другого на разум не наставит.** *v.* К151, 276
[He that is not master of himself, cannot bring others to reason.] He is not fit to command others, that cannot command himself.

305* **Кто спешит, позже оканчивает.** *v.* С155,258
[He that hurries finishes later.] Always in a hurry, always behind. *Cf.* More haste, less speed. Good and quickly seldom meet.

306* **Кто спит с собаками, встает с блохами.**
If you lie down with dogs, you will get up with fleas.

307*   **Кто старее, тот и правее.**   *v.* В483, С265, Ч42
          [He that is older is righter.] Older and wiser.

308*   **Кто тонет, ухватится и за соломинку (за острый мечь).**   *v.* У111
          A drowning man will clutch at a straw [(sharp sword)].

309   **Кто торгует, тот всегда горюет.**
          [He who trades, sorrows.] A dozen trades, thirteen miseries.

310   **Кто тороват, тот не будет богат.**
          [The generous will never be rich.] *Cf.* Generosity is more charitable than wealth. The higher the hill, the lower the grass.

311   **Кто умеет нищету свою скрыть, тот умеет ей пособить.**
          [He that knows how to conceal his poverty, knows how to relieve it.] He bears misery best that hides it most.

312*   **Кто (что) умеет, тот то и делает.**
          Those that can, do.

313   **Кто умнее, тот достанет поскорее.**   *v.* Д467
          [The smarter finish sooner.] He acts well who acts quickly. *Cf.* What the fool does in the end, the wise man does at the beginning.

314*   **Кто хорошо живет, тот долго живет.**   *v.* Д350
          He lives long that lives well.

315   **Кто хочет искать чести, тот не живи на одном месте.**
          [He that desires honour, must not live in one place.] He that stays in the valley shall never get over the hill.

316*   **Кто часто за шапку берется, тот не скоро уйдет.**   *v.* Р37
          [They that often grab their hats, seldom leave quickly.] They that are booted are not always ready.

317   **Кто что любит, тот то и купит.**   *v.* Т42
          [What one likes, one buys.] Pleasing ware is half sold. *Cf.* Better buy than sorrow.

318*   **Кто что посеет (сеял), то и пожнет (жнет).**   *v.* В160, К88,287, Ч97
          As you sow, so you reap.

319   **Куда ворона летит, туда и глядит. (Куда сова глядит, туда и летит.)** *v.* К40,321, Л108
          [Wherever the crow flies, that's where it looks.] [Where the owl looks, there it flies .] To plow a straight furrow, never look back. *Cf.* Where the crow flies, her tail follows. Look high and light low. Look to the future and you will always look up.

320   **Куда дерево подрублено, туда и валится (повалилось).**
          [The tree falls they way it's hewn.] *Cf.* Where the tree falls, there shall it lie.

321*   **Куда иголка, туда и нитка. (Куда клинья, туда и рукава.)**
          (Куда передни колеса, туда и задни.) (Куда поп, туда и приход).
          (Куда пятки, туда и носки.)   *v.* Б333, К40,319, П23
          [The thread must follow the needle.] [The sleeves go wherever go the gussets.] [Where the front wheels go, the rear ones follow.] [Where the parson goes, the parish follows.] [Where the heels go, the socks follow.] **The appurtenance must follow the main part.** *Lat.* res accessoris sequitur suam principalem.

322* **Куда конь с копытом, туда и рак с клешней.** *v.* K24, M130
[Where the steed plants its hooves, there the crab sticks its claws.] Jump on the bandwagon.

323* **Куда ни кинь, все (везде) клин.** *v.* B372,446, H566
[Whichever way you turn, a dead end.] Up the creek without a paddle.

324 **Куда низко, туда и вода течет.**
Water always flows down, not up. *Cf.* Water will always find its level. Don't try running water up a hill. All water that goes up has to come down.

325* **Куда одна овца (один баран), туда и все стадо.** *v.* Б434
One sheep follows another. If one sheep leap o'er the dyke, all the rest will follow.

326* **Куй железо пока горячо (кипит).** *v.* У106
Strike while the iron is hot. *SPL.* ferrum quando calet cudere quisque valet. ferrum, dum ignis candet, tuntendum.

327* **Кулик не велик, а все-таки птица.** *v.* H243
[The sandpiper is small, but a bird just the same.] Every fish is not a sturgeon. All flesh is not venison. Not everyone can be first.

328 **Купи хату крыту а шубу шиту.**
[Buy finished houses and woven furs.] He that buys a house ready wrought has many a pin and nail for nought. *Cf.* Choose a horse made and a wife to make.

329 **Купил бы сало да денег не стало.** *v.* Ж148
[I'd have bought some lard but I had no dough.] *Cf.* If it wasn't for the "ifs" you would be rich. Jack would be a gentleman if he had money.

330 **Курица кудахчет на одном месте, а яйца кладет на другом.** *v.* Б202, E29
[The hen prates in one spot and lays her eggs in another.] A cackling hen doesn't always lay. *Cf.* If a hen does not prate, she will not lay. †A good hen does not cackle in your house and lay in another's.

331 **Курица (курочка) зернышку клюет, да сыта живет (бывает).**
[The hen plucks at grains, yet lives not hungry.] Grain by grain and the hen fills her belly. *Cf.* One grain fills not a sack, but helps his fellow.

332 **Курица по одному яичку носит.** *v.* P92
[A hen lays one egg at a time.] One at a time is good fishing. *Cf.* Little by little does the trick. One thing at a time (+ and that done well, is a very good thing as many can tell).

333* **Курице не петь петухом.**
[A hen can never crow like a cock.] If you are a cock, crow; if a hen, lay eggs. *Cf.* You cannot make a crab walk straight.

334 **Курице уступи гряду, она возьмет и весь огород.** *v.* Д26

335* **Курицу яйцы (не) учат.** *v.* Я20

336 **Кушанье познавается по вкусу, а мастерство по искусству.** *v.* B602,636, Д145, Л99,
[A good dish is known by its flavour, and and a master's skill by his art.]   O7, X87
The proof of the pudding is in the eating. A workman is known by his work.

Л

1* **Ладил мужичок челночок, а свел на уховертку.** *v.* Д122,461, Ж26, И78
[He began fashioning a canoe, and ended with a toothpick.] *i.e. hopes deceived.*
Expectation always surpasses realization. He will make a spoon or spoil a horn.

2 **Лаком гость к меду.** *v.* Г51
[The guest with a sweet-tooth goes for the honey.] *Cf.* A fly follows the honey.

3 **Лакомый без прибыли всегда в убыли.** *v.* В10
[The gourmet without gain will always show a loss.] If it were not for the belly, the back
might wear gold. *Cf.* Gluttony makes the body sting as well as the pocket.

4 **Лакомство пьянству брат.**
[Gluttony is the brother of drunkenness.] As well to eat the devil as drink his broth.

5 **Лапа в лапу, а задаток в лавку.** *v.* Д137,437, И64, Х25
[Shake on it, but the deposit goes into the till.] Brotherly love for brotherly love, but
cheese for money.

6 **Лапти плетет (сплел), а концы хоронить не умеет (схоронил).**
[He weaves bast sandals but knows not how to hide the ends of the strands.] *Cf.* If the
knot is loose, the string slips.

7 **Ласковое слово лучше сладкого пирога.** *v.* Д312,315,351, О163
[A kind word is better than pastry.] A kind word goes a long way. A soft word is often
worth more than a house and a lot. Fair words hurt not the mouth. *Cf.* A soft answer
turneth away wrath. †Words never filled a belly.

8 **Ласковое слово не трудно, а споро (пуще дубины).** *v.* В249, Д312,315, Л147, М49,215
[A kind word is simple, yet effective (worse than a truncheon).] *Cf.* A good tongue is
a good weapon. Kindness is the noblest weapon to conquer with. There is great force
hidden in a sweet command.

9* **Ласковый теленок две матки сосет (+ а упрямый ни одной).**
[A loving calf is suckled by two mothers (+ but an obdurate one gets none).] Be friendly
and you will never want friends. *Cf.* No friend to a bosom friend (no enemy to a bosom
enemy).

10 **Лбом красится, а затылок вши едят.** *v.* Х44
[Made-up face, lice-infested nape.] The peacock has fair feathers but foul feet. *Cf.* The
face is a mask, look behind it. A clean glove may hide a dirty hand.

11 **Лбом стены не разобьешь (двери не прошибешь).** *v.* В690, И57, Н546
[You can't use your head to break down the wall (door).] Better bend the neck than
bruise the forehead. To run one's head against a stone wall.

12 **Лгать мягко, язык ворочается, а свидетелей нет.**
[Whisper a lie and ther will be no witnesses.] Where there is whispering, there is lying.

13* **Лгать не устать, лишь бы верили.**
[The liar tires not, as long as he is believed.] He that tells a lie must invent twenty more to maintain it. *Cf.* One lie makes many. A lie runs until it is overtaken by the truth.

14 **Лгать - так людей обегать.** *v.* Л104, Н48
[Lying is a subterfuge.] Truth gives a short answer but lies go round about. *Cf.* Liars can go around the world but can't come back. You can get far with a lie but not come back.

15 **Лгачь лгачу надежный свидетель.**
[A liar is a liar's best witness.] The wolf knows what the ill beast thinks. *Cf.* There is honour among thieves.

16 **Лебедь летит к снегу, а гусь к дождю.** *v.* И128, М201, П107, У15
[The swan flies towards snow, the goose towards rain.] *Cf.* Tastes differ.

17* **Лев мышей не давит, орел мух не ловит.** *v.* О99
Eagles don't catch flies [and lions don't crush mice].

18 **Левая рука, правое сердце.**
[Left hand, right heart.] *Cf.* Cold hands, warm heart.

19* **Левая рука правой помогает.** *v.* Р78
[The left hand helps the right.] One hand washes the other.

20* **Лег медведь и игра легла.**
[The game ends when the bear lies down.] The opera isn't over till the fat lady sings.

21 **Лег - свернулся, стал встряхнулся.** *v.* О50
[Go to bed when you want, get up when you want.] *said of a single, carefree lifestyle.* He travels fastest who travels alone.

22* **Легко друзей найти, да трудно сохранить.**
A friend is not so soon gotten as lost.

23* **Легко здоровому болезнь рассуждать.** *v.* С142
The healthful man can give counsel to the sick. *Lat.* facile cum valemus recta consilia aegrotis damus. *Cf.* Easy to keep the castle that was never besieged.

24* **Легко мнится бремя на чужом раме.** *v.* Н115,572
The burden is light on the shoulders of another. *Cf.* Everyone thinks his own sack heaviest.

25 **Легко на чужие гроши ехать.** *v.* Д28,222, И110, Ч130
[It is easy to travel at another's cost.] It is easy to cry Yule at other men's cost. *Cf.* The wholesomest meat is at another man's cost.

26* **Легко очернить, нелегко обелить.** *v.* Л106, Н465, Ч17,54
[Easy to tarnish, difficult to whitewash.] Reputation is hard to make, easy to lose. It's easier to pull down than to build up.

27 **Легко сказать, да нелегко доказать.** *v.* В512, Г186, Н231, С156
Easier said than done [proven].

28* **Легко чужими руками жар загребать.** *v.* Х73

194

29   **Легок по помине.**   *v.* †К18, Н49, П270, Т47
        [Responds quickly to the call]. Quick on the uptake. Talk of the devil and he is sure to
        appear. *SPL.* lupus in fabula.

30   **Легонько поел, легко и сделал.**   *v.* С338
        [Light meal, light work.] A swift eater, a swift worker. *Cf.* A full belly neither fights nor
        flies well.

31   **Легче в драке нежели в бесчестье мириться.**
        A just war is better than an unjust peace. He that makes a good war, makes a good peace.

32*   **Легче готовое нежели искать новое.**
        Old pottage (porridge) is sooner heated than new made. Use the old before getting the
        new.

33*   **Легче начать нежели кончать.**
        [It's easier to begin than to end.] *Cf.* Good to begin well, better to end well. Better
        never begin than never make an end. †The beginning is the hardest.

34   **Легче отомстить обиду чем перенести ее.**
        ['Tis easier to avenge an injury than to endure it.] *Cf.* It costs more to revenge than to
        bear with injuries. †Neglect will kill an injury sooner than revenge.

35*   **Легче работать руками чем головою.**   *v.* Н467
        ['Tis easier to use your hands than your head.] Tasks require a strong back and a weak
        mind. *Cf.* To be wise behind the hand.

36*   **Легче сказано (сказать) чем сделано (сделать).**   *v.* В512, Г186, Н231, С156
        Easier said than done.

37*   **Легче счастье найти нежели удержать.**
        'Tis easier to find happiness than to keep it. *Lat.* P.Syr. fortunam facilius reperias
        quam retineas.

38   **Лежа и кнута не наживешь.**
        [A sluggard won't even earn enough for goad.] *Cf.* A lazy ox is little better for the goad.
        Sloth, like rust, consumes faster than labour wears.

39   **Лежа, пищи не будет (добудешь).**   *v.* Б380, В396, Д12,127, К75, Р7
        If you won't work, you shan't eat. The man with the lazy hand has an empty mouth.
        Cf. They must hunger in frost that will not work in heat.

40*   **Лежачего не бьют.**   *v.* П45
        You don't kick a man when he is down.

41   **Лежачий товар не кормит.**
        [Idle goods won't put food in your mouth.] Never open your pack and sell no wares.
        Cf. When goods lie a long time, the price is forgotten.

42   **Лезет в волки, а хвост собачий (телячий).**   *v.* В361, И74, О105, С31,54,227
        [You cannot be a wolf if you have a dog's tail.] An ape's an ape, a varlet's a varlet, be
        they clad in silk or scarlet. What good can it do an ass to be called a lion.

43   **Ленивому болит в хребте.**   *v.* Д256, К252
        [The sluggard's back always hurts.] Idle folks lack no excuses. A lazy man always
        finds excuses. *Cf.* A lazy man works the hardest.

44* **Ленивому всегда праздник.** *v.* Б152,205, Д237, Е18
Every day is a holiday with sluggards. *Gr. Theocrit.* ἀεργοῖς αἰὲν ἑορτά. *Lat. EA.* ignavis semper feriae.

45* **Ленивому гриб не стоит поклона.** *v.* К181, Н376, П273, Р91, Ч107
[For the sluggard, a mushroom isn't worth the effort to stoop.] Sloth makes all things difficult. He that will not stoop for a pin shall never be worth a pound.

46 **Ленивому и одеться труд.** *v.* Д244, Х109
[Dressing is a chore for the sluggard.] A lazy sheep thinks its wool heavy.

47 **Ленивый вдвое делает.** *v.* С163
[The sluggard does everything twice.] A sluggard takes a hundred steps because he would not take one in time. *Cf.* He that does nothing, does ever amiss.

48 **Ленивый и по платью знать.**
[The sluggard is known by his clothes.] The sluggard must be clad in rags.

49 **Ленивый к работе, ретивый к обеду.** *v.* В122, К1, Н80, Р4
[Sluggish to work, avid to eat.] He has two stomachs to eat and one to work. Lazy folks' stomachs don't get tired.

50 **Ленивый ложится с курами, а встает с свиньями.**
[The sluggard lies down with the chickens and rises with the swine.] Sluggard's guise, slow to bed and slow to rise.

51 **Леность наводит бедность.** *v.* С245
Idleness is the key of beggary. Laziness travels so slow that poverty overtakes him.

52 **Лень добра не делает. (Лень до добра не доводит.)** *v.* Б150, П225
Of idleness comes no goodness. Trouble springs from idleness.

53 **Лес по дереву (топорищу) не тужит (плачет).** *v.* В683
[The forest grieves not for the tree (axe).] The axe goes to the wood from whence it borrowed its helve. *Cf.* Never grieve for what you cannot help.

54* **Лес рубят - щепки летят.** *v.* Б106, В369, Г35, Д410, И71, Н396, У65
[When trees are felled, the chips will fly.] You can't make an omelette without breaking eggs. Hew the log and let the chips fall where they may.

55* **Лесом шел а дров не видал.**
[He walked through the wood but saw no logs.] Send him to the sea and he will not get (salt) water. *Cf.* Don't walk through the woods and pick up a crooked stick.

56 **Лестницу надо мести сверху, а не снизу.** *v.* К115
[Stairs must be swept from the top, not the bottom.] Never tear a building down from the bottom up. Begin at the beginning (not at the end).

57 **Лестное слово что вешний день.** *v.* Л194
[A compliment is like a vernal day.] A flatterer has a venal tongue. *Cf.* Do not let flattery throw you off your guard against an enemy.

58 **Летает хорошо, а садиться не умеет.**
[He flies well but doesn't know how to land.] If you must fly, fly well.

59   **Лето работает на зиму, а зима на лето.**   *v.* K79
       [Summer prepares for winter, and winter for summer.] *Cf.* Winter is summer's heir.

60   **Лето родит а не поле.**
       [Summer bears forth, not the field.] *Gr.* Theophrast. ἔτος φέρει, οὐκ ἄρουρα.

61   **Лето сбирает, а зима поедает.**   *v.* Ч81
       Winter eats up what summer lays up.

62   **Лжецов сума всегда пуста.**
       [Liars' purses are always empty.] Liars never prosper. *Cf.* Deceivers have full mouths
       and empty hands.

63   **Лжецу надо(бно) добрая память.**   *v.* B455
       A liar should have a good memory. *Lat.* Quint.4.2.91 mendacem memorem esse oportet.

64*   **Лжецу и в правде не верят. (Лживый хоть правду скажет, никто не поверит.)**
       A liar is not believed when he speaks the truth.   *v.* B453,666, K224, C215
       Lat. Cic.*De.div.*2.71.146. mendaci homini, ne verum quidem dicenti, credere solemus.

65   **Лжив охоч хвастать.**
       [A liar likes to brag.] A vaunter and a liar are near akin. Boasters are cousins to liars.
       A boaster and a liar are much about the same thing.

66*   **Либо (или) грудь в крестах, либо (или) голова в кустах.**   *v.* И123, Л67
       [Either a cross on your chest or your head in shrubs.] *i.e. decoration or burial.* All or
       nothing. It's either win all or lose all. Either win the saddle or lose the horse. Either
       behind your shield or on it.

67*   **Либо (или) рыбку съесть, либо (или) на мель сесть.**   *v.* Б459, И123, Л66
       [Either run aground or have fish for dinner.] Either sink or swim. Win or lose.

68   **Либо (или) сена клок, либо (или) вилы в бок.**   *v.* И123
       [Either a wisp of hay or a prod of the fork.] *Cf.* One had better or else.

69   **Лизав нож, порезать и язык.**   *v.* Б405, Н421
       [You may cut your tongue licking a knife.] A man may cut himself on his own knife.
       Cf. The same knife cuts bread and fingers.

70   **Лизнув перстом, задеть и горстью.**   *v.* B291,342, Ж14, C84
       [Brush with a finger, strike with the hand.] In for a penny, in for a pound.

71*   **Лиса (кошка) спит, а кур (мышей) видит.**   *v.* Г228, C80,174,226, Ч84
       [The fox (cat) sees chickens (mice) in her sleep.] Pigs dream of acorns, and the goose
       of maize. The net of the sleeper catches fish. All thoughts of a turtle are turtle, of a
       rabbit, rabbit.

72   **Лисица всегда свой хвост прячет.**
       [The fox always hides its tail.] The tail does often catch the fox.

73   **Лисица старая льстица.**   *v.* Н360, C266,268,275
       [The fox is an old flatterer.] *Cf.* Old foxes want no tutors. An old fox needs not to be
       taught tricks.

74   **Лисий хвост да волчий рот.**
       [A fox's tail but a wolf's maw.] *Cf.* The wolf and fox are of one counsel.

75* **Лиха беда начало.**   *v.* Б642, Д308, З106, П17,199, С292
    The first step is the hardest. The first blow is half the battle.

76 **Лихо будет тому кто неправду делает кому.** *v.* Б377, Ж153,К238, П154, С81, Х95, Ч72
    [Ill-doers get ill-done by.] He who does evil comes to an evil end. *Cf.* The biter is
    sometimes bit. Evil deeds do not prosper. Avoid evil and it will avoid you.

77* **Лихо не лежит тихо.**   *v.* Л83
    [Ill never lies still.] An evil deed won't stay hid. Bad pennies always turn up. Small evils
    hatch quick.

78 **Лихо жить в нужде, а в горе и того хуже.**
    [Bad enough to be poor, even worse to be miserable.] *Cf.* Patience with poverty is all a
    poor man's remedy.

79* **Лихо помнится а добро забывается.**   *v.* Д311, Н102, Р16, †Д280
    [Evil is remembered, but good is forgotten.] A bad deed never dies. *Cf.* Shakesp.*J.C.*
    The evil that men do lives after them, the good is oft interred with their bones.

80 **Лихое лихим избывают (называют), а доброе добрым наживают (поминают).**
    [Fight evil with evil, and reward good with good.]   *v.* А13, З122, К106
    SPL.   dolor est dolori medicina. malum malo medicari. *Cf.* Fight fire with fire.
    Diamond cut diamond. *Gr.* Thuc.5.65: κακὸν κακῷ ἰᾶσθαι.

81 **Лихое лихому, а доброе доброму.**   *v.* Б379
    [Evil unto evil, and good unto good.] Be good with the good and bad with the bad.
    Gr. κακὰ κακοῖς. *Cf.* Plaut.*Bacch.*659: bonus sit bonis, malus sit malis.

82 **Лихое споро, не умрет скоро.**   *v.* Б218, С133,160
    Ill vessels seldom miscarry. *SPL.* vas malum non frangitur, optima cum pereant deteriora
    manet. *Cf.* †Nothing evil or good lasts a hundred years.

83 **Лихому (человеку) вина не надобно.**   *v.* Л77
    [Ill intention needs no pretext.] Any excuse will serve a tyrant. Wrong has no warrant.
    Weeds want no sowing.

84* **Лицо - зеркало души.**   *v.* Ч65
    The face is the index of the mind (heart).

85 **Лицом хорош, а душой не пригож. (Личиком гладок, а делами гадок.)** *v.* В99, Г112,
    Fair face, foul heart. An angel on top but a devil underneath.   С51,211

86 **Личико беленько (беленек), да разума меленько (да умом простенек).** *v.* К195,196,
    Beauty and wisdom seldom agree. Beauty has no brains.   Р65
    A pretty face may hide an empty head.

87 **Личиком скрасила, а нравом подгадила.**   *v.* С51,211
    Fair without, false within. *Cf.* A fair woman without virtue is like palled wine. Female
    is one head with two faces.

88 **Лишнего не бери, а кармана не дери.**   *v.* В91, Д99, Т85, Ч96
    [Take no more than you need - your pocket won't tear.] Take no more than you're able to bear.

89 **Лишнего пожалеешь, последнее потеряешь.**   *v.* П116
    [Spare the extra and lose all.] Don't spoil the ship for a ha'porth of tar. Penny wise and
    pound foolish.

90 **Лишнее говорить, себе вредить.** *v.* Б318, В67,229,357,521, Г176, О196, С126
Talk much and err much. Many words, many buffets. Loose talk costs lives. *Cf.* A fool's tongue is long enough to cut his own throat. The tongue talks at the head's expense. Least said, soonest mended.

91 **Лишнее слово досаду приносит.** *v.* М108
Much babbling is not without offense.

92 **Лишнему лишнее и надобно.** *v.* Б275, М128, Н8
Much would have more.

93 **Лишние догадки бывают гадки.**
Too much consulting confounds.

94 **Лишняя денежка карману не тягость.** *v.* З86, П111, Х19
[Extra money is no burden in the pocket.] A little saving is no sin. Store is no sore.

95* **Лови (ищи) ветер в поле.** *v.* И143

96 **Ловит волк, да ловят и волка.** *v.* Н374
[The wolf hunts and is himself hunted.] Long runs the fox but at last is caught. *Cf.* At length the fox is brought to the furrier. The smartest fox is caught at last.

97 **Ложась спать, думай как встать.** *v.* Н161
[Before you sleep, think of waking.] Think of the end before you begin.

98* **Ложка дегтю портит бочку меда.** *v.* В7, К8,203, О54,148, Ш3
[A spoonful of tar will mar a keg of honey.] One drop of poison infects the whole tun of wine.

99 **Ложка едоком, а лошадь ездоком.** *v.* В636, О7
[An eater makes the spoon, a rider the horse.] The proof of the pudding is in the eating. The worth of a thing is what it will bring. *Cf.* Use the means, God will give the blessing.

100 **Ложный друг подобен кошке, спереди ласкает, а сзади царапает.**
Flatterers are cats that lick before and scratch behind. *Cf.* The most deadly of wild beasts is a backbiter, of tame ones - a flatterer. To stroke with one hand, stab with the other. *Lat.* altera manu scabit, altera ferit.

101* **Ложь конь во спасение.** *v.* И125, Л138,144, У94
[A lie is a horse to the rescue.] *Cf. Psalm* 32.17: fallax equus ad salutem. A necessary lie is harmless. White lies save your soul.

102 **Ложь ложью погоняет.** *v.* В461, К292
One lie makes many.

103 **Ложь ходит на гнилых ногах.** *v.* Б100, В456
[A lie walks on rotten feet.] A liar is sooner caught than a cripple. *Cf.* A blister will rise upon one's tongue that tells a lie.

104* **Ложью свет пройдешь, да не воротишься.** *v.* Д274,286, Л14
A liar can go round the world but cannot come back. You can get far with a lie, but not come back.

105* **Локоть близок, да не укусишь.** *v.* К41
The elbow is near, but try and bite it. *Cf.* A horse cannot lick its own ear. A man can do no more than he can.

106*   **Ломать - не строить.**   *v.* Л26
       It is easier to pull down than to build.

107*   **Ломи дерево пока молодо.**   *v.* Д196, И137
       Bend the willow while it's young.   Bend the twig while it is still green. *Cf.* To nip in the bud. Destroy the lion while he is yet but a whelp.

108*   **Лошадь быстра, да не уйдет от хвоста.**   *v.* Г21, К40,319, П23
       [A horse is swift, but cannot outstrip its tail.] A bird never flies so far that his tail doesn't follow. *Cf.* When the crow flies, her tail follows.

109   **Лук от семи недуг.**
       [An onion wards off seven illnesses.] *a pun («лук» also means «bow»)* An apple a day keeps the doctor away.

110   **Лукавство не велико, а осторожность есть.**   *v.* М113, Н241
       [The evil is not as great as the precaution.] Apprehension of evil is often worse than the evil itself. *Cf.* Our worst misfortunes are those which never befall us.

111   **Лукавством жить не хочется, а правдою не умеется.**
       [Unwilling to live dishonestly, unable to live honestly.] If a man wishes to know the strength of evil, let him try to abandon it.

112   **Лукавых людей не надобно иметь за друзей.**   *v.* Б162
       [Ill men should not be befriended.] *Cf.* Books and friends shall be few but good. The best remedy against an ill man is much ground between. He who is no friend to the good cause is no friend of mine.

113   **Лучше бедность да честность нежели прибыль да стыд.**   *v.* В673, Д273,305,
       (Лучше убожество с добром нежели богатство со грехом.)   Х75,78
       [Better honest poverty than shameful gain.] Better be poor with honour than rich with shame. Better go to heaven in rags than to hell in embroidery. *Cf.* Unsullied poverty is always happy, while impure wealth brings with it many sorrows.

114*   **Лучше бить чем битым быть.**   *v.* Л117
       [Better to beat than to be beaten.] All the world loves a winner. *Cf.* †Better to be beaten than be in bad company.

115   **Лучше брать нежели давать.**   *v.* Д13,71
       [Taking is better than giving.] Some are always giving, others are always taking. *Cf. Acts.*20.35: †It is more blessed to give than to receive. †It is better to give than to receive.

116   **Лучше бессчастным нежели дураком.**
       [Better unlucky than a fool.] Of all poverty, that of the mind is the most deplorable. *Cf.* †Better be happy than wise.

117*   **Лучше быть молотком чем наковальней.**   *v.* Л114
       It is better to be the hammer than the anvil.

118*   **Лучше быть у других (жить) в зависти нежели (чем) в кручине (жалости).**
       Better envied than pitied.   *Gr.* Hrdt.3.52: κρεῖσσόν ἐστιν φθονεῖσθαι ἢ οἰκτειρείσθαι.   *SPL.* malo invidiam quam misericordiam.   *EA.*4.4.87: praestat invidiosum esse quam miserabilem.

119* **Лучше в малом да удача, чем в огромном да провал.** *v.* Л139, М20
[Better a small success than huge failure.] Better to be small and shine than to be great and cast a shadow. It's a whole lot better to be a little wheel turning than a big wheel standing still. A little along is better than a long none. Better a big fish in a little puddle than a little fish in a big puddle. *Cf.* Better a mischief than an inconvenience.

120* **Лучше в обиде быть (мучиться), чем в обидчиках (мучить).**
(Лучше терпеть самому нежели беду сделать кому.) *v.* Л148
Better to suffer ill than to do ill. Better to be a martyr than a confessor. Better to lose with a wise man than win with a fool.

121 **Лучше в утлой ладье по морю ездить чем злой жене тайну поверить.** *v.* В261
[Better to trust a frail dingy on the seas than a mean wife with a secret.] *Cf.* He knows little who will tell his wife all he knows. He may be trusted with a house full of unbored millstones.

122 **Лучше век терпеть нежели в миг (теперь) умереть.** *v.* И138
[Better long to endure than to die immediately.] Better bend (bow) than break.

123* **Лучше видеть нежели слышать.** *v.* Г113,115, Л146, Н210
[Seeing is better than hearing.] Seeing is believing. One eye has more faith than two ears. *Cf.* Better known than trusted.

124* **Лучше воду пить в радости нежели мед в кручине (печали).**
(Лучше малые крохи с тихостью чем большие куски с лихостью).
(Лучше есть хлеб с водой чем калач с бедой.) *v.* Д324, У24, Ч2
[Better to drink water in contentment than mead in misery.]
[Better bread and water than cake and sorrow.]
A crust of bread in peace is better than a feast in contention.
Cf. Lean liberty is better than fat slavery. An ounce of mirth is worth a pound of sorrow.

125 **Лучше воротиться нежели далече блудить.**
[Better to return than to get lost further.] Better to sit still than rise and fall.

126* **Лучше даровое лыко чем купленный ремень.**
[Better a rope for free than a strap purchased.] Nothing freer than a gift. *Cf.* Why buy the cow when you can get the milk for free.

127 **Лучше деньги пропить чем худое купить.**
[Money is better drunk than ill-spent.] *Cf.* He who buys what he does not need steals from himself. †Better spared than ill spent.

128* **Лучше десять виновных простить чем одного невинного наказать.**
Better ten guilty than one innocent suffer. *Cf.* Justice will not condemn even the devil himself wrongfully.

129* **Лучше друг вдали чем враг вблизи.** *v.* Г325
[Better a friend afar off than an enemy at hand.] Better good afar off than evil at hand.

130* **Лучше друг верный чем камень драгоценный.** *v.* В251, Д298,413
[A true friend is better than a precious gem.] Friends are like jewels. A faithful friend is as rare as a diamond. *Cf.* True friends are like diamonds, precious and rare; false ones like autumn leaves found everywhere. A true friend is the best possession. Better a friend on the road than gold or silver in your purse. A virtuous woman is as rare as a diamond.

131 **Лучше железо варить нежели с злою женою жить.** *v.* З138, Л135
[Better work in a forge than be ill-tethered.] Better be half-hanged than ill-wed. *Cf.* Better hand loose than an ill-tethering.

132* **Лучше жениться чем волочиться.** *v.* Ж74
[Better marry than tarry.] *Cf.*He who marries might be sorry, he who does not, will be sorry.

133* **Лучше из двух зол легчайшее выбирать.** *v.* И77
Of two evils choose the least. *Lat.* e duobus malis minus eligendum est.

134 **Лучше кума чем злая жена.**
[Better a godmother than an ill wife.] *Cf.* Next to no wife a good wife is best.

135 **Лучше камень долбить нежели злую жену учить.** *v.* Л131
[Better to break a stone than to teach a mean wife.] Better be half-hanged than ill wed.

136* **Лучше красоты ищи достоинства.** *v.* Ж61,87, Н255,316,475
[Choose virtue over beauty.] Choose not a wife by the eye only.

137* **Лучше лишиться яйца чем курицы.**
[Better to lose the egg than the hen.] Better give the wool than the sheep.

138* **Лучше ложь ко спасению нежели правда к погибели.** *v.* И125, Л101,144, О13, У94
Better a lie that heals than a truth that wounds.

139* **Лучше маленькая рыбка чем большой таракан.** *v.* В111, Л119, М20, Н281
[Better a small fish than a large roach.] Better are small fish than an empty dish.
Cf. Better a louse (mouse) in the pot than no flesh at all. Better a mischief than an inconvenience.

140 **Лучше мера нежели вера.** *v.* Д143, М62
[Moderation is better than faith.] Measure is a treasure. *Cf.* Moderation is the best means.

141 **Лучше молчать чем пустое врать.** *v.* Д306, М157, Н436, У101
[Better be silent than tell empty lies.] Be silent if you have nothing worth saying.
Cf. Better say nothing, than not to the purpose.

142 **Лучше на убогой жениться нежели с богатою всегда браниться.** *v.* Б194,285, Ж48,
[Better a poor wife than a rich scold.] Better a portion (fortune) Н402
in a wife than with a wife. *Cf.* A great dowry is a bed full of brambles.

143 **Лучше не свыкаться, нежели расставаться.**
(Лучше с милым не видаться нежели скоро расстаться.)
[Better not to grow accustomed (to see one's love) than to have to part (quickly).] She will as soon part with the crock as the porridge. *Cf.* Tennys.*Mem.*1.20: †'Tis better to have loved and lost than never to have loved at all.

144 **Лучше неправда прямая нежели правда кривая.** *v.* Г325, И125, Л138, У94
[Better a straight lie than a crooked truth.] False friends are worse than open enemies.
Cf. Open rebuke is better than secret love. †Better speak truth rudely than lie covertly.

145* **Лучше неучен да умен нежели учен да глуп.** *v.* Б217, В536, Д362, У86
[Better untaught but clever than taught and a fool.] Experience without learning is better than learning without experience. *Cf.* Learning without thought is labour lost, thought without learning is dangerous. A handful of common sense is worth a bushel of learning. Better untaught than ill taught.

146* **Лучше один раз увидеть чем сто раз услышать.** *v.*Б317,Г113,115,Л123, Н210,215, О194
[Better to see once than to hear a hundred times.] One eyewitness is better than two hearso's (ten hearsays).

147 **Лучше одного доброго похвала нежели многих злых.** *v.* В249, Д312, Л8, М49
[Better one kind word of praise than many unkind.] A spoonful of honey will catch more flies than a gallon of vinegar. *Cf.* Good words anoint us and ill do unjoint us.

148 **Лучше от добрых хулу терпеть нежели от злых хвалу иметь.**
(Лучше умная хула чем дурацкая хвала.) *v.* Л120
[Better the censure of the good than the praise of the evil.] [Better the censure of a wise man than the praise of a fool.] Praise by evil men is dispraise.

149* **Лучше плохо ехать чем хорошо пешком идти.** *v.* Б487, П129, Х92
[Better to ride poorly than to walk well.] Better to be a good runner than a bad stander. *Cf.* Better ride on an ass that carries me than a horse that throws me.

150* **Лучше поздно чем никогда.**
Better late than never. *Lat.* praestat sere quam numquam.

151 **Лучше просить нежели красть.** *v.* Г203, Л162, Х104
Better beg than steal.

152* **Лучше рябчик (синица) (голубь) в руках (руке) (тарелке)** *v.* Б231, Д393, Ж169,
чем два на ветке (журавль в небе) (глухарь на току). С122
[One grouse (titmouse)(pigeon) in the hand(s)(plate) is better than two on the branch (than a crane in the sky)(than a grouse in a rookery).] **A bird in the hand is worth two in the bush.** Better a sparrow in the hand than a pigeon on the roof.

153 **Лучше свое отдать нежели чужое взять.** *v.* Г152
Better give [your own] **than take** [others']. *Cf.* Better to pay and have little than have much and be in debt.

154* **Лучше «слава Богу» нежели «дай Бог.»** *v.* Г166
[Better say "Thank God" than "God willing."] Better to have than to wish. *Cf.* Better say "here it is," than "here it was."

155 **Лучше смерть нежели позорный живот.** *v.* Л164
Better to die with honour than to live with shame. *Gr.* κρεῖσσον θανεῖν ἤ ζῆν αἰσχρόν. *Lat.* Tac.*Agric.*33: honesta mors turpi vita potior.

156 **Лучше спать нежели колобродить.** *v.* Х105
[Better sleep than loaf about.] Better be idle than badly employed. Better rue sit than rue flit.

157* **Лучше споткнуться ногою нежели словом.**
Better the foot slip than the tongue.

158* **Лучше старик семерых молодых.**
[Better an old man than seven lads.] *Cf.* An old wise man's shadow is better than a young buzzard's sword.

159* **Лучше страдать брюхом нежели духом.** *v.* В285, М168
[Better to be hungry than depressed.] Better be poor than wicked. *Cf.* Better go away longing than loathing.

160* **Лучше старый друг нежели новых двух (новый).** *v.* В283, Д415
One old friend is better than two new ones. Old friends are best.

161* **Лучше тихо да вперед, чем скоро да назад.**   *v.* К305, С155
[Better to go forward slowly than back quickly.] Speed will get you nowhere if you're going in the wrong direction. Don't take two steps and slide back three. *Cf.* More haste, less speed. Better to go about than fall into a ditch.

162 **Лучше торговать нежели воровать.**   *v.* Г203, Л151, Х104
[Better to bargain than to steal.] *Cf.* Better to beg than steal, but better to work than to beg.

163 **Лучше умереть нежели горе терпеть.**   *v.* Л155
[Better to die than grieve.] Better to die than live in shame.

164 **Лучше умереть в поле чем в бабьем подоле.**   *v.* Л155
[Better to die in battle than behind womens' skirts.] *Cf.* Better to die with honour than to live with shame.

165 **Лучше хромать чем сиднем сидеть.**   *v.* Н285
[Better to limp than to sit and stay home.] Better a bare foot than none. One foot is better than two crutches. Better wear out shoes than sheets.

166* **Лучшее - враг хорошего.**   *v.* Д266, О125, П294
Best is the enemy of the good.

167* **Льва сонного не буди.**
Wake not a sleeping lion. *Cf.* Let sleeping dogs lie.

168* **Любви все возрасты покорны.**
Love conquers all [ages]. Love knows no season. *Cf.* Love hits everyone. The heart that loves is always young.

169* **Люби(шь) взять (ездить), люби и отдать (повозить).**
Люби(шь) кататься, люби и саночки возить.   *v.* Л173,200, П67, С201, У88,89
[If you like to take (ride), learn to give (drive).] [If you like riding, learn to enjoy carrying the sleigh.] To give as good as one gets. They that dance must pay the fiddler.

170 **Люби не люби, да почаще взглядывай.**
[Look carefully no matter how much you love.] Love all, trust few. *Cf.* Keep your eyes wide open before marriage and half shut afterwards.

171 **Люби смородинку, люби и оскоминку.**   *v.* Б344, Г281,297, К256, Н221,363
[If you like currants, you should enjoy the bitter after-taste.] Take the sweet with the sour. Deserves not the sweet that will not taste the sour.

172 **Люби спорщика, не люби потаковщика.**   *v.* Н50, С253
[Prefer the wrangler to the flatterer.] Better speak the truth rudely than lie covertly. *Cf.* Better suffer for truth than prosper by falsehood.

173* Люби ссору, люби и мир.
Любить в людях - люби и дома.
Любишь жену, люби и детей кормить.
Любишь кашу - люби и щи.
Любишь лето, люби и зиму.
Любишь много, люби и мало.   *v.* Б49,127, В20,616, Г281, Л169,
Любишь пить, люби и потчевать.   Н229, С201, У89, Х63
    [Those that quarrel must make peace.]
    [If you like to go out you must also stay home.]
    [If you love your wife, enjoy feeding the children.]
    [If you like *kasha*, you have to like the cabbage soup.]
    [If you like summer, like winter.]
    [If you like much, like little.]
    [If you like to drink, enjoy entertaining.]
    You must take the fat with the lean. Take the evil with the good. *Cf.* They that dance must pay the fiddler.

174 Любит жена и старого мужа коли не ревнив.
    [A wife loves even an old husband if he's not jealous.] Better to have a husband without love than with jealousy. Better be an old man's darling than a young man's warling.

175 Любить жену - держать грозу.   *v.* Н519
    He that has a wife has strife.

176 Любить барыш, любить и наклад.   *v.* Б18,80, Г58, Д73,246, Е10, К273
    Nothing venture, nothing gain. Nothing stake, nothing draw.

177 Любить себя - любить и друга (других).   *v.* В68, Ч11
    [Loving yourself means loving your friend (others).] To be loved, love and be lovable. *Cf.* Love your neighbour as yourself. He that knows himself, knows others.

178* Любить тепло, потерпеть и дым.   *v.* В20, Г281, Ж36, М43, Н94,397, О97, П201
    [He who likes the heat shall bear the smoke.] If you don't like the heat get out of the kitchen.

179* Любишь найти, люби и потерять.   *v.* В463, К268
    You win a few, you lose a few. Easy come, easy go.

180 Любишь рай, люби и муку.   *v.* В125, Л173
    [If you like heaven, enjoy suffering.] Crosses are ladders that lead to heaven. There is no going to heaven in a sedan. To go to heaven in a featherbed. *Lat.* non est e terris mollis ad astra via.

181 Люблю долго спать, а стыжусь поздно встать.
    [I like to sleep late but am ashamed to get up late.] Don't find pleasure without conscience. *Cf.* To take hares with foxes.

182 Люблю молодца за обычай.
    There's a man after my own heart.

183 Люблю тебя, да не как себя.   *v.* В567,658
    [I love you, but not like myself.] Every man is nearest himself. All men love themselves more than another. *Lat.* omnes sibi melius esse malunt quam alteri.

184 Любовь братская лучше каменных стен.
    [A brother's love is better than stone walls.] Love will go through stone walls.

185   **Любовь зла - полюбишь и козла.**   *v.* Л193, П132
[Love is unkind - you may fall for a goat.] Love makes the ugly beautiful. Love is blind. *Cf.* In the eyes of the lover, pock-marks are dimples. Love sees no faults.

186   **Любовь и голод правят миром.**
[Love and hunger rule the world.] *Cf.* Love makes the world go round. They that would lie down for love should rise for hunger.

187   **Любовь и малое принимает за великое.**
[Love sees the small as great.] *Cf.* Affection blinds reason. A credulous thing is love. Ov.*Met.*7.826: credula res amor est.

188*   **Любовь, кашель, дым и деньги не будут долгое время скрытны.**
Love, a cough,[smoke and money] **cannot be hid.** Love and smoke cannot be hidden. *Lat.* amor tussique non celantur.

189   **Любовь кольцо - а у кольца нет конца.**   *v.* В253
[Love is a ring, and a ring has no end.] **Love is a circle and an endless sphere.** Love without end has no end.

190*   **Любовь начинается с глаз.**
Loving comes by looking. Looks breed love. *Gr. Diog.* 4.49: ἐκ τοῦ ὁρᾶν γίγνεται τὸ ἐρᾶν. *Lat.* ex aspectu nascitur amor.

191*   **Любовь не картошка - не выбросишь (выкинешь) в окошко.**
[Love is not a potatato you can just toss out the window.] You can't control your love. *Cf.* Love can neither be bought nor sold.

192*   **Любовь покрывает множество грехов.**   *v.* О160, П132
Love covers many infirmities.

193   **Любовь слепа, доведет до беды и попа.**   *v.* К250, Л185, П132
Love is blind [it will lead you to trouble and to a priest].

194   **Любовь холостого как вешний лед.**   *v.* Л57
[A bachelor's love is like spring ice.] *Cf.* Love of lads and fire of chats (chips) is soon in and soon out.

195   **Любопытному на базаре нос прищемили.**   *v.* З93, М109
[The nosy buyer's nose got pinched at market.] Curiosity killed the cat.

196   **Любя жену потерпеть стыду.**
[Love of wife will suffer shame.] *Cf.* Love is never without jealousy.

197*   **Людей много, а человека нет.**   *v.* М122
[There are many people but few human beings.] A crowd is not company. *Gr. Plan.*50: πολὺς λαὸς, ὀλίγοι δὲ ἄμθρωποι.

198   **Людей не слушать, в добре не жить.**
[No good comes of not listening.] Present neglect makes future regret.

199*   **Людей слушай, а свой ум имей.**
[Listen to others but think for yourself.] Say as men say, but think to yourself.

200   **Люди ложь, и мы то ж.**
(Люди солгали, да и мы неправду сказали.)   *v.* В499,509, З51, К15, М118
[People lie and we do too.] To give as good as one gets. We're only human.

201* **Люди людьми и живут (людей и ищут).**
      People need people.

202 **Люди пьют, а мы похмелье принимаем.**   *v.* В207, З24, Н117, С1, Т8
      [They drink and we get the hangover.] One sows and another reaps. One does the scathe and
      another has the scorn. *Cf.* One may steal a horse while another may not look over a hedge.

203 **Люди тонут, а он веселую ломит.**   *v.* Д495,497
      [He laughs while people drown.] A fool will laugh when he is drowning. *Cf.* To be no
      laughing matter. He who laughs at others' woes finds few friends and many foes.

204 **Людность не делает убытка.**   *v.* В150
      [Crowdedness doesn't hurt.] The more the merrier.

205 **Людским речам вполовину верь.**   *v.* Н253
      [Believe only half of what people say.] Believe not all you hear. Believe not all that you
      see nor half what you hear.

206 **Людской стыд смех, а свой смерть.**   *v.* Ч110,114
      [Others' shame is laughable, one's own - fatal.] Everything is funny as long as it happens
      to someone else.

207 **Ляжешь подле огня, не хотя, ожжешься.**   *v.* О81, С26
      The fire which warms us at a distance will burn us when near.

208 **Лямкой богатства не вытянешь.**
      [You won't draw wealth with a towline.] *i.e. mere toil won't make you rich.* An ant may
      work its heart out, but it can't make honey. *Cf.* Ever busy, ever bare. No work is worse
      than overwork. The only work that hurts a man is hopeless work.

M

1   **Мал глаз, а весь Божий свет видит.**   *v.* Г110
[The eye is small yet can see the whole world.] *Cf.* One may see day at a little hole.

2   **Мал грех, да велика причина (да великую вину приносит).**   *v.* В587
[The sin is minor, but the cause (guilt) great.] The smaller the wrong, the greater the guilt. *Cf.* Little wrongs breed great evils. Injuries are written in brass.

3*   **Мал золотник, да дорог.**
[The *zolotnik* is small, but precious.] The best things come in small packages. *Cf.* A little body often harbours a great soul. A little man may have a large heart.

4   **Мал малышок, а мудрые пути кажет.**   *v.* У110
A child's service is little, yet he is a fool that despises it. From the mouths of babes springs truth.

5   **Мал муравей (муравей не велик), да горы копает.**   *v.* Б408, И41, Н206
[The ant is small yet digs mounds.] A small leak will sink a great ship.

6   **Мал родился, а выростет, всем пригодится.**   *v.* И89, К225, М25
[Born small, yet quite useful once grown.] *Cf.* Men are not to be measured by inches.

7   **Мал соловей да голос велик.**   *v.* М199, Н206
[The nightingale is small, but its voice great.] The buzz of a mosquito can drown out the ocean's roar.

8   **Мал чирей да гною полон.**   *v.* П297
[The boil is small yet full of puss.] No viper so little but has its venom.

9*   **Мал язык да всем телом (великими людьми) владеет.**   *v.* Я11,14
[The tongue is small yet rules the whole body (great men).] The tongue is a little thing but it fills the universe with trouble *Cf.* The tongue destroys a greater horde than does the sword.

10   **Мала(я) вина непокорством распространяется.**   *v.* Г316
[A minor fault, unchecked, will spread.] Submitting to one wrong brings on another.

11   **Мала дождевая капля жесток камень пробивает.**   *v.* В473,363, Д339,513, Т27
[A tiny raindrop can hollow a mighty stone.] Constant dripping wears away the stone.

12   **Мала иголка, а дырку делает.**   *v.* Д512
[A pin is small yet it makes a hole.] *Cf.* Of a little thing, a little displeases.

13   **Мала косточка, да в горле стала.**   *v.* К143, Н207, П297, Я25
[It only takes a small bone to lodge in one's throat.] A little stone may overturn a great wain.

14* **Мала(я) искра города пожигает.**   *v.* И143, О135,142
   [A small spark destroys entire cities.] Of a small spark, a great fire. *Lat.* Curt. parva saepe scintilla contemta magnum excitat incendium.

15* **Мала (невелика) птичка, да ноготок (носок) востер (остер).** *v.* Н206
   [The bird is small, yet its claws (beak) sharp.] Cats hide their claws. *Cf.* Little dogs have long tails.

16 **Малая (маленькая) собака и до старости щенок. (Маленькая птичка всегда воробей.)**
   [A small dog is ever a puppy.] [A small bird is ever a nightingale.] *Cf.* Little things are pretty. *Gr.* χάρις βαιοῖσιν ἀπηδεῖ. *Lat.* inest sua gratia parvis.

17 **Маленек да умненек.**
   [Small but sharp.] Little men have sharp wits. Small head, big ideas.

18 **Маленькая змейка да убивает большого быка.**   *v.* Д512, Н206
   [The viper is small yet can kill a bull.] No viper so little but has its venom. Little strokes fell great oaks.

19 **Маленькое деревцо в сук растет.**   *v.* К202
   [A small sapling grows into a great tree.] Timely crooks the tree that will good cammock be. How the sapling bends, so grows the tree.

20* **Маленькое дело лучше большого безделья.**   *v.* Л119,139, Н281
   [A small business is better than no business.] Better a little along than a long none. Better to be a little wheel turning than a big wheel standing still.

21 **Мало говоря больше услышишь.**   *v.* Б324
   [Speak less and hear more.] Hear much, speak little.

22 **Мало дать не хочется, а много дать - убыточно.**
   [To give little is a shame, to give much is a loss.] The little alms are the good alms. *Cf.* Small gifts make friends, great ones make enemies. There is no grace in a favour that sticks to the fingers. †Alms never make poor.

23 **Мало ль чего хочется да не сможется.** *v.* М129

24* **Мало по малу птичка свивает гнездо.**
   Little by little the bird builds his nest. *Cf.* Grain by grain the hen fills her belly. One by one the spindles are made.

25 **Мало родилось, да велико выросло.**   *v.* Б437, И89, М6, Н216
   Small is the seed of every greatness. Great oaks from little acorns grow.

26* **Малого пожалеешь да большое потеряешь.**   *v.* З22, Л89, О15, П116
   [Spare the little and lose tha great.] Penny wise and pound foolish. *Cf.* Nothing ventured, nothing gained.

27 **Малое не мало когда делает велико.**
   [Nothing's too small when the result is great.] *Cf.* From trifiling causes great results arise. *Lat.* ex minimis initiis maxima.

28 **Малое равенство лучше большого.**
   [Little equality is better than great equality.] *Cf.* If all were equal, if all were rich and if all were at table who'd lay the cloth?

29* **Малые дети малая печаль, болшие дети - большая печаль.**   *v.* Д218, С17
Little children, little troubles; big children, big troubles. *Cf.* Children when they are little make their parents fools, when they are great they make them mad.

30 **Малые от старых учатся (молодые от старых перенимают).**   *v.* Щ3
As the old cock crows, so the young one learns. *Lat.* a bove maiori discit arare minor.

31* **Малые птички свивают малые гнезда.**
Small birds make little nests. A small bird is content with a little nest.

32 **Малый барышъ лучше большого накладу.**
[Better a small gain than a large risk.] *Cf.* Men that venture little, hazard little. He that ventures too far, loses all.

33* **Маслом огонь не заливают (огня не потушишь).**   *v.* E13, 369, H405, O27
Pouring oil on the fire is not the way to quench it. *Gr.* ἐλαίῳ πῦρ σβεννύεις.
Lat. Hor.*Serm*.2.3: oleum camino addere. *SPL.* mala sunt in proclivi.

34 **Материн сын - отцов пасынок.**
[Mama's boy is father's stepson.] *Cf.* Mothers' darlings make but milksop heroes. A child may have too much of his mother's blessing.

35 **Материнская молитва со дна моря вынимает.**
[A mother's prayer can rescue from the ocean floor.] *Cf.* A mother's goodness is deeper than the sea.

36* **Материны глаза слепы.**
[A mother's eyes are blind.] *Cf.* No mother has a homely child.

37* **Мать всякому делу голова (конец).**
[The mother is the head (end) of any task.] Mother knows best.

38 **Мать кормит дитя так сохнет, а он об ней ни охнет.**
[The mother feeds the child till dry, but he won't return as much as a sigh.] *Cf.* How sharper than a serpent's tooth it is to have a thankless child.

39 **Мать перенять а отца не замять.**
[You can copy the mother but not the father.] *Cf.* No love to a father's. Ask the mother if the child be like the father.

40 **Мать плачет не над горсточкой а над пригоршенькой.**
[A mother cries not over a handful but over the full measure.] *Cf.* The good mother says not "Will you," but gives.

41 **Мать приветная - ограда каменная.**
[The good mother is a bulwark of stone.] *Cf.* A mother's breath is aye sweet. A boy's best friend is his mother.

42 **Мачеха добра, да не мать родна.**
[A kindly stepmother is still no mother.] *Cf.* Take heed of a stepmother: the very name of her suffices. There are as many good stepmothers as there are white ravens.

43 **Мед есть, в улей лезть.**   *v.* Ж36, H94,397, O97, П273
[He that would eat honey must enter the hive.] If you want to gather honey, you must bear the stings of bees. *Cf.* He that would have fruit must climb the tree. He that will eat the kernel, must crack the nut.

44 **Мед капнет от уст жены блудницы.**
[Honey flows from the lips of the wayward wife.] *Cf. Prov.*5.3: favus enim distillans labia meretricis. The lips of the consort drop as an honeycomb.

45 **Мед сладок в меру.**
[Honey is sweet in moderation.] *Cf.* Too much honey cloys the stomach. Eat your honey, but stop when you are full. Lick honey with your little finger.

46 **Медведь не умывается да здоров живет (все его боятся).**
[The bear does not bathe, yet lives healthy (people fear him).] *Cf.* A crow is never the whiter for washing herself often.

47 **Медведя бояться - от белки бежать.**
[He that is afraid of bears, runs from squirrels.] *Cf.* A man once bitten by a snake will jump at the sight of a rope. He that fears every bush must never go a-birding.

48* **Медведя не убил, а кожу запродал. (Медведь еще в лесе, а медведину продал.)**
Don't sell the skin till you have caught the bear. *v.* В260, Д126, Н373,477, Т45, Ц10
[The bear is still alive (in the woods), but his hide has already been sold.]

49* **Медом больше мух наловишь чем уксусом.**   *v.* В249, Д312,315, Ж40, Л147
Honey catches more flies than vinegar.

50* **Меж(ду) волками быть - волком и выть.**   *v.* З315, П152, С2,123
Who keeps company with the wolf, will learn to howl.

51 **Меж(ду) глаз да нос пропал (деревня сгорела).**
[Lose sight of the nose for the eyes.] [The village burned before anyone noticed.] Invisible, as a nose on a man's face. Lose sight of the forest for the trees.

52 **Меж дверей пальца не клади.**   *v.* Н319
[Slip not your finger between the doors.] Don't put your finger in too tight a ring. If you want your finger bit, stick it in a possum's mouth.

53* **Меж мудрыми и дурак умен будет.**
[In the company of wise men a fool will be wise.] Keep good men company, and you shall be of their number. *Prov.*13.20: He that walketh with wise men shall be wise.
Cf. If the fool knew how to be silent, he could sit amongst the wise.

54* **Меж слепых и кривой зрачий.**   *v.* В167, З30
Among the blind, the one-eyed man is king. *Gr.* ἐν τοῖς τόποις τῶν τυφλῶν λάμαν βασιλεύς. *EA.* inter caecos regnat strabus.

55 **Между большими колоколами малых не слышно.**   *v.* Б314, К249
[When great bells toll, small ones are not heard.] Great trees keep down the little ones.

56 **Между женских «да» и «нет» не проденешь иголки.**   *v.* Б5, Д110, С105
Cervantes *D.Q.*2.19: Between a woman's yes and no I wouldn't venture to stick the point of a pin. *Cf.* Maids say nay and take it. Nineteen nay-says of a maiden are half a grant.

57 **Мелева много, да помолу нет.**   *v.* Г57, Д233, С101
[Much grinding but no grounds.] Big talking but little saying. A flow of words is not always a flow of wisdom. *Cf.* The mill that is always going grinds coarse and fine.

58   **Мелка река да круты берега.**
      [Shallow river, steep banks.] *Cf.* Where wills are lofty, rivers are deep. Shallow streams make the most din.

59   **Мельница сильна водой, а человек едой.**
      [Water drives the mill, food the man.] *Cf.* The belly carries the legs. Mills will not grind if you give them not water.

60   **Меньше болтай, больше делай.**   *v.* Б316, Д116, Н270
      Speak little, do much.

61*   **Меньше говорить, меньше греха.**   *v.* Б318, Л90,О196, Ч37
      Least said soonest mended. Talk much and err much.

62   **Мера всякому делу вера.**   *v.* Д143, Л140
      Moderation in all things.

63   **Мерзлой роже да метель в глаза.**   *v.* Б418, К118, Н284, П265
      [It always snows in your eyes when your face is frozen.] When it rains, it pours.
      Cf. Bread never falls but on its buttered side. Wind in one's face makes one wise.

64   **Мерить воду, не спрашивать меду.**
      [Those who measure water must not ask for honey.] *Cf.* Nothing enters into a close hand.

65*   **Мертвая собака не кусает.**
      [Dead dogs don't bite.] Dead dogs bark not. Dead men don't bite. *RA*1.31: νεκρὸς οὐ δάκνει.

66   **Мертвец у ворот не стучится.**
      [Dead men do not knock at the door.] Dead men tell no tales.

67*   **Мертвому помины а живому именины.**
      [Memorials for the dead, namesdays for the living.] *Cf.* Speak only what is true of the living and what is honourable of the dead. The life of the dead is placed in the memory of the living. Cic.*Phil.*9.5: vita mortuorum in memoria posita est vivorum.

68   **Мертвый без гроба не живет.**   *pun*
      [The dead live in their graves.] *Cf.* The dead have a world of their own. Earth is the best shelter.

69*   **Мертвый лев хуже живой собаке.**   *v.* Г233, Ж97,125, П33
      Better a live dog than dead lion. *Lat.* melior est canis vivus leone mortuo.

70   **Мертвый не без могилы, а живой не без места.**
      [The dead have their grave, the living their place.] To the grave with the dead and the living to the bread (loaf). *Cf.* We must live by the living, not by the dead.

71   **Мертвый от церкви не ворочается. (Мертвых с погоста не носят.)**   *v.* П279, Ч100
      [The dead do not return from church(yard).] It's only the dead who do not return.

72   **Мертвый пес зайца не погонит.**
      [Dead dogs chase no hares.] *Cf.* Dead dogs bark not.

73*   **Мертвым на тот свет отовсюду дорога одна.**
      [The dead all travel the same road.] Death is one for all. *Lat.* mors omnibus una.
      Cf. Death meets us everywhere. Death has a thousand doors.

74 **Мертвым соколом ворон не травят.**
[Crows are not baited with dead falcons.] To go rabbit hunting with a dead ferret.

75 **Мертвым телом хоть забор подпирай.** *v.* O143
[The dead are good for nothing but perhaps to prop up fences.] Dead men don't walk again. *Cf.* To dead men and absent there are no friends left. Stark dead hath no fellow.

76 **Месиво за коровой не ходит.** *v.* Ж21, O17, X21, Я23
[The feeding trough doesn't come to the cow.] Roasted ducks don't fly into your mouth. *Cf.* The mountain will not come to Muhammad.

77* **Место человека не просвещает, но человек место.** *v.* H289,302,331
It is not the place that honours the man, but the man that honours the place.
Cf. †'Tis the place that shows the man. Office shows the man. *Lat.* **homo locum ornat, non ornat hominem locus.** magistratus virum indicat.

78 **Месяц светит, да не греет.**
[The moon shines but gives no warmth.] Every light is not the sun.
Cf. The moon is a moon still, whether it shines or not.

79* **Метил в ворону (пятку) (сыча) (цель), да попал в корову (нос) (грач) (пень).**
[To aim at the crow (heel)(owl)(target) and hit the cow (nose)(rook)(stump).]
SPL. qui asinum non potest, stratum caedit. *Cf.* An inch in a miss is as good as a mile. Better aim at the moon than shoot into the well.

80 **Меха не надуть, а смерда не научить.** *v.* И109
[One cannot puff up a fur, nor teach a boor.] *Cf.* You cannot make a silk purse out of a sow's ear. He that teaches a scorner does an injury to himself.

81 **Меч туп а меченосец глуп.**
[A dull sword in the hands of a dim swordsman.] *Cf.* Don't put a sword in a madman's hands.

82* **Мечом золото добывают, а меч золотом покупают.**
[Gold is won with the sword, and the sword is bought with gold.] Gold and iron are good to buy gold and iron.

83 **Мешай дело (ум) с бездельем (безумием), проживешь с весельем (с ума не сойдешь).** *v.* †И64
[Mix business with leisure and you'll live in pleasure (you won't go mad).] All work and no play makes Jack a dull boy. *Cf.* †Do not mix business and pleasure.

84 **Мешканьем беды не избудешь.** *v.* Ч94
[Trouble is not averted by loitering.] You may delay but time will not. *Cf.* He who lingers is lost.

85 **Мзда глаза (и мудрых) ослепляет.** *v.* Г119, Д67,75
Gifts blind the eyes.

86 **Мздою что уздою, обратишь судью в твою волю.**
A bribe like a bridle constrains the judge to your will.] *Cf.* Who receives a gift, sells his liberty. Benefits bind.

87 **Милее всего кто любит кого.**
All the world loves a lover.

88   **Мило пока не (пр)остыло.**   *v.* Н63, С50
[Nice until stale.] Everything new is fine. *Cf.* Do not wear out your welcome.

89   **Мило тому у кого всего много в дому.**
A small house well filled is better than an empty palace.

90   **Милого побои недолго болят.**   *v.* Б319, М95
A lover's anger is short-lived.

91   **Милому дружку ото рта кусок.**   *v.* Д240,242, Р15
[Take food out of your mouth to feed a good friend.] Love locks no cupboards.
Among friends all things are common.

92   **Милому насильно не быть.**   *v.* И105, К199, С113
Love cannot be compelled. Love is free. *Lat.* amor cogi non potest.

93   **Милости прошу к нашему шалашу.**   *sarc.*
[Welcome to our little retreat.] *said humorously* Make yourself at home.

94   **Милые бранятся - только тешатся.**   *v.* Б319, М90
Lovers' quarrels are soon mended. *Cf.* Lovers' quarrels are the renewal of love.
Lat. Ter.*And.*3.3.23: amantium ira, amoris redingratio est.

95*   **Мимо яблони яблоко не падает.**   *v.* К84, Я4
The apple never falls far from the tree.

96   **Мир да любовь всему голова.**
Love [and peace] conquer all. *Cf.* Peace has won finer victories than war.

97*   **Мир думает - ветер будет, мир плюнет - море будет.**   *v.* В524, Е26, П58, С22
[If all blow, there'll be a wind; if all spit, there'll be a sea.] Add little to little and
there'll be a great heap.

98   **Мир (свет) не без добрых людей.**
Good folks are scarce.

99*   **Мир тесен.**
It's a small world.

100   **Мир, тишина - всего лучше. (Мир - велико дело.)**   *v.* Г89
If there is peace in your heart, your home is like a palace. *SPL.* pax optima rerum quas
homini novisse datum est.

101*   **Млад годами (летами) да стар бедами (делами).**   *v.* Г202,274, М139, Н225
[Young in years but old in sorrow.] Young in limbs, in judgment old. *SPL.* iuveni
parandum seni utendum. *Cf.* Old head on young shoulders.

102   **Младость не возвратить, а старости не избыть.**
[Youth cannot be revived, nor old age averted.] *Cf.* You can't have two forenoons in one
day. Youth comes but once in a lifetime.

103*   **Мне не дорог твой подарок, дорога твоя любовь.**   *v.* Н290
[I value not your gift, but your love.] It's not the gift that counts, but the thought behind
it.

104   **Мни лен доле, волокна будет боле.**
[The longer you brake flax, the longer the cloth.] *Cf.* The more there's in it, the more there's of it.

105   **Мнит убог в гордости место обрести.**   *v.* Н555, П266
[The pauper's pride schemes of advancement.] Pride may lurk under a threadbare coat.

106   **Многие глаза более видят нежели один.**
[Many eyes see more than one.] *SPL.* oculi plus vident quam oculus.

107*   **Многие за столом храбры.**   *v.* Б345,В231, М130, П165
Many are arm-chair generals. *Cf.* It is easy to be brave from a safe distance. Every dog is a lion at home.

108   **Многие речи ссорам доводят.**   *v.* Л91, М108
Much babbling is not without offense. Many words, many buffets.

109*   **Много (все) будешь знать, скоро состаришься. (Меньше знать, больше спать.)**
[If you know too much, you'll get old before your time.]   *v.* Б321, Н250, С34, Ч15
[The less you know, the more you sleep.] What you don't know can't hurt you. Increase your knowledge and increase your griefs. Curiosity killed the cat. Much science, much sorrow.

110*   **Много воды с тех пор утекло.**
There's been much water under the bridge since then.

111   **Много (долго) выбирать - женатым (замужем) не бывать.**
(Много невест разбирать так женатому век не бывать.)   *v.* З46
[Be too discriminating and remain unmarried.] If you always say "No" you'll never be married. *Cf.* The girl that thinks no man is good enough for her is right, but she's left. If you wish for too much, you will end up with nothing. Who seeks a faultless friend rests friendless.

112*   **Много добра не надоест.**   *v.* Д264, К102, Х51
One can never have too much of a good thing.

113*   **Много думается, да не все то сбудется.**   *v.* В260, Г108, Д126, Л110,
[Not all that one imagines comes to pass.]   Н98,233,477, П228, Ц10
It is one thing to plan a deed and another to carry it out. No ideal is as good as a fact. Dearths foreseen come not. *Cf.* Thinking is far from knowing. It is ill fishing before the net. †There are more things than are thought of in heaven and earth.

114   **Много есть ума да разуму недостает.**   *v.* Д112,228
Knowledge and wisdom are far from being one.

115*   **Много желать, добра не видать.**
Covetousness is the root of all evil.

116   **Много званых, да мало избранных.**
Many are called but few are chosen. *Matt.*20.16 multi enim sunt vocati, pauci vero electi.

117   **Много знай, да меньше говори.**   *v.* З149, У97
A wise head makes a close mouth. *Cf.* He knows most who speaks least. An intelligent person is one who knows when to keep his mouth shut.

118   **Много (сколько) милости, а вдвое (боле) лихости.**
       (Много разумных а больше безумных.)   *v.* Д267, Л200
       [There's much good, but twice as much evil.] [Many are wise, but more are foolish.] Virtue and vice divide the world, but vice has the greater share. *Cf.* It is a good world, but they are ill that are on it.

119   **Много мясо, да все шейна.**
       [There's a lot of meat, but it's all gristle.] All flesh is not venison. *Cf.* All meat pleases not all mouths.

120   **Много на уме да мало на гумне.**
       [Much on your mind but little in the barn.] *Cf.* Good words fill not a sack. If you're so smart, why ain't you rich?

121   **Много начинают да мало совершают.**   *v.* К217,260, С103
       He who begins many things finishes but few.

122*   **Много народа да мало людей.**   *v.* Л197
       A crowd is not company.

123   **Много путей ко спасению.**
       [There are many ways to salvation.] *Cf.* There's more than one way to skin a cat.

124*   **Много слов а мало дел.**   *v.* Г180, 181,184,185, К207, Р25
       All talk and no action.

125   **Много соседов да мало обедов.**
       [Many neighbours but few meals.] *Cf.* Many kinsfolk and few friends. No one can love his neighbour on an empty stomach. Neighbours are good when they are neighbourly.

126   **Много сулит да мало дает.**   *v.* Е33, К302, Р25
       [Promises much but delivers little.] A long tongue is a sign of a short hand.

127   **Много сытно мало честно.**
       [Overabundance is short of honesty.] *Cf.* Too much of ought is good for nought. Virtue is found in the middle.

128*   **Много хорошо а больше лучше.**   *v.* Л92, У84
       [Much is good but more is better.] Much would have more.

129   **Много хочется да не все сможется.**
       Will is no skill. *Cf.* Covetousness breaks the sack.

130*   **Много храбрых после рати.**   *v.* В231, К24, М107, П169
       [Many are brave after the battle.] Hares may pull dead lions by the beard. When the ox is down, many are the butchers. It's easy to be brave from a safe distance. After dinner everyone is wise.

131   **Много яства, да брюха жаль.**
       [Many victuals, but spare the stomach.] Much meat, much malady.

132   **Многого захочется, последнее потеряешь.**   *v.* В522, Д246, 34,
       (Многого искать станешь, ничего не достанешь.)   К222, Н338,
       Grasp all, lose all. All covet all lose.

133 **Многого захочешь, пораньше с постели вскочишь.** *v.* К262, Р35
He that will deceive the fox must rise betimes. *Cf.* She who wishes to keep ahead of her neighbour must go to bed at sundown and get up at dawn.

134 **Многое говоря всегда стыда доводит.** *v.* Л91, М108
Much babbling is not without offence.

135 **Многое учение трудов потребует.** *v.* В645
There is no royal road to learning.

136 **Мокрая курица, а тоже петушится.** *v.* П307
[Even a wet hen may act haughty.] A humble bee in a cow-turd thinks himself a king.

137* **Мокрый дождя не боится. (Мокрому дождь не страшен.)** *v.* М211, Н271,387
[A wet man fears no rain.] Those that have wet their feet care not how deep they wade. He that is down need fear no fall. The anvil fears no blows.

138 **Молитвой квашню не заменишь.** *v.* Б20, З68, Н13
[Prayers are no substitute for the kneading trough.] Prayers plough not. Prayers reap not. *Cf.* Fair words will not make the pot boil.

139 **Молод годами, да старые книги читал.** *v.* Г100, М101
[Young in years, but well-read in old books.] A man may be young in years but old in hours. *Cf.* Out of old books comes new science.

140 **Молод князь (муж), молода и дума (мысль). (Молодой молодое и думает.)**
[Young prince (husband), young ideas.] You cannot put an old head on young shoulders.

141 **Молод, кости гложи, а стар - кашу ешь.** *v.* М147
[The young can gnaw bones, but the old must eat *kasha*.] Youth is nimble, age is lame. *Cf.* He wrongs not an old man that steals his supper from him.

142 **Молоденький умок что вешний лед.** *v.* К3
[A young mind is like spring ice.] *Cf.* Unbridled youth. Youth and white paper take any impression. Youth is the springtime of beauty. †Age writes in the sand.

143* **Молодец на (против)(среди) овец, а на (против)(среди) молодца, (и) сам овца.**
[Bold among the meek, but meek among the bold.] *v.* Г249, П313, Ш10
Who takes a lion when he is absent, fears a mouse present. A bully is always a coward.

144 **Молодец что огурец, а огурец - его едят свиньи.**
[Youth is a cucumber eaten by swine.] *Cf.* Time is the rider that breaks youth.

145 **Молодецкое сердце не уклончиво.**
[The intrepid are not meek.] A brave man's wounds are seldom on his back. *Cf.* There's no such word as can't (fail) in the lexicon of youth.

146 **Молодо - зелено, погулять велено. (Молодость горами шатает.)**
Youth will have its course (swing) (fling). Young colts will canter.

147 **Молодой - игрушки, а старый - подушки.** *v.* В175, М141, Н54, С280, Ч8
[Toys for the young, pillows for the old.] Youth is a crown of roses, old age a crown of willows. Youth is full of vitamins, age is full of germs. *Cf.* An old man is a bag full of bones.

148   **Молодой на битву, а старый на думу.**   *v.* Е23

[The young man is prompt to fight, the old man - to think.] Youth is hasty of temper, but weak in judgment. Age should think and youth should do. *Cf.* Reckless youth makes rueful age.

149*   **Молодому жениться рано, а старому поздно.**

A young man should not marry yet, an old man not at all.

150   **Молодому крепиться, вперед пригодится.**

What youth is used to, age remembers. *Cf.* The best horse needs breaking, and the aptest child needs teaching.

151*   **Молодость и молодостью провожай.**

[Set the young to lead the young.] Youth will to youth. *Gr.* Ar.*Rhet.*1.11.25: νέος νέῳ. *Cf.* Youth and age will never agree.

152   **Молодые дерутся, тешатся - а старые дерутся, бесятся.**

[The young quarrel and make up, the old quarrel and go mad.] Young men soon give and soon forget affronts; old age is slow in both. *Cf.* Old and tough, young and tender.

153*   **Молодые люди могут умереть, старики должны.**

Young men may die, but old must die.

154   **Молоко у корове на языке.**   *v.* У38

155   **Молча пришел, молча и пошел.**   *v.* П258

Lightly come, lightly go. *Cf.* Quiet sow, quiet mow.

156*   **Молчание знак согласия.**   *v.* Д307, П282

Silence means consent. *SPL.* qui tacet consentire videtur. silentio comprobare dicitur.

157   **Молчание лучше пустого болтания.**   *v.* Д306, Л146, У101

Silence is wisdom when speaking is folly. *Gr.* ἐνίοις τὸ σεγᾶν ἔστι κρεῖττον τοῦ λέγειν.

158   **Молчанием прав не будешь.**   *v.* Г190, Д229

[One cannot be correct if silent.] The lame tongue gets nothing. *Cf.* There is a time to speak and a time to be silent. Sometimes silence itself is criminal. *Lat.* turpe silere.

159   **Монах праздный есть тать лестный.**   *v.* И70, П146

[An idle friar is a adulating thief.] A friar is a liar. *Cf.* The friar preached against stealing, and had a goose in his sleeve.

160   **Море ковшом (песком) не вычерпаешь (засыпешь).**   *v.* В320, Г286, Ч32

You cannot empty the sea with a spoon. [(You cannot bury the sea in sand.)] *Cf.* †Many sands will sink a ship.

161*   **Море по рыбке не тужит. (Море - рыбачье поле.)**

[The sea grieves not for fish.] [The sea is a fishing field.] The sea has fish for every man.

162   **Море похвальбы не любит.**   *v.* Х3

[The sea bides no boasts.] Praise the sea but keep on land.

163   **Моту деньги подарить, что в воду пустить.**

[Money on extravagance is like money in the water.] Extravagance is the pitfall of the rich man. *Cf.* Who will not keep a penny, never shall have many.

164 **Мочалка с мочалкой и вяжется.** *v.* В602, К266, Н418, П109, Р9,77, С66, *Ap*.1.5
[Wisp will to wisp.] Birds of a feather flock together. Like will to like. It takes one to know one.

165 **Мошна туга - всяк ей слуга.**
[The purse is a strict monarch.] **All things are obedient to money.** Let your purse be your master. A full purse has many friends. *Cf.* Be ruled by him that bears the purse.

166 **Мошна туже, меньше тужит.** *v.* Б59,290, Г243, К278
Little wealth, little care. Less gear, less care.

167 **Мошна не говорит, а чудеса творит.**
[Money is silent yet works wonders.] Money is miraculous. Talk is but talk, but 'tis money buys land.

168 **Мошна пуста, да душа чиста.** *v.* В285, Л113,159
[Empty purse, clean conscience.] *Cf.* The poor sit on the front benches in Paradise. As the purse is emptied, the heart is filled.

169* **Моя хата (изба) с краю, (+ я ничего не знаю).** *v.* Н164,335, Я2
[It's next door and has nothing to do with me.] It's none of my business. *Cf.* I'm not my brother's keeper. Don't ask me.

170 **Мудрому совет всякий полезен.**
[All advice is useful for the wise.] Though old and wise, yet still advise. Many receive advice but only the wise profit from it.

171* **Мудрость в голове, а не в бороде.** *v.* Б340,342, П60, *Ap*.1.1
The brains don't lie in the beard. It is not the beard that makes the philosopher.

172* **Мудрость старости честнее.**
[Wisdom is more honoured than age.] *Cf.* Wisdom goes not always by years.

173* **Мудрый слышит в полслова.** *v.* В630, Д323, О39, Р32, У98
A word to the wise is sufficient.

174* **Муж в долгу (голах) (по деревням), а жена в шелку (серьгах) (ожерелье).** *v.* Б382,
[The husband's in debt while the wife's in silk (in beaded earings).] В10, Г88
Silks and satins put out the fire in the chimney. *Cf.* A nice wife and a back door will soon make a rich man poor. Many a man sees a wolf at the door because his wife saw a mink in the window.

175 **Муж в полях пахать, а жена руками махать.**
[The husband ploughs, the wife raves.] The better workman, the worse husband.

176 **Муж в тюрме а жена в сурьме. Муж пашет (в шанцах) а жена пляшет (в танцах).**
[The husband is dying in jail while the wife is dyeing her her.] *v.* Х86
[The husband ploughs while the wife dances.] It is an ill husband who is not missed.

177* **Муж глава, а жена душа.** *v.* Ж54,58
[The husband is the head, the wife - the heart.] In the husband wisdom, in the wife gentleness.

178 **Муж жену лозою (бьет), а она ему грозою (свое поет).** *v.* М181
[The husband lashes, the wife scolds.] Rutting wives make rammish husbands.

179* **Муж и жена - одна сатана.**
[Husband and wife share the same life.] Man and wife are one fool. They are finger and thumb. *Cf.* Most men and women are merely one couple more.

180 **Муж любит жену здоровую, а брат сестру богатую.**
[A husband wants a robust wife, a brother a rich sister.] *Cf.* The brother had rather see his sister rich than make her so.

181 **Муж пьет а жена горшки бьет.**   *v.* Л175, М178, Н519
[The husband drinks and the wife breaks the crockery.] *Cf.* He that has a wife has strife.

182 **Муж с женой брянись (бранятся), а третий не вяжись (а под одну шубу ложатся).** Д129, С60
[When husbands and wives quarrel - don't butt in (they'll still sleep under the same fur).] Put not the hand between the bark and the tree.

183 **Муж согрешит, так в людях грех - жена согрешит, домой принесет.**
(Мужнин грех за порогом останется, а жена все домой несет.)
[The husband's sin is the talk of the town, the wife's is a private matter.] If a husband is unfaithful, it is like spitting from the house to the street; but if a wife is unfaithful, it is like spitting from the street into the house. *Cf.* The wrongs of a husband are not reproached.

184 **Муж того не знает что жена гуляет.**
The husband is always the last to know. *Lat.* ille solus nescit omnia.

185 **Мужа чтут за разум, а жену по уму.**   *v.* Ж60
[The husband is respected for his reason, the wife for her sense.] *Cf.* Men get wealth and women keep it. Seldom does a husband thrive without the leave of his wife.

186 **Мужество - это сило.**   *v.* О172
[Courage is strength.] *Cf.* The weapon of the brave is in his heart. A man of courage is never in need of weapons.

187 **Мужество рождается в борьбе.**
[Bravery is born in battle.] Valour delights in the test. Courage comes through suffering.

188 **Мужество создает победителей.**   *v.* Г107
[Valour shapes victors.] Fearless courage is the foundation of victory. *Cf.* A brave man may fall, but he cannot yield.

189 **Мужик богатый, что бык рогатый.**   *v.* П160
[A rich boor is like a horned bull.] The higher the ape goes, the more he shows his tail. *Cf.* A gentleman never makes any noise.

190 **Мужик богатеет - в баре идет, барин беднеет - к мужику идет.**
[A *muzhik* gets rich and walks with the lords, but an impoverished lord must walk with the *muzhiks*.] *Cf.* From clogs to clogs are three generations.

191* **Мужик всегда мужиком.**
[Once a *muzhik*, always a *muzhik*.] You can take a man (boy) out of the country, but you can't take the country out of the man (boy). *SPL.* rustica turba suos nescit deponere mores.

192 **Мужик сосну рубит, а по грибам щепа бьет.**   *v.* Д467
[The lout fells the pine, and the chips splinter the mushrooms.] *Cf.* What the fool does in the end the wise man does in the beginning.

193 **Мужик что мешок, что положат, то и несет.**
[The *muzhik* is like a bag that will carry anything.] *Cf.* An easy fool is the knave's tool. A fool believes everything.

194 **Мужика (свинью) посади за стол, а он и ноги на стол.** *v.* Д25,31, К333, С54
[Invite a *muzhik* (pig) to table, and he'll put his feet on it.] *Cf.* Give him an inch and he'll take a yard. Give a dog (him) your finger and he'll want your hand.

195* **Мука всему наука.** *v.* Н149,378, О92
Misfortunes make us wise. Experience is the mother of wisdom. *Cf.* Trouble brings experience and experience brings wisdom. Aes.*Ag*.164: πάθει μάθος.

196 **Мукá не мýка, а без мукú - мýка.** *v.* Б144
[No grief with wheat, but without wheat much grief.] All griefs with bread are less.

197 **Мутную воду пьют в невзгоду.** *v.* В11, Е56, Н31
[Turbid water can be drunk in adversity.] All's good in a famine.

198 **Муха не боится обуха.** *v.* 327
[Flies don't fear truncheons.] You cannot kill flies with a spear. *Cf.* Don't use a cannon to shoot a sparrow.

199 **Муха не велика, да ворчит.** *v.* М7,203, Н206
[The fly is not big, yet buzzes loudly.] *Cf.* Fair and foolish, long and lazy, little and loud.

200 **Муха убивает-ли орла, а муравей льва?**
[Do flies kill eagles, or ants lions?] *Cf.* †A fly may conquer a lion.

201 **Мухи к свету, а мышь во тьму.** *v.* Л16, П107, У15
[The fly is attracted to light, the mouse to darkness.] *Cf.* A mouse in pitch. *Lat.* mus picem gustans. Tastes differ.

202* **Мучилась гора родами да родила мышь.** *v.* Г247, Д453
The mountains have brought forth a mouse. *Lat.* Hor.*AP*.139: parturiunt montes, nascetur ridiculus mus.

203 **Мушиный обычай - приставать.** *v.* Н77, О101
[The property of the fly is to intrude.] Flies look for ulcers. *Cf.* Flies come to feasts unasked. A fly follows the honey.

204 **Мы пахали.** *sarc.* *v.* В319
[We did our share of ploughing too.] *Cf.* Great braggers, little doers. They can do least who boast loudest. *Lat.* minima possunt qui plurima iactant.

205 **Мы с тобою как рыба с водою - ты на дно а я на берег.** *v.* Б391
[We're like fish and water: you to the bottom, and I to shore.] Friends agree best at a distance.

206 **Мы (и) сами с усами.** *sarc.* *v.* Н361
[We have whiskers too.] We weren't born yesterday.

207 **Мы сварили а другие съели.** *v.* О35
[We did the cooking and others did the eating.] I kill the boar and another eats the flesh. *SPL.* praestitis laboribus alius partam expungit gloriam.

208 **Мыло серо да моет бело.** *v.* Б173, К173
[Soap is grey yet washes white.] A black hen lays a white egg.

209   **Мышей огонь не жжет, ни палит.**   *v.* О103, Р41
[Fire neither burns nor singes mice.] *i.e. because they run away.* Burn the house to get rid of the mice.

210* **Мыши выбрали кота за попа.**   *v.* Г326
[The mice made the cat their priest.] It is a foolish sheep that makes the wolf his confessor. It is a bold mouse that breeds in the cat's ear.

211* **Мышь копны не боится.**   *v.* М137, Н271
[A mouse is not afraid of haystacks.] The anvil fears no blows.

212* **Мышь сыта, мука горька.**   *v.* В516, И30,116, С341
[Flour tastes bitter to a sated mouse.] When the cat is full, the milk tastes sour. *SPL.* satietas fastidium parit.

213* **Мягки руки чужие труды любят.**   *v.* Б126
[Tender hands prefer the labours of others.] Ill workers are good onlookers.   To the bystander, no work is too hard. A cat in gloves catches no mice.

214   **Мягко стелет, да жестко спать.**   *v.* К96
[He makes the bed soft, yet it's hard to sleep.] An iron hand in a velvet glove.   Velvet paws hide sharp claws. *Cf.* A honey tongue, a heart of gall. Speak softly and carry a big stick.

215* **Мягкое слово кости (не) ломит.**   *v.* Д312,346, Л8, П135, У99
[Kind words break (no) bones.] There is great force hidden in a sweet command. *Cf.* Sticks and stones may break my bones, but words will never hurt me. The tongue breaks bone and itself has none.

216   **Мясо не довари, а рыбу перевари.**
[Cook meat medium-rare, fish well-done.]   *Cf.* Raw poultry, veal and fish make churchyards fat.

217   **Мясоед с постом побранился.**
[Lent and meat-lovers don't agree.] It's ill speaking between a full man and a fasting man.

Н

1* **На бедного везде капнет.** *v.* Б31,32,271,*Ар.*1.34
[It will always rain on the poor.] The poor suffer all the wrong. The poor man pays for all. The poor man is aye put to the worst.

2* **На безлюдье и баба человек (и сидень в честь).** *v.* Н3, *Ар.*1.99
[When there's nobody around, a woman (recluse) is company.] For want of company, welcome trumpery. *Cf.* A crust is better than no bread. A bad bush is better than the open field. Better a lean jade than an empty halter.

3* **На безрыбье и рак рыба.** *v.* В448,498, З63, И32, К152,Н2,348, О18, *Ар.*1.99
[When there's no fish, a crab is considered a fish.] Who cannot catch fish, must catch shrimps. *Cf.* All's fish that's come to net. The gravest fish is an oyster. Better are small fish than an empty dish. Every fish is not a sturgeon. Something is better than nothing.

4* **На бешеный вопрос да круговой ответ.** *v.* К15,72, Н21, Я16
Ask a silly question and you'll get a silly answer.

5* **На битой (торной) дороге трава не растет.** *v.* Г66, Р52
Grass grows not on the highway. A trodden path bears no grass. Grass doesn't grow on a busy street.

6* **На Бога надейся (положись) (уповай), а сам не плошай.** *v.* Б265,297, Ж16
[Trust in God but rely on yourself.] Work as if everything depended on you, pray as if everything depended on God. *Cf.* Trust in God and do something. Pray to God, but keep hammering. Trust in God but keep your powder dry.

7 **На брань слово купится (слова прикупают) (слова ищут).** *v.* Д43
Wranglers never want words.

8* **На брезгливого не угодишь.** *v.* Б275, Д35, Ж3, Л92, Н19, П122
[The fastidious are never satisfied.] *Cf.* None says his garner is full.

9* **На брюхе(-то) шелк, а в брюхе(-то) щелк.** *v.* В10

10* **На весь мир мягко не постелешь (и солнышку не угреть).** *v.* З159, Н19,74, П95
[You cannot make a soft bed (the sun cannot shine) everywhere.] It is hard to please all parties. You can't please everybody.

11 **На весь свет и Бог не угодит.** *v.* Н19
[Not even God can please everyone always.] All things fit not all persons.

12 **На ветер живота не напасешься.** *v.* В215, З5
A man cannot live on air. You cannot reap the wind.

13   **На ветер надеяться - без помолу быть.**   *v.* Б88, Ж29, З68, М138
[To wait for the wind is to defer the grinding.] *i.e. the mill is idle.* He that lives on hope has a slender diet. Hope is the poor man's bread. He that lives on hope will die fasting. *Cf.* Oft expectation fails. Expect nothing and you won't be disappointed.

14   **На вино есть деньги, на хлеб нет.**
[To have money for wine, not bread.] *Cf.* Everyone has a penny to spend at a new ale house. It is better to have bread left over than to run out of wine.

15*   **На вкус (на любовь), на цвет товарища (спора) (образца) нет.**   *v.* И128, К253, О1,
There is no accounting for tastes [love] [colours].   П107, У15
Lat. de gustibus non est disputandum.

16   **На вожжах и лошадь умна.**
[Even a horse is smart when bridled.] It is the bridle and spur that makes a good horse.

17*   **На волке волчья и шерсть.**   *v.* В392, Е46, К23, Ч50,98
[The wolf has a wolf's hide.] Whoever is a wolf behaves as a wolf. The wolf must die in his own skin. A leopard cannot change his spots.

18*   **На воре (тате) шапка горит.**   *v.* В321,334,426, З133,145, У10
[The thief's cap is on fire.] A guilty conscience needs no accuser. The thief does fear every bush an officer. *SPL.* conscientia mille testes. *Cf.* He that commits a fault, thinks everyone speaks of it. When you have committed a crime, the whole world is a looking glass. Who has skirts of straw, needs fear the fire.

19   **На всех не угодишь.**   *v.* В525, Д82, З159, Н8,10,11, О30,74, П233
You can't please everyone. *SPL.* condire recte non est cuiusvis.   laudatur ab his, culpatur ab illis.

20   **На всяк день готовься к смерти.**   *v.* Ж158, С194
[Every day prepare for death.] Live mindful of death. *Lat.* memento mori. *Cf.* Eat, drink and be merry, for tomorrow you die. Death meets us everywhere.

21   **На всякие приветы надобно иметь ответы.**   *v.* К21,72, Н4,35, Я16
Like question, like answer. Every why has a wherefore.

22*   **На всякий горшок найдется покрышка.**   *v.* К87, Н39, П49
Every pot has its cover. Like (such) cup, like (such) cover.

23   **На всякий час не обережешься.**   *v.* Н58, Ч18
[One cannot provide for every contingency.] Least expected, sure to happen. The unexpected always happens.

24*   **На всякого (каждого) мудреца довольно простоты.**   *v.* Б167,420, В160,353, Е9
No man is wise at all times. *Gr.* Theognid. οὐδεὶς ἀνθρώπων αὐτὸς ἅπαντα σοφός.
SPL. etiam bonus nonnunquam dormitat Homerus. nemo horis omnibus sapit.

25   **На всякое ремесло по злыдням.**   *v.* Л77
[Every trade has its rascals.] There's no pack of cards without a knave. The plague and the hero are both of a trade.

26*   **На всякое чихание (всякий чох) не наздравствуешься.**   *v.* В525, Н10,11,19,74,
[One can't respond to every sneeze.]   О30,74, П95
You cannot please the whole world and his wife. *Cf.* He that all men will please shall never find ease.

27   **На всяком дереве птица сидела.**
[The bird has sat on every tree.] *Cf.* He's been around.

28   **На всякую долю Бог посылает.**   *v.* Б252,260, Д38, Р63
[God provides for every contingency.] *Cf.* God never sends mouth but he sends meat.
God sends cold after clothes. God makes the back for the burden. God tempers the wind
to the shorn lamb.

29   **На высоком месте сидеть - пространные надобно очи иметь.**   *v.* Б323, Ч7,54
[To sit in high office means having far-seeing eyes.] A post of honour is a post of
danger. Mickle power makes many enemies. High places have their precipices.

30   **На гнилой товар слепой купец.**
[Bad wares want blind buyers.] If fools went not to market, bad wares would not be sold.

31   **На голую ногу всякий башмак впору.**   *v.* В111, Е56, М197, Н62
[Any shoe will do for a bare foot.] Beggars can't be choosers. When in great need,
anything will do.

32*   **На грех мастера нет.**   *v.* Б149, И36, Н43,495, Ч30
[There is no master of error.] *SPL.* mala sunt in proclivi. To err is human. *Cf.* He who
makes no mistake is a fool.

33   **На грош амуниции, да на рубль амбиции.**   *v.* Б88
[A penny's worth of resources but a dollar's worth of ambition.] Poor by condition, rich
by ambition. *Cf.* Hope is the poor man's bread.

34   **На дворе мороз, а денежка в кармане тает.**
[It's freezing outside, yet money melts in your pocket.] *Cf.* Money can burn a hole in
your pocket.

35*   **На добрый привет добрый ответ.**   *v.* К21,72, Н21, Я16
As you salute, you will be saluted. Like question, like answer.

36*   **На живом все заживет.**   *v.* Ж98
[Everything will heal on the living.] There is aye life for a living man.

37*   **На зеркало нечего пенять, коли рожа крива.**   *v.* З116, К205, Н337, Р9:
[Blame not the glass for the crooked face.] *Cf.* What your glass tells you will not be told
by counsel. †A looking glass never tells a woman she is homely.

38   **На зло молящим нет события.**
The prayers of the wicked won't prevail.

39   **На каждую дыру найдется по затычке.**   *v.* К87, Н22, П4*
[One can find a plug for any hole.] *Cf.* Every light has its shadow. Such cup, such cover
A homely patch is better than a hole.

40   **На кнуте далеко не уедешь.**
[You will not ride far on a whip.] Untimeous spurring spoils the steed. *Cf.* A running
horse needs no spur.

41*   **На кого Бог, на того и добрые люди.**   *v.* С20
[Whom God smites, so do the righteous.] When a man is down, everyone runs over him
When a man is going downhill, everyone gives him a push.

42   **На кого игумен, на того и братья.**   *v.* З52,И69, К67
        Such as the abbot is, such is the monk. To a bad chaplain, a bad sacristan. *Cf.* Like priest, like people.

43*   **На кого грех (лень) (ложь) (напасть) (ошибка) (печаль) (проруха)**
     не бывает.   *v.* В582, Г312, И36, Н32,495, Ч26,30, *Ap.*1.36
        No man is infallible.

44   **На красивую глядеть хорошо, а с умной жить легко.**   *v.* Б363, С16
        [A beauty is fine to look at, but a clever woman is easy to live with.] Beauty is a fine thing but you can't live on it. *Cf.* Beauty won't make the pot boil.

45   **На крепкий сук острый топор.**   *v.* Н171, О108, Т75
        [A hefty bough requires a mighty axe.] The greater the obstacle, the more glory in overcoming it. *SPL.* duro nodo durus quaerendus est cuneus. *Cf.* The bigger the tree, the harder she falls.

46   **На кривой суд образца нет.**
        [There is no example for an unjust court.] *Cf.*We live by laws, not by example. A corrupt judge weighs truth badly.

47   **На кукушкиных яйцах цыплят не выведешь.**   *v.* З139, Н402, О96,156,166
        [You cannot breed chicks from the eggs of a cuckoo.] *Cf.* Of an evil crow, an evil egg.

48*   **На лес и поп вор.**   *v.* Г72, Н320,579
        [In the woods, even the priest is a thief.] When the house is open, an honest man sins. The righteous man sins before an open chest. The hole calls the thief.

49   **На ловца (и) зверь бежит.**   *v.* Л29
        [The prey runs to meet the hunter.] *i.e. falls into his hands.* The ball comes to the player.

50   **На льстивы речи не мечись, на грубую правду не сердись.**   *v.* Л172
        [Don't fish for compliments, nor anger at the rude truth.] *Cf.* Better speak truth rudely than lie covertly.

51   **На людей законы, а на себя рассуждение.**
        [Laws are for others, reason for yourself.] Laws govern the man, and reason the law.

52   **На милость образца нет.**   *v.* Н15
        [There's no recipe for kindness.] Kindness comes of will.

53   **На миру (людях) и смерть красна.**   *v.* В343,546, Г266, С21
        [With company, even death loses its sting.] Trouble shared is trouble halved. It is good to have company in trouble.

54   **На молодого смотрят, а на старого и глядеть нехотят.**   *v.* М147
        [Youth attracts and age averts the eyes.] *SPL.* contemnunt spinas, cum cedire rosae.

55*   **На молоке ожегшись (и) на воду дуешь.**   *v.* Б220,349, В394
        [He who has been scalded by milk will blow on water.] A scalded cat fears hot water. A man once bitten by a snake will jump at the sight of a rope. *SPL.* qui semel laesus fallaci piscis ab hamo, omnibus unca cibis aera subesse putat. piscator ictus sapit. *Cf.* Once bitten, twice shy. The burnt child dreads the fire.

56   **На море погоду видишь да едешь, сам себе убийца.**   *v.* B317
[The suicidal sail the sea despite bad weather.] Never go to sea when a storm is coming. *Cf.* He complains wrongfully on the sea that twice suffers shipwreck.

57*   **На мысле запрета нет.**   *v.* B528, Г213, C23
    Thought is free. *SPL.* cogitationis poenam nemo patitur.

58   **На напасть не напрясть.**   *v.* H23, Ч18
[One cannot prepare for all misfortunes.] It is the unforeseen that always happens. Nothing is so certain as the unforeseen. *Lat.* Plaut.*Most.*1.3.40: insperata accidunt magis quam speres.

59*   **На начинающего Бог.**
[God helps the beginner.] God helps the industrious. *Cf.* For a web begun God sends the thread.

60   **На наш век дураков хватит.**
[There are enough fools in our own lifetime.] The world is full of fools. *Cf.* There's a sucker born every minute.

61*   **На (одной) неделе семь пятниц.**
[His (her) week has seven Fridays.] *i.e. is indecisive or moody.* Changeful as the moon. *Cf.* As changeable as a chameleon. Neither here nor there.

62*   **На нет и суда нет.**   *v.* H31, P13
What cannot be cured must be endured. Beggars can't be choosers. A man cannot give what he hasn't got. *Lat.* nil dat quod non habet. *SPL.* cantabit vacuus coram latrone viator.

63   **На новоселье всегда бывает веселье.**   *v.* K279, M88, C50
[There's always mirth in a new home.] Everything new is fine.

64   **На обеде все соседи, а пришла беда - они прочь как вода.**   *v.* Б372,467,Г50, Д448,
[Trencher friends disperse like water when trouble appears.]   З16, K132, П236, X23
Trencher friends are seldom good neighbours. Cupboard love is seldom true love. While the pot boils, friendship lasts. Dinner over, away go the friends. *Cf.* When one has a good table, he's always right.

65   **На одного сердит, а на всех косо глядит.**   *v.* Г167
[Angry with one, sullen with all.] Angry men make themselves beds of nettles. *Cf.* To be on the house-top in anger. Anger profits nobody.

66*   **На одном гвозде всего не повесишь.**   *v.* B94,503
    Do not hang all on one nail.

67   **На одном месте и всяк бы сидел.**   *v.* H73
[All would prefer to sit in one place.] *Cf.* Laziness has no boosters but many pals. Nature hates all sudden changes.

68*   **На одном месте и камень мохом обростет.**   *v.* П9?
The rolling stone gathers no moss. Too much rest is rust. *Gr.* Apost.10.72: λίθος κυλινδόμενος τὸ φῦκος οὐ ποιεῖ. *Lat.* saxum volutum non obducitur musco.

69   **На опальный товар много купцов.**   *v.* З91, Ч19
[Forbidden goods find many buyers.] Everything forbidden is sweet. Forbidden frui tastes sweeter.

70* **На охоту ехать - собак кормить.** *v.* В347, Ж156, Н252, Х14
[Feed the dogs when it's time for the hunt.] *i.e. too late.* Fed hounds never hunt. Thatch your roof before the rain begins. Have not thy cloak to make when it begins to rain.

71 **На первой встрече да азартные речи.** *v.* П12
[Passionate talk at the first encounter.] The first dish is best eaten.

72* **На песке дом построен.**
[House built on sand.] *Cf. Matt.*7.26: A foolish man which built his home upon the sand. *Gr.* εἰς ἄμμον οἰκοδομεῖς.

73 **На печи сидя, генерал не будешь.** *v.* Б49,127, В616, Г281, Н67
[You'll never be general if you stay in bed.] Of idleness comes no goodness.

74* **На погосте жить, всех (мертвых) не оплачешь.** *v.* Н10,19,26, П233
[He who lives by the churchyard cannot mourn all the dead.] *said in justification of apparent indifference.* He who weeps for everybody soon loses his eyesight. Tears bring nobody back from the grave. *Cf.* He that would please all and himself takes more in hand than he's like to do.

75 **На посуле как на стуле - посидишь да встанешь.** *v.* К261, О11
[Promising is like sitting: after a while you get up.] A man apt to promise is apt to forget.

76 **На посуле тороват, а на дело скуповат.** *v.* В118, Н430
[Liberal to promise, miserly to perform.] Great promises and small performance. He promises mountains and performs molehills. He promises like a merchant and pays like a man of war.

77 **На потливую лошадь всегда овод садится.** *v.* М203
[Gadflies always go to a sweaty horse.] Flies haunt (go to) lean horses.

78 **На правду мало слов.** *v.* Б483, Л14, П223
Truth needs not the ornament of many words. The language of truth is simple. Truth gives a short (has no) answer (+ but lies go round about). *Cf.* Truth needs no rhetoric.

79 **На провальную яму не наберешь хламу.**
[A bottomless pit can never be filled.] *Cf.* Covetousness is always filling a bottomless vessel.

80 **На работу боком, а с работы скоком.** *v.* В122, К1, Л49, Р4
[Slow to work, quick from work.] *Cf.* You run to work in haste, as if nine men held you. A lazy man goes to his work like a thief to the gallows.

81 **На разливе пиво пьют, на разборе ягодки едят.**
[Much beer is drunk while bottling, and many berries eaten during sorting.] *Cf.* Nurses put one bit into the child's mouth and two in their own.

82* **На резвом коне жениться не езди.** *v.* Ж73
[Don't ride a fast horse to your wedding.] A young trooper should have an old horse. Before you marry 'tis well to tarry.

83 **На ретивую лошадь не кнут а вожжи (больше кладут).** *v.* Б101,244, 383
A boisterous horse must have a rough bridle [rather than the whip]. *SPL.* equo currenti non opus est calcaribus. A running horse needs no spur. *Lat. Ov.A.A.*2.732: nolle admisso subdere calcar equo.

84* **На рогоже сидя, о соболях не рассуждают.**   *v.* В548,563,569, З153,154, Н197, *Ap.*1.21
[Those who sit on bast mats should not judge sable.] *Cf.* Let the cobbler stick to his last. Blind men can judge no colours.

85* **На руку не кричи.**   *v.* Д131
[Don't blame the hand.] A bad workman always blames his tools. *Cf.* The fox condemns the trap, not himself.

86* **На свете ничего нового нет.**   *v.* Н554
Nothing new under the sun. *Lat.* nihil novum sub sole. *SPL.* nihil novi et peregrini sol videt.

87* **На свой аршин не меряй.**   *v.* В187,559, З53,107
Measure not another's corn by your own bushel.

88 **На себя работать не стыдно.**   *v.* В570, *Ap.*1.13
[Be not ashamed to work for yourself.] *Cf.* A man is a lion in his own cause. He that is ill to himself will be good to nobody.

89 **На сердитых воду возят.**   *v.* Е32
[The angry lug water.] *i.e. do the hard work.* He that is angry is seldom at ease. Anger punishes itself. Anger profits nobody. *Cf.* An angry man never wants woe. An angry beggar gets a stone instead of a handout.

90 **На сердце ненастье, то и в ведро дождь идет.**
[For the grieving heart it rains amid good weather.] *Cf.* In whose heart there is no song, to him the miles are many and long. When your heart's on fire, smoke gets in your eyes. An evil heart can make any doctrine heretical.

91* **На словах (говорить без дела), что на воде (писать).**   *v.* Ч101
[Words (without deeds) are like (writing on) water.] Words, like feathers, are carried away by the wind. Good words without deeds are like rushes and reeds. *Cf.* To write on water. *Gr.* εἰς ὕδωρ γραφεῖν. *Lat.* in aqua scribere.

92 **На словах медок а на сердце ледок.**   *v.* К171, Н122, С246
[Words of honey, heart of ice.] A honey tongue, a heart of gall. Plaut.*Truc.*1.1: in melle sunt linguae sitae vestrae - corda felle sunt sita.

93 **На суд идти, прежде самому осудиться.**   *v.* З17, О116, Ч136
[Judge yourself before venturing into court.] Judge others by what you do. Judge well before you criticize. *Cf.* He who will have no judge but himself condemns himself. No man ought to be judge in his own cause. *Lat.* nemo debet esse iudex in propria causa. If you judge your own case, you are judged by a fool.

94* **На сухом берегу рыбу не ловят.**   *v.* Ж36, М43, Н397, О97, П273
[There is no fishing on a dry shore.] You can't catch fish on a dry line. He who would catch fish must not mind getting wet. *Cf.*It's in vain to cast your net where there's no fish.

95 **На тебе Боже (небоже) что нам негоже.**
Good riddance to bad rubbish.

96 **На то щуке зубы (щука в море), чтобы карас не дремал.**   *v.* Б314
[The pike have teeth (live in the sea) to keep the carp from dozing.] A careless watch invites the vigilant foe. *Cf.* The big fish catch the little ones.

97 **На урода (все) не угода.**
Ungirt, unblessed.

98* **На (всяком) хотение живет (есть) терпение.**   *v.* В503, Ж23, Н233
[Wishful thinking invites patience.] From word to deed is a great space. *Cf.* If wishes were horses, beggars might ride.

99 **На худо добрые люди не учат.**   *v.* Х95
[The righteous do not teach evil.] Never do evil that good may come of it. *Lat.* quod non sunt facienda mala ut veniant bona.

100* **На час ума не стало, навек дураком прослыыл.**
[Err once without amends and remain a fool forever.] One foolish mistake can undo a lifetime of happiness.

101 **На человеческую глупость есть Божья премудрость.**   *v.* Ч27
[Man's folly is parried by God's wisdom.] Man proposes, God disposes. There is God when all's done.

102* **На чертей только слава.**   *v.* Д311, Л79, Р16
[Only devils are famous.] A bad deed never dies. Mankind bestows more applause on her destroyer than on her benefactor. *Cf.* Bad men leave their mark wherever they go. Marble busts are made of those who "raised Cain," not corn. Infamy is the livery of bad deserts.

103 **На что за тем гоняться кто не хочет знаться?**   *v.* В103
Friendship cannot stand always on one side.

104 **На что и клад коли в семье лад?**   *v.* В267, Д360, Н195
[What good is a treasure when there's contentment at home?] Content is more than a kingdom. Happiness is more than riches.

105 **На что корова, былаб жена здорова.**   *v.* Д270
[What good is a cow when your wife is sick.] *Cf.* A poor man's cow dies, a rich man's child. A good wife and health are a man's best wealth.

106 **На что того хуже, как дураку своя воля.**
[Nothing worse than a fool at large.] Fools and madmen ought not to be left in their own company. *Cf.* The fool asks much, but he is a fool that grants it.

107 **На чужих детей не указывай - у самого полон рот зубов.**   *v.* Д431, Н413, Т13, Ч47
[Don't point at others' children when you have plenty of your own.] Those who live in glass houses should not throw stones. Point not at others' spots with a foul finger.

108 **На чужих жен не заглядывай, а за своею прогляди.**   *v.* Х50
[Look not at others' wives, but mind your own.] *Cf.* Who has a fair wife needs more than two eyes. He who loves his wife should watch her.

109 **На чужое богатство не надейся, свое береги.**   *v.* З54, И134, Н112,338
[Covet not the wealth of others but preserve your own.] *Cf.* Catch not at the shadow and lose the substance. He that waits for dead mens' shoes may go a long time barefoot.

110* **На чужое горе не наплакаться.**   *v.* Г267, П300, Ч114
[One doesn't grieve excessiviely over others' misfortunes.] One always has strength enough to bear the misfortunes of one's friends. Another's cares will not rob you of sleep. To bear other people's afflictions, everyone has courage enough and to spare.

111 **На чужое пиво не надуешь рыло.**   *v.* В180,200, Г128, Ч122
[Of another's beer, you'll not get your fill.] He that is fed at another's hand (table) may stay long ere he be full. You can't get warm in another's fur.

112 **На чужой каравай рот (рта) не разевай (+ а пораньше вставай да свой затевай).**
(На чужой пир не надейся.)   *v.* З354, И134,Н109,338
[Don't crave another's pie (+ but rise earlier and make your own.] [Rely not on another's feast.] Scald not your lips in another man's pottage. Thrust not your feet under another man's table.

113* **На чужой рот пуговицы не нашьешь (не накинешь платок.)**   *v.* В191,404,528
[One cannot button (gag) peoples' mouths.] People will talk.

114 **На чужой сарай (стог) (своими) вилами не показывай (указывай).** *v.* В189,190,201,
(На чужую кучу глаза не пучи.) (На чужом гумне нет корысти мне.) Н303,318, Х97
[Point not your pitchfork at another's store (stack).] [Crave not another's store.] [There's nothing of interest to me in another's barn.] Covet not that which belongs to others. Pluck not where you never planted.

115* **На чужой спине (бремя) легко. (На чужом хребте легко работать.)** *v.*Б311, Л24,Н572
The burden is light on the shoulders of another. *Cf.* Ill workers are good onlookers.

116 **На чужой стороне и весна не красна.**   *v.* В139, Д386, С61, Ч128
[Even Spring loses its charm abroad.] Dry bread at home is better than meat abroad.
Cf. Better a friend's frown than a foe's smile.

117* **На чужом пиру похмелье.**   *v.* В207, З24, Л202, О188, С1, Т8
[To suffer a hangover from another's binge.] One does the scathe and another has the scorn. Adam ate the apple and our teeth still ache.

118* **На чужом столе хорош обед.**   *v.* В178,583, Д222, Ч118,129
The wholesomest meat is at another man's cost. Another man's food is sweeter.

119 **На чужую кашу надейся, а своя бы в печи была.**   *v.* Б297, Д442, Н6
[Hope for another's *kasha*, but keep your own on the stove.] Put your trust in God, but keep your powder dry. Trust me, but look to thyself.

120* **На чьем возу едешь (чей хлеб соль ешь), того (тому) и песеньку поешь.** *v.* В623, Г39,
[To the man submit on whose wagon you ride (at whose board you sit).] Н409, Ч24
Whose bread I eat, his song I sing. He who pays the piper calls the tune.

121 **На язык пошлины нет.**   *v.* О153
Talking pays no toll.

122 **На языке мед а в сердце лед.**   *v.* К171, Н92, С246
A honey tongue, a heart of gall. *SPL.* mel in ore, fel in corde.

123 **Наглого обычая не переменишь.**   *v.* Б440
It is hard to break a hog of an ill custom.

124 **Наглому дай волю, он захочет боле.**   *v.* Д25,31, М194
Give the devil an inch and he'll take an ell.

125* **Нагой разбою не боится.**   *v.* В121, Г241, З9, Н559, С5, У71
No naked man is sought after to be rifled. *Cf. Lat.* Plaut.*As.*1.1: nudo vestimenta detrahere.

126 **Над кем пословица не слывается.**   *v.* П184
Common proverb never lies.

127* **Над нами не капнет.**
[It won't drip on us.] *i.e. there's no need to hurry.* It will keep.

128 **Наделала синица славы, а море не зажгла.** *v. B601*
[The titmouse bragged but didn't set the sea on fire.] Brag is a good dog but dares not bite. *Cf.* Every bird loves to hear himself sing. Old brag is a good dog, but hold fast is a better one.

129 **Надеяться и ждать - одураченным стать.** *v. Ж29, 368, Н13*
[Hope and expectation will make a fool of you.] *Cf.* Hope often deludes the foolish man.

130 **Надсаженный конь, надломленный лук, да замиренный друг всегда ненадежен.**
[A horse broken-in, a bow loosened, and a reconciled friend are all unreliable.]
Cf. A reconciled friend is a double enemy. †Choose a horse made and a man to make.

131 **Наживать долго, а прожить скоро.**
Narrow gathered, widely spent.

132 **Нажил богатство, забыл братство.** *v. Б278*

133* **Назвался груздем (грибом), полезай в кузов.** *v. B291, K213, Н440, C84*
[If you call yourself a mushroom, get into the basket.] Don't say go but gaw. In for a penny, in for a pound. *Cf.* Throw the helve after the hatchet.

134* **Назови (называй) хоть горшком, только в печку не ставь (сажай).** *v. Б356, Я19*
[You may call me a pot, but put me not on the stove.] Words may pass but blows fall heavy. Sticks and stones may break my bones but names will never hurt me.

135 **Называет другом а обирает кругом.** *v. Д416*
[He calls me a friend but strips me bare.] When two friends have a common purse, one sings and the other weeps. *Cf.* All are not friends who speak us fair.

136 **Найдено делить легко.** *v. И110*
[It is easy to share found goods.] *Cf.* To be free at another man's cost. Nothing freer than a gift. He is free of fruit that wants an orchard.

137 **Наказал Бог народ - наслал воевод.**
[God punishes a people by sending a politician.] *Cf.* Where the devil can't come, he'll send.

138 **Нам добро и никому зло, то законное житье.** *v. И12, K146*
[Justice is what is good for us and not bad for others.] *Cf.* Justice pleases few in their own house.

139 **Нам чужого дерьма не надо, своего много.** *vulg.*
[We don't need others trash, we've enough of our own.] *Cf.* Good riddance to bad rubbish.

140 **Написано пером, не вырубишь и топором.**
[What the pen has writ, not even an axe can rend.] The pen is mightier than the sword. The written word (letter) remains. *SPL.* Litera dicta perit. Litera scripta manet.

141 **Напрасно о том рассуждают чего сами не знают.**
A person should not meddle with what he doesn't understand.

142 **Напрасно тот больной лечится, кто здоровый бесится.** *v. K298*
[It is futile to treat a man who is reckless with his health when he falls ill.] That sick man is not to be pitied who has his cure in his sleeve.

143* **Наружность обманчива.**   *v.* B316, H237,251, K191, П53
Appearances are deceiving.

144* **Наряди пень, и пень будет хорош.**   *v.* B78
Dress up a stick and it does not appear to be a stick.

145* **Наступи на черва - извиваться будет.**
Tread (step on) a worm and it will turn. *SPL.* non solum taurus feri uncis cornibus hostem: verum etiam instanti laesa repugnat ovis.

146* **Натура волка в лесу гонит.**   *v.* Г79
[Nature drives the wolf into the woods.] A frog cannot out of her bog. *Cf.* Nature is stronger than education.

147 **Натура - дура, судьба - индейка, а жизнь - копейка.**   *v.* Ж164, †H148
[Nature's a botcher, fate's a turkey, and life's just tow bits.] Life's a bitch. Life is a bubble on a stream.

148 **Натура не дура.**
Nature (God) is no botcher.

149* **Наука - мука.**   *v.* Б321, М109, H250,378, C34
Much science (learning), much sorrow.

150* **Наука переменяет природу.**
Art improves nature.

151 **Наука хлеба не просит а хлеб дает.**   *v.* P51
[Learning provides bread without requiring any.] He that learns a trade has a purchase made. *Cf.* Education is an investment never to be lost nor removed.

152 **Наука хороша по природе.**   *v.* П263
Nature surpasses nurture. *Cf.* Nature is conquered by obeying her. *Lat.* natura non nisi parendo vincitur.

153 **Науку в голову не вобьешь, как охоты не будет.**   *v.* И48
[Learning cannot be forced against one's will.] A man doesn't learn to understand anything unless he loves it. Nothing is easy to the unwilling. You can lead a horse to water, but you can't make it drink.

154 **Находчивость - великая сила (приносит победу).**   *v.* H269
[Resourcefulness is a great strength (brings victory) .] Cunning surpasses strength.

155* **Начали гладью, а кончали гадью.**   *v.* Б300, B287, З103, П202
[Began smoothly, ended rudely.] To go up like a rocket and come down like a stick.

156 **Начало благо, а конец потребен.**   *v.* Д303, З103, П201
Such beginning, such end.

157* **Начало половина дела.**   *v.* Д308, З106, Л75, П199
Well begun is half done. *Lat.* Hor.*Ep.*1.2.40: dimidium facti qui coepit habet.

158 **Начало премудрости - страх.**   *v.* O89
[Fear is the beginning of prudence.] Fear is one part of prudence.

159 **Начальнику первая чарка и первая палка.**
[The chief gets the first praise and the first reproach.] *Cf.* The first faults are theirs who commit them, the second theirs that permit them. The buck stops here.

160 **Начинаем духом а кончим брюхом.** *v.* Б136
[Begin with the spirit and end with the belly.] *Cf.* Not where one is bred but where he is fed. Better fed than taught. *Lat.* non ubi nascor, sed ubi pascor.

161 **Начинаючи (начиная) дело о конце размышляй (думай).** *v.* Л97, Н417
Think on the end before you begin.

162 **Наш грех больше всех.** *v.* Б311, В657
[Our sin is greatest.] Everyone thinks his sack (pack) heaviest.

163 **Наша горница с Богом не спорится.**
[Our hearth doesn't argue with God.] *said of homes with little or no heating. the temperature being about the same as outdoors;* *Cf.*Wind and weather, do thy worst.

164* **Наше дело сторона.** *v.* М169, Н335, Я2
It's none of our business.

165 **Наше дело маленькое.**
[Our job is small.] *Cf.* Cogs on a wheel.

166 **Наше дело телячье (+ поел да в закут).**
[We only do what we are told (+ and eat in the scullery).] Ours is not to question why, ours is but to do or die. Orders must not be challenged. *Cf.* He that serves, must serve.

167* **Нашего (своего, их, его, ее), поля ягода.** *v.* К266
[A berry of the same field.] *i.e. a kindred spirit.* Birds of a feather flock together.

168 **Нашел да не объявил - все равно что утаил.** *v.* К220
[Finding without revealing is the same as stealing.] The receiver is as bad as the thief.

169 **Нашел молчи, потерял молчи.** *v.* Н394
[Hush when you find, hush when you lose.] Finders keepers, losers weepers.

170 **Нашел черт на дьявола.**
[The devil happened upon his like.] Let one devil ding another.

171* **Нашла коса на камень.** *v.* Н45, О108
[The scythe has struck a stone.] *Lat.* **novacula in cotem incidit.** The irresistible force has met the immovable object. *Cf.* When Greek meets Greek, then comes the tug of war.

172* **Не бей в чужие ворота плетью, не ударили бы в твои дубиною.** *v.* Д432, Т80, Ч11
[Knock not at others' doors with a lash, lest they strike yours with a club.] Before you flare up at anyone's faults, take time to count ten of your own. *Cf.* Do as you would be done by.

173 **Не бей мужика дубьем (кнутом), бей его рублем.** *v.* Б364, И51
[Don't lash a lout - use cash.] A dog will not howl if you beat him with a bone.

174* **Не бить кума, не пить пива.** *v.* Б106, Г130,250, Д410
[If you you don't hit him, you won't have your beer.] You can't make an omelette without breaking eggs. *SPL.* phrynx non nisi plagis emendatur.

175 **Не богатый пиво варит, а тороватый.**
[It's the skilful and not the rich man who brews the beer.] Knowledge is better than riches (wealth). *Cf.* There are some things money can't buy.

176* **Не боги горшки обжигают.** *v.* C315
[It is not the gods who fashion pots.] Whatever man has done, man can do. God reaches us good things by our own hands.

177 **Не бойся барина, а бойся слуги.**
[Fear not the master but the servant.] *Cf.* Fear keeps and looks to the vineyard, not the owner.

178* **Не бойся врага умного, бойся друга глупого.** *v.* C253, У109
A rash friend is worse than a foe. A wise enemy is better than a foolish friend.
Cf. God deliver me from my friends, from my enemies I can defend myself.
Lat. Ov.*A.A.*1.751: non est hostis metuendus amanti, quos credis fidos effuge.

179 **Не бойся горького, бойся сладкого.**
[Beware not the bitter, but the sweet.] Beware the flatterer. *Cf.* Bitter pills may have blessed effects. Beauty may have fair leaves but bitter fruit. Beware of those who get familiar quickly.

180 **Не бойся палки, да бойся греха.**
[Fear not the rod but the sin.] Fear to do ill and you need fear nought else. Fear nothing but sin. *Cf.* The fox condemns the trap, not himself.

181 **Не бойся собаки что лает, а той что молчит да хвостом виляет.** *v.* И139, Н234, C223,
[Fear not the dog that barks but the one that wags its tail silently (bites slyly).] T28
Don't be afraid of a dog that barks. Barking dogs seldom bite. Beware of a silent dog and silent water. The silent dog is the first to bite. *SPL.* timidi canes vehementius latrant quam mordent. *Cf.* †A wagging tail dog never bites.

182 **Не бойся суда, бойся судьи.**
[Fear not the court but the judge.] *Cf.* †He whose father is judge goes safely to trial.

183 **Не брюхом слушай, а ухом.**
[Listen with your ears, not your belly.] We need brain more than belly food. *Cf.* The belly wants ears. Hungry bellies have no ears. *Lat.* venter auribus caret. It's a good story that fills the belly.

184 **Не будь гостью запасен (запаслив), а будь ему рад.**
[Welcome your guest and begrudge him not.] Be hospitable one to another without grudging. *Lat.* hospitales invicem sine murmuratione. *Cf.* It is a sin against hospitality to open your doors and shut up your countenance. *Lat.* nil interest habere ostium apertum et vultum clausum. Welcome the coming and speed the parting guest.

185 **Не будь изряден, будь пригоден.**
Be useful as well as ornamental.

186* **Не будь правды, не стало бы и лжи.** *v.* Г42, Е24, П227, C296
[If there were no truth, there would be no lies.] Without knowledge there is no sin or sinner. *Cf.* Tell a lie and find a truth. The more laws, the more offenders.

187 **Не будь тороплив, а будь памятлив.**
[Be not hasty but mindful.] Haste and wisdom are things far odd. *Cf.* Speed gets you nowhere if you're going in the wrong direction.

188 **Не бывать калине малиной.**
[A cranberry will never be a raspberry.] *Matt.*7.16: Of a thorn springs not a fig.
Cf. A rose is a rose is a rose.

189 **Не бывать плешивому кудрявым.** *v.* П122
[Bald cannot be curly.] You cannot pull hair where there is none

190 **Не было ни гроша, да (и) вдруг алтын.** *v.* Б448, В663, К118, Н408, С86
[Penniless, and suddenly a half-crown.] *i.e. a windfall.* From rags to riches. It never rains but it pours.

191 **Не было заботы, да дал Бог печаль.** *v.* Г270
[We were carefree until the Lord brought us sorrow.] *Cf.* †Suffering is better than care.

192* **Не было (бы) счастья, да несчастье помогло.** *v.* В355, Н531
[There would be no good fortune had misfortune not helped.] A blessing in disguise. There's no great loss without some gain.

193* **Не было у бабы хлопот (горя), купила порося.** *v.* В568
[The woman had no worries (problems), so she bought some pigs.] We carry our greatest enemies within us. Every man is his own worst enemy. Make not two sorrows of one. Bad is called good when worse happens. *Cf.* He that loves noise must buy a pig.

194 **Не быть курице петухом, а бабе мужиком.** *v.* В398,439, И74,106, С227
[A hen can never be a cock, nor a woman - a man.] *Cf.* A carrion kite will never be a good hawk. It's a sad house where the hen crows louder than the cock. When the hen crows, the house goes to ruin.

195* **Не в деньгах счастье.** *v.* В263,267, Д360, Н104
Money can't buy happiness. *Cf.* Money isn't everything.

196 **Не в коня корм (травить).**
[Don't waste the oats on the horse.] *i.e. a hopeless case.* A jade eats as much as a good horse. Don't throw (send) good money after bad.

197 **Не в свои оглобли не впрягайся.** *v.* В189,190,548,563,569, Н84,198
[Don't hitch yourself to another's harness.] Cultivate your own garden. Mind your own business. *Cf.* Hitch your wagon to a star. He who rides the tiger can never dismount.

198* **Не в свои сани не садись.** *v.* Н84,197,222,440, П293, Ч66
[Don't try to ride in another's sleigh.] *i.e. fill another's shoes.* Paddle your own canoe.

199 **Не в том кусте сидишь, не те песни поешь.** *v.* Н406
[You're sitting by the wrong bush and singing the wrong tunes.] To bark up the wrong tree. To beg at the wrong door.

200 **Не ваш дом, не ваша и печаль. (Не ваш конь, не ваш и воз.)** *v.* М169, Н164,
[If it's not your house, it's not your problem.] Н335,459, Я2
[If it's not your horse, it's not your load.] Let every peddlar carry his own burden (pack).

201* **Не ваша земля, не ваша и пашня.** *v.* В189, Н114,283,400, Х97
[If it's not your land, it's not your ploughed field.] Pluck not where you never planted. Every man should take his own.

202   **Не ваши то сани подламываются.**   *v.* B657, K10, H349, X71
     [It's not your sledge that breaks.]   *i.e." it's easy for you to say."* We have better counsel to give than to take. Advice is cheap. *Cf.* Every man can rule a shrew save he that has her. Nothing is given as freely as advice. Who has no children brings them up well.

203   **Не везде все родится.**   *v.* H248
     You can't have everything. *SPL.* non omnis fert omnia tellus.

204*   **Не везет в картах, везет в любви.**
     Unlucky at cards, lucky in love.   †Lucky at cards (life), unlucky in love.

205   **Не вели казнить, вели слово вымолвить.**
     [Let a man speak before he is punished.]   No man should be condemned unheard. Everyone is presumed innocent until proven guilty.

206   **Не велик сверчок да громко поет.**   *v.* M7,15,18,199
     [The cricket is small but loud.]   Little and loud.

207*   **Не велика блоха, да спать не дает.**   *v.* Ж15, M13, П297, Я25
     [A flea is small yet can keep you awake.] A little stone in the way overturns a great wain.

208   **Не велика семья, а все едоки.**
     [However small, a family means mouths to feed.]   *Cf.* A little house has a wide mouth.

209   **Не велика чекушка, а без нее не уедешь.**   *v.* M13
     [A cotter-pin may be small, yet you cannot ride without it.] Great businesses turn on a little pin. Great engines turn on small pivots.

210   **Не верь брату родному, а верь глазу кривому.**   *v.* H215
     [Believe rather your bad eye than your own brother.]   *Cf.* Seeing is believing.

211   **Не верь козлу в капусте, а волку в овчарне.**   *v.* Б385, B395, Д359, H389, П303
     [Don't trust a goat in the cabbage-patch nor a wolf in the sheepfold.]   Don't set a wolf to watch the sheep. Send not a cat for lard. *Cf.* Give the wolf wether to keep. It's better to keep a wolf out of the fold than to trust to drawing his teeth and talons after he shall have entered. The doghouse is no place to keep a sausage.

212   **Не верь коню в поле (дороге), а жене в воле (подворье).**   *v.* K245
     [Trust neither your horse in a field nor your wife in the townhouse.]   *Cf.* He that lets his horse drink at every lake and his wife go to every wake, shall never be without a whore and a jade.

213   **Не верь коню в узде.**   *v.* Б184
     [Trust not a horse in a bridle.]   *Cf.*Trust not a horse's heel. *Lat.*ab equinis pedibus procul recede.

214   **Не верь морю, а верь кораблю.**
     [Trust not the sea but the ship.]   *Cf.* †Praise (commend) the sea, but keep on land.

215*   **Не верь (чужим) речам, верь (своим) очам.**   *v.* Б317, Г113,165, Л123,146, H210, O194
     It is better to trust the eye than the ear. *SPL.* qui audiunt, audita dicunt; qui vident plane ssciunt. *Cf.* Seeing is believing. Believe nothing of what you hear and only half of what you see. One eye has more faith than two ears.

216*   **Не взять малого, не видать большого.**   *v.* Б437, И89, M25
     [Take not up the small and you'll never see the great.]   Small is the seed of every greatness. The highest towers begin from the ground.

217 **Не видались сем лет, а поговорить нечего.**
[After a seven years' absence, nothing to talk about.] *Cf.* Long absence changes a friend.

218 **Не видит, так и не бредит.**   *v.* В413, Д48, С4, Ч14
Unseen, unrued.

219 **Не вижу - душа мрет, увижу - с души прет.**   *v.* Б391, Е1, Р50
[Absent and longed-for, present and despised.] *i.e. a love-hate relationship.* Friends agree best at a distance. Intimacy breeds contempt.

220* **Не вино винит, но пьянство. (Невинно вино, виновато пьянство.)**   *v.* Н322,336,493
Intoxication is not the wine's fault but man's. *Cf.* Wine does not intoxicate men, men intoxicate themselves. One hates not the person but the vice.

221* **Не вкусив (вкусить) горького, не едать (видать) сладкого.**   *v.* Б344, В8, Г281, К256,
Suffering is bitter but its fruits are sweet.   Л171, Н363
Lat. dulcia non meruit, non gustavit arama.

222* **Не во все сани садись.**   *v.* В94, Н198, Ч66
[Do not ride in any sledge.] Every shoe fits not all feet. *Cf.* Don't bite off more than you can chew. A great shoe fits not a little foot.

223 **Не вознимайся высоко, так не спустишься низко.**   *v.* Б300,687, Н371
Climb not too high lest the fall be greater. The higher the aim, the higher the fall. The higher they go, the lower they fall. *Cf.* He sits not sure that sits too high. The highest tree has the greatest fall.

224* **Не волчий зуб, так лисий хвост. (Не всегда волчей рот имей - иногда и лисей хвост.)**   *v.* Б169, Г17
[If the wolf's tooth cannot, the fox's tail shall.] If the lion's skin cannot, the fox's shall. By hook or by crook. *EA.* si leonina pellis non satis est, vulpina addenda.

225* **Не время волос белит, а кручина.**   *v.* Г202,274, М101, Н390
[Misfortune, not age, greys hair.] **Many cares make the head white. Care brings grey hair.**

226 **Не все белит что бело, не все то чернит что черно.**   *v.* Б172, Н236,238,339
[Not all cleanses that is white, nor all tarnishes that is black.] Every white has its black, and every sweet its sorrow. *Cf.* A clean glove often hides a dirty hand. Dirty hands make clean money.

227 **Не все бьет что гремит.**   *v.* К259, Н431
[Not everything strikes that thunders.] There are more threatened than stricken. When the thunder is very loud, there's very little rain. *Cf.* It's the thunder that frights but the lightning that smites.

228 **Не все в слух, чаще на ухо.**   *v.* В565
[Not everything should be said out loud, but more often whispered.] All truths are not to be told.

229* **Не все в соборе поется.**   *v.* Л173, Н232, П8,187, С14
[It's not all singing in church.] *i.e. only part of the liturgy is sung.* There belongs more than whistling to going to plough. *Cf.* You must take the fat with the lean.

230 **Не все ври что знаешь. (Не все ворчат, надо и помолчать.)**   *v.* Н244,260
[Tell not all the lies you know (be silent also).] Don't tell all you know nor all you can. *Cf.* Tell not all you know, all you have, or all you can do.

231* **Не все всегда творится что просто говорится.**   *v.* В503,512, Г186, Л27, 36,О153, С156
[Not all is always done that is simply said.] Nothing happens from saying so. Saying so don't make it so. *Cf.* From word to deed is a great space. Saying and doing are two things.

232* **Не все коту масленица (+ бывает и великий пост).**   *v.* Д97, Ж141,164, Н229, О181
[Life's not just Carnival (Lent also comes).] Christmas comes but once a year. After Christmas comes Lent. Life is no bed of roses. *SPL.* minimis momentis maximae fiunt mutationes.

233 **Не все сбывается что желается.**   *v.* М113, Н98
[Not all materializes that is hoped for.] Better to have than to wish. Thinking is very far from knowing. If wishes were horses, beggars might ride.

234* **Не все собаки кусаются которые лают.**   *v.* Н181, С223, Т28
Barking dogs seldom bite.

235* **Не все сосны в лесу корабельные.**   *v.* В514, Н243
[Not all pines in the wood are fit for a ship.] Every block will not make a Mercury. *Lat.* ex quovis ligno non fit Mercurius.

236 **Не все то волк что серо.**   *v.* К144, Н226,238,570
[All that is grey is not a wolf.] All that shines is not silver. All cats are black at night.

237 **Не все то есть что видишь.**   *v.* В316, К191, Н143, П53
[Not everything you see is true.] Appearances are deceiving. *Cf.* To appear so does not prove thing to be so.

238* **Не все то золото что блестит.**   *v.* Б176, Н226
All that glitters is not gold.

239* **Не все те повары у кого ножи долгие.**   *v.* В574, И127
Not everyone who carries a long knife is a cook. All are not cooks who sport white caps and carry long knives. All are not hunters that blow the horn.

240* **Не все те русалки что в воду бросаются (ныряют).**   *v.* В574
[All are not mermaids who dive into the water.] All are not merry that dance lightly.

241* **Не всегда вор крадет (приходит), а (но) всегда берегись (его ждут).**   *v.* И8, Л110
[Thieves seldom come but are always expected.] Always figure for the worst and the best is bound to happen. All are not thieves that dogs bark at. *Cf.* He that has no ill fortune is troubled with good.

242 **Не всем сидеть на возу.**   *v.* Д105
[Not all can ride on top.] If two ride on a horse, one must ride behind.

243 **Не всем старцам (чернцам) в игуменах быть.**   *v.* К327, Н235
[Every elder (monk) cannot be an abbot.] Every man cannot be first (a master). Every fish is not a sturgeon.

244 **Не всему верь что слышишь, не всего желай что видишь.**
(Не все говори что знаешь, не все делай что можешь.)   *v.* Н230,253
Do not believe all you hear [do not crave all you see.] (Do not tell all you know [do not do all you can.]) *Cf.* Tell not all you know, all you have, or all you can do.

245   **Не вспоя (поя), не вскормя (кормя) ворога не наживешь.**   *v.* В391,538,676, Н528,
        [Nurse and nurture not and have no enemy.]   О130, П249
        To nourish a viper (snake) in one's bosom. *Cf.* Nothing worse than a familiar enemy.

246*   **Не всяк злодей кто часом лих.**   *v.* Б167, Е9
        [All are not wicked that once err.] He is good that failed never. *Cf.* No one is perfect.
        No man is wise at all times.

247*   **Не всяк игумен (монах) на ком клобук.**   *v.* Н295, Р94
        The cowl does not make the monk.

248   **Не всяк ко всему родился.**   *v.* К325, Н203,235,243
        [One isn't born for everything.] Not everyone can be first. Different strokes for different
        folks. One can't have everything. *SPL.* non ex quovis ligno fit Mercurius.

249   **Не всякая песенка до конца допевается.**   *v.* П95
        [Not every song is sung to the end.] *i.e. only good songs are.* *Cf.* A good song is none
        the worse for being sung twice.

250   **Не всякий кто думает счастье находит (и многое думанье в старость приводит).**
        [Not all thinkers find contentment (and too much thought ages).]   *v.* М109, Н149, С34
        Cf. Much science, much sorrow. Ignorance is bliss.

251   **Не всякий плут кто видом худ (приметы в свете часто лгут).**   *v.* Н143,237, Р65
        [Not all are swindlers who look sly,] **appearances are deceiving.** *Cf.* The face is no
        index to the heart. A homely form oft holds a handsome heart.

252*   **Не всякое лыко в строку.**   *v.* Н235
        [Not every cord is used in the weave.] An inch breaks no square. Mistakes don't make
        haystacks.

253*   **Не всякому (слуху) верь.**   *v.* Н244
        Believe not all you hear.

254*   **Не всякую правду жене сказывай.**
        [Don't tell your wife everything.] *Cf.* He that tells his wife news is but newly married.

255   **Не выбирай глазами, а выбирай ушами.**   *v.* Ж87, Л136, Н258,475
        Choose a wife by your ear rather than by your eye.

256*   **Не выноси из избы сору (+ так меньше вздору).**   *v.* И80, С242
        [Don't take your rubbish outside (+ and avoid ridicule).] Do not wash dirty linen in
        public.

257   **Не выдавай шумихи за золото.**   *v.* Б146, В348
        [Do not create a stir over gold.] To cry roast meat. *Cf.* Outside shoe, inside woe.

258   **Не гляди на лицо (рожу), гляди на обычай (душу).**   *v.* В99, Г112, Ж86, Н251,
        [Look not at the face but at the manner (heart).]   Н255,316, Р65
        Don't judge everyone by his looks. *Cf.* Fair face, foul heart. Fair without, false within.

259   **Не гляди под лесом, а гляди под носом.**   *v.* Д50, З20, П98
        [Look not under the trees but under your nose.] Don't lose sight of the forest for the trees.

260   **Не говори всего что знаешь.**   *v.* Н230,244
        Do not tell all you know.

261 **Не говори гоп, пока не перепрыгнешь (перескочишь).** *v.* Н395,477, Р38, Х6
[Don't cry "hurrah" until you're across.] Do not halloo till you're out of the wood.
Cf. Do not triumph before the victory.

262* **Не говори как что знать.**
Do not reveal your sources.

263 **Не говори правду, не теряй дружбу. (Не говорить было правды - не терять было дружбы.)** *v.* Г188
[Speak the truth and lose a friend.] Truth breeds hatred. All truths must not be told at all times. *Cf.* Flattery begets friends, truth begets enmity.

264 **Не говори что не могу, говори что не хочу.**
I can't means I won't.

265 **Не годится в страже вор, ни дурак на разговор.** *v.* Д479, О131, С10, У26
[Engage not a thief as a guard nor a fool in conversation.] *Cf.* It is a foolish sheep that makes the wolf his confessor. A fool is known by his conversation. †Set a thief to catch a thief.

266 **Не годы стареют (старят), горе.** *v.* Н225

267 **Не гони коня кнутом, а гони овсом.**
[Don't drive a horse with the whip, but with oats.] A good horse is worth its fodder.
Cf. A horse that will not carry a saddle must have no oats.

268* **Не гонись за простым вором, а лови атамана.** *v.* А18, Б330, З75, Ш6
[Don't go after the petty thief but the ringleader.] Laws catch flies but let hornets go.

269 **Не гонкой волка бьют, уловкой.** *v.* Н154
[The wolf will lose not in the chase, but in the ruse.] All the craft is in the catching.

270 **Не горлом а горбом.** *v.* Б316, Д116, М60, С230
[Not with the throat but the back.] *i.e. by action not talk.* Speak little, do much. Doing is better than saying. Say well is good, but do well is better.

271 **Не грози щуке морем, а нагому горем.** *v.* М137,211, Н387
[Don't threaten a pike with water nor a beggar with grief.] Mud chokes no eels. A dog will not howl if you beat him with a bone.

272* **Не давай голодному хлеба резать.** *v.* Н424
[Do not give a hungry man bread to cut.] The doghouse is no place to keep a sausage.
Cf. An open door may tempt a saint.

273 **Не давай повадки, чтобы не было оглядки.**
[Yield not to habit and have no regrets.] Fly that pleasure which pains afterward. *Cf.* Short pleasure, long repentance.

274* **Не давши слова - крепись, а давши - держись.** *v.* Д7,Н422, О10, Я18
Be slow to promise and quick to perform.

275 **Не дай Бог дел иметь с монастырями, со вдовами, да с малыми сиротами.**
[God forbid you should have to deal with the clergy, widows or young orphans.]
Cf. He that marries a widow with two children marries three thieves.

276 **Не дай Бог с дураком связаться.**
[God forbid anyone from becoming involved with a fool.] *Cf.* God keep me from the man that has but one thing to mind.

277 **Не дал Бог свинье рог(ов), а бодуща была бы.** *v.* Б163,298, С329
[God gave not horns unto pigs lest they butt.] *Cf.* God sends a curst cow short horns. *Lat.* dat deus immiti cornua curti bovi.

278 **Не даром старцы уроды.**
[Old men are ugly for a reason.] *Cf.* Old cattle breed not.

279 **Не дать - горе, а дать - вдвое.** *v.* Д150
[To refuse is bad, but to give - doubly so.] *Cf.* He who gives to the unworthy loses doubly.

280 **Не дают, не навязывайся, а дают - не отказывайся.** *v.* Г27, В541, Д79, О165, П196
[Insist not when refused, but refuse not when offered.] *Cf.* To sail with the wind and tide.

281 **Не делай своего хорошего, а делай мое плохое.** *v.* Л139, М20
[Better do what I tell you poorly than what you want to do well.] *Cf.* Do something, even if it's wrong. Don't do as I do, but as I say. My country, right or wrong.

282 **Не держи (имей) сто рублей, держи сто друзей.** *v.* Д422
[Better a hundred friends than a hundred rubles.] A friend in the market is better than money in the chest. *Cf.* One enemy is too many, and a hundred friends too few.

283 **Не дери дыру в чужом двору.** *v.* В189, Н201, Х97
[Do not dig a pit in another's yard.] *Cf.* To lay a block in another's way.

284 **Не до дела когда свинья щелок пролила.** *v.* С232, М63
[It doesn't help for the pig to spill the lye.] *Cf.* Nothing so bad but it might have been worse.

285* **Не до жиру, быть бы живу.** *v.* Л165
[Forget the fat and be glad you're alive.] *i.e. better alive than in luxury.* Better a bare foot than none. *Cf.* Better eye sore than all blind. I envied my neighbour's carriage until I met a man who had no feet.

286* **Не до поросят свинье, когда сама на огне.** *v.* С53

287 **Не добыча довод.** *v.* Д366, И121
[Denunciation doesn't pay.] The informer is the worse rogue of the two. *Cf.* An informer's money has a Judas ring. Treason is never successful, for when it is successful, men do not call it treason.

288 **Не доглядишь оком, заплатишь боком.** *v.* У34
He that looks not before, finds himself behind.

289* **Не дом хозяина красит, а хозяин дом.** *v.* Б147, В615, Д379, М77, П128
[It is not the house that adorns the master, but the master the house.] The master absent and the house dead. It is not the place that honours the man, but the man that honours the place.

290* **Не дорог час временем, а дорог уличкой.** *v.* Н449, У106
[The worth of an hour is what it will bring.] The only value of time is its use. *Cf.* The worth of a thing is what it will bring. The only way to save an hour is to spend it wisely.

291   **Не дорого ничто, дорого вежество.**   *v.* Б134,289, Д505,Н175, У118
        [Nothing is important, save knowledge.] Knowledge is better than riches (wealth).
        Cf. Knowledge is power.

292   **Не дорого пито, а дорого быто.**
        [What you possess is dear, not what you drink.] *Cf.* Have is have.

293   **Не думай быть нарядным, а думай быть опрятным.**
        [Try to be neat rather than elegant.] Neat (comely) but not gaudy.

294   **Не душой худ, а просто плут.**   *v.* И120
        [He's not all bad, he's just a crook.] One hates not the person but the vice. You may
        hate the things a person does, but never hate the person.

295*   **Не делает платье монахом.**
       The cowl does not make the monk.   *v.* Н247, Р94

296   **Не евши (поужинавши) легче (тоще) - а поевши (поужинавши) лучше.**
        [Skip a meal and feel lighter, but eat and feel better.] *Cf.* If I were to fast for my life,
        I'd take a good breakfast in the morning.

297*   **Не едином хлебом (будет) жив человек.**
       Man lives not by bread alone.

298   **Не жаль что выпито, а жаль что вылито.**   *v.* Г293
        [Regret not what is drunk, but what is spilt.] Spilt wine is worse than water.

299   **Не желай за женою богатства, а желай постоянства.**   *v.* Б194, Ж48, Л142, Н404
        [Seek not riches in a wife, but constancy.] Better a portion in a wife than with a wife.
        She that is good and fair needs no other dowry.

300*   **Не женат, не человек.**   *v.* Б65
        [A man without a wife is not a man.] A man without a wife is but half a man. He that
        has not a wife is not yet a complete man.

301   **Не жениться - чечениться.**
        [Not to marry is to remain a dandy.] Single long - shame at length.

302   **Не жупан пана красит, а пан жупана.**   *v.* Н289,324,331,443, Х9
        [It's not the cape that adorns the man, but the man the cape.] It's not the gay coat that
        makes the gentleman. *Cf.* Clothes make not the man. It is not the clothes that count, but
        the things the clothes cover.

303   **Не за свой кус хвататься, этим куском подавится.**   *v.* Н114,338
        [Take another's piece and choke.] *Cf.* He that eats the King's goose shall be choked with
        the feathers. Covet not that which belongs to others.

304   **Не за то волка бьют что сер, а за то что овцу сьел.**
        [The wolf is beaten not for being grey but for eating the stray.] *Cf.* Every sin brings its
        punishment with it.

305*   **Не заставляй дурака Богу молиться, он и лоб разобьет.** *v.* З97

306   **Не зачем в гости, и у нас хорошо.**   *v.* Д52,384
        [Why go out when home is nice.] He who would be well, needs not go from his house.

307   **Не земля родит, а небо (год).**
[It's not the earth that generates, but the sky (time).] *i.e. God and the weather.*
Cf. A field has three needs: good weather, good seed, and a good husbandman.

308   **Не знаем что вечер покажет.**
[We know not what night will bring.] *SPL.* nescimus quid serus vesper vehat. *Cf.* What is done in the night appears in the day.

309   **Не знаешь (угодаешь) где найдешь (найти), где потеряешь (потерять).**
(Не всегда возможно знать где найти, где потерять.)   *v.* Б460
[You never know where you may find nor where you may lose.] Whatsoever is somewhere gotten is somewhere lost. No telling which way luck (or a half broke steer) is going to run. *Cf.* Many things happen unlooked for. Take heed you find not what you do not seek.

310*   **Не зная (спросясь) броду, не суйся в воду.**   *v.* К129, Н380
[Wade not in the water unless you know the ford.]   Never wade in unknown waters. Look before you leap.

311   **Не идет место к голове, но голова к месту. (Не рок головы ищет, сама голова на**
рок   **идет.)** If the mountain will not come to Mahomet, Mahomet must go to the mountain. [Fate seeks not the man, but man goes out to meet it.]

312   **Не изведан - друг, а изведан - два.**   *v.* Д418, Н506
[A friend untried is a friend, a proven friend is two.] *Cf.* Try your friend before you trust.

313*   **Не имеющий раба, и сам по дрова.**   *v.* В629
[He who has no servant goes himself for firewood.]   Serve yourself if you would be well served. *Cf.* If you want a thing done - go; if not - send. If you would have a faithful servant and one that you like, serve yourself.

314*   **Не испортивши, дела не сделаешь.**   *v.* Б99, Н358, О197
Who makes no mistakes makes nothing. If at first you don't succeed, try again. *SPL.* qui nunquam male, nunquam bene. *Cf.* No man is his craft's master the first day. Things that are hard to come by are much set by. He that shoots oft at last shall hit the mark.

315   **Не ищи в другом правде когда нет ее в тебе.**   *v.* К74, Ч11
Those who betray their friends must not expect others to keep faith with them. *Cf.* Practise what you preach. Do as you would be done by.

316   **Не ищи красоты, ищи доброты.**   *v.* Ж61,87, Л136, Н255, Р65
[Look for kindness rather than beauty.] *i.e. in a wife.* Choose not a wife by the eye only.

317   **Не ищи мудрости (премудрости), ищи кротости.**
[Seek not wisdom (subtlety), but modesty.] The wisest man is he who does not fancy he is wise at all. *Cf.* He is wise that knows when he's well enough. The greatest wealth is contentment with a little.

318   **Не ищи что не твое.**   *v.* Н114
[Seek not what is not your own.] Be no seeker of other men's matters. Covet not that which belongs to others. *Cf.* Meddle not with another man's matter.

319   **Не клади волку пальца в рот.**   *v.* М52
[Put not your finger in the wolf's maw.] If you want your finger bit, stick it in a possum's mouth. *Cf.* He that has his hand in the lion's mouth must take it out as best he can.

320 **Не клади плохо, не вводи вора в грех.** *v.* Н48,444
[Do not leave things lying and tempt thieves.] Opportunity makes the thief. *Lat.* occasio facit furem.

321 **Не клин бы да не мох, (так) и плотник бы сдох.** *v.* К7

322 **Не копьем убивают - умом.** *v.* Н220,336,388,493, Р80
[It is the mind, not the spear that kills.] The wise man blames the archer, not the arrow. *Cf.* The dog bites the stone, not him that throws it. No bell is rung by accident.

323* **Не красна изба углами, красна пирогами.**
[The beauty of a house lies not in its walls but in its pies.] *i.e. hospitality.* A house is a fine house when good folks are within. *Cf.* Friendly house, best house. *Gr.* φίλος οἶκος, ἄριστος οἶκος.

324 **Не красна (складна) челобитная складом, складна указом.** *v.* Н302, П53
[It's not the seal that crowns a bill, but the decree.] A fancy cover doesn't make a fancy book.

325 **Не крепка тюрьма углами - крепка сторожем.** *v.* Д349
[It is the guards, not the walls that make a prison safe.] Men, not walls, make a city safe. *Gr.* Thuc.7.77.7: ἄνδρες γὰρ πόλις καὶ οὐ τείχη.

326 **Не крой чужих хором, как свой валится дом.** *v.* Ж93, С47,70, У42, Ч133
[Mend not others' roofs when your own house is tottering.] Do not neglect your own field and plough your neighbour's. *Cf. Matt.*7.3: You see a mote in another's eye but you cannot see the beam in your own. The paperhanger never papers his own house. Let us put our own house in order. The painter never paints his own house.

327* **Не купи двора, купи соседа.** *v.* К230
[Buy not the yard but the neighbour.] *i.e. the neighbour is more important than the property.* *Cf.* A good neighbour, a good morrow. Choose your company before your drink.

328* **Не лезь поперед батьки в пекло. Не суйся прежде (наперед) отца в петлю.** *v.* П239
[Rush not to hell (the gallows) before your father.] To run before one's horse to market.

329 **Не любо - не слушай, а врать не мешай.**
[If you don't like what you hear - don't listen, but don't interfere with my yarn.] Hold your tongue and let me talk. Ask no questions and hear no lies.

330 **Не мазан воз скрипит.**
[The ungreased cart will creak.] *Cf.* Who greases his wheels helps his oxen. The squeaking wheel gets the grease.

331* **Не место человека красит (просвещает), а человек место.** *v.* М77, Н289,302
It is not the place that honours the man, but the man the place.

332 **Не мечите бисер(а) перед свиньями.**
*Matt.*7.6: **Cast not pearls before swine.**

333 **Не мил и свет когда милого нет.**
[The world is grim when one's love is gone.] To live without love is really not living. *Cf.* To love is to live and to live is to love.

334 **Не может человек безгрешен быть в свой век.** *v.* Ч26
[No man can remain without sin in his lifetime.] Every man has his besetting sin. *Lat.* neque enim est homo qui non peccet. 11*Chron.*6.36: There is not a man which sinneth

not. None of us is without sin. Sen.*Ir*.2.28: neminem nostrum esse sine culpa. Many without punishment, but none without sin.

335 **Не мой (твой) (наш) (ваш) воз, не мне (тебе) (нам) (вам) его и везти.** *v.* M169, H164,
[It's not my (your) (our) load, so I (you) (we) needn't carry it.] H200,459, Я2
Let every peddlar carry his own pack. Let him that owns the cow take her by the tail.
Mind no business but your own.

336 **Не море топит корабли, а ветры.** *v.* H220,322,493
[It is not the sea that sinks ships, but the wind.] *Cf.* Every wind is ill to a broken ship.
Each man makes his own shipwreck.

337 **Не на карты пенять коли игрок худ.** *v.* H37
[Blame not the cards if the player is bad.] *Cf.* A bad shearer never had a good sickle.
The cards beat all the players, be they ever so skillful.

338 **Не надобно на чужое добро льститься, берегись своего лишиться.** *v.* 354, И134,
Covet not that which belongs to others [lest you lose your own.]M132,H109,112,303
Cf. Greediness overreaches itself. If you can't be good, be careful.

339 **Не называй дурное хорошим, а черное белым.** *v.* H226, C37
[Don't call bad good or black white.] Black's black and white's white. Say black is white.

340 **Не накладно сытого потчевать.** *v.* C337
[It is not disadvantageous to regale one who has had enough.] Give a bit of your cake
to one who is going to eat pie.

341 **Не нами началось (свет начался), не нами и кончится (скончается).** *v.* Ж154, H458
[We're not the first and we won't be the last.] *i.e. to make a mistake.*
I am not the first and shall not be the last. *Lat.* primus non sum nec imus.

342 **Не наряд жену красит, а домоустройство.** *v.* H442
[Good housekeeping embellishes a wife more than good clothes.] Housewifery is
woman's noblest fame. *Cf.* The foot on the cradle and the hand on the distaff is the sign
of a good wife.

343 **Не насытится око зрением, а ум богатством.** *v.* Г111,121,158
The eye is not satisfied with seeing [nor the mind with wealth.] *Cf. Eccles*.1.8 Non
saturatur oculus visu.

344 **Не начавши - думай, а начавши - делай.** *v.* Д372,458,459, У90
[Think before beginning and fulfill after.] Think twice before you act. Think - then
act. *Cf.* Be slow to promise and quick to perform. Better not to begin than never end.

345 **Не начинай дело выше меры.** *v.* У90
[Do not begin over your head.] Don't start anything you can't finish. Don't bite off
more than you can chew. *Cf.* Beware beginnings. Better never to begin than never to end.
Never begin anything on Friday that you are not able to finish that day.

346 **Не наше было, не к нам пришло.** *v.* H338
[It wasn't ours so we didn't get it.] *Cf.* Every man should take his own. Wish not to
taste what does not to you fall.

347* **Не наше дело горшки лепить, а наше дело их колотить.** *v.* О63,64
[Ours is not to make pots, but to shatter them.] *Cf.* One man sows and another man
reaps. Theirs is not to reason why, theirs is but to do and die. Stick to your own job.

348 **Не нашел гусь зернышка, глотает и камешка.** *v.* З29, И25, Н3,348, С107
[When the goose finds no grains, it swallows pebbles.] If thou hast not a capon, feed on an onion. *Cf.* The goat must browse where she is tied. Gnaw the bone which is fallen to thy lot. When in need, anything will do.

349 **Не наши сани подламываются.** *v.* Н202
[It's not our sleds that break down.] It's no sweat off our backs.

350 **Не ноги кормят брюхо, а брюхо ноги.**
[The legs don't carry the belly, but the belly carries the legs.] *Cf.* An army marches on its stomach. An empty belly bears no body. When the belly is full, the bones are at rest.

351 **Не обижай - сам не будешь обижен.**
[Offend not and be not offended.] *Cf.* None is offended but by himself. *Lat.* nemo laeditur nisi a seipso. Expect to be treated as you have treated others.

352* **Не обманешь - не продашь. (Не солгать - не продать.)** *v.* В622, Н383,486
[No swindle (lie) - no sale.] He praises who wishes to sell. *Cf.* Did you ever hear a fishwife cry stinking mackerel. A dealer in rubbish praises rubbish. *Lat.* scruta laudat.

353* **Не обманешь старого воробья на мякину.** *v.* С266

354 **Не опасайся начала злого, жди конца благого.**
[Don't bemoan the beginning of woe until good fortune ends.] Let your trouble tarry till its own day comes. *Cf.* Don't cross the bridge (river) (stream) till you get to it. Better come at the latter end of a feast than the beginning of a fray.

355 **Не от хлеба ходят, а ко хлебу.** *v.* Б474
[All run to bread and not away from it.] Feast and your halls are crowded. Everyone fastens where there is gain.

356 **Не отведав яблочка, не бросают.**
[Taste the apple before discarding it.] *Cf.* The husbandman ought first to taste of the new grown fruit.

357* **Не откладывай до завтра что можешь сделать сегодня.** *v.* О69
Never put off till tomorrow what may be done today. *Lat.* ne differas opus huius diei in crastinum diem.

358* **Не ошибается тот, кто ничего не делает.** *v.* Б99, Н314, О197
He who makes no mistakes makes nothing.

359 **Не пей за столбом, а пей за столом.** *v.* П7

360 **Не первая(ую) зима(у) волку зимовать.** *v.* Л73, С275
[It's not the wolf's first winter.] *i.e. inured to hardship.* Old foxes want no tutors. *Cf.* An old fox is not easily snared.

361 **Не первый снег на голову.** *v.* К55, М206
[Not the first snow on one's head.] *i.e. experienced, not unexpected.* I was not born yesterday. Not out of the blue.

362 **Не переливай из пустого в порожнее.** *v.* Б157, В128, Р56
[Don't pour from empty to empty.] *i.e. an exercise in futility.* *Cf.* To empty the sea with a spoon (nutshell). To carry water in a sieve.

363* **Не пить горького, не видать сладкого.**   *v.* Б344,353, В8, Г281, К256, Н221
He deserves not the sweet that will not taste the sour. *Cf.* Take the sweet with the sour. Sweet is the nut but bitter is the shell.

364 **Не плачь мати о чужом дитяти.**   *v.* П248
[The mother cries not for another's child.] *Cf.* The parson always christens his own child first. Another's cares will not rob you of sleep.

365* **Не плюй в (чужой) колодец, пригодится воды напиться.**   *v.* Н403
Do not spit into the well you may have to drink of. *Gr. Diog.*3.55: βορβόρῳ ὕδωρ λαμπρὸν μιαίνων, οὔποθ'εὑρήσεις ποτόν. *Cf.* Cast no dirt into the well that has given you water.

366 **Не по многу берет, больше набирет.**
[He who takes little, gathers more.] *i.e. over time.* He that eats least, eats most. *Cf.* Little and often fills the purse.

367 **Не по старости мрут, не по молодости живут.**   *v.* Ж144, С197
[People don't die just because they're old nor live because they're young.] Death devours lambs as well as sheep. *Cf.* Death keeps no calendar. Old men go to death, but death comes to young men.

368 **Не по хорошу мил, а по милу хорош.**
Fair is not fair, but that which pleases. Beauty is in the eye of the beholder. *Cf.* Jack is no judge of Jill's beauty.

369 **Не поглядев (посмотря) в святцы, да (и) бух в (большой) колокол (колокола).** *v.* В406
[Don't ring the churchbells before checking the calendar.] *Cf.* As the fool thinks, so the bell chinks. Think before you leap. Think twice before you act (once). A bell never rings by accident.

370 **Не подмажешь - не поедешь.**   *v.* К136, С304
[No grease, no ride.] *i.e. a bribe.* Who greases his way travels easily. *SPL.* plaustri rota male uncta stridet. Quisquis habet nummos, secura navigat aura.

371 **Не поднимай меня высоко, и не опускай низко.**   *v.* В686,687, Н223
[Neither raise me too high nor lower me too low.] *i.e. neither praise nor dispraise.* *Cf.* If you can't say something good about someone, don't say anything at all.

372 **Не поймав карася, поймаешь щуку.**   *v.* В373
[If the carp escapes, you'll catch a pike.] What we lose in the hake, we shall have in the herring.

373 **Не поймав (убивши) медведя, не продают шкуры.**   *v.* В260, Д126, Ж41, М48,
Don't sell the bear's skin before you have caught the bear.   Н477, Ц10

374 **Не поймали вора сегодня, изловят завтра.**   *v.* Л96, С136,139
[If the thief isn't caught today, he'll be caught tomorrow.] Long runs the fox, but at last is caught. *Cf.* We shall catch birds tomorrow. When every man gets his own, the thief will get the widdie.

375 **Не пойман - не вор (тать).**
[No man is a thief until he is caught.] A man is innocent until proven guilty. *Cf.* All are presumed good till found at fault. A blot's no blot unless it be hit.

376   **Не поклонясь грибу до земли, не поднять его в кузов.**   *v.* Л45, К181, П273, Р91, Ч107
[He that will not stoop for the mushroom will not have it in his basket.] He that would have the fruit must climb the tree.

377   **Не положа, не ищут.**   *v.* К38
Seek what may be found. He that hides can find. *Gr.* ἂν μὴ κατέθου μὴ ἀνελοῦ.
Lat. quae non posuisti, ne tollas.

378   **Не помучишься так не научишься.**   *v.* M195, H149, O92
[Without suffering you won't learn.] Experience bought by suffering teaches wisdom.
Cf. Once bitten, twice shy. Failure teaches success.

379   **Не попал волк в западню, увязнет в тенетах.**
[The wolf that falls not into the trap will be caught by the snare.] There are more ways to kill a dog than hanging it.

380   **Не посмотря в окно, не плюй.**   *v.* К129, H310
[Look before you spit out the window.] Look before you leap.

381   **Не посмотря товар, не покупают.**   *v.* Д124, 334,85, К187, Ч70
Never buy anything before you see it. *Cf.* Do not buy a pig in a poke. Keep your eyes open: a sale is a sale. Try it before you buy it.

382   **Не посылай холостого с сватаньем.**
[Do not send a bachelor to arrange a marriage.] *Cf.* Bachelors' wives and maids' children are always well taught.

383   **Не похваля товар не продашь.**   *v.* B622, H352,487
He praises who wishes to sell.

384   **Не пристало как седло корове (свиньи чепчик).**   *v.* Д499, К19, H594
As meet as a cow to bear a saddle (bonnet on a pig). **As a saddle becomes a cow.**
Lat. Amm.Marcellinus 16.5: clitellae bovi imposite sunt. *Cf.* A fifth wheel to a coach.

385*   **Не продажному коню и цены нет.**
[A horse that's not for sale has no price.] You cannot buy what is not for sale. *Cf.* There is a difference between "Will you buy" and "Will you sell."

386   **Не пройдет без грех у кого жена лиха.**   *v.* Б2
[A bad wife will make her husband a sinner.] A light wife makes a heavy husband.
Cf. Who has a wife has strife. A wife who tricks her husband wrecks the home.

387   **Не пугай сокола вороной.**   *v.* M137, H271
[Frighten not a falcon with a crow.] The anvil fears no hammer. *Cf.* No carrion will kill a crow.

388*   **Не пуля, а человек, из ружья убивает.**   *v.* H322,336,493
[It is not the bullet but the gunman who kills.] The wise man blames the archer, not the arrow. *Cf.* No bell is rung by accident. The dog bites the stone, not him that throws it.

389*   **Не пускай козла (обезьяну) сторожом в огород (к орехам).**   *v.* Б385, B395, Д359,
[Do not set a goat (monkey) to guard the orchard (nuts).]   H211, П303
To set the wolf to keep the sheep.

390   **Не работа сушит, а забота.**   *v.* H225
[Care dries one up more than work.] Worry kills more men than work. *Cf.* Sorrow is always dry. Nothing worries worry like work.

391 **Не равны бывают веки, не равны и человеки.**   *v.* Д429, К90
[Different times, different people.] Other times, other manners (customs). Times change and (people change their ideas) (we) with them.

392* **Не равны и пальцы на руках.**   *v.* В88, Г193, Д165, Р20
[Even the fingers of the hand are all unequal.] No like is the same. *Lat.* nullum simile est idem. *Cf.* There is a (some) difference between Peter and Peter.

393 **Не рад, да готов.**
[Not willing but ready.] *Cf.* †Ready and willing.

394 **Не радуйся нашедши, не плачь потерявши.**   *v.* Н169
[Exult not in finding nor cry in losing.] *SPL.* ad nullos fortunae ictus expallescere, pari suffragio stare in utraque fortuna. *Cf.* Easy come easy go. You win some, you lose some.

395* **Не радуйся (суди по) приезду, радуйся (суди по) отъезду.**   *v.* Н261,474,477,478
[Cheer (judge by) the departure, not the arrival.] Praise in departing. Don't cry "halloa" till you're out of the wood. It is not good praising a ford till a man be over.

396* **Не разбивши яиц, не сделаешь яичницу.**   *v.* Б106, В369, Д410, Л54
You cannot make an omelette without breaking eggs.

397 **Не разгрызешь (раскуся) ореха, так не съешь ядра (о зерне не толкуй).**   *v.* Ж36,
He that will eat the kernel, must crack the nut.   М43, Н94, О97, П273

398 **Не разевай рта, ворона влетит.**   *v.* В43
[Don't yawn too wide or a crow may alight.] A close mouth catches no flies.

399 **Не расти на вербе (елке) грушу (яблочку).**   *v.* Б168, В5, Д364, З101, О150, Я3
[Do not seek pears (apples) on a willow (spruce).] To ask pears of an elm tree. *Cf.* Look not for musk in a dog's kennel. Don't go to a buzzard's nest to find a dove.

400* **Не расти своего древа в чужом лесе.**   *v.* В189,196, Н201, Ч131
[Plant not your trees in another man's forest.] Hoe your own row. Skeer your own fire. *Cf.* Own is own. Every man should take his own.

401 **Не родись красив(ым) а родись счастлив(ым).**   *v.* П218, С306,323
Не родись ни хорош, ни пригож (ни умен) (ни красив), а родись счастлив.
[Better born lucky than pretty (good)(clever)(smart).] Better born lucky than wise (rich).

402 **Не родится от свиньи бобренок, всегда поросенок.**   *v.* З139, Н47, О96,156
[A beaver can never be born of a pig.] The litter is like to the sire and dam. Eagles do not breed doves.

403* **Не рой другому (для друга) яму - сам в нее попадешь (ввалишься).**   *v.* Н365,414,Ч72
To dig a pit for another and fall into it oneself. *SPL.* necis artifices arte pereunt. *Cf. Psalm* 7.15 (*Eccles.*10.8): He that diggeth a pit shall fall into it.

404 **Не с богатством (деньгами) жить, а с человеком (добрыми людьми)**   *v.* Л142, Н299, С20
[One lives with the person, not the wealth.] *i.e. said when one marries poor.* Better a fortune in a wife than with a wife. *Cf.* Riches alone make no man happy.

405* **Не с огнем к пожару соваться.**   *v.* Е13, 369, М33, О27
[Do not attend a fire with a flame.] To add oil to the fire.

406   **Не с той ноги, кума, плясать пошла.**   *v.* Н199
        [You're dancing on the wrong foot, godmother.] To start on the wrong foot.   *Cf.*
        You're barking up the wrong tree.

407   **Не сам пьяный ходит, черт его носит.**   *v.* П314
        [The drunkard walks not alone - the devil carries him.] The devil places a pillow for the
        drunken man to fall on.

408   **Не светило, не горело, да вдруг припекло.**   *v.* Б418, В663, К118, Н190, С86
        [Not a glimmer nor a flame and suddenly red hot.] *i.e. a windfall.* When it rains, it
        pours. It's either a feast or a famine.

409*   **Не свой дом, не своя и воля.**   *v.* Г39,307, Н120, У50, Х30, Ч24
        [Another's house, another's will.] To the man submit at whose board you sit. *Cf.* Be deaf
        and blind in another man's house.

410   **Не силою дерутся, умением.**   *v.* Б140, Р28, С119
        [Fighting requires skill, not strength.] Skill will accomplish what is denied to force. Skill,
        not strength, governs a ship. *SPL.* non corporis mole, sed ingenio certandum.

411   **Не сказывай жене у кого нос велик.**   *v.* Г183
        [Don't tell your wife whose nose is long.] Confide in an aunt and the world will know.
        Cf. If it's a secret, don't tell it to a woman. Blessed is the woman who can keep a secret
        and the man who will not tell his wife.

412   **Не слыть, а быть.**
        [To be, not seem.] Be what you appear to be.

413   **Не смейся братец чужой сестрице, своя в девицах.**   *v.* Д431, Н107, Т13, Ч47
        [The brother of a maid should not laugh at another's sister.] Those who live in glass
        houses shouldn't throw stones. Point not at others' spots with a foul finger.

414   **Не смейся, горох не лучше бобов.**   *v.* Н403, 431, Ч47
        (Не смейся горох над бобами, сам будешь валятся под ногами.)
        [Don't laugh, peas are no better than beans (you too may wind up on the ground).] *i.e.*
        "see if you can do any better." To laugh at someone is to be laughed back at. *Cf.* To
        give a pea for a bean. No more difference than between a broom and a besom.

415   **Не смейся над старым, и сам будешь стар.**   *v.* П200

416   **Не смейся слепому и хромому, чтоб не быть самому такому.**
        [Don't laugh at the blind nor the crippled, lest it befall you to join them.] He that mocks
        a cripple ought to be whole.

417   **Не смотри на начало, смотри на конец.**   *v.* Л97, Н161
        [Look not to the beginning] **look to the end.** *Lat.* respice finem. Begin nothing until you
        have considered how it is to be finished.

418   **Не сойдутся обычаи, не будут друзья.**   *v.* К266, М164, П109, Р9
        Sympathy of manners make the conjunction of minds. *Lat.* Cic. iucundissima est
        amicitia quam similitudo morum conciliavit. Likeness causes liking.

419   **Не солгать, так и правды не сказать.**   *v.* И29
        Tell a lie and find a truth.

420* **Не сотвори себе кумира.**
      Thou shalt not make unto thee any graven image.

421   **Не спеши на нож, будешь зарезан.**   *v.* Б405, Л69
      [Rush not at a knife if you don't want to get cut.] Never catch at a falling knife or a
      falling friend. They that play with edged tools must expect to be cut.

422   **Не спеши языком, а не ленись делом.** *v.* Я18

423* **Не спрашивай у старого, спрашивай у бывалого.**
      [Ask not an old man but an old hand.] He knows the way best who went there last. Ask not a
      blind man the way to the city. *Cf.* An ounce of practice is worth a pound of precept.

424* **Не спрашивай у кошки лепешки, у собаки блина.**   *v.* Н211,272, С220
      [Ask not a cat for a fritter nor a dog for a crepe.] A dog in a kitchen desires no
      company. A dog with a bone knows no friend. *Cf.* The doghouse is no place to keep a
      sausage. Send not a cat for lard.

425   **Не спрашивай у попа сдачи, у портного отдачи.**   *v.* Н526
      [Neither ask a priest for change nor a tailor for a refund.] *Cf.* A hundred tailors, a
      hundred millers, and a hundred weavers are three hundred thieves. Three things are
      insatiable: priests, monks and the sea.

426   **Не срывай яблока пока зелено, созреет и само упадет.**
      [Don't pick an apple while it's green; it will ripen and fall by itself.] Fruit unripe sticks
      on the tree. *Cf.* The time to pick berries is when they're ripe. You can't force a fruit to
      ripen by beating it with a stick.

427   **Не ставь недруга овцою, а ставь его волком.**
      [Make the wolf your enemy, not the sheep.] The fault of the ass must not be laid on the
      pack saddle. *Cf.* Put the saddle on the right horse.

428   **Не стало свечи, не палец зажечи.**   *v.* К323
      [You cannot use your finger when the candles run out.] Too late to spare when all is
      spent. *Cf.* Spare and have is better than spend and crave.

429   **Не стой там где дрова рубят.**
      [Don't stand about where logs are chopped.] Don't stick your neck out. Put your finger
      in the fire and say it was your fortune.

430   **Не столько дает сколько сулит.**   *v.* B118, Н76
      [He promises more than he delivers.] Great promises and small performances. *Cf.* To
      offer much is a kind of denial.

431   **Не столько смертей сколько скорбей.**   *v.* К259, Н227, Ш2
      [There is more mourning than dying.] There are more men threatened than stricken.

432* **Не страшны злыдни за горами.**   *v.* М130
      [The villains are not awesome whilst over the hills.] It is easy to be brave from a safe
      distance. Far shooting never killed bird.

433   **Не стращай дурака словами, грози ему кулаками.**
      [Intimidate a fool with your fists, not with your words.] For the wise man with a sigh,
      for the fool with a fist. *Cf.* Use soft words and hard arguments.

434* **Не строй церкви, пристрой сироту.** *v.* Б236
[Better to nurture an orphan than to build a church.] Good deeds are better than creeds.
Cf. Nearer the church, farther from God.

435 **Не стыдись говорить коли правду хочешь объявить.** *v.* З335
[If it's the truth, be not ashamed to speak.] *Cf.* Speak boldly and speak truly, shame the devil.

436 **Не стыдно смолчать коли нечего сказать.** *v.* Д306, Л141, М157
[It's all right to be quiet when there's nothing to say.] Better say nothing than not to the purpose.

437 **Не суйся в волки с телячьим хвостом.** *v.* Л42

438 **Не суйся вперед, чтоб не быть назади.**
The further we go, the further behind. The further you run, the further you are behind.

Cf. It is better to go back than go ahead badly. *Lat.* satius est recurrere quam currere male. It is often better to return than to go on, if you find you have taken the wrong road. †Not to go forwards is to go backwards.

439* **Не суйся пятница прежде четверга.**
[Friday must wait for Thursday.] Every day is not Friday, there is also Thursday.
Cf. Everything in turn.

440* **Не суйся в ризы коль не поп.** *v.* В291, Л42,178, Н133,198, П201, С84
[Don not the cloth unless you're a priest.] If you don't like the heat get out of the kitchen. *Cf.* The habit does not make the monk. *Lat.* cucullus non facit monachum. A holy habit cleanses not a foul soul. A broad hat does not always cover a venerable head.

441 **Не сули чужой полтины, дай свой алтын.** *v.* Д222, И110, Л25, Ч120
[Better to offer your own three *kopeks* than promise another man's half-ruble.] To be free at another man's cost. No greater promisers than those who have nothing to give.

442 **Не та хозяйка которая говорит, а та которая щи варит.** *v.* Н342
[The true housekeeper is not the talker but the one who cooks the soup.] *Cf.* There is but an hour in a day between a good housekeeper and a bad.

443 **Не та шинель что пуговицами блестит, а та что греет.** *v.* Д29, Н302, П64
[A fine coat is one that warms, not one whose buttons glitter.] Clothes and looks don't make the person.

444 **Не там вор крадет где много, а там где лежит плохо.** *v.* Г72, Н320
[Opportunity, not quantity, attracts the thief.] Opportunity makes the thief. The hole calls the thief. *Lat.* occasio facit furem. *Cf.* Ill herds make fat foxes.

445* **Не там родина где мать родила, а там (и) рай где добрый край.** *v.* В610,Г7,Ж113,Т9
[One's country is not one's birthplace, but where one is well treated.]
Where it is well with me, there is my country. *Lat.* ubi bene, ibi patria. *Cf.* Where men are well used, they'll frequent there. Home is where the heart is. A wise man esteems every place to be his country. *Gr.* πᾶσα γῆ πατρις.

446 **Не тебя стригут, так ты и молчи.** *v.* Б387
[Keep quiet unless it's your hair that's being clipped.] Don't cry before you are hurt.

447 **Не тем богат что есть, а тем богат чем рад.**   *v.* Б286, Е41, Т56,59, Х76
He is not rich that possesses much, but he that is content with what he has.

448 **Не тем моются чем грязнятся.**   *v.* О81,84
[What sullies cannot wash.] Brushing against dirt won't make you any cleaner. *Cf.* He that has to do with foul, never comes away clean. One clean sheet will not soil another.

449 **Не тем час дорог что долог, а тем что короток.**   *v.* Н290
[An hour is precious not because it's long but because it's short.] An inch of time is an inch of gold. *Cf.* Nothing is more precious than time, yet nothing is less valued.

450* **Не то забота что много работы, а то (забота) как ее нет.**   *v.* О144, С167
No work is worse than overwork. He has hard work indeed who has no work to do.

451 **Не то смешно что жена мужа бьет, а то смешно что муж плачет.**
[What's funny is not that a wife should beat her husband, but that he should cry.] It is a sour reek where the good wife dings the good man. *Cf.* It is a silly flock where the ewe bears the bell. It's a sad house where the hen crows louder than the cock.

452 **Не тогда искать стрел, как неприятель придет.**   *v.* Г304, Н70, П172, Х14
[Don't look for arrows when the enemy is at hand.] It is too late to learn to box when you're in the ring. *Cf.* When the devil comes, it is too late to pray. Have not thy cloak to make when it begins to rain. Thatch your roof before the rain begins.

453* **Не тогда плясать когда доски писать (тесать).**   *v.* П22,102, С214, Х2
[It's too late to dance when the time comes to inscribe (carve) your epitaph.] It's too late to stoop when the head is off. It's never too late until it is too late.

454 **Не только добра что много серебра.**   *v.* И19,58
[Much silver does not mean that all is well.] No silver without dross.

455* **Не только свету что в очью (окне).**
[There's more to the world than what you see (through the window).] More than meets the eye. Appearances are deceiving. *SPL.* mus non uni fidit antro. *Cf.* Can't keep up with the world by letting it roll by.

456* **Не тот вор кто крадет, а тот кто краденое принимает (кто потакает).**   *v.* В429, К220
[He is not the thief who steals, but he who receives what is stolen.] The receiver's as bad as the thief. If there were no receivers, there'd be no thieves.

457* **Не тот живет больше кто живет дольше.**   *v.* Ж159
[He who lives longest does not necessarily live most.] It's not how long but how well you live. Better to live well than long. *Cf.* Life lies not in living but in liking. *Lat.* Mart. non est vivere, sed valere vita. Wish not so much to live long as to live well.

458* **Не ты первый, не ты последний.**   *v.* Ж154, Н341
You're not the first and you won't be the last.

459 **Не тычь носа в чужое просо.**   *v.* З107, К161, Н335
A man should not stick his nose in his neighbour's pot. Keep your nose out of others' business.

460 **Не угадывай пива на сусле. (Не хвали пива в сусле, а ржи в озими.)**   *v.* В260,
[Don't judge the beer from the wort.][Don't praise winter rye   Ж34, Ц10
nor beer before brewing.] It is ill prizing for green barley. *Cf.* Don't count your chickens before they are hatched.

461 Не удариться лицом в грязь.
Don't fall on your face.

462* Не удержался за гриву, за хвост не удержаться.
[Seize not the tail if you have let slip the mane.] He who would not when he could, is not able when he would. *Cf.* Take time by the forelock (she is bald behind).

463 Не узнает корова новые ворота.   *v.* С264,273, Ч46
[The cow doesn't recognize a new gate.] You can't teach an old dog new tricks. *Cf.* He who leaves the old ways for the new, will find himself deceived.

464 Не умеет к ставцу лицом сесть.
[He doesn't know how to sit at a salad bowl.] *i.e. has no table manners.* (Not) to know a goose from a capon.

465 Не умеешь шить, так не пори.   *v.* Л26, Н347, Ч17
[If you don't know how to sew, don't tear.] It's easier to pull down than to build up. A man is not so soon healed as hurt.

466 Не умел играть комом, играй желвачком.   *v.* О91
[If you're not good at snowballs, be prepared for lumps.] Opportunity never knocks for persons not worth a rap. If you don't like it, you can lump it. *Cf.* Better bend the neck than bruise the forehead.

467* Не умел шить золотом, так бей молотом.   *v.* Л35
[If you can't embroider in gold, then learn to use a hammer.] Some tasks require a strong back and a weak mind. *Cf.* He that has not silver in his purse, should have silk on his tongue.

468* Не учи белого лебедя (рыбу)(щуку) плавать (+ щука знает свою науку).   *v.* С212,У121,
[Teach not the white swan (fish) (pike) to swim (+ the pike knows what it likes).] Я20 *Gr.* ἰχθὺν νήχεσθαι διδάσκεις. *Lat.* piscem natare doces. Teach your grandmother to suck eggs.

469 Не учи плясать (хромать), я сам скоморох (я сам умею).   *v.* В574
[Show me not how to dance (limp), I can be a clown on my own (I already know).]
To teach the cat the way to the kirn.

470 Не учили, покуда поперек лавки (лавочки) укладывался (лажился), а во всю вытянулся - не научишь.   *v.* К64, *Ap.*1.27
[He'll never learn full-grown what he wasn't taught when he could fit across a bench.] *Cf.* He who will not learn when he is young will regret it when he is old. What is learnt in the cradle lasts till the tomb. What we learn early we remember late.

471* Не учиться хромать когда ноги болят.   *v.* Н469
[When the legs ache you can limp without learning.] *Cf.* In doing we learn.

472 Не хвали в очи, не брани за глаза.
[Praise none to the face nor berate anyone behind the back.] *Cf.* Praise publicly, blame privately. Admonish your friends in private, praise them in public. *Lat.* P.Syr. secrete amicos admone, laude palam. A stab in the back is worse than a kick in the face.

473* Не хвали в три дни, а хвали в три года.
[Do not praise after three days but after three years.] He that passes judgment as he runs, overtakes repentance. *Cf.* Never praise your wife until you have been married ten years.

474   **Не хвали ветра не извеяв жита.**   *v.* H395, X4, Ц10
[Do not praise the wind before you scatter the grain.] It is no good praising a ford till a man be over.

475   **Не хвали жену телом, а хвали ее делом.**   *v.* Ж61, Л136, H316
[Praise a wife for her conduct, not her beauty.] *Cf.* A fair woman without virtue is like stale (palled) wine.

476   **Не хвали сам себя, есть много умнее тебя.**
[Don't praise yourself as there are many who know more.] Don't be boastful, someone may pass who knew you as a child. *SPL.* laus in ore proprio sordescit. *Cf.* Praise in one's own mouth stinks.

477*   **Не хвались идучи (шедши) на рать, хвались идучи (шедши) с рати.**   *v.* B260, Д262,
[Boast not on the way to the fray, but as you come away.]   M113, H261,395, Ц10
Do not triumph before the victory [but after].

478*   **Не хвались на коня садясь, а хвались когда слезешь.**   *v.* H261,395,474,477
[Boast not on mounting, but on dismounting.] Praise in departing. *Cf.* Do not halloo till you are out of the wood. Never praise your cider or your horse.

479*   **Не хвались началом, похвались концом.**   *v.* H477,482, X6
[Praise not the beginning, but the end.] Do not boast of a thing until it is done.
Cf. Praise a fair day at night.

480   **Не хвались породой - чужим хвастаешься.**
He who boasts of his descent, praises the deeds of another. Birth is but praise of ancestors. *Cf.* Gentility is but ancient riches. *Lat.* Sen.*H.F.*340: qui genus iactat suum, aliena laudat.

481   **Не хвались силою чтоб не заплатить спиною.**   *v.* X8
[Vaunt not your strength lest your back pay the price.] Such as boast much usually fall much.

482*   **Не хвальна похвала до дела.**   *v.* H479
Do not boast of a thing until it is done.

483   **Не хлопочи когда нет ничего в печки.**
[Don't fret when there's nothing in the oven.] Little goods, little care. *Cf.* Let the morn come, and the meat with it.

484   **Не хозяин тот кто своего хозяйства не знает.**
[He is no master that doesn't know his own housekeeping.] A man possesses only what he knows he posseses. *Cf.* The house shows the owner. Every man must pull his own weight. No man is free who is not master of himself.

485   **Не хочу в ворота, разбирай забор.**   *v.* Г174, K60,299, C75, X82
[I'll not use the gate - dismantle the fence.] *i.e. arrogant or whimsical behaviour.* A wilful man will have his way. As I will, so I command. *Lat.* Juv.*Sat.*6.223: hoc volo, sic iubeo. The strong man and the waterfall channel their own path.

486   **Не худое ремесло кто умеет сделать и весло.**   *v.* P51
[Even he who can make an oar knows a good craft.] Who has an art, has everywhere a part. They that cobble and clout shall have work when others go without.

487*   **Не хуля, не купишь - не хваля, не продашь.**   *v.* B622, H352,383
He praises who wishes to sell. He that blames would buy.

488   **Не человек гонит, время.**   *v.* B479
[Time, not man, is the driver.]   Time is a hard taskmaster.   *Cf.* Time is the rider that breaks youth. Time waits for no man.

489   **Не шути более рубля.**   *v.* Ш17
[Don't joke more than a ruble's worth.]   Bet a heap and begin to weep.   Long jesting was never good.   *Cf.* Leave a jest when it pleases lest it turn to earnest.

490   **Не шути над тем кто не бранится ни с кем.**
[Make not fun of the man who offends none.]   *Cf.* Jest not with the eye nor with honour. *Lat.* non (est) bonum ludere cum sanctis.

491*   **Не яйцам учить кур.**   *v.* Я20

492   **Невечно ж драться, и когти притупятся.**
[Fighting must end as even claws lose their edge.]   *Cf.* All that is sharp is short.   The harder the storm, the sooner it's over.

493*   **Невинен гвоздь что лезет в стену - обухом колотят.**   *v.* H322,336,388, P80
[Don't blame the nail for piercing the wall - it's being hammered.]   Clay replies not to the potter.   No bell is rung by accident.

494*   **Невозможного на свете нет.**
Nothing is impossible.

495*   **Невольный грех живет на всех.**   *v.* Б455, B582, Г312, 32, И18,36, H43, Ч26,30, *Ap.*1.36
No man is infallible. Every man has his faults. To err is human. Accidents will happen in the best regulated families.

496*   **Неволя всему научит.**   *v.* Г245, H591, П85, X81, Я21
Necessity is the mother of invention.

497   **Недалеко до песен когда струны готовы.**
[When the strings are tuned, the songs will follow.]   *Cf.* If winter's here can spring be far behind?

498   **Неделя в неделю, жди четверга.**
Thursday come and the week is gone.

499   **Неделя год копит.**
[The week makes the year.] One day at a time. He never broke his hour that kept his day.

500   **Недозрелый умок что весенный ледок.**
[An immature mind is like spring ice.]   Little minds, like weak liquors, are soon soured. *Cf.* Raw leather will stretch.

501*   **Недосол на столе, (а) пересол на спине.**
[Undersalted on the table, oversalted - on the cook's back.]   Salt cooks bear blame, but fresh bear shame.

502   **Недоученный хуже неученого.**   *v.* П140, X89
Better untaught than ill taught.

503   **Незван в пир не ходит.**
Don't go [to the feast] **if you're uninvited**.

504* **Незваные гости гложут и кости.**
[Unbidden guests must nibble bones.] Who comes uncalled, sits unserved. *Cf.* An unbidden guest must bring his stool with him.

505 **Незнаемая прямизна наводит на кривизну.** *v.* Б226
A shortcut is often a wrong cut. Don't go round the world for a shortcut. *Cf.* The farthest way about is the nearest way home.

506 **Неизведанный друг нехорош для услуг.** *v.* Д418, Н312
Try your friend before you trust.

507* **Нельзя объять необъятное.**
No one is bound to do impossibilities. *Lat.* nemo tenetur ad impossibilia. *Cf.* There are no absolutes that are livable.

508 **Нельзя солнышку по два раза в сутки обходить.** *v.* В86, Д83
[The sun cannot pass twice in one day.] You cannot have two forenoons in the same day.

509* **Ненужен как собаке пятая нога.** *v.* П320
[As unnecessary as a fifth leg on a dog.] A fifth wheel to a coach. As much needed as a toad of a side pocket.

510 **Неповинна душа смерти не боится.** *v.* З109
[A clear conscience does not fear death.] *Cf.* A good conscience makes a good couch (is a soft pillow).

511 **Непостоянный подобен ветру - куда ветер, туда и он.** *v.* Н61
[The fickle are like the winds - they go where they blow.] Changeful as the moon. *Cf.* Free as the wind. What wind blew you hither? If we go with the wind, we shall soon be gone with the wind.

512 **Неправ медведь что корову съел, а неправа и корова что в лес зашла.** *v.* В333
[The bear was wrong to eat the cow, but the cow was also wrong to wander off into the wood.] How can the cat help it if the maid be a fool? *Cf.* Two wrongs don't make a right.

513 **Неправедна корысть в прок нейдет.** *v.* З121, К188, Т49, Х96, Ч127
Ill-gotten goods never prosper. *Gr.* κέρδος αἰσχρὸν βαρὺ κειμήλιον. *Lat.* non habet eventus sordida praeda bonos. Cic.*Phil.*2.27: male parta, mala dilabuntur.

514 **Непригож лицом да хорош умом.** *v.* Л86
[A foul face yet a sharp mind.] The face is a mask, look behind it. *Cf.* It makes little difference what's on the outside of your head if there's something on the inside. You can't tell a book by its cover.

515 **Несчастным бывает кто много желает.** *v.* З61, Т62
[He is unhappy who desires much.] The pleasure of what we enjoy is lost by coveting more.

516 **Нет в голове, нет в мошне.** *v.* Б134,435, У118
[An empty head means an empty purse.] *Cf.* He that has no money in his pot, let him have it in his mouth. Better an empty purse than an empty head.

517 **Нет друга - так ищи, а есть - так береги.** *v.* Н564
[Seek a friend if you have none, and keep him if you have one.] Be slow in choosing a friend, but slower in changing him. Make new friends but keep the old. *Cf.* Have patience with a friend rather than lose him forever.

518* Нет дыму без огня.   v. Г37, Д510, О26
      No smoke without some fire.

519   Нет жены, нет и заботы.   v. Л175
      [No wife, no cares.] He that has a wife, has care (strife).

520   Нет милее (такого) дружка как родимая (родная) матушка (+ да родимый батюшка).
      [No better friend than one's own loving mother (+ and father).]   v. С334
      No love to a father's. A mother's love never ages. *Gr.* Theogn. οὐδὲν ἐν ἀνφρώποισι
      πατρὸς καὶ μητρὸς ἄμινον ἔπλεϑ.

521   Нет мошны, есть спина.
      [No money but a strong back.] *i.e. willing to work. Cf.* It may be hard to work, but it
      must be harder to want. Wrinkled purses make wrinkled faces.

522   Нет ничего тайного, что не стало бы явным.   v. В148
      [There is no secret that will not be revealed.] Secrets are never long-lived. *Cf.* Wherever
      there is a secret, there must be something wrong.

523* Нет правила без исключений.
      There is no general rule without some exception. *Lat.* nulla regula sine exceptione.

524* Нет розы без шипов (+ нет радости без печали).   v. Х45
      No rose without a thorn [+ nor happiness untinged by sorrow.]

525   Нет солнце, и месяц светел. *v.* И32

526   Нет таких воров как портных мастеров.   v. Н425
      There is knavery in all trades, but most in tailors.

527   Нет таких лавок где продавали мамок.
      [A nurse cannot be bought in a shop.] Love is not found in the market.

528   Нет такого вреда когда от домашних придет беда.   v. Д159,160,371
      Nothing worse than a familiar enemy. *Gr.* μᾶλλον πείζει πάν᾽ τογ᾽οικεῖον κακόν.

529* Нет такого дня за которым бы ночи не было.   v. Б371, Д159,160
      Every day comes night. *Cf.* It is never a bad day that has a good night. Be the day ever
      so long, at length comes evensong.

530   Нет такого зла которого неможно было бы прикрыть.
      [There is no evil that cannot be concealed.] *SPL.* nihil tam improbe factum quin
      patrocinium inveniat.

531* Нет худа без добра. (Никое добро без вреда.)   v. В355, Н192, Т17
      No evil without good. Nothing so bad in which there is not something of good.
      Gr. οὖΔεν κακὸν ἀμιγὲς καλοῦ. *SPL.* terra serpentes et ciconias fert.

532   Нетом не разживешься.   v. С192
      [One cannot get rich by saying no.] Success comes in cans, failure in can'ts. *Cf.* I can't
      died in the poorhouse. Never say can't. If you always say "No" you'll never be married.

533* Ни аза (в глаза) не знать.
      Not to know the first thing about anything.

534 **Ни в марте воды, ни в апреле травы.**
[March rain brings April grass.] *Cf.* April showers bring May flowers.

535 **Ни в мать, ни в отца, а в проезжого молодца.**
[To take after neither mother nor father, but the stranger passing through.] To take after the milkman.

536 **Ни к селу, ни к городу.** *v.* H544
[Neither to town nor to country.] *Cf.* Neither here nor there.

537* **Ни кожи, ни рожи (+ ни видение).**
[Neither body nor face (+ nor demeanour).] Ugly as sin.

538 **Ни кола, ни двора.**
[To have neither stake nor yard.] To have neither house nor home.

539 **Ни коня удержать без узды, ни богатства без ума.**
[You can't control a horse without a bridle nor prosperity without intelligence.] Command your wealth, else it will command you. *Cf.* Riches serve a wise man but command a fool. Prosperity lets go the bridle.

540 **Ни на что не уповай, скорее долг отдавай.**
[Rely on nothing and repay debts promptly.] Trust is dead, ill payment killed it.

541* **Ни печаль без утешения, ни радость без наказания.** *v.* Б125, П29, Р17
[No sorrow without consolation, nor happiness without a price.] Of sufferance comes ease. No pleasure without pain. *Cf.* Pain is the price that God puts upon all things.

542 **Ни пить бы, ни есть, лишь бы на милую глядеть.**
[Neither food nor drink, just the sight of one's love.] *Cf.* Lovers live by love, as larks live by leeks. Drink to me only with thine eyes.

543 **Ни радость вечна, ни печаль бесконечна.** *v.* Г80,263, Р18, С85
[Neither gladness nor sadness last forever.] Sadness and gladness succeed each other.

544* **Ни рак, ни рыба. (Ни рыба, ни мясо.) (Ни сиво, ни буро.)** *v.* H536
[Neither crab nor fish (fish nor meat) (grey nor chestnut).] *i.e. nondescript. Cf.* The gravest fish is an oyster, the gravest bird's an owl, the gravest beast's an ass, and the gravest man's a fool. To make fish of one and flesh (fowl) of the other.

545 **Ни с молоду молодец, ни под старость старик.** *v.* Б415
Old young and old long.

546* **Ниже носа не чихнешь, а выше головы не скочишь.** *v.* В690,691, Л11
[You cannot sneeze below your nose, nor jump above than your head.] However high the eye may rise, it will find the eyebrow above it.

547 **Никогда не надо чужой беде смеяться.** *v.* К186, Р10
Never rejoice about your neighbour's misfortunes.

548* **Никто на свою ногу топора не опустит.** *v.* H551
[No man will lower the axe on his own foot.] No man is hurt by himself. No man fouls his hands in his own business.

549* **Никто не знает где башмак давит, кроме того кто его носит.** *v.* В618, З142
[None knows better where the shoe pinches than he that wears it.] I know best where the shoe pinches (wrings) me. *Lat.* Jer.*A.Iov.*1.48: nemo scit praeter me ubi me (soccus) premat.

550 **Никто сам себе не лиходей.** *v.* Н548
No man fouls his hands in his own business. *SPL.* nemo est tam malus quin culpae suae speciem honestam inveniat. *Cf.* †He is his own worst enemy. †None is hurt but by himself. †*Lat.* nemo laeditur nisi a seipso.

551 **Никто того не ведает как бедный обедает.**
[None opines how the poor man dines.] A poor man's tale cannot be heard.

552* **Ничем ничего не сделаешь.** *v.* Д512
Nothing comes of nothing. *Lat.* ex nihilo nihil fit.

553* **Ничто не вечно под луной.** *v.* Б439,471, В480, Д371, К33, Т19
[There's nothing permanent under the moon.] Nothing can last forever. Everything has an end. The world will not last always.

554* **Ничто не ново под луной.** *v.* Г292, Н86
Nothing new under the sun [moon]. *Lat.* nil sub sole novum.

555 **Нищему гордость как корове седло.** *v.* П266
[Pride for a beggar is like a saddle for a cow.] Pride and poverty are ill met yet often seen together.

556 **Нищета не отнимает ни чести ни ума.**
[Poverty diminishes neither dignity nor intellect.] Poverty is no disgrace. *Cf.* Under a ragged coat lies wisdom. Pride may lurk under a threadbare coat. Poverty is not a shame, but being ashamed of it is. Poverty isn't a crime.

557 **Нищий везде сыщет.**
[The needy will find what he needs anywhere.] Poverty is the mother of all arts.

558* **Нищий вора не боится.** *v.* Б352, Г239
The beggar may sing before the thief.

559* **Нищий на нищем не ищет.** *v.* Г241, З9, Н125, С5, У71
[The poor seek not of the poor.] No naked man is sought after to be rifled.

560* **Новая метла (новый веник) чисто метет.**
A new broom sweeps clean.

561 **Новая труба гласно, а старая согласно.**
[A new horn is loud, but an old one harmonious.] There's many a good tune played on an old fiddle.

562 **Нового счастья ищи, старого не теряй.** *v.* Н517,564
[Seek new fortune without relinquishing the old.] *Cf.* Don't throw away your old shoes before you get new ones. Don't trade old friends for new.

563 **Новый друг что весенный лед (неуставный плуг).** *v.* Н506
[A new friend is like spring ice (an uncertified plough).] *i.e. unreliable. Cf.* What is new is not true (and what is true cannot be new).

564   **Новых друзей наживай, а старых не забывай.**   *v.* H517
       Make new friends but keep the old. *Apost.* 12.1: νέων φίλων εὐπορῶν, παλαιῶν μὴ ἐπιλανθάνου. *Cf.* Remember man and keep in mind, a faithful friend is hard to find.

565   **Ноги в тепле, голова в холоде, бегай докторов и будешь здоров.**   *v.* Д203
       [Keep your feet warm and head cold, avoid doctors, and you'll enjoy good health.] A cool mouth and warm feet live long.

566*   **Нос вытащит - хвост увязит (завязит), хвост вытащит - нос увязит (завязит).**   *v.* B446,
       [Free the beak and the tail gets caught, free the tail and the beak is caught.]   K323
       i.e. an inextricable situation. The farther in, the deeper. *Cf.* If it's not one, it's the other.

567   **Нос крив и нрав кажется неправ.**
       [A crooked nose argues a crooked nature.] A crooked stick will cast a crooked shadow.

568   **Ночная кукушка всегда дневную перекукует.**   *v.* Ж56, 326, П113, X101
       [The night cuckoo is always louder than the daytime cuckoo.] *said of a wife's influence on her husband.* The woman you keep, keeps you. Man has his will, but woman has her way. He that would thrive must ask leave of his wife. He that has a wife has a master. *Cf.* Night is the mother of counsel. *Lat.* in nocte consilium.

569   **Ночь все покрывает.**
       [Night conceals everything.] Darkness has no shame. *SPL.* nox nihil moderabile suadet.

570*   **Ночью все кошки черны (лошадки вороные).**   *v.* K144, H236
       All cats (horses) are black (grey) in the night.

571*   **Ночью все дороги гладки.**
       [All roads are smooth by night.] All shapes, all colours, are alike in the dark. *SPL.* nocte latent mendae.

572*   **Ноша легка на чужом плече.**   *v.* Л24, H115
       The burden is light on another's shoulder. *Cf.* Everyone thinks his own sack heaviest.

573   **Нужда беду родит.**
       [Poverty is the mother of woe.] Poverty breeds strife. Need makes greed. *Cf.* Poverty is the mother of crime.

574   **Нужда вежлива, а голь догадлива.**
       [Need is polite, poverty crafty.] *Cf.* Poverty is an enemy to good manners.

575   **Нужда говорлива.**   *v.* У37
       [Need is garrulous.] All complain.

576   **Нужда горбится и прямится.**
       [Need hunches over and straightens up.] *Cf.* Need makes an old wife trot.

577*   **Нужда дружит и кошку с собакой.**
       [Need makes friends of cats and dogs.] Adversity makes strange bedfellows.

578   **Нужда железо ломает.**
       [Need shatters steel.] Hunger breaks stone walls. *SPL.* durum (ingens) necessitatis telum.

579*   **Нужда закона не знает (свой закон пишет).**   *v.* Г222, Ж131, H48, П307
       Need (necessity) knows no law (obeys its own law). *Lat.* necessitas non habet legem.

580   **Нужда и голод погоняет на холод.**   *v.* В674, Г218
[Need and hunger drive men into the cold.]   Hunger drives the wolf out of the wood.

581   **Нужда и по воскресным дням постится.**   *v.* Г235
[Poverty also fasts on feast days.]   Necessity has no holiday.

582   **Нужда (камень) котел грызет.**
[Need gnaws at the kettle (a stone).]   Hungry enough to eat nails. *Cf.* Poor folks are glad of porridge.

583   **Нужда научит калачи есть.**   *v.* Б45, Н589, П246
[Need will teach a man to eat *kalachi*.] *kalachi were wheat loaves made in southern Russia where impoverished peasants from the north (accustomed to rye) would flee to escape famine.* *SPL.* optimus orandi magister est necessitas. *Cf.* Need makes the naked man run.

584   **Нужда научит кузнеца сапоги тачать.**   *v.* Г245
[Need will teach the blacksmith to stitch boots.]   Necessity teaches a naked woman to spin.   Sorrow makes websters spin. *Cf.* Necessity is the mother of invention.

585   **Нужда не ждет (ведреной) погоды.**
[Need does not await good weather.]   Need will have its course.

586   **Нужда нужду ведет, а горе сводничает.**
Need makes greed [as sorrow panders].   *Cf.* Two false knaves need no broker.

587   **Нужда обеты преступает.**   *v.* Ж131
[Poverty breaks vows.]   It is hard to be leal and poor.

588   **Нужда острит разум.**   *v.* Б45, Г220,223, П274
[Need sharpens the mind.]   Necessity sharpens industry. *Cf.* Hunger sharpens the wits. Hunger increases the understanding.

589   **Нужда скачет, нужда пляшет (плачет), нужда песеньки поет.**   *v.* П246,276
Need makes the naked man run [dance (cry), and sing.]

590   **Нужда счастье насилует.**   *v.* Ж131
[Poverty rapes happiness.]   *Cf.* There is no virtue that poverty destroys not.

591*   **Нужда учит родить (всему учит).**   *v.* Г245, Н496, Х81, Я19
Necessity is the mother of invention. *SPL.* gladiator in arena consilium capit. hominem experiri multa paupertas iubet.

592   **Нужда цены не знает.**   *v.* Г222
[Need knows no price.]   Necessity never made a good bargain. *Cf.* Need makes greed.

593   **Нужда чутьем идет.**
[Need walks by feel.]   *Cf.* Necessity is coal black.

594   **Нужно, как слепому зеркало.**   *v.* К19, Н384
[As necessary as a mirror to a blindman.]   *Cf.* As comely as a cow in a cage.

595   **Нынче я, завтра ты, всякому своя очередь.**
I today, you tomorrow [everyone in turn].   *Lat.* hodie mihi, cras tibi.

596   **Ныне на ногах а завтра в могиле.**   *v.* Ж152, С87
[On your feet today, in the grave tomorrow.]   Here today (one day), gone tomorrow (the next). Today a man, tomorrow none.

О

1* **О вкусах не спорят.**   *v.* И128, Н15, П107, У15
There's no accounting for tastes. There is no disputing about tastes. *Lat.* de gustibus non est disputandum.

2* **О мертвых (покойниках) - или хорошо, или ничего (плохо не говорят).**
Speak well of the dead. *Gr.* Diog.Laert.1.3.2.70: τὸν τεθνηκότα μὴ κακαλογεῖν. *Lat.* de mortuis nil nisi bonum.

3* **О чем две бабы говорят, вся деревня знает.**
[When two women talk, the whole town will know.] Tell a woman and you tell the world. *Cf.* Wherever there is a woman, there is gossip.

4 **О чем тому тужить чего нельзя воротить (кому есть чем жить).** *v.* А29, Б219, И140,
Never grieve for what you cannot help.   П278,279, С214, Ч105
It is too late to grieve when the chance is past. Things past cannot be recalled. It's no use crying over spilt milk.

5 **Оба лучше.**   *v.* З57
[Both are better.] *i.e. than one or either.* Never choose between two good things, take them both.

6 **Обед тогда варят когда дрова горят.**   *v.* Ж41
[Don't cook the meal till after you've started the fire.] Don't spread the cloth till the pot begins to boil.

7* **Обед узнаешь кушаньем, а ум слушанием.**   *v.* В636, Д145, К336, Л99
[Judge a meal by eating and intellect by listening.] The proof of the pudding is in the eating.

8* **Обедать в гостях, и к себе позвать.**   *v.* В21
[He must offer an invitation who accepts one.] A host's invitation is expensive. *Cf.* Serve a noble disposition, though poor, the time comes he will repay you.

9 **Обезьяна и в золотом наряде обезьяна.**   *v.* В361, С54
[A monkey dressed in gold is still a monkey.] An ape's an ape, a varlet's a varlet, though they be clad in silk or scarlet. A pig in the parlour is still a pig.

10 **Обещай рассудив, а давай не скупясь.**   *v.* Д7, Н274,422
[Promise prudently and perform unselfishly.] Be slow to promise and quick to perform.

11 **Обещанного три года ждут.**   *v.* Н75, П190
[One can wait three years for what is promised.] *sarc.* Promises are made to be broken. A man apt to promise is apt to forget. *Cf.* You can't live on promises.

12* **Обещать и слово держать как небо и земля.** *v.* Д117, О152
[Promise and performance are as different as heaven and earth.] It's one thing to promise, another to perform. *Cf.* Between promising and performing, a man may marry his daughter.

13* **Обман спасительный лучше истины гибельной.** *v.* И125, Л101,138, У94
Better a lie that heals than a truth that wounds.

14 **Обманом и города берут.** *v.* П284, Я17
[Entire cities may be taken by treachery.] Cities are taken by the ears.

15 **Обрадовался крохе, да и ломоть потерял.** *v.* Б191, З22, М26, П94,116
[Dropped the morsel for the crumb.] He who grabs at the shadow may lose the substance. Penny wise, pound foolish. *Cf.* Grasp no more than the hand can hold. Grasp a little and you may secure it, grasp much and you will lose everything.

16 **Обуха плетью не перешибешь (перестегаешь) (перебьешь).** *v.* П287, У54
[The lash cannot outdo the butt of an axe.] The weakest goes to the wall.

17* **Овес за лошадью не ходит.** *v.* М76, Х21, Я23
[Oats don't follow the horse.] Roasted ducks don't fly into your mouth.

18* **Овец не стало, и на коз честь.** *v.* З29, И25,32, Н3, С107, У113
[When the sheep are gone, the goats have the honour.] *i.e. will do, to substitute.* If you can't get a horse, ride a cow.

19 **Овин горит, а молотильщики есть просят.**
[The barn is burning and the threshers want to eat.] *Cf.* To play chess when the house is on fire.

20* **Овсяная (оржаная) (ржаная) каша сама себя хвалит.** *v.* Г317, Д301, К335, О7
[Oatmeal (barley) (buckwheat) porridge praises itself.] *i.e. also through flatulence.* The proof of the pudding is in the eating.

21 **Овца руно растит, а скупой деньги коптит, не для себя.** *v.* С165, 166
[A lamb's wool and a miser's money go to others.] He that hoards up money pains for other men.

22 **Овца не слушающая пастыря, корысть волку.** *v.* Б187
[A sheep that strays is the wolf's gain.] The wolf eats often of the sheep that have been told. The lone sheep is in danger of the wolf.

23 **Овцы мрут и ягнятся, пастухи жирятся.**
[While sheep die and multiply, the shepherds thrive.] He that has sheep, swine and bees - sleep he, wake he, he may thrive.

24 **Овце с волками худо жить.**
[Hard for a sheep to live amongst the wolves.] *Cf.* Two wolves may worry one sheep. Death of wolves is safety of sheep.

25* **Овчинка (шкура) выделки не стоит.** *v.* B545, И66, К172, П291
[The sheepskin is not worth the workmanship.] The game is not worth the candle.

26 **Огонь без дыму а человек без ошибок не бывает.** *v.* Г37, Д510, К18, Н518
No fire without smoke [nor man without fault].

27   **Огонь (огня) маслом заливать (не зальешь) (не тушат), лишь огня прибавлять.**
    Pouring oil on the fire is not the way to quench it.   *v.* E13, З69, М33, Н405
    Gr. ἐλαιῳ τὸ πῦρ σβεννύεις.

28*   **Один в поле не воин (ратник).**   *v.* В87, О38
    [One on the field is not a warrior.] One man is no man. *Gr.* εἷς ἀνήρ, οὐδεὶς ἀνήρ.
    Lat. unus vir, nullus vir.

29   **Один волк гоняет овец полк.**
    [One wolf can rout an entire flock.] It never troubles the wolf how many the sheep may be. One butcher doesn't fear many sheep. *Cf.* One, but a lion.
    Gr. Aes.*Fab.*240: ἕνα...ἀλλὰ λέοντα.

30*   **Один (одним) всем не услужишь.**   *v.* В525, Н19, О74
    None so good that it's good to all. It is hard to please all parties. He labours in vain who tries to please all parties. All feet tread not in one shoe.

31*   **Один глупый бросит (кинет) камень в воду, а сто умных не вынут.**   *v.*Г149,Д475,У102
    A fool may throw a stone into a well which a hundred wise men cannot pull out.

32*   **Один другому не указ.**
    No man is another's master.

33   **Один дурак, а умных пятерых ссорит.**   *v.* Б166, Г142, Д501, И17, С9
    One fool makes many (a hundred). *Lat.* unius dementia dementes efficit multos.

34*   **Один дурак в час спросит больше чем десять мудрецов сумеют ответить за год.**
    A fool can ask more in an hour than a wise man can answer in seven years.
    SPL. quaerit delirus quod non respondet Homerus.

35*   **Один женится, а семеро пьют.**   *v.* Б474, К117, М130,207, О44
    [One gets married and seven get drunk.] *i.e. seven benefit from the toil of one.*
    Cf. Everyone fastens where there's gain. I kill the boar, another eats the flesh.

36*   **Один за всех, все за одного.**
    One for all and all for one.

37   **Один и дома горюет, а двое и в поле воюют.**   *v.* В87, О28,38
    [The home's too big for one and the field's too small for two.] One's too few, two are too many. *Cf.* Two attorneys can live in a town when one cannot. Two keep counsel if one's away. Space is ample east and west, but two can't go abreast.

38   **Один и у каши не спор (загинет).**   *v.* В87, О28,37
    [One even at the table is at a loss.] One is no number. One body is no body. *Lat.* monas numerus esse non dicitur.

39   **Один намекнет, а другой смекнет.**   *v.* Д323, М173, Р32, У98
    [One hints, the other guesses.] A word to the wise man is enough. *Lat.* verbum sat sapienti.

40   **Один одного стоит.**
    One to one is odds.

41*   **Один пирог два раза не сьешь.**   *v.* А1, И84, С26
    You can't eat the same bread (pie) twice. You cannot have your cake and eat it.

42   **Один раб двум господам не служит.**
*Matt.*6.24: **No man can serve two masters.**

43*   **Один радуется а другой плачет.**   *v.* Б11, В410, Г84, И20,133, К157, *Ap.*1.23
[One laughs, the other cries.] Fortune to one is mother, to another is stepmother. Somewhere the sun is shining, somewhere a little rain is falling.

44   **Один с сошкой а семеро с ложкой.**   *v.* О35
[One with a plough and seven with a spoon.] *i.e. one works and others benefit.* *Cf.* One sows and another reaps. When the ox is down, many are the butchers. When the tree is fallen, everyone goes to it with a hatchet.

45   **Один советует - один и отвечает.**
He who follows his own advice must take the consequences.

46   **Один умен десять безумных водит.**   *v.* В27, З13, Р31, У93
[One wise man can command ten fools.] *Cf.* One man is worth a hundred and a hundred is not worth one. One good head is better than a thousand strong hands.

47   **Один сын - не сын, два сына - полсына, а три сына - сын.**
[One son is no son, two sons are half a son, but three sons are a son.] *i.e. less chance of disappointment. Cf.* He that has one son makes him a fool. †One boy's a boy, two boys are one half a boy, three boys are no boy at all *(i.e. the more boys that help, the less work is done).*

48*   **Одна беда минет, так десят придет.**   *v.* Б24,25, О58,67, Т1
[No sooner is one trouble past than ten appear.] Of one ill come many. Ill comes often on the back of worse. *SPL.* finis alterius mali gradus est futuri.

49   **Одна беда не приходит.** *v.* Б25

50*   **Одна голова не беда, а (и) беда, так одна.**   *v.* Л21
[Being single is not a problem, and if it were, it's only one problem.] *i.e. marriage has more responsibility. Cf.* †The married man has many cares, the unmarried man one more.

51   **Одна головня и в печи гаснет, а две и в поле курятся.**   *v.* В447, Г28
[One log will die in a stove, while two can smolder even in a field.] *Cf.* Two heads (hands) are better than one.

52   **Одна копейка и та ребром.**
[One *kopek* and it's the very last.] *ie. "to spend one's last penny (bottom dollar.)"*

53*   **Одна ласточка лета не делает (весны не приносит).**
One swallow makes not a summer [spring]. *Gr.* μία χελιδὼν ἔαρ οὐ ποιεῖ. *EA.* una hirundo non facit ver. *SPL.* ver non una dies, non una reducit hirundo. *Cf.* One woodcock does not make a winter.

54*   **Одна паршивая овца все стадо портит.**   *v.* В7,К8,203, Л98, Ш3
One scabbed sheep will mar a whole flock. *Lat.* morbida facta pecus totum currumpit ovile. *SPL.* Juv.*Sat.*2.79: grex totus in agris unius scabie cadit.

55*   **Одна речь не пословица.**   *v.* Б179, Г135,204, П183
[Words alone don't make a proverb.] A proverb comes not from nothing.

56　　**Одна рука в меду, другая в патоке.**
　　　　[One hand in honey, the other in molasses.] To be caught red-handed. *Cf.* One foot in the grave, the other on a banana peel.

57　　**Одна собака вернее господину двух служителей.**
　　　　[One dog is more faithful to a master than two servants.] A dog is a man's best friend.

58　　**Одна сорока с плоту а десять на плот.**　　　　　　　　　*v.* O48
　　　　[One magpie leaves the raft and ten fly onto it.] When one door closes another one opens. *Cf.* To grow like Hydra's heads. There is more than one frog in the puddle.

59*　　**Одна удача идет, другую ведет.**　　　　　　　　　　　*v.* C309
　　　　Nothing succeeds like success.

60*　　**Однажды отрежь а десятью примерь.**　　　　　　　*v.* Д213, C103
　　　　Measure twice [ten times] **but cut once.**

61　　**Одни выучились говорить, а другие узнавать.**
　　　　[Some have learned to answer, others to ask.] Some are wise and some are otherwise. *Cf.* Some have tact, others tell the truth.

62*　　**Одни плачут а другие скачут.**　　　　*v.* B71,210,211,218,611, K186, O76, C310
　　　　[Some cry, others jump.] There's no great banquet but some fare ill. Some have the hap, others stick in the gap.

63*　　**Одни сеют, другие жнут.**　　　　　　　　　　　　　*v.* B210,211
　　　　Some sow, others reap. *Lat.* alii sementem faciunt, alii metent(em). *Gr.* ἄλλοι μὲν σπείρουσιν, ἄλλοι δὲ ἀμήσονται.

64　　**Одни умеют строить, а другие разорять.**　　　　　*v.* Л26, H347,465
　　　　[Some know how to build, others to destroy.] *Cf.* It's easier to pull down than to build. *Lat.* facilius est destruere quam construere.

65*　　**Одним зарядом двух птичек убить.**
　　　　To kill two birds with one stone [cartridge].

66　　**Одним умным человеком дом стоит.**
　　　　[One wise man keeps a house standing.] Well goes the case that wisdom counsels. *Cf.* One good head is better than a thousand strong hands.

67　　**Одно горе идет по пятам другого.**　　　　　　*v.* Б24, O48, П265, T1, Ч51
　　　　[One trouble comes on the heels of another.] Ill comes often on the back of worse. *Cf.* Misfortunes never come singly.

68　　**Одно золото не стареется.**
　　　　[Only gold never grows old.] *Cf.* What cannot gold do?

69*　　**Одно «нынче» лучше двух «завтра».**　　　　　　　*v.* Л152, H357
　　　　One today is worth two tomorrows. One hour today is worth two tomorrow. Better a egg today than a hen tomorrow. *Cf.* An hour in the morning is worth two in the afternoon (evening). No time like the present. Never put off for tomorrow what you can do today.

70　　**Одно око, да видит далеко.**　　　　　　　　　　　*v.* B306, У40
　　　　[One eye, yet it sees far.] *Cf.* He that has but one eye, sees the better for it.

71* **Одного поля ягода.**   *v.* И98
[A berry of the same field.] *i.e. a kindred spirit, or two of the same.* A bird of the same feather. Tarred with the same brush. Made from the same mould.

72* **Одного семеро не ждут.** *v.* С97

73 **Одной рукой крестится, а другой в чужую пазуху лезет.**   *v.* Б236, И122, С43
[He crosses himself with one hand while picking a pocket with the other.] The friar preached against stealing and had a goose in his sleeve.

74 **Одному на всех не упакать (угодить).**   *v.* В525, Н19, О30
It is hard to please all parties. *Lat.* durum est omnibus placere.

75 **Одному против многих замышлять нельзя.**   *v.* В87
[One cannot conspire against many.] It is hard for one to withstand many.
Gr. Hom.*Od.*20.313: χαλεπον γὰρ ἐρυκακέειν ἕνα πολλούς. *Cf.* One is no number.

76 **Одному сбылось, а другому не удалось.**   *v.* Б460, В71,210,218, Д82, К186, С310,330
Some win, some lose.

77 **Ожидаем света а утрена отпета.**
[We're waiting for sunrise and matins are all sung.] Though you rise early, yet the day comes at his time and not till then.

78 **Око видит далеко, а мысль (ум) еще дальше.**
[The eye sees far, but the mind even farther.] The eye looks but the mind sees. *Cf.* My mind to me is a kingdom. *Lat.* Sen.*Thyest.*380: mens regnum bona possidet.

79* **Око за око, зуб за зуб.**
An eye for an eye and a tooth for a tooth. *Deut.*19.21: oculum pro oculo, dentem pro dente.

80 **Около печи нельзя не нагреться.**
[You can't help but warm up by the stove.] The fire is never without heat. *Cf.* †If you don't like the heat, get out of the kitchen.

81 **Около сажи (воды) (огня) (терна) ходить -**   *v.* В107, Г31,332, Д63, К271,
очернишься (обмочешься) (ожжешься) (уколишься).   Л207, С25, Х16, Ч38
He that handles pitch shall be defiled. If you play with fire you get burnt. He that handles thorns shall prick his fingers.

82* **Около святых черти водятся.**   *v.* Б339, Г73, П146
[Devils lurk near saints,] The devil lurks behind the cross. *Cf.* The devil can cite scripture to his purpose.

83 **Около хлеба и мыши водятся.**
No larder but has its mice.

84 **Около чего потрешься, того и наберешься.**   *v.* Г332, И1,119, Н448, О81, У38
[You pick up what you rub up against.] He that deals in dirt has aye foul fingers. He who goes into a mill comes out powdered. He that has to do with what is foul never comes away clean.

85 **Окоротишь, так не воротишь.** *v.* Ч93

86   Он дружбу ведет а после рожном в рот.   *v.* Б16,100, З336
To smile in one's face and to cut one's throat.

87   Он из воды сух выйдет.
[He'll come out of water dry.] *i.e. is invincible, indomitable.* *Cf.* To have nine lives like a cat. †The rain that rains on everybody else can't keep you dry.

88   Он пороху не выдумал.
[He didn't invent powder.] *i.e. he's no genius.* *Cf.* He didn't invent the wheel. Some people have brains and then there are others.

89   Опасенье половина спасенья.   *v.* Н158
[Apprehension is half of salvation.] Fear is one part of prudence. A word before is worth two behind. One good forewit is worth two afterwits. *Cf.* Prevention is better than cure. Providing is preventing.

90   Опрятная кухарка дороже повара.
[Better a neat cook than a fancy chef.] Better are meals many than one too merry. *Cf.* Durability is better than show.

91*   Опустя лето, да в лес по малину.   *v.* Н466, П169,267
[Having missed summer, to go off to the woods for raspberries.] *i.e. too late.* **Baskets after vintage.** To come a day after the fair. *Gr.* κατόπιν ἑορτῆς ἥκεις. *Lat.* post festum venisti.

92   Опыт - лучший учитель.   *v.* Б217, З2, Н149,378
Experience is the best teacher. *Cf.* Experience is the mother of wisdom (knowledge) (science). Experience is the mistress (teacher) of fools.

93   Опытность нередко заменяет ученье.   *v.* З2
Experience is often a substitute for learning.

94*   Опять двадцать пять. (Опять за рыбу деньги.)   *v. Ap.*1.107
[Back to twenty-five. (Pay again for the same fish.)] Back to square one. And (so) what else is new?

95   Орать пашню, копить квашню.   *v.* Б380, В113, Г131
[Plough the field and fill the trough.] Plough deep and you will have plenty of corn. *Cf.* Plough deep while sluggards sleep - you'll have corn to sell and to keep.

96   Орел орла плодит, а сова сову родит.   *v.* З139, Н47,402, О156
[Eagles breed eagles, and owls owls.] Eagles do not breed doves.

97*   Ореха не разгрызешь, так и ядра не съешь.   *v.* Н397, П273
He that will eat the kernel must crack the nut. *Lat.* Plaut.*Curc.* 1.1.55: qui a nuce nucleum esse vult, frangit nucem.

98   Орла узнаешь по полету, а молодца по обороту.   *v.* В310, З158
[The eagle is known by his flight, a clever man by his turn of phrase.] The bird is known by his note, the man by his words.

99*   Орлом мух не ловят (орел мух не ловит).   *v.* Л17
Eagles catch no flies. *Gr. Apost.*1.44: ἀετὸς μυίας οὐ θηρεύει. *Lat. EA.* aquila non captat muscas.

100* **Орлы бьются (дерутся) а молодцы перья (достаются).**
[Fighting eagles leave feathers for lucky men to find.] Two dogs strive for a bone and a third runs away with it. *Cf.* If the sky falls we shall catch larks.

101 **Освоила вошь коросту.**   *v.* M203
[The louse has alighted on a scab.] *i.e. found the sore spot.* Flies look for ulcers.

102 **Осень всклочет, да (а) как весна захочет.**
[Autumn may grumble, but spring commands.] *i.e. not autumn shoots but the spring weather determines a harvest.* No autumn fruit without spring blossoms.

103* **Осердясь на блохи (вши) да и шубу (одеяло) в печь.**   *v.* M209
[To burn one's cloak (blanket) to get rid of the fleas (lice).] To burn one's house to get rid of the mice.

104 **Осина и без ветра шумит.**
[Aspen rustle even without the wind.] To tremble (quake) like an aspen leaf.

105 **Осла и в львинной коже по крику узнаешь.**   *v.* И74,Л42
[Even in a lion's skin, the ass's bray will give him away.] What good can it do an ass to be called a lion. *Cf.* An ass in a lion's skin *(title of one of Aesop's fables).*

106 **Осла познаешь по ушам, а дурака по словам.**
An ass is known by his ears [and a fool by his words.] *SPL.* vox cicadam prodit.

107* **Осла пригласили на свадьбу - возить дрова и воду.**
[The ass was invited to the wedding - to haul logs and water.] The parrot has fine feathers but he doesn't go to the dance. *Cf.* An ass must be tied where the master will have him. A pig in a parlour is still a pig.

108 **Остер топор, да (и) сук зубаст.**   *v.* H45,171, O108
[The axe is sharp, but the bough too is tough.] *i.e. unyielding.* An old horse for a hard road.

109 **Остер язычок как бритва.**   *v.* Я14,22
[The tongue is razor-sharp.] The tongue is not steel yet it cuts. The tongue stings.

110* **Осторожно все делать можно.**
Everything may be done with care.

111 **Осторожного коня и зверь не вредит.**
[Wild beasts won't harm the wary steed.] Warned folks may live. *Cf.* There's no arrest for the wary.

112* **Осторожность - мать безопасности (мудрости).**   *v.* K221, O141, P33
Caution is the parent of safety. *Cf.* Caution is the eldest child of wisdom. He lives safely that lives closely.

113 **Острое слово с языка что пуля срывается.**
[A harsh word is like a bullet fired from the tongue.] A good tongue is a good weapon. *Cf.* Hard words cut the heart (enter the heart and lie there heavy as lead.

114 **Острым топором камня не перерубишь, лишь топор иступишь.**   *v.* И63, Ш8
[You will only dull the blade if you try to chop a stone with an axe.] No man can flay a stone. To cut blocks with a razor. *Cf.* If you can't make every edge cut, you can sure make it bruise.

115   Осудил горшок чугунку, а сам весь в саже.   *v.* Г288, И102
     The pot calls the kettle black.

116   Осуждая друга, посмотри за собою.   *v.* З17, Н93
     [Before you criticise your friend, look to yourself.] Judge well yourself before you
     criticize. *Cf.* Judge others by what you do. Reprove others but correct yourself.

117   От беды (горя) бежал, да в пропасть (беду) попал.   *v.* Б46,47, О129,146
   (От горя бегом, а кручина передом.)
     [To run from trouble (sorrow) and fall into an abyss (woe).] Out of the frying pan and
     into the fire. Shunning the smoke, they fall into the fire. *Lat. EA.* fumum fugiens, in
     ignem incidi.

118*   От великого до смешного один шаг.
     From the sublime to the ridiculous is but one step.

119*   От волка бежал, да на медведя напал.   *v.* Г324
     [To flee the bear and run into the wolf.] Escaped the thunder and fell into the lightning.

120   От вора, от разбойника остатки бывают (хоть стены останутся), а от пожару мало
   что (ничего) остается.
     [Thieves and bandits leave something (the walls) behind, but fires spares nothing.]
     Cf. Fire and water have no mercy.

121   От вражды любовь произойти не может.
     [Enmity cannot breed love.] *Cf.* Hate from hate is sure to grow. Seldom does the hated
     man end well. †Hate likely turns to love.

122   От всего вылечишься, кроме смерти.   *v.* А24, З40
     There is a remedy for everything but death. *Cf.* Death defies the doctor.

123   От греха не уйдешь а от беды не упасешься.
     [You cannot avoid harm nor escape misfortune.] Sin, sorrow and work are the things
     men can't shirk. *Cf.* Misfortunes find their way even on the darkest night.

124   От греха подальше.
     Stay clear of trouble. Don't meet troubles half way. Stay out of harm's way. Keep
     your nose clean.

125*   От добра добра не ищут.   *v.* Д266, Л166, О164, П294
     Leave (let) well (enough) alone. The best is the enemy of the good.

126*   От доброго житья толстеют, а от дурного худеют.   *v.* В265
     [One grows fat from the good life and lean from the bad.] *Cf.* Laugh and grow fat. Fat
     people are jolly people. The envious man grows lean.

127*   От доброго корени добрая и отрасль.   *v.* И109, К69,80,84, О167, П52
     [Of a good root, a good branch.] **It is good grafting on a good stock.** Of evil grain,
     no good seed can come. *SPL.* esquilla non nascitur rosa.

128   От доброго обеда и к ужину останется.
     [Of a good lunch there will be some left for dinner.] *Cf.* He that saves his dinner will
     have the more for his supper.

129 **От дождя не в воду, а от огня не в полымя.** *v.* О117,146
[Go not from the rain into water nor from the flame into fire.] *Cf.* Pour not water on a drowned mouse. To jump from the smoke into the flame. *Lat.* *EA.* fumum fugiens in ignem incidi.

130 **От домашнего (своего) вора не убережешься.** *v.* Д391, Н245,528
[There's no defense against the familiar thief.] Nothing worse than a familiar enemy.

131 **От дурака добра не жди.** *v.* Н265
[Expect no good of a fool.] He is a fool who expects sense from a fool. He who sends a fool expects one. *Cf.* What can you expect from a hog but a grunt?

132 **От жиру собаки бесятся.** *v.* С11

133 **От затирки бывают дырки.**
[Zeal may cause a weal.] Zeal without prudence is frenzy.

134 **От избытка сердца уста глаголют (говорят).**
[Words spring from the fulness of the heart.] When the heart is on fire, some sparks will fly out of the mouth. *SPL.* ex abundantia cordis os loquitur.

135 **От искры сыр бор загорается.** *v.* И136, М14, О142
[A spark will set fire even to a damp forest.] Of a small spark a great fire. A little spark kindles a great fire.

136 **От кого чают, того и величают.** *v.* В623, Г39, Н120,409, Ч24
[We honour those of whom we harbour expectations.] Every man bows to the bush he gets bield of. All flatterers live at the expense of those they flatter. Cic.*Off.*1.15: a quo plurimum sperant, ei potissimum inserviunt.

137 **От козла ни шерсти ни молока.** *v.* К45

138 **От курицы яйцо, а от яйца курица.**
[The chicken lays the egg and the egg hatches the chicken.] What came first, the chicken or the egg?

139 **От лихого не услышишь доброго слова.**
[You won't hear a kind word from a wicked person.] No gratitude from the wicked. Ill will never speak well or do well.

140 **От мала и до велика.**
From small beginnings come great things. *Cf.* From rags to riches.

141 **От малого опасения великое спасение.** *v.* Б183,186, К221, О112, Р33, Ш11
An ounce of prevention is worth a pound of cure.

142* **От малой искры велик пожар делается.** *v.* И91,136, М14, О135, У106
Of a small spark a great fire. *SPL.* parva scintilla neglecta magnum saepe excitat incendium. etiam capillus umbram habet.

143 **От мертвого худа не бывает (+ а от живого добра).** *v.* М75
[No ill comes from the dead (+ nor good from the living).] Dead men do no harm. *Cf.* Dead men don't bite. *Gr.* νεκρὸς οὐ δάκνει. *Lat.* mortui non mordent.

144 **От нечего делать надобно что нибудь делать.**   *v.* Б104, В505, Н450, С167
[When one has nothing to do, one has to do something.] It is more pain to do nothing than something. *Cf.* Anything is better than nothing.

145* **От одной матки да не одни ребятки.**   *v.* И126
[Not all children of the same mother are alike.] Many a good cow has an ill calf.

146 **От огня в полымя броситься.**   *v.* Б47, И76,93, О117,129
[From the flame into the fire.] Out of the frying pan into the fire.

147 **От одного берега отстал, а к другому не пристал.**
One foot in the sea and one on shore. *Cf.* One foot cannot stand in two boats. To burn one's bridges.

148* **От одного порченого яблока, целый воз загнивает.**   *v.* В7, К8,203, Л98, О54, Ш3
One bad (rotten) apple spoils the bunch (its neighbours). *Cf.* One scabbed sheep will mar a whole flock.

149 **От одного слова, да век ссора.**   *v.* В67,521, Ж95, С125
Small words sometimes grow into mighty strife. *Lat.* lis verbis minimis interdum maxima crescit. *Cf.* One year's seeding makes seven years weeding.

150 **От осины (овцы) яблочко (волк) не родится.**   *v.* В168, Д364, Н399, Я3
[Of an aspen (lamb) no apple (wolf) can spring.] Ask pears of an elm tree. One can't gather grapes of thorns or figs of thistles.

151 **От пословицы не уйдешь (укоешься).**   *v.* П186
[You cannot escape a proverb.] Proverbs cannot be contradicted.

152* **От слова до дела далеко (целая верста).**   *v.* Г180, Д117, О12
[From word to deed is a long way (one *verst*).] Saying and doing are two different things. *Cf.* Easier said than done. There's many a slip 'twixt the cup and the lip.

153* **От слова не сделается.**   *v.* В503,512, Н121,321, Э1
Saying so don't make it so. Talking pays no toll.

154 **От смерти не откупишься (уйдешь).**   *v.* З40
[There's no escaping death.] Death is deaf and will hear no denial. *Cf.* Every bullet has its billet.

155* **От смерти нет лекарства (не отлечишься).**   *v.* Б307
Death defies the doctor. *Lat.* contra vim mortis non est medicamen in hortis. There is a medicine for all things except death and taxes.

156 **От совы не родятся соколы.**   *v.* З139, Н47,402, О96
[Owls don't breed falcons.] Eagles do not breed doves. *SPL.* esquilla non nascitur rosa, nec hyacinthus.

157* **От судьбы не уйдешь.**   *v.* Г18, Р62,68, Ч45
No flying from fate.

158 **От сумы да от тюрьмы не отказывайся (отрекайся).**
[Don't make light of the beggar's pan nor the prison cell.] *i.e. the same fate may befall you; there's no guarantee against calamity.* No fence against a flail. *Cf.* Flee never so fast, you cannot flee your fortune.

159 **От того кто не мил и подарок постыл.**
A wicked man's gift has a touch of its master.

160 **От того терплю кого больше всех люблю.** *v.* Л192
[We most forbear those whom we most love.] Where there is no love, all faults are seen.
Cf. Love covers many infirmities. A true friend is one who knows all your faults and
loves you still. Love sees no faults.

161 **От трудов праведных не наживешь (не нажить) палат каменных.** *v.* П221
[Honest work won't earn mansions of stone.] Honesty is ill to thrive by. *Cf.* Honesty is
praised and starves. Virtue and riches seldom settle on one man.

162 **От умеренного расходу остатки бывают которые недостатки награждают.**
[Moderate spending's savings offset shortfalls.] Know when to spend and where to spare
and you needn't be busy, you'll never be bare.

163 **От учтивых слов язык не отсохнет.** *v.* Л7,8
[Kind words won't parch your tongue.] Fair words hurt not the mouth.

164 **От хлеба хлеба не ищут.** *v.* О125, П294
[Seek not bread when you have it.] Leave well enough alone.

165 **От хлеба-соли не отказываются.** *v.* Г27, Д79, Н280, Т43
[Do not refuse hospitality.] Never refuse a good offer. Throw no gifts at the giver's head.

166* **От худой курицы худые яйцы.** *v.* Н47
Of an evil crow [hen], **an evil egg.** Such bird, such egg. *Gr.*κακοῦ κόρακος κακὸν
ᾠόν.

167 **От худого семя не жди доброго племя.** *v.* И108, К69,84,89, О127, П52, Х95, Щ4
Of evil grain no good seed can come. *SPL.* mali corvi malum ovum.

168* **От черта крестом, от свиньи пестом, а от лихого человека ничем.** *v.* К147
[Ward off the devil with a cross, swine with a staff, but there's no defense against an
evil man.] Take heed of an ox before, a horse behind, and a man on all sides.

169 **От чужих ворот не стыдно сделать поворот.**
(От чужого стола не стыдно, не евши, встать.)
[There's no shame in turning away from others' gates.] [Be not ashamed to rise without
eating from another's table.] *Cf.* Leave off with an appetite (while the play is good).
Leave the court ere the court leave thee. At the table it becomes no one to be bashful.

170 **От щелчка доходит до кулака.** *v.* И117, П207, Ш17
[Taps lead to punches.] Fools (dogs) begin in jest and end in earnest. *Cf.* When push
comes to shove.

171* **Отвага - половина победы.** *v.* С191
A bold heart is half the battle.

172 **Отвага сердце в броню одевает.** *v.* М186
[Valour shields the heart with armour.] The weapon of the brave is in his heart. *Cf.* A
man of courage is never in need of weapons.

173 **Отдай мое, а со своим как хочешь.** *v.* Б182
[Do what you want with your own, but give back mine.] Be bold with what is your own.

174   **Отец наказывает, отец и хвалит.**
[The father both punishes and praises.] *Cf.* One father is more than a hundred schoolmasters. He who loves well chastises well. Love well, whip well.

175*   **Отец рыбак - дети в воду смотрят.**   *v.* B398
[A fisherman's children look to the sea.] He that comes of a hen must scrape.

176*   **Отзвонил, (да) и с колокольни долой (проч).**
[Once the bell is rung, leave the belfry.] *i.e. finish your job and forget about it.* When the job is well done, you can hang up the hammer. *Cf.* The thing that's done is not to do (has an end). Live your life, do your work, then take your hat.

177*   **Отзовутся (отольются) кошке (волку) (медведью) мышкины (овечьи) (коровьи) слезки.**   *v.* З28, K238, Л76, П154,T13, Ч72
[The cat (wolf) (bear) will cry for the mouse's (sheep's) (cow's) tears.] He that mischief hatches, mischief catches. Curses, like chickens, come home to roost. *Cf.* We cannot do evil to others without doing it ourselves.

178*   **Откладывай веселье до праздника.**   *v.* X68
[Do not celebrate before the holiday.] *Cf.* He laughs best who laughs last.

179   **Откуда ветер, оттуда счастье.**
[Whence the wind, thence fortune.] *Cf.* Fortune is fickle. You never know your luck. Cast your fate to the wind.

180   **Отложи блины до иного дни.**   *v.* Б174,180, X60
[Save some *bliny* for another day.] *Cf.* Lay up for a rainy day.

181   **Отошла коту масленица.**   *v.* H232
After Christmas [Carnival] comes Lent.

182   **Отрезанный ломоть (к хлебу) не пристанет (приставишь).**
[A loaf once cut cannot be made whole.] It's easy to steal from a cut loaf. *Cf.* What's done cannot be undone.

183   **Отруби ту руку по локоть, которая добра себе не желает.**
[If your hand betrays you, cut it off.] *Cf. Matt.*18.9: If thine eye offend thee, pluck it out. Better eye out than always ache.

184*   **Отскочил чтобы дальше прыгнуть.**
We must recoil a little to the end we may leap the better. *Cf.* One step back, two steps forward.

185   **Отсталых бьют.**   *v.* 370, K285, П124,127,179
[Those who fall behind are whipped.] Late-comers are shent (ruined).

186   **Оттерпимся и мы люди будем.**   *v.* T21
[With patience we too can become like everyone else.] They that have patience may accomplish anything. He conquers who endures. Patient men win the day. *Lat.* vincit qui patitur. He that can have patience, can have what he will.

187   **Отца с сыном и царь не рассудит.**   *v.* M182
[Not even the *tsar* can settle a dispute between father and son.] *Cf.* Put not thy hand between the bark and the tree.

276

188   Отцы ели клюкву а у детей оскомина на зубах.
(Отцы согрешили а детей наказывают.) *v. Н117*
[The fathers ate the cranberries and the children have the bitter aftertaste.] *i.e. the sons inherit the sins of the fathers.* Adam ate the apple and our teeth still ache. *Exod.* 20.5: The iniquity of the fathers is visited upon the children. *Cf.* The tongue offends and the ears get the cuffing. †The father to the bough, the son to the plough.

189*   Охота не работа. *v. И48, К247*
It is easy to do what one's self wills. *Cf.* One's own will is good food. A man's will is his heaven.

190*   Охота пуще неволи.
[Zeal is worse than need.]   *i.e. one undertakes more difficult tasks by choice than imposition.* Desire has no rest.

191   Охоту тешить, не беда (беду) платить.
[Pleasure is worth any price.] Satisfaction is the best payment. *Cf.* A burden of one's choice is not felt.

192   Охотник за семь верст ходил киселя есть.
[The hunter walked seven miles for his pudding.] Where your will is ready, your feet are light. *Cf.* A hungry man sees far.

193   Охотно тот служит кого хвалят.
[He that is praised works happily.] Praise a fool and you make him useful. *Cf.* Praise is a spur to the good.

194*   Очи ушей вернее. *v. Б317, Г113, Л123,146, Н215*
It is better to trust the eyes than the ears. *Gr. Apost.* 18.71: ὠτίων πιστότεροι ὀφαλμοί. *EA.* oculis magis habenda fides quam auribus. *Cf.* One eyewitness is better than two hear-so's. One eye has more faith than two ears.

195*   Ошибка в фальшь не ставится. (Ошибка не обман.)
Erring is not cheating. *Cf.* To err is human, to to persist in it is beastly (folly). *Lat.* humanum enim est peccare, diabolicum vero perseverare. Honest error is to be pitied, not ridiculed.

196   Ошибке в слове не спор, живет и на всех проговор. *v. Б318, Л90*
Talk much and err much. *Cf.* If wise men erred not it would be hard with fools.

197*   Ошибками учатся. *v. Б99, Н314,358, У72*
Failure teaches success. We learn by our mistakes.

П

1   **Падает на медведя желудь, и он рыкнет, а как целый дуб, и он не мигнет.**
[The bear roars when hit by a falling acorn, but doesn't flinch at a falling oak.] To stumble at a straw and leap over a block. To strain at a gnat and swallow a camel.

2   **Панихиду пели а кутьи не ели.**   *v.* B118
[To have the funeral service but not the wake.] *Cf.* More show than substance. Service without reward is punishment.

3   **Пар костей не ломит.**
[Steam breaks no bones.] *said when room or outdoor temperatures are high. Cf.* Head and feet keep warm and the rest will take no harm.

4   **Паны дерутся, а у холопов чубы трещат.**   *v.* Б16, К186, С185
The humble suffer from the folly of the great. The pleasures of the mighty are the tears of the poor.

5   **Пей да не пролей (да ума не пропей) (да дело разумей).**
[Drink but don't spill (but don't lose your mind) (but know your business).]
Cf. He that spills the rum loses that only, he that drinks it often loses that and himself. Nobody should drink but those that can drink.

6   **Пей до дна, а на дне добро.**
[Bottoms up - the best is at the bottom.] *Cf.* He was hanged that left his drink behind him. Drink like hell and be happy.

7*   **Пей за столом, а не пей за столбом.**
[Drink at the table, not at the lamp-post.] Do not drink between meals.
Cf. The one who drinks now and then is always drunk.

8   **Пению время а молитве час.**   *v.* B463, H229
[There's time for singing but only an hour for prayer.] There is a time to wink as well as to see.

9   **Пера не обманешь.**
[The pen will not be deceived.] *i.e. will only write the intention of the writer.* If you don't write, you're wrong. *Cf.* The written word remains. *Lat.* littera scripta manet.

10   **Перва чарка, перва и палка.** *v.* H159

11* **Первая брань лучше последней.**
[The first quarrel is better than the last.] *i.e. the first may be followed by reconciliation, but not the last.* The first blow makes the wrong, but the second makes the fray.

12   **Первая волвянка в кузов.**   *v.* H71, П18
[The first mushroom goes in the basket.] The first dish pleases all.

13　**Первая дорожка - всегда на людей.**
[The first trip is always out.] The greatest step is that out of doors. *Cf.* A journey of a thousand miles begins with one step.

14　**Первая жена как утренняя заря, а вторая как красное солнышко.**
(Первая жена от Бога, вторая от человека, а третья от дьявола.)
[The first wife is like the morning dawn, the second like the glorious sun.] [The first wife is from God, the second from man, and the third from the devil.] The first wife is matrimony, the second company, and the third heresy.

15　**Первая рюмка колом, другая соколом, а третья мелкими пташечками.**
[The first glass is a stake, the second a falcon, and the third a flutter of birds.] *i.e. drinking becomes easier with each glass. Cf.* The first glass for thirst, the second for nourishment, the third for pleasure, the fourth for madness. First is worst, second the same, the last is best of all the game.

16　**Первое счастье с малого кусочка сыту быть.**
The greatest happiness is to be content with little.

17*　**Первый блин (всегда) комом.**　　　　　　　　　　　*v.* Б99, В642, Л74, П20
[The first *blin* (pancake) comes out lumpy.] If at first you don't succeed, try again. *Cf.* Every beginning is hard. The first attempt is the most difficult.

18　**Первый кус разбойник.**　　　　　　　　　　　　　　　*v.* Н71, П12
[The first morsel is a criminal.] *i.e. it invites the hungry. Cf.* The first dish is best eaten.

19　**Первому гостью первое и место и красная ложка.**　　　　　　*v.* К283
[The first guest gets the best seat and the finest spoon.] He that comes first to the hill may sit where he will. First come, first served. *Lat.* qui primus venerit, primus molet.

20*　**Первую песенку зардевшись поют (спеть).**　　　　　　　　*v.* П17
[The first song is sung with a blush.] *i.e. a first attempt lacks confidence. Cf.* The beginning is the hardest. Beware beginnings.

21*　**Первый снег - не зима, первая зазноба - не невеста.**
[The first snow doesn't mean winter, nor the first love marriage.] Those whom we love first we seldom wed. *Cf.* Love and weather can never be depended on.

22　**Перед смертью не надышишь (некогда уж разживаться).**　　　*v.* Н453, П102
[It's too late to live when it's time to die.] It's too late to stoop when the head is off. *Cf.* Enjoy yourself, it's later than you think. †Better late thrive than never do well.

23　**Передние колеса везут (лошадь везет), а задние за ними едут (сами катаются).** *v.*Г21,
[Where the front wheels go, the rear wheels follow.] When the　　К40,321, Л108
crow flies, her tail follows. *Cf.* Wherever you go, you can never get rid of yourself.

24　**Передний заднему мост.**
[The first are a bridge for the last.] *Cf.* The wise man must carry the fool on his shoulders.

25*　**Перемелется, (все) мука будет.**　　　　　　　　　　　*v.* С59
[With time, it will be ground to fine flour.] It will all come right in the wash.

26　**Перерод хуже недороду.**
[A surplus is worse than a failed harvest.] *i.e. prices plummet.* Too much of a good thing is worse than none at all. *Cf.* Too much water drowns the miller.

27 **Перестань о том тужить, чему нельзя пособить.**   *v.* А29, Б219, И140, Ч92
    Never grieve for what you cannot help.

28 **Песня быль (ладом), а сказка складка (складом живет).**
    [A song is true, but tales are fabrication.] *Cf.* The tale runs as it pleases the teller. There are always two tales to a story. A song will outlive sermons in the memory.

29* **Печаль без радости, ни радость без печали не бывает.**   *v.* В174, Н541, Р17, С94
    No pleasure without pain. No weal without woe. No joy without annoy.

30 **Печаль не уморит, а здоровье повредит.**   *v.* Г269
    Sorrow kills not but it blights. *Gr.* λύπαι γὰρ ἀνθρώποισι τίκτουσι νόσος.

31* **Печаль человека не красит.**
    [Sorrow becomes no one.] Sorrow is good for nothing but sin.

32 **Печальному шутка на ум не идет.**
    [The sad man won't get the joke.] I am sad because I cannot be glad.

33 **Пешего сокола ворона бьет.**   *v.* Ж97, М69
    [Better a flying crow than a grounded falcon.] Better a live dog (rabbit) (trout) than a dead lion (tiger) (whale). *Cf.* One foot is better than two crutches. Better lame than always seated.

34* **Пешком ходить - долго жить.**
    [Walk much and live long.] *Cf.* The man who walks takes title to the world around him.

35 **Писал писачка, а имя ему собачка.**   *sarc.*
    [The secretary wrote it, initialed S.O.B.] *i.e. said contemptuously about officious red-tape. Cf.* It is the clerk makes the justice.

36 **Писали, не гуляли.**
    Work keeps you out of mischief. *Cf.* All work is noble.

37 **Пить воду, вода не смутит ума.**
    [Drink water and keep a clear head.] Drink only with the duck.

38* **Пить до дна - не видать добра.**
    [Drink it dry and bid virtue good-bye.] Good is the man who refrains from wine.
    Cf. Sweet is the wine, but sour the payment. Ever drunk, ever dry.

39 **Пить добро, а не пить - лучше того.**
    [Drinking is good, but not drinking is better.] *Cf.* †Drink wine and have the gout, drink no wine and have the gout too.

40* **Плата тою же монетою.**
    Repay in kind. *Cf.* Those who deceive may expect to be paid in their own coin.

41 **Платье на грядке, а дурак (урод) на руке.**   *v.* П250
    [She's got her dress in the wardrobe, but a fool on her arm.] Many a one for land takes a fool by the hand.

42 **Плачем горю не поможешь (пособишь).** *v.* С172

43 **Плеть обуха не перебьет.** *v.* О17

44* **Плох тот солдат кто не метит в генералы.** *v.* Х108
[It is a poor soldier who doesn't strive to be a general.] Every French soldier carries a marshall's baton in his knapsack. Every little fish would be a whale.

45* **Плохо того бить кто не противится.** *v.* Л40
Don't kick a man when he's down.

46 **Плюй (ему) (им) в глаза - все Божья роса.** *sarc.*
When you spit in a timid man's eye, he says it's raining.

47 **Пляшет по жениной дудке.**
He dances after his wife's pipe (whistle).

48* **По барину и говядина.** *v.* К61, П54, *Ap.*1.76,81
As the master is, so is his dog [meat].

49* **По горшку и покрышка.** *v.* К87, Н22, З9
Such pot, such pot-lid. *Lat.* patellae dignum operculum. Like cover like cup.

50 **По грибы не час, и по ягоды нет, так хоть по сосновы (еловые) шишки.** *v.* В498, К152
[If you can't pick mushrooms or berries, then at least get some pine (fir) cones.] He that may not do as he would must do as he may. There's a season for all things.

51* **По деньгам и товар.** *v.* Д221,226, К71, Ч12
You get what you pay for. *Cf.* If you pay peanuts, you get monkeys.

52 **По дрожжам пиво узнают.** *v.* К69,89, О127,167, Щ4
[Know the beer from the barm.] You may know from a penny how a shilling spends. Ill seed, ill weed. Of good seed, good corn.

53* **По дыму над баней пару не угодаешь.** *v.* В316, Н143,324
[You cannot judge the steam from the smoke of a bathouse chimney.] You cannot judge a tree by its bark. You cannot judge a book by its cover.

54* **По жильцу и квартира.** *v.* П48,70
The house discovers (shows) the owner. Such bird, such nest.

55* **По заслугам и честь.** *v.* В360, Д321, П72, Ч53
[You get what you deserve.] Give credit where credit is due. We get out of life exactly what we put into it. *Cf.*A good dog deserves a good bone.

56* **По заячьему следу доходят до медвежей берлоги.** *v.* Б170, П63,150, Х27
[The hare's tracks may lead you to the bear's den.] If you begin with a common pin, you will end up with a silver bowl. Use the little to get to the big. From small beginnings come great things. From trifling causes great results arise. *Lat.* ex minimis initiis maxima.

57 **По земли широко а до неба высоко.** *v.* С52
[The world is wide and the heavens are high.] *i.e. anything is possible.* The world is a wide place (parish).

58* **По капельке море, по зернышку ворох.** *v.* Б89, В244,524, Е26, И90, М97, П82, С22
[Many drops make an ocean, many grains a heap.] Many drops of water make an ocean. Little drops of water, little grains of sand make the mighty ocean and the pleasant land. Many drops make a shower (flood). *Gr.* ψεκάδες ὄμβρον γεννῶσαι.

59 **По косе жену узнают.** *v. К179*
[A wife is known by her braid.] *Unmarried girls wore their hair in twin braids; once married they would wear one single braid.*

60 **По косе не суди об уме (а суди о красе).** *v. Б341, В400, М171, У2*
[Judge not the brain from the braid.] *Cf.* Bush natural - more hair than wit. Long hair and short sense.

61 **По которой дороге шел, по той и пойди.**
По (при) которой (какой) реке плыть (плыл)(жить), по той и слыть (плыви).
[Choose the road (river) you have come by.] Every road leads in two directions. *Cf.* Whatever goes up must come down. †Never return by the same road.

62 **По малу и воз на горе становится.** *v. Б450*
[Little by little, the load gets up the hill.] Step by step the ladder is ascended.

63* **По нитке и (до) клубка дойдешь (доходят).** *v. Б450, П56*
[Start with a thread and soon you'll have a ball.] By the thread the ball is brought to light. *Cf.* A spider spins his web strand by strand. One by one the spindles are made.

64* **По одежде (по платью) встречают, по уму провожают.** *v. Д29, Н443*
[One is received according to one's dress and sent off according to one's wit.] Good clothes open all doors. *SPL.* discincta vestis, distinctus animus. *Cf.* Clothes make the man. *Gr. Hom.Od.*6.29: εἵματα ἀνήρ. *Lat.* vestis facit virum. Fine clothes may disguise, silly words will disclose a fool.

65* **По одежде (кроватке) протягивай ножки.** *v. К209, П69*
Stretch your legs according to your coverlet.

66* **По пению узнается птица.**
The bird is known by its note. *SPL.* avis plumis dignoscitur.

67 **По пляске на погудку не напасешься.** *v. Л169, У88*
[Dancing won't pay for the tune.] They that dance must pay the fiddler. *Cf.* The better dancer, the worse man.

68* **По привычке и в аду живут.** *v. Ж132, И3, П244,249*
[One can even get used to living in hell.] One can get used to everything, even hanging. *Cf.* Custom reconciles us to everything.

69 **По приходу и расход держи.** *v. П65*
[Keep your debit to your credit.] Whatever you have, spend less. Stretch your legs according to your coverlet. *SPL.* buccae noscenda est mensura tuae. *Cf.* Never spend money before you have it. Spend as you get. Pay as you go.

70* **По птичке и клетка.** *v. П54*
[Such bird, such cage.] Such bird, such nest. *SPL.* efficimus pro nostris opibus nostra moenia. parvum parva decent.

71 **По ране и пластырь.**
[Such wound, such bandage.] There's a salve for every sore. *Cf.* Desperate cuts must have desperate cures.

72 **По ремеслу и плата.** *v. П55*
[Such profession, such pay.] *Luke* 10.7: The workman (labourer) is worthy of his hire. *Cf.* Pay the piper his due. Every man must pay his Scot.

73   **По семени и плод.**   *v.* Д309, К88,318, П192, Ч97
[Such seed, such fruit.] *Galat.*6.7: quae seminaverit homo, haec et metet. As they sow, so let them reap. He that sows good seed, shall reap good corn. *Cf.* If you want to raise corn, plant corn seed, not cotton seed.

74   **По семье глядя, и кашу варят.**   *v.* 358, К209, Ч77
[Prepare the *kasha* to the size of your family.] *Cf.* Cut your coat according to your cloth.

75   **По сказанному как по писанному.**   *v.* С179
[Keep your word whether spoken or written.] Words bind men. *Lat.*verba ligant hominem.

76   **По сытому брюху хоть обухом.**   *v.* Ж128
[A man with a full belly can sustain any blow.] Stuffing holds out the storm. *Cf.* A full belly makes a brave heart. An army travels on its stomach.

77   **По твоему уму носить будешь суму.**
[Your burden will be equal to you wit.] *Cf.* Cunning is no burden. Intelligence seeks its own level.

78*   **По усам текло, а в рот не попало.**
[Poured down the whiskers but not in the mouth.] *The concluding rhyme in fairy tales: And there we were, drinking mead and beer, Which all poured not into our mouths, but down our beards.* All is lost that goes beside one's mouth. *Cf. Gr.* Hom. χείλια μεντ' ἐδίην δ'ὀκ ἐδιηνε. *Lat.* labra id, non palatum rigat.

79   **По утру нежится, а по вечерам бесится.**   *v.* В64, К301, С85
[Gentle in the morning, wild at night.] *Cf.* If you sing (laugh) before breakfast, you'll cry before supper. An angel on top but a devil underneath.

80   **По чужим словам, как по лестнице.**
[Going by others' words is like going up a ladder.] *i.e. shaky and unreliable. Cf.* A believer is a songless bird in a cage. Quick believers need strong shoulders.

81*   **По шерсти (собачка) имя (кличка) (дано).**   *v.* В668, К48
[A dog is named according to its fur.] When all men say you are an ass, it is time to bray. *Cf.* If the shoe (cap) fits, wear it.

82   **По ягодке собирай - наберешь кузовок.**   *v.* В524, Е26, П58, С22
[Pick one berry at a time and you'll fill the basket.] Add little to little and there will be a great heap. *Cf.* Grain by grain and the hen fills her belly. Little and often fills the purse.

83   **Победа требует прилежания.**
[Victory demands perseverance.] Victory belongs to the most persevering. *Cf.* Have at it and have it. Perseverance kills the game. Diligence can do all. *Lat.* cura potest omnia.

84*   **Победителей не судят.**
[The victors are not judged.] Success is never blamed. Vanquishers are kings, the vanquished thieves. *Cf.* Success makes a fool seem wise.

85*   **Побей мужика - часы сделает.**   *v.* Н174,496, Я21
[Beat the *mujik* and he'll fashion a watch.] A man can do a lot of things if he has to.

86*   **Повадился кувшин по воду ходить, там ему и голову сломить.**
        The pitcher goes so often to the well that it is broken at last. *SPL.* a teneris assuescere multum.

87　Повар и нюхая наестся.
　　[A cook may have his fill by sniffing.] *Cf.* Every cook knows to lick her own fingers.
　　He is a poor cook that cannot lick his own fingers.

88　Повар с голоду не умрет.　　　　　　　　　　　　　　　　*v.* К100
　　[A cook never starves to death.] A three years' drought will not starve a cook. *Cf.*
　　Millers are the last to die of a famine.

89*　Повинную голову (и) мечь не сечет.　　　　　　　　　　*v.* Я6
　　[The sword will not sever the penitent head.] A fault confessed is half redressed.
　　Cf. †Confess and be hanged.

90*　Повторение мать учения.
　　Repetition is the mother of learning (skill).　*Lat.* **repetitio mater studiorum
　　(memoriae).**
　　Cf. Knowledge without practice makes but half an artist.

91　Погибать (помирать), так с музыкой.
　　[If you must die, then die with music.] If you must go down, go down in flames. *Cf.*
　　As well be hanged for a sheep as a lamb.

92　Погнался за ломтем (малым) (сухарем), да (целый) хлеб (большое) потерял.
　　[Go after the morsel and lose the loaf.]　　　　　　　*v.* З22,54, О16
　　Catch not at the shadow and lose the substance.

93　Погодить не устать, было бы чего ждать.
　　[One doesn't mind waiting provided there is something to wait for.] Don't give up hope
　　till hope is dead.

94　Погонишься за шилом, топор потеряешь.　　　　　　　　*v.* З11,22, О15
　　[Look for the awl and lose the axe.] Lost with an apple and won with a nut. *Cf.* If you
　　run after two hares you will catch neither.

95　Под всякую песеньку не подпляшешь, под всяки нравы не подладишь.　*v.* Н10,26,249
　　[One cannot dance to every tune, nor adapt to every whim.]
　　Cf. He that would please all and himself to, undertakes what he cannot do. You cannot
　　run and bark at the same time.

96*　Под каждой крышей свои мыши.　　　　　　　　　　　　*v.* У29
　　[Every house has its own mice.] There is a skeleton in every house (cupboard).

97*　Под лежачий камень (и) вода не течет (плывет).　　　　　*v.* Н68
　　[Water never flows under a settled stone.] A rolling stone gathers no moss.

98*　Под лесом видить а под носом не видить.　　　　　*v.* Д50, З20, М51, Н259
　　[To see under the trees but not under one's nose.] *SPL.* non videmus id manticae, quod
　　in tergo est. Lose sight of the forest for the trees. *Cf.* Stretching out the hand to catch the
　　stars, he forgets the flowers at his feet. Plin.*Ep.*8.20: proximorum incuriosi, longinqua
　　sectemur.

99　Под старое тулово, да молодые ноги.　　　　　　　*v.* Б343, В401, Г214, Р64, С89
　　[Young legs under an old torso.] An old head on young shoulders.

00　Под старость человек либо умный, либо глупый бывает.　　　*v.* Д260
　　[On the threshold of old age one is either smart or stupid.] Every man is a fool or a
　　physician at forty. *Cf.* A fool at forty is a fool indeed.

101   **Под толстым сукном не хуже согреешься как под бархатом.**
      [A coarse cloth warms no worse than velvet.] As good broth may come out of a wooden ladle as out of a silver spoon. *Cf.* Under a ragged (threadbare) coat, lies wisdom.

102   **Подавай теплой рукой, а холодной не успеешь.**   *v.* H453, П22
      [Lend a hand while it's warm, it will be too late when it's cold.] *i.e. dead. Cf.* One of these days is none of these days. It's too late to stoop when the head is off.

103*   **Подальше положишь, поближе возмешь.**
      [The farther you put it, the nearer you'll find it.] Fast (safe)(sure) bind, fast (safe)(sure) find.

104   **Поделом (по делам) вору и мука.**   *v.* K86, Ч40
      Like fault, like punishment.

105   **Поди в гости смело, когда нет дома дела.**   *v.* И64
      [Go out boldly once your homework is finished.] Work (business) before pleasure (play).

106   **Подле гор не ходи, и ты сапоги не искривишь.**   *v.* K125
      [If you walk alongside a hill, your shoes will wear unevenly.] He that dwells next door to a cripple will learn to halt.

107   **Подле пчелки медок, а подле жучки навоз.**   *v.* И128, Л16, М201, H15, O1, У15
      [The bees like their honey, and the mongrel *Zhuchka* his dung.] *Cf.* Every man to his taste, quoth the man when he kissed his cow.

108   **Подлезь там где перескочить нельзя.**
      [Creep when you cannot jump.] *Cf.* First creep, then go. If you cannot go over or under, then go through.

109*   **Подобный подобного любит.**   *v.* B620, K266, М164, H418, P9,76, T7, *Ap.*1.5
      Likeness causes liking. Like will to like. *Gr.* ὅμοιον ὁμοίῳ. *Lat.* similis simili gaudet (aequalis aequalem delectat).

110   **Подперто не валится.**
      [Propped up stays put.] Bind fast (safe)(sure), fast (safe)(sure) find. *Cf.* He that repairs not a part, builds all. Better safe than sorry.

111   **Подпора сена не ест.**   *v.* Б68, З87, Л94
      [A brace won't eat your hay.] *i.e. costs nothing.* Store is no sore. *Cf.* Fast (sure) bind, fast (sure) find. Forecast is better than work-hard. It is better to be safe than sorry.

112   **Подумай, обдумай, да и молви.**
      [Think once, think twice, then speak.] First think, then speak.

113   **Подумаю с подушкою, а после спрошусь с женушкою.**   *v.* H568, X101
      [I'll think on my pillow and then I'll ask my wife.] He that will thrive, must ask leave of his wife.

114*   **Поезжай на день а бери хлеба на неделю.** *v.* E6

115*   **Пожалел волк кобылу, оставил хвост да гриву.**
      [The wolf pitied the mare so he left its tail and mane.] Crows weep for the dead lamb and then devour him.

116   **Пожалеть алтына, потерять полтина.**   *v.* B594, З22, Л89, М26, O15, C163
      [Save three *kopeks* and lose a half-ruble.] **Penny wise and pound foolish.**

117* **Пожелать скатертью дорогу.**   *v.* С132
Good riddance! Get lost!

118 **Поживешь подоле, увидишь по боле.**   *v.* В222, Д254
Live and learn.

119 **Поживешь - увидишь, подождешь - услышишь.**
Live and learn [see], wait and see [hear].

120* **Поживи на свете, погляди чудес.**   *v.* Ч44,109
Wonders will never cease.

121 **Пожили в нужде, да нажили хуже.**   *v.* †Б395
The poor get poorer. He that has little shall have less.

122 **Позавидовал плешивый лысому.**   *v.* В178,583, Н189, С49, Ч129
[One bald man envies another.] One potter envies another. None says his garner is full.

123 **Позавидовала кошка собачью житью.**   *v.* П122
[The cat envies the dog's life.] No man is content with his lot. The grass is always greener on the other side.

124 **Поздний гость гложет и кость.**   *v.* П127,275
[A guest who is late must nibble the bone.] He that comes last to the pot is soonest wroth.

125* **Поздно беречь вино когда бочка пуста.**   *v.* К214, Ч76
[Too late to spare the wine once the barrel is empty.] Better spare at brim than at bottom. When the wine is run out, you stop the leak. *Lat.* Sen.*Ep.*1.5: sera est in fundo parsimonia. *Cf.* We never know the worth of water till the well is dry.

126 **Поздно дать - все равно что отказать.**
[To give late is the same as denying.] The thing that is fristed (delayed) is not given. *Cf.* Justice delayed is justice denied.

127 **Поздно пришел - только кости нашел.**   *v.* 370, К28, О185, П124,179,275
[To the latecomer go the bones.] *Lat.* tarde venientibus ossa. Who comes late lodges ill. *Cf.* The absent saint gets no candle.

128 **Пойдешь со двора, дома поростет трава.**   *v.* Б147, В615, Д379, Н289
[Leave home and the garden gets overgrown with grass.] The master absent and the house is dead.

129* **Пой лучше хорошо щегленком чем дурно соловьем.**   *v.* Б487, Г285, Л149
[Better sing best among the finches than worst among the nightingales.] Better be the head of a dog (fox) (mouse) (lizard) than the tail of a lion. Better be first in a village than second at Rome. Better be the head of an ass (the yeomanry) than the tail of a horse (the gentry). *Cf.* It is better to hear the lark sing than the mouse cheep.

130* **Пока дышу (живу) - надеюсь.**   *v.* Г38
While there is life, there is hope. *Lat.* dum vivo, dum spero. *Cf.* Never say die.

131 **Пока солнце взойдет, роса глаза выест.**   *v.* П163, Э2
[Until the sun rises, the dew will blind your eyes.] While the grass grows, the horse starves. Don't hold your breath.

132* **Покажется (полюбится) сатана (сова) лучше (пуще) ясного сокола.** *v.* Л185,192,193
[Love makes a devil (owl) seem prettier than a white falcon.] Love is blind. Love covers many infirmities. *Cf.* In the eyes of the lover, pock marks are dimples.

133 **Поклон человека не портит.** *v.* B117, П135
[Respect spoils no one.] A smile goes a long way. Respect a man, he'll do the more. A smile costs nothing but gives much.

134* **Поклонами шубы не подшить.** *v.* B376, C244
[Compliments won't finish the fur.] Talking will not make the pot boil. *Cf.* Fair words won't fill a sack (bucket) (belly). Flattery butters no parsnips.

135 **Поклониться - голова не отвалится.** *v.* Д346, M215, П133
[Your head won't fall off from bowing.] *i.e. it doesn't hurt to show respect.* A kind word never hurt anyone. *Cf.* Soft words break no bones (hurt not the mouth).

136 **Покой пьет воду, а беспокойство - мед.**
[The relaxed drink water, the anxious - mead.] *Cf.* Good wine engenders good blood.

137 **Покорное слово сокрушает кости.** *v.* B249
[Words of respect may shatter bones.] *Cf.* Kindness is the noblest weapon to conquer with. Sometmes clemency is cruelty and cruelty clemency. Full of courtesy, full of craft.

138* **Полегче (легче) на поворотах.**
Easy on the curves. Take time in turning a corner. *Cf.* If you want to live on the square, don't cut the corners.

139 **Полон дом, полон рот.**
[A full house, a full mouth.] Where there is a store of oatmeal, you may put enough in the crock. *Cf.* They that have got a store of butter, may lay it thick on their bread.

140* **Полузнание хуже незнания.** *v.* Д498, H502, X89
A little knowledge (learning) is a dangerous thing. Better untaught than ill-taught.

141 **Ползком где низко, тишком где склизко.** *v.* T35
Slow and steady wins the race.

142 **Помолчи боле, поживешь доле.**
[Talk less and live longer.] Silence does seldom harm. Be silent and safe: silence never betrays you. *Cf.* Hear, see and be silent if you wish to live in peace. *Lat.* audi,vide, tace, si vis vivere in pace.

143 **Помутя воду, не скоро устоится.**
[Stirred water takes long to still.] It is easier to raise the devil than to lay him. *Cf.* The more you stir a stink, the louder it smells.

144 **Понедельник тяжелый день.**
St. Monday. *Cf.* Monday is the key of the week.

145 **Поп бездонный мешок. (Попого брюхо не наполнится.)**
[A priest is a bottomless sack.] [A priest's belly is insatiable.] *Cf. Lat.* Persius *Sat.*6.72: popae venter. Three things are insatiable: priests, monks and the sea.

146 **Поп людей учит, а сам грешит.** *v.* Б339, Г73, Д258, И70, M159, O82
[The priest who preaches to others sins himself.] The devil lurks behind the cross. Wher the fox preaches, take care of your geese.

147 **Поп едет дорогою, а черт целиком.**
[The priest travels by road, but the devil goes everywhere.] The devil is never far off.

148 **Поп обедни не отпел, а дурак шапку надел.** *v.* Д483
[The fool dons his cap before the priest ends his service.] Fools never perceive where they are ill-timed or ill placed.

149 **Попа знают и в рогоже.** *v.* З160

150 **Попадешь в корень, доберешься и до вершины.** *v.* Б170, П56, Х27
[If you can hit the root, you can reach the top.] He that's always shooting must sometimes hit. Use the little to get to the big. *Cf.* He who aims at the moon may hit the top of a tree, he who aims at the top of the tree is unlikely to get off the ground. We aim above the mark to hit the mark.

151 **Попадешься в руки, натерпишься муки.**
Just wait till I get my hands on you!

152 **Попал в стаю, лай не лай, а хвостом виляй.** *v.* Ж135, З315, М50, С2,123
Whe keeps company with wolves will learn to howl. He who live with cats will get a taste for mice.

153* **Попал из кобыл да в клячи.** *v.* И82

154 **Попался, который кусался.** *v.* Д456, Л76, О177, Т13, Ч72
The biter bit.

155* **Попытка не пытка (шутка), (+ а спрос не беда).** *v.* 392
There's no harm in trying, [+ and it doesn't hurt to ask]. To inquire is neither a disaster nor a disgrace.

156 **Пора гостям по дверям.**
Time for the guests to go home.

157 **Пора и честь знать.**
[Time to know what is respectable.]*i.e. and not overstay one's welcome.* The bewitching hour.

158* **Поработаешь до поту, так и поешь в охоту.** *v.* П177, С146
[Work till you sweat and you'll eat better.] Work well done makes pleasure more fun. Work makes life pleasant.

159* **Порядок душа всякого дела.**
[Order is the soul of any enterprise.] *Lat.* **ordo anima rerum.** Good order is the foundation of all good things. *Cf.* Order is heaven's first law. *Lat.* ordine pervenies quo non licet ire laborare.

160 **Посади деревенскую овцу в почет, хуже городской козы будет.** *v.* М189
[Pamper a country lamb and it will act worse than any town goat.] The higher the ape goes, the more he shows his tail.

161* **Посади дурака (свинью) за стол, и он(а) ноги на стол.** *v.* М194
[Sit a fool (pig) at the table and he'll put his legs up.] Give him an inch and he'll take an ell.

162 **Посади мужика в порогу, а он под святые лезет.** *v.* Г150, Ж30
[Sit the *muzhik* by the door and he'll rush to the altar.] Fools always rush to the fore.

163   **Посиди у моря, да подожди погоды.**   *v.* Д205, П131
[One may as well wait for the weather at the seashore.] Don't hold your breath. *Cf.* Wait for things to blow over.

164*   **Посконная рубаха не нагота, хлеб с половой не голодня.**
[A hemp shirt's no destitution, nor bread off the floor a famine.] Hard work is not easy and dry bread is not greasy. All things are less dreadful than what they seem.

165   **Посла ни секут, ни рубят, только милуют.**
Messengers should neither be beheaded nor hanged. *Gr.* Schol.Hom.*Il.*4: πρέσβυς οὐ τύπτεται, οὐδὲ ὑβρίζεται. *Lat.*legatus non caeditur, neque violabitur.

166*   **После грозы (ненастья) и ведро будет.**   *v.* Б384, Г23, Ж32
After black clouds clear weather. After a storm comes a calm. *SPL.* post nubila phoebus.

167   **После дела за советом не ходят.**
When a thing is done, advice comes too late. *SPL.* utile non est consilium post facta dari, quod oportuit ante.

168*   **После дождичка в четверг.**   *v.* В11
[After Thursday's drizzle.] *i.e. one of these days.* One of these days is none of these days.

169*   **После драки кулаками не машут.**   *v.* М130, О91
[Don't wave your fists after the fight.] When the war is over, then comes help. *Lat.* post bellum auxilium. *Cf.* After death the doctor.

170   **После нас хоть потоп.**
After us, the deluge. [*Fr. Après nous le déluge.*]

171   **После обеда да с ложкой пришел.**
[He came with a spoon after supper.] After dinner, mustard. To arrive after the feast. *Gr.* κατόπιν ἑορτῆς ἡκέσθαι. *Lat.* post festum venire.

172*   **После поры не точат топоры.**   *v.* Н452
[Too late to sharpen the axe after the event.] When all is done and nothing left, what avails the dagger with the dudgeon-haft. *Cf.* The putting-off man sharpens his arrows when he sees the bear.

173   **После свадьбы всякий тысяцкий.**   *v.* У83, Х15, *Ap.*1.68
[Anyone can be master of ceremonies after a wedding.] It's easy to be wise after the event.

174   **После скобели топором (не тешут).**   *v.* З105
[After the adze with an axe.] *i.e. too late; the adze is used after the axe to finish shaping timber.* There's little left for the broom after the besom. Put the cart before the horse.

175*   **После смерти не каются (нет покаяния).**   *v.* П22, С214, Х14
[Too late to repent after death.] Too late to stoop when the head is off. Late repentence is seldom true. *Lat.* poenitentia sera raro vera.

176   **После супу вина выпить, у врача червонец украсть.**
[Wine after a meal steals the doctor's money.] *Cf.* If you drink in your pottage, you'll cough in your grave.

177   **После трудов, сладок покой.**   *v.* П158, С146
[Rest is sweet after hard work.] Rest is the sweet sauce of labour. The sleep of a labouring man is sweet. *SPL.* grata quies post exhaustum solet esse laborem.

178* После ужина (гриппа) горчица.   *v.* П171
      After meat (dinner) [the ague] mustard.

179 Последнего и собаки рвут.   *v.* 370, К285, О185, П124,127, Р49
      [The last goes to the dogs.]   The race is to the swift. Late-comers are shent. *Cf.* Last
      come, worst served.

180 Последняя спица в колеснице.
      [The last spoke in the wheel.]   Just a cog in the machine.

181 Пословица ввек (вовек) не сломится.
      Time passes away, but sayings remain.

182 Пословица - всем делам поперечница.
      A good maxim is never out of season.

183 Пословица говорится - масло само не родится.   *v.* Б179, Г135,204, О55
      A proverb comes not from nothing.

184 Пословица не мимо ходит.   *v.* Н126, С263
      Common proverb seldom lies. Old saws speak truth.

185 Пословица не покормица, а с нею добро.
      [A proverb may not put food in your mouth, but it consoles.]   Great consolation may
      grow out of the smallest saying. Patch griefs with proverbs.

186 Пословицу не обойти и не объехать.   *v.* О151
      Proverbs cannot be contradicted.

187 Послушание паче поста да молитвы.   *v.* Н229, С14
      [There's more to penance than fasting and prayer.]   There's more to riding than a pair of
      boots. *Cf.* Pretended holiness is double iniquity. There belongs more to whistling than
      going to plough.

188* Поспешишь, да людей насмешишь.   *v.* Б300, Г90, Д123,146, С159, Ч102
      [Make haste and make people laugh.]   Haste makes waste. Haste trips up its own heels.

189* Поспешность нужна только блох ловить.   *v.* С251
      Nothing must be done hastily but killing of fleas.

190 Посуленное ждется.   *v.* Н75, О11
      [One must wait for what is promised.]   Promise is debt.

191 Посулил пан шубу, так и слово его греет.
      [When a man promises a fur, his word may keep you warm.] A nod from a lord is a
      breakfast for a fool. Mankind lives on promises. Fair promises make fools fain.

192 Посеянное взойдет.   *v.* В360, К88,287, П73, Ч97
      [What is sown will grow.]   You reap what you sow. *Cf.* You can't have the ear unless
      you plant the corn. No sowing, no reaping. †Many things grow in the garden that were
      never sown there.

193 Потерял честь хмелем.
      [Respect is lost through drink.]   Wine wears no breeches.

194* Потерянного времени не воротишь.   *v.* B466
Time lost cannot be recalled.

195 Потужи по себе, а потом о других.   *v.* Д119,424, Ж17
Mind other men, but most yourself.

196 Потчевать можно, неволить грех.   *v.* Н280
[To offer is fine but to force is a crime.] *said when one's offer is declined, as with the phrase " I won't twist your arm.". Cf.* Force is no argument.

197 Похвала молодцу (мужу) пагуба.   *v.* Б161
[Praise is the clever man's (husband's) undoing.] Praise a fool and slay him. Praise none too much for all are fickle.

198* Похожа свинья на быка, только шерсть не така.   *v.* Г96,192
[A pig's like a bull, just the hide is different.] *said of incongruous comparisons.* If a pig had wings, it might fly.

199 Почин дороже дела (денег) (всего дороже).   *v.* Д308, З106, Л75, Н157
[Beginnings are paramount.] A good beginning is half the task. A good beginning makes a good ending.

200 Почитай старших, сам будешь стар.   *v.* Н415
[Respect the old since you will be old yourself.] Who honours not age is not worthy of it. *Cf.* Old age is honourable. He that respects not is not respected. †Kindness is lost that's bestowed on children and old folks.

201* Пошел в попы, (так) служи и панихиды.   *v.* B291, K213, Л178, Н440
[If you've become a priest, you must also officiate funeral sevices.] If you don't like the heat, stay out of the kitchen.

202* Пошел (зашел) к куме, да засел в тюрьме.   *v.* Б300, З103, Н155
[Set out to my godmother's, but wound up in jail.] A bad end from a good beginning. *Lat.* coepisti melius quam desinis. You began better than you end. Sweet beginning with a sour end. Hell is paved with good intentions.

203 Пошехонцы в трех соснах заблудились.   *v.* B155
[The hicks couldn't find their way around three pines.] *Cf.* Not to see the city for the houses. To get lost in a fog. A prating fool shall fall.

204 Пошла изба по горнице, сени по полатям.   *v.* Б438, B273
To throw (fling) the house out of the windows. *i.e. create pandemonium.*

205* Пошли дурака за водой, он огня несет.   *v.* Н305
[Send a fool to fetch water and he'll bring back a flame.] I ask for a fork and you bring me a rake. *Cf.* Forbid a fool a thing, and that he'll do.

206 Пошлины взяты, а товар утонул.   *v.* B372, Ц8
[Duties paid, but the cargo sank.] The operation was a success but the patient died.

207 Пошутить во время умей, да и перестать разумей.   *v.* 356, И117, Т16, X98, Ш15,1
[Know when to jest and when to stop.] Leave a jest when it pleases lest it turn to earnest. Long jesting was never good.

208* **Прав дракою не будешь.** *v.* Б299, К206, Х98, Ш13
Force is no argument. *Cf.* Those who are right need not talk loudly. Where force prevails, right perishes.

209* **Правда в огне не горит и в воде не тонет.**
[Neither fire nor water can destroy the truth.] Truth is mighty and will prevail.

210 **Правда глаза колет.**
[Truth stings the eyes.] Home truths are unpalatable. The sting of reproach is in the truth of it. *Cf.* Truth and roses have thorns about them. Truth has a scratched face.

211 **Правда далеко, кривда под боком.**
[Truth is far, falsehood by your side.] Falsehood is common, truth uncommon. *Cf.* Truth lies at the bottom of a well. Falsehood flies and truth comes limping after it.

212 **Правда диковиннее вымысла.**
Truth is stranger than fiction.

213 **Правда милости не ищет.**
[Truth seeks no favour.] *Cf.* Truth seeks no corners. Truth begets hatred. *Lat.* veritas odium parit.

214 **Правда ныне изгнана.**
[Today truth has been banished.] Trust is dead (ill payment killed it).

215 **Правда сама себя очистит.** *v.* Б209,257
Truth will come to light. The truth will out. Truth ever honourably declares itself. *Lat..* res se vera quidam semper declarat honeste.

216* **Правда суда не боится.** *v.* К241
Truth fears no trial.

217 **Правда ходит в лаптях, а неправда в кривых сапогах.**
[Truth walks in sandals, and falsehood in worn-out boots.] Craft must have clothes, but truth loves to go naked.

218* **Правда хорошо, а счастье лучше.** *v.* Н401, С318
Better to be happy than right. Better be born lucky than wise. *Cf.* †Fortune is the companion of virtue.

219* **Правда шутки не любит.**
[Truth bides no jest.] It's ill jesting with the truth. The truest jests sound worst in guilty ears.

220 **Правдивая рука всегда правдою живет.**
[The righteous hand can do no wrong.] A good heart cannot lie.

221 **Правдою не обуешься, сыт не будешь.** *v.* О161
[Truth won't fill your stomach nor buy you shoes.] Honesty is ill to thrive by. *Cf.* The devil dances in an empty pocket.

222 **Правду всяк хвалит, да не всяк ее хранит.**
[All praise the truth but few practice it.] Many a one says well that thinks ill.

223* **Правду красить нет нужды.** *v.* Д275, Н78
Truth has no need of rhetoric (figures). Truth needs not the ornament of many words.

224 **Праведному закон не писан.** *v.* †Б159, 378

I *Timoth.*1.9: **The law is not made for a righteous man.** *Cf.* He who is a law to himself no law does need. Good men must not obey the laws too well. Good men want laws for nothing but to protect themselves. Good laws often proceed from bad manners.

225* **Праздность есть мать пороков.** *v.* Б150, Л52

Idleness is the root of all evil [mother of all vices].

226 **Предупреждение - то же бережение.** *v.* Б186

Forewarned is forearmed. *Cf.* Prevention is better than cure.

227 **Прежде закон нежели (а потом) грех.** *v.* Г42, Е24, Н186, С296

[The law precedes the offence.] We enact many laws that manufacture criminals. *Cf.* The more laws, the more offenders. Laws are made to be broken.

228 **Прежде невода рыбы не ловят.** *v.* М113

It is ill fishing before the net.

229* **Прежде отца в петлю не суйся.** *v.* Н328

[Rush not before your father to the noose.] To run before one's horse to market.

230 **Прежде смерти не должно умирать.** *v.* Р39

231 **Прежде хвалити а после хулити.**

[Praise first then censure.] *SPL.* prius creta, mox carbone notare.

232 **При горести терпение лучше спасения.** *v.* В641, Д375, Т23

Patience is a remedy for every grief.

233 **При дороге жить, всех не угостить.** *v.* Б233, Н10,11,19,74

[If you live by the roadside, you cannot treat everyone.] *Cf.* Choose not a house near an inn or in a corner.

234 **При корыстех друг познавается.**

[Self-interest reveals friends.] As frost to bud, self-interest is to friendship. *Cf.* Poverty parts fellowships.

235* **При матке все детки гладки.** *v.* В647, С57, *Ap.*1.6

No mother has a homely child. *Cf.* The crow thinks her own birds fairest (whitest).

236 **При пиве (пире), при бражке, много братьев (все дружки - при горе все ушли).**

(При счастье приятелей много везде, а прямого друга узнаешь в беде.) *v.* Б372,467,

In time of prosperity, friends will be plenty, in time of adversity, Г50, З16, Н64
not one amongst twenty. *Gr.*Theognid.πολλοί τοι πόσιοις καὶ βρώσιοις εἰσὶν
ἑταίροι.

237 **При светле сидеть более стыду.** *v.* Х61, Ч20

[More light, more shame.] He that does ill, hates the light. *John* III.20 *Cf.* The light is nought for sore eyes.

238 **При сытости помни голод, а при богатстве не забывай убожества.**

[Remember hunger when you're full, and indigence when rich.] *Cf.* Remember the poor - it costs nothing.

239 **Прибирай остаток, меньше будет недостаток.** *v.* Б19, У72
[Save what is left and you'll seldom run short.] Of saving comes having. Spare well and have well.

240 **Прибыль с убылью на одном живут дворе.**
[Profit and loss live at the same address.] Where profit is, loss is hidden nearby.
Cf. No pain, no gain.

241 **Привыкла собака за возом ходить, и за пустой телегой бежит.**
[A dog accustomed to following laden wagons will chase an empty cart.] It is hard to break a dog of an ill custom.

242* **Привыкнешь, и в аде живешь.** *v.* Ж132, И3, П68, С282
[One can even get used to living in hell.] One can get used to everything, even hanging. It's nothing when you're used to it.

243* **Привычка вторая натура (другая природа).**
Custom is a second nature. *Gr.* τὸ ἔθος ἑτέρα φύσις. *Lat.* consuetudo est altera natura.

244 **Привычка печаль утоляет, а тягость облегчает.** *v.* Ж132, И3, П68, С282
[Custom soothes sorrow and relieves woe.] Custom reconciles us to everything.

245 **Пригляди за своим а потом за чужим.** *v.* Д119,425, Ж17, П195
Yourself first, others afterward. Self-preservation is the first law of nature. Mind other men, but most yourself.

246 **Пригнала нужда к поганой луже.** *v.* Н583,589
[Need will drive you to a filthy puddle.] *i.e. to drink.* Need makes the naked man run. *Cf.* They have need of a blessing who kneel to a thistle. They are scarce of horseflesh where two and two ride on a dog.

247 **Пригожее яблоко бывает никогда горько.**
[A comely apple is never bitter.] A fair face cannot have a crabbed heart.

248 **Приготовь домашним пищу, а потом давай и нищим.** *v.* Н364
[Feed your family first, then the poor.] Charity begins at home.

249* **Пригрели змейку, а она тебя за шейку.** *v.* В414,676, Н245, З6
To nourish a snake (viper) in one's bosom. Save a thief from the gallows and he'll be the first to cut your throat.

250 **Приданое в сундуке, а урод на руке.** *v.* П41
[A dowry in the bag and an eyesore on the arm.] Many a one for land takes a fool by the hand. Better a portion (treasure) in a wife than with a wife. A great dowry is a bed full of brambles.

251* **Придет беда, отворяй ворота.** *v.* Б25
[When misfortune comes, open the gates wide.] Misfortunes never come singly. It never rains but it pours.

252 **Придет время, все лягут в могилку.** *v.* В650, Ц5
[When the time comes, all will go to their grave.] We shall lie all alike in our graves.

253 **Придет время, прорастет и семя.** *v.* В535,646
[The seed will grow, with time.] *Cf.* All in good time. Everything has its time.

254 **Придет кручина, как нет ни дров, ни лучины.**
[When troubles come, there's neither firewood nor kindling.] *Cf.* Trouble makes every sad accident a double evil. Of one ill come many. Trouble (misfortunes) never come singly.

255 **Придет нужда, сама скажется.**   *v.* Б27, Г4,260,270
Misfortunes come of themselves. *Lat.* mala ultro adsunt. Mischief (evils) come without calling for.

256* **Придет солнышко и к нашим окошечкам.**   *v.* А7, Б373, В288, И20
[The sun will shine in our window too.] Every dog has his day. The sun shines on all the world.

257 **Придет старость, будет слабость.**   *v.* С271
A hundred disorders has old age. Age breeds aches.

258* **Приехал, не здоровался, поехал не простился.**   *v.* М155
[He came without a greeting and took French leave.] Lightly come, lightly go.

259 **Признание - сестра покаяния.**
[Confession is the sister of repentance.] Confession is the first step to repentance. Confession is good for the soul.

260 **Прикрытый грех не явен.**   *v.* Т5
[A sin concealed is less manifest.] *Cf.* Sin that is hidden is half-forgiven.

261 **Приласкаешь собаку, не пойдет с тобой в драку.**
[Treat a dog kindly and it won't bite you.] *Cf.* If you would wish a dog to follow you, feed him.

262 **Прилежание все преодолевает.**
Perseverance conquers all things. *SPL.* labor (improbus) omnia vincit.

263* **Природа натуру одолевает.**   *v.* Н152
Nature passes nurture.

264 **Присяга насильная у Бога не сильна.**
[Oaths coerced are not binding with God.] *SPL.* per vim iurata non sunt rata.

265 **Приходят стужи на наши нужды.**   *v.* Б418, М63, О67, Т1
[Frosts descend upon our want.] On the snow add frost. *Cf.* It never rains but it pours. Ill comes often on the back of worse.

266 **Прихоти господские, а житие нищенское.**   *v.* М105, Н555
Pride may lurk under a threadbare coat. Pride and poverty are ill met yet often seen together.

267* **Пришел коня ковать а кузня сгорела.**   *v.* О91, П311
[Come to shoe the horse after the forge has burned.] It's too late to lock the stable door once the horse has been stolen. It's too late to husband when all is spent. A dry well pumps no water.

268 **Приятельское слово не должно быть сурово.**
A good friend never offends.

269 **Про ваше здоровье и говорить скромно.**
[Speak cautiously about your health.] You must not pledge your own health. *Cf.* Praise no man till he be dead.

270* **Про волка речь, а волк на встречь.**   *v.* Л29, Т47
Talk (speak) of the devil [wolf] and he is sure to appear. *Apost.*6.50: εἰ καὶ λύκου ἐμνήσθης καὶ εὐθὺς παραγινομένον.

271 **Про старые (одни) дрожжи не говорят дважды (трижды).**   *v.* Б457,482, О94, Ч62
[Don't speak twice of old yeast.] It's no use to flog a dead horse. Let bygones be bygones. *Lat.* rem actam agas.

272 **Провожают гостя богатого чтоб не упал, а бедного - чтоб не украл.**
[A wealthy guest is escorted lest he stumble, a poor guest - lest he steal.] Shame goes with poverty, confidence with wealth. *Cf.* There's one law for the rich, and another for the poor.

273* **Проглотить-то хочется, да пожевать лень.**   *v.* Л45, Н376,397, О97, Р91, Ч107
[Eager to swallow but too lazy to chew.] He wants his corn shelled. He that will eat the kernel must crack the nut.

274 **Проголодаешься, догодаешься.**   *v.* Б45, Г223
[Hunger will find a way.] Hunger sharpens the wits. *Lat.* acuit ingenium fames.
Cf. Hunger is the handmaid of genius. Hunger teaches many things. *Gr.* πολλῶν ὁ λιμὸς γίγνεται διδάσκολος. *Lat.* multa docet fames.

275 **Прозеваешь бражку, так и водицу хлебай.**   *v.* К285, П124,127
[He that misses the malt must settle for water.] He that comes last to the pot is soonest wroth. Last come, worst served.

276 **Проймет голод, проявится и голос.**   *v.* Г220, Д402, Н589, Ч22
[He that is gripped by hunger will find his voice.] *Cf.* He that cannot ask, cannot live.

277* **Пролив (пролитую) воду, не поймаешь (соберешь).**   *v.* В216
Spilled water cannot be gathered up.

278 **Пролита посудина не бывает полна. (Пролитое полно не живет.)**   *v.*А29,Б219,И92,
[An spilled bowl cannot be refilled. (What's spilt is gone.)]   И111,О4,П279,Ч69,93
It is no use crying over spilt milk. A cracked bell can never sound well. Nothing seems quite as good as new after being broken. *Lat.* quod factum est, infectum fieri non potest. *Cf.* Past cure, past care.

279 **Пролитого да прожитого не воротишь. (Пролитое не поднять, а битого не поворотить.)**
(Прошедшего не возвратишь.)   *v.* Б219, М71, О4,85, П278, Р55, Ч93,105
Things past cannot be recalled. [You can't restore what's spilt or broken.] What's done cannot be undone.

280* **Промах есть промах.**   *v.* Ч134
A miss is as good as a mile.

281* **Промедление смерти подобно.**   *v.* Д30, З99
[Delay is like death.] Delays are dangerous. Kill time and time will kill you. *Cf.* Defer not till tomorrow to be wise, tomorrow's sun to you may never rise. Killing time is not murder, it's suicide.

282   **Промолчал, не отвечал, поэтому согласен стал.**   *v.* Д306, М156
Silence means consent. *Lat.* qui tacet clamat.

283   **Пропадает птичка от своего язычка.**   *v.* Д78, 347, О14
[Many a bird is lost through its song.] The tongue talks at the head's cost. *Cf.* Birds are entangled by their feet, men by their tongues.

284*   **Пропал мех и (а) на батьку грех.**
[The fur's gone and even the father's suspected.] Suspicion breeds phantoms.

285*   **Пропала коровка, пропадай и веревка.**
[If the cow is gone, so is the halter.] The tail goes with the hide. You cannot sell the cow and drink the milk.

286   **Простота хуже воровства.**   *v.* В12
[It is worse to be a fool than a thief.] Most of us would rather be taken for knaves than for fools. Better be a rogue than a fool. *Cf.* †Better be a fool than a knave.

287*   **Против ветра не подуешь.**   *v.* Б208, О16
Puff not against the wind. *Cf.* Blow against the hurricane.

288   **Против жара и камень треснет.**
[Even a stone will crack under heat.] Weight can break a bridge.

289   **Против рожна не попрешь.**   *v.* Б196, Т25,74
*Acts.*14.5: **You cannot kick against the pricks.** *SPL.* contra torrentem non est nitendum.

290*   **Противное лекарство приятнее болезни.**   *v.* Г291
[A bitter physic is preferable to a disease.] Bitter pills may have blessed effects. Good medicine always tastes bitter.

291*   **Прошва дороже шубы.**   *v.* В545, И66, К172, О25
[The fur is not worth the sewing.] The game is not worth the candle.

292   **Прошла молодость - не попращалась, пришла старость - не поздоровалась.**   *v.*Ж111
[Youth has gone with no good-byes, and old age has come with no hello's.] Life is half spent before we know what it is.

293   **Пряди всяк свою пряжу.**   *v.* В563, З154, Н197,198, *Ap.*1.21
[Let each spin his yarn.] Let the cobbler stick to his last. Every man to his trade. Every man should cultivate his own garden. Hoe your own row. Paddle your own canoe.

294   **Прямо (только) вороны летают.**   *v.* В85
[Only crows fly straight.] A horse never goes straight up a hill. The farthest way around is the shortest way.

295   **Прямое прямее не будет.**
(Прямое нечего править.)(Прямое править - испортить.)   *v.* Л166, О125,164
[Straight cannot be straighter.] [Straight requires no straightening.] [Straight is spoiled by straightening.] *Cf.* Let well enough alone.

296   **Птицу кормом, а человека словом обманывают.**   *v.* Я13
[A bird is caught with seeds, a man with words.] Birds are entangled by their feet, men by their tongues.

297* Птичка не велика, да ноготок востер.   *v.* Ж15, М8, Н207, Я25
   [The bird is small, but its claws are sharp.] No viper so little, but has its venom. *Cf.*
   Velvet paws hide sharp claws.

298 Пугана (пуженая) ворона (и) куста боится.   *v.* Г106
   Birds [crows] once snared fear all bushes. *SPL.* qui semel est laesus fallacis piscis ab
   hamo, omnibus unca cibis aera subesse putat.

299* Пуля найдет виноватого.   *v.* Р69
   Every bullet has its billet.

300 Пускай излает собака чужая, да больно как лает своя домовая.   *v.* Б311,В657, Г267,
   [We don't mind others' dogs barking, but worry when our own do.] К10, Н110, Ч114
   Another's cares will not rob you of sleep. *Cf.* Wake not at every dog's bark.

301* Пусти бабу в рай, а она и корову ведет.
   [Let a woman into heaven and she'll bring her cow.] Women, priests and poultry never
   have enough.

302 Пусти на ноготок, пролезет на локоток. *v.* Д31

303* Пустили козла в огород.   *v.* В395, Д359, Н211,389
   [They let the goat into the orchard.] They let a bull in a China shop. They have set the
   wolf to guard the sheep.

304 Пустился в драку, хохла не жалей.   *v.* В38, К124
   [If you fight, don't worry about your hair.] Never wear your best trousers when you go
   out to fight (for freedom).

305 Пустого места нечего искать.   *v.* Д512, З9
   Where nothing is, nothing can be had.

306 Пустой голове все трын-трава.   *v.* Д495,500
   [It is all the same for a fool.] Fools are fain of nothing. Fools are never uneasy.

307* Пустой колос голову кверху носит.   *v.* В119, Г136, М136, Х103,
   [An empty head carries itself high.] A humble bee in a cow turd thinks himself king.
   Empty vessels make the greatest noise.

308 Пустой мешок введет в грешок.   *v.* Б34, Г222, Ж131
   [An empty purse drives one to sin.] Poverty is the mother of crime.

309 Пустой церкви пономарь.
   [A sexton in an empty church.] *i.e. an empty distinction.* A big frog (toad) in a small
   puddle.

310* Путь к сердце мужчины лежит через (его) желудок.
   The way to a man's heart is through his stomach.

311 Пущенной голубь из рук к рукам не возвратится.   *v.* С214
   [A pigeon let go will not return to your hand.] It's too late to shut the stable door when
   the horse has bolted.

312 Пьют для людей, а едят для себя. *v.* Е94

313 **Пьян напьется и с царем дерется, а проспится и свиньи боится.** *v.*B231,Г249,М143
[The drunk who would fight the *Tsar* fears even his swine once sober.] П316,Ш10
He that is drunk is as great as a king. *Cf.* Who takes (kills) a lion when he is absent,
fears a mouse present.

314 **Пьян об угол не ударится.** *v.* H407
[The drunk won't stumble over corners.] Drunken folks seldom take harm.

315* **Пьян проспится, а глуп (дурак) - никогда.**
A drunk man will sober up, but a damn fool never. A drunken man will get sober,
but a fool will never get wise.

316* **Пьяному (и) море по колено (+ а лужа по ушам).** *v.* B231, П313
[The sea is knee-deep for a drunk.] *i.e. false bravery.* Whiskey made rabbit hug the lion.
SPL. vino cura fugit, tunc pauper cornua sumit, tunc dolor et luctus rugaque frontis abit.
Cf. When wine is in, wit is out.

317 **Пьяный что бешеный.** *v.* T48
[A drunk is like a madman.] Nothing more than a fool a drunken man. *Cf.* A spur in the
head is like two in the heel.

318* **Пятая (седьмая) (десятая) вода на киселе.**
[Jelly watered down five times.] *i.e. a very distant relation.*

319 **Пятого игрока под стол.** *v.* П320
[The fifth player goes under the table.] *i.e. is superfluous.*

320* **Пятое колесо на телеге.** *v.* H509
A fifth wheel to a coach.

Р

1* **Работа дураков любит.**
    [Hard work loves fools.] Only fools and horses work. Cheapest is the dearest labour.

2* **Работа хвалит мастера.**   *v.* Д135
    Work commends the master. *SPL.* opus commendat artificem. *Cf.* A workman is known by his work.

3* **Работа черна, да денежка бела.**
    [Work may be black but money is white.] *i.e. grimy toil earns clean money.* Dirty hands make clean money. *Cf.* Muck and money go together. Great gain makes work easy.

4   **Работает как ребенок а ест как детина.**   *v.* В122, К1, Л49, Н80
    [He works like a child but eats like a man.] He has two stomachs to eat and one to work.

5   **Работай до поту, покушаешь в охоту.** *v.* П158

6   **Работай покуда руки гнутся.**
    [To work as long as your arms can bend.] *Cf.* Work till you drop. To work like a horse. To work hand and foot. *Lat.* conari manibus pedibus.

7   **Работать не заставят, и есть не поставят.**   *v.* Б380, В113, Д12,127,К75, Л39
    He that will not work, shall not eat. *Cf.* A man eats so he works.

8   **Работнику алтынь, а подрядчику рубль.**
    [Three *kopeks* for the labourer, a ruble for the contractor.] *Cf.* Good workmen are seldom rich. Be an employee and work eight hours, be a boss and your work is never done.

9   **Равные обычаи, крепкая любовь.**   *v.* К266,М164, Н418, П109, *Ар.*1.5
    Likeness causes liking.

10 **Рад безумный видя дурака при напасти.**   *v.* Н547
    [The knave delights in a fool's misfortune.] Rejoice not at another'sorrow. Make not another's misfortune your joy. *Lat.* P.Syr.421: malum ne alienum feceris tuum gaudium.

11* **Рад будешь как долг избудешь.**   *v.* 372,90
    [A debt paid will make you happy.] A borrowed loan should come laughing home.

12* **Рад бы в рай да грехи не пускают.**   *v.* В690,691,692, Д503
    [I'd love to go to heaven but my sins won't let me.] The spirit is willing but the flesh is weak. No man must go to heaven who has not sent his heart there before. *Cf.* There's no going to heaven in a sedan.

13 **Рад бы дал (дружку) пирожка, да (хлеба) у самого ни куска.**   *v.* Н62
    [I'd gladly give you a *pirozhok*, but I haven't got any (bread) myself.] A man cannot give what he hasn't got. *Cf.* Charity begins at home.

14   **Рад дурак что пирог велик.**   *v.* Д500
[A fool delights in a big pie.] A little thing pleases a fool. *Lat.* parva leves capiunt animos.

15*   **Ради милого дружка и сережка из ушка.**   *v.* Д240,242, М91
[I'll give a dear friend even the earing from off my ear.] Anything for a friend.

16*   **Радости забываются, а печали никогда.**   *v.* Д311, Л79, Н102
[Happines is forgotten, but sorrow never.] Good deeds are easily forgotten, bad deeds never.

17*   **Радость без печали не бывает. Радость с горем живет (рядом ездят).**
      No pleasure without pain. No cross, no crown.   *v.* Б125, Н541, П29, С94
No weal without woe. No joy without annoy. *SPL.* miscentur tristia laetis.

18   **Радость не вечна и печаль не бесконечна.**   *v.* Г80,263, Н543, С85
[Neither happines nor sorrow last forever.] Sadness and gladness succeed each other.
Cf. No happiness lasts for long. *Lat.* nulla longi temporis felicitas.

19   **Радость прямит, кручина крючит.**   *v.* Г276
[Happiness straightens, grief contorts.] Misfortunes hasten age. *Cf.* Joys are our wings,
our sorrows - our spurs.

20*   **Раз на раз не приходится.**   *v.* В88, Г193, Д165, Н392, *Ap.* 1.93
No like is the same.

21   **Развеешь ворохами, не собирешь крохами.**
[What you scatter by bushels, you won't gather by bits.] Scatter with one hand, gather
with two. Waste not, want not.

22   **Разговор дорогу короче делает.**   *v.* Б199, В25,213, У103
[Talking shortens the journey.] Cheerful (pleasant) company shortens the miles. Good
company on the road is the shortest cut. *Cf.* A merry companion is a wagon in the way.

23*   **Разговор серебро, молчание - золото.**   *v.* С128,181
Speech is silvern, silence is golden.

24*   **Разговорами сыт не будешь.**   *v.* Б21, В376,367, Г184,226, Е45, И101, С236, У7, Ш14
Fair words fill not the belly. *Cf.* Fine (fair) words butter no parsnips (cabbage). Many
words will not fill a bucket. Good words fill not a sack.

25   **Разговоры больши, а хлеб-соль маленька.**   *v.* Е33, К207,302, М126, Х10
Great boast and small roast.

26*   **Разные головы, разные и мысли.**   *v.* С140,283, Ч89
So many heads (men), so many minds (wits). *Lat.* Ter.*Phorm.*2.4.14: quot homines,
tot sententiae.

27   **Разные обычаи - крепкая любовь.**   *v.* †Р9
[Different ways strengthen love.] Opposites attract.

28   **Разум силу преодолеет (победит).**   *v.* Б140, И49, С120
[Reason surpasses strength.] Wisdom is better than strength. Reason rules all things.

29   **Разумный видит что за чем идет.**   *v.* З141,146
[The wise man knows what goes after what.] He knows on which side his bread is
buttered. He knows how many beans make five.

30 **Разумный любит научиться, а глупый любит всех учить.**
[The wise man seeks to learn and the fool seeks to teach.] The wise seek wisdom, the fool has found it. *Cf.* The wise man questions himself, the fool others.

31* **Разумный согрешит, многих глупых соблазнит.** *v.* В27, Г210, О46, У93
[When the wise man sins, he takes many fools with him.] The greater the man, the greater the crime. *Cf.* One wise man is worth ten thousand fools.

32 **Разумный только свиснет, а кто догадлив смыслит.** *v.* Д323, М173, О39, У98
[The wise man need only whistle for the shrewd man to catch on.] A word to a wise man is enough. *Lat.* verbum sat sapienti.

33 **Ранний сев к позднему в амбар (закрома) не ходит.** *v.* Б183, О112,141, Ш11
[Who sows early needn't go to the silo a second time.] *i.e. for seed for late sowing* A stitch in time saves nine.

34* **Ранняя женитьба видимая беда.** *v.* В294, Ж70,79, К119
They that marry in green their sorrow is soon seen. Early wed, early dead.

35 **Ранняя птичка носок прочищает, а поздняя глазки продирает.** *v.* К223, М133
[The early bird cleans its beak while the late one rubs its eyes.] The early bird catches the worm. *SPL.* aurora musis amica.

36 **Рано затеял да поздно свел.**
[Started early but ended late.] First up, last down. *Cf.* Early up and never the near.

37 **Рано оседлали да поздно поскакали.**
(Рано снарядились, да поздно в путь пустились.) *v.* В315, К316
[Saddled up early but got off to a late start.] They that are booted are not always ready. *SPL.* dantur ultimi saepe fiunt primi.

38 **Рано пташечка запела, как бы кошечка не съела.** *v.* Н261,474
[The bird shouldn't sing to too soon lest the cat get her.] It's not good praising a ford till a man be over. Don't halloo till you're out of the woods. He that laughs on Friday shall weep on Saturday.

39* **Раньше смерти не умрешь.** *v.* Г299, Д91,107, П230
[You cannot die before your time.] A man can die but once.

40 **Раскрасилась клевета во все махровые цвета.** *v.* В566, С124
[Arrant calumny assumes all shades and hues.] *Cf.* The tale runs as it pleases the teller.

41 **Рассердясь на вши, да шубу в печь.** *v.* О103

42 **Рассказчики не годятся в приказчики.** *v.* Б329, Г184, Д210
[Great talkers don't sell many wares.] The greatest talkers are always the least doers.

43 **Рассуждай или нет, а сто рублей деньги.**
[Think what you like, but 100 rubles is still money.] Money is money.

44 **Расходы подытожить - душу растревожить.** *v.* 332, С147
[To add up expenses is a sure way to get upset.] Merry is the feast-making till we come to the reckoning.

45 **Рваться не рвись, а крепче берись.**
What is worth doing at all is worth doing well.

46   Ревность, яко ржа, губит сердце.   *v.* Ж43
Envy eats nothing but its own heart.

47*   Редко да метко.   *v.* Г176, К176
[Rare but apt.] Few words are best.

48*   Редкое свиданье, приятный гость.   *v.* Х41, Ч9
[A rare guest is a good guest.] A constant guest is never welcome. *Cf.* Absence makes the heart grow fonder. That thing which is rare is dear. *Lat.* rara praeclara.

49   Резвого жеребца и волк не берет.   *v.* П179
[Not even a wolf can take a swift stallion.] The race is to the swift.

50*   Реже видишь, милее будешь.   *v.* Е1, Н219
Absence makes the heart grow fonder. *Cf.* Familiarity (intimacy) breeds contempt.

51   Ремесло за плечами не висит, а ко времю годится.   *v.* Н151,486, Т54
Who has a trade, has a share everywhere.

52   Репу да горох не сей подле дорог.   *v.* Б233, Г66, Н5
[Do not plant turnips or peas near a roadway.] He that sows in the highway tires his oxen and loses his corn. *Cf.* Choose not a house near an inn or in a corner.

53   Ретивая лошадка не долго живет.   *v.* Р54
[A frisky horse is short-lived.] A horse that draws best is most whipped.

54   Ретивому коню всегда работы вдвое, а тот же корм дают.   *v.* В206, К184,218
[The willing horse does twice the work for the same feed.] All lay load on the willing horse.

55   Решено - вершено.   *v.* Б459, П279, Ч62,93
[Decided is done.] Settled once, settled forever. A decision made cannot be recalled. *Cf.* The resolved mind has no cares. The die is cast. *Lat.* alea iacta est.

56   Решетом воду мерять - потерять время. (Решетом воды не вычерпаешь.)   *v.*Б157,В128,
[Measuring (bailing out) water with a sieve is a waste of time.]   320,К22,Н362,Х13
To carry (draw)(fetch) water in a sieve. *Apost.*9.91: κοσκίνῳ ὕδωρ φέρειν. *EA*. cribro aquam haurire. *Cf.* The wind cannot be caught in a net.

57*   Ржаная каша сама себя хвалит. *v.* О20

58   Риск - благородное дело.   *v.* Г58, С100
[Risk is a noble business.] The more danger, the more honour. *Cf.* Nothing ventured, nothing gained. Everything is sweetened by risk.

59   Рогом о козел, а родом осел.
[A goat by his horns, but an ass by his birth.] *Cf.* He wears the bull's feather. *i.e. a cuckold.*

60   Род, племя близко, а свой рот ближе.   *v.* В658, Е17, Р73, С74
[Near is my family and kin, but nearer still my skin.] Near is my shirt, but nearer is my skin.

61*   Родинку не смыть, обычая не изжить.   *v.* Н123
[One can neither wash off a birthmark nor shake a habit.] It's hard to break a hog of an ill custom.

62   **Родись плясуном и будешь плясать.**   *v.* Г18, К160, О157, Р68
[If you're born to dance you'll be a dancer.] He that is born to be hanged shall never be drowned. No flying from fate.

63   **Родится роток - родится и кусок. (Родись человек, краюшка хлеба готова.)**   *v.*Б252,
God never sends mouth but he sends meat.   435, Д34,38, 38

64   **Рожа стара - сердце молодо.**   *v.* Б343, В401, Г214, П99, С89
[Old face, young heart.] To have a hoar head and green tail. A grey head is often placed on green shoulders.

65*   **Рожею хорош (кувяка) (орел) (сокол), да делами не пригож (разумом ни мака) (умом тетерев).**   *v.* В99, Г112, К195, Л86, Н258, У11
[Fair (babe's) (aquiline) (falcon's) face but incompetent (no wit) (the mind of a grouse).] The face is no index of the heart. A pretty face may hide an empty head. Pretty face, poor fate. Trust not the face. *Lat.* fronti nulla fides.

66   **Розга хоть нема, да придает ума.**
[Birchen twigs don't speak, yet they instruct.] *Prov.*29.15: The rod and reproof give wisdom. *Lat.* virga atque correptio tribuit sapientiam. Birchen twigs break no ribs.

67*   **Розню тошно а вместе тесно.**   *v.* Г275, Д440
[Either pining whilst apart or fighting when together.] Those we love, we can hate. Love and hate are blood relations. The greatest hate springs from the greatest love.

68   **Рокового (суженого) на коне не объедешь.**   *v.* О157, Ч45
[Even on horseback you won't escape your destiny.] No flying from fate. You cannot escape your fate.

69*   **Рок головы ищет.**   *v.* П299
[Fate seeks its victim.] Each cross has its inscription. Every bullet has its billet.

70   **Роса мочит по зорям, а дождь по порам.**
[The dew dampens by dawn, but rain from time to time.] *i.e. rain is not as predictable as dew.* When God pleases, it rains with every wind.

71   **Роскошные и скупые меры довольства не знают.**   *v.* С161, Т62
[Extavagance and avarice are never content.] Poverty wants some things, luxury many things, avarice all things. Avarice is never satisfied. *Cf.* Lechery and covetousness go together.

72   **Ртом болезнь входит, а беда выходит.**   *v.* Я9
[Diseases enter by the mouth and troubles exit.] The mouth is the executioner and doctor of the body.

73*   **Рубашка к телу ближе.**   *v.* В658, Р60, С74
Near is my shirt, but nearer is my skin.

74   **Рубаха кафтана ближе.**   *v.* Р73
Near is my coat but nearer is my shirt. *SPL.* tunica pallio propior.

75   **Руби дерево здоровое, а гнилое и само свалится.**
One needs cut only healthy trees, the rotten ones fall of themselves.] Never take a stone to break an egg when you can do it with the back of your knife.

76* **Руби дерево по себе.** *v.* К209,266, П109, Ч96
[Cut a tree according to your size.] *said about marriage and choosing one's partner, or starting a task within one's abilities.* Marry your like (equal)(match). *Lat.* aequalem tibi ducito. Ov.*Her.*9.32: nube pari. Don't bite off more than you can chew. Cut your coat (sail) to your cloth.

77* **Рука руку знает.** *v.* М164, P88
[One hand knows another.] It takes one to know one.

78* **Рука руку моет, а обе хотят быть белы (и обе чисты бывают).** *v.* Л19
One hand washes the other (and both the face) [and both come clean]. *Apost.*1.36a: χεῖρ χεῖρα νίζει. *Lat.* manus manum lavat. *Cf.* Scratch my back and I'll scratch yours. One good turn desrerves another.

79 **Рука руку чешет, а обе свербят.**
[When one hand scratches the other, both will itch.] Scratching is bad because it begins with pleasure and ends in pain.

80 **Рука согрешит, голова отвечает.** *v.* Н322,493, И88
[The hand errs at the head's cost.] *Cf.* Nothing is stolen without hands. The tongue talks at the head's cost.

81 **Рука чиста, да дельцо маховато.**
[The hand is clean but the deed rash.] Have not only clean hands, but clean minds.

82 **Руками не складешь чего нельзя.** *v.* И92,118, П28
[Hands cannot repair what cannot be mended.] A cracked bell can never sound well (is never sound).

83 **Руки как грабли.** *v.* P84
[Rakish hands.] He is better with a rake than with a fork.

84* **Руки крюки.** *v.* P83
[Hooks for hands] *i.e. sticky fingers, thievish.* Sailors fingers are all fish hooks. *Cf.* His fingers are lime twigs. Nothing is stolen without hands.

85 **Рыба ищет где глубже, а человек где лучше.** *v.* Д60
[Fish move to deeper water, man towards what is better.] Change of pasture makes fat calves. *Cf.* To an optimist, every change is for the better.

86 **Рыба мелка, да уха сладка.** *v.* Ж101
[Even small fish may make a good soup.] The greatest crabs be not all the best meat.

87* **Рыба с головы гниет (начинает портится).**
Fish begins to stink at the head. *Apost.*9.18: ἰχθὺς ἐκ κεφαλῆς ὄζειν ἄρχεται. *Lat.* Piscis primum a capite foetat.

88* **Рыбак рыбака (дурак дурака) (свой свояка) видит из далека.** *v.* М164, P77
[One fisherman (fool) knows another from afar.] It takes one to know one. *Cf.* Deep will call unto deep.

89 **Рыба рыбою сыта, а человек человеком.** *v.* Б314, К249, Ч31
[Fish devour fish, and men other men.] The great fish eat up the small. Man is to man a wolf. *Lat..* homo homini lupus.

90   **Рыбка да рябки - потеряй деньки.**
[Fishing and hunting are thieves of time.] Time spent in folly is doubly lost. *Cf.* Hunting, hawking, paramour - for one joy, a hundred displeasures.

91*   **Рыбка хочется, а в реку не вскочется.**   *v.* K181, Л45, H376, П273, Ч107
[He wants the fish but won't wade in the river.] You can't catch trout with dry trousers (breeches).

92*   **Рыболова одна тоня кормит.**   *v.* K332, C284
[It takes only one cast to feed a fisherman.] *i.e. one successful cast.* One at a time is good fishing. *Cf.* Still he fishes that catches one.

93   **Рябая рожа зеркала не любит.**   *v.* З116, H37
[A pock-marked face shuns the looking-glass.] An ugly woman dreads the mirror.

94*   **Ряса монаха не делает.**   *v.* H247,295
The cowl (habit) (hood) does not make the monk. *Lat.* cucullus (tonsura) non facit monachum.

С

1* **С больной головы, да на здоровую.**   *v.* В197,207, Л202, Н117, Т8, *Ap.*1.77
[To shift the blame from the guilty to the innocent.] One has the scathe and another has the scorn. *Cf.* He that cannot beat the ass, beats the saddle. The tongue offends and the ears get the cuffing.

2* **С волками жить, по волчьи выть.**   *v.* З15, М50, С123
Who keeps company with wolves will learn to howl.

3 **С возу упало, пиши - пропало.** *v.* Ч100

4* **С глаз долой - из сердца.**   *v.* В413, Д48, Н218, Ч14
Out of sight, out of mind.

5 **С голого, что с мертвого - взятки гладки.**   *v.* Г241, З9, Н125,559, У71
[Meager are the scrapings off a dead man or a beggar.] No naked man is sought after to be rifled. *Cf.* Sue a beggar and get a louse.

6 **С горы видней.**
[One can see better from a hilltop.] *i.e. learn from those wiser and more experienced.* Learn from your betters. A dwarf on a giant's shoulders sees further of the two.
Cf. Learn from the mistakes of others.

7 **С горы на заднице съедешь, а на гору и ногами не скоро взойдешь.**
[You can slide on your rump down a hill that your feet take a long time to climb.] It is easier to run down a hill than up one. *Cf.* Make no more haste when you come down than when you went up. Up hill spare me, down hill bear me. All downhill it is easy to descend. *Lat.* omnia proclivia sunt, facile descendere.

8 **С добрым другом и прожиток после будет не в убыток.**
[Among good friends, even expenses are not a loss.] Friends tie their purse with a cobweb thread. True friends share both the bad and good.

9* **С дураком пива не сваришь.**   *v.* Б166, Г142, Д485, И17, О33
[You can't brew beer with a fool.] Fools never prosper. It takes the foolish to confound the wise.

10* **С дураком свяжешься, сам дурак будешь.**   *v.* В451, Д479, Н265
[Deal with fools and become one of their number.] When you argue with a fool, that makes two. He's not the fool that the fool is, but he that with the fool deals. One fool makes many. *Lat.* unius dementia dementes efficit multos. *Cf.* It takes a fool to know a fool.

11 **С жиру собаки бесятся.**
[Fat drives dogs mad.] A swine over fat is the cause of his own bane. *Cf.* Greed killed the wolf. Covetousness breaks the sack. On fat land grow foulest weeds.

12* **С кем поведаешься, от того и наберешься (тем и прослывешь).** *v.*В359,З15,С28,123
A person is reflected in the friends he chooses. A man is known by his friends. *Cf.* Show me your friend and I'll tell you who you are. If you lie down with dogs, you will get up with fleas.

13* **С косым не толкуй о кривом.** *v.* В36
[Speak not of a hunchback to a cross-eyed man.] It's ill halting before a cripple. *Cf.* Name not a halter (rope) in his house that was hanged.

14 **С курицы хозяйство не наберешь.** *v.* Н229, П187
[It takes more than chickens to make a farm.] There belongs more than whistling to going to plough. There's more to riding than a pair of boots.

15 **С лихой (паршивой) собаки (овцы) хоть шерсти клок.**
[Even a bad sheep gives a bit of wool.] Take what you can get. Make the best of a bad situation. If worst comes to worst, make the best of it. You can have no more of a cat but her skin.

16 **С лица не воду пить.** *v.* Б363
Prettiness makes no pottage. *Cf.* Beauty has no brains. Beauty is only skin deep.

17* **С малыми детками горе, а с большими - вдвое.** *v.* Д218, М29
Little children, little troubles; big children, big troubles. A little child weighs on your knee, a big one on your heart.

18 **С медом съешь и осметок.** *v.* К102
[Honey makes filth palatable.] Anything is good with strawberries and cream. *Cf.* To sugar (gild) the pill (word).

19* **С милым годок покажется часок.** *v.* С308
[A year seems like an hour in good company.] When a man is happy, he does not hear the clock strike.

20 **С милым рай в шалаше.** *v.* Б431, В97, Н404
Love lives in cottages as well as in courts.

21* **С миром и беда (смерть) не убыток (страшна).** *v.* В343,546, Г266, Н53
[With company, even misery (death) loses its sting.] Company in misery makes it less. Company in distress makes trouble less. Misery loves company. Grief is lessened when imparted to others.

22* **С миру по нитке - голому рубаха.** *v.* В524, Е26, М97, П58,82
[A thread from everyone makes a shirt for one.] Add little to little and there will be a great heap. *Cf.* Every little (bit) helps. Many a little makes a mickle (nickel). Many littles make a lot.

23 **С мыслей (со вранья) пошлин не берут.** *v.* Д252, Н57
Thought is free.

24* **С неумения руки не болят.**
[Your arms won't hurt if you don't know how.] *i.e. to use ignorance as an excuse for not working.* It pays to be ignorant.

25* **С огнем шутить не надо. (С огнем не шути и воде не верь.)** *v.* В115, О81
Don't play with fire (nor trust water). *Cf.* Fire and water are good servants but bad masters.

26* С одного вола двух шкур (две шкуры) не дерут.   *v.* O41
[You cannot skin the same ox twice.] *i.e. double jeopardy.* You can't eat the same bread twice. You cannot have your cake and eat it. *Diog.*5.85: κύνα δέρειν δεδαρμένην. *Lat.* ab uno bove bina pellis non trahitur.

27* С одного удара дуба не свалишь.   *v.* Д200, 333
An oak is not felled with one stroke. *Gr. Diog.*7.77a: πολλαῖσι πληγαῖς δρῦς δαμάζεται. *SPL.* multis ictibus dejicitur quercus.

28 С пчелкой водиться - в меду находиться, а с жуком связаться - в навозе оказаться.   *v.* B359, 315, C12,123
[Go with a bee and be in honey, but go with a bug and you'll be in a dung heap.] Tell me with whom you go and I'll tell you what you do.

29* С разговоров сыт не будешь.   *v.* P24

30 С рожи болван, а во всем есть талан.   *v.* Д251,489, Ф4
Fortune favours fools.

31 С суконным рылом (да) в калачный ряд (не суйся).   *v.* B592,606, Л42
[Go not among finery in homespun.] Every little fish would become a whale. Never put a churl upon a gentleman. They don't put marble tops on cheap furniture.

32 С трубами свадьба, и без труб свадьба.
[With or without fanfare, a wedding's a wedding.] Ceremony is not civility, nor civility ceremony.

33 С умным речи к разговору, с безумным лишь на ссору.   *v.* Г145, Д493
[Wise men converse, fools argue.] Fools bite one another, but wise men agree together.

34 С умом жить - мучиться, а без ума жить тешиться.   *v.* Б321, M109, H149,250
[Wise men live in torment, fools in ease.] Increase your knowledge and you increase your griefs.

35 С чем в колыбельку, с тем и в могилку.   *v.* K64, H470, У104, Ч46
[As in the cradle, so to the grave.] You can't take it with you. *or* What is learned in the cradle lasts to the grave. *Cf.* Between the cradle and the grave.

36* С чужого коня среди грязи долой.   *v.* 373, K286,Ч67
[One must dismount another's horse, even into the mud.] *i.e. one must relinquish one's unrightful place even under the worst of circumstances.* **If you are on a strange horse, get off in the middle of the road.** The borrower is a slave to the lender. *Cf.* He that borrows must pay again with shame or loss.

37 Сажу мукой не сделаешь.   *v.* H339, Ч50
[You cannot make soot out of flour.] To make white black.

38* Сам заварил кашу, сам и расхлебай.   *v.* K34, Ч77
As you brew, so must you drink.

39* Сам живи и другим не мешай. (Сам не согрешай, а людям не мешай.)   *v.* Ж116
Live and let live.

40 Сам нож точит, а говорит не бось.   *v.* C43
[He sharpens his knife and tells you not to worry.] Do as I say, not as I do. *Cf.* He looks one way and rows another.

41   **Сам огни и воды и медныя трубы прошел.**   *v.* Б441, И4
[He's gone through fire and water and copper piping.] He's gone through thick and thin.

42   **Сам поет, сам и слушает.**   *v.* К9
[Who sings alone must listen to his own music.] Who eats his cock alone must saddle his horse alone.

43   **Сам пьет а людей за пьянство бьет.**   *v.* И122, О73, С40
[He drinks and censures others for drinking.] The friar preached against stealing and had a goose in his sleeve. Don't do as I do, but as I say.

44   **Сам себя ни хвали ни хули.**   *v.* К153
Neither praise nor dispraise thyself (+ thy actions serve thy turn).

45   **Самовольное признание лучшее свидетельство.**
[Confession is the best form of testimony.] *Cf.* Open confession is good for the soul. A generous confession disarms slander.

46   **Самолюб никому (Богу) не люб.**
[None loves an egotist.] He is unworthy to live who lives only for himself. *Gr.* πολλοί σε τοὶ μισοὺσιν, ἂν σαυτὸν φιλεῖς.

47*   **Сапожник без сапог.**   *v.* Ж93, Н326, У42, Ч133
A shoemaker's son always goes barefoot.

48   **Сбережешь - что найдешь.**   *v.* Г331, П239, Т55
A penny saved is a penny got. Of saving comes having.

49   **Сват свату холодный друг.**   *v.* Д93, П122
[One matchmaker dislikes another.] One potter envies another. Two of a trade seldom agree.

50*   **Свежее всегда лучше.**   *v.* К270,279, М88, Н63
Newer is truer. *SPL.* scopae recentiores, semper meliores. grata est novitas.

51   **Сверху мило, внутри гнило.**   *v.* В99, К196, Л87, С210,211
Fair without, false within. An angel on top but a devil underneath. Beauty is only skin deep. Fair face, foul heart.

52*   **Свет не клином сошелся.**   *v.* В96, И127, П57
[The whole world doesn't hinge on one thing.] The world is a wide parish (place). There are more ways to the wood than one. *Cf.* There are more fish in the sea. Not the only game in town. There's more than one way to skin a cat.

53*   **Свинье не до поросят коли ее палят.**   *v.* Н286
[The sow forgets the piglets when she's on the spit herself.] A bletherin' cow soon forgets her calf.

54*   **Свинья и в золотом ошейнике - все свинья.**   *v.* В49,361, Л42, М194, О9
[A pig in a golden collar is still a pig.] A pig in the parlour is still a pig. *Cf.* Wash a pig, scent a pig; a pig still is a pig. Pigs are pigs. An ape's an ape, a varlet's a varlet, though they be clad in silk or scarlet. Dress a monkey as you will, it remains a monkey still.

55*   **Свинья не знает в апельсинах вкусу.**
[A pig cannot judge the taste of oranges.] A pig used to dirt turns up its nose at rice boiled in milk. *Cf.* What can you expect from a pig but a grunt?

56   **Свободный человек ничего не боиться.**   *v.* В335, Д276, К241
      [A free man fears nothing.] All fear is bondage. *Cf.* Mountaineers are always freemen.
      A clear conscience fears no accuser.

57   **Свое дитя и горбато, да мило.**   *v.* В647, П235, С67, *Ap.*1.6
      [Even if it is crippled, one loves one's own child.] No mother has a homely child.
      Cf. The crow thinks her own bird(s) the fairest (whitest).

58   **Своего спасибо не жалей, а чужого не жди.**
      [Wait not for others' thanks nor be sparing of your own.] One never loses anything by
      politeness. *Cf.* Gratitude is a lively expectation of favours yet to come.

59*   **Свои люди, (небось) сочтемся (сочтутся).**   *v.* Б362, Д242, П25
      [Friends will be even some day.] Friends have all things in common. It will all come
      right in the wash.

60   **Свои (две) собаки дерутся (грызутся), чужая (третья) не приставай!**   *v.* Г29, М182
      [When your own (two) dogs fight, a third had better keep away.] Put not your hand
      between the bark and the tree.

61*   **Свои сухари лучше чужих пирогов.**   *v.* В139, Г280, Н116, Ч128
      Dry bread at home is better than roast meat [pies] **abroad.**

62   **Свой глаз - алмаз (а чужой стекло) (лучше чужого).**   *v.* Х34
      [Your own eye is like a diamond, others'- mere glass.] The master's eye makes the horse
      fat (fattens the herd). *SPL.* urget praesentia Turni. fertilissimum in agro oculum domini.
      Cf. The eye of the master does more than his hand. If the owner keeps his eye on the
      horse, it will fatten. If you want a thing well done, do it yourself.

63   **Свой домишка хоть худ, да лучше чужого.**   *v.* С71, Х18
      Home is home, though it never be so homely. *SPL.* domus propria (amica), domus
      optima.

64   **Свой дурак дороже чужого умника.**   *v.* Ж113, С67
      [Your own fool of a kinsman is better than a smart stranger.] You may choose your
      friends but your family is thrust upon you. Blood is thicker than water.

65   **Свой кошель припаси, да как хошь и тряси.**   *v.* В138
      [He who fills his purse may shake it as he wills.] Own is own.

66*   **Свой своего (свояка) видит издалека.**   *v.* К266, М164, П109, Т7
      Like will to like. *Cf.* Scabby donkeys scent each other over nine hills. One swine
      recognizes another. A wood seller knows a wood buyer.

67*   **Свой своему по неволе друг (брат).**   *v.* В647, П235, С57,64
      [One naturally prefers one's own kin(d).] Blood is thicker than water. An ass to an ass
      is beautiful. *SPL.* asinus asino pulcherrimus.

68   **Свой ум царь в голове.**   *v.* Д505, Ц3
      [The mind is king.] My mind to me a kingdom is. A good mind possesses a kingdom.
      Lat. mens regnum bona possidet. A man's will is his heaven.

69   **Своя воля страшней неволе.**
      [One's own willpower is worse than bondage.] Will is the cause of woe. *Cf.* Men are
      blind in their own cause. The willing horse carries the load (gets the whip).

70   Своя голова болит, чужой не лечат.   *v.* Н326, Ч132,133

[When your own head aches, don't treat others.] Physician, heal thyself. *Cf.* People who live in glass houses shouldn't throw stones.

71*   Своя земля и в горсти мила.   *v.* С63, Х18,19

[A handfull of soil is pleasing if it's your land.] Home is home though it ever be so homely.

72   Своя избушка, свой простор.   *v.* В136,194,404,579, Т14

A man's house is his castle.

73*   Своя ноша не тянет (тяжела).

A burden of one's choice is not felt.

74*   Своя рубашка (сорочка) к телу ближе (свой рот ближе).   *v.* В567,658, Р60,73, С225

[One's own shirt is nearer to one's skin.] Near is my shirt, but nearer is my skin. *SPL.* omnes sibi melius esse malunt quam alteri.

75*   Своя рука владыка.   *v.* Г174, К60,299, Н485, Х82

[A man can do as he pleases.] Man is his own master. A strong man and waterfall channel their own path. *Cf.* Every man is architect of his own fortune.

76   Своя своих не познаша.

Mistake friend for foe. Not to know who your friends are. *inspired from John.1.10-11: in propria venit et sui eum non receperunt (he entered his own realm and his own would not receive him).* *Cf.* See me and see me not.

77   Своя худоба никому не кажется худа.   *v.* В309, Ч116

[Each is blind to his inadequacies.] We see not what is in the wallet behind. The hunchback doesn't see his own hump.

78   Связался с чертом, пеняй на себя.   *v.* Б377, В20

[If you deal with the devil, you have only yourself to blame.] He needs a long spoon that sups with the devil. He that takes the devil into his boat must carry him over the sound.

79   Свято место пусто не бывает (будет).

Nature abhors a vacuum.   A vacuum is always filled.

80*   Святому святое и снится.   *v.* Л71, С174,226, Ч84

[A saint has saintly dreams.] Names and natures often agree. The net of the sleeper catches fish. The pig dreams of acorns and the goose of maize. All thoughts of a turtle are of turtle, of a rabbit, rabbit.

81   Сделав худо, не жди добра.   *v.* Б377, Ж153, Л76, С224, Х95

[An evil-doer shouldn't expect any good.] Evil to him who evil does. He who does evil comes to an evil end. Roots of evil bear evil fruits. *Cf.* The deed comes back upon the doer.

82   Сделавши добро, не кайся.

Never be weary of well-doing.

83*   Сделайся овцою а волки будут.   *v.* Б398, Н437

He that makes himself a sheep shall be eaten by the wolf.

84   Севши в пиру на ряду, не говори что плясать не могу.   *v.* В291, Е32, Л70, Н133,

[Don't say you don't know how to dance if you've come to the ball.]   Н440, П202
Don't say go but gaw. He that has shipped the devil must make the best of him.

85* **Сегодня в цветах, а завтра в слезах.** *v.* Г22,80,263, К301, Н543, Р18
[Flowers today, tears tomorrow.] Laugh before breakfast, cry before sunset. Sadness and gladness succeed each other.

86 **Сегодня густо а завтра пусто.** *v.* Б418, К118, Н408
[Plenty today, nothing tomorrow.] Either a feast or a famine. *Cf.* Here today, gone tomorrow.

87 **Сегодня в порфире, а завтра в могиле.** *v.* Ж152, Н596
[In purple today, in the grave tomorrow.] Today a man, tomorrow none.

88 **Сегодня на деньги а завтра в долг.** *v.* Д166
[In the black today, in the red tomorrow.] What you lose today you cannot gain tomorrow. *Cf.* Never spend tomorrow counting yesterday's empty bottles.

89 **Седина в бороду (а) бес в ребро.** *v.* Б343, В401,402, Г214, П99, Р64
Hoar head and green tail. *Cf.* A grey head is often placed on green shoulders. Grey hairs are often nourished with green thoughts.

90 **Седина напала, счастье пропало.**
[Grey appears and happiness disappears.] Grey hairs are death's blossoms. *Cf.* Age makes a man white but not better.

91 **Сей в решето когда в сито не прошло.**
[Sift through the screen what has been caught by the sieve.] He that deals in the world needs four sieves.

92 **Сей день не без завтраго.** *obs.*
Every day hath a tomorrow.

93 **Сей свет дом всех людей.**
[The world is everyone's common home.] We're all in the same boat. The world is what people make it. *Cf.* The world is a stage and all the people in it its actors.

94* **Сей слезами, радостью пожнешь.** *v.* Н221,541, П29
They that sow in tears shall reap in joy. Of sufferance comes ease. *Cf.* Suffering is bitter but its fruits are sweet.

95 **Семеро капралов, один рядовой (+ да и тот кривой).** *v.* Г303
[Seven corporals and one private (+ and a buck-private at that).] Too many chiefs and not enough braves. Too many eskimos, too few seals.

96* **Семеро одного не ждут.** *v.* Б332, Я23
[Seven don't wait for one.] The majority rules. The absent are always in the wrong. The tail goes with the hide.

97 **Семеро сватаются а одному достанется.**
[Of seven suitors one will wed.] The last suitor wins the maid.

98* **Семи смертям не бывать, одной не миновать.** *v.* Г299, Д91,107, С291, Ш2
A man can die but once [not seven times.]

99 **Семь бед миновал, а на одну наскочил.**
[Seven times lucky, but not the eighth.] It's the last straw that breaks the camel's back. The last drop makes the cup run over.

100 **Семь бед, один ответ.** *v.* Г58, Р58
[Seven crimes, the same punishment.] As well be hanged for a sheep as for a lamb. Over shoes, over boots. *Cf.* A man can die but once. In for a penny, in for a pound.

101* **Семь верст до небес, да все лесом.** *v.* Г57, Д233, М57
[Seven miles to the heights, but all through the woods.] *said of long senseless talk.* Big talking but little saying. Beat around the bush. *Cf.* A flow of words is no proof of wisdom.

102 **Семь дел в одни руки не берут.** *v.* Т85
[Two hands cannot perform seven tasks.] Grasp no more than the hand will hold. *Cf.* One foot cannot stand in two boats. Do not bite off more than you can chew. He that sips many arts drinks none. Jack of all trades and master of none. Grasp all, lose all.

103* **Семь раз примерь (отмерь) (отмеряй), один (однажды) отрежь.** *v.* Д213, О60
Measure twice [seven times], cut once. *SPL.* praestat Prometheum esse quam Epimetheum.

104* **Семь топоров вместе лежат, а две прялки врозь.**
[Seven axes can lie together, but two spinning wheels clash.] *i.e. men get along better than women.* Two women cannot live under one roof. Two women in the same house can never agree.

105 **Семьдесят семь коз женская душа.** *v.* Б5, Д110, М56
[Seventy seven she-goats make a woman's mind.] A woman is a weathercock. *Cf.* A woman's mind and winter change oft.

106 **Семью пестами в ступе не полезешь.** *v.* Д84,94,103
[Seven pestles won't fit in one mortar.] Too many hands spoil the pie. *Cf.* A round peg in a square hole.

107 **Сена нет - так и солома съедома.** *v.* З29, И25, Н348, О18
[When there's no hay, the straw is edible.] If though hast not a capon, feed on an onion. *Cf.* The goat must browse where he is tied. All's good in a famine.

108* **Сера овца, бела овца - один овечий запах.** *v.* В511, Е14, К277, Х85, Ч64,69
[White or grey, all sheep smell the same.] It's six of one or half a dozen of the other.

109* **Сердитому палка сыщется.** *v.* Б454, Г302, К122
It is easy to find a stick to beat a dog.

110 **Сердце вещун (+ учет добро и худо).**
[The heart is a seer (it sees both good and evil).] The heart has eyes that the brain knows nothing of.

111* **Сердце не камень.**
[The heart is not a stone.] A gentle heart is tied with an easy thread.

112 **Сердце сердцу весть подает.**
Two hearts beat as one.

113* **Сердцу не прикажешь. (Силой милому не быть.) (Сильно мил не будешь.)** *v.* И105, К199, М92
Love cannot be forced (compelled).

114 **Сидением (стоянием) города не берут.**
[Sitting (standing) still never captured a city.] Action is the basis of success. *Cf.* Successful people do what failures put off until tomorrow. Don't sit around and talk about what you are going to do - do it. Easy to keep the castle that was never besieged.

115   **Сиди криво а суди прямо.**   *v.* С287
[It's all right to sit askew as long as you think straight.] He that sits well thinks ill.
Cf. Crooked logs make straight fires.

116   **Сидя на колесе, думай чтоб не быть под колесом.**
[Sitting at the wheel, take heed lest you get run over.] He sits not sure that sits too high.
Cf. A man who flings a stone up a mountain, may have it rolled back upon himself.

117   **Сидячий стоячего перетянет.**   *v.* Б332, Х105
[A sitter prevails over one who stands.] Sit a while and go a mile.

118   **Сило закон ломит (преступает). (Сило солому ломит.)**   *v.* Г76,87, У54, Ч136
[Force prevails over law (breaks straw).] Might is right. *SPL.* ius vi obruitur.

119   **Сило и слава богатству послушны.**   *v.* Д180
[Money rules power and glory.] *Cf.* Money is the only monarch.

120*   **Сило уму уступает.**   *v.* Б140, И49, Р28
Wisdom is better than strength. Policy goes beyond strength.

121   **Сильна правда да деньги сильней.**
[Truth is potent but money is omnipotent.] Beauty is potent but money is omnipotent.
Money is the ace of trumps.

122*   **Синица в руках лучше соловья в лесе.**   *v.* Б231, Д393, Ж169, Л152
A bird [titmouse] in the hand is better than two [a nightingale] in the bush.

123*   **Скажи с кем ты друг, а я скажу кто ты таков.**   *v.* В359, З15, С12,28
Tell me who your friends are and I'll tell you who you are. *Cf.* Tell me with whom
you travel (thou goest) and I'll tell you who you are (thee what thou doest). A man is
known by the company he keeps.

124   **Скажи свинье, свинья борову, а боров всему городу.**   *v.* В566, Р40
[Tell the pig and the pig tells the hog and the hog tells the whole town.] Those who
bring gossip will carry it. *Cf.* Tell a woman and you tell the whole world. A tale never
loses in the telling. Scandal grows with the telling.

125*   **Сказавши, слово не воротишь.**   *v.* В681, С178,182
A word spoken is past recalling. Words once spoken can never be recalled. Words
have wings and cannot be recalled.

126   **Сказал бы словечко, да волк недалечко.**   *v.* Л90, О149, У62
[I'd have told you but the wolf is near.] *Cf.* Loose talk costs lives. Walls have ears.

127   **Сказано - не доказано, надо делать.**   *v.* В561, Г185, Д294
Deeds will show themselves and words will pass away. Don't sit around talking about
what you're going to do - do it. *Cf.* Good words without deeds are but rushes and reeds.

128*   **Сказанное слово серебяное (медное), а несказанное золотое.**   *v.* Р23, С181
Speech is silver, silence is golden.

129*   **Сказано - сделано.**
No sooner said than done. *Lat.* dictum, factum.

130   **Скакать корова не родилась.**   *v.* И86, К200
[The cow was not born to gallop.] You cannot make a crab walk straight.

131* Скандал и в благородном семействе.   *v.* B140,159, И18
      Accidents will happen in the best regulated families.

132* Скатертью дорога.   *v.* П117
      Good riddance. Good riddance to bad rubbish.

133* Склеенная посуда два века живет.   *v.* Б218, Л82, С160
      [A broken dish repaired can last forever.] Ill vessels seldom miscarry. *Lat.* malum vas
      non frangitur.

134   Сколь часто падаешь, столь часто вставай.   *v.* X78
      [As often as you fall, get up.] Success comes in rising every time you fall. Never say die.

135   Сколько б утка не бодрилась, а гусем не бывать.   *v.* B398,439, И74,106, С227
      [Try as it will, the duck cannot be a goose.] A buzzard never makes a good hawk.

136* Сколько веревку не вить, а концу быть.   *v.* Б471, E37, К33, Н374,553, С139, Т14
      [Regardless of how long you make a rope, it will always have an end.] *said of crime,*
      which "will out." Everything has an end. At length the fox is brought to the furrier. The
      longest day has an end.

137   Сколько воды не пить, а пьяному не быть.   *v.* B368, Г296, К50
      [You won't get drunk no matter how much water you drink.] Whether you boil snow or
      pound it, you can have but water of it.

138* Сколько волка ни корми, а он все к лесу глядит.   *v.* B392, У8
      [The wolf still looks to the wood no matter how much you feed him.] The wolf may lose
      his teeth, but never his nature. The wolf may change his coat but not his nature.
      SPL. lupus pilos mutat, non animum (mores). *EA.* lupus pilum mutat, non mentem.

139   Сколько вору ни воровать, (а) кнута (виселице) не миновать.   *v.* B422, Н374, С136
      [No matter how much he steals, the thief will not escape the lash (gallows).] The end of
      the thief is the gallows. *Cf.* All thieves come to some bad end. He that does what he
      should not, shall feel what he would not.

140* Сколько голов, столько умов.   *v.* P26, С142,283, Ч89
      So many men (heads), so many minds (wits). *Lat.*Ter.*Phorm.*2.4.14: quot homines, tot
      sententiae.

141* Сколько лет, сколько зим.   *v.* С278
      [So many years, so many winters.] Long time no see.

142   Сколько людей, столько и лекарей.   *v.* Л23, С140
      So many men, so many minds[physicians]. The healthful man can give counsel to the
      sick. *Lat.* facile cum valemus recta consilia aegrotis damus.

143   Сколько милости, а вдвое лихости. *v.* M118

144   Сколько ни ликовать, а без слез не миновать.
      [You cannot escape tears no matter how happy you are.] Tears and trouble are the lot of
      all. *Cf.* Laugh at leisure, you may weep ere night.

145   Сколько ни петь, а амином вершить.   *v.* Д160, Н529
      [No matter how much you sing you will end on amen.]*i.e. all church choruses in the*
      Russian Orthodox liturgy end with "amen." Be the day never so long, at last comes
      evensong. All things must end.

146 **Сколько ни служить, а в отставке быть.** *v.* П158
[No matter how much you work, eventually you must retire.] There's a good time coming.

147 **Сколько пива, столько и песен.** *v.* З32, Р44
[As long as there's beer, there's song.]*Cf.*Merry's the feast making till we come to the reckoning.

148 **Сколько сможет, столько и сгложет.**
[He will gnaw as much as he can.] Once you start eating, it's hard to stop.

149 **Сколько сможется (хочется), столько и хочется (сможется).**
[One wants (has) as much as one has (wants).] *Cf.* You want the thing you have. Take all you want, but eat all you take.

150 **Сколько с быком ни биться, а молока от него не добиться.** *v.* К52

151 **Сколько цвету и цвести, а быть опадать.** *v.* Х46
[As much as a flower may bloom, it must whither.] The fairest flowers must soonest fade. *Cf.* All good things must end.

152* **Скорая женитьба - видимый рок.** *v.* Ж70, К119, Р34
[A hasty marriage has a foreseeable fate.] *Cf.* Marry in haste and repent at leisure.

153 **Скорее дело вершишь, коли судью подаришь.** *v.* М85, Н370, С300,304
[Bribe the judge and gain a speedier judgment.] *Cf.* Who greases his way travels easily.

154 **Скорее можно осла плясать (медведя грамот) научить.** *v.* Б207
[It's easier to teach an ass to dance (bear to read).] *SPL.* facilius asinum docere freno currere. *Cf.* He that teaches a scorner does an injury to himself.

155* **Скоро да не споро.** *v.* Б300, К235,305, С258
More haste, less speed.

156* **Скоро (сказка) сказывается, да не скоро (дело) делается.** *v.* Г186, Л27,36, Н231
Sooner said than done. *originally a refrain in traditional folk tales.*

157 **Скорость нужна, а поспешность вредна.** *v.* Д47
[Speed is needed, not haste.] Make haste slowly.

158 **Скоротишь, не воротишь.** *v.* О85

159 **Скорый поспех людям на смех.** *v.* Б300, Г90, Д123,146, П188
Haste trips up its own heels.

160 **Скрипучее дерево два века стоит.** *v.* Б218, Л82, С133,269
A creaking door (gate) hangs long on its hinges.

161 **Скуп, себе добра хочет.** *v.* Р71, Т62
[The miser seeks good for himself.] The more you get, the more you want. Avarice (greed) overreaches itself. Avarice is never satisfied. The greedy never know when they have had enough. *Cf.* Poverty wants many things, and avarice all.

162 **Скупой богач беднее нищего.** *v.* Д487, Ж150,163, З160
A rich miser is poorer than a poor man. Fools live poor to die rich.

163   **Скупой больше платит, а ленивый больше ходит.**   *v.* Л47, П116
[Avarice spends more and sloth walks farther.] The covetous spend more than the liberal.

164   **Скупой запирает крепко и подносит редко.**   *v.* Б192, Д13,71
[Misers hoard fast and give seldom.] Some have a short arm for giving and a long arm for getting.

165   **Скупые умирают, а дети сундуки отпирают.**   *v.* О21
[Misers die and their sons pry open their bags.] Covetous mens' chests are rich, not they. A miser's son is a spendthrift. *SPL.* tenacem sequitur prodigem. *Cf.* He that hoards up money takes pains for other men.

166   **Скупые что пчелы - всегда мед собирают а после сами умирают.**   *v.* О21
[Misers gather like bees and then die.] Covetous men live drudges to die wretches.

167   **Скучен день до вечера, коли делать нечего.**   *v.* Б55,104, В505, Н450, О144
[It's a dull day when there's nothing to do.] It's more pain to do nothing than something.

168   **Славны бубны за горами.**   *v.* Б227, В178,583, Ч118,129
[Tambourines are fine over the hills.] *i.e. things seem better at a distance.* The grass is always greener on the other side of the fence. Hills are green (blue) far away. Distant hills look greener. Faraway cows have long horns. Wonderful in appearance are the horns of a cow beyond the sea.

169   **Сладкое с излишеством сделается горьким.**   *v.* В514,591, И40,116, М211, С341
[Excessive sweet tastes bitter.] When the cat is full, the milk tastes sour. Too much pudding will choke a dog. Too much sweet spoils the best coffee.

170   **Сладок мед, да не по две ложки в рот.**   *v.* И40, С169,341
[Honey is sweet a little at a time.] Too much honey cloys the stomach.

171*   **Слеза скоро сохнет.**
Nothing dries sooner than tears. *Gr.* οὐδὲν ϑᾶσσον ξηραίνεται δακρίου. *Lat.* lacrima nihil citius arescit.

172*   **Слезами горю не поможешь.**   *v.* А28, О4, П27, Ч92
[Tears do not relieve sorrow.] Two barrels of tears will not heal a bruise. Tears bring nobody back from the grave. Tears never yet wound up a clock nor worked a steam engine. *Cf.* Never grieve for what you cannot help.

173*   **Слепой зрячего ведет.** *sarc.*   *v.* Н423
[The blind man leads the sighted.] The blind man wishes to show the way. *Gr.* τυφλὸς ὁδηγεῖ. *Lat.* caecus monstrat viam (iter monstrare vult).

174   **Слепой курице - все пшеница.**   *v.* Г228, Л71, С80,226
[Everything is wheat to a blind chicken.] The blind eats many a fly. *Cf.* Better to be blind than to see ill.

175*   **Слепой слепца водит, оба в яму (ни зги не видят).**   *v.* Д470
If the blind lead the blind, both shall fall into the ditch.

176   **Слепой сказал «посмотрим».**
Let me see, as the blind man said. *said as an expression of doubt.*

177   **Словам тесно, да мыслям просторно.**   *v.* Г178
[Words are binding, thoughts free.] I say little, but I think the more. *Cf.* It's hard to find modest words to express immodest things.

178   **Слово выпустишь, так и вилам не втащишь.**   *v.* В689, Ч83
A word and a stone let go cannot be called back. *Cf. Gr.* ῾ΡίΨας λόγον τις οὐκ ἀνερεῖται πάλιν.

179*   **Слово давать и слово держать должно быть одно и тоже.**   *v.* П75
[Giving and keeping one's word ought to be one and the same.] A man's word is as good as his bond. *Cf.* To be as good as one's word. Let deeds correspond with words. Plaut.*Pseud.*108: dictis facta suppetant.

180   **Слово не стрела, да пуще стрелы.**   *v.* Б158, Я22
[Words are not arrows, but worse.] Words cut more than swords. A word spoke is an arrow let fly. *Lat.* plaga linguae est hastae ictus.

181*   **Слово серебро - молчание золото.**   *v.* Р23, С128
Speech is silvern, silence golden.

182*   **Слово что воробей, вылетит - не поймаешь.**   *v.* В689, С125, Ч83
Words have wings and cannot be recalled. *Cf.* A word spoken is past recalling. A word and stone let go cannot be recalled.

183   **Словом поспешен, скоро посмешен.**
[He that is quick to talk is quick to appear silly.] Said first and thought after makes many a disaster.

184   **Слон родился, слон и есть.**
[Born an elephant, ever an elephant.] An elephant is an elephant, whether on high or on low ground.

185*   **Слоны трутся, а между собой комаров давят.**   *v.* Б16, К186, П4
[When elephants rub, mosquitos are crushed.] The Indian elephant cares not for a gnat. *Lat. EA.* indus elephantus haud curat culicem. *Cf.* The pleasures of the mighty are the tears of the poor.

186   **Слухом земля полнится (слух землю полнит).**   *v.* С243
[Rumour sweeps the world.] *said to conceal one's source of information.* Rumour is a great traveller. *Cf.* A little bird told me. Gossip needs no carriage.

187   **Слушай ухом а не брюхом.** *vulg.*   *v.* Б368, Г227, У7
[Listen with your ears, not your belly.] *remonstrance when asked to repeat; as in the phrase "unplug your ears." Cf.*The belly wants ears. Sen.*Ad.Luc.*21.11: venter praecepta non audit. The belly will not listen to advice.

188   **Служить бы рад, да прислуживаться тошно.**   *v.* В444
[Eager to work but loathe to take orders.] He that serves, must serve. They that are bound must obey.

189*   **Смелому Бог помогает.**   *v.* Х84
Fortune favours the bold. *Lat.* Verg.*Aen.*10.284: audentes fortuna iuvet.

190   **Смелому горох хлебать, а робкому и (пустых) щей (редьки) не видать.**   *v.* С192
[The bold get peas, while the timid - not even plain broth.] None but the brave deserves the fair.

191   **Смелый приступ не хуже победы.**   *v.* O171
        A bold heart is half the battle.

192   **Смелый там найдет где робкий потерял.**   *v.* Б109, Н532, С190
        [The bold will win where the timid lose.] He most prevails who nobly dares. Success comes in cans, failures in can'ts. *Cf.* Faint heart never won fair lady.

193*   **Смерть, да жена, Богом суждена. (Смерть да женитьба животы окажут.)**
        [Death and marriage are fated.] Marriages are made in heaven.   *v.* З110, С302
        Cf. Nothing is certain but death and taxes. Death is prepared for everyone. *Lat.* mors omnibus parata.

194   **Смерть дорогу сыщет (найдет причину).**   *v.* Г101, Н20, Х74
        [Death will find the way (a reason).] One excuse is as good as another. Where there's a will, there's a way. *Cf.* Nothing so certain as death. Death meets us everywhere. *Lat.* mors aliquam causam semper habere solet.

195   **Смерть злым, а добрым вечная память.**   *v.* Д279,332, Х53
        [The evil die, but the good live on in mens' memories.] Good men must die, but death cannot kill them quite.

196   **Смерть мужу покой.**
        [Death is a husband's rest.] *Cf.* Death is a remedy for all ills. Earth is the best shelter.

197*   **Смерть не за горами, а за плечами.**   *v.* Б445, Д463, Н367, Ч3
        [Death is not over the hill, but over the shoulder.] At every hour death is near. Death keeps no calendar.

198   **Смерть не разбирает чина (+ а ведет равно и крестьянина и дворянина).**   *v.* Ж152,
        [Death does not recognize rank (but treats peasants and nobles alike).]   У57, Ц5
        Death is the great leveller. Death is no respecter of persons. Death and the grave make no distinction of persons. *Lat.* omnia mors aequat.

199   **Смерть о саване не тужит.**   *v.* С214
        [Death grieves not for the shroud.] *Cf.* Our last garment is made without pockets.

200*   **Смерть терпеть легче нежели ждать.**   *v.* Ж161
        Fear of death is worse than death itself.

201   **Сметану любить, корову кормить.**   *v.* В616, Л169,173, У88
        [If you like cream, feed your cow.] If you want roasted bananas, you must burn your fingers first. If you put nothing into your purse, you can take nothing out.

202*   **Смех и грех (горе).**
        [Both tragic and comic.] One doesn't know whether to laugh or cry.

203   **Смирение девушке (девичья) ожерелье.**
        Silence is the best ornament of a woman.

204   **Смирного человека всегда дураком зовут.**
        [A quiet man is always called a fool.] It is better to be silent and be thought a fool than to speak and remove all doubt.

205   **Смирную собаку и кочет побьет.**   *v.* Н41, Х66
        [Even a cock can beat a docile dog.] A coward is more exposed to quarrels than a man of spirit. Everyone gives a push to a tumbling man. *Cf.* The weakest goes to the wall.

206 **Смола к дубу не пристанет.** *v.* Д287
[Sap won't stick to the oak.] Virtue is a thousand shields. Virtue is the safest helmet.

207 **Смолоду охотно, а под старость перхотно.** *v.* В173, Ч39
Young mens' knocks old men feel. *Lat.* quae peccamus iuvenes ea luimus senes. *Cf.*
If you lie upon roses when young, you'll lie upon thorns when old.

208* **Смолоду прореха - под старость дыра.** *v.* С23, Ч8
[A tear in youth becomes a hole in old age.] He that corrects not small faults will not
control great ones. The excesses of our youth are draughts upon our old age. *Cf.* Reckless
youth makes rueful age. Where there's a mouse hole there'll soon be a rat hole.

209 **Смотри дерево по плодам, а человека по делам.** *v.* Б316, Д198,409
Judge a tree by its fruit [and a man by his deeds.] Judge a man by his deeds, not by
his words. *Cf.* Deeds are fruits, words but leaves.

210* **Снаружи красота, внутри пустота.** *v.* Д310, Л87, С51
Beauty is only skin deep. An angel on top but a devil underneath.

211 **Снаружи мило, а внутри гнило.** *v.* Г112, Л85, С51
Fair face, foul heart. Fair without, false within.

212* **Снизу не учат, а сверху.** *v.* Н468,491, Ч106, Я20
[Veterans, not beginners must teach.] You have to be smarter than the dog to teach him
tricks. *Cf.* †Children can teach old folks.

213 **Сноп без перевясла - солома.** *v.* Б86,203, Д441, Е31
[A sheaf without a strap is just a bundle of straw.] *i.e. organisation requires leadership.*
Thirteen staves and never a hoop will not make a barrel. *Cf.* In union strength. Willows
are weak, yet they bind.

214* **Снявши голову по волосам не плачут.** *v.* Н453, П175,311, С199
[It's too late to care for the hair when the head is off.] It's no time to stoop when the
head is off. It's no use crying over spilt milk. *Cf.* It's too late to shut the stable door after
the horse has bolted.

215* **Со лжи люди не мрут, а впредь им не верят.** *v.* В453,666, К224, Л64
[A lie doesn't kill people, only their credibility.] He that once deceives is ever suspected.
A liar is not believed when he speaks the truth. Tell a lie once and you are always a liar
to that person.

216 **Со стороны виднее.**
Lookers-on see most of the game.

217 **Со счастьем хорошо и по грибы ходить.**
[It's good to go gathering mushrooms when you're lucky.] Good luck beats early rising.

218 **Собака и на владыку лает.**
[Dogs bark even at bishops.] A little dog will run a lion out of his own yard.

219 **Собака лает, ветер носит.**
[The dog barks and the wind carries it.] The moon does not heed the barking of dogs.
Cf. The braying of an ass does not reach heaven.

220* Собака на сене лежит, сама не ест и другим не дает. *v.* Н424
The dog in the manger won't eat the oats nor let anyone else eat them. *Cf.* A dog in the kitchen desires no company. While the dog gnaws bone, companions would be none. *Gr. Aesop.*404: κύων ἐν φάτμῃ. *Lat.* dum canis os rodit, sociari pluribus odit.

221* Собака собаку не съест. *v.* Б240, В389,435, И21, К155
Dog does not eat dog. *Lat.* canis caninum non edit.

222 Собака хватлива была, так и волки съели. *v.* Х16
[The dog was frisky until the wolves got it.] *Cf.* If you play with the bull you'll get a horn in the eye. A bad dog never sees the wolf.

223* Собака что лает редко кусает. *v.* Н181,234
Barking dogs seldom bite.

224 Собаке собачья и смерть. *v.* Б377, Ж153, К29, С81
[A dog dies a dog's death.] An ill life, an ill death. Such life, such death.

225 Сова о сове, а всяк о себе. *v.* В527,551, С74, Х12
[An owl for an owl] and every man for himself.

226* Сова спит, а куры видит. *v.* Г228, Л71, С80,174, Ч84
[A sleeping owl dreams of chickens.] The pig dreams of acorns, the goose of maize. The net of the sleeper catches fish. *Lat.* dormientis rete trahit.

227 Сова хоть бы под небеса летала, а все соколом не будет. *v.* В398,439,И74,106,
[However high the owl may fly, it cannot be a falcon.] Л42, Н194, С135
A carrion kite will never be a good hawk. A buzzard never makes a good hawk.

228 Совестливый и изза сытого стола голодным встает.
[The shy man even leaves a full table hungry.] At the table it becomes no one to be bashful. *Cf.* Shameful leaving is worse than shameful eating. Never be ashamed to eat your meat.

229 Совесть паче тысячи свидетелей.
Conscience is a thousand witnesses. *SPL.* conscientia mille testes.

230* Совет - хорошо, а дело лучше (а два лучше). *v.* Д116,355, Н270
Actions speak louder than words.

231 Согласного стада и волк не берет. *v.* Б156, Е31, У105
[Not even the wolf can take a united flock.] A lone sheep is in danger of the wolf. *Cf.* In concord there is strength.

232 Сокол с места, а ворона на место. *v.* Н284, Х85
[A crow to succeed a falcon.] Nothing so bad that it couldn't be worse. Bad is called good when worse comes along. *Cf.* New prince, new bondage. If you leave your place, you lose it.

233 Солдат в отпуску - рубаха из порток. *v.* Г63
[A soldier on furlough lets his shirt out of his trousers.] A little nonsense now and then is relished by the best of men. *Cf.* Rules were made to be broken. When the cat's away the mice will play.

234* Солнце сияет на злые и благия. *v.*Д365, И20,56
*Matt.*5.45: **The sun shines upon all alike.**

235   **Солнышко нас не дожидается.**   *v.* Г199, Д356
[The sun won't wait on us.] Time and tide wait for no man.

236   **Соловья баснями не кормят.**   *v.* Б21,367, В376, Г226,227, Е45, И101, У7, Ш14
[You can't feed a nightingale with talk.] Fair words fill not the belly. Fine words butter no parsnips.

237   **Солома с огнем не улежит.**   *v.* В141, Ш7
Fire cannot be hidden in flax.

238*   **Сон лучше всякого лекарства.**
Sleep is better than medicine.

239   **Сон не обогатит.**   *v.* С245
[Sleep won't make you rich.] Sleep is the poor man's treasure. Love not sleep, lest thou come to poverty. *Prov.*20.13: noli diligere somnum, ne te egestas opprimat. *Cf.* A sleeping fox catches no poultry. Sleeping cats catch no mice.

240*   **Сон смерти брат.**
Sleep is the brother of death. *Gr.*ὁ ὕπνος θανάτου ἀδελφός. *Lat.* consanguineus Let sopor.

241   **Сонный что мертвый.**
Sleep is the image of death.

242*   **Сор из избы не выносят.**   *v.* И80, Н256
Do not wash dirty linen in public.

243   **Сорока на хвосте принесла.**   *v.* С186
A [magpie] little bird told me.

244*   **Спасибо в карман не кладут. (Спасибом сыт не будешь.)**   *v.* З43, И100, П134
You can't put "thanks" into your pocket. [Thanks won't fill your belly.] *Cf.* Thanks is poor pay. Keep your thanks to feed your chickens (cat).

245   **Спать долго - жить с долгом.**   *v.* Л51, С239
[Sleep late and wake with debt.] *Cf.* He that lies long abed, his estate feels it.

246   **Спереди лижет а сзади царапает.**   *v.* З130, К171, Н92,122
[Licks your hand but claws your back.] A honey tongue, a heart of gall. He has honey in the mouth and a razor at the girdle.

247   **Спесивому хвала лучше дара.**
[The proud treasure praise more than gifts.] Fair words make fools fain. *Cf.* A nod from a lord is breakfast for a fool.

248   **Спесивый высоко мостится да низко ложится.**
[Pride reaches high but falls low.] Pride goes before a fall. Pride goes before and sham follows after.

249   **Спесивый не взглянет, а слепой не рассмотрит.**
[The proud will not look as the blind will not see.] The proud will rather lose than as their way. *Cf.*It is good beating proud folks for they'll not complain.

250   **Спесь в добро не вводит.**   *v.* С24
[Pride leads to no good.] Pride goes before a fall (destruction). *Cf.* Pride joined wit many virtues chokes them all.

251   Спешить хорошо лишь блох ловить.   *v.* П189
        Nothing must be done hastily but the killing of fleas.

252   Спи в ненастье а жни в ведро.   *v.* В30, К180
        Make hay while the sun shines [and sleep in bad weather].

253   Спорник лучше потаковщика.   *v.* Л172, Н178, У109
        [Better to dispute than to indulge.]   A wise enemy is better than a foolish friend.

254*   Справит горбатого могила, а упрямого дубина. *v.* Г250

255*   Спустя лето (да) по малину в лес не ходят. *v.* О91

256   Ссора до добра не доводит.   *v.* Б358
        [Quarrels never come to any good.]   *Cf.* From one quarrel comes a hundred sins.
        Quarrelers do not live long. Disputing and borrowing cause grief and sorrowing.

257   Ссуды пишут на железной доске, а долги на песке.   *v.* Д369, У23
        [Loans are engraved in metal, debts are written on sand.] Creditors have better memories
        than debtors.

258   Стань торопиться, из рук все повалится.   *v.* К305
        More haste, less speed. Haste trips up its own heels.

259   Стар (старый конь) (старая кобыла) борозды не испортит.
        [The old mare won't spoil the furrow.]   An old ox makes a straight furrow.

260   Стар козел да крепки рога.   *v.* У61
        Old oxen [goats] have stiff horns.

261*   Старая любовь долго помнится (не ржавеет).
        Old love will not be forgotten. Old love does not rust.

262   Старая погудка на новый лад.   *v.* Т3,26
        [The same tune in a new arrangement.] *i.e. the same old story.* A new tout in an old horn.

263   Старая пословица не мимо молвится (во век не сломится).   *v.* П184
        Old saws speak truth.

264*   Старая собака не привыкнет ощейника носит. (Старую собаку приучить к цепи
   трудно.)   *v.* Н463, С273, Ч46
        An old dog won't be easily brought to wear a collar. *Lat.* **canis antiquus catenae**
        assuefieri non potest. You cannot teach an old dog new tricks. *SPL.* psittacus senex
        spernit ferulam.

265   Старина с мозгом.   *v.* В483, К307, Ч42
        Older and wiser. The essence of age is intellect.

266*   Старого воробья на мякине не обманешь.   *v.* Л73, С268
        You cannot catch old birds with chaff. *Diog.*4.7: γέρων ἀλόπηξ οὐχ ἁλίσκεται.

267*   Старого дурака ничем не исправить.   *v.* К141
        There's no fool to the old fool.

268   **Старого орла трудно на гнезде поймать. (Старому в зеркале калач не продашь.)**
[An old eagle is not easily caught.] [You won't sell an old   *v.* Л73
man a cake through a looking glass.] An old fox is not easily snared.

269   **Старое дерево скрипит да стоит, а молодое да валится.**   *v.* Б185,415, C160
[An old tree screeches but stands, while the young sapling falls.] Old and tough, young
and tender. An old cart well used may outlast a new one abused. *Cf.* †An old horse slips
quicker than a young one.

270*   **Старость не радость.**
[Age is no rage.] Age brings grief. *Lat.* aetas male habet. *Cf.* Old and cold. Life
protracted is protracted woe.

271   **Старость приходит не с радостью, но со слабостью.**   *v.* П257
A hundred disorders has old age. Age breeds aches. Old age is a sickness of itself.
Lat. Ter.*Ph.*4.1: senectus ipsa morbus est.

272   **Старую собаку не батькой звать.**
[Don't call every old dog "gramps."] *i.e. not every elder deserves respect.* Age makes a
man white but not better. *Cf.* Old springs give no price. †Old age is honourable.

273*   **Старую собаку новым фокусам не научишь.**   *v.* Н463, C264, Ч46
You cannot teach an old dog new tricks.

274   **Старые немощи трудно лечить.**
Old age is a malady of which one dies. Old age is an incurable disease.
Lat. Sen.*Lucil.*108.28: senectus insanabilis morbus est.

275   **Старый волк знает толк.**   *v.* Л73, Н360
Old foxes want no tutors.

276   **Старый ворон даром не каркнет.**
An old dog barks [crow croaks] not in vain.

277*   **Старый друг лучше новых двух.** *v.* Л160

278   **Старый старится, молодой растет.**   *v.* C141
[The old get older, the young grow.] Age lasts, youth devours. *Cf.* The old one crows,
the young one learns.

279*   **Старый что малый.**
[An old man is like a child.] Old men are twice children. *Lat.*   *EA.* bis pueri senes.

280   **Старый хочет спать, а молодой играть.**   *v.* B175, M147
[The old seek sleep, the young crave play.] *Cf.* Nothing more playful than a young cat,
nor more grave than an old man. *Lat.* Sen.*Hipp.*453: laetitia iuvenem, frons decet tristis
senem.

281   **Старыми руками трудно кошелек развязывать.**   *v.* Ч103
[Old hands do not easily untie purse-strings.] The older the bird, the more unwillingly
it parts with its feathers. The older, the more covetous. *Cf.* When all sins grow old,
covetousness is young. *Lat.* cum omnia vitia senescunt, avaritia iuvenescit.

282   **Стерпится, слюбится.**   *v.* Ж132, И3, П68,244
[Once you're used to it, you'll like it.] *often said of a loveless marriage.* Once a use,
ever a custom. Custom reconciles us to everything.

283 Сто голов, сто умов. *v.* С140

284 **Стоит выиграть чтоб не бояться проиграть.** *v.* А8, Р92
[One must win in order not to fear losing.] Still he fishes that catches one. *Cf.* Win at first and lose at last. Success has ruined many a man.

285 **Стоит овца барана.** *v.* Н414
[One lamb is worth a sheep.] To give a pea for a bean.

286 **Стоит человек по горло в воде, а просит напиться.**
[Up to his neck in water and still asks to drink.] *Gr.* ἐν θαλλάσσῆ ζητεῖς ὑδῶρ. *Lat.* medio fluminis queris aquam. The sea complains it wants water.

287 **Стой криво, да прямую речь держи.** *v.* Б404, Г126, Д411, И23, С115, У75
[Stand crooked but speak straight.] *Cf.* Crooked furrows grow straight corn.

288* **Стоячая вода плеснеет.**
Standing pools gather filth.

289 **Стоячему с сидячим трудно говорить.**
[A standing man cannot converse easily with one who is sitting.] *Cf.* Little knows the fat man what the lean does mean.

290 **Страх путь кажет.** *v.* И142
[Fear shows the way.] Fear is a great inventor. Fear gives wings. *Lat.* timor addidit alas.

291 **Страхов много а смерть одна.** *v.* Г299, С98, Ш2
[There are many fears but only one death.] A man can die but once. Cowards die often.

292* **Страшно дело до начину.** *v.* В642, З106, Л75
[The job is dreadful before beginning.] Every beginning is hard.

293 **Стреляй в куст - виноватого Бог сыщет.**
[Aim for the bush - God will smite the guilty.] Revenge is a morsel for God.
Gr. Theocrit. εὑρὲ θεὸς ἀλιτρόν.

294 **Стриженая девка косы не заплетет (не успеет стриженая девка косы заплести).**
[Faster than a short-haired girl can do her braid.] Before you could say Jack Robinson. Quicker than boiling asparagus. *Lat. EA.* velocius quam asparagi coquntur.

295 **Строгая власть всем ненавистна.**
Mickle power makes many enemies.

296 **Строгий закон виноватых творит.** *v.* Г42, Е24, Н186
[Harsh laws create offenders.] The more laws, the more offenders. Wrong laws make short governance.

297 **Стыд не дым, глаз не выест.** *v.* Б356,357
[Shame is not like smoke that will sting your eyes.] *i.e. can be tolerated. Cf.* Sticks and stones may break my bones but names never hurt me. Conscience like a cheverel skin (kid-leather).

298 Стену лбом нельзя проколотить. *v.* Л11

299 **Суд крив, коли судья лжив.**
[It is a crooked trial whose judge is dishonest.] *Cf.* From a foolish judge, a quick sentence. A corrupt judge weighs truth badly. *Lat.* Hor.*Sat.*2.2.8: male verum examinat omnis corruptus iudex.

300 **Судейские ворота без серебра не отворяются.** *v.* M85, C153,301
[A judge's doors open only to silver.] *Cf.* No lock will hold against the power of gold. *Lat.* Syr.85: bene perdit nummos iudici cum dat nocens.

301 **Судьям то и полезно, что им в карман полезно.** *v.* C153,300
[What's good for the judge is what's good for his pocket.] A pocketful of right needs a pocketful of gold.

302 **Суженого и конем не объедешь (и водой не обойдешь).** *v.* З110, C193
[You cannot escape your fated husband either on horseback or over seas.] Marriages are made in heaven. *SPL.* coniugia sunt fatalia. *Cf.* There's no flying from fate.

303 **Сума да тюрьма дадут ума.**
[Poverty and jail instruct.] Adversity comes with instruction in its hand.

304 **Сухая ложка рот дерет.** *v.* H370
[A dry spoon sticks to your mouth.] *said of "buttering someone up."* Who greases his way travels easily.

305 **Сущее имя давать.** *v.* X26, *Ap.*1.7
To call a spade a spade. *SPL.* scapha scapha est appellanda.

306 **Счастливое дитя и без сорочки счастливо.** *v.* H401, C323
[The fortunate child is lucky without wealth.] It is better to be born lucky than rich. Better to have good fortune than to be a rich man's child.

307 **Счастливому везде добро (хорошо) (счастится).** *v.* K162, T65
[A lucky man does well anywhere.] He dances well to whom fortune pipes.

308* **Счастливые часов не наблюдают.** *v.* C19
When a man is happy he does not hear the clock strike.

309 **Счастливый и в огне не сгорит и в воде не потонет.** *v.* K39, O59
[Neither fire nor water can harm the fortunate.] Give a man fortune (luck) and cast him into the sea. *Cf.* Nothing succeeds like success. Like a cat, he always falls on his feet. He is like a cork, nothing will sink him. *EA.* tanquam suber.

310* **Счастливый скачет, а несчастный плачет.** *v.* B71,210,218, Д82, K186, O62,76
[The lucky dance while the unlucky cry.] Some have the hap, some stick in the gap.

311 **Счастливый ходит, на клад набредет, а несчастный пойдет и гриба не найдет.**
[The lucky stumble upon treasures; the unlucky cannot even find a mushroom.]
Some people would fall down a sewer and find a ring.

312* **Счастливым быть - всем досадить.** *v.* Г95, Ч121
[Being happy makes others miserable.] Envy doesn't enter an empty house.

313* **Счастливым прежде смерти назваться нельзя.** *v.* B204, T44, X4
Praise no man till he is dead. Call no man happy till he is dead.

314   **Счастье бедному алтын, богатому миллион.**   *v.* К269
        [Three *kopeks* make a poor man happy, but it takes a million for the rich.] Poor folk are
        fain of little. *Cf.* Luck and halfpenny are goods enough.

315   **Счастье в воздухе не вьется, а руками достается.**   *v.* Н176, С322
        Luck is often pluck. Diligence is the mother of good luck. There is no luck in laziness.
        God reaches us good things by our own hands. *Cf.* Good luck is a lazy man's explanation
        of another's success.

316   **Счастье без ума ничто (дырявая сума).**
        [Luck without wisdom is worthless (like a purse with a hole).] *Cf.* †You don't need
        brains if you have luck.

317   **Счастье зови а горе терпи.**
        The worse luck now, the better another time. Bad luck often brings good luck.

318   **Счастье и дураку помогает, а от несчастья и умный погибает.**   *v.* П218
        [Good luck helps a fool while bad luck may ruin even a wise man.] An ounce of luck
        is worth a pound of wisdom.

319   **Счастье и несчастье на одном коне (полозу) ездят (едут).**   *v.* Б326, В675, С328
        [Fortune and misfortune ride the same steed (sled).] Great fortune brings with it great
        misfortune.

320   **Счастье идет на костылях, а несчастье летит на крыльях.**   *v.* Б42, Г271, З123
        [Luck limps on crutches while misfortune flies on wings.] Misfortune arrives on
        horseback but departs on foot.

321   **Счастье, как и стекло, легко разбивается.**
        Fortune is like glass, it breaks when it is brightest. *SPL.* fortuna vitrea est, tum cum
        (maxime) splendet, frangitur.

322   **Счастье крепких ног требует.**   *v.* С315
        [Fortune requires strong legs.] There is no luck in laziness. *SPL.* difficile est aequa
        commoda mente pati.

323*   **Счастье лучше богатства.**   *v.* Н401, С306
        [Luck is better than wealth.] It is better to be born lucky than rich. Better be fortunate
        than rich.

324   **Счастье многих обманывает.**   *v.* К148
        Fortune is fickle.

325   **Счастье на коне, а несчастье под конем.**
        [Fortune rides upon the saddle and misfortune upon the crupper.] *Cf.* Marriage rides upon
        the saddle and repentance upon the crupper.

326   **Счастье - на мосту с чашкой.**
        [Fortune - panhandling by the bridge.] *said of beggars. Cf.* Bad luck is good luck for
        someone.

327   **Счастье скоро оставит, а добрая надежда никогда.**
        [Luck is quick to abandon, but hope never.] If fortune torments me, hope contents me.

328* Счастье с несчастьем двор обо двор живут (об межу живут).   *v.* В675, С319
Fortune and misfortune are next-door neighbours. Danger is next neighbour to security.

329 Счастье, что Бог не дал медведю волчей смелости, а волку медвежьей силы.
[Lucky that God didn't give the bear a wolf's wiles and the wolf   *v.* Б298, Н277
a bear's stength.] A curst cow has short horns. *Lat.* dat deus immiti cornua curta bovi.

330 Счастье - что палка, о двух концах.   *v.* В71,210,211,218, О76
[Luck is a stick with two ends.] Some have the hap, some stick in the gap.

331 Счастья не поймаешь, счастье не придет.
[Fortune comes to him who goes out to meet it.] *Cf.* Fortune favours the bold. Luck is a good word if you put a "p" before it.

332* Счет дружбы не мешает (портит).   *v.* Б225, Д44, К175, Ч10
[Accounts don't hinder friendship.] Short reckonings make long friends.

333* Счет правды любит.   *v.* Б120
[Accounts brook no error.] Misreckoning is no payment.

334 Сын запоет, и отец не уймет.   *v.* Н520
[A father won't stop his son from singing.] *Cf.* No love to a father's.

335 Сыпь коню мешком, так не будешь ходить пешком.
[Feed your horse well and you won't go on foot.] Corn him well and he'll work better.

336 Сыто, человек спит довольно, а голодно, спит мало.   *v.* Б128
[A man sleeps well on a full stomach, but poorly when hungry.] Who goes to bed supperless, all night tumbles and tosses.

337 Сытого гостя легко потчевать.   *v.* Н340
[It is easy to regale a guest who is full.] Give a bit of cake to one who is going to eat pie. *Cf.* Eat and welcome, fast and heartily welcome.

338* Сытое брюхо к учению глухо (туго).   *v.* Л30
A belly full of gluttony will never study willingly. *Gr.* παχεῖα γαστήρ λεπτὸν οὐ τίκτει. *SPL.* a studii venter nimium distentus abhorret.

339 Сытый волк смирнее ненасытного человека.
[A sated wolf is calmer than a hungry man.] A hungry man is an angry man.

340* Сытый голодного не разумеет.   *v.* Д234
He whose belly is full believes not him who is fasting. He that is warm thinks all so. *Cf.* It takes one to know one.

341 Сытому и мед не мил.   *v.* И30,40,116, М212, С129,170
[Even honey isn't sweet to one who is full.] Too much honey cloys the stomach. When the cat is full, the milk tastes sour.

Т

1   Та беда еще не угасла, а другая и загорелась.   v. Б24, О48,67, П265, Ч51
[One trouble hasn't subsided before another erupts.] Ill comes often on the back of worse.

2* Та ведь хороша была корова к молоку, которая умерла.   v. А1, У91, Ч76
[The better milk cow always dies.] The worth of a thing is best known by the want of it. The fish that escapes is the biggest fish of all. *Cf.* Blessings brighten as they take their flight. He could have sung well before he broke his left shoulder with whistling.

3   Та же щука, да под хреном. (Те же щи, да в другую тарелку.)
(Тот же блин, да на другом блюде.)   v. В487,506, 37,18, С262, Т26
[The same old pike but with horseradish.] [The same soup in a different dish.] [The same *blin*, but on a different plate.] The more it changes, the more it remains the same. *Cf.* To be served with the same sauce. Man changes often but gets better seldom.

4   Та не овца которая с волком гулять пошла.
[It is no sheep that has ambled off with the wolf.] Keep not ill company lest you increase the number.

5   Тайный грех в половину прощен.   v. П260
Sin that is hidden is half forgiven.

6   Так печка печет.   v. В444
[That's how the oven bakes.] That's how the cookie (biscuit) crumbles.

7   Там глупому и ужина где дураков дюжина.   v. В620, К266, П109, С66
[The fool seeks dinner where there are a dozen of his number.] Fools go in crowds. *Cf.* Like will to like. A merry man is usually a fool.

8* Там дрова рубят, а к нам щепки летят.   v. В197,207, 324, Л202, Н117, С1, *Ар.*1.77
[They hew logs and we get the chips.] One does the scathe and another has the scorn. One does the harm and another hears the blame. One beats the bush and another has the bird. *Cf.* Hew not too high lest the chips fall in thine eye.

9* Там и отечество где жить добро (там добро где хлеба довольно).   v. В610,
Where it is well with me, there is my country.   Г7, Ж113, Н445
SPL. patria est ubicunque bene est.

10* Там хорошо где нас нет.   v. В186,583, Д57
[It's always better where we happen not to be.] Some people can see no good near home. The grass is always greener on the other side of the fence. Distance lends enchantment.

11 Твердо крепку брать.
A hard nut to crack.

12   **Твое хоть дороже, краснее - а свое мне милее.**   *v.* B555,622,652, T38, Ч28
[Though yours is dearer and prettier, I prefer my own.] Every man likes his own thing best. Every peddlar thinks well of his pack. Every peddlar praises his own needles.

13   **Твой приговор да тебе же во двор.**   *v.* Д431,456, H107,413, O177, П154, Ч47,72
Curses like chickens come home to roost. *Cf.* Judge not lest ye be not judged.

14*   **Твой дом, твоя и воля.**   *v.* B136,404,579, C72
[Your house, your realm.] Every man is a master in his home. A man is king in his own house. *Lat.* domi suae quilibet rex.

15   **Тебе смешно, а мне к сердцу дошло.**   *v.* 356, И117
Better lose a jest than a friend. *Lat.* Quint.6.3.28 potius amicum quam dictum perdere. *Cf.* The truest jests sound worst in guilty ears.

16   **Телу простор - душе теснота.**   *v.* B2
[What may be spacious for the body is constraining for the soul.] The body is sooner dressed than the soul. *Lat.* corporis delicium, animi exitium.

17   **Теля умерло, хлева (хлеба) прибыло.**   *v.* Б312, B355, H192
[The calf died so there was more food.] There's no loss without some gain. Nothing so bad in which there is not something of good.

18   **Тем люди не играют, от чего умирают.**
It is ill jesting with edged tools.

19   **Темная ночь не навек.**   *v.* B480,Д371, K33, H553, C136
The longest night will have an end.

20*   **Теперь еще цветки, а ягодки впереди.**   *v.* Э4
[Flowers today, berries tomorrow.] Flowers are the pledges of fruit.

21   **Терпение дает умение.**   *v.* O186
[Patience begets skill.] Diligence makes an expert workman. They that have patience may accomplish anything. *Cf.* Only those who have the patience to do simple things perfectly will acquire the skill to do difficult things easily.

22   **Терпение и труд все перетрут.**
[Patience and hard work overcome everything.] Patience conquers. Labour overcomes all things. Care and diligence bring luck. *Lat.* labor omnia vincit. patientia victrix.

23   **Терпение - лучшее спасение.**   *v.* B641, Д375, П232
Patience is the best remedy for every trouble. *SPL.* animus aequus optimum aerumnae condimentum.

24*   **Терпи казак (горе), атаман(ом) будешь.**
[The patient Cossack shall become a chieftain.] Patient men win the day. *Lat.* vincit qui patitur.

25   **Терпя, и камень (железо) треснет.**   *v.* Д339, K98, П288
[With time, stone (steel) will fissure.] Patience wears out stones (pierces the rock). Time devours all things.

26   **Тех же щей, да пожиже влей.**   *v.* C262, T3
[The same soup but watered down.] *i.e. the same thing but worse.* The nature of things does not change.

27   **Тихая вода берега подмывает.**   *v.* К98, М11
[Still waters erode the shores.] *SPL.* altiora flumina, minimo sono labuntur.
The still sow eats up all the draff. The quiet hog drinks the most swill. *Cf.* Constant
dripping wears the stone. *Lat.* gutta cavat lapidem. Still waters are the deepest.

28   **Тихая собака пуще кусает.**   *v.* И139, Н181,234
[Silent dogs bite worse.] The silent dog is the first to bite. *Cf.* Beware of a silent dog
and still water. *Lat.* cave tibi a cane muto et aqua silenti.

29*   **Тихие воды глубоки.**   *v.* В152, Е2, Ч112
Still waters run deep.

30   **Тихий воз будет на горе.**   *v.* Т35
[The slow load will make it up the hill eventually.] To climb steep hills requires slow
pace at first.

31   **Тихо не лихо, а смирнее прибыльнее.**   *v.* Е5
Slow but sure.

32   **Тихо озеро, а чертей полно.**   *v.* В152, Ч112
[A still lake teems with devils.] The stillest humours are always the worst.

33   **Тихое молчание ничему не ответ.**
[Tacit silence is no answer.] Good listening does not mean sitting dumb. Silence is a
still noise. Silence is the ornament of the ignorant.

34   **Тише воды, ниже травы.**   *v.* В154
[Stiller than water, lower than the grass.] *i.e. a meek person.* *Cf.* Study to be quiet.
Lat. quieti sitis.

35*   **Тише едешь, дальше будешь.**   *v.* П141, Т30
Slow and steady wins the race. Make haste slowly. *Gr.* σπεῦδε βραδέως. *Lat.* festina
lente. *SPL.* paulatim longius itur.

36   **То (не) грешно что в моду вошло.**
[If it's fashionable, it's not sinful.] One is not smelt where all stink.

37   **То и полезно что в дом полезло.**   *v.* Д320
Everything is of use to a housekeeper.

38   **То лучше всего что есть у кого.**   *v.* В555,581,595,652,656, К11, Т12, Ч28
Every man likes his own thing best.

39   **То не беда что на деньги пошла, а то беда что на деньги нейдет.**   *v.* К182

40   **То пропало что с возу (в море) упало.**   *v.* Ч100

41*   **Товар лицом продается.**   *v.* Х59
Pleasing ware is half sold.

42   **Товар полюбится, и ум (карман) расступится.**   *v.* К317
Good wares make quick markets.

43*   **Тогда бери, когда дают.**   *v.* Г27, Д79, Н280, О165
[Take upon offer.] Never refuse a good offer. Get it while the getting's good.

44   **Тогда похвались когда в гроб вселись.**   *v.* B204, C313, X4
      Praise no man till he is dead.

45*   **Тогда сон хвали как (когда) сбудется.**   *v.* B260,Ж34, M48, H477
      [Praise a dream when it comes true.] It is no good praising a ford till a man be over.

46   **Толкуй больной с подлекарем.**   *v.* T77
      [Let the intern explain to the patient.] *i.e. it is futile to talk to someone who doesn't*
      understand. Arguing with a fool shows there are two. *Cf.* Let Joe do it. Ask me no
      questions and I'll tell you no lies. Explain an ill saying and you make it worse.
      Lat. Syr.372: male dictum interpretando facias acrius.

47   **Только заведи речь о мутной воде, так он и пустился рыбу ловить.**   *v.* П270, Л29
      [Just mention water and he's off fishing.] Talk of an angel and you'll hear his wings.

48   **Тому нельзя помочь, кто вина пить охоч.**   *v.* П317
      [He who loves drink is beyond help.] Who is master of his thirst is master of his health.

49   **Тому не прожить без убытка, кто богатится от зла прибытка.**   *v.* З121, K188,
      [He will incur a loss, whose gains are ill-gotten.]   H513, X96, Ч127
      Ill-gotten goods never prosper.

50   **Тому нечего бояться, кого все страшатся.**
      [He that's feared by all need not himself fear.] *Cf.*†Whom many fear must need fear many.

51   **Тому тяжело кто помнит зло.**
      [Life is hard for those who remember ill.] He lives unsafely that looks too near on
      things. *Cf.* A retentive memory is a good thing, but the ability to forget is the true token
      of happiness.

52*   **Тонул топор сулил - а вытащили и топорища жаль.**   *v.* Г327, K134
      [He that promises an axe while drowning will begrudge the helve once saved.] Vows
      made in storms are forgotten in calms.

53   **Тонут больше в луже, а не в море.**
      [More drown in puddles than in the sea.] He came safe from the East Indies and was
      drowned in the Thames. *Cf.* Wine has drowned more men than the sea.

54   **Торговать, не горевать (не попа звать).**   *v.* P51
      [He does not grieve who trades.] *Cf.* He who has a trade has a share everywhere.

55   **Тот без нужды живет, кто деньги бережет.**   *v.* Б84,189, З86,89, C48
      [He who saves lives not in want.] Of saving comes having. Thrift is a great revenue.

56   **Тот богат кто своим счастьем доволен.**   *v.* Б286, E41, H447, T59, X76
      He is not rich that possesses much, but he that is content with what he has. To be content
      with little is true happiness. *SPL.* dives est qui vivit sua forte contentus. *Cf.* He who is
      content in his poverty is wonderfully rich.

57   **Тот дурак кто говорит не так (кто пирогу не рад).**
      [He is a fool that denies it.] He who thinks he is wise is a fool (+ he who knows he is
      a fool is wise). *Cf.* The first degree of folly is to hold oneself wise, the second to profess
      it, the third to despise counsel.

58   **Тот замок трудно уберечь, к которому все ключи подходят.**   *v.* K107
      [It is difficult to preserve a lock that all keys open.] *Cf.* There's a key to every lock.

59 **Тот и богат кто нужды не знает.** *v.* Б286, Е41, Н447, Т56
He is not rich that possesses much, but he that is content with what he has.

60 **Тот и господин кто все может сделать один.**
[A true master can do everything himself.] A good workman can use any kind of tools. *Cf.* †A fool thinks nothing is right but what he does himself.

61 **Тот не кается кто с разумом справляется.**
[He who heeds reason repents not.] Planning your future saves you from regretting your past.

62 **Тот ни чем не веселится кто на деньги льстится.** *v.* Н515, Р71, С161
[He who hungers for money can never be happy.] The pleasure of what we enjoy is lost by coveting more.

63 **Тот скоро разбогатеет кто всегда от ремесла потеет.** *v.* Д403
[He will soon be rich who sweats at his work.] Unless you work hard, you cannot succeed. Trade is the mother of money. *Cf.* No sweet without some sweat. The harder you work, the more luck you have.

64 **Тот смел кто на коня сел.** *v.* Б91
He was a bold man that first [mounted a horse] ate an oyster.

65 **Тот счастлив будет кого фортуна не забудет.** *v.* К162, С307
[Happy is he whom fortune has not forgotten.] He dances well to whom fortune pipes.

66* **Треску бояться, и в лес не ходить.** *v.* Б355, В393, Д451
He that fears leaves [crackling] **must not go into the woods.**

67* **Третий - лишний.** *v.* Г30
Two is company, three is a crowd. One's too few, three's too many.

68 **Три дни молол, а в полтора дни съел.**
[He ate in one and a half days what took three days to grind.] One year's seeding makes seven years' weeding.

69* **Три к носу (и) все пройдет.**
[Rub your nose and it will go away.] *said as a consolation. Cf.* Keep your nose clean.

70* **Точность - вежливость королей.**
Punctuality is the politeness of princes. *Cf.* Punctuality is the soul of business.

71* **Трою числом лучше.** *v.* Б124,263
[Three is a better number.] All things thrive at thrice. Third time's lucky. Number three is always fortunate.

72 **Труд при учении скучен, да плод от учения вкусен.** *v.* Б78,93, У120
[The labour of learning is tiresome, but its fruit sweet.] Lessons hard to learn are sweet to know. *Cf.* Sweet is the nut but bitter (hard) is the shell.

73 **Труд человека кормит, а лень портит.**
[Work nourishes man, idleness spoils him.] *Cf.* An idle brain is the devil's workshop. Sloth wears out the body while it corrodes the mind.

74 **Трудно против рожна прати.** *v.* Б196, П289
It is hard to kick against the pricks. *Acts.*9.5: durum est contra stimulum calcitrare. *Gr.* Pind. ποτὲ κέντρον λακτίζειν.

75* Трудным путем высокая честь достижается.
The greater the obstacle, the more glory in overcoming it. No flowery road leads to glory. *SPL.* ardua per praeceps gloria tendit iter.

76* Турусы на колесах.
[Nonsense on wheels.]*ie. rubbish, twaddle.* Cock and bull story. A tale of a roasted horse.

77 Ты ближе к делу, а он про козу белу. *v.* Г180, Т46, *Ap.*1.19,28
[You say one thing and he's on about white goats.] *i.e. cannot or will not understand; changes the subject. Cf.* You tell a tale to a deaf man. To whistle (sing) psalms to the taffrail (dead horse). A fool talks when he should be listening.

78* Ты - мне, я - тебя. *v.* Д27,367,369
Scratch my back and I'll scratch yours. *Lat.* serva me, servabo te.

79 Ты на гору, а черт за ногу.
[You go up the hill and the devil grabs your foot.] *i.e. no luck in overcoming difficulties.* Life is just one damned thing after another.

80* Ты пожалей - и тебя пожалеют. *v.* Д368, З12, К15,74, Н172, У108, Ч11
One good turn deserves another. Do as you would be done by.

81* Ты черта крести, а он в воду лезет. *v.* Д77
[Christen the devil and he'll get into the water.] Better fleech the devil than fight him. *Cf.* He that takes the devil into his boat must carry him over the sound. †The devil loves no holy water.

82 Тяжба не деньги, а потрава не хлеб. *v.* Д363, З21
[As easy to gain money from a lawsuit as to reap a harvest after a stampede.] Agree, for the law is costly.

83 Тяжела ты шапка мономаха. *v.* К219
Crowns have cares. Uneasy lies the head that wears the crown.

84* Тяжело молоту, тяжело и наковальне. *v.* И113, Ч68,82
[It's just as hard on the hammer as it is on the anvil.] What's sauce for the goose is sauce for the gander.

85 Тяжело нагребешь - домой не отнесешь. *v.* Б312, В91, Д86, К177, Л88, С102, Ч96
[Don't take more than you can carry home.] Take not up more than you can bear. Don't bite off more than you can chew. Covetousness breaks the bag. *Cf.* Catch no more fish than you can salt. Enough is as good as a feast. Too much pudding will choke a dog.

86* Тяжело против воды плыть. *v.* В154,541
It is ill (evil) striving against the stream. No striving against the stream. *Cf.* It's best to sail with the wind and tide. It is ill shaving against the wool.

87* Тяп да ляп - и (вышел) корабль (не выйдет корабль). *v.* В513, Д142
[One, two, three and it's a finished ship.] *i.e. shoddy work. Cf.* Speed gets you nowhere if you're headed in the wrong direction.

У

1   У баб да у лукавых (и) слезы готовы.   *v.* Ж82
    [Women and knaves have ready tears.] Trust not a woman when she weeps. *Cf.* A
    woman's tears are her strongest weapon.

2   У бабы волос долог да ум короток.   *v.* В400, П60
    [Women are] **long of hair, short of wit.** Long hair, little brains. Long hair and short
    sense. *Cf.* You can't grow hair and brains in the same head.

3   У богатого груз в корабле, у бедного хлеб на уме.
    [The rich man has cargo on his ship and the poor man has bread on his mind.] Poor men
    seek meat for their stomachs, rich men stomachs for their meat. The rich man thinks of
    the future, the poor man of today. *Cf. Prov.*15.15: Better is little with the fear of the
    Lord than great treasure and trouble therewith.

4   У богатого мужика уродил Бог сына дурака.
    [God gave the rich man a fool for a son.] *Cf.* A wise man commonly has foolish
    children.

5* У богатого телята, у бедного ребята.   *v.* Ж24
    [The rich man has cattle, the poor man has children.] A rich man for dogs and a poor
    man for babies. Children are poor men's riches. The rich get richer and the poor have
    children. *Cf.* A poor man's cow dies, a rich man's child.

6   У богатого черт детей качает.
    [The devil rocks the rich man's children.] *Cf.* He that cockers his child provides for his
    enemy. Happy is the child whose father went to the devil.

7* У брюха нет ушей. (У голодного брюха нет уха.)   *v.* Б367,Г227, Ш8
    The belly wants ears. Plut.*Cat.*8: γαστὴρ οὐκ ἔχει ὦτα.

8   У волка всегда одна песенька.   *v.* В392, С138
    [The wolf is always of one mind.] The wolf and fox are both of one counsel. *Cf.* A wolf
    may lose his teeth but never his nature.

9   У волка из зубов не отнимешь.
    [You can never snatch anything back from a wolf's mouth.] As irrevocable as a lump of
    butter in a greyhound's (dog's) mouth.

10 У вора заячье сердце, и спит и боится.   *v.* В426, Н18
    [Thieves have a coward's disposition, they sleep in fear.] A guilty conscience feels
    continuous fear. Once a thief, ever in danger. *Cf.* The thief doth fear each bush an
    officer. †He that fears the gallows shall never be a good thief.

11 У вора ремесло на лбу не написано.   *v.* Р65, У39
    [Thieves don't wear their identity for all to see.] Nobody calls himself a rogue.
    SPL. nemini ex fronte eminet nequitia.

12* **У всякого барона своя фантазия. (У всякого своя дурь в голове.)** *v.* В554, К12,211
[Every baron has his fantasy.] **Every man is mad on some point**.

13 **У всякого молодца своя ухватка.** *v.* В558,626,628, У17, *Ap.*1.90
Every man after his fashion. *SPL.* pectoribus mores tot sunt quot in ore figurae.

14 **У всякого плута (разбойника) свой расчет.** *v.* В558,626,628, У17, *Ap.*1.90
[Every thief (rogue) keeps his own accounts.] Every man has his price.

15* **У всякого свой вкус, а у осла ослиный. (Один другому не указчик - кто любит
арбуз, кто любит свиной хрящик.)** *v.* И128, Л16, М201, Н15, О1, П107
Every man to his taste (and an ass has an ass' taste). [One likes melon while another
prefers pigs knuckles.] Every man to his taste, quoth the man when he kissed his cow.

16 **У всякого скота своя пестрота.** *v.* В60,69
[Every herd has its variety.] It takes all kinds to make the world.

17* **У всякой пташки свои замашки.** *v.* В626,628, У13, *Ap.*1.90
[Every bird has its ways.] Every man after his fashion.

18* **У всякой собаки своя кличка.**
[Every dog has its name.] No stone without its name. *Lat.* Lucan.*BC.*9.973: nullum est
sine nomine saxum. *Cf.* Names and natures often agree.

19 **У денег глаз нет (нету глаз).**
Money is blind.

20 **У добра всегда ноги кривы.** *v.* Х44, Ш21
[Goodness always walks with a limp.] Truth has a scratched face. Head of gold, feet of clay.

21 **У доброго дядьки добры и дитятки.** *v.* К84,91
[A kind father has kind children.] Of good parents come good children. *Cf.* Parents
are patterns.

22 **У доброго (милостиво) мужа всегда жена досужа (и худая жена).**
[A kind husband always has a capable wife.] A good husband makes a good wife.

23 **У долгу и век долог.** *v.* Д369, С257
[A debt lasts a long time.] Creditors have better memories than debtors. Sins and debts
are always more than we think them to be. *Cf.* Debt is better than death.

24* **У друга пить воду лучше неприятельского меду.** *v.* Б232, Д324, Л124
[Water from a friend is better than mead from an enemy.] A friend's frown is better than
a foe's smile. Better little with content than much with contention. A crust of bread in
peace is better than a feast in contention. Dry bread with love is better than fried chicken
with fear and trembling. *Cf.* The smoke of a man's country is better than fire of
another's. Dry bread at home is better than roast meat abroad.

25 **У дурака в горсти дыра.** *v.* Б139, В576, Г137
[A fool has a hole in his hand.] A fool and his money are soon parted.

26* **У дурака дурацкая и речь.** *v.* Г146, Н265
The mouth of fools pours out foolishness. *Gr.* Eur.*Bacch.* μωρᾶ γάρ μωρὸς λέγει.
Lat. stultus stulta loquitur. *Cf.* A fool is known by his speech.

27   У зависти глаза велики.   *v.* Б197, З64
         Nothing sharpens sight like envy.

28   У завтра нет конца.
         [Tomorrow has no end.] There is always a tomorrow. Tomorrow is untouched.

29*   У каждой избушки есть погремушки.   *v.* П96
         There is a skeleton in every house.

30*   У каждой медали есть оборотная сторона.   *v.* В584, У47
         Every medal has its reverse.

31   У кого во рту желчь, тому все горько.   *v.* Г294, *Ap.*1.56
         [Who has a tongue of gall finds everything bitter.] An ill stomach makes all the meat bitter. *Cf.* Who has bitter in his mouth, spits not all sweet.

32   У кого деньги есть, тот на закон не смотрит.
         [A man with money need not heed the law.] There's one law for the rich and another for the poor. *SPL.* aurum lex sequitur, datur venia corvis.

33   У кого детей много, тот не забыт от Бога.   *v.* Б66, Х57
         [God remembers those with many children.] Children are the keys of paradise. *Cf.* Whom God loves, his bitch brings forth pigs. Where children are not, heaven is not.

34   У кого много дел впереди, тот назад не оглядывается.   *v.* Н288
         [He who has much to do ahead never looks behind.] He that will not look before him, will have to look behind him. *Cf.* He who looks behind will never get ahead. He who never goes forward, goes backward.

35   У кого много остатку, тот не боится недостатку.   *v.* Б68, *Ap.*1.17
         [He fears no shortage who has a surplus.] They that have a store of butter may lay it thick on their bread. *Cf.* Provision in season makes a rich house.

36*   У кого пропало, тому вдвое грех.
         [He that has lost a thing suffers doubly.]*i.e. for the loss and object.* Lose both pot and water. *Cf.* All's lost, both labour and cost. He that is not sensible of his loss has lost nothing.

37*   У кого что болит (что кого веселит), тот о(б) том и говорит.   *v.* Ч60
         [All complain about their own pain.] *said of people who always talk about the same thing.* To have a bee in one's bonnet. Everyone speaks of his own interest. Everyone has a complaint of some kind. What the heart thinks, the tongue speaks. *Cf.* Each priest praises his own relics.

38   У корове молоко на языке.   *v.* Д221, К71
         [A cow's milk is on its tongue.] *i.e. cows must be fed well to give milk.* You don't get more out of a thing than you put into it. *Cf.* Butter is once a year in a cow's horn.

39   У корысти всегда рожа бескорыстна.   *v.* Г180, У11
         [Interest always has a disinterested face.] Fine words dress ill deeds. He that will slight my horse will buy my horse.

40   У кривого один глаз, да видит больше всех нас.   *v.* В306, О70
         He that has but one eye, sees the better for it [sees more than all of us.]

41   **У лицемера хвалы горшок, а у завистливо хулы мешок.**
[Flatterers have a potful of praise, and the envious a bagful of abuse.] *Cf.* The most deadly of all beasts is a backbiter, of tame ones a flatterer.

42   **У ленивой пряхи нет и про себя рубахи.**   *v.* Ж93, Н326, С47,70, Ч133
[The lazy seamstress has nothing to wear herself.] The tailor's wife is worst clad. The tailor's sons wear patched pants. *Cf.* A shoemaker's son always goes barefoot.

43   **У лжеца на одной неделе семь четвергов.**
[A liar's week has seven Thursdays.] *a pun on the idiomatic expression "seven Fridays to one's week," which is said of a fickle or indecisive person.*

44*   **У плохого мужа жена всегда дура.**
A bad husband makes a bad wife. Many a one blames his wife for his own unthrift.

45*   **У повешенного в доме о веревке не говорят.**   *v.* Б153
Name not a rope (halter) in his house that was hanged (hanged himself).

46*   **У одной матки разные детки.** *v.* О145

47*   **У палки (одной кишки) два конца.**   *v.* В584, У30
[Every stick has two ends.] When you pick up a stick at one end, you also pick up the other end. *Cf.* There are two sides to every question.

48   **У пьяного басен (басней) не переслушаешь.**
When wine sinks, words swim.

49   **У пьяного речи а у трезвого мысль.**   *v.* Ч104
[The drunk speaks, the sober man thinks.] What soberness conceals, drunkeness reveals.

50*   **У себя как хочешь, а в гостях как велят.**   *v.* В22, Г307, Н409, Х30, Ч24
[Do as you like at home but as you're told as a guest.] To the man submit at whose board you sit. *Cf.* When in Rome, do as the Romans. Be deaf and blind in another man's house. A man is king in his own house.

51*   **У семи дворов один топор (да и тот без топорища).**   *v.* †А27
[Seven yards and one axe (and that one lacks a handle).] A pot that belongs to many is ill stirred and worse boiled. The common horse is worse shod.

52*   **У семи нянек (маток) дитя без глазу.**   *v.* Д212, У52
With seven nannies a child will be without eyes. *SPL.* multi duces Cariam perdiderunt. multi medici Caesarem perdiderunt. non potest bene geri res publica multorum imperiis.

53   **У семи пастухов не стадо.**   *v.* Д212, У51
[Too many shepherds spoil the flock.] Too many eskimos, too few seals. Too many chiefs and not enough braves. Too many commanders cause confusion in the ranks.

54   **У сильного всегда бессильный виноват.**   *v.* Б332, Г87, О16, С118, Ч136
[Against the stronger, the weaker are always wrong.] Might is right. The weakest goes to the wall.

55   **У скупого всякая копейка алтынным гвоздем прибита.** *v.* В594

56*   **У случая на затылке нет волосов.**
[The nape of opportunity is bare.] Take time (occasion) by the forelock, for she is bald behind. *Lat.* post est occasio calva.

57* У смерти все равны.   *v.* Б442, Ж152, С198, Ц5
    Death is the great leveller.

58 У сотни безумных найдешь и умных.
    [Among a hundred fools you may find some who are wise.] *Cf.* No man is always a fool, but every man is sometimes. A fool's bolt may sometimes hit the mark. All men are fools, but the wisest of fools are called philosophers.

59 У спесивого чины более законов.
    [The haughty prefer rank to justice.] An ounce of vanity spoils a hundred weight of merit.

60 У старого жена молода, беда не мала.   *v.* В303, М149
    [An old man and a young wife spell great trouble.] *Cf.* A young maid married to an old man is like a new house thatched with old straw. Old men when they marry young women, make much of death.

61 У старого козла крепка рога.   *v.* С260
    Old oxen [goats] have stiff horns.

62* У стен (бывают) уши.   *v.* С126
    Walls have ears.

63 У страха глаза велики.
    Fear has magnifying eyes.

64 У тороватого скупость на дне.   *v.* Ч76
    [The generous have greed at the bottom.] *i.e. if depleted.* The generous mind least regards money and yet most feels the want of it. *Cf.* Liberality consists less in giving much than in giving at the right time. †Bounty has no bottom. *Lat.* Cic.*Offic.*2.15.55: largitionem fundum non habere.

65* У хлеба не без крох.   *v.* Г130, Л54
    [No bread without crumbs.] He who wishes a fire must put up with smoke. He that would have eggs must endure the cackling of hens.

66* У худой рожи и худой обычай.
    There is never a foul face but there's a foul fancy.

67 У языка зубы да губы два замка.   *v.* Г333, Д209
    [The tongue has teeth but the lips are a lock.] Good that the teeth guard the tongue.

68 Убил Бог лето мухами.   *v.* Г51
    [God ruined summer with flies.] A fly in the ointment. There's good and bad in everything.

69 Убогий что уродливый, что есть то и носит.
    [With beggars and ugly people, what you see is all they have.] *Cf.* He carries all his wardrobe on his back.

70 Убогим Бог прибежище.
    [God is the poor man's last resort.] *Cf.* Man's extremity is God's opportunity.

71 Убогого убить добычи не добыть.   *v.* Г241, 39, Н125,559, С5
    [There's no gain in killing a beggar.] No naked man is sought after to be rifled.

72 Убыток учит нажит прибыток.   *v.* Б19, О197, П240
    We learn (profit) from our mistakes. No great loss but some profit.

73 **Уговор дороже (лучше) денег.** *v.* Д6
[A man's word is better than money.] An honest man's word is as good as his bond.

74 **Удалой долго не думает.**
[The bold think quickly.] He who hesitates is lost.

75 **Удица крива, да рыбица пряма.** *v.* Б404, Г126, Д411, И23, К204, С287
[A bent rod will catch a straight fish.] Crooked logs make straight fires. Straight trees have crooked roots.

76 **Уехали с орехами.**
[They left with the goods.] To be left in the lurch. *Cf.* To take the money and run.

77 **Ужин не нужен, был бы обед.**
[As long as there's dinner, forget about supper.] *Cf.* He sups ill who eats all at dinner.

78 **Узнавай человека не год, не два, а семь лет.** *v.* Б390, В214, Ч108
[Know a man not a year or two, but seven.] Before you make a friend, eat a bushel of salt with him.

79* **Улита едет (да) когда-то будет.**
To go at a snail's gallop (pace).

80* **Уломали (умыкали) (укатали) бурку (сивку) крутые горы.** *v.* Б439
[Steep hills have worn out the old steed.] The old grey mare isn't what she used to be. *Cf.* Time is the rider that breaks youth. Everything is the worse for wear.

81 **Ум без разума беда.** *v.* У86,92
[Mind without reason is dangerous.] There's no fool like a learned fool. *Cf.* Knowledge is folly, except where grace guide it.

82 **Ум любит простор.** *v.* Б336, Д504, К68, Н57, С68
[The mind loves space.] A good mind possesses a kingdom. *Cf.* Thought is free. †Small minds are lured by trifles.

83 **Ум пришел, да пора прошла.** *v.* Д484, П173, Х15, *Ap.*1.68
It's easy to be wise after the event. When a fool has made up his mind, the market's over.

84* **Ум хорошо, а два лучше.** *v.* М128, О5,51
Two heads are better than one.

85* **Ума за морем не купишь коли его дома нет.** *v.* В19, Г337
[You cannot order brains abroad if you haven't got them at home.] They who cross the seas change their skies but not their natures. *SPL.* coelum, non animus mutant, qui trans mare currunt. *Cf.* If an ass goes a travelling, he'll not come home a horse. No change in circumstances will change a defect in character.

86 **Ума много да разуму нет.** *v.* В536, Д362, Л145, У81,92
[Much learning but little sense.] No man is the wiser for his learning. *Cf.* A handful of common sense is worth a bushel of learning. Mother wit is better than book education.

87 **Умей взять, умей и отдать.** *v.* Д80, Л169
[Know how to give, not just take.] Give and take. Give a little, take a little. *Cf.* Give and you shall receive.

88 **Умей в саночках кататься, умей и саночки возить.** *v.* Л169, П67
[If you like to ride the sleigh, you must also pull it.] They that dance must pay the fiddler.

89 **Умел дитя родить, умей и научить.** *v.* Л169,173
[If you were able to have children, you should be able to bring them up.] *Cf.* He that takes the devil into his boat must carry him over the sound.

90 **Умел начать, умей и окончить.** *v.* Н344,345
[Finish what you begin.] Don't start anything you can't finish. Better not to begin than never make an end. *Cf.* He who begins many things, finishes but few.

91 **Умерла та курица коя несла золотые яйца.** *v.* А1,Т2, Ч76
The hen (goose) that lays the golden eggs [is dead].

92 **Умная голова да дураку досталась.** *v.* Д498, В536, У86
[He may be smart yet he acts like a fool.] A little learning is a bad thing. *Cf.* Learning in the breast of a bad man is as a sword in the hand of a madman.

93 **Умная голова сто голов прокормит (кормит) (+ а сама по миру ходит).** *v.* В27, З13, О46, Р31
[One wise man may feed a hundred other men.]One wise man is worth more than ten thousand fools. *Gr.* Pl.*Gorg.*490A: εἷς φρονῶν μυρίων μὴ φρονούντων κρεῖττον ἐστί. *Cf.* A single day in the life of a wise man is worth more than the lifetime of a fool.

94 **Умная ложь лучше правды.** *v.* И125, Л101,138,144, О13
[An intelligent lie is better than the truth.] *Cf.* A great lie is best. It is better to lie a little than to be unhappy much. Better a lie that heals than a truth that wounds.

95* **Умного иногда и глупый на разум наставит.** *v.* В465, И16,129
A fool may give a wise man counsel.

96 **Умного послав - ожидай, а за безумным сам ступай.** *v.* Д488
He that sends a fool means to follow him.

97 **Умного не достает ушей, а у глупого один язык слишком.** *v.* Б249, Д208, З149, М117, У101
[The wise man is short of ears while the fool has one tongue too many.] An open ear and a closed mouth is the best substitute for wisdom. Foolish tongues talk by the dozen. *Cf.* Give every man your ear but few your voice.

98* **Умному не много слов. (Умный понимает и полуслово.)** *v.* В630, Д323, М173, О39, Р32
A word to the wise is sufficient. *Lat.* verbum sat sapienti.

99 **Умные (хорошие) речи приятно слушать.** *v.* Д346, М215
[It's nice to hear intelligent talk.] *said to show approval of what is said, as in the phrases:* *"You can say that again!" "Now you're talking!"* Smooth words make smooth ways.

100 **Умный грешит, да поправить спешит.**
[The wise man rushes to correct his error.] Show a good man his error and he turns it to a virtue (but an ill, it doubles his fault).

101 **Умный молчит а дурак ворчит.** *v.* Д306, Л141, М157, У97
Wise men silent, fools talk.

102* **Умный не всегда развяжет что глупый завяжет.** *v.* Г149, Д474,475, О31
Fools tie knots [which wise men may not always untie] **and wise men loose them.**
Cf. A fool may throw a stone into a well which a hundred wise men cannot pull out.

103   **Умный товарищ - половина дороги.**   *v.* Б199, В213, Р22

A good companion is a wagon in the way [is half the journey]. No road is long with good company.

104   **Умрем, ничего с собою не возьмем (так все останется).**   *v.* С35

You can't take it with you.

105   **Упрямая овца волку корысть.**   *v.* Б156,187

[Wolves love stubborn sheep.] The lone sheep is in danger of the wolf.

106   **Упустишь огонь - не потушишь.**   *v.* О142

[Neglect the spark and you won't extinguish the fire.] An occasion lost cannot be redeemed.

107*   **Ус в честь, а борода и у козла есть.**   *v.* Б340, М171, *Ap.*1.1

If the beard were all, the goat might preach.

108*   **Услуга за услугу.**   *v.* Д369, З12, К15, Т80

One good turn deserves another.

109*   **Услужливый дурак опаснее врага.**   *v.* Н178, С253

[An obliging fool is more dangerous than an enemy.] A rash friend is worse than a foe. A wise enemy is better than a foolish friend. *Cf.* Hell is paved with good intentions.

110*   **Устами младенца глаголет истина.**   *v.* М4

From the mouths of babes springs truth (come words of wisdom). From the mouth of babes and sucklings come great truths.

111*   **Утопающий за соломинку хватается.**   *v.* К308

A drowning man will catch (clutch) at a straw.

112   **Утопший пить не просит.**

[The drowning man won't ask for a drink.] *Cf.* A fool would ask for a drink if he were drowning. When a dog is drowning, everyone offers him a drink.

113*   **Утративши корову, козы стеречь.**   *v.* О18

[If you lose your cow, you must guard your goat.] He that has but one eye, must be afraid to lose it.

114*   **Утро вечера мудренее.**   *v.* Д457

[Morning is wiser than evening.] Night brings counsel.

115   **Уха лучше рыбы.**   *v.* †Д221

[The soup is better than the fish.] The whole is greater than the sum of its parts.

116*   **Ученье атаман (красота) (свет) - а неученье комар (сухота) (тьма).**

[Education is king (best)(illumination) - ignorance is a sting (worst)(darkness).] Knowledge is better than ignorance. There is only one good - knowledge, there is only one evil - ignorance. *Gr.* D.Laert.*Socr.*2.31: μόνον ἀγαθὸν εἶναι, τὴν ἐπιστήμην, καὶ ἓν μόνον κακόν, τὴν ἀμαθίαν.

117   **Ученье в счастье украшает, а в несчастьи утешает.**

[Learning is an ornament in fortune and a consolation in misfortune.] Learning is a treasure which accompanies its owner everywhere. *Cf.* Knowledge is the treasure of the mind. Knowledge is no burden.

118   **Учение лучше богатства.**   *v.* Б134,284,289, Г140, Д505, Н175,291
       Better wit than wealth. Knowledge is better than riches (wealth).

119   **Учение - человеку ожерелье.**
       [Education is man's ornament.] *Cf.* Education polishes good natures and corrects bad
       ones.

120*   **Учения корень горек, да плод сладок.**   *v.* Б78, Т72
       [Bitter is the root of learning, but sweet is the fruit.] Lessons hard to learn are sweet to
       know. *Cf.* Bitter pills may have blessed effects. Sweet is the nut, but bitter is the shell.

121   **Ученого учить, лишь (только) портить.**   *v.* Н468, Я20
       [Teaching only spoils the scholar.] *Cf.* Teach your grandmother to suck eggs.*Lat.* doctum
       doces.

122   **Учи жену без детей, а детей без людей.**
       [Instruct not a wife in front of her children, nor children in front of others.] Teach your
       son in the hall, your wife on the pillow. Admonish your friends in private, praise them
       in public.

123   **Учись смолоду - не умрешь с голоду.**   *v.* Б181, Ч46
       [Learn young and you won't die hungry.] Learn young, learn fair.

124*   **Учить иных - научиться и сам.**   *v.* Д132, Ч106
       To teach another is to learn yourself. *Lat.* docendo discimus (homines dum docent,
       discunt.) *Cf.* In doing, we learn.

Ф

1*   **Факты - упрямая вещь.**   *v.* Б481
      Facts are stubborn things.

2   **Февраль воду подпустит, март подберет.**
      [March dries up the February rains.] *Cf.* February fill ditch. February makes a bridge and
      March breaks it.

3*   **Философ смерти не боится.**
      [A philosopher does not fear death.] The whole life of a philosopher is a preparation for
      death. *Lat.* Cic.*TD*.1.30.74: tota philosophorum vita commentatio mortis est.

4   **Фортуна велика да ума мало.**   *v.* Д251,489, С30
      Fortune favours fools.

X

1   **Хата бела да без хлеба беда.**
    [A bare house, however pretty, means trouble.] Bare walls make giddy housewives.

2*   **Хвали день до заката.**   *v.* H453, †X6
    [Praise the day before the sunset.] *i.e. before it's over.* *Cf.* Evening praises the day.

3   **Хвали море, а сиди на берегу.**   *v.* Д45, E11, M162
    Praise the sea but keep on land.

4   **Хвали рожь в стогу, а барина в гробу.**   *v.* B204, H474, C313, T44
    Praise [rye in the stack, and] **no man till he be dead.**

5   **Хвали сон коли сбудется.** *v.* T45

6*   **Хвали утро (день) вечером.**   *v.* H479, †X2
    Praise a fair day at night.

7   **Хвалился черт всем миром овладеть, а Бог ему и над свиней не дал власти.**   *v.* K302
    [The devil bragged he would rule the world, but God didn't even grant him dominion over swine.] They brag most that can do least.

8   **Хвались да не поперхнись.**   *v.* H481
    [Praise, but don't choke on it.] Such as boast much usually fall much.

9*   **Хвалят на девке шелк, когда в самой девке есть толк.**   *v.* H302
    [Praise a girl's dress only if she herself is sensible.] It is not the clothes that count, but the things that clothes cover. *Cf.* Clothes don't make the woman, but they help.

10   **Хвастать - не косить, спина не болит.**   *v.* E33, K302, P25
    [Boasting isn't like mowing - your back doesn't hurt.] Great braggers, little doers. They brag most that can do least. *Lat.* minima possunt qui plurima iactant.

11   **Хвастливое слово гнило.**   *v.* Д81, K296
    [Rotten is the word of praise.] Man's praise in his own mouth stinks. Where boasting ends, dignity begins.

12   **Хватайся сам за доску, пускай другой тонет.**   *v.* B527,551, C225
    [Seize the life raft yourself - let the next man drown.] Every man for himself and the devil take the hindmost.

13   **Хватил шилом патоки.**   *v.* Б157, В128,320, К22, Р56
[Seize syrup with an awl.] *i.e. get nothing.* To carry water in a sieve.   *Lat.*   *EA.*
cribro aquam haurire.

14*   **Хватился каяться монах, как уж смерть в головах.**   *v.* А20, Н70,452,453, Р56
[The monk repents at death's door.] When the devil comes, it's too late to pray. *Cf.* Late
repentance is seldom true. It is no time to stoop when the head is off.

15   **Хватился, когда с горы скатился.**   *v.* Д485, П173, У83, *Ар.*1.68
[He took hold only after falling down the hill.] It is easy to be wise after the event.

16   **Хватлива собака скорее околеет.**   *v.* О81, С222, Ч38
[A coverous dog will perish sooner.] *Cf.* He that handles thorns shall prick his fingers.

17   **Хвост голове не указка.**   *v.* Я23
[The tail does not command the head.] The tail cannot shake the dog.

18   **Хижа своя лучше каменных хором чужих.**   *v.* С63,71
[One's own hut is better than others' stone mansions.] A hut is a palace to a poor man.
Cf. A small house well-filled is better than an empty palace. Home is home, though it
never be so homely.

19   **Хлеб в пути не тягость (тяжесть).**   *v.* Е6, З87, Л94, П114
[Bread is no burden on a journey.] Meat and matins hinder no man's journey. *Cf.* Store
is no sore. Who goes for a day into the forest should take bread for a week.

20*   **Хлеб всему голова.**   *v.* К99, Щ5
Bread is the staff of life.

21*   **Хлеб за брюхом не ходит.**   *v.* М76, О17, Я23
[Bread doesn't come to the stomach.] Roasted ducks don't fly into your mouth.

22   **Хлеба не будет, станем пряники есть.** *sarc.*   *v.* Е52
[When we run out of bread, we will eat cake.] If they can't eat bread, let them eat cake.
Cf. Bread today is better than cake tomorrow.

23   **Хлеба нет и друзей не бывало.**   *v.* Б372,467, Е42, К132, Н64
Poverty parts fellowship. No longer foster, no longer friend. *Cf.* When poverty comes in
at the door, love flies out of the window.

24*   **Хлебом люди не шутят.**   *v.* В386
[Do not joke with bread.] Do not jest in serious matters. Clumsy jesting is no joke. To
quarrel with one's bread and butter.

25   **Хлеб-соль вместе, а табачок врозь.**   *v.* Д136,И64, Л5, *Ар.*1.25
[Bread and salt in common, but tobacco apart.] *i.e. said of common and private expenses,
mixing business with pleasure.* Brotherly love for brotherly love, but cheese for money.
Don't mix business with pleasure. *Cf.* A woman's a woman, but a good cigar's a smoke.

26*   **Хлеб-соль ешь, а правду режь.**   *v.* С305, *Ар.*1.7
[Break bread as you like, but speak the truth bluntly.] To call a spade a spade. Tell it
like it is. To speak from the shoulder.

27   **Ходил за зайцем, а видел волка.**   *v.* Б170, П56,150
[To hunt rabbits and see wolves.] Use the little to get to the big.

28   **Ходить по льду, поскользнуться.**   *v.* B20
     [If you walk on ice, expect to slip.] He that fears leaves, let him not go into the wood.
     Cf. Try the ice before you venture upon it.

29* **Ходячего на сидячего не меняют.**   *v.* X92
     [Don't exchange a walker for a sitter.] We don't always gain by changing. Do not change
     horses in midstream. *Cf.* You give me bread for cake. I will not change a cottage in
     possession for a kingdom in reversion. Better a devil you know than one you don't know.

30* **Хозяину в дому не указывай.**   *v.* B22,194, Г307, H409, У50, Ч24
     [Don't command the master in his own house.] He that reckons without his host must
     reckon again. *Cf.* When in Rome, do as the Romans.

31   **Хозяину и стены помогают.**   *v.* B135, Д387
     [Even the walls help the master of the house.] At home everything is easy. Everything
     is of use to a good housekeeper.

32   **Хозяйка лежит, и все лежит - хозяйка на ногах, и все на ногах.**   *v.* Ж50
     [When the housewife slumbers, so does the house; when she's up and about, so is
     everyone else.] A gentle housewife mars the household. *Cf.* The house goes mad when
     women gad.

33* **Хозяйкою дом стоит.**   *v.* B553,Д271,318, Ж54,91
     [The homemaker makes the home.] The wife is the key of the house. *Cf.* Woeful is the
     household that wants a woman. Master absent and the house is dead.

34   **Хозяйский глаз смотрок.**   *v.* Г100, C62
     [The eye of the master is discerning.] One eye of the master sees more than ten of the
     servants. *Lat.* Phaedri *Fab.*11.8: dominum plurimum videre in rebus suis. The eye of the
     housewife (master) makes the cat (horse) fat.

35   **Хозяйство водить, не разиня рот.**
     [Housekeeping means not yawning.] *Cf.* There is but an hour in a day between a good
     housewife and a bad. The real housewife is at once a slave and a lady. The finger of the
     housewife can do more than a yoke of oxen.

36   **Хозяюшка в дому, как оладьейка в меду.**
     [A housewife at home is like a fritter in honey.] *Cf.* Woeful is the house that wants a
     woman. Good housewifery is a great revenue.

37   **Холоден сентябрь, да сыт.**
     [September is cold, but full.] *Cf.* September blow soft till fruit be in loft.

38   **Холостого сватом не посылают.**   *v.* K54
     [Do not send a bachelor to arrange a marriage.] *Cf.* Bachelors' wives and maids' children
     are well taught. Bachelors' wives are always best managed.

39   **Холостой где ни свернулся - спит.**
     [A bachelor can sleep anywhere.] An ox, when he is alone, licks himself at pleasure.

40   **Холя всему хороша.**
     [All things are better with care.] Care saves ware. An ounce of care is worth a pound of cure.

41* **Хорош гость когда редко ходит.**   *v.* P48, Ч9
     [The rarer the guest, the better the welcome.] A constant guest is never welcome. Short
     visits make long friends.

42   **Хорош и лунный свет как солнца (на небе) нет.**   *v.* В448, И32, Н525
       [Moonlight will do when the sun is gone.] *Cf.* The moon is not seen where the sun shines.

43   **Хорош кус, да не для наших уст.**   *v.* В178, Н118, Х49, *Ap.*1.37
       [It's a fine morsel, but it's not for us.] *said of something unattainable.* It's a good fish if
       it were caught.

44*   **Хорош павлин, да ногами худ.**   *v.* Л10, У20
       The peacock has fair feathers but foul feet.

45   **Хорош цветок, да остер щипок.**   *v.* Н524
       There is no rose without a thorn.

46   **Хорош цветок, да скоро вянет.**   *v.* С151
       The fairest flowers soonest fade.

47   **Хороша деревня, да слава худа.**   *v.* Г313, И60
       [Many a good village has a bad name.] Give a dog a bad name and hang him. The devil
       is not so black as he is painted. *Cf.* Common fame is but a common liar. You can't tell
       a book by its cover.

48   **Хороша книга, да начетчик плох.**
       [The reader is bad, not the book.] 'Tis the good reader that makes the book good.
       Cf. A book that is shut is but a block.

49   **Хороша рыба, да на чужом блюде.**   *v.* В179,583, Н118, Х43, Ч129
       [Fish is fine on another's plate.] Neighbour's fare is always counted the best.

50   **Хорошая жена лишняя сухота.**   *v.* Н108
       [A fair wife is an extra headache.] Who has a fair wife needs more than two eyes.

51*   **Хорошего ненадолго, и сладкого недосыта.**   *v.* Д264, М112
       [Good is ephemeral, and sweets never suffice.] You can never have too much of a good
       thing.

52*   **Хорошего понемногу (хорошенького понемножку).**   *v.* В516, И40
       [Take what is good a little at a time.] *said when enough is enough.* Enough of a good
       thing is plenty. You can have too much of a good thing. *Cf.* Too much pudding will
       choke a dog. Too much is good for nought. Make haste slowly. Too good is stark nought.

53   **Хорошее дело два века живет.**   *v.* Д279,300,332,442, Ж142, С195
       A good deed is never lost. *Cf.* Virtue never grows old.

54   **Хорошему вору все в пору.**
       [Everything is of use to a good thief.] *Cf.* Everything is of use to a housekeeper.

55*   **Хороши вести что нечего ести.**   *v.* Д317
       No news is good news.

56   **Хороши займы с отдачею.**   *v.* Д368, З72, Р11
       [Loans are good in the repayment.] *Cf.* A borrowed loan should come laughing home.

57*   **Хорошие дети - отцу и матери утешение.**   *v.* Б66, Д219, У33
       [Good children are a consolation to their parents.] Happy is he who is happy in his
       children. Children are the parents' riches. It takes children to make a happy home.
       Cf. Where children are not, heaven is not.

58 **Хороший совет стоит десяти изрядных.**
[One good piece of advice is worth ten fair ones.] Good counsel has no price. Good advice is beyond price. *Lat. EA.* bono consilio nullum est munus pretiosus.

59* **Хороший товар сам себя хвалит.**   *v.* Д299,301, Р57, Т41
[Pleasing ware praises itself.] Pleasing ware is half sold. Good wine needs no bush.

60 **Хорошо белую денежку беречь на черный день.**   *v.* Б174,180, В83, О180
[It's good to save a bright penny for a dark day.] Lay up for a rainy day. *Plan.*244: καλά μου χρήματα ἐν κακῷ μου καιρῷ.

61 **Хорошо вору красть коли ночь темна.**   *v.* П237, Ч20
[The robber loves to steal by night.] He that does ill hates the light. Night is the cloak of sinners.

62* **Хорошо и собачке своя конурка.**   *v.* В621,652, Т38, Ч28
[Every dog likes its kennel.] The bird loves her nest. A dog returns to his own home. *Cf.* Every man likes his own thing best. The hare returns to her form.

63 **Хорошо и честь и гроза.**   *v.* Л169,173, Н229, У88
You must take the good with the bad. You must take the fat with the lean.

64* **Хорошо лгать на мертвого.**   *v.* О72
[It is easy to lie about a dead man.] The dead (absent) are always wrong. *Cf.* Dead men tell no tales. The dead have no rights.

65 **Хорошо на друга калач купить, не полюбится - сам съешь.**
[It's good to buy cake for a friend - you can always eat it yourself if he doesn't like it.] *Cf.* A good saver is a good server.

66 **Хорошо на того грозиться, кто гроз боится.**   *v.* Д285, С205
[It's easy to threaten those who fear threats.] A coward is much more exposed to quarrels than a man of spirit. It's nice to beat proud folks for they'll never complain. *Cf.* Everyone give a push to a tumbling man. Cowards are made to be trampled on, unless their wit cover them.

67* **Хорошо около костра щепы подбирать.**
[It's nice to gather chips near the fire.] It is best to sit near the fire when the chimney smokes.

68* **Хорошо смеется тот кто смеется последним.**   *v.* О178
He laughs best who laughs last.

69 **Хорошо тому добро делать кто помнит.**
[It is good to do good for those who remember.] To a grateful man give money when he asks. The grateful man gets more than he asks.

70 **Хорошо тому жить у кого бабушка (мать) ворожит.**   *v.* Д422, Н282
[Lucky is he whose (grand)mother can cast a spell.] A friend at (in) court. He whose father is judge goes safely to court. A friend in the market is better than money in the purse.

71* **Хорошо тому смеяться, кто на сухом берегу.**   *v.* В145,151, Н202
[He can laugh who has his feet planted firmly on shore.] In a calm sea every man is a pilot. Nothing is more delightful than to look upon danger from a place of perfect safety.

72 **Хорошо худо не живет (бывает).**   *v.* Д118,137,263,283,319, К137,233,289
     Do well and have well.

73* **Хорошо чужими руками жар загребать.**
     It's good to take the chestnuts out of the fire with the cat's (dog's) paw. It is good to learn at other men's mens' cost. To have others do one's dirty work. To use another's foot to kick a dog.

74* **Хотение найдет причину.**   *v.* Б452, Г101, Д76, С194
     Where there is a will there is a way.

75* **Хоть гол, да прав.**   *v.* Г203, Д151,153,273, Л113, Х77
     [Broke, but honest.] Better be poor with honour than rich with shame. *Cf.* It is better to be a rich man than an honest man.

76 **Хоть есть нечего, да жить весело.**   *v.* Б286, Н447, Т56
     The greatest wealth is contentment with a little. *Cf.* He who is content in his poverty is wonderfully rich.

77 **Хоть нет барыша, да слава хороша.**   *v.* В673, Д151,153,273,305, Л113, Х75
     A good name is better than riches.

78* **Хоть падать, да не лежать.**   *v.* Б169, С134
     [Though you may fall, get up.] Success comes in rising every time you fall. Our greatest glory consists not in never falling, but in rising every time we fall. If at first you don't succeed, try again. To fall into sin is human, to remain in sin is devilish.

79 **Хоть святых вон понеси (выноси).**
     [You may as well remove the icons.] *i.e. not to offend them; said of rude conduct.* *Cf.* The man who curses, prays to the devil.

80 **Хоть тяжелая доля, да все своя воля.**   *v.* В407,411
     [Though my lot be difficult, still I am free.] A poor freedom is better than rich slavery.

81* **Хоть яловая, а (да) телись.**   *v.* Н496,591, Я21
     [Though barren, yet calve.] *i.e. do the impossible.* Do or die. A man can do a lot of things if he has to.

82 **Хочу с кашей ем, хочу масло пахтаю.**   *v.* Г174, К299, Н485, С75
     [If I feel like it, I'll eat it with *kasha*, or I'll whip it up into butter.] *i.e. I'll do whatever I like.* A wilful man will have his way. *Cf.* That which will not be butter, must be made into cheese.

83 **Храброму не нужна длинная шпага,**
     A brave arm makes a short sword long.

84 **Храбрым счастье помогает.**   *v.* С189
     Fortune favours the bold. *Lat.* Ter.*Phorm.*1.4: fortes fortuna adiuvat.

85* **Хрен редьки не слаще.**   *v.* В511, К277, С108,232, Ч64
     [Horse radish is no sweeter than garden radish.] There's little choice in rotten apples. It's six of one to half a dozen of the other.

86 **Худ муж помрет, добрая жена по миру пойдет.**   *v.* М176
     [When a wicked husband dies, his good wife comes into her own.] He is an ill husband who is not missed.

87   **Худ пирог, да съелся.**   *v.* К336
[A bad pie is eaten just the same.] The proof of the pudding is in the eating. No good horse of a bad colour.

88   **Худа та мышь которая одну лазейку знает.**   *v.* В504
The mouse that has but one hole is quickly taken. *Lat.* mus miser est antro qui tantum clauditur uno. *Cf.* Don't put all your eggs in one basket.

89   **Худая грамота - только пагуба.**   *v.* Д498, Н502, П140
Better untaught than ill-taught.

90*   **Худая жена и хорошего мужа портит.**   *v.* Ж80, К78
[A bad wife will ruin even a good husband.] *Cf.* A good wife makes a good husband. Fat wives make lean husbands.

91   **Худая молва на крыльях летит.**   *v.* Д235,330, Х110
Ill news comes apace [has wings]. **Bad news travels fast.**

92   **Худая стоянка лучше доброго похода.**   *v.* †Б487, †Л149, †Х29, Х105
[A poor halt is better than a good march.] *Cf.* †A good run is better than a bad stand.

93*   **Худая та птица которая гнездо свое марает.**   *v.* Х106
It is an ill bird that fouls its own nest.

94   **Худо в карты играть а козырей не знать.**   *v.* А12, В54
[It's tough to play cards without knowing the trumps.] Many can pack the cards yet cannot play well.

95*   **Худо до добра не доведет.**   *v.* В63, Л76, Н99, О167, С81
Good can never grow out of evil.

96*   **Худо нажитое в прок нейдет.**   *v.* З121, К188, Н513, Т49, Ч127
Ill-gotten goods never prosper. *Gr.* Hes.*OD.* κακὰ κέρδεα ἰσ'ἄτῃσι.

97*   **Худо ходить с серпом на чужую жниву.**   *v.* В189,190, Н2,114,201,283
[Do not go to another's harvest with your own sickle.] Pluck not where you never planted. *Cf.* You can't get warm in another's fur coat. Scald not your lips in another man's pottage.

98*   **Худого не хвали, а хорошего не кори.**
[Neither praise the bad nor blame the good.] *Cf.* Praise makes a good man better and a bad man worse. Praise-all and blame-all are two blockheads. Reward and punishment are the walls of a city.

99   **Худое дворянство хуже пономарства.**
[Wicked nobility is even worse than the clergy.] Gentility without ability is worse than plain beggary.

00   **Худое долго помнится, а хорошее скоро забудется.**   *v.* Д311

01   **Худое дело когда жена не велела.**   *v.* Ж56, З26, Н568, П113
['Tis an ill thing indeed when the wife's unwilling.] He that will thrive must ask his wife.

02   **Худое дело коли сам истец судья.**
No man ought to be judge in his own cause. *Lat.* nemo debet esse iudex in propria causa.

103* **Худое колесо больше (громче) скрипит.**   *v.* В119, Г136, К206, П307, Ш13
The worst wheel of a cart creaks most (makes the most noise).

104 **Худое ремесло лучше хорошего воровства.**   *v.* Г203, Л151,162
[A bad job is better than a good theft.] Better beg than steal.

105* **Худое сидение лучше хорошего хода.**   *v.* Х92, С117
[A bad sit is better than a good walk.] **Better rue sit than rue flit.** *Cf.* Better ride on an ass that carries me than a horse that throws me. Better sit still than rise and fall. Better ride a poor horse than go afoot.

106 **Худой вор который в своей деревне ворует.**   *v.* Б234, Х93
[It is a wicked thief who steals in his own village.] The fox (wolf) preys furthest from his home (den).

107* **Худой мир лучше доброй брани (ссоры).**   *v.* Д138
Better a lean peace than fat victory. *Gr. Plan.*132: συμφόνημα, νίκημα.

108* **Худой солдат который не надеется быть генералом.**   *v.* П44
[It is a poor soldiear who doesn't dream of becoming a general.] Every French soldier carries a marshall's baton in his knapsack. Every little fish would be a whale.

109 **Худой солдат который свое ружье носить ленится.**   *v.* Д244, И71, Л46
[It's a poor soldier who is loathe to bear his gun.] A lazy sheep thinks its wool heavy. *SPL.* marti arma non sunt oneri.

110* **Худые вести не лежат на месте.**   *v.* Д330, Х91
Bad news travels fast. *SPL.* posterio solent esse deteriora.

Ц

1   **Царев гнев посол смерти.**
[The *tsar's* wrath is death's emissary.] He whom the prince hates is as good as dead.

2   **Царские глаза далеко видят.**
[The *tsar* sees far.] Kings have many ears and many eyes (long arms).

3* **Царствует ум головою.**   *v.* С68
[The mind governs the head.] My mind to me is a kingdom.

4   **Царь думает а народ ведает.**
[The *tsar* supposes and the people disposes.] *Cf.* What the king wills, the law wills.

5   **Царь и народ, все в землю пойдет.**   *v.* Ж152, П252, С198, У57
[The *tsar* and the people all lie alike in the ground.] We shall all lie alike in our graves.

6   **Царь птицам орел, а сокола боится.**
[The eagle is the king of birds yet he fears the falcon.] A lion may come to be beholden to a mouse.

7   **Цветы надо собирать (собирают) а не выбирать (выбирают).**   *v.* Х87
[Flowers are gathered, not selected.] *i.e. all are beautiful.* Fair flowers are never left standing by the wayside. No good horse of a bad colour.

8* **Целы сани и лошади пропали.**   *v.* И95, П206
[The sleigh is fine but the horse's are lost.] The operation was a success but the patient died. Uncover not the church to mend the choir. Do not cut the sheet to mend the dishcloth. Oft times for sparing of a little cost man has lost the large coat for the hood.

9* **Цель оправдает средства.**
The end justifies the means. *Lat.* cum finis est licitus, etiam media sunt licita.

10* **Цыплят осенью считают.**   *v.* В260, Д126, Ж34,41, М48,113, Н460,477, Т45
[Count your chicks in autumn.] Don't count your chickens till they hatch.

Ч

1   **Чарка вина прибавит ума.**
[A glass of wine will improve your mind.] *Cf.* Good wine engenders good blood.

2   **Час в добре проживешь (пробудешь) - все горе (по)забудешь.**   *v.* Л124
[An hour of goodness and you'll forget your sorrow.] An ounce of mirth is worth a pound of sorrow. One day of pleasure is worth two of sorrow.

3*   **Час от часу, а к смерти ближе.**   *v.* Б445, Д160,169, С197
[Each hour brings death nearer.] *Cf.* As soon as man is born he begins to die. †At every hour death is near.

4   **Час терпеть (минешь), (а) век жить (живешь).**   *v.* Д162
[Endure for an hour and live ever after.] *i.e. tolerate temporary inconvenience for long-term gain.* We can crowd eternity into an hour or stretch an hour into eternity. *Cf.* A man may lose as much in an hour than he can get in seven.

5   **Час упустишь, годом не наверстаешь.**
An hour wasted can never be regained.

6*   **Часом с квасом, порой с водой.**
[Sometimes some *kvas*, sometimes just water.] *i.e. so-so; humorous reply to the query "How are you?"* Feast today and fast tomorrow.

7   **Часто приходит беда и напасть, кому дана большая власть.**   *v.* Б323, В234,686, Н29
[Trouble and grief often befall those in great power.] High places have their precipices. *Cf.* Out of office, out of danger. Wealth and power do not give peace of mind.

8   **Часто радость во младости, кручина во старости.**   *v.* В175, М147, С23,208
[Many are the joys of youth, the woes of old age.] *Cf.* Reckless youth makes rueful age. The excesses of our youth are draughts upon our old age. Every dissipation of youth has to be paid for with a draught on old age.

9*   **Частые гости наскучат.**   *v.* Р48, Х41
A constant guest is never welcome.

10*   **Чаще счет так дольше дружба.**   *v.* Б225, Д44, К175, С332
Short reckonings make long friendship.

11* Чего в другом не любишь, того и сам не делай.   *v.* Д434, К74, Л177,
Чего сам не любишь (хочешь), того и другому не желай.   Н73,315, Т80
       Do as you would be done by. [Do not wish upon others what you dislike yourself.]

12 Чего в товаре не доплатишь, того и не получишь.   *v.* П51
       [You cannot have what you have not paid for.] Take all and pay all. You get what you
       pay for.

13 Чего не варишь, нечего того и в горшок класть. (Что не варят, то и в горшок не
кладут.) (Чего не ешь, того ножом не режь.)   *v.* В573, Г160, Ч96
       [Don't put in the pot what you don't plan to cook.] [Don't cut what you don't eat.] Take
       all you want, but eat all you take. *Cf.* Take not up more than you can bear. Do not bite
       off more than you can chew. To cut one's thongs according to one's leather.

14* Чего не видишь, того и не бредишь.   *v.* В413, Д48, Н218, С4
       What the eye sees not, the heart rues not. *Lat.* quod non videt oculus, cor non dolet.
       What the eye doesn't see, the heart won't crave (grieve for). *Cf.* If the eye won't admire,
       the heart won't desire.

15* Чего не знаешь, того и (не) желаешь.   *v.* М109, Ч14
       [You (do not) covet what you do not know.] Better to know nothing than to know it isn't
       so. What you don't know can't hurt you. *Cf.* Blue are the far away hills. He that knows
       knows least presumes most.

16 Чего не поищешь, того верно не сыщешь.
       Nothing seek, nothing find.

17* Чего не положил - не руши.   *v.* Л26, Н465
       [Do not destroy what you have not put together.] It is easier to pull down than build.

18* Чего не чаешь, то получаешь.   *v.* В44, Н23,58
       [That which you do not hope for, happens.] Least expected, sure to happen. It is the
       unforeseen that always happens. *SPL.* insperata saepius accidunt. *Cf. Lat.*
       Plaut.*Most.*1.3.40: insperata accidunt magis quam speres. A watched pot never boils.

19* Чего нельзя, того и хочется.   *v.* Г315, З391, Н69
       Forbidden fruit is sweet.

20 Чего стыдимся, того и таимся.   *v.* В148, П237, Х61
       [We keep secret whatever we are ashamed of.] Wherever there is a secret, there must be
       something wrong. A vice lives and thrives by concealment.

21 Чего хвалить не умеешь, того не хули.   *v.* Ч17
       [Do not criticize what you know not how to praise.] Unless you can do better, don't
       criticize. *Cf.* He may find fault that cannot mend. *Gr.* Ulpian.*Rhet.* οὐκ ἔχω πῶς
       ἐπαινέσω,ψέγειν δ'οὐβούλομαι. †Blame is safer than praise.

22 Чего хочется, того и просится.   *v.* Г220, Д402, П276
       Ask and have.

23* Чей берег, того и рыба. (Чей двор, того и хоромы.) (Чей конь, того и воз.)
(Чья земля, того и хлеб.)   *v.* Ч67
       [Who owns the shore, pwns the fish.] [Who owns the yard, owns the house.] [Who owns
       the horse, owns the load.] [Who owns the land, owns the bread.] *Cf.* Possession is nine
       points of the law.

24* **Чей хлеб ешь, того и обычай тешь. (Чье кушаю, того и слушаю.)** *v.* В623, Г39,
To the man submit at whose board you sit. Whose bread   Н120,409, О136, У50
I eat, his song I sing. *SPL.* utendum est foro. *Cf.* When in Rome, do as the Romans.

25* **Человек не для себя родится (трудится).** *v.* Ж107, К222
We are not born for ourselves.

26* **Человек не без греха.** *v.* И36, Н43,334,495, Ч30
Every man has his besetting sin. *SPL.* peccare humanum facinus est. *Cf.* Many without
punishment, none without sin.

27* **Человек предполагает а Бог располагает.** *v.* Н101
Man proposes, God disposes. *SPL.* homo proponit, deus disponit.

28 **Человек чем богат, тем и рад.** *v.* В575,581,600,652, Т12,38
[A man is happy with whatever wealth he has.] *Cf.* The greatest wealth is contentment
with a little.

29* **Человека родят не спросивши.** *v.* Б75
[Man is born unasked.] We weeping come into this world (and weeping hence we go),

30* **Человеку свойственно ошибаться.** *v.* Б149, И39, Н32,43, Ч26
To err is human. *Lat.* errare est humanum.

31* **Человек человеку волк.** *v.* Р89
Man is to man a wolf. Dog eat dog.

32 **Челном море (океана) не переехать.** *v.* Г286, М160, *Ap.*1.8
It is hard to cross the sea in an egg-shell [canoe]. *Cf.* To empty the sea with a spoon.

33 **Чем больше гвоздей, тем крепче.**
[The more nails, the more solid.] *Cf.* Hard as nails.

34* **Чем бы дитя не тешилось (играл), лишь бы не плакал(о).** *v.* Б364
[Anything so long as the child keeps still.] Anything for a quiet life.

35* **Чем дальше в лес, тем больше дров.** *v.* Д60

36 **Чем дарят, тем не корят.**
[Don't rub a gift in the recipient's face.] *Cf.* Rich gifts wax poor when givers prove unkind.

37 **Чем меньше разговоров, тем лучше для дела.** *v.* М61
Least said, soonest mended.

38* **Чем поиграешь, тем и ушибешься (зашибешься).** *v.* Г332, О81, Х16
[Whatever you play with may hurt you.] They who play with edged tools must expect
to be cut. You may play with the bull till you get his horn in your eye. He who plays
with a cat must expect to be scratched.

39 **Чем с молода похвалится, тем под старость покается.** *v.* В173, С207
If you lie upon roses when young, you'll lie upon thorns when old. Young men's knocks
old men feel.

40* **Чем согрешил, тем и накажешься.** *v.* К86, П104
Like fault, like punishment. *Cf.* Every sin carries its own punishment. He who has
sinned has already punished himself.

41   **Чем сосуд наполнен, то из него и льется.**   *v.* Д221, К71, У38
      [Whatever is in a vessel is what will pour out.] You don't get more out of a thing than
      you put into it. *Cf.* You get out of life what you put into it.

42*   **Чем старее, тем правее.**   *v.* В483, К307, С265
      Older and wiser. The older the better. *Luke.*5.39: ὁ παλαιὸς χρηστός ἐστιν.   *Lat.*
      vetus melius est. *Cf.* An old ox makes a straight furrow. *Lat.* quo antiquius, eo melius.

43*   **Чем ушибся, тем и лечись.**   *v.* A13, В169, Г24, З122, К106
      Seek your salve where you get your sore. *Lat.* similia similibus curantur.

44   **Чем черт не шутит (пока Бог спит).**   *v.* Г97, П120, Ч109
      [The devil may play any trick (while God's asleep).] *i.e. anything can happen.* The devil
      is master of all arts. The sky's the limit. Wonders will never cease.

45   **Чему быть, тому не миновать.**   *v.* O157, P68
      What will be, will (shall) be. There's no flying from fate.

46*   **Чему с молоду не научился, того и под старость не будешь знать.** *v.* Б181,К64,Н463,
      [What you haven't learnt in youth, you won't learn in old age.]   С35,273,У123,*Ap.*1.6
      You cannot teach an old dog new tricks. Young learn, learn fair.

47   **Чему посмеешься (позавидуешь), тому сам поработаешь (того сам берегись).** *v.* Д431,
      To laugh at someone is to be laughed back at.   Н107,413,414, Т13, *Ap.*1.103
      Cf. He finds fault with others and does worse himself. Those who live in glass houses
      shouldn't throw stones.

48*   **Через пень колоду валить.** *idiom.*
      [To do something] **in a slipshod manner.**

49   **Через сноп не молотят.**
      [No threshing after stacking.] *i.e. everything in turn.* *Cf.* Don't jump the gun.

50   **Черного кобеля не вымоешь до бела.**   *v.* Н17,339, С37
      [You cannot wash a black mare white.] A crow is never the whiter for washing herself
      often. *Cf.* The leopard cannot change his spots.

51   **Черт на черте едет.**   *v.* Б24, О67, Т1
      [One devil rides on another's back.] Ill comes often on the back of worse. *Cf.* One devil
      is like another.

52   **Черт своих не берет.**
      [The devil does not take his own.] The devil is good (kind) to (protects) his own.

53   **Честному мужу честен и поклон.**   *v.* Д19,292, З14, П55
      [An honest husband deserves an honest bow.] Honour will honour meet. Honour to
      whom honour is due.

54   **Честь на волоске висит, а потеряешь так и канатом не привяжешь.** *v.* Л26, Н29
      [Honour hangs by a thread, but once it drops - not even a cable will fasten it.]
      The post of honour is the post of danger. A broken reputation is never mended. Glass,
      china and reputations are easily cracked and never well mended.

55   **Честь переменяет нравы, (+ а редко на добро).**   *v.* 380
      Honours change manners (but rarely improve them). *Lat.* honores mutant mores.

56   **Честь честью, а дело делом.**   *v.* Б295, Г32
            [Honour is one thing, but business another.] Honour and profit lie not in one sack.
            Cf. Honour buys no beef in the market.

57   **Чечетка отлетит а гнездо останется.**   *v.* Г173
            [The redpoll may fly away but the nest remains.] The great wall stands; the builder is
            gone. There are no birds of this year in last year's nests.

58   **Чистое к поганому не пристанет.**   *v.* Г310, О84, Н449
            [Cleanliness will not abide filth.] *SPL.* Quin dicant de te homines, non est in manu tua:
            id tamen est, merito ne dicant. *Cf.* Scandal will rub off like dirt when it is dry.

59*   **Чистота человека к Богу приводит (половина спасения).**
            Cleanliness is next to godliness.

60   **Что ближе к сердцу, то скорее и на языке.**   *v.* У37, Ч78
            What the heart thinks the tongue speaks.

61   **Что Бог послал, то и наше.**   *v.* Б251, Д79
            [That which God has given is ours.] *Gr.* τὸ φέρον ἐκ θεοῦ καλῶς φέρειν χρεί. *Lat.*
            quod dii dant, fero.

62*   **Что было, то сплыло (то былью поросло).**   *v.* Б457,482, П271,279, Ч93,105
            What's done is done. Let bygones be bygones. *Lat.* quod periit, periit.

63   **Что в деревне (поле) родится, то в городе (доме) пригодится.**   *v.* Г320
            [What's born in the country comes in handy in town.] The chicken is the country's but
            the city eats it.

64   **Что в лоб, что по лбу.**   *v.* В511, Е14, К277, С108, Х85, Ч69
            [Either hit your head or bump it.] *i.e. same difference.* It's either six of one or half a
            dozen of the other. *Cf.* By river come, by water go.

65   **Что в сердце варится, то в лице не утаится.**   *v.* Л84
            The face is the index of the heart (mind).

66   **Что в те сани садиться, в которых не кататься?**   *v.* Н198,222
            [Why climb into a sled if it's going nowhere?] *Cf.* Never do things by halves.

67   **Что взято, то свято.**   *v.* С36, Ч23
            [That is sacred which is taken.] Possession is nine points of the law. *Cf.* Who accepts
            nothing, has nothing to return.

68   **Что всем, то и одному.**   *v.* И113, Т84, Ч82
            [What's good for all, is good for one.] What's good for the goose is good for the gander.
            SPL. pari iure sumus, aequales inter nos sunt calculi.

69*   **Что выпито (дурно), что вылито (худо), все равно.**   *v.* В511, Е14, О4, П278, С108,
            [Drunk or spilt, it's all the same.] *Cf.* It's no use crying over spilt milk.   Ч64,105

70   **Что глазами не доглядишь, то мошной доплатишь.**   *v.* Д124, З334,85, Л187, Н381
            [What your eyes miss, your purse will pay.] *i.e. look before you buy.* Keep your eyes
            open - a sale is a sale. The buyer needs a thousand eyes, the seller wants but one.

71*   **Что говорит большой, слышит и малый.**
            Little pitchers have long ears.

72* **Что другу желаешь, то сам себе получаешь.** *v.* Л76, К14, Н403, О177, П154, Т13
[What you wish upon another shall befall you too.] Curses, like chickens, come home to roost. Dig a pit for another and fall into it yourself.

73 **Что есть, вместе - а чего нет, пополам.** *v.* Д397
[Let's share what we have and split what we don't.] Share and share alike. Heads - I win, tails - you lose.

74 **Что за честь коли нечего есть.**
[What good is honour when there's nothing to eat.] Honour buys no beef in the market.

75* **Что из дуба масло.** *v.* З101, И83, К45, Щ7
[Like oil from an oak.] Like water (milk) (blood) from a stone.

76* **Что имеем - не храним, а потерявши - плачем.** *v.* В409, К215, П125, Т2, У64,91
[We do not preserve what we have, yet we cry at its loss.] The worth of a thing is best known by the want of it. You never miss water till the well runs dry.

77 **Что испек, то и кушай.** *v.* К34, П74, С38
As you bake, so shall you eat.

78 **Что кого веселит (у кого болит), тот об этом и говорит.** *v.* У37

79 **Что кота больше гладишь, то он больше хвост подымает.**
[The more you pet a cat, the more it raises its tail.] *Cf.* It is in his own interest that the cat purrs.

80* **Что легко наживается, легко и проживается.** *v.* Б479, В662, К47
Easy come, easy go.

81 **Что летом родится, то зимою пригодится.** *v.* Л61
Winter eats what summer lays up.

82 **Что миру, то и бабину сыну.** *v.* И113, Т84, Ч68
[What's good for all, is good for one.] What's sauce for the goose is sauce for the gander.

83* **Что муж возом не навозит, то жена горшком наносит.**
[What the husband doesn't haul in his cart, the wife brings in her jug.] *i.e. the wife is resourceful. Cf.* Who finds a wife, finds a good thing. †A wife can throw out with a spoon faster than a husband can bring in with a shovel.

84* **Что на уме думается, то во сне видится.** *v.* Г228, Л71, С80,226
[Dreams are about what's on your mind.] The net of the sleeper catches fish. The pig dreams of acorns and the goose of maize.

85 **Что написано пером, то не вырубишь топором.** *v.* Н140

86 **Что не властен ты давать, то бесчестно обещать.**
[It's dishonest to promise what you can't deliver.] Never promise what you can't perform. To offer much is a kind of denial. *Lat.* quod pare non possis, verbis promittere noli.

87 **Что не наше, того нам и не надо.**
[We have no need for whatever is not ours.] Wise men care not for what they cannot have.

88 **Что не складно то и не ладно.**
You can't drive a square peg into a round hole. *SPL.* asino et bove non est arandum.

89   **Что ни город, то норов (+ что ни деревня, то обычай).**   *v.* Р26, С140
[The city has its habits (and the country has its customs).] Every country has its own customs.

90*   **Что ни делается, все к лучшему.**   *v.* Б259
Whatever happens is for the best. All's for the best in the best of all possible worlds.

91   **Что ни делаешь, а на хвост осматривайся.**
[Whatever you do, mind your tail.] Make not thy tail broader than thy wings.

92   **Что о том тужить, чего нельзя воротить.** *v.* О4

93*   **Что окоротишь, того не воротишь.**   *v.* Б219, О85, П278,279, Р55, Ч62,105
What's done cannot be undone.

94   **Что откладывается, не отставляется.**   *v.* М84
[What is deferred is not averted.] You may delay, but time will not. *SPL.* quod dissertur non aufertur.

95   **Что по морю (реке) плывет, всего не переловишь (+ а что люди говорять, всего не переслушаешь).**   *v.* В523,533
[You can't catch all the fish in the sea (river), (+ nor pick up all that people say).] There's a limit to everything. *Cf.* You can't have everything (No one has everything).

96   **Что поднял, то и понес.**   *v.* В91, Д86, Л88, Т85, Р76, Ч13
[Whatever you pick up, you must carry.] Take not up more than you can bear. *Cf.* He that takes the devil into his boat, must carry him over the sound.

97*   **Что посеешь, то и сожнешь. (Что припасешь, то и сосешь.)**   *v.* В160, К88,287,318,
As you sow, so shall you reap.   П73,192

98   **Что природа дала, то и мылом не вымоешь.**   *v.* Г246, Н17, Ч50
[What nature has given, not even soap will wash out.] Drive nature out of the door and it will return by the window. You can drive out nature with a pitchfork, but she keeps on coming back. A crow is never the whiter for washing herself often.

99*   **Что родится, то годится.**   *v.* Б103, В649, Г15, К225, М6
[Whatever has been born into the world has a purpose.] There is no man born into this world whose work is not born with him. There's reason in all things. *Cf.* Everyone has his lot and a wide world before him.

100   **Что с возу упало, то (давно) пропало.**   *v.* Г74, Д4, К59, М71, П279, С3,
[Whatever has fallen off the cart is lost forever.] For a lost thing, care not. *SPL.* rosam, quae praeteriit, ne quaeras iterum.

101   **Что с гуся вода, небылые слова.**   *v.* Н91
[Empty words are like water off a duck's back.] Words, like feathers, are carried away by the wind. Words are but wind.

102*   **Что скоро, то хворо (не споро).**   *v.* В539, Г90, К235, П188
Haste makes waste. *SPL.* festina lente.

103   **Что старее, то скупее.**   *v.* С281
The older, the more covetous. *SPL.* senecta ad rem est atenta nimium. *Cf.* The older the bird, the more unwillingly it parts with its feathers.

104* **Что у трезвого на уме, то у пьяного на языке.** *v.* У49
What soberness conceals, drunkenness reveals. *Gr. Diog.*8.43: τὸ ἐν τῇ καρδίᾳ τοῦ νήφοντος ὑπερ γλώττης ἐστὶ, τοῦ μεθύοντος. *Lat.* quod in corde (animo) sobrii, id est in lingua ebrii. *SPL.* in vino veritas.

105* **Что ушло, того не воротишь.** *v.* Б219, О4, П279, Ч69,93
Things past cannot be recalled.

106* **Чтоб других учить, надо свой разум наточить.** *v.* Н468, С212, У124, Я20
[To teach others, you must sharpen your own wits first.] You have to be smarter than the dog to teach him tricks.

107* **Чтобы рыбку съесть, надо в воду лезть.** *v.* К181, Л45, Н376, П273, Р91
[To taste of the fish, one must wade in the water.] You can't catch trout with dry trousers (breeches). *Cf.* The cat would eat fish and would not wet her feet. Fish are not caught with a bird call.

108* **Чтобы узнать человека, надо семь (три) пуд(а) соли с ним съесть.** *v.* Б390, В214,У78
Before you make a friend, eat a bushel of salt with him.

109 **Чудеса не колеса, сами катятся.** *v.* П120, Ч44
[Wonders, unlike wheels, turn by themselves.] Wonders will never cease.

110 **Чужая беда людям смех.** *v.* Л206, Ч114,132
Everything is funny as long as it happens to someone else.

111 **Чужая денежка карман прожжет.**
Your [others'] money burns (a hole) in your pocket.

112 **Чужая душа - потемки (темный лес) (что дремучи бор).** *v.* В142,152,184, Е3, Т29,32
[Dark is the mind of the stranger.] You can look in the eyes, but not in the heart. *Cf.* Still waters run deep. You can't tell a book by its cover.

113 **Чужая похвала жене часовая, а мужнина вековая.**
[A husband's praise is forever, while the stranger's is but a passing whim.] *Cf.* Praise from a wife is praise indeed.

114* **Чужая рана не больна. (Что у тебя болит, то у друга не свербит.) (Чужая слеза - вода.) (Чужое горе в половину горевать.)** *v.* В657, Г267, Л206, Н110,П300, Ч110,132
[Another's wound does not hurt.] [Your pain doesn't bother your friend.] [Others' tears are mere water.] [Others' sorrow is only half-bad.] It's easy to bear the misfortunes of others.

115* **Чужая сторона прибавит ума.**
He that travels far knows much.

116* **Чужие грехи пред очами, а свои за плечами.** *v.* В309,659, С77
The hunchback sees not his own hump, but his companion's. We see not what is in the wallet behind. The eye that sees all things sees not itself. *SPL.* nemo videt id manticae quod in tergo est.

117 **Чужие дети шалят - нам смех, а свои - так горе.** *v.* Д431, Л206, Ч47
[We laugh when others' children misbehave, but cry when ours do.] *Cf.* To laugh at others is to be laughed back at.

118* **Чужие хлебы приедчивы. (Чужой хлеб всегда слаще.)**   *v.* B178,583, H118, C168, Ч129
[Others' bread is sweet.] The wholesomest meat is at another's cost. Our neighbour's ground yields better corn than ours. *SPL.* fertilior seges est alienis semper in agris.

119 **Чужим богат не будешь. (Чужое добро не в корысть.)**   *v.* B185, Г128, H111, Ч122
[You cannot prosper with others' goods.] *Cf.* Ill-gotten goods never prosper.

120* **Чужим добром подносить ведром.**   *v.* И110, H441
[To offer others' goods by the bushel.] He is free of fruit that wants an orchard. He is free of horse that never had one.

121 **Чужим здоровьем болен.**   *v.* Г95, B181, З65, C312
[He is ill from others' health.] *i.e. envious.* An envious man waxes lean with the fatness of his neighbour.

122 **Чужим ртом сыту не быть.**   *v.* B180, H111, Ч119
[You cannot satisfy your hunger vicariously.] He that is fed at another's hand (table) may stay long ere he be full.

123* **Чужим умом умен не будешь (не выстроишь дом).**   *v.* B556
[You cannot be smart (build a house) with another's wits.] Every man is the architect of his own fortune. *Cf.* Every tub must stand on its own bottom.

124 **Чужими руками хорошо жар загребать.** *v.* X73

125 **Чужое беречь пуще своего.**
[Caring for others' belongings is worse than caring for your own.] *i.e. because it is more difficult Cf.* When interest is lost, memory is lost.

126* **Чужое взять (любить), свое потерять.**   *v.* A19, B522, З4, K222, M132
[Take another's and lose your own.] Avarice loses all in seeking to gain all. *Cf.* If you run after two hares, you will catch neither.

127 **Чужое добро (чужой кус) впрок (в рот) нейдет.**   *v.* З121, K188, H513, T49, X96
Ill-gotten goods seldom prosper.

128* **Чужое и хорошее - постыло, а свое и худо - да мило. (Чужое не прочно и большое, а свое и малое, да правое.) (Чужой обед сладок, да не прочен.)**   *v.* B130, Г280, Д386,
Dry bread at home is better than roast meat abroad. [Better a little of   H116, C61
your own than a lot of another's.] [Another's board may be savoury but it's unreliable.]

129* **Чужой ломоть больше всегда.**   *v.* B178,583, П122, C168, Ч118
The grass is always greener. Our neigbour's ground (cow) yields better corn (more milk) than ours. *SPL.* vicinium pecus grandius uber habet. *Cf.* Your pot broken seems better than my whole one.

130 **Чужой мошне не будь указчик.**   *v.* B188, Д28
Do not be liberal (free) of another man's cost (pottage).

131 **Чужому товару цены не уставишь.**   *v.* B199, H400
[You cannot price another's wares.] Skeer your own fire.

132* **Чужую беду руками (бобами) разведу, а к своей ума не приложу.**   *v.*Г267,H110,П300,
[Others' problems are easy to solve, it's one's own that are insoluble.]   C70,Ч110,114
It is easy to bear the misfortunes of others. We can always bear our neighbours' misfortunes.

133* **Чужую кровлю кроешь, а в свою капает (течет).** *v.* Ж93, Н326, С47,70, У42
[Repair not another's roof when your own is leaking.] The door of the carpenter is loose. Look to thyself when thy neighbour's house is on fire. Do not neglect your own field and plough your neighbour's. *SPL.* alienos agros irrigare, suis sitientius.

134* **Чуть-чуть не считается.** *v.* П280
A little doesn't count. Almost is not good enough. Almost was never hanged (never killed a fly.) *Cf.* †Every little bit counts.

135 **Чья бы корова мычала, а твоя бы молчала.** *v.* 317, О116
[Better let others' cows bellow and your's keep still.] Sweep before your own door before you sweep before others'. Point not at others' spots with a foul finger. *Cf.* Judge well yourself before you criticise.

136 **Чья сторона сильнее, та и правее.** *v.* Г87, С118, У54
[Whichever side is stronger shall prevail.] Might is right. The stronger always succeeds. Plaut.*Truc.*812: plus potest qui plus valet. The weakest goes to the wall. *SPL.* corvi lusciniis honoratiores.

Ш

1   **Шапочно знакомство не пойдет в потомство.**
[Casual friendship is ephemeral.] *Cf.*A short acquaintance brings repentance.

2*   **Шахания много, да мат один.**   *v.* Г299, Н431, С98,291
[There may be many checks, but only one mate.] A man can only die once. There are more threatened than stricken.

3*   **Шелудивая (паршивая) овца все стадо портит.**   *v.* В7, К8,203, Л98, О54,148
One scabbed sheep will mar a whole flock.

4   **Шемякин суд.**
[An unfair trial.] A kangaroo court.

5*   **Шепчет с уха на ухо, а слышно с угла на угол.**   *v.* Г183, Н411
Whispered words are heard far. *Cf.* Confide in an aunt and the world will know.

6*   **Шершень паутину пробьет, а муха явязнет.**   *v.* А18, З75, Н268
[Webs catch flies but let hornets go.] Laws catch flies but let hornets go free. We hang little thieves and take off our hats to great ones.

7*   **Шила в мешке не утаишь.**   *v.* В49,141, С237
[An awl cannot be hidden in a sac.] An eel cannot be hidden in a sac. Fire cannot be hidden in a flax (straw).

8   **Шилом воду (моря) не нагреешь.**   *v.* И63,79,111, О114
[You cannot heat water with an awl.] You cannot make a silk purse out of a sow's ear. You can't make a whistle out of a pig's tail. You cannot saw wood with a hammer.
Cf. To cut blocks with a razor.

9   **Широка в ад дорога, а попадешь, так нет поворота.**   *v.* В157
The descent to Hell is easy [and there's no returning once you're there.]
Cf. Lat. Virg.*Aen.*6.126: facilis descensus Averni.

10   **Шкодлив как кошка, а труслив как заяц.**   *v.* Г249, М143, П313
[Mischievous as a cat but fearful as a rabbit.] A bully is always a coward.

11*   **Штопай дыру пока невелика.**   *v.* Б183, Р33, О141
[Plug a hole while it is small.] A stitch in time saves nine. Prevention is better than cure. Thatch your roof before the rain begins. *Cf.* A patch is the sign of thrift, a hole the sign of negligence. Where there's a mouse hole, there will soon be a rat hole.

12   **Шуба за кафтаном тянется.**
[The fur trails close behind the cape.] *i.e. said of autumn in general and of mid-september in particular.*

13*   **Шумом праву не быть.**   *v.* В119, Г136, Д407, К206, Х103
[Shouting won't make one right.] Those who are right need not talk loudly. Some think that the louder they shout, the more persuasive their argument is. Striking manners are bad manners. *Cf.* Knowledge talks lowly, ignorance loudly. One who talks the loudest says the least.

14   **Шуму уши полны, а перекусить нечего.**   *v.* Б21,367, Г226, Е45, Р24,236, У7
[The ears are full of promises yet there's nothing to eat.] Fair (fine) words butter no parsnips (fill not the belly). Hungry bellies have no ears.

15   **Шути да оглядывайся!**   *v.* И117, П207, Т16
Leave a jest when it pleases lest it turn to earnest.

16*   **Шутить над другом, любить шутку и над собою.**   *v.* Д431, Ч47, *Ap.*1.103
If you give (make) a jest, you must take a jest.

17   **Шутить хорошо до краски.**   *v.* И117, Н489, П207
Leave a jest when it pleases lest it turn to earnest. Long jesting was never good. *Cf.* Don't carry a joke too far. When your jest is at its best, let it rest.

18*   **Шутка в добро не введет.**
[Joking leads to no good.] True jests breed bad blood. *Cf.* Dogs begin in jest and end in earnest. He makes a foe who makes a jest.

19*   **Шутка, минутка - а заражает на час.**
[A joke lasts a minute but is remembered an hour.] A laugh a day makes the world seem gay. *Cf.* The most utterly lost of all days is that on which you have not laughed.

20   **Шуту в дружбе не верят.**
[Friendship brooks no jest.] Fall not out with a friend for a trifle. A friend must not be wounded, even in jest. *Syr.*54: amicum laedere ne ioco quidem licet. Better lose a jest than a friend. *Lat.*Quint.6.3.28: potius amicum quam dictum perdere. *Cf.* Some had rather lose their friend than their jest. A joke never gains over an enemy, but often loses a friend.

21   **Шутя мед пьют, а в правду кандалы трут.**   *v.* Г188, У20
[Jest is sweet, truth stifling.] *Cf.* The truth always hurts. Flattery begets friends but the truth begets enmity.

Щ

1   **Щеголял с молоду, а под старость умирает с голоду.**   *v.* Г335
       An idle youth, a needy age.

2*   **Щей горшок, да сам большой.**   *v.* Д172
       [A store of soup and strength to go with it.] *said of someone who is independent and self-sufficient.* Health and money go far. *Cf.* When the stomach is full, the heart is glad.

3   **Щенок лает, от больших слышит.**   *v.* М30
       [The pup barks as it hears its elders bark.] As the old cock crows, the young cock learns. *Cf.* Like dogs, when one barks, all bark. One barking dog sets all the street a barking. *Lat.* latrante uno, statim et alte canis. Dogs bark as they are bred.

4*   **Щеня злое от злой суки.**   *v.* К69,89, О167, П52
       We may not expect a good whelp from an ill dog.

5*   **Щи да каша - пища наша.**   *v.* К99, Х20
       [Cabbage soup and *kasha* is our staple diet.] *Cf.* Bread is the staff of life.

6   **Щука то умерла, да зубы остались (живы).**
       [The pike's dead, but its jaws remain (live).] Though the wound be healed, yet a scar remains.

7   **Щупает петуха, не будет ли яйца.**   *v.* З101, И83, К45, Ч75
       [To expect eggs from a rooster.] You go to a goat (ass) for wool. *EA.* de lana caprina. *Cf.* If you are lucky even your rooster will lay eggs.

Э

1   **Это вилами на воде написано.** *v.* Б8, В503
    [That's written on the water with a pitchfork.] He wags a wand in water. *Cf.* To be still up in the air. That remains to be seen. *Gr.* ὕδατος γράφειν. *Lat. EA.* in aqua scribis.

2   **Эта ворона нам не оборона.** *v.* Д205, П131
    [That raven is not our haven.] *rhyme signifying unreliable help.* Don't hold your breath.

3   **Это еще (все) присказка, а сказка (будет) впереди.**
    [This is only the introduction, the story is yet to come.] *used in a positive sense.* You haven't seen anything yet.

4   **Это еще (только) цветочки, а ягодки впереди.** *v.* Т20
    [These are but the blossoms, the berries are yet to come.] *used negatively.* Flowers are the pledges of fruit. The worst is yet to come. This is only the beginning.

5   **Этот номер не пройдет.**
    [That ploy won't work.] That won't wash. You won't get away with this.

Я

1* **Я его выручил, а он меня выучил.**
[I helped him and he taught me a lesson.] *i.e. ungrateful.*

2 **Я не я, и лошадь не моя (и я не извозчик).** *v.* M169, H164,335
[Don't look at me, it's not my horse (I'm not the driver).] *Cf.* Let him that owns the cow take it by the tail. To be clean.

3 **Яблок на сосне не бывает. (Яблоки на осине не растут.)** *v.* Б168, Д364, H399, O150
[Ask not apples of a pine (asp).] To ask pears of an elm tree.

4* **Яблоко от яблони не далеко откатывается (падает).** *v.* K84, M95
The apple never falls far from the tree.

5 **Яблочное семя знает свое время.**
[An apple seed knows its time.] Harvest follows seed time.

6 **Явен грех малу вину творит.** *v.* П89
[A sin avowed diminishes blame.] A fault confessed is half redressed.

7 **Язык без костей, мелет что хочет.**
[The tongue has no bones and rattles any which way.] The tongue is an unruly member. *Cf.* The tongue breaks bone, and itself has none.

8 **Язык враг, прежде ума глаголет.** *v.* Я13
Your tongue runs before your wit.

9 **Язык голову кормит, он же и спину портит (до беды доводит) (до добра не доведет).** *v.* Р72
[The tongue both feeds the head and breaks the back (gets you into trouble).]
Cf. The mouth is the executioner and doctor of the body.

10 **Язык лепечет, а голова не ведает.** *v.* Я8
The tongue runs before one's wit. *Cf.* The fool's tongue is long enough.

11* **Язык мал, великим человеком шатает.**
[Small tongues may move great men.] Under the tongue men are crushed to death. The tongue is a little thing, but it fills the universe with trouble.

12   **Язык мой, а речи не свои говорю.**
[I speak with my tongue but not with my own words.]   Wise men make proverbs, fools repeat them.

13* **Язык мой - враг мой.**   *v.* П296, Я8
My tongue is my enemy.

14   **Язык не стальной, а режет.**   *v.* М9, О109
The tongue is not steel yet it cuts.

15   **Язык разум открывает.**
[The tongue reveals the mind.]   Your thoughts go no further than your vocabulary. Style is the dress of thought.   *Cf.* Be careful of your thoughts, they may become words at any time. The heart thinks what the tongue speaks.

16   **Язык языку ответ дает (даст).**   *v.* К21,72, Н4,21,35, *Ap.*1.33
[One tongue (may) answer(s) another.]   Make use of your tongue and you will find out. Like question, like answer.   Such answer as a man gives, such will he get.

17* **Языком и грады ниспадают.**   *v.* О14
[Cities fall by the tongue.]   Cities are taken by the ears. A city that parleys is half gotten.

18* **Языком не спеши, а делом не ленись (спеши делом).**   *v.* Д7, Н274,422, О10
[Be slow to speak but quick to act.]   Be slow to promise and quick to perform.   *Cf.* Let your actions be equal to your promises.

19   **Языком что хочишь болтай, а рукам воли не давай.**   *v.* Б356, Н134
[Let your tongue run at rover but keep your hands still.]   Words may pass but blows fall heavy. Sticks and stones may break my bones, but names will never hurt me.

20* **Яйца курицу не учат.**   *v.* Н468, С212, У121
Eggs can't teach the hen. Do not teach your grandmother to suck eggs.   Teach your father to get children.   *SPL.* ante barbam doces senem.

21   **Ямщик в дороге пайщик.**   *v.* Г245, Н496,591, П85, Х81
[The coachman is a welder on the road.]   A man can do a lot of things if he has to. *Cf.* Necessity is the mother of invention. Necessity does everything well.

22   **Ярко слово смущает сердце.**   *v.* Б158, С180
[Pointed words stir the heart.]   The tongue stings. The tongue wounds more than the arrow. The tongue is sharper than the sword.

23   **Ясли к лошади не ходят.**   *v.* М76, О17, С96, Х21
[The manger will not go to the horse.]   The tail does not shake the dog.   *Cf.* If the mountain will not come to Mahomet, Mahomet must go to the mountain.

24   **Ястреб ловит что хочет, а ратай что может.**
[The hawk may catch whatever it likes, but the ploughman whatever he can.]   Since we cannot get what we like, let us like what we can get.   *Cf.* A man must plough with such oxen as he has.

25   **Ящерка маленька, да зубы остреньки.**   *v.* Ж15, М13, Н207, П297
[A lizard may be small, but its teeth are sharp.]   No viper so little but has its venom. *Cf.* A thorn is small, but he who has felt it doesn't forget it.

APPENDIX 1: PROVERBS & SAYINGS WITH PERSONAL &
GEOGRAPHICAL NAMES

Авраам

1   **По бороде Авраам, а по делам хам.**   *v.* Б340, М171, У107
    [He has the beard of an Abraham but the manners of a ham.] It is not the beard that makes the philosopher. *Cf.* If a beard were a sign of smartness, the goat would be Socrates.

Агафья   *v.* Фадей 85

Адам

2*   **Женою и Адам из рая изгнан.**   *v. Ap.*1.59
    [Even Adam was expelled from paradise because of his wife.] No mischief but a woman is at the bottom of it. *Lat.* Juv.*Sat.*6.242: nulla fere causa est in qua femina litem moverit.

Аксен

3   **Всяк Аксен про себя умен.**
    [Every Bart thinks he's smart.] *rhyme* Our own opinion is never wrong.

Азовское море   *v.* Дон 16

Ананья

4   **В людях Ананья (Илья), а дома каналья (свинья).**   *v.* В64, Д390
    A saint abroad and a devil at home.

5   **Каков Ананья, такова у него Маланья.**   *v.* В599, К266, М164, П109, Р9
    [Every Ananya has his Melanie.] Every Jack has his Jill. Likeness causes liking. Birds of a feather flock together.

Анна

6   **Хороша дочь (дочка) Аннушка, коли (когда) хвалит мать да бабушка.**   *v.* В647,
    [Annie's a fine girl according to her mother and grandmother.]   П235, С57
    No mother has a homely child.

Варвара

7   **Варвара мне тетка, а правда сестра.**   *v.* С305, Х26
    [Ruth may be my aunt, but truth is my sister.] *rhyme meaning truth is paramount.*

Волга

8   **В ложке Волги не переедешь.**   *v.* Ч32
    [You won't cross the Volga in a dingy.] It is hard to sail over the sea in an egg-shell.

9   **Волгу плыть долго, а Дунай широко.**
    [The Volga's too long to swim, the Danube too wide.]

Вологда   *v.* Москва 39

Георгий

10   **Что у волка в зубах, то Егорий послал.**
    [What the wolf has in his jaw is a gift from St. George.] *historically, St. George's day (3 April) was the first day of the year that sheep were let out to pasture, and hence, were vulnerable to wolves.* Cf. God never sends mouth but he sends meat. To hold is to have.

Герасим

11   **Возьмем да покрасим и выйдет Герасим.**
    [Add some colour and it looks like Jerome.] *rhyme* Everything is according to the colour of the glass with which one views it.

Гриша

12   **У всякого Гришки свои делишки.**   *v.* З153
    [Every Bob has his job.] *rhyme* Every man knows his own business best.

Демид

13   **Всякий Демид себе норовит.**   *v.* В570, И34, Н88
    [Every Demid strives in his own interest.] A man is a lion in his own cause. Every man draws water to his own mill.

14   **Два Демида, да оба не видят.**
    [Two fools and neither can see.] Two fools in one house are too many.

Дон

15   **Живет на Дону, оставя дома жену.**
    [He lives on the Don, having left his wife at home.] *rhyme*

16*   **Рассказывать Донскому казаку Азовские вести.**
    [Tell a Cossack from the Don news of the Azov.] *i.e. futile effort, he's been there.*

17   **У кого много всего в дому, тот не будет в лямке на Дону.**   *v.* Б446, У35
    [He whose house is full will never end up towing on the Don.]

Егор

18   **Про горького Егорку поют и песню горьку.**
    [A bitter song for bitter Egor.] *rhyme*

Емеля

19   Ему говори про попа, а он про Емелью дурака.   v. T77, Ap.1.28
       [Talk to him about the priest, and he responds about Emile the fool.]

20*   Мели Емеля твоя неделя.   v. Ap.1.107
       [It's Emile's turn to bend our ear.] To talk the hind leg off a donkey.

Еремей

21*   Всяк (сам) Еремей про себя разумей.   v. В563, З17,154, П293
       [Every Jerry of himself should be wary.] Point not at other's spots with a foul finger. The
       cobbler should stick to his last. Every man to his trade

22   По Ереме колпак.   v. Ap.1.81
       [Every Jerry gets his cap.] *i.e. what he deserves.* If the cap fits wear it.

Еремин   *v.* Фома 93,97

Иван

23   Иван в дуду играет, а Мария с голоду умирает.   v. И133, К157, О43
       [Ivan's piping while Mary's starving.] Some have the hap, others stick in the gap.

24   Кабы не кабы, так бы Ивана Великого в кувшин заткнул.   v. А5, Е21,25
       [If ifs were not ifs, I'd have put away Ivan the Great.] If my aunt had been a man, she'd
       have been my uncle. If is the epitaph on the tomb of opportunity.

25   Люби Ивана а береги кармана.   v. В32, Д426,437, Х25
       [Love your John but watch your pocket.] Lend money and lose a friend. *Cf.* Love your
       neighbour, but do not pull down the fence.

26   Не надейся на Ивана, а бери из своего кармана.
       [Don't count on John, but reach in your own pocket.] *Cf.* He that is fed at another's
       hand, may stay long ere he be full.

27   Чему Ваня не научился, того Иван не выучит.   v. К64, Н470
       [You cannot teach old John what little Johnnie hasn't learned.] What Johnny will not
       teach himself, Johnny will never know. What's learnt in the cradle lasts till the tomb.
       Cf. You cannot teach an old dog new tricks.

28   Я говорю про Ивана, а ты про болвана.   v. T77, Ap.1.19,31
       [I'm talking about John and you're on about some fool.] Don't change the subject.

Илья   *v.* Ананья 4

Камчатка

29   Камчатная наволочка соломою набита.
       [Kamchatka pillowcases are stuffed with straw.]

Казань   *v.* Фома 95

30   Казань осетрами а Сибир соболями.
       [Kazan for sturgeon and Siberia for sable.] *Cf.* Oxford knives and London wives.

Киев

31*   **В огороде бузина а в Киеве дядька.**   *v. Ap.*1.28
[Elderberries in the yard and an elder uncle in Kiev.] *i.e. a non-sequitur.* That is for that and butter is for fish.

32   **Осел в Киеве (Царьграде) конем не будет.**   *v.* В438, Г337, *Ap.*1.61
[The ass may go to Kiev, but he still won't be a horse.] If an ass goes a-travelling, he'll not come back a horse.

33*   **Язык до Киева доведет.**   *v. Я*16
[Your tongue will get you to Kiev.] *i.e. by asking the way.* Who has a tongue will find his way. He who uses his tongue will reach his destination.

Макар

34*   **На бедного Макара все шишки валятся.**   *v.* Н1
[All the cones fall on poor Makar.] An unhappy man's cart is easy to overthrow. The Tracys have always the wind in their faces. He would fall on his back and break his nose. *SPL.* arbore deiecta quivis ligna colligit.

Марина

35   **Князью княгиня, боярину Марина, а всякому (мила) своя Катерина.**
[The prince has his princess, the lord his Marina and the yeoman his Katrina.] *Cf.* To each his own.

Мария

36*   **И на Машку промашка. (На всяку Машка бывает промашка.)**   *v.* Ж102, И35, К165,
[Even Masha can mess up.] [Every *Masha* may err.]   Н43,495
Even Homer sometimes nods. It is a good horse that never stumbles. No man is infallible.

37   **Хороша Маша да не наша.**   *v.* Х43
[Masha's fine though she's not mine.] It's a good fish if it were caught.

Москва

38*   **В Москве все найдешь кроме птичьего молока.**
[One can find everything in Moscow except pigeon's milk.] All things are to be bought at Rome [Moscow]. *Lat.* omnia venalia Romae.

39   **В Москве к заутрене звонили, а в Вологде звон слышали.**
[Moscow churchbells chiming matins are heard in Vologda.]

40*   **Все дороги ведут в Москву.**
All roads lead to Rome [Moscow].

41*   **Говорят в Москве кур доят.**   *v.* Г192
[They say you can milk chickens in Moscow.]

42   **Деревня родина краше Москвы.**
[One's country hometown is lovelier than Moscow.]

43   **Живучи (жить) в Москве, пожить и в тоске.**
[Live in Moscow, live in sorrow.] *Cf.* See Naples and die.

44*   **Москва всем городам мать.**
        [Moscow is the mother of all cities.]

45   **Москва деревне не указ.**
        [Moscow is no model for the country village.]

46   **Москва кому мать, кому мачеха.**
        [Moscow is mother to some, stepmother to others.]

47   **Москва людна и хлебна.**
        [Moscow is populous and lucrative.]

48*   **Москва молодцов видала.**
        [Moscow has seen her share of clever people.]

49   **Москва не клином сошлась (не сразу строилась). (Не вдруг Москва строилась.)**
        Moscow wasn't built in a day.

50*   **Москва не плачет (слезам не верит).**
        [Moscow doesn't cry (believe in tears).]

51   **Москва от копеечной свечки сгорела.**
        [A penny candle burned down Moscow.] *twice: 28 July 1493 and 30 May 1737*

52*   **Москва - сердце России.**
        [Moscow - the heart of Russia.]

53   **Москва царство, а деревня рай.**
        [Moscow is a kingdom, but the countryside is heaven.]

54   **Мужик для поговорки шел до Москвы.**
        [The *muzhik* went to Moscow for a proverb.] *Cf.* Wise men make proverbs, fools repeat them.

55   **Не хвались в Москву, а хвались из Москвы.**   *v.* H261,477,478
        [Boast not as you go to Moscow, but as you return.] *Cf.* Triumph not before the victory.

Наталья   *v.* Фадей 85

56   **У злой Натальи все люди канальи.**   *v.* У31
        [Cruel Natalia thinks everyone is vicious.] *rhyme* Ill doers are ill thinkers. An ill stomach
        makes all the meat bitter. *Cf.* A gossip speaks ill of all and all of her.

Николай

57*   **Хвали зиму после Николина дня.**
        [Praise winter after St. Nicholas' day.] *i.e. after 6 December, when winter arrives.*

Новгород

58   **Новгород нижний сосед Москве ближний.**
        [Nizhnyi Novgorod is Moscow's next-door neighbour.] *rhyme*

Олоферн

59   **Жена Олоферну главу отсекла.**   *v. Ap.*1.2
        [A wife beheaded Holophernes.] No mischief but a woman is at the bottom of it.
        Lat. Juv.*Sat.*6.242: nulla fera causa est in qua non femina litem moverit.

Павел   *v.* Петр 63

60   **У всякого Павла своя правда.**
[Every Paul heeds his own call.] Every man to his own opinion. *Cf.* Every man in his way.

Париж

61   **Осла хоть в Париж, все будет рыж.**   *v.* В438, Г337, *Ap.*1.32
[Send an ass to Paris, it won't change colours.] If an ass goes a-travelling, he'll not come back a horse.

Петр

62*   **Далеко кулику до Петрова дня.**
[The snipe has a long wait till St. Peter's day.] It's a long way to Tiparary.

63*   **Каков Петр, таков и Павел.**   *v.* Ч82
[Such Peter, such Paul.] *Cf.* What's sauce for the goose, is sauce for the gander.

64*   **С деньгами Петр Петрович, а без денег - паршивая сволочь.**   *v.* Д193, Ж148
Jack would be a gentleman if he had money.

Петрак

65   **Было у Петрака четыре батрака, а нынче Петрак сам батрак.**   *rhyme*
[Four stewards had Stuart, but now Stuart is himself a steward.]

Рим (Римский)

66   **В Риме был и папы не видал.**
[Went to Rome but didn't see the Pope.]

67   **Римская лесть мнимая честь.**
[Roman flattery is false adulation.] *Cf.* Fear the Greeks bearing gifts. †To speak with Roman bluntness. *Lat.* Mart.*Ep.*11.20: Romana simplicitate loqui.

Россия (русский)

68*   **Русак (русский человек) задним умом крепок (живет).**   *v.* П173, У83, Х15
[The Russian is] **wise after the event.**

69*   **Руси есть веселие пити (не может без того быти).**
[Russia delights in (cannot live without) drink.] *reputed to have been said by Vladimir I upon embracing Christianity rather than Islam as the state religion.*

70   **Русский глазам не верит, все надо пощупать.**
[A Russian cannot believe his eyes and must touch everything.]

71   **Русский и с горя и с радости пьет.**
[A Russian will drown his sorrow and his joy.] *i.e. in drink.*

72*   **Русский месяц подождет.**
[A Russian can wait a month.] *i.e. a pun on patience, lethargy and the Julian calendar observed by the orthodox church.*

73   **Русский ни с мечом ни с калачом не шутит.**
[A Russian never jests with swords or cake.]

74*   Русского мужика без каши не накормишь.
         [Without his *kasha*, the Russian *mujik* hasn't eaten.]

75*   У русского железная грудь и каменные кулаки.
         [A Russian has a chest of iron and fists of stone.]

Рязань   *v.*   Фома 95

Сава

76   Каков Сава, такова ему слава.   *v.* П48, *Ap*1.81
        [Such name, such fame.] If the cap fits, wear it.

77*   На волки (только) слава, а овец таскает (ест) Сава.   *v.* B197, 324, C1, T8, *Ap*.1.101
        [Sava steals the lamb and the wolf gets the blame.] One does the scathe and another has
        the scorn.

Саксония

78   Молода, в Саксонии не была.   *v.* П48, *Ap*.1.81
        [She's young and hasn't been to Saxony yet.] *Cf.* Like a young bear with all his troubles
        before him.

Семен (Сенька)

79   Грозен Семен, а боится Семена одна ворона.
        [Simon the terrible, of whom only a crow is terrified.]

80*   Не по Сеньке шапка.
        [The hat's too big for little Simon.] *i.e. he's not fit for the job.* To bite off more than one
        can chew.

81*   По Сеньке и шапка.   *v.* П48, *Ap*.1.22,76
        [The cap fits Simon.] If the cap fits, wear it. You get what you deserve.

Сибирь

82   Сибирь золотое дно.
        [Siberia is a gold mine.]

Синай

83   Свой вертеп лучше Синайской горы.   *v.* B23, Д51
        [A cave of your own is better than even Sinai.] East or West, home is best.

Тарас

84   Женился Тарас, не спросился у нас.   *v.* Б75
        [Taras got married without consulting with us.]

Тула

85*   В Тулу со своим самоваром не ездят.   *v.* B59,377,378
        [One doesn't bring *samovars* to Tula.] To carry coals to Newcastle.   Owls to Athens.
        Pepper to Hindustan.

Фадей

86   **Владей Фадей своей Агафьей (Натальей).**
[Every Teddy should rule his Mrs.]

87   **Проживет Фадей и без затей.**
[Teddy is ready to live without pretension.]

Фалья

88   **Всякая Фаля сама себя хвалит.**   *v.* B572,590,595
[Every Thalia likes to flatter herself.] Every ass likes to hear himself bray.

Федор

89   **У лентяя Федорки одни отговорки.**   *v.* K252, Л43
Idle folks lack no excuses.

Федот

90   **Всяк Федот по своему гнет.**   *v.* B558,626, У13,17
Every man after his own fashion.

91   **Голодному Федоту и репа в охоту.**   *v.* Б383, Г230, K227
[Hungry Fedot will be glad to eat turnips.] Hunger makes hard beans sweet.

92   **Для нашего Федота не страшна работа.**
[When it comes to work, Teddy's ready.] *rhyme*

93   **Федот, да не тот.**   *v.* B88, P20
[Worse than Fedot himself.] *rhyme* No like is the same. *Cf.* They are so alike that they
are the worse for it.

Филат

94*   **У каждого Филатки свои ухватки.**
Every man has his hobby horse.

Филя (Филемон) (Филипп)

95   **У Фили пили, да Филю и побили.**
[Dined with Phil then did him in.] *i.e. repay kindness with evil.*

Фома

96*   **Говорят про Фому, а он про Ерему.**
[The subject is Tom and he's on about Jerry.]

97   **Горюет Фома что пуста у него сума.**
[Thomas wines that his purse is empty.]

98   **Ехал к Фоме (в Казань) а заехал к куме (в Рязань).**
[Took off for Tom's (Kazan) but ended up at Ron's (Razan).]

99*   **На безлюдье и Фома дворянин.**   *v.* H2,3
      [When there's no one around, even Thomas is royalty.] For want of company, welcome trumpery. *Cf.* Better a lean jade than an empty halter. A bad bush is better than the open field. A crust is better than no bread.

100*   **Начал про Фому, а свел про Ерему.**
      [He began about Tom and wound up with Jerry.] *i.e. got off the subject, digressed.*

101*   **Не наказывай Фому за Еремину вину.**   *v. Ap.*1.77
      [Don't blame Tom for Jerry's fault.] Tobiah sinned and Sigud is beaten.

102   **Фома плачет а жена скачет.**   *v.* O43
      [Tom cries while his wife flies.]

103   **Шутить над Фомой, так и люби над собой.**   *v.* Ч47, Ш16
      If you give a jest, you must take a jest.

Христос

104*   **Дорого яичко к Христову (великому) дню.**   *v.* Д348,394
      [An egg in time for Christmas is nice.] Slow help is no help.

105*   **Живет как у Христа за пазухой.**
      [He lives as if under Christ's protective mantle.] Well thrives he whom God loves.

Юрий

106   **Вот тебе бабушка, и Юрев день.**
      [So much for St. Yuri's day.] *an expression of disappointment. Refers to the repeal of a law of 1497 that had allowed peasants to change landlords once a year in the two-week period around St. Yuri's day (26 November, Julian calendar).*

Яков

107   **Заладила сорока Якова.**   *v.* O94, *Ap.*1.20
      [The magpie's calling Jacob again.] To sing the same old tune.

APPENDIX 2   Table 1:   **PROVERB STRUCTURE**

[Based on A.Dundes, "The Structure of the Proverb," *Proverbium* 25 (1975), pp. 961-973.]

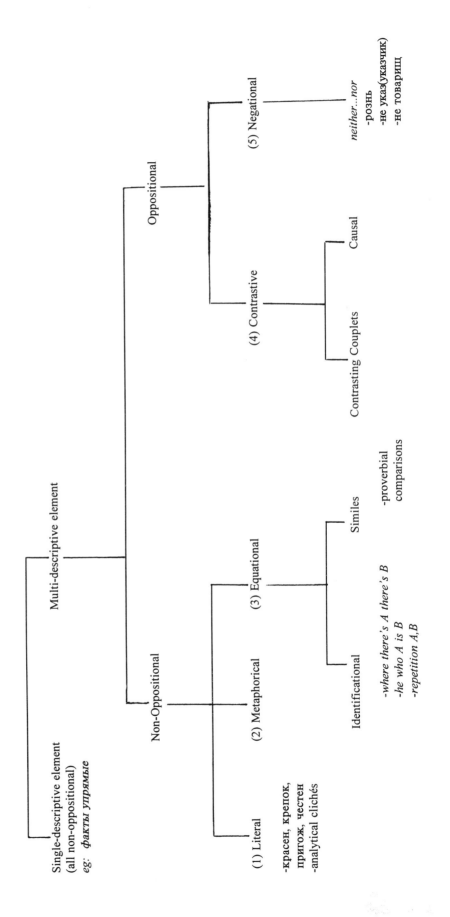

APPENDIX 2: THE STRUCTURE OF THE RUSSIAN PROVERB[1]

with

examples of common types of
Russian proverbs and sayings
unparalleled in other languages

Russian proverbs are essentially of the multi-descriptive element type. They are bipartite and consist of two propositions, the one compared with or weighed against the other. For even those proverbs which appear to be tripartite, it can be shown that the three parts are always patterned so that the first two are opposed to the third, thus forming in fact a bipartite structure.[2]

In non-oppositional proverbs, the basic elements of the proverb, *i.e.* the topic and comment, are arranged in linear agreement with a view to indicating common identificational features or similarities. In oppositional proverbs, the parts stand in contrast to delineate differences.

1. Literal Proverbs

These are non-oppositional "practical" sayings which have a concrete meaning. They may be truisms, platitudes, nonce communications, or analytical clichés, *i.e.* legal, economic, medical sayings or omens and superstitions which often take the form of observations, recommendations or rules.[3] Their essential property is that they have only one direct meaning and permit no extended interpretation. This

---

[1] The structural analysis of Russian proverbs outlined in this Appendix is based on the general structural scheme for proverbs developed by Alan Dundes in his study "On the Structure of the Proverb" *Proverbium* 25 (1975) pp. 961-973, and seeks to integrate Russian proverbs, with their specificities, within that scheme.

[2] M.I.Levin, "Structure of the Russian Proverb" in *Studies Presented to Professor R.Jacobson,* ed.C.E.Gribble (Cambridge,Mass: Slavica, 1968), p. 184.

[3] Permiakov, *From Proverb to Folk Tale* (Moscow: Nauka, 1979), pp. 85ff., does not consider these as proverbs because they do not admit of extended interpretation. But this is precisely a characteristic of literal proverbs as described here. Depending on the referent circumstances in the real world at the time of their use, they may certainly demonstrate a *de facto* extended interpretation and thus perform the general function of serving as *signs* for encoded communication.

direct meaning is the sum of the meanings of the component words making up the literal proverb, and any change in these components will immediately change the meaning of the proverb.

An important Russian linguistic sub-group of this category is made up of proverbs and sayings with the adjectives **красен**, **крепок**, **пригож**, and **честен**. For non-native speakers of Russian, these expressions may be best understood if they are not construed literally, but instead taken as variants of the idea conveyed by the English saying *the proof of the pudding is in the eating.*

Analytical Clichés

Арык не вырить - поле не полить.	*You cannot water a field without digging furrows.*
Без веретена пряжи не спрядешь.	*You cannot spin yarn without a spindle.*
Без клиньев кафтана не сошьешь.	*You cannot sew a garment without gores.*
Без музыки не танцуют.	*No dancing without music.*
В огне и железо плавко.	*Even iron melts in fire.*
В сухой год зайцев больше, в сырой - мышей.	*Dry years beget more rabbits, wet years - more mice.*
Весна не мясна, осень не молочна.	*Spring without meat means autumn without milk.*
Весна отмыкает ключи и воды.	*Spring unlocks the springs and waters.*
Вода вымоет, хлеб выкормит.	*Water cleanses, bread nourishes.*
Где лишняя навозу колышка, там лишняя хлеба коврижка.	*An ounce of fertilizer will yield a pound of grain.*
Даст небо дождь, а земля рожь.	*If heaven grants rain, the earth will provide rye.*
Иглой шьют, чашей пьют, а плетью бьют.	*A needle for sewing, a cup for drinking and a lash for flogging.*
Клей на бумажку а игла на рубашку.	*Glue paper, but stitch clothes.*
На испорченном (кривом) коне не много передешь. На леченой кобылке (клячке) не далеко уедешь.	*You won't get far on a lame horse (sickly mare) (jade).*
Наездом хлеба не напашешь.	*You cannot harvest bread with scarce tillage.*
Ноги носят, а руки кормят.	*The legs walk, the hands feed.*
Одной рукой (и) узла не завяжешь.	*You cannot (even) tie a knot with one hand.*
Озимы в закром не сыплют.	*Winter crops are not stored in the granary. i.e. are not kept for the next year.*
Окунь осетра волочит.	*The perch takes the sturgeon.*
От лося лосята, от свиньи поросята.	*Elks beget elk calves and pigs piglets.*
От ненависти вражда рождается.	*Hatred breeds hostility.*
От яблонки яблочко, от елки шишка.	*Apple trees grow apples, fir trees - cones.* P33
Ранний сев к позднему в амбар (закрома) не ходит.	
Рыба вода, репа земля, а ягода трава.	*Fish need water, turnips soil, berries grass.*
Скотину гладь не рукой, а мукой.	*Stroke the stock with fodder, not your hand.*
Слепой не увидит, гордый не взглянет, дурак не рассудит, умный не осудит.	*The blind won't see, the proud won't look back, the fool won't know and the wise won't condemn.*
Старое старится а молодое растет.	*As the young grow, the old get older.*
Трудно найти, легко потерять.	*Easier lost than found.*
Убитого зверя в поле не оставляй.	*Don't leave dead game in an open field.*
Чего стыдимся, того и таимся.	Ч20

Красен, Крепок, Пригож and Честен

Весна днем красна.	*Spring's beauty is in her days.*
Весна красна цветами, а осень снопами.	*Spring vaunts her flowers, autumn - her haystacks.*
Всякая ссора красна миром.	*Every dispute is redeemed by settlement.*
Долг платежом красен (а займы отдачею).	Д368
Женихом брак честен.	*The groom makes a wedding true.*
Красна беседа смиреньем.	*Humility embellishes conversation.*
Красна брань дракою.	*Pugnacity embellishes abuse.*
Красна дорога ездоками.	*Travellers adorn a road.*
Красна пава перьем, а жена мужем.	*Feathers decorate a hen and a husband embellishes a wife.*
Красна река берегами, а обед пирогами.	*Banks adorn a dinner as pies embellish dinner.*
Красна речь слушаньем.	*Listening embellishes discourse.*
Красно поле пшеном (рожью), а беседа умом.	*Wheat (rye) embellishes a field, wit a conversation.*
Крепка лавка сидельцем.	*The sitter makes the bench.*
Неделя середою крепка, жизнь половиною.	*The week hinges on Wednesday, life on middle age.*
Обед красен не ложкой, а едеоком.	*A guest, not a spoon, adorns the dinner table best.*
Пригож лук стрелами, а обед пирогами.	*What good is a bow without arrows, or a meal without pies.*
Речь красна слушаньем.	*The beauty of speech is in the listening.*
Честны свадьба гостями, похороны слезами, а пьянство дракой.	*Guests make the wedding, tears the funeral, and a brawl a drinking bout.*

2. Metaphorical Proverbs

These non-oppositional proverbs are structurally similar to literal proverbs but their general meaning does not stand or fall with that of their component words, which may function as signs or signals denoting broader concepts. These proverbs may therefore display two meanings: a direct literal meaning and an extended interpretative meaning.

Борщ без каши вдовец, каша без борща - вдова.	*Borsch without kasha is a widower, and kasha without borsch is a widow.*
В платье моль, а в сердце печаль.	*Grief plagues the heart as a moth gnaws a dress.*
Вьется ужом а топорщится ежом.	*Slithers as a snake but bristles like a hedgehog.*
Глотка шире котла, а сердце уже заячей лапы.	*A gullet bigger than a boiler, but a heart smaller than a rabbit's foot.*
Деньги - прах, а жизнь - золото.	*Health is better than wealth.* Cf. Д188
Добрый человек лучше каменного моста.	*A kind man is better than a stone bridge.*
Не сади дерево корнем к верху.	*Do not plant a tree with roots upward.*
Непродажному коню нет цены.	*The horse that is not for sale is priceless.*
Панциря за кожею не бывает.	*There's no armour beneath the skin.*
Пить пиво а не брагу - любить девку да не бабу.	*To drink beer instead of home brew is like preferring girls to women.*
По потраве не хлеб, по суду не деньги.	*A blight won't yield bread, nor the courts money.*
Ржа ест железо а печаль сердце.	*Rust eats steel as sorrow corrodes the heart.*
Рысь пестра сверху (снаружи) а человек (лукав) изнутри.	*A lynx is motley on the outside, a man on the inside.*
Слезами моря не наполнишь, кручиною поля не изъездишь.	*One cannot fill the sea with tears nor trample a field with sorrow.*
Слепого в вожаки не берут.	*Don't take a blind man as a guide.*
Слепые в карты не играют.	*Blind men should not be cardplayers.*
Судья праведный - ограда каменная.	*An honest judge is like a protective stone wall.*
Хлеб за брюхом не ходит.	X21
Я тебе голублюсь, а ты от меня тетеришься.	*I approach you like a dove and you back away like a grouse.*

3. *Equational Proverbs*

Russian equational proverbs are predominantly of the identificational type following the pattern "Where there's A, there's B," and "he who is A is B." [4]   Truly equational proverbs of the type A = B exist, but are less common than the oppositional negational type described in (5) below. A large subclass of this category is made up of proverbial comparisons which take the form of similes. Such identificational comparisons occur more frequently as sayings than proverbs.[5]

Identificational

Булат не гнется, а золото не ржавеет.	*Steel does not bend but gold will not rust.*
Был бы лес, будет и леший.	*Where there's a forest, there's a lumberjack.*
Был бы ловец, а ружье будет.	*Where there's a hunter, there's a rifle.*
Глупый умного не любит, а пьяный - трезвого.	*Fools dislike the wise as drunkards the sober.*
Для друзей пироги, для врагов кулаки.	*Offerings for friends, clobbering for foes.*
Сколько пива, столько песен.	C147
Туча не без грому, а хозяин не без содому.	*A cloud has its thunder and a master his temper.*
У девки догадка, а у парня смысл.	*Women have intuition, men - reason.*
Умей воровать, умей и концы хоронить.	*He that steals must know how to erase clues.*

Similes - Proverbial Comparisons

Бежит как сумасшедщий.	*To act like one possessed.*
Белый как снег (мел).	*As white as snow.*
Бледный как полотно.	*As white (pale) as a sheet.*
Блудлив как кошка, труслив как заяц.	*Profligate as a cat, cowardly as a rabbit.*
Боится, как огня.	*To fear like fire.*
Бьется, как рыба об лед.	*Like a fish struggling against ice.*
В жизни как в картах выигрывают не тузы а козыри.	*In life as in cards, it's the trumps not the aces that win.*
Вертится, как белка в колесе.	B256, K16
Вестовщик как мостовщик.	*A gossip is like a bridgebuilder.*
Визжит, как поросенок.	*To squeal like a pig.*
Водою плывучи что со вдовою живучи.	*Who sails the seas lives with a widow.*
Волный, как ветер.	*As free as the wind.*
Выступает, словно пава.	*As proud as a peacock.*
Глуп, как пробка.	*As stupid as a cork.*
Глухой что слепой: чего недослышит, то выдумает.	*What the deaf and blind don't hear, they imagine.*
Горе что полая вода - все затопит а потом сойдет.	*Grief, like floodwaters, drenches everything then runs off.*
Глядит, словно кот на сало.	*Stares like a cat at cream [lard].*

---

[4]   See *Dictionary, supra,* Г2 - Г106 and К212 - К318.

[5]   The examples listed in this section include the most common proverbial comparisons identified by G.L.Permiakov on the basis of a field survey among native Russian speakers, and published in «75 Найболее употребительных русских сравнительных оборотов типа присловии» *Proverbium* 25 (1975) 974-978.

Глянет (точно) рублем подарит.	As if looks were enough.
Голодный, как собака (волк).	As hungry as a dog.
Горький, как полынь.	As bitter as wormwood.
Грызутся, как собаки (изза кости).	To fight like dogs over a bone.
Дело без конца что кобыла без хвоста.	An unfinished job is like a mare without a tail.
Держится как репей за кожух.	Grips like a burdock onto a sheepskin.
Длинный, как жердь.	As tall as a beanpole.
Дрожит, как осиновый лист.	As shaky as an aspen leaf.
Дурное слово что смола - пристанет, не отлепишь.	An ill word is like tar, once it sticks you can't get it off.
Жарко, как в бане.	As hot as a bath.
Живут (дружат) как кошка с собакой.	(To agree) like cats and dogs.
Жирный, как свинья.	As fat as a pig (hog).
Здоров (силен), как бык.	As strong as an ox.
Злой, как собака.	As vicious as a dog.
Знает, как своих пять пальцев.	To know like the back of one's hand.
Красивый, как рак.	As red as a boiled lobster.
Кричит, будто его режут.	To scream bloody murder.
Легкий, как перышко (пушинка).	As light as a feather.
Липнут, как мухи на мед.	To stick like flies to honey.
Лопнул, как мыльный пузырь.	To burst like a (soap) bubble.
Льет, как из ведра.	To rain (pour) buckets.
Молчит, точно воды в рот набрал.	Cat got his tongue.
Мягкий, как пух.	As soft as down.
Надоел, хуже горькой редьки.	To grow sick and tired of...
Надулся, как индюк.	As cocky as a bantam rooster.
Не видать, как своих ушей.	To see no more than one's own ears.
Недобрые слова как с гуся вода.	Unkind words are like water off a goose's back.
Нем, как рыба.	As mute as a fish.
Неповоротлив, как медведь.	As cross as a bear.
Несолоно хлебать что немилого целовать.	Eating without salt is like kissing without love.
Носится, как дурак с писаной торбой.	To make a great song and dance about...
Носиться, как курица с яйцом.	As busy as a hen with one chick.
Нужен, как прошлогодный снег.	To need something as much as last year's snow.
Нужен, как собаке пятая нога.	To need like a dog needs a fifth leg.
Остров в море а сердце в горе.	The grieving heart is an island in the sea.
Острый, как бритва.	As sharp as a razor.
От него пользы как от козла молока.	Like milk from a he-goat.
Плавает, как топор.	To swim like a rock [axe].
Подскочил, как ужаленный.	To start as if stung.
Ползет, как черепаха.	As slow as a turtle.
Поможет, как мертвому припарки.	As helpful as a poultice for a dead man.
Похожи, как две капли воды.	Like two peas in a pod [drops of water].
Пристал, как банный лист.	To stick like a leech [leaf].
Прицепился, как репей(ник).	To stick like a burdock.
Работает как лошадь (вол).	To work like a horse.
Разбирается, как свинья в апельсинах.	As snug as pigs in pease-straw [oranges].
Разошлись, как в море корабли.	Passed like ships in the sea.
Распоряжается, как у себя дома.	Acts like a master at home.
Растет, как на дрожжах.	Rises like yeast.
Растут, как грибы после дождя.	To grow like mushrooms [after the rain].
Свеженький, как огурчик.	As cool as a cucumber.
Светло, как днем.	As bright (clear)(plain) as day.
Сидит, как на шпильках (иголках).	To be on pins and needles.
Сказал, как отрезал (отрубил).	Said is like done.
Скачет, как коза.	To leap like a goat.
Сойдет, как с гуся вода.	Like water off a duck's back.
Спит, как убитый.	To sleep like a dead man.
Стал, как вкопанный.	Stood as if rooted to the ground.
Старо, как мир.	As old as the hills.

Твердый, как алмаз.	*As hard as a diamond.*
Толстый, как бочка.	*As big (stout) as a barrel.*
Труслив, как заяц.	*As fearful as a hare (as scared as a rabbit).*
Упрямый, как осел.	*As stubborn as a mule.*
Уставился, как баран на новые ворота.	*To stare like a lamb at a new gate.*
Хитрый, как лиса.	*As cunning (clever) as a fox.*
Худой (тощий), как жердь	*As skinny (thin) as a beanpole (rail).*
Чавкает, как свинья.	*To eat like a hog (pig).*
Черный, как ворон.	*As black as a raven.*
Чувствует себя, как рыба в воде.	*Like a fish in water.*
Шатается, как пьянный.	*Totters like a drunkard.*

4. *Contrastive Proverbs*

Whereas non-oppositional Russian proverbs establish an equation by identifying points of comparison or similarity among the propositions of a proverb, oppositional proverbs underscore their differences. This is achieved either by contrast or outright negation. Contrasts can be drawn by the use of semantic pairs of antonyms or contrastive words that exist within the lexical arsenal of the language, or they can be made conceptually by contrasting the cause and effect in a proverb's propositions, as in «от искры сыр бор загорается». Frequently, both of these techniques are used together, as in «от малой искры велик пожар делается», and many examples of this can be found in all languages. In Russian, however, the pattern of contrastive couplets is equally typical and occurs perhaps more often than in other modern languages.

Contrasting Couplets

Бары липовые а мужики дубовые.	*Bluebloods are linden, rednecks are of oak.*
Батька - горбом, а сынок - горлом.	*The father performs, the son promises.*
Белое - венчальное, черное - печальное.	*White for weddings, black for wakes.*
Богу свечка, черту кочерга.	*A candle for God and a poker for the devil.*
В радости сыщут, а в горести забудут.	B123
Где умному горе, там глупому веселье.	*A fool laughs when the wise man would cry.*
Годное на сварку, негодное - на свалку.	*Throw what's good in the pot and what's bad in the dump.*
Обычай бычий, а ум телячий.	*To have the manner of a bull but the brains of a calf.*
Один радуется а другой плачет.	O43
Один шьет, другой порет.	*One sews, another tears.*
Одному с женою утеха и радость, другому печаль и горесть.	*Some find comfort and happiness in a wife, others sorrow and strife.*
Печка нежит, дорожка учит.	*The hearth spoils, the road disciplines.*
Попы поют над мертвыми, комары над жывими.	*Priests sing over the dead, mosquitos over the living.*
Потоп кораблям, песок журавлям.	*Floods for boats, sands for cranes.*
Радость прямит, кручина крючит.	P19
С чем приехал, с тем поехал.	*Go as you have come.* Cf. C35
Совет свет, а несовет тьма.	*Harmony is like day, discord like night.* Cf. У116
Стыдливый покраснеет, а бесстыдный побледнеет.	*The shy blush but the shameless pale.*

Счастливый скачет, а несчастный плачет.   C310
У счастливого умирает недруг, а у   *The lucky lose an enemy, the unlucky a friend.*
  бессчастного друг.
Хороша веревка длинная, а речь короткая.   *A long string and a short speech are good.*
Юному хвастать а старому хрястать.   *The young man brags, the old man nags.*
Юный с игрушками, а стар с подушками.   M146

5. *Negational Proverbs*

The most common Russian negational proverbs form a pattern of negative identification by describing what objects or situations are *not*. Some may be tempted to infer from this some profound insight into the Russian psyche, but such indulgence is beyond the purpose here.

There are four important idiomatic and/or linguistic subgroups in this category: proverbs with **neither ... nor**, with **рознь, указ (указчик** or **указывать)**, and with the phrase **не товарищ**. All these produce opposition through explicit negation.

Аркан не таракан - зубов нет а шею ест.   *A noose is no moose [roach]: no jaws yet it breaks*
                                                  your neck just the same.
Беда не дуда - станешь дуть и слезы идут.   *Trouble's not a pipe: puff on it and tears flow.*
Бобы не грибы - не посеяв не взойдут.   *Beans are not like mushrooms: unless you sow they*
                                                  won't grow.
Брехать - не цепом мотать.   *There's a difference between spinning lies and*
                                                  rolling dough.
Брюхо не гусли - не евши не уснет.   *The belly's no zither: unfed it won't keep still.*
Брюхо не лукошко - под лавку не сунешь.   *The belly's no basket: you can't tuck under a*
                                                  bench.
Век жить - не мех шить (не нитку исшить).   *To live a lifetime is not just sewing a fur nor using*
                                                  up your thread. Cf. B227, Ж147
Веру переменить - не рубашку переодеть.   *Converting religion is not just switching shirts.*
Вешний лед не дорога, а с пьянным речь не   *Spring ice is no roadway, nor is a drunkard's talk*
беседа.   *conversation.*
Вино не пшеницп - прольешь, не соберешь.   *Wine isn't like wheat that can be gathered up once*
                                                  spilt.
Воровать - не блины подавать.   *Stealing is not just serving up blini.* Cf.B432
Время не деньги, потеряешь - не найдешь.   B478
Гармонь не огонь - а разогревает.   *An accordion's no flame, yet it warms just the*
                                                  same.
Год (жизнь) прожить - не реку (море)   B227, Ж147
переплыть (не поле перейти).
Годы не птицы - улетят, не поймаешь.   *Years are not birds: once flown they cannot be*
                                                  caught.
Голова не карниз - не приставишь.   *The head is not a cornice that can be reattached.*
                                                  Cf. Г212
Горе горевать - не пир пировать,   *Bearing grief is not like going to a feast.*
Горе не море - выпьешь до дна.   *Sorrow is not the sea: you can drink it dry.*
Горе не плуг, бороздки прокладывает.   *Sorrow is no plough yet it digs furrows.*
Горе не сухарь - в стакане не размочишь.   *Grief is not a biscuit: you can't soften it by*
                                                  dunking.
Гость не кость - за дверь не выкинешь.   *A guest is not a bone you can just toss out.*
Грамота не болезнь - годы не уносят.   *Education cannot be dissipated by time like a*
                                                  disease.
Грязь не сало, высохла и отстало.   *Mud is not like grease: it dries then flakes off.*
Дар не купля - не хают а хвалят.   *A gift is not like a purchase - no complaints, only*
                                                  compliments.

Дело не волк - в лес не убежит.
Дело не воробей (голуби) - не улетит (разлетятся).
Дело не малина - в лето не опадет.

Дело не сено - пять лет не сгниет.
Деньги не грибы (рожь) - и зимой растут.

Деньги не люди - лишними не будет.
Деньги не щепки - на полу не подымешь.

Детишек воспитать, не курочек пересчитать.

Дождь не дубина - не убьет.
Долг не веревка - не сгниет.
Долг не крыша - не обвалится.
Долг не рана - не заживет.
Долг не ревет, а спать не дает.
Дом вести - не бородой трясти (не лапти плести).
Дома не в гостях - посидев не уйдешь.

Дрова сечь - не желать плеч.
Дружба не гриб - в лесу не найдешь.

Душа не одежда - наизнанку не вывернешь.
Душа не яблоко - ее не разделишь.

Его ласка не коляска - не садешь и не поедешь.
Жена не горшок - не разобьется.
Жена не гусли - поиграв, на стену не повесишь.
Жена не коза - травой кормить не будешь.
Жениться - не воды напиться (не все веселиться) (не лапоть надеть) (не чихнуть, можно повременить).
Жизнь не камень - на одном месте не лежит а вперед бежит.
Закон не кол - обтешешь.
Капусту садить - не разиня рот ходить.

Любовь не картошка - не выбросишь в (за) окошко.
Мост не великий пост - можно объехать.
Наука не пиво - не нальешь.

Обычай не клетка - скоро не переставишь.
Отказ не обух - шишек на лбу не будет.

Работа не коза - в лес не убежит.

Рот не ворота - клином не запрешь.

С другом знаться - не редьку есть.
Сердце не лукошко - не прошибешь окошко.
Хвастать - не колеса мазать.
Язык не лопатка - знает что горько, что сладко.

Д136
Work, unlike sparrows (pigeons), won't fly away.

Work is not a raspberry: it won't drop off in summer.
Work won't decay like hay in five years.
Money is not like mushrooms (rye): it grows in winter too.
Д186
Money is not like chips: you won't find it on the ground.
Raising children is more than just counting heads like chickens.
Rain is not like a club: it won't kill you.
A debt is not like a rope that will rot away.
A debt is not like a roof that will collapse.
A debt is not a wound that will heal.
A debt doesn't shriek, but won't let you sleep.
Keeping house is not just a flick of your whiskers (weaving slippers).
At home is not like visiting: one can't just stay awhile.
Splitting logs means not sparing one's shoulders.
Friendship is not a mushroom you can find in the woods.
The heart is not a garment you can turn inside-out.
The heart is not an apple you can cut up and divide.
His tender nature is not a buggy you can ride.

A wife's not a crock: she won't break.
A wife's not a psaltery: you can't put her away when you've finished playing.
A wife's not a goat: she eats more than grass.
Marriage is not just drinking one's fill of water (all laughs) (slipping on a slipper) (a sneeze - you can put it off).
Life is not a stone that lies still, it speeds forward.

The law is not a picket: one cannot get around it.
Planting cabbage is not just walking about yawning.
Л191

A bridge is not like Lent: one can bypass it.
Learning is not like beer: you can't just pour a glass.
Custom is a cage that cannot be easily moved.
A refusal is not a blow on the head: no bumps spring up.
Work is no goat: it won't run into the woods.
Cf. Д136
The mouth is not a portal: you cannot stop it with a wedge.
Knowing a friend's not as easy as eating a radish.
The heart is not like a basket: you can't just see in.
Boasting is not like just greasing the wheels.
The tongue is not just a scoop: it knows the sweet from the bitter.

Neither ...Nor   *see also* H 536-545

Ни солоно, ни сладко,	*Neither savoury nor sweet.*
Ни стрижено, ни брито.	*Neither trimmed nor shaven.*
Ни усов, ни бороды, ни сохи, ни бороны.	*Neither whiskers, nor beard, nor plough nor furrow.*
Ни шьет, ни порет.	*Neither sews nor rends.*

Рознь

Вина вине рознь.	*No two faults alike.*
Воз возу рознь.	*There are no two loads alike.*
Гость гостью рознь.	*No two guests alike.*
Грех греху рознь.	*No two sins alike.*
День дню рознь - нынче тепло, а завтра мороз.	*No two days are alike: hot today, cold tomorrow.*
Дерево дереву рознь.	*No two trees are the same.*
Жизнь жизни рознь.	*One life is different from another.*
Талант таланту рознь.	*All skills are different.*

Указ, указчик, указывает.

Век веку не указывает.	*One age orders not another (i.e. history does not necessarily repeat itself).*
	Г307
Гость хозяину не указчик.	
День дню не указчик.	*One day does not pre-ordain another.*
Мастер мастеру не указ.	*One craftsman does not command another.*
Один другому не указ.	О32
Среда и пятницу четвергу не указчица.	*Wednesday and Friday do not command Thursday.*
Ум разуму не указ.	**The mind does not command reason.**

Не товарищ

Гусь свинье(и) не товарищ.	Г338
Пеший конному не товарищ.	*A horseman and a footman see not eye to eye.*
Слепой зрячему не товарищ.	*The blind man is no friend to the sighted man.*

BIBLIOGRAPHY

RUSSIAN PUBLICATIONS

1. Аникин В.П. *Русские народные пословицы, поговорки, загадки и детский фольклор.* Москва, 1957.

2. Ашукин Н.С. и Ашукина М.Г. *Крылатые слова.* Москва, 1960.

3. Бабичев Н.Т. и Боровский Я.М. *Словарь латинских крылатых слов.* Москва: Русский язык, 1986.

4. Богданов А.И. *Сборник пословиц и присловиц Российских.* 1741.

5. Буковская М.В. *et al. Словарь употребительных английских пословиц.* Москва: Русский язык, 1990.

6. Гуревич В.В. и Дозорец Ж.А. *Краткий русско-английский фразеологический словарь.* Москва: Русский язык, 1988.

7. Даль В.И. *Пословицы русского народа.* Москва, 1861-1862.

8. Дубровин М.И. *Английские и русские пословицы и поговорки в иллюстрациях.* Москва: Просвещение, 1993.

9. Жуков В.П. *Словарь русских пословиц и поговорок.* Москва, 1966.

10. _____ *Словарь русских пословиц и поговорок.* 4е изд. испр. и доп. Москва: Русский язык, 1991.

11. Княжевич Д.М. *Полное собрание русских пословиц и поговорок, расположенных по азбучному порядку.* Москва, 1822.

12. Кузьмин С.С и Шадрин Н.Л. *Русско-Английский словарь пословиц и поговорок.* Москва: Руский язык, 1989.

13. Кусловская С.Ф. *Сборник английских пословиц и поговорок.* Минск: Вышэйшая школа, 1987.

14.   Мартынова А.Н. и Митрофанова В.В. *Пословицы, поговорки, загадки.* Москва: Современник, 1986.

15.   Молоткова А.И. ред. *Фразеологический словарь русского языка.* Москва: Русский язык, 1978

16.   Пермяков, Г.Л. *От поговорки до сказки - заметки по обшей теории клише.* Москва, 1970.

17.   _____ «О смысловой структуре и соответсующей классификации пословичных изречений.» *Перемиологический Сборник* Москва, 1978, 105-135.

18.   _____ transl. Filippov, Y.N. *From Proverb to Folk-Tale. Notes on the General Theory of Cliché.* Moscow: "Nauka" Publishing House, 1979.

19.   Снегирев И.М. *Русские народные пословицы и притчи.* Москва, 1848.

20.   Соболев А.И. *Русские пословицы и поговорки.* Москва, 1983.

21.   Тарланов, З.К. «Особенности синтаксиса русских пословиц.» *Русская Речь,* no. 4(1977), 56-59.

22.   Фелицина, В.П. «О пословицах и поговорках как материалы для фразеологического словаря.» *Проблемы фразеологии. Исследования и материалы.* Ed. А.М. Бабкина. Москва, 1964. 200-204.

23.   _____ и Прохоров Ю.Е. *Русские пословицы, поговорки, и крылатые выражения, Лингвострановедческий словарь.* Москва: Русский язык, 1988.

24.   Шейдлин, Б. *Москва в пословицах и поговорках.* Москва, 1929.

OTHER PUBLICATIONS

1.   *(anonymous).*   "Russian Proverbs." *The Quarterly Review,* 139 (1875).

2.   Altenkirch, R. "Die Beziehungen zwischen Slaven und Griechen in ihren Sprichwörten." *Archiv für slavische Philologie,* 30 (1908-1909), 1-47; 321-364.

3.   Aroutunova, Bayara. "Gesture and Word: A Semiotic Treatment of Russian Phraseologic Expressions and Proverbs." *Folia Slavica,* 3, nos. 1-2 (1979), 48-79.

4.   Bauer-Czarnomski, F. *Proverbs in Russian and English.* London, 1920.

5.   Carey, Claude. *Etude des proverbes russes recueillis et non publiés par Dal' et Simoni.* Diss. Harvard University, 1966. Published under the title *Les proverbes érotiques russes. Etudes de proverbes recueillis et non-publiés par Dal' et Simoni.* The Hague: Mouton, 1972.

6.   Disraeli, Isaac. *Curiosities of Literature.* London: Routledge, 1834.

7. Dundes, Alan. ed. *The Study of Folklore.* Englewood Cliffs, 1965.

8. _____ "On the Structure of the Proverb." *Proverbium* 25 (1975), 961-973.

9. Fuller, T. *Gnomologia: Adagies and Proverbs; Wise Sentences and Witty Sayings, Ancient and Modern, Foreign and British.* London, 1732.

10. Georges, Robert A. & Dundes Alan. "Toward a Structural Definition of the Riddle." *Journal of American Folklore.* 76 (1963) 117.

11. Geyr, Heinz. *Sprichwörter und sprichwortnahe bildungen im dreisprachigen Petersburger Lexikon von 1731.* Bern: Peter Lang, 1981.

12. Guershoon, Andrew. *Certain Aspects of Russian Proverbs.* Diss. University of London, 1941. London: Frederick Muller, 1941.

13. Hazlitt, W.C. *English Proverbs and Proverbial Phrases.* London: Reever and Turner, 1869.

14. Henderson, A. *Scottish Proverbs.* Edinburgh, 1832.

15. Jaszczun W., Krynski, S. *A Dictionary of Russian Idioms and Colloquialisms.* University of Pittsburgh Press, 1967.

16. Kuznetsova A. *Без пословицы речь не молвится.* Munich, 1964.

17. Levin, Maurice Irwin. *Repetition as a Structural Device in the Russian Proverb.* Diss. Harvard University, 1964.

18. _____ "The Structure of the Russian Proverb." *Studies Presented to Professor Roman Jacobson.* Ed. Charles E. Gribble. Cambridge, Mass.: Slavica Publishers, 1968. 180-187.

19. Mawr, E.B. *Analogous Proverbs in Ten Languages.* London: Elliot Stock, 1885.

20. Mieder, Wolfgang. *International Proverb Scholarship: An Annotated Bibliography.* New York: Garland Publishing, 1982.

21. _____ *International Proverb Scholarship: An Annotated Bibliography. Supplement I.* New York: Garland Publishing, 1990.

22. Mieder W., Kingsbury S.A., Harder K.B. *A Dictionary of American Proverbs.* Oxford: Oxford University Press, 1992.

23. Milner G.B. "What is a Proverb?" *New Society* 332 (6 Feb.69), 199-202.

24. _____ "Quadripartite Structures." *Proverbium* 14 (1969), 379-383.

25. Otto, H. *Die Sprichwörter und sprchwörtlichen Redensarten der Römer.* Leipzig, 1890.

26. Permiakov G.L. "О логическом аспекте пословиц и поговорок." *Proverbium* 10 (1968), 225-235.

27. _____ "О лингвистическом аспекте пословиц и поговорок." *Proverbium* 11 (1968), 276-285.

28. _____ "О предметном аспекте пословиц и поговорок." *Proverbium* 12 (1969), 324-328.

29. _____ "On Paremiological Homonymy and Synonymy." *Proverbium* 24 (1974), 941-943.

30. _____ "Наиболее употребительных русских сравнительных оборотов типа присловий." *Proverbium* 25 (1975), 974-979.

31. Rothe, Richard. "Russische Sprichwörter." *Sprachpflege*, 11 (1962), 210-11.

32. Rothstein, Robert A.   "The Poetics of Proverbs." *Studies Presented to Professor Roman Jacobson.* Ed. Charles E. Gribble. Cambridge, Mass.: Slavica Publishers, 1968. 265 -274.

33. Seiler, F. *Deutsche Sprichwörterkunde.* Handbuch des deutschen Unterrichts IV.III. München, 1922.

34. Sigal, Georges. "Dictons et proverbes russes: Reflets d'une psychologie collective toute différente de celle des français." *Revue de psychologie des peuples*, 25 (1970), 308-324.

35. Stevenson, Burton. *The Macmillan (Home) Book of Proverbs, Maxims and Familiar Sayings.* New York: Macmillan, 1948.

36. Strafforello, Gustavo. "Filosofia dei proverbii russi." In G. Strafforello. *Curiosità ed amenità letterarie.* Firenze: L.Niccolai, 1889. 126-132.

37. Taverner, R. *Proverbs or Adagies with newe addicions gathered out of the Chiliades of Erasmus.* London, 1539.

38. Taylor, Archer. *The Proverb.* Hatboro, Pennsylvania, 1962.

39. Wilson, F.P. *The Oxford Dictionary of English Proverbs.*   3rd ed. Oxford: OUP, 1970.

40. Yermoloff. *Die Landwirtschaftliche Volksweisheit in Sprichwörtern, Redensarten und Wettergeln.* Leipzig, 1905.

ENGLISH PROVERB INDEX

NB.   This index lists only those proverbs in English for which there are corresponding or equivalent Russian proverbs. For the purposes of this dictionary, *equivalent* means complete lexical parity, while *corresponding* denotes conceptual parity, in which there is correspondence in the usage of the proverbs, although the words, syntax and imagery may differ. The arrangement of Index entries is by *key word*, by which is meant the sequentially first noun most closely associated with the meaning of the proverb and/or having greater linguistic range or frequency. For proverbs without nouns, key words are verbs, adjectives or adverbs, taken again on the basis of the same criteria. Numbers in **bold** indicate the closest corresponding Russian proverb for entries with more than one listing.

Able	He who would not when he could, is not able when he would. H462
Absence	Absence makes the heart grow fonder. P50
Absent	The absent are always wrong. Б75, C96, X64
Accident	Accidents will happen in the best regulated families. B140, H495, **C131**
Acquaintance	Short acquaintance brings repentance. Ш1
Acorn	Acorns were good until bread was found. K270
	Out of little acorns, mighty oak trees grow. Б437, M25
Action	Action is the basis of success. C114
	Actions speak louder than words. Д116, C230
	Our actions are our security, not others' judgment. B561
	'Tis action makes the hero. **B632**, Д145
Adam	Adam ate the apple and our teeth still ache. H117, O188
	We are all Adam's children. B499,625
Advantage	In spending lies the advantage. Д66
Adversity	Adversity comes with instruction in its hand. C303
	Adversity is the touchstone of friendship. Б48
	Adversity makes men wise. Б45
	Adversity makes strange bedfellows. H577
Advice	Advice is cheap. H202
	After advice is a foll's advice. B302
	He who follows his own advice must take the consequences. O45
	Many receive advice, but only the wise profit from it. M170
	The best advice is found on the pillow. Д457
	When a thing is done, advice comes too late. П167
Advisement	Advisement is good before the need. Б183

The shortest answer is doing.   Д139

Ant	A coconut shell full of water is an ocean to an ant. Д247
	An ant may work its heart out, but it can't make honey. Л208
Anvil	An iron anvil should have a hammer of feathers. Д312
	The anvil fears no hammer. Н271, M137,211
Ape	An ape's an ape, a varlet's a varlet, though they be clad in silk or scarlet. В361, Л42, **О9**
	The higher the ape goes, the more he shows his tail. M189, П160
Appearances	Appearances are deceiving. **H143**, H237,455
Appetite	Appetite comes with the eating. А21
Apple	An apple a day keeps the doctor away. Л109
	Lost with an apple and won with a nut. П94
	No good apple on a sour stock. К84
	One bad (rotten) apple spoils the bunch. В7, К203, **О148**
	The apple never falls far from the tree. К84, **M95**, Я4
	The apples on the other side of the wall are the sweetest. В178,583, H118, Ч118,129
Appurtenance	The appurtenance must follow the main part. К321
April	April showers bring May flowers. А22
Arm	Some have a short arm for giving and a long arm for getting. Б192, Д13,71, С164
	Stretch your arm no further than your sleeve will reach. Д238
Arrow	Straight as an arrow. К32
	The wise man blames the archer, not the arrow. H322,388
Art	Art improves nature. H150
	It is not strength but art that obtains the prize. Б140
	Who has an art has everywhere a part. H486
Ask	Ask and have. Ч22
Asparagus	Quicker than boiling asparagus. С294
Ass	An ass is known by his ears. О106
	An ass laden with gold still eats thistles. Д487, Ж150,163
	An ass to an ass is beautiful. С67
	Every ass likes to hear himself bray. В590, *Ap.*1.88
	Every ass thinks himself worthy to stand with the king's horses. В592
	If an ass goes a travelling, he'll not come home a horse. В438, Г337, *Ap.*1.32
	The fault of the ass must not be laid on the pack saddle. H427
	What good can it do an ass to be called a lion. И74, Л42, О105
	When all men say you are an ass, it is time to bray. К48, П81
	Wherever an ass falls, there he will never fall again. Б301
Assembly	A learned assembly is a living library. В379
Aunt	Confide in an aunt and the world will know. Г183, H411, Ш5
	If my aunt had been a man, she'd have been my uncle. Е21, *Ap.*1.24
Autumn	No autumn fruit without spring blossoms. О102
Avarice	Avarice is never satisfied. Р71, С161

Bed	As you make your bed, so you must lie on it. K35, K81
	Better go to bed supperless than rise in debt. B285
	He that lies long abed, his estate feels it. C245
	Too much bed makes a dull head. K154,262
	Who goes to bed supperless, all night tumbles and tosses. **Б128**, C336
Bee	A humble bee in a cow turd thinks himself king. M136, **П307**
	To have a bee in one's bonnet. У37
Beggar	A beggar can never be bankrupt. Б347
	Beggars can't be choosers. E56, H31,62
	Give a beggar a horse and he'll ride it to death. Д23
	Great as beggars. B233
	The beggar ennobled does not know his own kinsman. Б278
	The beggar may sing before the thief. Б352, **Г239**, **H558**
Begin	Begin nothing until you have considered how it is to end. H417
	Better not to begin than never make an end. У90
	He who begins many things, finishes but few. **K260**, M121˙
	Well begun - half done. **Д308**, 3106, Л75, H157
	Whatever begins also ends. Б83
	You began better than you end. П202
Beginning	A good beginning is half the task (makes a good ending). П199
	All beginnings are hard. **B642**, П17
	Begin at the beginning, not the end. K115, Л56
	From small beginnings come great things. O140
	Such beginning, such end. H156
	Sweet beginning with a sour end. П202, 3103
	Where there's no beginning, there's no end. **Б83**
Believe	Believe not all that you see nor half of what you hear. Л205
	We soon believe what we desire. K5
Bell	A cracked bell can never sound well. И92,118, П278, P82
	No bell is rung by accident. H493
	When thou dost hear a toll or knell, then think upon thy passing bell. Г321
Belly	A belly full of gluttony will never study willingly. C338
	Better fill a man's belly than his eye. Г111
	He whose belly is full believes not him who is fasting. **C340**, Д234
	Hungry bellies have no ears. Г227
	If it were not for the belly, the back might wear gold. B10, Л3, H9
	Never good that mind the belly too much. Б369
	The belly hates a long sermon. Г229
	The belly teaches all arts. Б365
	The belly wants ears. У7
Bellyful	A bellyful is a bellyful, whether it be meat or drink. B9
Benefit	Benefits bind. B549
Betray	Those who betray their friends must not expect others to keep faith with them. H315
Better	Better a little along than a long none. M20
	Better be half-hanged than ill-wed. Л131,135
	Better beg than steal. Г203, **Л151**
	Better bend than break. И138, Л122
	Better envied than pitied. Л118
	Better fed than taught. Б136, H160
	Better never begin than never make an end. Л33

Better ought than nought. E40
Better rue sit than rue flit. Л156, X105
Better to have than to wish. Л154
Better to sit still than rise and fall. Л125

Bird
A bird in the hand is worth two in the bush. Ж169, Л152, C122
A bird is known by its note. B311, K49, П54
A bird may fly high, but he must come down for water. Ж168
A bird never flies so far that his tail doesn't follow. Л108
A bird of the same feather. И98, O71
A little bird told me. C243
A small bird is content with a little nest. M31
Birds are entangled by their feet, men by their tongues. П296
Birds of a feather flock together. K266, **M164**, H167, **П109**, *Ap.*1.5
Birds once snared fear all bushes. П298
Every bird likes his own nest best. B600
Every bird likes to hear himself sing. B572, 590, **B601**
Far shooting never killed bird. H432
It is an ill bird that fouls its nest. X93
Little by little the bird builds his nest. M24
Small birds make little nests. **M31**
Such bird, such egg. O166
Such bird, such nest. П54
The bird is known by his note, the man by his words. B310, 3158, O98
The early bird catches the worm. K223, **P35**
The older the bird, the more unwillingly it parts with its feathers. C281
There are no birds of this year in last year's nests. Г173, Ч57
To kill two birds with one stone. O65
You cannot catch an old bird with chaff. C266

Birth
Birth is but praise of ancestors. H480

Bite
Don't bite off more than you can chew. P76, Ч96

Biter
The biter is sometimes bit. Д456, **П154**

Bitter
That which is bitter to endure may be sweet to remember. B8
The bitter must come before the sweet. Б344, **Г281**, H221,363
Who has bitter in his mouth, spits sweet. Г294

Black
Black is black and white is white. H339
Black will take no other hue. B156
Spice is black but it has a sweet smack. Б172
To say black is white. H339, C37, Ч50

Blame (n)
Deaf men go away with the blame. Г156

Blame (v)
He that blames would buy. H487

Blessing
A blessing in disguise. H192

Blind
Blind men can judge no colours. K54
Don't ask a blind man the way to the city. H423
If the blind lead the blind, both fall into the ditch. C175
In the kingdom of the blind, the one-eyed man is king. **M54**
Let me see, as the blind man said. C176
Men are blind in their own cause. B547
The blind eat many a fly. C174
The blind man wishes to show the way. C173

Box	It's too late to learn to box when you're in the ring. H452
Boy	Boys will be boys. Д216
Brag	They brag most that do least. X7,10
Bragger	Great braggers, little doers. X10
Brain	Better brains than brawn. Б401
	The brains don't lie in the beard. Б342, **M171**
	We need brain more than belly food. H183
	You don't need brains if you have luck. Д251
Branch	The highest branch is not the safest roost. Г323
Brave	A brave man may fall, but he cannot yield. Г107
	A brave man's wounds are seldom on his back. M145
	It is easy to be brave from a safe distance. M130, H432
	None but the brave deserves the fair. C190
	'Tis more brave to live than to die. Ж161
Bread	A crust is better than no bread. E52
	A crust of bread in peace is better than a feast in contention. Л124, У24
	A hungry man often talks of bread. B380, **Г232**
	All griefs with bread are less. **Б144**, B679, Г224, **M196**
	Ask for bread and be given a stone. B345, K93
	Bitter is the bread of charity. Г280
	Bread is the staff of life. K99, X20
	Dry bread at home is better than roast meat abroad. B139, Д386, H116, **C61**, Ч128
	Dry bread with love is better than fried chicken with fear and trembling. Д324, У24
	Eaten bread is soon forgotten. A1, Б366
	He knows on which side his bread is buttered. 3141, P29
	If they can't eat bread, let them eat cake. X22
	It is better to have bread left over than to run out of wine. H14
	Lacking bread, tarts are good. K95
	Man lives not by bread alone. H297
	To quarrel with one's bread and butter. X24
	Whose bread I eat, his song I sing. H120, **Ч24**
	You can't eat the same bread twice. A1, O41, C26
	You give me bread for cake. X29
Breakfast	Laugh before breakfast, cry before sunset. C85
Breath	Don't hold your breath. Д205, П131, Э2
	Keep your breath to cool your soup. E50
Breed	Breed is stronger than pasture. B168
	Not where one is bred but where one is fed. Г7
Brevity	Brevity is the soul of wit. K197
Bridge	Weight will break a bridge. П288
Broad	It's as broad as it is long. B507
Broom	A new broom sweeps clean. H560
	There's little left for the broom after the besom. 3105, П174
Broth	A good broth may come out of a wooden ladle as out of a silver spoon. П101
Brother	Not his brother's keeper. Б359

Cake	All our cakes are dough. K93
	Give a bit of your cake to one who is going to eat pie. H340, C337
	It's a piece of cake. B513
	You can't have the cake and eat it. **O41**, C26
Canoe	Paddle your own canoe. H198, П293
Cannot	I can't means I won't. H264
Cap	If the cap fits, wear it. *Ap.*1.22,76
Capon	If thou hast not a capon, feed on an onion. И25, 329, H3,348, C107
	Not to know a goose from a capon. H464
Card	A card which never appears neither wins nor loses. K273
	Many can pack the cards yet cannot play well. B54, X94
	Unlucky at cards, lucky in love. H204
Care	Another's cares will not rob you of sleep. П300
	Care brings grey hair. Г274, **H225**
	Care saves ware. X40
	Crowns have cares. T83
	Hang care. 358
	Many cares make the head white. H225
	Much coin, much care. Б290, **Д179**
Careless	Such as are careless of themselves are seldom mindful of others. Г174
Cart	An old cart well used may outlast a new one abused. Б185, C269
	An unhappy man's cart is easy to overthrow. *Ap.*1.34
	Put the cart before the horse. П174
Case	A clear case brings the right verdict with it. K86
	Well goes the case that wisdom counsels. O66
Cask	The cask savours of the first fill. Б348
Cat	A cat in gloves catches no mice. Б126
	A cat may look at a king. B405
	A scalded cat fears hot water. **H55**
	All cats are black (grey) in the night. K144, **H570**
	Cats hide their claws. M15
	He is like a cat, fling him which way you will and he'll light on his legs. K39
	How can the cat help it if the maid be a fool. B333, H512
	Send a cat for lard. H211
	The cat knows whose beard she licks. 3145
	The cat shuts its eyes while it steals cream. Ж165
	The cat would eat fish and would not wet her feet. **K181**, Л45
	There's more than one way to skin a cat. C52
	To agree like cats and dogs. **Д435**, Ж104
	To teach the cat the way to the kirn. H469
	When the cat is full, the milk tastes sour. M212, C169
	When the cat's away, the mice will play. Г63
	Who lives with cats will get a taste for mice. П152
	Who plays with cats must expect to be scratched. Ч38
	You can have no more of a cat than her skin. C15
Caution	Caution is the parent of safety. O112
Ceremony	Ceremony is not civility, nor civility ceremony. C32

Chute	Chatting to chiding is not worth a chute. Б328
City	A city that parleys is half gotten. Я17
	A great city, a great solitude. B238
	Cities are taken by the ears. O14, Я17
Claw	Velvet paws hide sharp claws. M214
Clay	Clay replies not to the potter. H493
	Unless the clay is well-pounded, no pitcher can be made. Г130
Cleanliness	Cleanliness is next to godliness. Ч59
Clerk	It is the clerk makes justice. Г11
	The greatest clerks are not the wisest men. B177
Cloak	Have not thy cloak to make when it begins to rain. B347, Г304, H70,452
Clock	When a man is happy, he does not hear the clock strike. C19,**308**
Cloth	Don't spread your cloth till the pot begins to boil. Ж41, O6
	The best cloth may have a moth in it. B163
Clothes	Clothes and looks don't make the person. H443
	Clothes don't make the woman, but they help. X9
	Clothes make not the man. H302
	Good clothes open all doors. Д29, П64
	It is not the clothes that count, but the things the clothes cover. X9
Cloud	After black clouds, clear weather. Б384, Г23, Ж32, **П166**
	Every cloud has a silver lining. Г26
Clover	In clover. K56
Clown	Give a clown your finger and he will take your hand. Д25, Д31
Coat	Cut your coat according to your cloth. K209
	If the coat fits, wear it. B668
	It is not the gay coat that makes the gentleman. Б350, **H302**
	Near is my coat but nearer is my shirt. P74
	You can't get warm in another's fur coat. B180,185, Г128, H111
Coal	To carry coals to Newcastle. B59,377, *Ap.*1.85
Cobble	They that cobble and clout shall have work when others go without. H486
Cobbler	Let the cobbler stick to his last. **B563**,569, З154, *Ap.*1.21
Cock	A cock and bull story. T76
	A cock is master of his coop. B137
	A cock is bold on his own dunghill. B562, Д389, И43
	As the old cock crows, so the young one learns. **M30**, Щ3
	If you are a cock, crow; if a hen, lay eggs. K333
	There's many a good cock that's come out of a tattered bag. Д288
	Who eats his cock alone must saddle his horse alone. K9, C42
Cog	Just a cog in the machine. П180
Coin	Where coin is not common, commons must be scant. 345

Salt cooks bear blame but fresh cooks bear shame. H501
Too many cooks spoil the broth. Д212, У52,53

Cookie
Cookie today, crumb tomorrow. B662
That's how the cookie crumbles. B443, T6

Corn (n)
Crooked furrows grow straight corn. C287
He that sows in the highway tires his oxen and loses his corn. P52
He wants his corn shelled. П273
Measure not another man's corn by your own bushel. B187,559, **H87**
Plough deep and you will have plenty of corn. Г131,O95
You can't have the ear unless you plant the corn. Ж167

Corn (v)
Corn him well and he'll work better. C335

Cost
Do not be liberal (free) of another man's cost (pottage). Д28, Л25, H441, Ч130
Often for sparing a little cost a man has lost the large coat for the hood. Ж20

Cottage
I will not change a cottage in possession for a kingdom in reversion. X29

Counsel (n)
An enemy may chance to give good counsel. Г314
Come not to counsel uncalled. B171
Counsels in wine seldom prosper. B331
Good counsel has no price. X58
Good counsel never comes amiss. B630
The healthful man can give counsel to the sick. Л23, C142
We have better counsel to give than to take. H202

Counsel (v)
He that will not be counseled cannot be helped. K275

Counsellor
The land is never void of counsellors. B302

Country
A wise man esteems every place to be his own country. B610
It's a free country. B404,406
Where it is well with me, there is my country. H445, **T9**
You can take the man out of the country, but not the country out of the man. M191

Courage
Courage comes through suffering. M187
Fearless courage is the foundation of victory. K237, M188

Covet
Covet not that which belongs to others. H338

Covetousness
Covetousness breaks the bag. T85
Covetousness is always filling a bottomless vessel. Ж7
When all sins grow old, covetousness is young. C281

Cow
A bawling cow soon forgets her calf. H286, C53
As a saddle becomes a cow. K19, H384
Curst cow has short horns. Б298
Faraway cows have long horns. C168
If you buy the cow, take the tail into the bargain. B292
It isn't the cow that lows the most that will milk the most. E29
Let him that owns the cow take her by the tail. H335
Many a good cow has an evil calf. И126, O145
You cannot sell the cow and drink the milk. П285

Coward
A coward is more exposed to quarrels than a man of spirit. C205, X66
Cowards prattle more than men of worth. B631

Crab
The greatest crabs be not the best meat. Ж101, **P86**
You cannot make a crab walk straight. **K200**, C130

Cradle What is learnt in the cradle lasts to the grave. K64, H470, *Ap.*1.27

Craft All the craft is in the catching. H269
Craft must have clothes but truth loves to go naked. П217
Of all crafts, theft is the worst. B433
Too much courtesy, too much craft. Г180

Cream It is not well for a man to pray cream and live skim milk. Ж26

Credit Give credit where credit is due. П55

Creditor Creditors have better memories than debtors. Д369, C257

Creek Up the creek without a paddle. B372, K323

Cripple He that dwells next door to a cripple will learn to halt. K125, П106
He that mocks a cripple ought to be whole. H416
It's ill halting before a cripple. C13

Criticise Unless you can do better, don't criticise. Ч21

Crock She will as soon part with the crock as with the porridge. Л143

Crook There is a crook in the lot of everyone. И39

Crooked That which is crooked cannot be made straight. И86

Cross Crosses are ladders that lead to heaven. Л180
Each cross has its inscription. P69
We all have our cross to bear. Б400

Crow A crow is never the whiter for washing herself often. Ч50
Carrion crows bewail the dead sheep, then eat them. B391
Crows are black the world over. B440
Crows weep for the dead lamb and then devour him. П115
Crows will not pick out crows' eyes. B435, И21, K155
He has brought up a crow to pick out his own eyes. B538
Of an evil crow, an evil egg. H47, **O166**
The crow thinks her own birds the fairest. C57,67
To shoot at a pigeon and kill a crow. И124
When the crow flies, her tail follows. П23

Cry Do not cry before you are hurt. Б387, Г120, H446
Great cry and little wool. B319, K207
The cautious seldom cry. K221

Cunning Cunning surpasses strength. **H154**,269

Cup Like (such) cup, like (such) cover. **K87**, H22,39, П49
There's many a slip 'twixt the cup and the lip. B362, Г109, И2

Cur A cur will bite before he barks. И139
Brabbling curs never want sore ears. Д408

Cure Past cure, past care. И140
That sick man is not to be pitied who has his cure in his sleeve. H142
What cannot be cured must be endured. H62

Curiosity Curiosity is ill manners in another's house. B193
Curiosity killed the cat. 393, Л195, M109

Custom   Custom is a second nature. П243
Custom reconciles us to everything. П244
Custom takes the taste from the most savoury foods. И30
Every country has its custom. Ч89
It is hard to break a hog of an ill custom. H123, P61
Once a use, ever a custom. C282

Dam   Where the dam leaps over, the kid follows. Д201

Damned   Damned if you do, damned if you don't. Д9

Danger   Danger is the next neighbour to security. C328
Danger makes men devout. Г91, Д334
Nothing is more delightful than to look upon danger from a safe place. X71
The more danger, the more honour. P58

Dark   All shapes, all colours are alike in the dark. H571

Darkness   Darkness has no shame. H569

Darling   Better an old man's darling than a young man's warling. Л174

Daughter   A diamond daughter turns to glass as a wife. Д406

Day   A day will come will pay for all. Б386
Another day, another dollar. 396
As sure as night follows day. Б371, Д160
Be the day ever so long, at last comes evensong. Д159, H529, C145
Drunken days have all their tomorrows. B14,15,322
Every day come night. Б371, Д160
Every day is not yesterday. Д165
Lay up for rainy day. Б174,**180**, B83, X60
One day at a time. H499
One may see day at a little hole. Г110, M1
One of these days is none of these days. П168
Our day too will come some day. A7, Б373, И24, П256
Praise a fair day at night. B280, **Д171**, X6
The day is short and the work is much. Д147
Though you rise early, yet the day comes at its time and not till then. O77
You can tell the day by the morning. K193

Dead   Dead dogs bark not. M65
Dead men do no harm. O143
Dead men don't bite. M65
Dead men don't walk again. M75
Dead men tell no tales. M66
It is only the dead who do not return. M71
No man is dead till he's dead. Ж124
Speak well of the dead. O2
The dead are always wrong. (The dead have no rights.) X64

Dearth   Dearths foreseen come not. M113

Death   At every hour death is near. Д463, C197
Better death than dishonour. **Б210**, Г289
Death defies the doctor. Б307, O155
Death devours lambs as well as sheep. Ж144, H367
Death hath not so ghastly a face at a distance as it hath at hand. B304

Death is deaf and will hear no denial. 340, O154
Death is one for all. M73
Death is the great leveller. C198, **У57**
Death keeps no calendar. C197
Death makes no distinction of person. C198
Death meets us everywhere. H20, C194
Fear of death is worse than death itself. C200
Like death upon wires. B80
Live mindful of death. H20
There is a remedy for everything but death. 340, **O122**

Debt
A man in debt is a man caught in a net. B34
Debt is a heavy burden to an honest mind. Д367
Debt is the worst poverty. 374

Deceive
He that once deceives is ever suspected. B453,666, **K224**, C215

Deed
A bad deed never dies (will not stay hid). Д311, Л77,79, H102
A good deed is never lost. Д300, **X53**
An ill deed cannot bring honour. И81
Deeds, not words. Б316, M60, **H270**
Deeds will show themselves and words will pass away. C127

Good deeds are better than creeds. H434
Good deeds are easily forgotten, bad deeds never. **Д311**, P16
It is one thing to plan a deed and another to carry it out. Г108, M113
The deed comes back upon the doer. C81

Delay
Delays are dangerous. П281
Delay breeds loss. 399
Delays are dangerous but they make things sure. Д30
You may delay, but time will not. M84, Ч94

Deluge
After us the deluge. П170

Descent
He who boasts of his descent, praises the deed of another. H480

Desire
Desire has no rest. O190

Devil
As well to eat the devil as drink his broth. Л4
Better fleech the devil than fight him. T81
Between the devil and the deep blue sea. B446
Give the devil an inch and he'll take an ell. H124
Give the devil his due. B375
He needs a long spoon that sups with the devil. C78
He that takes the devil into his boat must carry him over the sound. C78
It is easier to raise the devil than to lay him. П143
Let one devil ding another. H170
Talk (speak) of the devil and he is sure to appear. П270
The devil is good (kind) to (protects) his own. Ч52
The devil is good when he is pleased. Д77
The devil is master of all arts. Ч44
The devil is never far off. П147
The devil is not so black as he is painted. Г313, **И60**, X47
The devil lurks behind the cross. Б339, Г73, **O82**, П146
The devil places a pillow for the drunken man to fall on. H407
The devil wipes his tail with the poor man's pride. B158
To hold a candle to the devil. B289
Truth may sometimes come out of the devil's mouth. Г314
When the devil comes, it's too late to pray. A20, H452, X14
When the devil can't go, he sends his grandmother. K138

When the devil prays, he has booty in his eye. И13
Where the devil cannot come, he will send. К138

Diamond   Diamond cut diamond. А13, **А14**

Die   A man can die but once. Г299, **Д91**, Д107, Р39, С98, С101, С291, Ш2
                  Never say die. Ж124, С134
                  Young men may die, but old men must die. M153

Difference   No more difference than between a broom and besom. H414

Dinner   A dinner lubricates business. Б85,113
                  After dinner everyone is wise. M130
                  After dinner, mustard. П171,**178**
                  At dinner, my man appears. **Б467**, Д447, Е42
                  Dinner over, away go the friends. H64

Dirt   Brushing against dirt won't make you any cleaner. H448
                  Fling enough dirt and some will stick. К105
                  Who deals in dirt has foul fingers. **Г332**, И1, И119
                  You can't play in dirt without getting dirty. Г332

Disaster   To inquire is neither a disaster nor a disgrace. П155

Disease   A deadly disease neither physician nor physic can ease. З98
                  Diseases come on horseback but depart on foot. Б303,304

Dish   Pay with the same dish you borrow. К31
                  The first dish is the best eaten. H71,П12

Distance   Distance lends enchantment. Д57, Т10

Do   A man can do a lot of things if he has to. П85
                  Do as I say, not as I do. С40,43
                  Do as you would be done by. К74, H315, Т80, **Ч11**
                  Do well and have (fare) well. Д118,263, К137, **К289**, Х72
                  Doing is better than saying. Д116, H270, С230
                  He that may not do as he would must do as he may. К152, П50
                  I do as I please. **К60**, H485, С75
                  In doing we learn. Д132, У124
                  Those that can, do. К312
                  To tremble at doing and to sweat at eating. **B122**, К1

Doctor   Better pay the butcher than the doctor. Д343
                  Every doctor thinks his pills the best. B581
                  The more doctors, the more diseases. Г55

Dog   A bad dog never sees the wolf. С222
                  A beaten dog escheweth the whip. Б220
                  A dog in the kitchen desires no company. H424, С220
                  A dog is a man's best friend. О57
                  A dog returns to his home. Х62
                  A dog returns to where he has been fed. Б389, **И51**
                  A dog scourged can bid a lion fear. Б171, Г329
                  A dog will not bark (howl) if you beat him with a bone. H271
                  A dog with a bone knows no friend. H424
                  A grateful dog is better than an ungrateful man. Д340
                  A little dog will run a lion out of his own yard. С218
                  A mischievous dog must be tied short. Б244
                  A staff is quickly found to beat a dog. Б454
                  An old dog barks not in vain. С276

An old dog won't be easily brought to wear a collar. C264
Barking dogs seldom bite. H181,234, **C223**
Better a live dog than a dead lion. Ж97, **M69**, П33
Brag is a good dog but dares not bite. H128
Cut off a dog's tail and he will be a dog still. B688
Dog does not eat dog. Б240, B389, И21, K155, **C221**
Don't be afraid of a dog that barks. H181
Even a dog is a lion at home. B607
Every dog has his day. A7, Б373, П256
For every dog there is a leash. Б456
Give a dog a bad name and hang him. X47
Greedy dogs never have enough. Ж3
If you lie down with dogs you will get up with fleas. **K306**
It is easy to find a stick to beat a dog. **Б454**, Г302, C109
It's a poor dog that's not worth the whistling. B545, K172
It's hard to break a dog of an ill custom. П241
Like a dog in a wheel, always moving but never advancing. K16
Look not for musk in a dog's kennel. B5, З101, H399
Quarreling dogs come halting home. Г253, Д408
Short-tailed dog wags his tail same as a long one. Б387
The dog in the manger won't eat the oats nor let anyone else eat them. C220
The dog that trots about finds the bone. B396
The hindmost dog may catch the hare. Д49
The mad dog bites his master. **Б211**, З125
The silent dog bites first. И139, H181, **T28**
The tail cannot shake the dog. Б332, **X17**, Я23
There are more ways to kill a dog than hanging it. H379
Two dogs strive for a bone and a third runs away with it. O100
Wake not at every dog's bark. П300
We may not expect a good whelp from an ill dog. Щ4
When the dog is beaten, the lion is tamed. Б171
You cannot teach an old dog new tricks. **C273**, Ч46
You have to be smarter than the dog to teach him tricks. C212, **Ч106**

Done

Done and forgotten. Б477, Д140
No sooner said than done. C129
What's done cannot be undone. Б219, O85, П279, **Ч62**,93

Door

A creaking door hangs long on its hinges. C160
At open doors dogs come in. **B98**, K126
Sweep before your own door before you sweep before others'. Ч135
To beg at the wrong door. H199
When one door closes, another one opens. O58

Dowry

A great dowry is a bed full of brambles. Б285, Ж48, Л142
She that is good and fair needs no other dowry. H299

Dream

Dreams are what you hope for, reality is what you plan for. B358
Dreams give wings to fools. Д501

Drink

As you brew, so must you drink. C38
Drink does not drown care but waters it and makes it grow. B336, Г298
Drinking and thinking don't mix. B338
The more one drinks, the more one may. Б469

Driver

The best drivers have wrecks. И18

Drop

Many drops of water make an ocean. П58
The last drop makes the cup run over. C99

Drunk   A drunk man will sober up, but a damn fool never. П315
                   Ever drunk, ever dry. B337
                   Drunken folks seldom take harm. П314
                   He that is drunk is as great as a king. П313
                   Nothing more than a fool, a drunken man. П317

Drunkenness   Drunkenness does not produce faults, it discovers them. B329
                   What soberness conceals, drunkenness reveals. У49, Ч104

Duck   Drink only with the duck. П37
                   Roasted ducks don't fly into your mouth. **Ж21**, M76, X21

Dumb   Good listening does not mean sitting dumb. T33

Dwarf   A dwarf on a giant's shoulders sees further of the two. C6

Eagle   Attempt not to fly like an eagle with the wings of a wren. B430
                   Eagles do not breed doves. З139, H47,402, O96,156
                   Eagles don't catch flies. Л17, **O99**

Ear   In one ear and out the other. B89
                   Wide ears and a short tongue. Д208, У97
Early   Early wed, early dead. P34
                   He who rises early makes progress in his work. K223

Ease   Of sufferance cometh ease (rest). Б125, H541, C94
                   Think of ease but work on. Д129

Easy   Easier said than done. B512, **Г186**, Л27, Л36, H231, **C156**
                   Easy as pie. Д142
                   Easy come, easy go. Б444,479, B662, **K47**, Ч80
                   It is easier to pull down than to build up. Л106
                   It is easy to do what one's self wills. O189
                   Tis easier to find happiness than to keep it. Л37
                   Tis easy to sigh, but it's better to pray. Ж16

Eat   All he does is just eat and sleep. Ж109
                   As you bake, so shall you eat. З358, K34, **C38**, **Ч77**
                   Eat to please yourself but dress to please others. E44
                   He that eats least, eats most. H366
                   Man must eat to live, not live to eat. Б145
                   Once you start eating, it's hard to stop. C148

Education   Education makes the man. K63

Eel   An eel cannot be hidden in a sack. Ш7
                   As slippery as an eel. B693
                   Mud chokes no eels. H271

Egg   As sure as eggs is eggs. B250
                   Better an egg today than a hen tomorrow. O69
                   Eggs can't teach the hen. H491, **Я20**
                   He that would have eggs must endure the cackling of hens. Г130, У65
                   Teach your grandmother to suck eggs. H468, У121, Я20
                   To have both the egg and the hen. K146
                   To put all your eggs in one basket. B504, X88
                   You cackle often but never lay an egg. Б202

Everyone ought to know his own business best. 3151,153, *Ap.*1.12
Everyone speaks of his own interest. У37
Everyone thinks his sack heaviest. Б311, B657, H162
Everyone to his own opinions. B191,528
When everyone is wrong, everyone is right. Г19

Everything   A place for everything and everything in its place. B586
Everything comes to him who waits. **B510**, И24
Everything forbidden is sweet. З91, Ч19
Everything gives cause for either laughter or tears. B611
Everything has a beginning. B495
Everything has an end. E37, H553, C136
Everything has its time. B535, **B646**
Everything in turn. B494
Everything is according to the colour through which one views it. *Ap.*1.11
Everything is funny as long as it happens to someone else. Л206, Ч110
Everything is good in its season. A4, **B635**,655
Everything is of use to a housekeeper. T37
Everything is sweetened by risk. P58
Everything may be done with care. O110
Everything must have a beginning and an end. Б471
Everything that happens, happens for the best. B517
One can get used to everything, even hanging. И3, П68,242
You (one) can't have everything. B95,523, H203,248

Evil   Apprehension of evil is often worse than evil itself. Л110
Bear with evil and expect good. Ж110
Choose the lesser of the two evils. И77, Л133
Covetousness is the root of all evil. M115
Evil doers are evil dreaders. 3127
Evil to him who evil does. C81
He that helps evil hurts the good. **Д352**, K243
He who does evil comes to an evil end. Л76
He who speaks evil, hears worse. Г191
If a man wishes to know the strength of evil, let him try to abandon it. Л111
Never do evil for evil. 3131
Never do evil that good may come of it. H99
No evil without good. H531
Take the evil with the good. Л173

Example   A good example is the best sermon. B441

Excuse   One excuse is as good as another. C194

Experience   A thimbleful of experience is worth a tubful of knowledge. 32
A thorn of exprerience is worth a wilderness of advice. 32
Experience bought by suffering teaches wisdom. H378
Experience is often a substitute for learning. Б217, 32, **O93**
Experience is the best teacher. O92
Experience is the master of wisdom. M195
Experience without learning is better than learning without experience. Л145

Expectation   Expectation always surpasses realization. Ж26

Extravagance   Extravagance is the pitfall of the rich man. M163

Extreme   One extreme follows another. K43

Eye	Far from the eye, far from the heart. Д48
	He that has but one eye, must be afraid to lose it. У113
	He that has but one eye, sees the better for it. О70, У40
	However high the eye may rise, it will find the eyebrow above. B691, H546
	It is better to trust the eyes than the ears. Б317,H210,**215**, О194
	Little troubles the eye, but far less the soul. Г125
	Neither eyes on letters nor hands on coffers. Г117
	One eye has more faith than two ears. Л123
	The buyer needs a thousand eyes, the seller one. Ч70
	The eye is the mirror (window) of the soul. **Г118**, K77
	The eye is a shrew. Г124
	The eye is the pearl of the face. Б54
	The eye looks but the mind sees. О78
	The eye that sees all things sees not itself. **B309**, Ч116
	The eyes are not satisfied with seeing. Г121,158, H343
	The eyes are bigger than the belly. Б368,B275, Г111,**116**
	There's more than meets the eye. H455
	To cry with one eye and laugh with the other. Г127
	What the eye sees not, the heart rues not. Ч14
	When you spit in a timid man's eye, he says it's raining. П46
	You can look into the eyes but not in the heart. B142, Ч112
Eyesight	He who weeps for everybody soon loses his eyesight. H74
Eyewitness	One eyewitness is better than two (ten) hearsays. Л146
Face	A fair face cannot have a crabbed heart. П247
	A good face is a letter of recommendation. K189
	A pretty face may hide an empty head. Л86, P65
	Don't fall on your face. H461
	Fair face, foul heart. B99, Г112, **Л85**, C51, C211
	The face is a mask, look behind it. Л10, H514
	The face is the index of the mind (heart). Л84
	The face is no index of the heart. P65
	There is never a foul face but there is a foul fancy. У66
	To smile in one's face and cut one's throat. **B16**, О86
	Trust not the face. P65
Fact	Facts are stubborn things. Ф1
	No ideal is as good as a fact. M113
Failure	Failure teaches success. О197
Fair	Fair and foolish, long and lazy, little and loud. M199
	Fair is not fair, but that which pleases. H368
	Fair without, false within. Л87, **C51**
Fall	Climb not too high lest the fall be greater. H223,371
	Hasty climbers have sudden falls. Б300
	He that is down need fear no fall. M137
	The higher the standing, the lower the fall. B686
	The higher they go, the lower they fall. H223
Falsehood	Falsehood is common, truth uncommon. П211
Famine	Anything's good in a famine. B111, M197, H31

Far	Far fowls have fair feathers. Б227
	Far from court, far from care. K272
	He that travels far, knows much. Ч115
	Soft pace goes far. K236
	You go far about seeking the nearest. Д50
Farther	Go farther and fare worse. Д52,60
	The farther in, the deeper. Д60, H566
Fast	He that runs fast will not run long. Б484,486
Fat	Fat paunches have lean pates. Ж129
	Little knows the fat man what the lean does mean. C289
	You must take the fat with the lean. Л173, X63
Fate	Cast your fate o the wind. O179
	Fate leads the willing but drives the stubborn. Ж39
	No flying from fate. O157, P62,68
	You cannot escape your fate. **P68**
Father	Like father, like son. 351, **K62**
	Many a good father has a bad son. Д37, И126
	No love to a father's. H520
	No man is responsible for his father. Б411
Fault	A fault confessed is half redressed. П89, Я6
	Before you flare up at anyone's faults, take time to count ten of your own. H172
	Every man has his faults. H495
	He finds fault with others and does worse himself. Д431
	He that commits a fault thinks everyone speaks of it. B334
	He that corrects not small faults will not control great ones. C208
	It's always someone else's fault. B70
	Like fault, like punishment. K86, П104, **Ч40**
	We tax our friends with faults but see not our own. Д432
	Who is in fault suspects everybody. B419,425
	Wink at dmall faults. И75
	You would find fault if you knew how. Б455
Faulty	The faulty stands on his guard. B587
Favour	Great mens' favours are uncertain. Б351
Fear	All fear is bondage. C56
	Fear gives wings. И142, C290
	Fear has magnifying eyes. У63
	Fear is beyond all arguments. И132
	Fear is one part of prudence. H158, O89
	Fear is stronger than love. B575
	He that fears you present will hate you absent. K139
	It was fear first created gods in the world. Г91
Feast	Feast and your halls are crowded. H355
	Feast today and fast tomorrow. Ч6
	It's either a feast or a famine. K118
	To arrive after the feast. П171
Feather	Fine (fair) feathers make fine birds (fair fowl). Б142, B310
	You could have knocked him (me) down with a feather. E2
Fence	No fence against a flail. O158

Fiddle   There's many a good tune played on an old fiddle. E36, **H561**

Fiddler   They that dance must pay the fiddler. Л169, П67, У88

Field   Do not neglect your own field and plough your neighbour's. H326, C70, Ч133

Find   Fast (safe) (sure) bind, fas (safe) (sure) find. П103
He that hides can find. H377

Finder   Finders keepers, loosers weepers. H169

Finger   Don't put your finger in too tight a ring. M52
If you want your finger bit, stick it in a possum's mouth. M52, H319
Put your finger in the fire and say it was your fortune. H429
Sailor's fingers are all fish hooks. P84
They are finger and thumb. M179

Fire   A fire which warms us at a distance will burn us when near. Л207
Don't play with fire. C25
Fight fire with fire. K106, 3122
Fire cannot be hidden in flax. **B141**, C237, Ш7
From (out of) the frying pan (and) into the fire. Б47, И87,93, O117,146
He who plays with fire could get burned. 310, **K281**
He who wishes a fire must put up with smoke. У65
If you play with fire you get burnt. B115, O81
In the coolest flint there is hot fire. И7
It is best to sit near the fire when the chimney smokes. X67
It's good to take chestnuts out of the fire with the cat's paw. X73
No smoke without fire. **Д510**, O26
Skeer your own fire. H400, Ч131
The fire is never without heat. O80
Where there's smoke, there's fire. Г37, Г68

First   Be the first at a feast and the last at a fight. Д79
First come, first served. **K283**, П19
First try then trust. Д358,**508**
First up, last down. P36
He that comes first to the hill may sit where he will. П19
I am not the first and shall not be the last. Ж154, H341
If at first you don't succeed, try again. H314
Not everyone can be first. K327, **H243**,248
The first blow is half the battle. Л75
The first is worst, the second same, the last is best of all the game. П15
The first step is the hardest. Л75
You're not the first and you won't be the last. H458
Yourself first, others afterward. Д119, Ж17, П195, **245**

Fish (n)   Anything is fish that comes to net. B605
Bait the hook well and the fish will bite. B672
Better a big fish in a little puddle than a little fish in a big puddle. Л119
Better a small fish than an empty dish. Л139
Big (great) fish eat (up) little fish (the small). Б314, K249
Every fish is not a sturgeon. K327, H243
Every fish would be a whale. П44, X108
Fish and guests smell after three days. Г305
Fish begin to stink at the head. P87
He who would catch fish must not mind getting wet. H94
It's a good fish if it were caught. X43
Like a fish out of water. K51
The best fish swim near the bottom. Д60, P85
The fish that escapes is the biggest fish of all. T2

A fool can ask more questions in an hour than a wise man can answer in seven years. О34
A fool can dance without a fiddle. Д477
A fool is ever laughing. Д497
A fool is known by his speech. У26
A fool may throw a stone into a well that a thousand wise men cannot pull out. Д475, **О31**
A fool may give a wise man counsel. У95
A fool says I can't, a wise man says I'll try. Г151
A fool will laugh when he is drowning. Л203
A fool may sometimes speak the truth. Б412, **В465**, **И16**, И129
A fool would ask for a dring if he were drowning. У112
A fool's bell is soon rung. Д482
A fool's bolt may sometimes hit the mark. И129
A fool's tongue is long enough to cut his own throat. В608
A little thing pleases a fool. Д500, Р14
An easy fool is a knave's tool. В576
As the fool thinks, so the bell clinks. В406, Д490, Н369
Better be a rogue than a fool. В12, П286
Every fool likes his own bauble best. В555
Every man is a fool or a physician at forty. П100
Everyone is a fool sometimes. Б167
Fools and madmen ought not to be left in their own company. Н106
Fools are fain of flitting. Д466
Fools are fain of nothing. Д500, П306
Fools are never uneasy. Д483,495, П306
Fools are wise as long as silent. Г138
Fools begin in jest and end in earnest. О170
Fools bite one another, but wise men agree together. **Г145**, Д493, С33
Fools build houses, wise men buy them. Д468
Fools fight one another and wise men agree. Г145
Fools go in crowds. Т7
Fools grow without watering. Д494
Fools live poor to die rich. Ж150, **С162**
Fools make feasts, wise men eat them. Д481
Fools never perceive when they are ill-timed or ill-placed. П148
Fools never prosper. Д485, С9
Fools rejoice at promises. Д478
Fools tie knots and wise men loose them. **Г149**, У102
Fools will be fools still. Д472
For the wise man with a sigh, for the fool with a fist. Н433
Forbid a fool a thing and that he'll do. Д490
Give a fool enough rope and he'll hang himself. Д10
He is a fool who expects sense from a fool. О131
He is a fool who makes a hammer of his fist. В51
He is a fool who is not melancholy once a day. Д495
He is not a wise man who cannot play the fool on occasion. Б396
He is not the fool that the fool is but he that with the fool deals. В451, Д479, С10
He that is born a fool is never cured.   Д486
He that knows he is a fool is not a big fool. Д473
He that sends a fools means to follow him. **Д488**, У96
He who thinks he is wise is a fool (+ he who knows he is a fool is wise.) Т57
If fools went not to markets, bad wares would not be sold. Н30
It is better to be silent and thought a fool than to speak and remove all doubt. С204
Many a one for land takes a fool by the hand. П41,250
More fools, more fun. Б64
One fool makes a hundred. О33
One fool makes many. Б166, Г142, О33
One fool praises another. Б198, **Д469**,471
One fool scrubs another. Д471
Only a fool is positive. Д495
Only fools and horses work. Р1
Only fools speak or fiddle at the table. Д466

Praise a fool and slay him. П197
Praise a fool and you make him useful. O193
Send a fool to market and a fool he will return. B19,496
The family of fools is very old. B130
The fool asks much, but he is more the fool that grants it. Д24
The fool errs alone whereas the wise man corrupts many. Г154
The fools do more hurt in this world than the rascals. Б414
The higher the fool, the lower the fall. Д56
There's no fool like a learned fool. У81
There's no fool like an old fool. K141, C267
Two fools in one house are too many. *Ap.*1.14
What the fool does in the end, the wise man does in the beginning. B577, Д467
When a fool has bethought himself, the market's over. Д484
When you argue with a fool, that makes two. C10

Foot

A going foot is aye getting. Д130
All feet tread not in one shoe. B88, O30
Better a bare foot than none. Л165, H285
One foot is better than two crutches. Л165
One foot cannot stand in two boats. C102
One foot in the sea and one on shore. O147
Those that have wet their feet care not how deep they wade. M137
To start on the wrong foot. H406
To use another's foot to kick a dog. X73

Forbidden

Forbidden fruit is sweet. **391**, H69, Ч19

Force

Force is no argument. П208
Force without forecast is of little avail. Б140
The irresistible force has met the immovable object. H171

Ford

It's no good praising a ford till a man be over. H474

Forest

To lose sight of the forest for the trees. 320, H259, П98
Who goes for a day into the forest should take bread for a week. E6, П114

Forewarn

Forewarned is forearmed. Б186, П226

Forgive

Forgive and forget. Б457

Fork

I ask for a fork and you give me a rake. П205

Fortune

Build not up a fortune on the labours of others. B180,185
Every man is the architect of his own fortune. B556, Ч123
Fortune and misfortune are next-door neighbours. C328
Fortune favours fools. Д251,489, C30, Ф4
Fortune favours the bold. C189, **X84**
Fortune is fickle. C324
Fortune is like glass, it breaks when it is brightest. C321
Fortune knocks at least once at every man's gate. И24
Fortune to one is mother, to another is stepmother. **И133**, O43
Give a man fortune and cast him into the sea. C309
Great fortune brings with it great misfortune. Б326, B675, C319
He dances well to whom fortune pipes. **K162**, C307, T65
If fortune torments me, hope contents me. C327
One man's fortune is another man's misfortune. B410, **K157**
The wheel of fortune is forever in motion. K148

Foul

He that has to do with what is foul never comes away clean. H448, **O81**,84

Fox	An old fox is not easily snared. C268
	He that will deceive the fox must rise. M133
	Long runs the fox but at last is caught. Л96, H374, C136
	Old foxes want no tutors. H360, C275
	The fox condemns the trap, not himself. H180
	The fox may grow grey but never good. B392
	The fox preys farthest from home. Б234
	The tail does often catch the fox. Л72
	When the fox preaches, take care of your geese. Б302, П146
Freedom	A poor freedom is better than rich slavery. B407, X80
	Freedom comes before silver and gold. B408
Friar	A friar is a liar. M159
	Do as the friar says, not as he does. И70
	The friar preached against stealing and had a goose up his sleeve. И122, O73
Friday	Every day is not Friday, there is also Thursday. H439
Friend	A faithful friend is as rare as a diamond. Л130
	A friend in need is a friend in deed. **Д412**
	A friend in the market is better than money in the chest. Д422, H282, X70
	A friend is best found in adversity. Д419
	A friend is not so soon gotten as lost. Л22
	A friend is never known until needed. **Б48**, Д420
	A friend to all is a friend to none. B530
	A friend's frown is better than a foe's smile. Б232, У24
	A good friend is my nearest relation. Б63, Д336,**450**, K234
	A good friend never offends. Д240, П268
	A near friend is better than a far-dwelling kinsman. Б224
	A person is reflected in the friends he chooses. C12
	A rash friend is worse than a foe. У109
	A true friend is the best possession. Д298, Д413
	A true friend is forever a friend. Д444
	Admonish your friends in private, praise them in public. У122
	All are not friends that speak us fair. Д416, H135
	Any friend of my friend is a friend of mine. Д449
	Anything for a friend. **Д242**, M91, P15
	Be friendly and you will never want friends. Л9
	Be slow in choosing a friend but slower in changing him. Д427
	Before you make a friend, eat a bushel of salt with him. B214, У78, **Ч108**
	Bought friends are not friends indeed. Д425
	Fall not out with a friend for a trifle. Ш20
	For a good friend, the journey is never too long. Д241, K2
	Friends agree but at a distance. **Б391**, Д58, H219
	Friends are like jewels. Л130
	Friends are thieves of time. Ж28
	Friends have all things in common. **Б362**, C59
	Friends may meet but mountains never greet. Г248
	Friends tie their purse with a cobweb thread. C8
	Have but few friends, though many acquaintances. З156
	Have no friends not equal to yourself. И114
	He makes no friend that never made a foe. Б320
	He that has friends has no friends (He who has many friends has none). Д446
	I cannot be your friend and your flatterer too. Д439
	In time of prosperity, friends will be plenty; in adversity, not one amongst twenty. П236
	Make new friends but keep the old. H564
	Mistake friend for foe. C76
	No longer foster, no longer friend. Б372, E42, **Ж10**, X23
	Old friends are best. Л160, C277
	One old friend is better than two new ones. Л160

Sunshine friends. Д448
Tell me who your friends are and I'll tell you who you are. 315, C12,123
Those who betray their friends must not expect others to keep faith with them. K282
To a friend's house, the trail is never long. Д241, E30, K2
Trencher friends are seldom good neighbours. Д448, **H64**
True friends share both the good and the bad. C8
Try your friend before you trust. H506
When a friend asks,there is no tomorrow. Д423
When good cheer is lacking, your friends will be packing. Г50, H64
When two friends have a common purse, one sings and the other weeps. H135
You may choose your friends, your family is thrust upon you. Ж113, C64

Friendship   As frost to bud, self-interest is to friendship. П234
Friendship cannot always stand on one side. H103
Friendship is a plant which must often be watered. Д255
One may mend a torn friendship but it soon falls tatters. Д438
Real friendship does not freeze in winter. Д248,414

Frog   The frog cannot out of her bog. Г79, H146

Fruit   Domestic fruit will not grow on a wild tree. Д392
Fruit unripe sticks on the tree. H426
He is free of fruit that wants an orchard. Ч120
He that would have the fruit must climb the tree. H376
The fruit of a good tree is also good. K84

Furniture   The best furniture in a house is a virtuous woman. B374

Further   The further you go, the further behind (The further you run, the further you are behind). H438

Future   Planning your future saves you from regretting your past. T61

Game   Lookers-on see most of the game. C216
Not the only game in town. C52
The game is not worth the candle. B545, **И66**, O25, П291

Gamester   The better the gamester, the worser man. И68

Garbage   Garbage in, garbage out (GIGO). Д221

Garden   A rich man's garden is his servant's prison. Б12
Cultivate your own garden. H197,198, П293
No garden without its weeds. B352

Garment   Our last garment is without pockets. C199

Gate   If you don't like my gate, don't swing on it. K213

Gather   Narrow gathered, widely spent. H131

Gear   Less gear, less care. M166
The gear that is gifted is never so sweet as the gear that is won. Д70

Gem   Don't value a gem by what it's set in. 359

General   General today, common soldier tomorrow. И82,101
Many are arm-chair generals. B231, M107

Gentility	Gentility without ability is worse than beggary. X99
Gentleman	I will never put a churl upon a gentleman. C31
Get	Get it while the getting's good. T43
	Since we cannot get what we like, let us like what we can get. Я24
	The more you get, the more you want. C161
Gift	A gift is better than a promise. B208
	A small gift usually gets small thanks. K66
	A wicked man's gift has a touch of its master. O159
	Fear the Greeks bearing gifts. *Ap.*1.67
	Gifts blind the eyes. Г119, M85
	It is not the gift that counts, but the thought behind it. M103
	Nothing freer than a gift. Б17, Л126
	Small gifts make friends, great ones make enemies. M22
	Throw no gifts at the giver's head. O165
Give	A man cannot give what he hasn't got. K52, H62, P13
	Better give than take. Л153
	Give a little, take a little. У87
	Give and take. Д80
	He gives twice who gives quickly. Д95, K300
	He that gives to be seen will relieve none in the dark. B65
	No one can give what he hasn't got. K52
	To give as good as one gets. K15, Л169,200
Gladness	A man of gladness seldom falls into madness. K216
Glory	No flowery road leads to glory. T75
Gnat	To strain at a gnat and swallow a camel. П1
Goat	You go to a goat for wool (milk a he-goat). **K45**, Щ7
God	Danger (river) past, God is forgotten. Г327, И27
	God builds the nest for the blind bird. Б254
	God comes with leaden feet but strikes with iron hands. Б253
	God gives the milk but not the pail. **Б447**, B292, Д39, K303
	God helps the industrious. H59
	God helps them that help themselves. **Б188**, K295
	God is always opening his hand. Б251, 38, Ч61
	God makes and the tailor shapes. Б448
	God never sends mouth but he sends meat. Б252, **Д38**, P63
	God reaches us good things by our own hands. H176, C315
	God send you joy, for sorrow will come fast enough. Д121
	God shapes the back for the burden. Б260
	He to whom God gave no sons, the devil gives nephews. Б250
	Nothing with God is accidental. Б259
	Pray to God but keep hammering. Б265
	Spend and God will send. Б251
	To whom God gives the task, he gives the wit. K158
	Trust in God and do something. Б297, H6
	Trust in God but keep your powder dry. Б297, H6,119
	Well thrives he whom God loves. *Ap.*1.105
	When God pleases, it rains with every wind. P70
	When God will punish, he will first take away the understanding. K142
	Where God has made his church, the devil will have his chapel. Г8,103
	Work as if everything depended on you, pray as if everything depended on God. H6

Gold   All that glitters is not gold. Б176, Н226,238
An old woman's gold is not ugly. Б392, З167
Gold and iron are good to buy gold and iron. М82
Gold doesn't shine around diamonds. З163
Gold is an unseen tyrant. З165
Gold is tested by fire, men by gold. И141
Gold is tried in the fire. З164
Pour gold on him and he'll never thrive. Д21
When gold speaks, other tongues are dumb. Е28

Good   Be good with the good and bad with the bad. Л81
Better (do) a little good than a great deal of bad. Б222
Better good afar off than evil at hand. Л129
Do good, thou doest it for thyself. Д283
Good can never grow out of evil. С81, **Х95**
Good folks are scarce. М98
Good is good, but better carries it. Д282
Good is to be sought and evil attended. Д265,278
He is good that failed never. Н246
It's never too late to do good. Б221
None is so good that it's good to all. В491, **В552**, И19, О30
There is no good that does not cost a price. **В661**, И9
What is good for one may be bad for another. К186
What's good was never plentiful. Д264

Goodness   Goodness is better than beauty. Д310
Goodness is not tied to greatness, but greatness to goodness. В685

Goods   Conceited goods are quickly spent. К240
Ill-gotten goods never prosper. К188, **Н513**, Т49, Х96, Ч127
Little goods, little care. Н483

Goose   As is the gander, so is the goose (What's sauce/good for the goose is sauce/good for the gander). И113, Т84, Ч82, *Ар.*1.63
Goose, gander, gosling are three sounds but one thing. З19
He that has a goose will get a goose. К164

Gossip   A gossip speaks ill of all and all of her. Г191
Those who bring gossip will carry it. С124

Grain   Every grain has its bran. В354
Go not against the grain. Б196
Grain by grain and the hen fills her belly. К331
Of evil grain, no good seed can come. И109, К69,89, О127,**167**
Sift him grain by grain and he proves but chaff. В129

Grass   A trodden path bears no grass. Н5
Grass doesn't grow on a busy street. Г66, Н5
Grass grows not on the highway. Н5, Р52
Grass is immortal. Г82
He that fears every grass must not walk in a meadow. Б355
The grass is greener on the other side of the fence. В178,179,186,583, П122, С168, Ч129
While the grass grows, the horse starves. П131

Gratitude   No gratitude from the wicked. О139

Grave   Graves are of all sizes. В651
If you drink in your pottage you'll cough in your grave. П176
Tears bring nobody back from the grave. С172
To the grave with the dead and the living to the bread. М70

We shall all lie alike in our graves. П252

Great   Great without small makes a bad wall. Б388
            The great and little have need of one another. З111

Green   Bend the twig while it is green. Л107
            They that marry in green, their sorrow is soon seen. Р34
            Thraw the wand while it is green. Д196

Grey   Grey hairs are death's blossoms. С90
            He is grey before he is good. В403

Grief   Grief is lessened when imparted to others. С21
            Grief pent up will break the heart. Ж42
            No day passes without some grief. Д167

Grieve   Never grieve for what you cannot help. **П27**, Ч92

Guest   A constant guest is never welcome. Р48, Х41, **Ч9**
            Guests, like fish, spoil after three days. В102, Г305
            Time for the guests to go home. П156

Guilt   Secret guilt by silence is betrayed. К288

Guilty   Better ten guilty than one innocent suffer. Л128

Gun   Stand by your guns. Г65

Habit   Habit is overcome by habit. Е43
            Pursuits become habits. К239

Hail   Hail brings frost in the tail. Д87

Hair   A woman's hair is her crowning glory. К179
            Long hair, short wit (sense). В400
            More hair than wit. Б341
            No hair so small but has its shadow. И31
            You cannot pull hair where there is none. Н189

Halter   Name not a halter in the house of the hanged. В36

Hammer   It is better to be the hammer than the anvil. Л117
            You can't saw wood with a hammer. И63, Ш8

Hand   An iron hand in a velvet glove. М214
            Better hand loose than an ill tethering. Л131
            Dirty hands make clean money. Р3
            Do not stick your hand in burning water to see if it's hot. З10
            Grasp no more than the hand will hold. С102
            He that is fed at another's hand (table) may stay long ere he be full. Н111, Ч122
            He'd reach out his hand if he were dying. В24
            Just wait till I get my hands on you. П151
            Many hands make light work. Д443
            Many kiss the hand they wish cut off. З36
            Never let your left hand know what your right hand is doing. Д120
            No man fouls his hands in his own business. Н549,551
            One hand washes the other. Л19, Р78

Put not the hand between the bark and the tree. Г29, М182, **С60**
Scatter with one hand, gather with two. Р21
The man with the lazy hand has an empty mouth. Л39
To catch (caught) red-handed. О56
Too many hands spoil the pie. С106

Hap   Some have the hap, others stick in the gap. *Ap.*1.23

Happiness   Happiness and gladness succeed each other. И5
Happiness is more than riches. В267, Д360, Н104
He that talks much of his happiness summons grief. В348
One doesn't appreciate happiness unless one has known sorrow. К280
The greatest happiness is to be content wih little. П16

Hare   First catch your hare. Б422, Ж41
Hares may pull dead lions by the beard. М130
If you run after two hares, you will catch neither. З11
The hare returns to her form. И34
To run with the hare and hunt with the hounds. И12,38
To take hares with foxes. Л181

Harm   One does the harm and another hears the blame. В207, 324, Н117, С1, Т8
Stay out of harm's way. О124
There's no harm in trying. З92, П155

Harvest   Harvest follows seed time. Я5

Haste   Haste and wisdom are things far odd. Н187
Haste makes waste. Г90, Д123, П188, **Ч102**
Haste not, rest not. Д115
Haste trips up its own heels. Б300, Г90, П188, С155,159
Make haste slowly. К236, **С157**
More haste, less speed. **С155**, С258

Hate   The greatest hate springs from the greatest love. Г275, Р67

Have   Better to have than to wish. Н233
Have at it and have it. П83
It's not what you have but how you use it. Д433
To hold is to have. *Ap.*1.10

Hawk   A buzzard never makes a good hawk. И106
A carrion kite will never make a good hawk. В398,**439**, И106, Н194, С227

Hay   Make hay while the sun shines. К180, С252

Head   A good head does not want for hats. Е27
A grey head is often placed on green shoulders. В402
A wise head makes a close mouth. З149, **М117**
An empty head, like a bell, has a long tongue. Д233
An idle head is a box for the wind. **Б132**, Г205
Better be the head of a dog (fox)(mouse)(lizard) than the tail of a lion. П129
Better be the head of an ass (the yeomanry) than the tail of a horse (the gentry). Г285, П129
Don't use your feet, use your head. Г215
Head of gold, feet of clay. У20
Hoar head and green tail. **В401**, Г214, П99, Р64, С89
If you don't use your head, you must use your feet. Б131, Г134
It makes little difference what's on the outside of your head if there's nothing inside. В18
It takes a level head to win. Е32
It's too late to stoop when the head is off. Н453, П22,**175**, С214

Mickle head, little wit. Г209
My cap is better at ease than my head. Г208
Old head on young shoulders. Б343
One good head is better than a thousand hands. **B27**, 313, O46
Small head, big ideas. M17
So many heads (men), so many minds (wits). P26, **C140**, C142, C283
To have a soft place in one's head. B230
To run one's head against a stone wall. Л11
Two heads are better than one. У84
Uneasy lies the head theat wears the crown. T83
Use your head for something besides a hat rack. Г212
Use your head. Ж122
What you haven't got in your head, you have in your heels. Г134
What your head forgets, your heels remember. Г134
When the head aches, all the body is worse. Г206
You cannot put an old head on young shoulders. M140

Health   He that wants health, wants all. Ж128
Health and wealth go far. Д172, Щ2
Health is better than wealth. Б310, **3114**
Health is not valued till sickness comes. Б50
Health is the first muse. 3113
You must not pledge your own health. П269

Heap   Bet a heap and begin to weep. H489

Hear   Believe not all you hear. H244, **H253**
Hear much, speak little. Б324, M21

Heart   A big heart is better than a big house. B238
A bold heart is half the battle. **O171**, C191
A gentle heart is tied with an easy thread. C111
A good heart conquers ill fortune. Д287
A good heart cannot lie. П220
Faint heart never won fair lady. **Б109**
The heart's letter is read in the eye. Г85
The way to a man's heart is through his stomach. П310
There's a man after my own heart. Л182
Two hearts beat as one. C112
What the heart thinks the tongue speaks. Ч60
When the heart is on fire, some sparks will fly out of the mouth. O134
Where there is room in the heart there is room in the house. B150

Heaven   Better go to heaven in rags than to hell in embroidery. Л113
No man should go to heaven who has not sent his heart there before. P12
There's no going to heaven in a sedan. B125, Л180

Hell   Hell is paved with good intentions. A11
Hopers go to hell. B126
Rake hell and skim the devil. Б377
The descent to hell is easy. Ш9
The road to hell is paved with good intentions. Д353

Help   Self-help is the best help. B629, 346
Slow help is no help. Д348, 394, *Ap.*1.104

Hen   A black hen lays a white egg. Б173, K173
A cackling hen doesn't always lay. Б202, K330
He that comes of a hen must scrape. B398, O175
It is a sad house where the hen crows louder than the cock. Г277

Hercules	Not even Hercules could contend against two. B87
Heresy	Heresy may be easier kept out than shook off. E20
Hero	'Tis action that makes the hero. B632
Herring	What we lose in the hake, we shall have in the herring. B373, H372
Hill	It is easier to run down a hill than up one. C7 Looking at a hill won't move it. Г**158**, Г114 The higher the hill, the lower the grass. K310 The hills are green far away. Б227, В178,583, Д57, C168, Ч118,129 To climb steep hills requires a slow pace at first. T30
Hindsight	Hindsight is better than foresight. 371
Hog	He who does not kill hogs will not get black puddings. Б106, B369
Hole	No one can dig up a hole. Д512 You can't drive a square peg into a round hole. Ч88
Holiday	Every day is a holiday with sluggards. Б205, Л**44**
Home	At home, everything is easy. B135, Д387 East or west, home is best. B23, *Ap*.1.83 Every man is a master (king) in his home (house). B136, **B579**, T14 Home is home, though it never be so homely. C63,71, X18 Make yourself at home. M93 The farthest way about is the nearest way home. Д53
Homer	Even Homer sometimes nods. Ж102, *Ap*.1.36
Honesty	Honesty is ill to thrive by. O161, П221 No honest man ever repented of his honesty. B116, **349**
Honey	He has honey in the mouth and a razor on the girdle. K171, C246 He that has no honey in his pot, let him have it in his mouth. Б294 He that steals honey should beware of the sting. E49, Ж13 Honey catches more flies than vinegar. B249, Л147, **M49** If you want to gather honey, you must bear the stings of bees. Ж36, **M43** Make yourself honey and the flies will devour you. Г290 Too much honey cloys the stomach. И40, C170
Honour	A post of honour is a post of danger. H29, Ч54 An ill deed cannot bring honour. B63, X95 Better to die with honour than to live with shame. Л155 Great honours are great burdens. Б323, B234 Honour buys noo beef in the market. Ч74 Honour is the reward of virtue. Д292 Honours and profit lie not in one sack. Б295, **Ч56** Honour will honour meet. Ч53 Honours change manners. **Ч55** We cannot come to honour under coverlet. B148
Hope	Don't give up hope till hope is dead. П93 Hope is a slender reed for a stout man to lean on. 341 Hope is the poor man's bread. Б88, H13,33 Hope springs eternal in the human breast. Ж96 Who lives by hope will die of hunger. Ж29, **368**, H13

Horn　　　A new tout in an old horn. C262
He that blows best, bears away the horn. B653
Let the horns go with the hide. Б10
Toot your own horn. B200

Horse　　　A boisterous (scary) horse must have a rough (stout) bridle. Б101, **383**, H83
A good horse is worth its fodder. H267
A horse never goes straight up a hill. П294
A horse stumbles that has four legs. Б117, **K165**
A lazy horse thinks its harness heavy. Д244
A running horse needs no spur. H83
A short horse is soon curried. K114
All lay load on the willing horse. B206, **K184**,218, P54
An old horse for a hard road. O108
Don't look a gift horse in the mouth. Д68
Don't ride the high horse. Д19
Have a horse of your own and you may borrow another. K164
He is free of horse that never had one. И110
He that cannot beat the horse beats the saddle. Б214
He that has a white horse and a fair wife never wants trouble. K245
He that lets his horse drink at every lake and his wife go to every wake... H212
He that will slight my horse will buy my horse. У39
If two ride on a horse, one must ride behind. Д105, H242
If you can't get a horse, ride a cow. З29, И25, O18,C107
If you're on a strange horse, get off in the middle of the road. C36
It is a good horse that never stumbles. И35, K165, *Ap.*1.36
It is the bridle and spur that makes a good horse. H16
It's too late to shut the stable door once the horse has bolted. П267,311, C214
No good horse of a bad colour. X87, Ц7
Pedigree won't sell a lame horse. Г166
The horse that draws best is most whipped. P53
To a greedy eating horse, a short halter. Б312
Trust not a horse's heels. H213
Where the horse lies down, there some hairs will be found. Г46
You can lead a horse to water but you can't make it drink. H153
You may break a horse's back, be he never so strong. K166
You may know a horse by its harness. Б90

Hospitable　　　Be hospitable to one another without grudging. H184

Host　　　A host's invitation is expensive. B21, O8
He that reckons without his host must reckon again. B22

Hot　　　Over hot, over cold. B201

Hound　　　Fed hounds never hunt. Ж156, H70
Many hounds may soon worry one hare. Г54
The good huntsman must follow the hounds and not give up the chase. Д356

Hour　　　An hour in the morning is worth two in the evening. K185
An hour wasted can never be regained. Ч5
At every hour, death is near. C197
He never broke his hour that kept his day. H499
It chances in an hour that happens not in seven years. И130
One hour today is worth two tomorrow. O69
The bewitching hour. П157
We can crowd eternity into an hour and stretch an hour into eternity. Ч4

House　　　A house is a fine house when good folks are within. H323
A little house has a wide mouth. H208

A man's house is his castle. B136, **B579**, C72, T14
A small house well-filled is better than an empty palace. M89
Choose not a house near an inn nor in a corner. Б233
Every house has its dirty corner. Г283
He that buys a house ready wrought has many a pin and nail for nought. K328
He that would be well need not go from his house. Д384, H306
In an orderly house, all things are always ready. Д65
Name not a halter in the house of the hanged. B36
The house discovers (shows) the owner. Д378, П54
The house goes mad when women gad. Г53, **Ж50**
Those who live in glass houses shouldn't throw stones. Д431, H107,413, Ч47
To have neither house nor home. H538
To throw (fling) the house out of the window. Б438, **B273**, П204
When the house is open, an honest man sins. H48

Housewife   A gentle housewife mars the household. X32
Bare walls make giddy housewives. X1

Housewifery   Housewifery is a woman's noblest fame. H342

How   No matter how but whether. З18

Human   We're only human. B499, Л200

Humour   The stillest humours are the worst. T32

Hunchback   The hunchback sees not his own hump, but his companion's. B659, C77, Ч116

Hunger   Hunger breaks stone walls. H578
Hunger drives the wolf out of the woods. Г218, H580
Hunger finds no fault with the cookery (Hunger never saw bad bread). Б383, Г231, **K227**
Hunger increases the understanding. Г223
Hunger is the best sauce (chef). Г219
Hunger knows no friend. Г221
Hunger makes hard beans sweet. Г230, *Ap.*1.91
Hunger sharpens the wits (teaches many things). П274

Hunter   All are not hunters that blow the horn. И127

Hurry   Always in a hurry, always behind. K305

Hurt   A man is not so soon healed as hurt. Б303, H465
He that hurts another, hurts himself. K291
No man hurts himself. H548
We often hurt those whom we love (You always hurt the one you love). K140,212,248

Husband   A bad husband makes a bad wife. У44
A good husband makes a good wife. У22
Better to have a husband without love than with jealousy. Л174
Husband, don't believe what you see, but what I tell you. Ж57
If a husband is unfaithful, it is like spitting from the house to the street; but if a wife is
      unfaithful, it is like spitting from the street into the house. M183
If the husband be not at home, there is nobody. Б77
In the husband wisdom, in the wife gentleness. Ж58, M177
It is an ill husband who is not missed. M176, X86
The husband is always the last to know. M184
The wrongs of the husband are not reproached. M183

Husk   The husk often tells what the kernel is. B73, Г94

Hut	A hut is a palace to a poor man. X18

Idiot	The idiot bakes snow in the oven and expects ice-cream pie. H305
Idle	Better be idle than badly employed. Л156
	Idle folks lack no excuses. Б152, K252, Л43, *Ap.*1.89
	Idle men are dead all their life long. Б55
Idleness	Idleness is the key of beggary. Л52
	Idleness is the mother (root) of all evil (vice). Б150, П225
	Of idleness comes no goodness. H73, Л52
If	If ifs and ans were pots and pans there'd be no trade for tinkers. A5, E21, *Ap.*1.24
	If it weren't for the ifs, you'd be rich. E25
Ignorance	Ignorance and pride grow on the same wood. Г252
	Ignorance is bliss. Б133
	Ignorance is blister. Б82
	Ignorance is the mother of impudence. Г143
	Quickest way to show ignorance is to talk about something you know nothing about. K231
Ignorant	It pays to be ignorant. C24
Ill	An ill life, an ill end. **Ж153**, K29
	Better to suffer ill than to do ill. Л120
	Fear to do ill and you need fear nought else. H180
	For ill do well, then fear no hell. Д303
	He that does ill hates the light. П237, X61
	Ill comes in by ells and goes out by inches. Б42, Г271, 3123
	Ill comes often on the back of worse. Б24,29, O48,67, T1
	Ill doers are ill thinkers. *Ap.*1.56
	Ill seed, ill weed. K89, П52, O167
	Ill will never speak well or do well. O139
	Ill-gotten, ill-spent. 3121
	Of one ill come many. O48
	Who would do ill, never wants an occasion. K123
Image	Thou shalt not make unto thee any graven images. H420
Impossibility	No one is bound to do impossibilities. H507
Impossible	Few things are impossible to diligence and skill. Д253
	Nothing is impossible. H494
Inch	An inch breaks no square. H252
	Give him an inch and he'll take an ell. Д26,31,33
Informer	The informer is the worse rogue of the two. H287
Innocent	A man is innocent until proven guilty. H375
Insult	Don't add insult to injury. B302
Intelligence	Intelligence seeks its own level. П77
	Where intelligence ends, folly begins. Г45

Interest	Interest will not lie. Б92
Intimacy	Intimacy breeds contempt. H219
Intoxication	Intoxication is not the wine's fault, but man's. H220
Iron	An iron fist in a velvet glove. Ж40 Iron not used rusts. Ж44 Strike while the iron is hot. K326
Itch	Scratch where it itches. Г43
Jack	All work and no play makes Jack a dull boy. M83 Every Jack must have his Jill. B599, *Ap.*1.5 Jack would be a gentleman if he had money. Д193, Ж148, *Ap.*1.64
Jade	A jade eats as much as a good horse. H196
Jest (n)	Better lose a jest than a friend. T15 If you give (make) a jest, you must take a jest. Ш16, *Ap.*1.103 Leave a jest when it pleases lest it turn to earnest. **П207**, Ш15 Many a true word is spoken in jest. B48,202 Truest jests sound worst in guilty ears. П219
Jest (v)	Do not jest in serious matters. B386, X24 It is ill jesting with edged tools. T18 Long jesting was never good. H489, Ш17
Job	When the job is well done, you can hang up the hammer. O176
Johny	What Johny will not teach himself, Johny will never know. *Ap.*1.27
Joke	Don't carry a joke too far. И67
Joy	God send you joy, for sorrow will come fast enough. Д265 No joy without annoy. B174, П29 Our greatest joys and our greatest sorrows grow on the same vine. Г22
Judge (n)	He whose father is judge goes safely to court. X70 No man ought to be judge in his own cause. X102
Judge (v)	Don't judge everyone by his looks. H258 Judge a man by his deeds, not by his words. Б316, C209 Judge others by what you do. H93 Judge well (yourself) before you criticize. З17, H93, O116, Ч135
Judgment	He that passes judgment as he runs overtakes repentance. H473
Justice	Fear no man and do justice to all men. B633
Keep	It will keep. H127
Key	A golden key opens every door. Д156 The used key is always bright. Ж44 There's a key for every lock. K107

Life means strife. B68
Life without a friend is death without a witness. Ж112
Life's a bitch. H147
Life's race is either forward or backward. Ж141
Make your life, don't copy it. Ж130
Plan life as though to live forever, but live today as if to die tomorrow. Ж158
Such a life, such a death. K29
There's aye a life for a living man. Ж98, **H36**
There's life in the old dog yet. E36
We get out of life exactly what we put into it. П55
We're living the life of Reilly. Ж99
While there's life, there's hope. **Г38**, П130

| **Light** | Every light has its shadow. H39 |
| | Little is the light that can be seen on a murky night. B149 |

Like (adj) Like will to like. B620, K266, M164, **П109**, C66,
No like is the same. B88, Д165, H392, **P20**, *Ap.*1.93

Like (v) If you don't like it, you can lump it. H466
Likeness causes liking. П109, P9, *Ap.*1.5

Limit There's a limit to everything. B533, Ч95

Limitation Know your limitations and go not beyond them. B550, З152

Linen Do not wash your dirty linen in public. И80, H256, C242

Lion A lion may come beholden to a mouse. Ц6
A man is a lion in his own cause. H88, *Ap.*1.13
Destroy the lion while he is yet but a whelp. И137
If the lion's skin cannot, the fox's shall. Г17, H224
Wake not a sleeping lion. Л167
Who takes a lion when absent fears a mouse present. M143, П313

Lips Scald not your lips in another man's pottage. H112

Lip-service Lip-service costs little yet may bring in much. Д314

Litter The litter is like to the sire and dam. 3147, **H402**

Little A little along is better than a long none. Л119
A little thing pleases a fool. Д500
Add little to little and then there will be a great heap. B524, E26, M97, П82, C22
He that has little shall have less. П121
Little and loud. H206
Little men have sharp wits. M17
Little sticks kindle the fire. Б98
Many a little makes a mickle. Б89, E26, И90
Out of little acorns mighty oak trees grow. Б437
Use the little to get to the big. Б170, П56,150, X27

Live He is unworthy to live who lives only for himself. C46
He lives in his element. Ж108
He lives long that lives well. Д350, K314
He lives unsafely that looks too near on things. T51
It is not how long but how well you live. (Better to live well than long.) H457
Let all live as they would die. Ж115
Live and learn, Wait and see. П119
Live and learn. **B222**, П118

Live and let live. **Ж116**, C39
Live happy, live long. B225
Live within your means. Ж117
May we all live happily ever after. Ж136
One should live to build, not to boast. Д378
To live from hand to mouth. Ж103
To live long is to suffer long. B223
To live in clover. Ж100
We must live by the quick. Ж126
You only live once. Д90,433

Loaf   It's easy to steal from a cut loaf. O182

Loan   A borrowed loan should come laughing home. 372,90, P11

Lock   Lock, stock and barrel. B274

Log   A crooked log (rod) is not to be straightened. Г250, И86
              Crooked logs make straight fires. Б404, Г126, **Д411**, И23, **К204**, У75

Look (v) He that looks not before, finds himself behind. H288
              He that will not look before him, will have to look behind. У34
              Look before you leap. H310,380

Lord   A nod from a lord is breakfast for a fool. П191
              Nothing agrees worse than a lord's heart and a beggar's purse. B239
              The Lord giveth and the Lord taketh away. Б248
              The Lord is merciful. Б258

Lose   Those that have must lose. K268
              You cannot lose what you never had. Д400

Loss   A man cannot have but one loss, more will follow. Б44
              One man's loss is another man's gain. Г69
              There's no great loss without some gain. B355, H192, T17

Lost   What(so)ever is somewhere gotten is somewhere lost. H309

Lot   No man is content with his lot. П123

Love (n) Brotherly love for brotherly love, but cheese for money. Д437, Л5, X25
              Cupboard love is seldom true love. H64
              Hot love, hasty vengeance (is soon cold). B114
              Looks breed love. Л190
              Love and a cough cannot be hid. Л188
              Love and hate are blood relations. Д440, P67
              Love and smoke cannot be hidden. Л188
              Love cannot be compelled. Б354, K199, **M92**, C113
              Love conquers all. Л168
              Love covers many infirmities. Л192, П132
              Love is a circle and an endless sphere. Л189
              Love is blind. Л185,193, П132
              Love is free. M92
              Love is not found in the market. H527
              Love lives in cottages as well as in courts. Б431, C20
              Love locks no cupboards. M91
              Love makes the ugly beautiful. Л185
              Love knows no season. Л168
              Love will go through stone walls. Л184
              Love without end has no end. Л189
              Old love does not rust. **C261**

Old love will not be forgotten. C261
One love expels another. Д101
There are no ugly loves nor handsome prisons. B237, K198
There's no love lost between them. Д93
They that would lie down for love should rise for hunger. Л186
To live without love is not really living. H333
Where there is no love, all faults are seen. O160
You can't control your love. Л191

Love (v)   Love all, trust few. Л170
Love me, love my dog. Б378, **K128**,254
Loving comes by looking. Л190
Those whom we love first we seldom wed. П21
To be loved, love and be lovable. Л177

Loyalty   Loyalty is worth more than money. B251

Luck   An ounce of luck is worth a pound of wisdom. C318
Diligence is the mother of good luck. C315
Good luck beats early rising. C217
Good luck disappears like our hair, bad luck lasts like our nails. C320
Luck is often pluck. C315
No telling which way luck or a half broke steer is going to run. Б460, H309
The worse luck now, the better another time. C317
There is no luck in laziness. C315,**322**

Lucky   It is better to be born lucky than rich. H401, **C323**
It is better to be born lucky than wise. П218
The more wicked, the more lucky. 3118

Lurch   Left in the lurch. У76

Maiden   Maidens should be meek till they be married. Д109

Majority   The majority rules. C96

Malice   Malice hurts itself most. K291

Man   A discontented man knows not where to sit easy. E16
A hungry man is an angry man. K228, C339
A man can do a lot of things if he has to. X81, Я21
A man can do no more than he can. И57
A man doesn't learn to understand anything unless he loves it. H153
A man is king in his own house. C72, T14
A man surprised is half beaten. B127
A married man turns his staff into a stake. Б443
A wilful man will have his way. H485, X82
All men love themselves more than another. Л183
An old man in a house is a good sign. Б118
An old wise man's shadow is better than a young buzzard's sword. Л158
As a man is, so he sees. K13
As soon as a man is born he begins to die. Ч3
As the man is, so is his talk. K92
Call no man happy till he is dead. C313
Covetous men live drudges to die wretches. C166

Every man after his own fashion. **B558**,626, У13,17, *Ap*.1.90
Every man drags water to his own mill. И34
Every man for himself and the devil take the hindmost. X12
Every man for himself and God for us all. **B551**, C225
Every man has his delight. K211
Every man has his hobby horse. *Ap*.1.94
Every man has his price. У14
Every man has his proper gift. B548
Every man is a king (master) in his own house. B136,**579**, T14
Every man is his own worst enemy. B568,H193
Every man is nearest himself. **B567**, Л183
Every man is mad on some point. B554, K12,211, **У12**
Every man knows his own business best. *Ap*.1.12
Every man likes his own thing best. B555,581,**652**,656, T12,**38**, Ч28
Every man must walk in his own calling. B548
Every man should take his own. H201,400
Every man thinks his own geese swans. B656
Every man to his own opinion. *Ap*.1.60
Fear no man and do justice to all men. B633
Good men must die, but death cannot kill them quite. Д332, C195
Man and wife are one fool. M179
Man has his will and woman has her way. H568
Man is the measure of all things. Д506
Man is to man a wolf. P89, Ч31
Man proposes, God disposes. H101, Ч27
Men are best loved farthest off. E1
Men are not to be measured by inches. M6
Men get wealth and women keep it. Ж60, M185
No man is infallible. И36, H43, H495
One man is worth a hundred and a hundred is not worth one. O46
Patient men win the day. T24
Rather a man without money than money without a man. K182
Seldom is a long man wise. Б331
Some men die before they begin to live. B77
The covetous man is his own tormentor. 361
The grateful man gets more than he asks. X69
The greater the man, the greater the crime. Б326, P31
The strong man and the waterfall channel their own path. Г174, K299, H485, C75
There is no man born into the world whose work is not born with him. B649, K225, Ч99
To the man submit at whose board you sit. H409, У50, **Ч24**
Today a man, tomorrow none. Ж152
Whatever man has done, man can do. H176
When a man is down, everyone runs over him. H41
Wise men care not for what they cannot have. Ч87
You can't keep a good man down. E36

Mankind

Mankind bestows more applause on her destroyer than on her benefactor. H102

Manner

Evil communications corrupt good manners. 3136
Striking manners are bad manners. Б313, K206
Sympathy of manners make the conjunction of minds. H418

Many

Many are called but few are chosen. B370

Marble

They don't put marble tops on cheap furniture. B52,120, C31

Mare

The old grey mare isn't what she used to be. Б439, У80

Market

A moneyless man goes quick through market. Б58
He that cannot abide in a bad market deserves not a good one. K256

Marriage
An ill marriage is a spring of ill fortune. K242
Keep your eyes wide open before marriage. 381
Marriage is a game best played by two winners. Г261
Marriage is a lottery. Ж88
Marriage makes or mars a man. Ж72
Marriage rides upon the saddle and repentance upon the crupper. 382, C325
Marriages are made in heaven. **3110**, C193,302

Marry
A young man should not marry yet, an old man not at all. M149
Before you marry, be sure of a house wherein to tarry. Ж92
Before you marry, 'tis wise to tarry. Ж73, H82
He who marries might be sorry, he who does not will be sorry. Ж74, Л132
It is unlucky to marry for love. Ж75
Marry in haste, repent at leisure. B294, **Ж70,79**, K119, P34, C152
Marry your like. P76
They that marry in green, their sorrow is soon seen. Ж78
Who marries for love without money has good nights and sorry days. Б33

Martyr
Better to be a martyr than a confessor. Л120

Master
A falling master makes a standing servant. Б11
An ill master, an ill scholar. Д470
As the master is, so is his dog. П48
Every man cannot be a master. H243
Everyone is a master and a servant. Б13
He that is master of himself will soon be master of others. Г301
Man is his own master. C75
Many a man serves a thankless master. B488
No man can serve two masters. Д106, И38
No man is another's master. O32
The master absent and the house is dead. Б147, H289, П128
The master's eye makes the horse fat. C62
The master's footsteps fatten the soil. Г100
The master's wish is his command. Б14
Who is master of his thirst is master of his health. T48

Matrimony
Matrimony is a school in which one learns too late. Ж65

Maxim
A good maxim is never out of season. П182

May
A May flood never did any good. Ж31
Marry in May, repent alway (rue for aye). B66

Maybe
Every maybe has a may not be. A6, K232

Meal
Better are meals many than one too merry. O90
Do not drink between meals. П7

Measure (n)
Measure is treasure. Д143, Л140
There is a measure in all things. B534

Measure (v)
Every man should measure himself by his own foot rule. B559,580
Measure not another man's corn by your own bushel. B187, H87
Measure twice, cut once. Д213, O60, C103
To measure everyone by your own yard. **B559**, H87

Meat
After meat, mustard. П178
All meat's to be eaten, all maids to be wed. И128
Do not cry roast meat. Б146, H257
It is better to want meat than guests or company. E39
It's good to be merry at meat. Б85

Meat and matins hinder no man's journey. X19
Much meat, much malady. M131
One man's meat is another man's poison. B170
The wholesomest meat is at another man's cost. H118, Ч118
They that have no other meat, bread and butter are glad to eat. E53, K101

Medal

Every medal has its reverse. У30

Medicine

Good medicine always tastes bitter. Г291, П290
Medicines are not meant to live on. A25
There is no medicine against death. **A24**, O122

Messenger

Messengers shall be neither beheaded nor hanged. П165

Middle

A middle course is safest. Ж119

Might

Might does not make right. Ж94
Might is (makes) right. C118, У54, Ч136

Milk

It's no use crying over spilt milk. A29, O4, П27,278, C214, Ч69

Milkman

To take after the milkman. H535

Mill

Every man draws water to his own mill. **B604**,624
He who goes into a mill comes out powdered. O84
Mills and wives are ever wanting. Ж66

Mind (n)

A good mind possesses a kingdom. Д505, C68
A sound mind in a sound body. B45, З112
Great minds think alike. B240
Little minds, like weak liquors, are soon soured. H500
My mind to me a kingdom is. **C68**, Ц3
Out of sight, out of mind. B413
The generous mind least regards money and yet most feels the want of it. У64

Mind (v)

Mind no business but your own. З37
Mind other men, but most yourself. Д119, Ж17, **П195, П245**

Mint

Long mint, little dint. B224

Minute

Here one minute, gone the next. Б444
There's a sucker born every minute. Б470

Mirth

An ounce of mirth is worth a pound of sorrow. Л124, Ч2
The mirth of the world dureth but a while. B268, Д290

Mischief

Better a mischief than an inconvenience. Л119,139
He that mischief hatches, mischief catches. O177
Mischief comes by the pound and goes away by the ounce. Б28
Mischief comes without calling for. П255
Mischief has swift wings. Б30
No mischief but a woman is at the bottom of it. *Ap.*1.2,59

Miser

A miser is an ass that carries gold but eats thistles. З166
A rich miser is poorer than a poor man. C162

Misery

He bears misery best that hides it most. K311
Misery loves company. **B343**,546, C21

Misfortune   It is easy to bear the misfortunes of others. Г267, Н110, **Ч114**
Misfortune hastens age. Г276, Р19
Misfortunes come of themselves. Г4, Г270, П255
Misfortunes come on wings but depart on foot. Б42, Г271, З123
Misfortunes make us wise. М195
Misfortunes never come alone (singly). Б25
Never rejoice about your neighbours misfortunes. Н547, Р10
Our worst misfortunes are those that don't befall us. Л110

Miss   A miss is as good as a mile. П280, Ч134

Mistake   He who makes no mistakes, makes nothing. Б99, **Н314,358**
Mistakes don't make haystacks. Н252
One foolish mistake can undo a lifetime of happiness. Н100
We learn by our mistakes. **О197**, У72

Moderation   Moderation in all things. М62

Molasses   Slow as molasses. К18

Monday   St. Monday. П144

Money   All things are obedient to money. Д178
Don't throw good money after bad. Н196
He that has money has what he wants. К27
He that hoards up money pains for other men. О21, С165
He that loves money has what he wants. К27
He that wants money, wants everything. Б56
It's the principle, not the money. Д137
Lend your money and lose your friend. В32, Д426, *Ap.*1.25
Many means to get money. И131
Money begets money. Б272, Д173,183, К164
Money can burn a hole in your pocket. Н34
Money can't buy happiness. В263, Н195
Money can't buy happiness, but it can go a long way in helping you. Д158, К182
Money evaporates. Д195
Money has no smell. Д187
Money has wings. Д157
Money is blind. У19
Money is miraculous. М167
Money is money. Р43
Money is round, it rolls away. Д154,**176**
Money is the root of all evil. Б464
Money is the sinews of war. Д192
Money is the only monarch. Д180
Money is wise, it knows the way. А16
Money makes the pot boil. Д155, Е35
Money recommends a man everywhere. А16, Б273
Money wants no followers. Б462
Money will do anything. Д182
More money, more sin. Б281, Д150
Ready money is ready medicine. А26
Ready money will away. Д189
Rich mens' spots are covered with money. Д181
The abundance of money ruins youth. Б280
To the grateful man give money when he asks. Х69

Monk   The cowl does not make the monk. Н247, Н295, **Р94**

Monkey   Monkey see, monkey do. К210

Moon	As if just landed from the moon. K53
	Changeful as the moon. H61,511
	The moon does not heed the barking of dogs. C219
	The moon is a moon still, whether it shines or not. K36
	The moon is not seen where the sun shines. H525, **И32**
More	The more the merrier. B150, Л204
Mosquito	The buzz of a mosquito can drown out the ocean's roar. M7,199
Mother	A mother's love never ages. H520
	Good mother asks not "will you?" but gives. Г2
	Like mother, like daughter. K80
	Mother knows best. M37
	No mother has a homely child. B647, П235, C57, *Ap.*1.6
Mother-in-law	Mother-in-law and daughter-in-law are a tempest and a hailstorm. 3170
	The mother-in-law remembers not that she was a daughter-in-law. Б243
Mould	Made (cast) from the same mould. И98, O71
Mountain	If the mountain will not come to Mahomet, Mahomet must go to the mountain. Я23
	To make a mountain of a molehill. Б458, B684, Д125, И73
	The higher the mountain, the greater the descent. B687
	The mountain has brought forth a mouse. Г247, Д453, M202
Mouse	It's a bold mouse that breeds in a cat's ear. Г326, M210
	No larder but has its mice. O83
	Pour not water on a drowned mouse. O129
	To burn one's house to get rid of the mice. M209, O103
	The mouse that has one hole is quickly taken. X88
Mouth	A closed mouth catches no flies. **B43**, H398
	A cool mouth and warm feet live long. H565
	All is lost that goes beside one's mouth. П78
	An intelligent person is one who knows how to keep his mouth shut. M117
	From the mouths of babes springs truth. M4, У110
	Keep your mouth shut and your ears open. 3149, M117
	The mouth is the executioner and doctor of the body. P72
	The mouths of fools pour out foolishness. У26
Much	Much would have more. Л92, M128
	Too much of a good thing is worse than none at all. П26
	You can have too much of a good thing. B516, И40
	You can never have too much of a good thing. K102, M112, X51
Music	Great strokes make not sweet music. B232
Nail	Do not hang all on one nail. B94,504, **H66**
	For want of a nail, the shoe is lost. Б86
	Hungry enough to eat nails. H582
	One nail (peg) drives out another. **K106**, Л80
	The loss of a nail, the loss of an army. Б86
	To hit the nail on the head. B442
Naked	No naked man is sought after to be rifled. Г241, 39, H125,559, C5
	There's no trying to strip a naked man. Г237, **39**

Name   A good name is better than riches. **B673**, Д153,273,305, X77
            That's my name, ask me again and I'll tell you the same. K26

Nature   He that follows nature is never out of his way. Б196
            Nature abhors a vacuum. C79
            Nature has given us two ears and one tongue. Б249
            Nature (God) is no botcher. H148
            Nature (sur)passes nurture. H152, **П263**
            Self-preservation is the first law of nature. 338, П245
            The nature of things does not change. T26
            You can drive nature with a pitchfork, but she keeps on coming back. Г246

Near   Near is my shirt, but nearer is my skin. B658

Neat   Neat but not gaudy. H293

Necessity   Necessity has no holiday. Г235, H581
            Necessity is the mother of invention. Г245, H496, H591
            Necessity never made a good bargain. H592
            Necessity sharpens industry. H588
            Necessity teaches a naked woman to spin. H584
            Needs must when necessity drives. B82, Г220

Neck   Better bend the neck than bruise the forehead. Л11
            Don't stick your neck out. H429

Need   Need knows no law. H48,579
            Need makes greed. H586
            Need makes the naked man run. H583,589, П246
            Need will have its course. H585
            When in great need, anything will do. H31
            When need is highest, help is nighest. B492

Needle   A needle in a haystack. **И61**,143

Neglect   Present neglect makes future regret. Л198

Neighbour   Love your neighbour but do not pull down the fence. *Ap.*1.25
            Our neighbour's ground yields better corn than ours. B178,583, H118, Ч118,129
            Neighbours' fare is always counted the best. X49
            We can live without our friends but not our neighbours. Б51

Nest   A shrewd man feathers his own nest. B578
            Feather your own nest. B609

Net   The net of the sleeper catches fish. Л71, C80,226, Ч84

New   Everything new is fine. M88, H63
            Newer is truer. K279, **C50**
            So what else is new? O94

News   Good news may be told at any time. Д268
            Ill news comes apace (Bad news travels fast). X91, X110
            News spreads like wildfire. Д330
            No news is good news. X55

Night   As sure as night follows day. Б371
            Night brings counsel. У114
            Night is the cloak of sinners. X61
            The longest night will have an end. T19

Noise	The noise is so great one cannot hear God thunder. B162
None	None of us are perfect. Б149, И39
	None says his garner is full. B523, Д**35**, П122
Nonsense	A little nonsense now and then is relished by the best of men. C233
Nose	A man should not stick his nose in his neighbour's pot. H459
	He would fall on his back and break his nose. 397, *Ap.*1.34
	Invisible, as a nose on a man's face. M51
	Keep your nose clean. O124
	See no farther than the tip of one's nose. Д62
Nothing	Be silent if you have nothing worth saying. Л141
	Better to say nothing than not to the purpose. Д306, H436
	If you wish for too much, you will end up with nothing. 347, M111
	It costs nothing to ask. **344**
	It is more pain to do nothing than something. O144, C167
	Nothing can last forever. Б439, H553
	Nothing comes of nothing. H552
	Nothing comes out that is not put in. Ж8
	Nothing dries sooner than tears. C171
	Nothing happens from saying so. H231
	Nothing in this life is free. Д73, **331**
	Nothing is certain but the unforeseen. B44
	Nothing is easy to the unwilling. И48, H153
	Nothing is good or bad but by comparison. B509
	Nothing is stolen without hands. И88, P81,**84**
	Nothing new under the sun. H86, H554
	Nothing seek, nothing find. Ч16
	Nothing seems quite as good as new after being broken. И118, П278, P82
	Nothing so bad but it might have been worse. H284, C232
	Nothing so certain as death. C194
	Nothing so contagious as a bad example. Д502
	Nothing so necessary for travellers as languages. Г295
	Nothing stake, nothing draw. Л176
	Nothing venture(d), nothing gain(ed). Б18,**80**, Г61, Д73, Д246, К273, Л176
	Something is better than nothing. B448,**498**, H3
	There is nothing permanent except change. B532
	Where nothing is, nothing can be had. П305
Nought	Nought is never in danger. Б218
	To come from little good to stark nought. К143
Nut	A hard nut to crack. T11
	He that will eat the kernel must crack the nut. **H397**, **O97**
	Sweet is the nut but bitter (hard) is the shell. T72
	The gods gave nuts to those that have no teeth. Д54
Oak	An oak is not felled by one stroke. Д200, 333, **C27**
	Every oak has been an acorn. B613
	Little strokes fell great oaks. Д513
	Oaks may fall when reeds stand the storm. Д464
Obey	The vessel that will not obey her helm will have to obey the rocks. И123
	They that are bound must obey. C188
Obstacle	The greater the obstacle, the more glory in overcoming it. H45, **T75**

Occasion   An occasion lost cannot be redeemed. У106

Ocean   It always rains in the ocean. Г14

Offense   Much babbling is not without offense. Л91, M108, M134

Offer   Never refuse a good offer. O165, T43

Oil   Oil and water don't mix. Г338, З117
                      Pouring oil on the fire is not the way to quench it. E13, 369, M33, **O27**
                      To add oil to the fire. H405

Old   None so old that he hopes not for a year of life. Ж105
                      Old and cold. C270
                      Old and tough, young and tender. C269
                      Old pottage is sooner heated than new made. Л32
                      Older and wiser. В483, K307, C265, **Ч42**
                      The older, the more covetous. C281, **Ч103**
                      Though old and wise, yet still advise. M170
                      Use the old before getting the new. Л32

Omelette   You can't make an omelette without breaking eggs. Б106, В369, Д410, И71, Л54, H174,**396**

One   It is hard for one to withstand many. O75
                      It takes one to know one. M164, P77,88
                      One body is no body. O38
                      One for all and all for one. O36
                      One is no number. В87, O38
                      One is not smelt where all stink. T36
                      One is too few, two is too many. O37
                      One less, one lighter. Б4
                      One man is no man. В87, O28
                      One to one is odds. O40
                      One's too few, three's too many. T67

Opera   The opera isn't over till the fat lady sings. Л20

Operation   The operation was a success but the patient died. П206, Ц8

Opinion   Every man to his own opinion. *Ap.*1.60
                      Our own opinion is never wrong. *Ap.*1.3

Opportunity   Opportunity makes the thief. H320, H444
                      Opportunity never knocks for persons not worth a rap. H466
                      The hasty leaps over his opportunities. K235

Opposite   Opposites attract. P27

Orchard   It is easy to rob an orchard when none keeps it. Б67

Order   Good order is the foundation of all good things. П159
                      Order makes for peace. Г89
                      Orders must not be challenged. H166

Others   Be that which you would make others. K130
                      Covet not that which belongs to others. A19, H114,318
                      If we can tell others what to do, we should know what to do ourselves. В182
                      If you wish to see the best of others, show the best of yourself. K130
                      To have others do one's dirty work. X73

Peace
A bad peace is better than a good quarrel. Д138
Better a lean peace than a fat victory. X107
If there is peace in your heart, your home is like a palace. M100
If you want peace, prepare for war. E34

Peacock
A peacock has fair feathers but foul feet. Л10, **X44**

Pear
The man who plants pears is a-planting for his heirs. Д202
To ask (seek) pears of an elm tree. Б168, Д364, **H399**, O150, Я3

Peddlar
A small pack becomes a small peddlar. K61
Every peddlar praises his needles. **B622**, T12
Let every peddlar carry his own burden (pack). H200,335

Pen
The pen conveys one's meaning a thousand miles. B242
The pen is mightier than the sword. H140

Penny
A bad penny always turns up. Л77
A penny at a pinch is worth a pound. Б228,417
A penny in the purse will bid me drink. Б410
A penny saved is a penny got. C48
Everyone has a penny to spend at an new alehouse. H14
In for a penny, in for a pound. B291, B342, Ж14, Л70
Penny and penny laid up will be many. Г330, K167
Penny wise and pound foolish. Б191, B594, 322, Л89, M26, O15, **П116**
Take care of the pence and the pounds will take care of themselves. Б70, Д164, K168
You may know from the penny how the shilling spends. П52
There is no companion like the penny. Д186

People
People condemn what they do not understand. H141
People need people. Л201
People will talk. H113
Some people can see no good near home. T10
Some people would fall down a sewer and find a ring. C311

Perseverance
Perseverance conquers all things. П262

Person
A person should not meddle with what he doesn't understand. H141
One hates the person, not the vice. H294
You may hate the things a person does, but never hate the person. И120, H294

Philosopher
The whole life of a philosopher is a preparation for death. Ф3

Physician
Physician, heal thyself. C70

Pie
An apple pie without cheese is like a kiss without a squeeze. Б115

Pig
A pig in the parlour is still a pig. C54
A pig used to dirt turns up its nose at rice boiled in milk. C55
He that loves noise must buy a pig. H193
One doesn't buy a pig in a poke. K187
Pigs dream of acorns, and the goose of maize. Г228, Л71, C226
Pigs might fly if they had wings. Г96, П198
The voice of a pig cannot be disguised. B49
You can't take the grunt out of the pig. B49

Pill
Bitter pills may have blessed effects. Г291, П290

Pillar
From pillar to post. Б46

Pin	If you begin with a common pin, you will end up with a silver bowl. П56,150
	You have a head and so has a pin. Г211
Pipe	He dances after his wife's pipe. П47
Piper	He who pays the piper calls the tune. H120
	Pay the piper his due. Б488
Pit	To dig a pit for another and fall into it oneself. **H403**, Ч72
Pitch	He that touches (handles) pitch shall be defiled. Г332, K271, **O81**
Pitcher	Little pitchers have long ears. Ч71
	The pitcher goes so often to the well that it is broken at last. П86
Place	A man cannot be in two places at once. З1
	A place for everything and everything in its place. B649, Г15
	High places have high precipices. Б323, H29, **Ч7**
	If you leave your place, you lose it. C233
	It is no play where one weeps and another laughs. K186
	It is not the place that honours the man, but the man that honours the place. M77, **H331**
Please	He that would please all and himself takes more in hand than he is like to do. H74
	It is hard to please all parties. H10,19,26, O30, O74
	You can't please everybody (everyone). B525, H10, H11, **H19**
Pleasure	Don't find pleasure without conscience. Л181
	Fly that pleasure which pains afterward. H273
	No pleasure without pain. H541, П29, P17
	One day of pleasure is worth two of sorrow. Ч2
	Short pleasure, long repentance. Г319
	The pleasure of what we enjoy is lost by coveting more. H515, T62
	The pleasures of the mighty are the tears of the poor. Б16, K168, П4, C185
	You can't mix business with pleasure. Д141
Plenty	Plenty makes poor. И115
Plough	Plough deep and you will have plenty of corn. B113, Г131, O95
	There belongs more than whistling to going to plough. H229, C14
	To plough a straight furrow, never look back. K319
Pluck	Pluck not where you never planted. B189,190, H114,**201**, X97
Pocket	As much needed as a toad in a side pocket. H509
	You can't put "thanks" into your pocket. C244
Poison	One drop of poison infects the whole tun of wine. K8, **Л98**
Policy	Policy goes beyond strength. C120
Politeness	One never loses anything by politeness. C58
Politics	In politics a man must learn to rise above principle. Д344
Pool	Standing pools gather filth. C288
Poor	A poor man's table is soon spread. Ж133
	A poor man's tale cannot be heard. H551
	Better be poor than wicked. Л159
	Better be poor with honour than rich with shame. **Л113**, X75
	It is hard to be leal and poor. H587

Poor and liberal, rich and covetous. Б376
Poor as a churchmouse. Б267
Poor by condition, rich by ambition. Н33
Poor folk are fain of little. К269, С314
Poor men seek meat for their stomachs and rich men stomachs for their meat. У3
Remember the poor, it costs nothing. П238
The poor get poorer. П121
The poor man is aye put to the worst. Б31,32, Н1
The poor man pays for all. Н1
The poor must dance as the rich pipe. Б40
The poor suffer all the wrong. Б32, Н1

Possession   Possession is nine points of the law. Ч23,67

Pot   A pot that belongs to many is ill stirred and worse boiled. У51
A watched pot never boils. Ж27
Better a louse (mouse) in the pot than no flesh at all. В111, Л139
Every pot has its cover (There's a lid for every pot). К87, **Н22**, П49
Neither pot broken nor water spilt. В397, **И12**, К146
The earthen pot must keep clear of the brass kettle. Г287
The pot calls the kettle black. Г288, **О115**, Ч135
To lose both pot and water. У36
While the pot boils, friendship lasts. Н64
Your pot broken seems better than my pot whole. В178,179

Potter   One potter envies another. П122, **С49**

Poverty   Bashfulness is an enemy to poverty. Г220
Of all poverty, that of the mind is most deplorable. Л116
Poverty and wealth are twin sisters. Д401
Poverty and wealth do not agree. Б287,288,350
Poverty breeds strife. Н573
Poverty is no crime (sin). Б35
Poverty is no vice (shame). Б36
Poverty is no disgrace. Н556
Poverty is the mother of all arts. Н557
Poverty is the mother of crime. Г222, Ж131, П308
Poverty is the mother of health. Ж121
Poverty parts fellowship. Х23
Poverty shows us who are our friends and our enemies. Б39
There is no virtue that poverty destroys not. Б34
Unsullied poverty is always happy, while impure wealth brings sorrow. Л113

Power   Power itself has not one half the might of gentleness. В249

Practice   Practice what you preach. А15, **Г189**, П146

Praise (n)   Man's praise in his own mouth stinks. К296, Х11
Praise by evil men is dispraise. Л148
Praise is a spur to the good, a thorn for the evil. Д281
Praise is the reflection of virtue. Д292, **314**
Praise makes good men better and bad men worse. Х98

Praise (v)   He who praises wishes to sell. Н352,**383**,487
Neither praise nor dispraise thyself. К153, **С44**
Praise a fair day at night. Х6
Praise in departing. Н395,478, *Ap.*1.55
Praise no man till he is dead. В204, **С313**, Т44, Х4
Praise none too much for all are fickle. Б161, П197

Prayer   He has much prayer and little devotion. Б122
Prayers plough not (reap not). А20, М138
The prayers of the wicked won't prevail. Н38

Prettiness   Prettiness makes no pottage. Б363, С16

Prevent   Prevent rather than repent. Б183

Prevention   An ounce of prevention is worth a pound of cure. О141
Prevention is better than cure. Б186

Prick   It is hard to kick against the pricks. Т74
You cannot kick against the pricks. П289

Pride   Pride and poverty are ill met yet often seen together. Н555, П266
Pride goes before a fall. С248,250
Pride goes before and shame follows after. С248
Pride may lurk in a threadbare coat. М105, П266

Priest   Each priest praises his own relics. В581
Like priest, like people. З52, И69, К67, Н42
Once a priest, ever a priest. З160

Prince   He whom the prince hates is as good as dead. Ц1

Proclamations   To whisper proclamations is ridiculous. Г10

Profit   No great loss but some profit. У72
Those who take the profit should also bear the expense. Б18
Where profit is, loss is hidden nearby. П240

Promise (n)   A promise is a promise. Д6
Fair promises make fools fain. П191
Great promises and small performance. В118, **Н76,**Н430
Promise is debt. П190
Promises are made to be broken. О11

Promise (v)   A man apt to promise is apt to forget. Н75
Be slow to promise and quick to perform. Д7, Н274, Н422, О10, Я18
He promises like a merchant and pays like a man of war. Н76
He promises mountains and performs molehills. В118, **Н76**
He that promises much, means nothing. К261
It's one thing to promise, another to perform. О12
Never promise what you cannot perform. Ч86

Promiser   No greater promisers than those who have nothing to give. Н441

Prophet   No man is a prophet in his own country. В133

Proud   The proud will rather lose than ask their way. С249

Proverb   A proverb comes not from nothing. Б179, Г135,204, О55, П183
A proverb is an ornament to language. Г204
Common proverb never lies. Н126, П184
Patch grief with proverbs. П185
Proverbs cannot be contradicted. О151, П186
Wise men make proverbs, fools repeat them. Я12

Providence   Providence is better than rent. Б189

Provision   Provision in season makes a rich house. Б68,446

Psalm   To sing (whistle) psalms to the taffrail (a dead horse). Г157, Д236

Pudding   Better some of a pudding than none of a pie. Б222, И55
                   The proof of the pudding is in the eating. В636, К336, Л99, О7,20
                   Too much pudding will choke a dog. И40, С169

Pump   He was christened with pump water. В47

Punctuality   Punctuality is the politeness of princes. Т70

Punishment   The punishment should fit the crime. В172

Purse   A full purse begets a stout stomach. В74, Д155, Е35
                   A heavy purse makes a light heart. В74
                   As the purse is emptied, the heart is filled. Ж160
                   Better an empty purse than an empty head. Б134
                   If you put nothing into your purse, you can take nothing out. С201
                   Let your purse be your master. М165
                   You cannot make a silk purse out of a sow's ear. И79, И111

Push   When a man is going downhill, everyone gives him a push. Н41

Quarrel   An old quarrel is easily renewed. К4
                   Lovers' quarrels are soon mended. М94
                   The quarrels of lovers are the renewal of love. Б319

Quart   You cannot get a quart into a pint box. И85

Question   Ask a silly question and you'll get a silly answer. Н4
                   Ask me no questions and I'll tell you no lies. Т46
                   Like question, like answer. Н21,35
                   Shoot first, ask questions later. К104
                   Theirs is not to question (reason) why, theirs is but to do and die. Н347

Quick   Quick on the uptake. Л29

Quickly   He acts well who acts quickly. К313
                   Whatsoever is well resolved should be quickly performed. Д460

Rabbit   To go rabbit hunting with a dead ferret. М74
                   Whiskey made the rabbit hug the lion. П313,316

Race   The race is to the swift. П179, Р49

Rain   Rain falls alike on the just and the unjust. Д365
                   When it rains, it pours. Б418, К118, М63, Н408

Rainy   Lay up for a rainy day. Б180

Rake   He is better with a rake than with a fork. Р83
                   There's little left for the rake after the besom. В529

Rascal There isn't a rascal or a thief that doesn't have his devotion. Б403, И13

Rat Don't throw water on a drowned rat. В302
Like a rat in the wheel. К16

Raven The croaking raven bodes death. В436

Ready They that are booted are not always ready. К316, Р37

Reason Reason rules all things. И10, Р28
There is a reason for everything (in all things). Б103
There is reason in the roasting of eggs. Б102, И10

Reckoning Merry is the feast-making till we come to the reckoning. З32, Р44
Short reckonings make long friends. Б225, Д44, **К175**, С332, Ч10

Recoil We must recoil a little to the end we may leap the better. О184

Reed Where there are reeds, there is water. Г79

Relative A lot of relatives, a lot of trouble. К149

Remedy The best remedy against an ill man is much ground between. Б162

Repentance Late repentance is seldom true. П175

Repetition Repetition is the mother of learning. П90

Reputation A good reputation stands still, a bad one runs. Д274
A man's best reputation for his future is his reecord of the past. К46
Glass, China and reputations are easily cracked and never well-mended. Ч54
Reputation is hard to make and easy to lose. Л26, Ч54

Respect Respect a man and he will do the more. В117, П133

Rest Rest is the sweet sauce of labour. П177
Too much rest is rust. Н68

Revenge Revenge is a morsel for God. С293

Rich A rich man for dogs, and a poor man for babies. У5
A rich man's foolish sayings pass for wise ones. Б282
He's not rich that possesses much, but that's content with what he has. Б286, **Н447**, Т56, Т59
Rich folk have many friends. Д184
Rich men may have what they will, poor men what they can. Б293
The rich feast, the poor fast, dogs dine and and the poor pine. Б37
The rich get richer. Б272
The rich man has the world by the tail. Б274
The rich man knows not his friends. Б39
The rich man thinks of the future, the poor man of today. У3
They are rich who have true friends. В252

Riches Enough is great riches. Б286
From rags to riches. В663, Н190
Riches and virtue do not often keep each other company. Б295
Riches bring cares and fears. Д175
Riches have wings. Д157,194
Small riches hath most rest. Б276, **Д152**

Riddance Good riddance! П117, С132

Right   A pocketful of right needs a pocketful of gold. C301
It will all come right in the wash. П25, C59
Those who are right need not talk loudly. Б299,313, Д407, К206, П208, **Ш13**

River   Even the weariest river winds somewhere safe to sea. Г47
Where there's a river, there's a bridge. И59

Road   Every road leads in two directions. П61
No road is long with good company. B589

Rogue   Little rogues easily become great ones. К143
No rogue like to the godly rogue. B665
Nobody calls himself a rogue. У11

Roof   Thatch your roof before the rain begins. Г304, H70,452,

Rome   All roads lead to Rome. *Ap.*1.40
Better be first in a village than second at Rome. П129
When in Rome, do as the Romans. B50,154,187, Г39

Room   Where there is room in the heart, there is room in the house. B150

Rope   Name not a rope in his house that was hanged. У45
To make a rope of sand. И99

Rose   If you lie upon roses when young, you'll lie upon thorns when old. Ч39
No roses without a thorn. **H524**, X45

Row   Hoe your own row. B196, **H400**, П293

Rub   Do not rub him the wrong way. E17
There's the rub. B442

Rubbish   Good riddance to bad rubbish. H95, C132

Rule   There is no general rule without some exception. H523

Ruler   No man can be a good ruler unless he has first been ruled. К276

Rumour   Rumour is a great traveller. C186

Run   You cannot run and bark at the same time. 31

Runner   It's better to be a good runner than a bad stander.   Л149

Sad   I am sad because I cannot be glad. П32

Saddle   As a saddle becomes a cow (sow). К19, H384
Either win the saddle or lose the horse. **И123**, Л66

Sadness   Sadness and gladness succeed each other. Г80, Г263, H543, P18, C85

Sail   Cut your sail according to your cloth. B573, К209
Make not your sail too big for the ballast. B52, Г160

The sea cannot be scooped up in a tumbler. Г286
The sea complains it wants water. C286
The sea has fish for every man. M161
You cannot empty the sea with a spoon. Г286, **M160**

Season   There's a season for all things. П50

Secret   If it's a secret, don't tell it to a woman. H411
Secrets are never long-lived. H522
Whenever there is a secret, there must be something wrong. B148, Ч20

See   Better seen than heard. **B300**, Г165
One is not bound to see more than he can. Г159
Seeing is believing. Г115, Л123
Seen one, seen them all. B487,506, E14
The eyes are not satisfied with seeing. Г121, Г158
We shall see what we shall see. Б8
What we see depends mainly on what we look for. B307
You haven't seen anything yet. Э3

Seek   Seek and ye shall find. 348, И144, K246
Seek what may be found. K38, H377

Seeker   Be no seeker of other men's matters. H318

Sell   He praises who wishes to sell. **H383**,486

Serve   He that serves, must serve. B444, C188
If you would be well served, serve yourself. H313

Settle   Settled once, settled forever. P55

Shadow   Catch not at the shadow and lose the substance. П92, 322
He that grabs at the shadow shall lose the substance. O15
Stand in the sunshine and the shadow will fall behind. И107

Shame   Better to die than live in shame. Л163
He who has no shame, has no honour. B56
He who is without shame, all the world is his. Б204

Share   Share and share alike. Д397, Ч73

Sheep   A lazy sheep thinks its wool heavy. Д244, Л46, X109
As well be hanged for a sheep as for a lamb. C100
Better give the wool than the sheep. Л137
He that has sheep, swine and bees - sleep he, wake he, he may thrive. O23
He that makes himself a sheep shall be eaten by the wolves. **Б398, C83**
If the sheep leap o'er the dyke, all the rest will follow. K325
It is a foolish sheep that makes the wolf his confessor. M210
One scabbed sheep will mar a whole flock. K203, O54, Ш3
One sheep follows another. K325
The lone sheep is in danger of the wolf. Б156, O22, C231, У105
There is a black sheep in every flock. B159
Where every hand fleeces, the sheep goes naked. B529

Sheet   Do not cut the sheet to mend the dishcloth. И95, Ц8

Shepherd   It is the part of a good shepherd to shear the flock, not flay it. Д291

Shield   Either behind your shield or on it. Л66

Skeleton   There's a skeleton in every house. П96, **У29**

Skill   All things require skill but appetite. Б111
Few things are impossible to diligence and skill. Д253
Skill and assurance are an invincible army. B203
Skill, not strength, governs a ship. H410
Skill will accomplish what is denied to force. Б140, H410

Slander   Slander leaves a scar (score) behind it. K105

Sleep   Sleep is better than medicine. C238
Sleep is the brother of death. C240
Sleep is the image of death. C241
Sleep is the poor man's treasure. C239
The sleep of the just. Б201
The sleep of the labouring man is sweet. П177

Sloth   Sloth makes all things difficult. Л45

Slow   Slow and steady wins the race. П141, T35
Slow but sure. E5, T31
Slow but sure wins the race. K236

Sluggard   A sluggard takes a hundred steps because he would not take one in time. Л47, C163
Sluggard's guise, slow to bed and slow to rise. Л50
The sluggard must be clad in rags. Л48
The sluggard's convenient season never comes. E18

Small   Better to be small and shine than to be great and cast a shadow. Л119
Many small make a great. Б89, B244, **И90**, П58
Small is the seed of every greatness. И89, M25, H216

Smile   A smile goes a long way. П133

Smoke   No smoke without fire. Д510, H518
Shunning the smoke, they fall into the fire. O117

Snake   He that has been bitten by a snake (serpent) is afraid of a rope. Б349, B394
To nourish a snake in one's bosom. **B676**, H245, П249
When a snake (serpent) has bitten, a lizard alarms. B394

Snow   On the snow add frost. П265
Whether you boil snow or pound it, you can have but water out of it. B368, K50, C137
You cannot strike fire from snow. Г300

Soldier   Every French soldier carries a marshall's baton in his sack. П44, X108
Many soldiers are brave at the table who are cowards in the field. B231
Soldiers fight and kings are the heroes. B383

Some   Some are always giving, others are always taking. Л115
Some are wise, some are otherwise. O61
Some have the hap, some stick in the gap. B71,**210**,211,218, O62, C310
Some like it hot, others prefer it cold. Ж2

Son   A foolish son is the calamity of his father. B17
A miser's son is a spendthrift. C165
Teach your son in the hall, your wife on the pillow. У122

Song   A good song is none the worse for being sung twice. H249

Spoon
He will make a spoon or spoil a horn. Д122, Л1
To fill the mouth with an empty spoon. И103

Sports
In sports and journeys men are known. В46

Spot
Point not at others spots with a foul finger. **317**, Н107, Ч135, *Ap.*1.21

Sprat
Every sprat nowadays calls itself a herring. В592
Throw out a sprat to catch a mackerel. Д246

Square
Back to square one. О94

Stand
Stand by your guns. Г65

Start
Don't start anything you can't finish. Н345

Steed
Untimeous spurring spoils the steed. Н40

Step
Step after step the ladder is ascended. Б450, П62
The greatest step is that out of doors. П13

Stick
A crooked stick will cast a crooked shadow. Н567
A straight stick is crooked in the water. В58, К205
Dress up a stick and it does not appear to be a stick. В78, Н144
It's easy to find a stick to beat a dog. **Б454**, Г302, К122, С109
Speak softly and carry a big stick. К96
Sticks and stones may break my bones but names will never hurt me. Н134, Я19
To go up like a rocket and to come down like a stick. Б300, В287, З103, Н155
When you pick up a stick at one end, you also pick up the other end. У47

Sting
After your fling, watch for the sting. Г196

Stitch
A stitch in time saves nine. Б183, Р33, Ш11

Stock
It is good grafting on a good stock. О127

Stomach
A stomach like an ostrich. В75
An ill stomach makes all the meat bitter. У31, *Ap.*1.56
To have two stomachs to eat and one to work. В122, К1, Л49, Н80, Р4

Stone
A little stone in the way overturns a great wain. К143, М13, Н207
Boil stones in butter and you may sup the broth. К102
Constant dripping wears away the stone. В363, Д339, **К98**, М11
Like water (milk)(blood) from a stone. Ч75
Never take a stone to break an egg when you can do it with the back of your knife. Р75
No land without stones, no meat without bones. **Б71**, В101
No man can flay a stone. О114
No stone without its name. У18
The rolling stone gathers no moss. **Н68**, П97

Stool
Between two stools one falls to the ground. К244

Store
Store is no sore. **387**, Л94, Х19
Where there is a store of oatmeal, you may put enough in the crock. П139

Storm
A storm in a teacup. Б409
After a storm comes a calm. Б384, Г23,26, Ж32, **П166**
Stuffing holds out the storm. П76
Vows made in storms are forgotten in calms. Г327

Stovewood	Distant stovewood is good stovewood. Д60
Straw	A drowning man will clutch at a straw. К308, У111
	Straws show which way the wind blows. В277
	To stumble at a straw and leap over a block. П1
Strawberry	Anything is good with strawberries and cream. К102, С18
Stream	Cross the stream where it is ebbest. К129
	It is ill striving against the stream (No striving against the stream). Т86
	The stream cannot rise above its source. В692
Stroke	Different strokes for different folks. Н248
	Great strokes do not make sweet music. Б313, В164,**232**
Style	Style is the dress of thought. Я15
Subject	Don't change the subject. *Ap.*1.28
	The subject's love is the king's lifeguard. В254
Sublime	From the sublime to the ridiculous is but one step. О118
Succeed	If at first you don't succeed, try again. Б169, П17, Х78
	The stronger always succeeds. Ч136
Success	Great success is always preceded by great preparation. В497
	Nothing succeeds like success. О59
	Success comes in cans, failure in can'ts. Н532, С192
	Success comes in rising every time you fall. С134, Х78
	Success does not depend on size. Г251
	Success is never blamed. П84
Suffering	Suffering does not manifest itself. З143
	Suffering is bitter but its fruits are sweet. Н221
Suitor	The last suitor wins the maid. С97
Sun	Every light is not the sun. М78
	Somewhere the sun is shining, somewhere a little rain is falling. Г69, И20
	The same sun that will melt butter will harden clay. И94
	The sun is never the worse for shining on a dunghill. И52
	The sun shines on all alike. В640, **И24**, С234
	The sun shines on all the world. А7, Б373, В288, П256
	Two suns cannot shine in one sphere. Д103
Suspicion	Suspicion breeds phantoms. П284
Swallow	One swallow makes not a summer. О53
Sweet	Every sweet has its bitter. В591
	He deserves not the sweet that will not taste the sour. К256, Л171, Н363
	No sweet without some sweat. Т63
	Short and sweet. Р47
	Take the sweet with the sour. Л171
	Too much sweet spoils the best coffee. И116, **С169**
Swift	A swift eater, a swift worker. Л30
Swine	A swine over fat is the cause of his own bane. С11
	One swine recognizes another. В278

Swing   What you lose on the swings, you gain on the roundabouts. B373, H372

Sword   A brave arm makes a short sword. X83
                 One sword keeps another in the sheath. Д16

Table   At the table it becomes no one to be bashful. C228
                 Thrust not your feet under another man's table. H112

Tail   The tail goes with the hide. Б332, П285, C96

Tailor   A tailor must cut three sleeves to every woman's gown. **A28**, Д345
                 A tailor's sons wear patched pants. У42
                 A tailor's wife is worst clad. У42
                 A hundred tailors, a hundred millers, and a hundred weavers are three hundred thieves. H425
                 There is knavery in all trades, but most in tailors. H526

Take   Take all you want, but eat all you take. Ч13
                 Take not up more than you can bear. B91, **Ч96**
                 Take what you can get. C15
                 Take while the taking's good. Г27
                 You can't take it with you. C35, **У104**

Tale   A tale never loses in the telling. B566
                 A tale of a roasted horse. T76
                 The tale runs as it pleases the teller. P40
                 There are two tales to every story. И97
                 You tell a tale to a deaf man. T77

Talk   All talking and no action. M124
                 Big talking but little saying. M57, C101
                 By talking, people understand one another. Г190
                 Loose talk costs lives. B67, C126
                 Talk is talk, but 'tis money buys land. M167
                 Talk much and err much. **Б318**, Л90, M61, O196
                 Talking pays no toll. H121, O153
                 Talking will not make the pot boil. П134

Talker   Great talkers fire too fast to take aim. Г187
                 The greatest talkers are the least doers. **Б329**, Д210, P42

Taste   Every man to his taste, quoth the man when he kissed his cow. П107, У15
                 There is no accounting for tastes. И128, H15, **O1**

Tear   Tears bring nobody back from the grave. C172
                 Tears and trouble are the lot of all. C144
                 Two barrels of tears will not heal a bruise. C172

Tell   Tell it like it is.   351
                 Tell me with whom you go and I'll tell you what you do. C123

Temptation   Who avoids temptation avoids sin. B571

Thanks   Thanks is poor pay. И101

Thick   To go through thick and thin. Б441, И4, C41

Thief   All are not thieves that dogs bark at. И8, H241
                 All thieves come to some bad ends. B422, C139

Trade is the mother of money. T63
Who has a trade has a share everywhere. P51

Traveller   A traveller may lie with authority. Д59,**286**
Travellers and poets have leave to lie. Д398
Travellers may change climates, not conditions. 325

Treachery   Treachery will come home to the traitor. Д456

Treason   We love the treason but hate the traitor. И121

Tree   A tree is known by its fruit. Д198,409
Great trees are good for nothing but shade. Д452
Great trees keep down the little ones. M55
He that loves the tree, loves the branch. K254
It takes all kinds of trees to make a forest. B60
Judge a tree by its fruit. C209
Straight trees have crooked roots. У75
The bigger the tree, the harder she falls. H45
Timely crooks the tree that will good cammock be. **K202**, M19
To bark up the wrong tree. H199
When the tree is fallen, everyone runs to it with an axe. K24
You cannot judge a tree by its bark. П53

Trooper   A young trooper should have an old horse. H82

Trouble   Don't meet troubles half way. O124
He that seeks trouble never misses. Г5, 328, K238
Let your trouble tarry till its own day comes. H354
Never trouble trouble till trouble troubles you. Г273
Sing your troubles away. Г70
Stay clear of trouble. **O124**
Tears and trouble are the lot of all. Г256
Trouble arises when you least expect it. Г260
Trouble breeds trouble. Б22
Trouble enters unannounced. Б26,27
Trouble shared is trouble halved. B343, Г266
Trouble springs from idleness. Л52

Trousers   Never wear your best trousers when you go out to fight. B38, K124, П304

Trout   A live trout is better than a dead whale. П33
You can't catch trout with dry trousers. P91, Ч107

True   If it were only true. B212

Trust (n)   In trust is treason. B41
Trust is dead, ill payment killed it. H540

Trust (v)   I will trust you no further than I can see you. B261
Trust me, but look to thyself. Д442, H119

Truth   All truths are not to be told. B565, H228
All truths must not be told at all times. H263
Better speak truth rudely than lie covertly. Л172, H50
Home truths are unpalatable. П210
If you tell the truth you won't have to remember what you said. K290
In too much dispute, truth is lost. Б358
It is ill jesting with the truth. П219
Live truth instead of professing it. Г189
Old saws speak truth. П184, **C263**

Speak the truth bravely. 335, H435
The language of truth is simple. H78
The truth always hurts. Ш21
To tell the truth, the whole truth, and nothing but the truth. И100
Truth and oil are ever above. B209
Truth and roses have thorns about them. П210
Truth fears no trial. П216
Truth finds foes where it makes none. Г188
Truth gives a short answer (+ but lies go round about). Л14, H78
Truth has a scratched face. У20
Truth has no need of rhetoric. П223
Truth is dead. П214
Truth is mighty and will prevail. П209
Truth is stranger than fiction. П212
Truth may be blamed, but cannot be shamed. Б482
Truth needs not the ornament of many words. H78, П223
Truth never grows old. B500
Truth will come to light (Truth will out). П215
Truth's best ornament is nakedness. Д275,302
Without truth there can be no virtue. B55, Г77

Tub   Let every tub stand on its own bottom. B580

Tune   To sing the same old tune. *Ap.*1.107

Turn   Every man will have his own turn served. B560, B604
                 One good (ill) turn deserves another. Д**368**, 312, K15, T80, **У108**
                 One never loses by doing a good turn. Б221

Two   It takes two birds to make a nest. Б94
                 It takes two to quarrel (tango). B109, Д250
                 Never choose between two things, take them both. O5
                 No man can do two things at once. Д86
                 There are two sides to every question. B584
                 Two attorneys can live in a town when one cannot. O37
                 Two bigs will not go into one bag. B91, Д86,**99**
                 Two dogs over one bone seldom agree. Д108
                 Two good days in a man's life: when he weds and when he buries his wife. Д96
                 Two hands are better than one. B447, O51
                 Two in distress make sorrow less. B**343**,546
                 Two of a trade seldom agree. Д93, C49
                 Two to one is odds. Д**89**,102
                 Two's company but three's a crowd. Г30
                 You cannot have two forenoons in the same day. B86, Д83, **H508**

Tyrant   Any excuse will serve a tyrant. Л83

Uncalled   Who comes uncalled, sits unserved. H504

Unexpected   It is the unexpected that always happens. H23,**58**, **Ч18**

Ungirt   Ungirt, unblessed. H97

Uninvited   Don't go if you're uninvited. H503

Union   Union is strength. Б203, E31, C213

United	United we stand, divided we fall. Д441, C213
Unseen	Unseen, unrued. H218
Untaught	Better untaught than ill taught. **B643, H502**, X89
Up	Whatever goes up must come down. B627
Useful	Be useful as well as ornamental. H185

Vacuum	A vacuum is always filled. C79
Valley	He that stays in the valley shall never get over the hill. K315
Valour	Valour delights in the test. M187
Vanity	An ounce of vanity spoils a hundred weight of merit. У59
Vanquisher	Vanquishers are kings, the vanquished thieves. П84
Venison	All flesh is not venison. K327
Vessel	Empty vessels make the greatest noise. П307 Ill vessels seldom miscarry. **Б218**, Л82, **C133** The vessel that will not obey her helm will have to obey the rocks. И123
Vice	A vice lives and thrives by concealment. Ч20 Every vice fights against nature. З132 Vice is often clothed in virtue's habit. З134
Victory	Do not triumph before the victory. H261,**477**, *Ap.*1.55 Victory belongs to the most persevering. П83
Vine	Take a vine of a good soil and a wife o a good mother. B671, **Г162**
Viper	No viper so little but has its venom. Ж15, M8,18, П297
Virtue	He that sows virtue, reaps fame. Д321 Virtue and vice divide the world, but vice has got the greater share. Д267, M118 Virtue is a jewel of great price. Д293 Virtue is a thousand shields (the safest helmet). C206 Virtue will triumph. Д287
Virtuous	He cannot be virtuous that is not rigorous. Б433
Voice	The voice of the people, the voice of God. Г129
Vows	Vows made in storms are forgotten in calms. K134, T52

Wall	Hard and hard makes not the stone wall. Д88 Men, not walls, make a city safe. Д349, **H325** Talking to him is like talking to a wall. E15 The great wall stands, the builder is gone. Ч57

Weapon The weapon of the brave is in his heart. M186, O172
When weapons speak, the muses are silent. K116

Weary Never be weary of well-doing. C82

Weather In fair weather prepare for foul. Г309
Take the weather as it comes. B467

Wedding One wedding brings on another. Ж77

Wedlock Wedlock is a padlock. Ж69

Weed Weeds want no sowing. Л83

Welcome He that is welcome fares well. K112
Welcome is the best dish. Г308

Well (adv) Leave well (enough) alone. Д266, Л166, **O125**,164, П294
Whatsoever is well resolved on shall be quickly performed. Д460

Well (n) Do not spit into the well you may have to drink of. H365
If you leap into a well, providence is not bound to fetch you out. B445
The deeper the well, the colder the water. B682

What What happens is for the best. Ч90

Wheel A fifth wheel to a coach. H509, **П320**
Better to be a little wheel turning than a big wheel standing still. Л119, M20
The worst wheel of a cart creaks most. X103

Whisper Where there is whispering, there is lying. Л12

Whistle Clean as a whistle. K156
You cannot make a whistle out of a pig's tail. Ш8

White A white wall is a fool's paper. Б175
Every white has its black, and every sweet its sour. H226
To make white black. C37

Whoever Whoever is not with us is against us. K274

Why Every why has a wherefore. H21

Wife A cheerful wife is the joy of life. Д329
A dead wife's the best goods in a man's house. Ж62
A good wife and health are a man's best wealth. Д270
A good wife makes a good husband. **Ж80**, K78
A light wife makes a heavy husband. Б2, H386
A man without a wife is but half a man. H300
A man's best fortune or his worst is a wife. Д269
A neat maiden often makes a dirty wife. Д111
A quiet wife is mighty pretty. Ж52
A true wife is her husband's flower of beauty. Ж47
A wife cannot testify against her husband. Ж59
An obedient wife commands her husband. Ж56
Better a portion (treasure) in a wife than with a wife. Б194, Л142, H299,404
Choose a wife by your ear rather than by your eye. **Ж87**, H255
Choose not a wife by the eye only. Ж61,87, Л136, H316
Choose wife on a Saturday rather than a Sunday. B669, Ж86
He that has a wife has strife. Л175, H519
He that has a wife has a master. 326
He that has not a wife is not yet a complete man. Б65, **H300**

He that tells his wife news is but newly married. Ж68
He that will thrive must ask leave of his wife. Н568, П113, Х101
If you sell your purse to your wife, give your breeks into the bargain. Ж67
It is a sour reek where the good wife dings the good man. Н451
Next to no wife a good wife is best. Л134
No lack to lack a wife. Б65
Rutting wives make rammish husbands. М178
Take a vine of a good soil and a wife of a good mother. В671
The cunning wife makes her husband her apron. Ж56
The first wife is matrimony, the second company, the third heresy. П14
The wife is the key of the house. В553, Ж54,91, **Х33**
There is a good wife in the country and every man thinks he has her. В654
Who has a fair wife needs more than two eyes. Х50
Wife and children are bills of charges. Ж69

Will

Be still and have thy will. Б397, **Ж123**
Good will and welcome is the best cheer. Б195
One's own will is good food. К247
Where there's a will, there's a way. **Б452**, **Г101**, Д76, С194, **Х74**
Where your will is ready, your feet are light. О192
Will is no skill. М129
Will is the cause of woe. С69

Willow

Bend the willow while it's young. Л107

Win

Some win, some lose. В210, **О76**, С310
Win or lose. Л67
You win a few, you lose a few. К268, Л179

Wind

Great winds blow upon high hills. Б337
Puff not against the wind. Б208, П287
Sail with the wind and tide. В541
The wind is fresh and free. Д74
To catch the wind in a net. В132,215, И143
To know which way the wind blows. З146
You cannot hinder the wind from blowing. В217
You can't reap the wind. З5, Н12

Wine

Counsels in wine seldom prosper. В331
Good is the man who refrains from wine. П38
Good wine engenders good blood. Ч1
Good wine needs no bush. **Д299**, Х59
In wine there is truth. Б52, **В544**
Spilt wine is worse than water. Г293, Н298
When the wine is run out you stop the leak. П125
When wine is in, wit is out. **В325**, Д55
When wine sinks, words swim. У48
Wine does not intoxicate men, men intoxicate themselves. Н220
Wine is a turncoat. В332
Wine is the best liquor to wash glasses in. В366
Wine is the whetstone to wit. В323
Wine on beer brings good cheer. В326
Wine wears no breeches. П193
You cannot know the wine by the barrel. В188

Wing

Make not your tail broader than your wings. Ч91
No flying without wings. Б73,74
Unused wings cannot soar. Б74

Winter

A good winter brings a good summer. К79
Winter eats up what summer lays up. Л59, Ч81

Wisdom   The wise seek wisdom, the fool has found it. P30
                The rod and reproof give wisdom. P66
                Wisdom is better than strength. Б140, И49, **P28**, C120
                Without wisdom, wealth is worthless. **Б289**, Г140, У118

Wise   A wise man commonly has foolish children. У4
                For the wise man with a sigh, for the fool with a fist. H433
                He is wise that is rich. Д177
                He is wise that is ware in time. B301
                It is easy to be wise after the event. П173, У83, X15, *Ap.*1.68
                It takes the foolish to confound the wise. И17, C9
                It's good to be merry and wise. B262
                No man is wise at all times. Б167, B160,353, E9, И37, H24
                None is so wise but the fool overtakes him. Б420
                One wise man is worth a thousand fools. P31
                The wise man may sometimes play the fool. И37
                Wise men learn by other's harms, fools by their own. Д496
                Wise men propose and fools determine. Г153
                Wise men silent, fools talk. У101

Wisest   The wisest man is he who does not fancy himself wise at all. H317
                The wisest men may fall. И35,37

Wish   If a man could have all his wishes, he would double his trouble. Д150
                If wishes were horses, beggars might ride. H98,233

Wit   After wit comes ever late. Д361
                Better wit than wealth. Д505, У118
                Little wit in the head makes much work for the feet. Б131
                Want of wit is worse than want of gear. Д149

Wive   First thrive, then wive. K297
                It is hard to wive and thrive in one year. Б216

Woe   No weal without woe. П29
                Woe to him that is alone. Б62

Wolf   A wolf may change his mind but never his fur. E46, H17
                A wolf may lose his teeth but never his nature. **B392**, E46, K23, H17
                It never troubles the wolf how many the sheep may be. O29
                Set the wolf to keep the sheep. Б385, B395, Д359, H211,389, П303
                The only good wolf is a dead wolf. B399
                The wolf and fox are of one counsel. Л74, У8
                The wolf eats often of the sheep that have been told. O22
                The wolf knows what the ill beast thinks. Л15
                The wolf must die in his own skin. H17
                Who keeps company with a wolf will learn to howl. Ж135, 315, **M50**, П152, **C2**
                Whoever is a wolf, behaves like a wolf. H17
                Wolf in sheep's clothing. B388
                Wolves rend sheep where shepherds fail. Б187

Woman   A fair woman without virtue is like palled wine. Б1
                A wicked woman is worse than the devil. З138
                A woman at home and the flies are gone. Б3
                A woman is a weathercock. Б5, Д110, C105
                A woman's instinct is often truer than mens' reasoning. Ж84
                A woman's mind and winter change oft. Б5
                A woman's place is in the home. Б7, Д318, Ж60
                A woman's strength is in her tongue. Ж64,85
                A woman's tears are her strongest weapon. Б6, Ж83

A woman's work is never done. Д381
A worthy woman is the crown of her husband. Ж47
An ugly woman dreads the mirror. Р93
If a woman were satisfied she wouldn't be a woman. Ж81
It's no more pity to see a woman weep than to see a goose go barefoot. Д112
Play, women, and wine undo a man laughing. Д113
Tell a woman and you tell the world. О3
The more women look to their glass, the less they look to their home. Г3
Three women and a goose make a market. Г336
Three women make a market. Д98
Trust not a woman when she weeps. Ж82
Two women can't live under one roof (Two women in the same house never agree). С104
Women, priests, and poultry never have enough. П301
Women will have their wills. Ж45

Wonder   Wonders will never cease. П120, Ч44,109

Wood   All wood is worth logs. Е14
Do not halloo till you're out of the wood. **Н261**,395
Green wood makes a hot fire. И91
He that fears leaves must not go into the woods. В393, Т66
To carry wood into the forest. В59,**377**
To live too near the wood to be frightened by owls. К214
You can always cut more wood off, but you cannot put it on again. И92

Word   A flow of words is not always a flow of wisdom. Г57, Д233, М57
A kind word goes a long way. Д312, Л7,8
A kind word never hurt anyone. Д346, У99
A man's word is as good as his bond. С179
A soft word is often worth more than a house and a lot. Д351, Л8
A thousand words won't fill a bushel. Б20
A word and a stone let go cannot be recalled. В689, С178
A word spoke is an arrow let fly. С180
A word spoken is past recalling (Words once spoken cannot be recalled). **С125**
A word to the wise is sufficient. В630, Д323, **М173**, О39, Р32, **У98**
An honest man's word is as good as his bond. Д6, У73
Bare words buy no barley. Б20
Fair words fill not the belly. Б21,**367**, Г226, Е45,Р24, С236, У7, Ш14
Fair words hurt not the mouth. Д313, **О163**
Fair words make fools fain. С247
Few words are best. Г176, К176, Р47
Fine words butter no parsnips. И101, С236
Fine words dress ill deeds. Г180
For mad words, deaf ears. Г155
From words to deeds is a great space. В503, Н98
Good words cost nought. Д351
Good words without deeds are like rushes and reeds. Н91
Good words won't fill a sack. В376
Hard words break no bones. Б357
He who gives you fair words feeds you with an empty spoon. Г184, К192
Many words, many buffets. В229, Л90
One word cannot be changed but for the worst. И100
Small words sometimes grow into mighty strife. О149
Smooth words make smooth ways. У99
Take a man by his word and a cow by her horn. Б421
The written word (letter) remains. Н140
There is a great difference between word and deed. Д117
Whispered words are heard afar. Ш5
Words are but wind. Ч101
Words bind men. П75
Words cut more than swords. С180

Words have wings and cannot be recalled. B681, C125, C182
Words, like feathers, are carried away by the wind. H91
Words may pass but blows fall heavy. Б356, H134, Я19

Work (n)   Hard work is not easy and dry bread is not greasy. П164
He has hard work indeed who has nothing to do. H450
Never was good work done without much trouble. Б53
No work is worse than overwork. H450
The best way to get rid of work is to do it. Д136
Work commends the master. P2
Work is afraid of a resolute man. B638, Д135
Work keeps you out of mischief. П36
Work makes life pleasant. Б104, B505, П158
Work well done makes pleasures more fun. П158

Work (v)   He that will not work shall not eat. Б380, P7
If you won't work, you shan't eat. Д12, Л39
Unless you work hard, you cannot succeed. T63
Work till you drop (work hand and foot). P6

Worker   Ill workers are good onlookers. M213

Workman   A bad workman quarrels with his tools. Д131, H85
A good workman can use any kind of tools. T60
Diligence makes an expert workman. T21
The better workman, the worse husband. M175
The work shows the workman. **B602**, Д145, K336
The workman is worthy of his hire. П72
What's a workman without his tools. Б69,110,123,200

World   All the world loves a lover. M87
All the world loves a winner. З16, Л114
All's for the best in the best of all possible worlds. Ч90
He that deals with the world needs four sieves. C91
It takes all sorts to make a world. B60,69, У16
It isn't what you want in this world, it's what you get. Д461
It's a good world but they are ill that are on it. C143
It's a small world. M99
One half the world doesn't know how the other half lives. Б266
The world is a ladder for some to go up and some to go down. B71
The world is a wide parrish (place). П57, C52
The world is full of fools. H60
The world is what people make it. C93
The world is wiser than it was. B84
We come weeping into this world. Ч29
You cannot please the whole world and his wife. H26

Worm   Tread on a worm and it will turn. H145

Worry   If you can do nothing about it, don't worry; if you can do something, do it - don't worry. Г259
Worry kills more than work. H390

Worst   Always figure for the worst and the best is bound to happen. H241
If worst comes to worst, make the best of it. C15
The worst is yet to come. Э4

Worth   His worth is warrant for his welcome. Г306, Ж38
The worth of a thing is best known by the want of it. T2, Ч76
The worth of a thing is what it will bring. Л99
What is worth doing is worth doing well. P45

Wound   The wound that bleeds inwardly is the most dangerous. 379
                   Though the wound be healed, yet a scar remains. Щ6

Wrangler   Wranglers never want words. Д43, Н7

Wren   Every wren is loud in its fen. B612

Write   Easy writing makes hard reading. Г310
                   If you don't write, you're wrong. П9

Wrong   He who owes is in all the wrong. 373
                   Submitting to one wrong brings on another. Г316, М10
                   The smaller the wrong, the greater the guilt. B587, М2
                   Two wrongs don't make a right. Г311, З131, К201
                   Wrong has no warrant. Л83

Year   A man may be young in years but old in hours. М139
                   It takes a year to make a friend. Б390, **B214**
                   One year's seeding makes seven years' weeding. Т68
                   Our years roll on. Г198

Yesterday   Every day is not yesterday. B667
                   In search of yesterday. И135
                   Not born yesterday. М206, Н361

Young   Old young and young old. Н545
                   Young in limbs, in judgment old. М101
                   Young learn, learn fair. Б181, У123, Ч46
                   Young men soon give and soon get affronts, old age is slow in both. М152

Youth   An idle youth, a needy age. Г335, **Щ1**
                   If youth but knew and age but could do. E23
                   If youth only had the experience and old age had the strength. E23
                   Reckless youth, makes rueful age. C207,208
                   The excesses of our youth are draughts upon our old age. C208, Ч8
                   The mark must be made in youth. Б181
                   What youth is used to, age remembers. М150
                   Youth comes but once in a lifetime. Д83
                   Youth is a crown of roses, old age a crown of willows. М147
                   Youth is full of vitamins, age is full of germs. М147
                   Youth is hasty of temper but weak in judgment. М148
                   Youth is nimble, age is lame. М141,147
                   Youth is reckless. B597
                   Youth will have its course (swing)(fling). М146
                   Youth will to youth. М151

Yule   It is easy to cry Yule at other mens' cost. Л25

Zeal   Zeal without prudence is frenzy. O133

* * *